Lecture Notes in Artificial Intelligence

T0238519

Subseries of Lecture Notes in Computer Science

LNAI Series Editors

Randy Goebel
University of Alberta, Edmonton, Canada
Yuzuru Tanaka
Hokkaido University, Sapporo, Japan
Wolfgang Wahlster
DFKI and Saarland University, Saarbrücken, Germany

LNAI Founding Series Editor

Joerg Siekmann
DFKI and Saarland University, Saarbrücken, Germany

Patrick Brézillon   Patrick Blackburn
Richard Dapoigny (Eds.)

Modeling
and Using Context

8th International and Interdisciplinary Conference
CONTEXT 2013
Annecy, France, October 28 - 31, 2013
Proceedings

 Springer

Volume Editors

Patrick Brézillon
University Pierre and Marie Curie (UPMC)
Paris, France
E-mail: Patrick.Brezillon@lip6.fr

Patrick Blackburn
University of Roskilde
Roskilde, Denmark
E-mail: patrickb@ruc.dk

Richard Dapoigny
University of Savoie, LISTIC - Polytech'Savoie
Annecy-le-Vieux Cedex, France
E-mail: richard.dapoigny@univ-savoie.fr

ISSN 0302-9743   e-ISSN 1611-3349
ISBN 978-3-642-40971-4   e-ISBN 978-3-642-40972-1
DOI 10.1007/978-3-642-40972-1
Springer Heidelberg New York Dordrecht London

Library of Congress Control Number: 2013947785

CR Subject Classification (1998): I.2, F.4.1, H.4, J.3, J.4

LNCS Sublibrary: SL 7 – Artificial Intelligence

Typesetting: Camera-ready by author, data conversion by Scientific Publishing Services, Chennai, India

Printed on acid-free paper

Springer is part of Springer Science+Business Media (www.springer.com)

Preface

Sixteen years after the first conference was held in 1997, the 8th International and Interdisciplinary Conference on Modeling and Using Context (CONTEXT 2013) continues the tradition of extending foundational research on context, evaluating the status and consequences of context-related research, and addressing new issues and applications. CONTEXT is not only the oldest conference series devoted to context, it is also unique in the emphasis it places on interdisciplinary research and the interplay between theory and application. Previous editions of the series were held in Rio de Janeiro, Brazil (CONTEXT 1997), Trento, Italy (CONTEXT 1999, LNCS 1688), Dundee, UK (CONTEXT 2001, LNCS 2116), Palo Alto, USA (CONTEXT 2003, LNCS 2680), Paris, France (CONTEXT 2005, LNCS 3554), Roskilde, Denmark (CONTEXT 2007, LNCS 4635), and Karlsruhe, Germany (CONTEXT 2011, LNAI 6967). Each of these brought together researchers and practitioners from a wide range of fields to report on and discuss progress on context-related research.

CONTEXT 2013 was held during 28th October – 1st November, 2013, at Annecy, France. The first day was devoted to three workshops:

Smart University
> organized by Thomas Roth-Berghofer, S. Oussena (University of West London, UK), and M. Atzmüller (University of Kassel, Germany).

Context-based Information Retrieval for E-science(CIRE'2013)
> organized by C. Cote (University LYON III, France) and J. Jose (University of Glasgow, UK).

Context for Business Process Management
> organized by Xiao Liu (East China Normal University, China) and Xiaoliang Fan (Lanzhou University, China).

The main conference brought togetherpaper and poster presentations. The conference call for papers invited researchers and practitioners to share insights from the wide range of disciplines concerned with context, including computer science, cognitive science, linguistics, psychology, philosophy, computer science, the social sciences and organizational sciences, and all application areas. The call succeeded, and a wide range of papers were accepted, the acceptance rate for conference papers was roughly 50%.

The selected papers cover eight themes that were used as the eight sections of this book and the eight conference sessions: Context and Meaning, Context in Context, Contextual Methodologies, Conceptual Approaches to Context, Formal Approaches to Context, Contextual Methodologies, and two sessions on Applying Context. The Poster Session (only nine posters were accepted, to enable fruitful exchanges among participants) was held at the end of the third day, just before the social event. The 23 main session papers and the 9 shorter papers presented in the poster session can be found in this volume.

The two keynote speakers at the conference were:

Craige Roberts (Ohio State University), and

Matthew Stone (Rutgers)

Moreover, to link more intimately research and applications, for this eighth edition of the CONTEXT Series, there was a special industrial talk (Context management in a lightly instrumented smart home) given by:

Frédéric Weis and Michèle Dominici (IRISA, University Rennes 1).

We would like to thank all our invited speakers for their inspiring talks and contributions to the conference.

CONTEXT 2013 was organized under somewhat difficult circumstances. It was originally due to take place in Norway, but unexpected difficulties meant this plan had to be abandoned late in the day, and new arrangements made. It is an excellent testimonial to the underlying strength of the CONTEXT community that it was possible to restart the organizational work and run the conference on schedule. We are deeply grateful to the members of the Organization and Program Committees for their willingness to work under such tight time constraints, and would also like to say a special thank you to Henning Christiansen who was always ready and willing to help out when the going got tough.

This experience has led to an overhaul of the organization for the conference series, and the future is bright. Arrangements are close to finalization for both the 2015 and 2017 editions, and it is hoped to help rebuild the Community of Context on a more interactive footing with the aid of social media (indeed, 2013 was the first time there was Facebook presence concerning the CONTEXT conference). All in all, things look healthy for both the CONTEXT conference series and its associated research community, and we look forward with optimism to future developments on Modeling and Using Context.

August 2013

Patrick Brézillon
Patrick Blackburn
Richard Dapoigny

Organization

Program Chairs

Patrick Blackburn   Roskilde University, Denmark
Patrick Brezillon   Université Pierre et Marie Curie, France

Program Committee

Patrick Barlatier	University of Savoie, France
Luciana Benotti	National University of Cordoba, Argentina
Yolande Berbers	Katholieke Universiteit Leuven, Belgium
Patrick Blackburn	University of Roskilde, Denmark
Marcos Borges	Federal University of Rio de Janeiro, Brasil
Patrick Brezillon	University of Paris 6, France
Sylvie Calabretto	INSA Lyon, France
Jörg Cassens	University of Hildesheim, Germany
K. Cheverst	Lancaster University, UK
Henning Christiansen	Roskilde University, Denmark
Richard Dapoigny	University of Savoie, France
Klaus David	University of Kassel, Germany
Bruce Edmonds	Manchester Metropolitan Univ Business School, UK
Jérôme Euzenat	INRIA and University of Grenoble, France
Xiaoliang Fan	Lanzhou University, China
Christian Freksa	University of Bremen, Germany
Chiara Ghidini	FBK-irst, Italy
Fausto Giunchiglia	University of Trento, Italy
Avelino Gonzalez	University of Central Florida, USA
Patrick Humphreys	London School of Economics, UK
Anders Kofod-Petersen	NTNU, Norway
David Leake	Indiana University, USA
Thomas R. Roth-Berghofer	University of West London, UK
Flavia Maria Santoro	Universidade Federal do Estado do Rio de Janeiro, Brazil
Hedda R. Schmidtke	Carnegie Mellon University, USA
Roy Turner	University of Maine, USA
Kristof Van Laerhoven	Technische Universität Darmstadt, Germany
Elisabetta Zibetti	University Paris 8, France

Local Organization at Université de Savoie (France)

Patrick Barlatier
Richard Dapoigny
Eric Benoit
Lamia Berrah

Additional Reviewers

Ciara Di Francescomarino   Fondazione Bruno Kessler, Italy
Alessander Botti Benevides   University of Trento, Italy
Emma Norling   Manchester Metropolitan University, UK
Sylvie Cazalens   Université de Nantes, France
Arne Kreutzmann   University of Bremen, Germany

Chairs of the Community of Context

Patrick Brezillon   Université Pierre et Marie Curie, France
Henning Christiansen   Roskilde University, Denmark
Thomas R. Roth-Berghofer   University of West London, UK
Hedda R. Schmidtke   Carnegie Mellon University, US
Richard Dapoigny   Université de Savoie, France

Sponsors

association française pour le Contexte

Table of Contents

Section 1: Context and Meaning

Section 2: Context in Context

Section 3: Contextual Methodologies

Section 4: Conceptual Approaches to Context

Section 5: Formal Approach to Context

Section 6: Contextual Technologies

Section 7: Applying Context

Short Papers

A Typed Approach for Contextualizing the Part-Whole Relation

Richard Dapoigny and Patrick Barlatier

LISTIC/Polytech'Annecy-Chambéry
University of Savoie, P.O. Box 80439, 74944 Annecy-le-vieux cedex, France
`richard.dapoigny@univ-savoie.fr`

Abstract. In the domain of knowledge representation as well as in Conceptual Modeling, representing part-whole relations is a long-stand-ing challenging problem. Most approaches addressing this issue rely on a set-theoretical framework, but many difficulties remain especially for disambiguating transitivity. In mathematical logic and program checking, dependent type theories have proved to be appealing but so far, they have been little applied in the formalization of knowledge. To bridge this gap, we represent part-of structures in a dependently-typed framework with the purpose of enhancing expressiveness through an explicit introduction of properties characterizing the context. We show that the dependently typed language easily captures the notion of contextualized part-of with many examples.

1 Introduction

In this paper, we provide an analysis of the transitive (meta)property for the so-called *part-of* relation which is of fundamental importance in many disciplines including cognitive science [26], linguistics [31], ontology [5] and conceptual modeling [16]. There is a growing interest towards the definition of a typology of *part-of* relations depending on the different types of entities they relate [21,31]. These classifications involve several sorts of relations whose the more discussed are subQuantity-of, functional part-of, member-of (organizational part-of) and the challenging spatial part-of dependent on a numerical predicate [20]. The development of suitable foundational theories for addressing unambiguously the transitivity of these relations is an important step towards the definition of precise real-world semantics. However, while the transitive (meta)property of *part-of* relations has been widely discussed (see e.g., [6,20,30,21,16] most solutions are either highly complex or far from being consensual. We address this problem in a unified way based on the explicit introduction of the properties characterizing the context. This led to an expressive specification of what is called a "contextualized part-of" based on contextual properties.

Furthermore, in [15] the author pointed out that most modeling languages that have been proposed so far to express formal constraints (or rules) over relations are based on very simple meta-conceptualization and lack expressiveness. For that purpose, we use a highly expressive language built on a solid logical background. It is a two-layered language referred to, as KDTL (Knowledge-based Dependently Typed Language) which includes a higher-order dependent type theory as a lower layer and an ontological layer

P. Brézillon, P. Blackburn, and R. Dapoigny (Eds.): CONTEXT 2013, LNAI 8175, pp. 1–14, 2013.

as upper layer [1,10]. The logic in the lower layer operates on (names of) types whose meaning is constrained in the upper (ontological) layer. Dependent types are based on the notion of indexed families of types and provide a high expressiveness (see e.g., [8] for a formal comparison with basic Description Logics) since they can represent subset types, relations or constraints as typed structures. They will be exploited for representing knowledge in an elegant and secure way. This last aspect is analyzed in [7] where the authors investigate typing applied to reasoning languages of the Semantic Web and point out that dependent types ensure normalization. For example, type theory enjoys the property of subject reduction which ensures that no illegal term will appear during the execution of a well-typed query in a well-typed program. Alternatively, in [11], the authors have shown the ability of the type-theoretical approach to cope with scalability on the SUMO foundational ontology.

2   State-of-the Art

2.1   Mereology

In many papers, the *part-of* (or *part-whole*) relation often refers to mereology. Mereology is the most significant formal theory of *part-of* relations. It originates in the works of Husserl and Leśniewski [19,22] and should be thought as an attempt to lay down the general principles underlying the relationships between an entity (a whole) and its parts. A complete description of mereology can be found in [29,28]. The *part-of* relation cannot be understood by just making analogies to how people might express themselves in casual English conversation. Mereology, originally conceived as an alternative to set theory, sees the world as made up of lumps of anonymous stuff where these lumps are related with the *part-of* relation. The assertion "A is *part-of* B" means that if you "take" all of B, you must "take" all of A with it. However, it does not mean, you would say "A is *part-of* B" in normal idiomatic English. If we restrict ourselves to physical objects, then if one were to draw a spatio-temporal boundary around B, A would be wholly (i.e., spatio-temporally) included inside that boundary. The mereological relation is not based on set theory and requires multiple levels of granularity to make multiple *part-of* relations to co-exist in the same theory which is clearly not true of subsumption relations.

A mereological theory can be seen as a first-order theory with identity characterized by some basic principles. The common principle for mereology considers parthood as a partial ordering, i.e., a reflexive (1), antisymmetric (2) and transitive (3) relation.

$$\forall x \; P(x,x) \tag{1}$$

$$\forall x, y \; P(x,y) \wedge P(y,x) \rightarrow x = y \tag{2}$$

$$\forall x, y, z \; P(x,y) \wedge P(y,z) \rightarrow P(x,z) \tag{3}$$

where P denotes the *part-of* relation. Some mereological theories take the *proper-part-of* (a both asymmetric and transitive relation) as the basic primitive. However, even postulating axioms (1)-(3) to form the Ground Mereology (GM) is not uncontroversial. Many authors (see e.g., [21]) argue that transitivity does not systematically hold and an important distinction is assumed between the mereological *part-of* relation which is always transitive. The limitations of classical mereology to model the *part-of* relations between functional complexes (the component-functional complex relation) has been underlined in [17]. Due to many problems, mereology can hardly be applied in concrete applications as a theory of conceptual parts [13]. The theory (i) postulates constraints that cannot generally hold for *part-of* relations and (ii) is unable to characterize the distinctions which arise with the different types of *part-of* relations. One of the most significant problem with ground mereology is the assumption of unrestricted transitivity for the *part-of* relation. In many cases, this position is not tenable and some solutions have been suggested [21,17] as it will be discussed below.

2.2 *Part-of* Relations in Set Theory

Another popular mathematical theory for supporting partitions is set theory. Kinds, types, species and the like are usually treated as sets of their instances and sub-kinds, as subsets of these sets. Set theory complies with the granularity levels that are involved in the classification of reality by giving us a means of considering objects as elements of sets. For example, objects are single whole units within which further parts cannot be discovered. However, as underlined in [5], set theory suffers from limitations for representing *part-of* relationships, mainly because (i) it does not distinguish natural totalities (e.g., *person*) from artificial totalities (e.g., $\{afemur, Russell, aggregation\}$), (ii) its extensional nature poses problems e.g., with biological species which may remain the same while their instances may change (e.g., metamorphosis) and (iii) its inability to address multiple levels of representation, e.g., an organism is a totality of cells while being a totality of molecules, but their corresponding sets are distinct, since they have distinct members. In an extensional perspective, a set can be simply postulated by enumerating its members (or parts). This assumption is called ontological extravagance and should be ruled out from an ontological system as advocated in [17].

2.3 Related Works

The analysis which has been investigated in [21] is the more complete and formal taxonomy described so far. It is first based on the distinction between transitive and intransitive part-whole relations. Then, the types of relations are refined by considering the categories of the entity types participating in the relation (i.e., the relata). These categories are extracted from the DOLCE ontology of particulars [12,24] where each category is disjoint from the others. The taxonomy of *part-whole* relations is described in figure 1 (*s-part_of* and *f-part_of* stand respectively for structural part-of and functional part-of). The general part-whole relation subsumes (i) a mereological *part-of* relation which is transitive and (ii) a meronymic *mpart_of* which is assumed non-transitive, that is, neither transitive nor intransitive. Then a further sub-level is proposed by refining relations according to their relata. For example, *constituted_of* is subsumed by the *mpart_of* relation while it constrains its relata to be of the respective categories POB and M (i.e., Physical OBject and amount of Matter). While this classification is appealing, we do not agree with the decision ascribing *f-part_of* to be a sub-relation of *s-part_of*. We discuss this point later. Furthermore, while the author has pointed out that a categorization of relata is an important issue, its representation relies on first-order theories which are

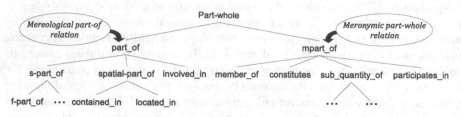

Fig. 1. A taxonomy of *part-of* relations (from [21])

less expressive than a dependently-typed system. In [6] a general and transitive *part-of* possibly non-transitive relation is suggested whose meaning is restricted to a ϕ-part where ϕ denotes a predicate modifier which formalizes additional conditions. However, as detailed in [20], such a view simply results in a ϕ-part which is non-transitive, i.e., some specific ϕ-part are transitive while some are intransitive. For that reason, the author suggests a different perspective to solve the issue of transitivity among part-of relations. According to his claims, x ϕ-*part-of* y should be described with a relative product of two binary relations, i.e., ϕ and *part-of* and should involve three relata. The proposed approach is interesting but suffers from insufficiencies since (i) the choice of an additional relation is quite arbitrary, (ii) the mechanism of ternary relation and "relative product" is not unified and the choice hands down to the user and (iii) the underlying first-order framework lacks expressiveness. In [31], the authors have tried to solve the ambiguities in *part-of* relations by providing six different kinds of meronymic relations (i.e., ϕ-part). Their work stem from an interesting idea, categorizing *part-of* relations, but it fails in many points due to a lack of formalization and precision.

3   Basis for the Support Language

In the conceptualization of information systems, [25] has pointed out that the related language should be able to "formally represent the relevant knowledge". This assertion yields that the conceptual language should (i) be expressive enough to represent the "relevant knowledge" and (ii) offer deduction capabilities to provide a valid (i.e., certified) model. For that purpose we use KDTL well-suited to comply with the constraint of expressiveness required for representing contextualized part-whole relations [1,10].

3.1   The KDTL Lower Layer

The lower layer of the language is a higher-order dependent type theory. It is intended to provide a certified and coherent map of a domain. More precisely, it relies on a dependent version of the simply typed λ-calculus which includes both a typing system and a higher order logic for reasoning. The constructive logic of KDTL is centered on the concept of proof rather than truth and follows the Curry-Howard isomorphism [18] in which proving is "equivalent" to computing (or querying a database). It enjoys the property of subject reduction which ensures that no illegal term will appear during the execution of a well-typed query in a well-typed conceptualization. Dependent types are based on the notion of indexed families of types and provide a high expressiveness since they can represent subset types, relations or constraints as typed structures. The typed mechanism distinguishes the universes[1] (for typing types themselves) $Type$ for data structures and $Prop$ for logic. In what follows, we denote by Γ an environment which formalizes the logical context. Each typing assertion is made with first checking its environment expressed as a finite sequence[2] of expressions of the form $x_i : T_i$ where x_i is a variable and T_i a term. The fundamental notion of typing judgment $\Gamma \vdash M : T$ where M and T are terms is read as "M has type T in Γ".

Definition 1. *Let Γ be a valid environment.*
  A term T is called a type in Γ if $\Gamma \vdash T : U$ for some universe U.
  A term M is called a proof object in Γ if $\Gamma \vdash M : T$ for some type T.
  A term M is well-typed if for some context Γ we have $\Gamma \vdash M : T$ for some T.
  A type T is inhabited in the context Γ if $\Gamma \vdash M : T$ for some M.
  A type T is well-formed if for some context Γ we have $\Gamma \vdash T : Type_i$ for some universe $Type_i$, $i \geq 0$.

To show that $M : T$ holds in a given context Γ, one has to show that either Γ contains that expression or that it can be obtained from the expressions in Γ with the help of type deduction rules i.e., type formation, introduction and elimination rules. The relation of instantiation (:) between a universal and its instance corresponds here to type inhabitation. The equality between terms in the ontological layer is ascribed to be coherent w.r.t. the Leibniz equality of the lower layer (two types are logically identical iff they have the same properties). It relates to the usual definition of the identity condition for an arbitrary property P, i.e., $P(x) \wedge P(y) \rightarrow (R(x,y) \leftrightarrow x = y)$ with a relation R satisfying this formula. This definition is carried out for any type in KDTL since equality between types requires the Leibniz equality. The major reason is that identity can be uniquely characterized if the language is an higher-order language in which quantification over all properties is possible. This property yields that Leibniz's Law, which is at the basis of identity in the lower layer of KDTL is expressible in this language.

A *dependent product type* is a function type where the range of the function changes according to the object to which the function is applied. The syntax for dependent function types is:

$$\Pi x : A \,.\, B(x)$$

Given a proof object a of type A, the product type asserts that there is a corresponding type $B[a]$[3] whose proofs are the result of its constructor. For instance, let us consider the product-type: $\Pi x : Person \,.\, Car[x]$ in which Car is a type constructor returning the cars which belong to a given person. It means that for a given instance x (e.g., $Peter$) of the type $Person$ it yields a set of proof objects whose type is $Car[Peter]$. In other words, we can manipulate the latter as an object which corresponds in fact to a "set" of values (here the cars which belong to $Peter$).

---

[1] Also called sorts.
[2] The sequence is ordered because any type in the sequence may depend on the previous variables.
[3] $B[a]$ means that all free occurrences of x have been substituted with a.

Given two types A and B, the type forming operation for the *dependent sum type* (or Σ-type) of $B[x]$ is expressed as $\Sigma x : A.B[x]$, x ranging over A. In other words,

$$\Sigma x : A . B[x]$$

is the type of pairs $\langle a, b \rangle$ where a is an object of type A and b is of type $B[a]$. Proof objects for dependent sums are pairs in which the second component depends on the first: $\langle a, b \rangle : (\Sigma x : A . B[x])$. For example let us consider the type $date : Type_i$ whose proof objects denote a particular year, month and day, i.e., a tuple [2]. Given N, the type of natural numbers, the dependent type $Nat[12]$, the type of natural numbers ranging from 1 to 12 and Nat(length of month m in year y), the type of natural numbers ranging from 1 to a maximum value itself depending on the value for the year y^4, then the *date* type could be defined with the sum-type:

$$date \triangleq \Sigma y : N . \Sigma m : Nat[12] . Nat[length\ of\ month\ m\ in\ year\ y]$$

A possible proof object for the type *date* is given by a tuple like $\langle 2011, \langle 2, 28 \rangle \rangle$. This exemplifies the capability of dependent types to describe in a concise way very expressive data structures. With $M : (\Sigma x : A.B)$, two operators extract the components of the pair such that $\pi_1(M) : A$ and $\pi_2(M) : B[\pi_1(M)]$. The interesting point is that available tools exist (e.g., the Coq theorem prover [3]) making more exploitable the theoretical picture.

3.2 The KDTL Higher Layer

In KDTL, kinds, properties and formal (ontological) relations are the basic components of the core ontology (see [1] for more details). A kind is considered as a canonical concept, assumption which is in line with the existence of "natural types", i.e., it can be identified as a type in isolation and relates to what is called an "atomic concept" in DL. Using kinds instead of unary predicates for the ontological categories (i) gives the possibility to find an unintended application of n-ary predicates during the type checking (e.g., for non well-typed kinds) and (ii) offers a rich structural knowledge representation by means of partially ordered kinds. Properties result from the aggregation of atomic properties depending on this kind (e.g., relational properties or predicates). For example we consider a kind hierarchy derived from the DOLCE taxonomy of particulars in which directly subsumed kinds are disjoint from each others [24,12][5]. The highest level denotes the kind *particular* (PT) which subsumes *endurants*[6] (ED), *perdurants* (PD), *qualities* (Q) and *abstract* entities (AB). In the following the is_a relation will be denoted $\leqslant$. We do not address here other issues such as existential dependence although it is easily accounted for with dependent types.

4 Contextualized Parthood

It is well-established that some *part-of* relations are always transitive (e.g., spatial and temporal *part-of*) while others are more problematic. In this paper, we claim that, fol-

---

[4] e.g., using a case construct.

[5] Without its logical apparatus.

[6] Endurants are in time and have a temporal extension.

lowing [20,28,6]: (i) the basic binary *part-of* relation is transitive, (ii) non-transitive *part-of* relations can be easily accounted for in the unified framework of dependent type theory. In order to capture a finer semantics of *part-of* relations, we will introduce a contextualized version of these relations.

4.1 Subsumption and *part-of* Relations

We assume the usual position adopted in most formal ontologies in computer science, that terms result from a general categorization into universals (i.e., general entities) which are further refined in subcategories (e.g., properties) and particulars. Particulars are specific entities which exemplify universals but which cannot have themselves instances. Usually in object-oriented frameworks, classes (representation of universals) are defined according to their set of properties. KDTL departs from this choice by introducing kinds for which the set of properties is implicit (atomic kinds) while properties result from the dependency upon the particular they depend on. In such a way, properties are attached to a given particular (see the example at the end of this section).

Before discussing the *part-of* relation, the formal distinction between the so-called *is_a* relation (also called subsumption) and the *part-of* relation must be clarified. We defend the position here that the differences between *is_a* and *part-of* relations rely on the notion of (ontological) properties persistence. Suppose that we have a mathematical proximity space S in which parts are ordered by the inclusion relation $\subseteq$. Given two parts U and V, they are assigned the respective collections $A(U)$ and $A(V)$ of ontological properties owned by each of them. The possession of primitive ontological properties is said to be persistent if $U \subseteq V \rightarrow A(V) \subseteq A(U)$. The transposition of this relation to the typed framework requires the introduction of universes (i.e., types of types which are closed under type-forming operations) together with their cumulative hierarchy i.e., $Univ_i \subseteq Univ_{i+1}$ (see e.g., [23]). Restricting ourselves to universes within a cumulative hierarchy instead of parts in a mathematical space is coherent as far as it relies on the Leibniz equality asserting that types (or universes) are equal iff they have the same properties. Then, ordering of universes extends the Leibniz equality to the inclusion relation using subsets of properties. Interpreting ontologies as universes, the *is_a* relation in a domain ontology is seen as an inclusion between collections of properties which inhere in parts in the universe.

Axiom 1. *Given two universals U, V and their respective collections of properties $Pr(U)$ and $Pr(V)$, if the relation is persistent that is, $Pr(V) \subseteq Pr(U)$, then $U\,is\_a\,V$ holds.*

Using a dependent type, it becomes possible to define a concept with a collection of properties. This collection is contextualized to a domain ontology and if we switch to another domain ontology, the collection may change as well. For example, the collection of properties $CP\_HumHeart$ for a given human heart is given by the parameterized nested Σ-type:

$$CP\_HumHeart[x : HumanHeart] := (x_1 : Volume \times x_2 : Age \times$$
$$\Sigma x_3 : Pump \,.\, FunctionAs[x, x_3])$$

Notice there must exist a proof (e.g., value in the table of a Database) for the collection of properties to be proved. It is important to see that the type which stands for the collection of properties depends on a particular heart, say $h1$, is $CP\_HumHeart[h1]$ and if we switch to another heart (e.g., $h2$) then we get another type $CP\_HumHeart[h2]$ reflecting distinct properties.

Clearly, the *part-of* relation is non-persistent (otherwise it would be a *is_a* relation). It follows that the collections of properties for each universal within a *part-of* relation are not in the inclusion relation but this property does not rule out a possible intersection between these collections. Assuming that the strong property of non-persistence for *part-of* relations is not sufficient then it must be refined in order to cope with the multiple constraints which inhere in the formalization of part-whole relations. For example, a classification such as the hierarchy of [21] is a first step in this direction.

4.2   Analysis of *part-of* Relations

A first attempt to distinguish different "kinds" of *part-of* relations has been to narrow the meaning of being a part with the introduction of a ϕ-*part-of* [6] where ϕ is intended to be a predicate modifier (e.g., "by requiring that parts make a direct contribution to the functioning of the whole"). However, as discussed in [20] this assumption is not sufficient to solve ambiguities and even, it cannot explain why some specific ϕ-parts are transitive and why others are intransitive. In [20], the author advocates for either a relative product of two relations (ϕ and *part-of*) or a ternary relation. First, which of these two alternatives should be applied in any situation is unclear and second, the additional relation lacks expressiveness and generality. We depart from the ϕ-part for modal reasons and rather argue that a proper modeling only requires a hierarchy of contextualized types. As a consequence more knowledge is required to clearly account for relations built on the transitive *part-of* relation. For that purpose the *part-of* relation is made more precise (i) by constraining the type of each argument (ii) using finer dependencies with dependent type and (iii) adding contextualized properties to refined types. Assuming that the context denotes conditions above which some assertion holds, we claim that a contextualized structure denoted C_Rel can be a possible candidate to solve this issue. The question arises now what can be the context for the *part-of* relation. By contextualized *part-of* relation, we mean (i) restricting the domain of arguments with a contextualized intent and (ii) ascribing a relevant (meta)property to the *part-of* relation according to its context of use. We first specify a necessary transitive relation denoted $PartOf$ using entities as arguments (PT is the root of the kind taxonomy). This relation formalizes a broad and basic sense of part.

$$C\_Rel \triangleq \Sigma x : Kind . \Sigma y : Kind . Relation[x, y]$$
$$PartOf \triangleq \Sigma x : PT . \Sigma y : PT . POR[x, y]$$

with POR denoting the partial order relation and assuming that $PartOf \leqslant C\_Rel$, $PT \leqslant Kind$ and $POR \leqslant Relation$. The contextualized relation C_PartOf first restricts the scope of the arguments with $K_1 \leqslant PT$ and $K_2 \leqslant PT$.

$$C\_PartOf \triangleq \Sigma x_1 : K_1 . \Sigma x_2 : K_2 . POR[x_1, x_2]$$
$$C\_PartOf \leqslant PartOf$$

The second restriction is achieved with the specification of a particular (meta)property MP (see section 4.1) for a C_PartOf relation:

$$C'\_PartOf \triangleq \Sigma u : C\_PartOf . MP[u]$$
$$C'\_PartOf \leqslant C\_PartOf$$

The latter formalizes a contextualized *part-of* relation both with restricted arguments and with an appropriate (meta)property. Once the *part-of* relation has been contextualized, there is a need to explain when their composition yields a transitive relation. The following axioms addresses this issue.

Axiom 2. *Given two C_PartOf relations with the respective (meta)properties MP and MP', then transitivity applies with their composition iff (i) their relata are co-ercible (i.e., relata of one part-of relation subsumes relata from the other) (ii) $MP = MP'$ and (iii) these properties are preserved in the composition.*

Notice that (i) and (ii) yield that the two relations are coercible. Let us investigate this result on some challenging $PartOf$ relations.

The $SubQuantityOf$ Relation. Using a typed framework will constrain the part and the whole to some types within a given environment. For example, assuming that M denotes some matter, the $PartOf$ relation can be restricted as follows:

$$\Sigma x : M . \Sigma y : M . POR[x, y]$$

However, one can observe that a smaller amount of matter (part) is related to a whole quantity of matter in which either the part and the whole may refer to identical or distinct type of stuff [14,21]. Two kinds of contextualized relations are appropriate for the case at hand, i.e., $ChemCompSubQuantityOf$ and $VolSubQuantityOf$, denoting respectively "sub chemical component of" and "sub volumes of" which are sub-relations of the *part-of* relation. There is inclusion between meta-properties of each of these relations and the *part-of* relation which means that each of them inherits the transitivity property from $PartOf$. Since what is expected to be described is a non-transitive relation [21], applying axiom 2 should provide a very simple solution relying on an application context. Then, let us show that transitivity occurs iff the two relations share the same application context.

$$ChemCompSubQuantityOf \triangleq$$
$$\Sigma u : (\Sigma x : M . \Sigma y : M . POR[x, y]) . ChemicalComposition[u] \quad (4)$$
$$VolSubQuantityOf \triangleq$$
$$\Sigma v : (\Sigma x : M . \Sigma y : M . POR[x, y]) . Volume[v] \quad (5)$$

with the obvious subsumptions:

$$ChemCompSubQuantityOf \leqslant PartOf$$
$$VolSubQuantityOf \leqslant PartOf$$

It yield that the transitivity requires the context preservation for the *part-of* relation. Let us consider the particular relations (the nested pair ensures that we are speaking about the same entity, i.e., $\pi_1 \pi_2 x$ in $R2$ is the same entity as y in $R1$):

$$R1 \triangleq \Sigma u : (\Sigma x : Salt . \Sigma y : SeaWater . POR[x, y]) . ChemicalComposition[u]$$
$$R2 \triangleq \Sigma u : (\Sigma x : R1 . \Sigma y : Ocean . POR[\pi_1 \pi_2 x, y]) . Volume[u]$$

We obtain two distinct relations $R1$ and $R2$ with $R1 \leqslant ChemCompSubQuantityOf$ and $R2 \leqslant VolSubQuantityOf$. When applying axiom 2, since $R1$ and $R2$ are not sub-relations of the same relation type ($R1$ holds within the context of a chemical composition while $R2$ is involved within the context of a volume assessment), then their instances cannot satisfy the transitivity rule. Since there is no preservation of the context of application for these relations, they are intransitive and the salt cannot be considered as a sub quantity of the ocean. Now, if we consider the relations:

$$R3 \triangleq \Sigma u : (\Sigma x : GlassOfWine . \Sigma y : BottleOfWine . POR[x, y]) . Volume[u]$$
$$R4 \triangleq \Sigma u : (\Sigma x : R3 . \Sigma y : BarrelOfWine . POR[\pi_1 \pi_2 x, y]) . Volume[u]$$

Using axiom 2 the premises say that $R3$ and $R4$ are subrelations of the same relation type, then their instances satisfy the law of transitivity. They hold within the same context of application i.e., the volume assessment. It follows that transitivity holds in that case according to the results in [21].

The $FunctionalPartOf$ Relation. According to many authors [16,30,20], there are both cases of transitivity and cases of non-transitivity for the functional *part-of*. As pointed out in [30], the functional *part-of* should be attached to the lexical categories that are used for representing the part and the whole. First using types will comply with this constraint. Second, the point here is that any functioning part is an endurant (ED) [21], and as such, it can have a temporal extension. We do not discuss temporal extensions here since we are mainly concerned with the correct (atemporal) conceptualization of *part-of* relations. We describe two distinct cases, one which illustrate transitive relations and the other which deals with intransitive relations.

(1): A given nucleus is *part-of* this cell, this cell is *part-of* the heart, but yet this nucleus is not *part-of* the heart.

(2): Any carburetor is a functional *part-of* an engine, and any engine is a functional *part-of* a machine, e.g., a car, therefore any carburetor is a functional *part-of* a machine, e.g., a car.

First, the $PartOf$ relation can be restricted as follows:

$$\Sigma x : ED . \Sigma y : ED . POR[x, y]$$

Two kinds of contextualized relations are then introduced, i.e., $IndFunctionalPartOf$ and $CollFunctionalPartOf$, denoting respectively individually-dependent functional *part-of* and collectively-dependent functional *part-of*, which are also sub-relations of the *part-of* relation. As previously stated, each of them inherits the transitivity property from $PartOf$. Then, let us show how the application context will disambiguate the issue of transitivity between the two relations.

$$IndFunctionalPartOf \triangleq$$
$$\Sigma u : (\Sigma x : ED . \Sigma y : ED . POR[x,y]) . IndividFuncDepend[u] \quad (6)$$
$$CollFunctionalPartOf \triangleq$$
$$\Sigma v : (\Sigma x : ED . \Sigma y : ED . POR[x,y]) . CollectivFuncDepend[v] \quad (7)$$

with the subsumptions:

$$IndFunctionalPartOf \leqslant PartOf$$
$$CollFunctionalPartOf \leqslant PartOf$$

Let us formalize the particular relations and check if the contextual property is preserved through their composition :

$$F1 \triangleq \Sigma u : (\Sigma x : Nucleus . \Sigma y : Cell . POR[x,y]) . IndividFuncDepend[u]$$
$$F2 \triangleq \Sigma u : (\Sigma x : F1 . \Sigma y : Heart . POR[\pi_1 \pi_2 x, y]) . CollectivFuncDepend[u]$$

with $F1 \leqslant IndFunctionalPartOf$ and $F2 \leqslant CollFunctionalPartOf$. The relation $F1$ holds within the context of an individual functional *part-of*, that is a single part is required in the whole (the nucleus). Alternatively, $F2$ needs the context of a collective functional *part-of* (a collection of cells contributes to the functioning of the heart). Then, applying axiom 2, instances of $F1$ and $F2$ are of different types which reflects the fact that there is no preservation of the context of application for these relations. It follows that, for $F1$ and $F2$ transitivity fails showing that a nucleus cannot be considered as a sub functional *part-of* the heart.

For case 2, we specify the following relations:

$$F3 \triangleq \Sigma u : (\Sigma x : Carburetor . \Sigma y : Engine . POR[x,y]) . IndividFuncDepend[u]$$
$$F4 \triangleq \Sigma u : (\Sigma x : F3 . \Sigma y : Car . POR[\pi_1 \pi_2 x, y]) . IndividFuncDepend[u]$$

Using axiom 2 it is easy to see that the two relations $F3$ and $F4$ are coercibles, i.e., they are composed within the same context of application (the $IndFunctionalPartOf$ relation). Then, transitivity holds in that case as explained in [30].

Organizational *part-of*. Another interesting case of problematic *part-of* relation is the organizational *part-of* [20] also called $memberOf$ (see e.g., [21]) with a sub-relation called $member - collective$ [17]. Let us consider the following well-known example. A person P is member of (*part-of*) the basketball club BC, and BC is member of (*part-of*) the National Federation of Basketball (NFB), but P is not a member of (*part-of*) of NFB. Here the *part-of* relation is restricted to the kinds SOB (social objects) or POB (physical objects. These two cases can be separately treated. For the sake of simplicity, we only describe the case of social objects and the *part-of* relation is written: $\Sigma x : SOB . \Sigma y : SOB . POR[x,y]$ Similarly to the previous subsection, and following [17], two relations can be specified, i.e., $IndOrganizationalPartOf$

and $IntegrOrganizationalPartOf$, with the respective meanings, individual organizational *part-of* and integral organizational *part-of* (integral whole). Using the same corresponding definitions and substituting the respective definitions, we get:

$$IndivOrganizationalPartOf \triangleq \Sigma u : (\Sigma x : SOB .$$
$$\Sigma y : SOB . POR[x, y]) . IndividOrgaDepend[u] \tag{8}$$
$$IntegrOrganizationalPartOf \triangleq \Sigma v : (\Sigma x : SOB .$$
$$\Sigma y : SOB . POR[x, y]) . IntegralOrgaDepend[v] \tag{9}$$

For the case at hand, we specify the relations:

$$O1 \triangleq \Sigma u : (\Sigma x : Person . \Sigma y : BC . POR[x, y]) . IndividOrgaDepend[u]$$
$$O2 \triangleq \Sigma u : (\Sigma x : O1 . \Sigma y : NFB . POR[\pi_1\pi_2 x, y]) . IntegralOrgaDepend[u]$$

The relation $O1 \leqslant IndivOrganizationalPartOf$ holds within the context of an individual organizational *part-of* (individual-integral whole), while $O2 \leqslant IntegrOrganiza$ *tionalPartOf* needs the context of an integral organizational *part-of* (integral whole-integral whole). Then, using axiom 2, there is no preservation of the context of application for these relations and the relation is intransitive (NFB has clubs as members, not individuals while BC has individuals as members). This result has been generalized for member-collective relations which are intransitive [17].

The Quantitative $PartOf$ Relation. Finally, a more challenging case is the large spatial *part-of* described in [20]. If the part x is a 60%-spatial *part-of* y and y is a 60%-spatial *part-of* z, then x cannot possibly be a 60%-spatial *part-of* z because x is necessarily a 36%-spatial *part-of* z. A $60\_spatialPartOf$ relation can be written as:

$$60\_spatialPartOf \triangleq \Sigma x_1 : S_1 . \Sigma x_2 : S_2\_60[x1] . POR[x1, x2]$$

The point here is that x_2 is not of kind S_2 but rather a constrained version of it with a numeric equation (for example if n denotes a natural number, $x < 5 * n$ is a type which represents the set of values that are less than $5 * n$). Therefore it is easy to built the type $S_2\_60[x1]$ which depends on x_1, i.e., $x_2 < 0.6 * x_1$. Here the contextualized form is achieved with dependent types. Due to the typing, the transitivity requires that the relations between x and y, y and z and x and z are of the same kind. This is clearly not the case since the relation between x and z has the kind:

$$36\_spatialPartOf \triangleq \Sigma x_1 : S_1 . \Sigma x_2 : S_2\_36[x1] . POR[x1, x2]$$

and then, for this numerical constraint, the particular relation is intransitive.

5   Conclusion

It is demonstrated that KDTL can model several non-trivial aspects of transitivity for *part-of* relations such as meta-level contextual properties. Types exploit regularities that can be used to make predictions about relational interactions. Usual representations of the *part-of* relation under-specify the categories of the entity types (relata) involved in the relation [21] and using a typed language solves this issue. We have suggested here a unified representation involving the high expressiveness of dependent type theory. Contextualizing the properties of the *part-of* relation is the major contribution of this work with the purpose of solving most challenges inherent in a correct representation. We have specified the most discussed relations such as $SubQuantityOf$, $FunctionalPartOf$, $memberOf$, and a more complex one such as the quantitative *part-of* relation. In each case it is shown how to take in consideration contextual properties in a simple an unified way. This result has been made possible due to the expressiveness of dependent types and type checking allowing to guarantee the consistency of typed expressions. KDTL has been implemented in Coq [10] and interfaced with a triple store database. Further work includes a reasoning system for automatic conceptualization of *part-of* relations.

References

1. Barlatier, P., Dapoigny, R.: A Type-Theoretical Approach for Ontologies: the Case of Roles. Applied Ontology 7(3), 311–356 (2012)
2. Jacobs, B.: Categorical Logic and Type Theory. Studies in Logic and the Foundations of Mathematics, vol. 141. Elsevier (1999)
3. Bertot, Y., Castéran, P.: Interactive Theorem Proving and Program Development Coq'Art: The Calculus of Inductive Constructions. Texts in Theoretical Computer Science. An EATCS series. Springer (2004)
4. Bittner, T., Smith, B.: A Theory of Granular Partitions. In: Duckham, M., Goodchild, M.F., Worboys, M. (eds.) Foundations of Geographic Information Science, ch. 7, pp. 124–125 (2003)
5. Bittner, R., Donelly, M., Smith, B.: Individuals, Universals, Collections: On the Foundational Relations of Ontology. Frontiers in Artificial Intelligence, vol. 114. IOS Press, Amsterdam (2010)
6. Casati, R., Varzi, A.C.: Parts and places: the structures of spatial representation. MIT Press (1999)
7. Cirstea, H., Coquery, E., Drabent, W., Fages, F., Kirchner, C., Maluszynski, J., Wack, B.: Types for Web Rule Languages: a preliminary study, technical report A04-R-560, PROTHEO - INRIA Lorraine - LORIA (2004)
8. Dapoigny, R., Barlatier, P.: Modeling Contexts with Dependent Types. Fundamenta Informaticae 104(4), 293–327 (2010)
9. Dapoigny, R., Barlatier, P.: Towards Ontological Correctness of Part-whole Relations with Dependent Types. In: Procs. of the Sixth Int. Conference (FOIS 2010), pp. 45–58 (2010)
10. Dapoigny, R., Barlatier, P.: Modeling Ontological Structures with Type Classes in Coq. In: Pfeiffer, H.D., Ignatov, D.I., Poelmans, J., Gadiraju, N. (eds.) ICCS 2013. LNCS, vol. 7735, pp. 135–152. Springer, Heidelberg (2013)
11. Angelov, K., Enache, R.: Typeful Ontologies with Direct Multilingual Verbalization. In: Rosner, M., Fuchs, N.E. (eds.) CNL 2010. LNCS(LNAI), vol. 7175, pp. 1–20. Springer, Heidelberg (2012)
12. Gangemi, A., Guarino, N., Masolo, C., Oltramari, A., Schneider, L.: Sweetening ontologies with DOLCE. In: Gómez-Pérez, A., Benjamins, V.R. (eds.) EKAW 2002. LNCS(LNAI), vol. 2473, pp. 166–181. Springer, Heidelberg (2002)
13. Gerstl, P., Pribbenow, S.: Midwinters, end games, and body parts: a classification of part-whole relations. International Journal of Human-Computer Studies 43(5-6), 865–889 (1995)

14. Guizzardi, G.: Ontological Foundations for Structural Conceptual Models, University of Twente, Centre for Telematics and Information Technology (2005)
15. Guizzardi, G., Masolo, C., Borgo, S.: In Defense of a Trope-Based Ontology for Conceptual Modeling: An Example with the Foundations of Attributes, Weak Entities and Datatypes. In: Embley, D.W., Olivé, A., Ram, S. (eds.) ER 2006. LNCS, vol. 4215, pp. 112–125. Springer, Heidelberg (2006)
16. Guizzardi, G.: The Problem of Transitivity of Part-Whole Relations in Conceptual Modeling Revisited. In: van Eck, P., Gordijn, J., Wieringa, R. (eds.) CAiSE 2009. LNCS, vol. 5565, pp. 94–109. Springer, Heidelberg (2009)
17. Guizzardi, G.: Representing Collectives and Their Members in UML Conceptual Models: An Ontological Analysis. In: Trujillo, J., et al. (eds.) ER 2010. LNCS, vol. 6413, pp. 265–274. Springer, Heidelberg (2010)
18. Howard, W.A.: The formulae-as-types notion of construction. In: To H.B. Curry: Essays on Combinatory Logic, Lambda Calculus and Formalism, pp. 479–490. Academic Press (1980)
19. Husserl, E.: Logische Untersuchungen. Zweiter Band, Untersuchungen zur Phänomenologie und Theorie der Erkenntnis. Niemeyer, Halle (1901); Eng. trans. by Findlay, J.N.: Logical Investigations, vol. 2. Routledge & Kegan Paul, London (1970)
20. Johansson, I.: On the Transitivity of the Parthood Relations. In: Relations and Predicates, pp. 161–181. Ontos-Verlag (2004)
21. Keet, C.M., Artale, A.: Representing and reasoning over a taxonomy of part-whole relations. Applied Ontology 3(1-2), 91–110 (2008)
22. Leśniewski, S.: Podstawy ogólnej teoryi mnogosci. I. Moskow: Prace Polskiego Kola Naukowego w Moskwie, Sekcya matematyczno-przyrodnicza (1916); English translation by Barnett, D. I.: Foundations of the General Theory of Sets. I, In: Leśniewski, S., Collected Works, Surma, S.J., Srzednicki, J., Barnett, D.I., Rickey, F.V. (eds.), vol. 1, pp. 129–173. Kulwer, Dordrecht (1992)
23. Luo, Z.: Computation and Reasoning, vol. 11. Oxford Science Publications (1994)
24. Masolo, C., Borgo, S., Gangemi, A., Guarino, N., Oltramari, A.: Ontology Library (D18), Laboratory for Applied Ontology-ISTC-CNR (2003)
25. Mylopoulos, J., Borgida, A., Jarke, M., Koubarakis, M.: Telos: Representing Knowledge About Information Systems. ACM Trans. on Information Systems 8(4), 325–362 (1990)
26. Pribbenow, S.: Meronymic Relationships: From Classical Mereology to Complex Part-Whole Relations. In: Green, R., Bean, C.A. (eds.) The Semantics of Relationships, pp. 35–50. Kluwer, Dordretch (2002)
27. Setzer, A.: Object-Oriented Programming in Dependent Type Theory. Trends in Functional Programming 7, 91–108 (2007)
28. Simons, P.: Parts: A Study in Ontology. Clarendon Press, Oxford (1987)
29. Varzi, A.C.: Parts, wholes, and part-whole relations: The prospects of mereotopology. Data and Knowledge Engineering 20(3), 259–286 (1996)
30. Vieu, L.: On the transitivity of functional parthood. Applied Ontology 1, 147–155 (2006)
31. Winston, M.E., Chaffin, R., Herrman, D.: A taxonomy of part-whole relations. Cognitive Science 11(4), 417–444 (1987)

Interpreting Vague and Ambiguous Referring Expressions by Dynamically Binding to Properties of the Context Set

Dustin A. Smith and Henry Lieberman*

MIT Media Lab; 20 Ames St. Cambridge, MA 02139 USA
{dustin,lieber}@media.mit.edu

Abstract. Referring expressions with vague and ambiguous modifiers, such as "a quick visit" and "the big meeting," are difficult for computers to interpret because their words' meanings are in part defined by context, which changes throughout the course of an interpretation. In this paper, we present an approach to interpreting context-dependent referring expressions that uses *dynamic binding*. During the incremental interpretation of a referring expression, a word's meaning can be defined in part by properties from the current candidate referents — its denotation up to the previous word for the tentative interpretation.

1 Referring Expressions in Context

For a hearer to understand the *intended meaning* of a speaker's utterance, he must make inferences based not only on evidence in the utterance's linguistically-encoded *surface meaning* but also on outside information, collectively referred to as **discourse context** (for an introduction, read [1, Ch. 1]). Nowhere is this more apparent than in linguistic *reference* — when a speaker attempts to use her utterance to convey the identity of some entities (or set of entities) to her audience. The speaker does so by producing a **referring expression**, namely: "a description of an entity [or entities] that enables the hearer to identify that entity in a given context" [2]. Consider the referring expression "<u>it</u>": it seems evident that for the hearer to resolve what meaning the speaker intended by using the pronoun, he must draw from information outside of the pronoun itself. We have found that by focusing on the ubiquitous task of **reference**, large portions of context can be constrained so that others can be investigated.

In general, it is the hearer's job to use information from the context to determine which of a presumed set of meanings the speaker intended when she chose to use a particular *lexical item* (e.g., a morpheme, word, or idiom). And although the lexical items in an utterance arrive in a linear order, the hearer may need to backtrack and revise his decisions based on subsequent information. If the hearer does not revise an incorrect decision, he will likely fail to arrive at the speaker's intended meaning. The linguistic phenomena of ambiguity and vagueness are

---

* We are grateful for the support from the sponsors of the MIT Media Lab.

P. Brézillon, P. Blackburn, and R. Dapoigny (Eds.): CONTEXT 2013, LNAI 8175, pp. 15–30, 2013.

two root causes of interpretive decision points. In certain contexts, these phenomena make linguistic communication efficient for humans [3, 4] and extremely challenging for computational models.

Our goal is to build a computational model of reference that is able to represent only the relevant linguistic choices, and then make the correct decisions. We approach the problem in two stages: (1) making the system *expressive* enough to capture desired linguistic phenomena by ensuring the system is capable of representing all choice points that lead to the desired output[1] and (2) finding a control algorithm that minimizes the number of choice points considered to produce the desired output.

Unfortunately, theories of discourse context are rarely defined precisely; and so it is difficult to separate the components of context that influence the meaning of lexical items from those that do not. We attempt to rectify this: in section 1.1, we summarize several ways context can influence the interpretation of referring expressions, and in section 1.3, describe a constrained communication task in which context's influence on lexical items can be modeled directly. Afterward, we present an incremental model of reference interpretation that defines the meanings of vague (gradable) and lexically ambiguous adjectives using information from the on-line interpretation.

1.1   What Components of Discourse Context Influence Reference Interpretation?

In the study of language, the term "context" has been used to connote a wide range of information that is available to the speaker or hearer. A skeptic might take it to mean *any information that outside the scope of the theory at hand.*

Tomasello described **discourse context** as "information that is available to [both speaker and hearer] in the environment, along with what is 'relevant' to the social interaction, that is, what each participant sees as relevant and knows that the other sees as relevant as well—and knows that the other knows this as well, and so on, potentially ad infinitum. This kind of shared intersubjective context is what we may call following [5] **common ground**...it takes [hearer and speaker] beyond their own egocentric perspective on things" [6, pp. 76].

Of course, common ground is a fiction: in addition to being paradoxically recursive, neither speaker nor hearer are omniscient so neither could ever know the true common ground. However, as a theoretical concept it may still be useful to envisage such an idealized state both the speaker and hearer's inferential processes work toward in order to make the reference task succeed. As such, the speaker and hearer each have their own notions of success. The speaker wants to convey the referents to the hearer, so it is useful for her to know what he knows or is capable of inferring. Similarly for the hearer, the speaker's act of reference contains "an implicit assurance that he has enough information to uniquely identify the referent, taking into account the semantic content of the

---

[1] Because our system is *incremental*, the "desired output" of a referring expression can be evaluated at intermediate stages.

referring expression and information from the context, whether situational (i.e. currently perceivable), linguistic, or mental (i.e. memory and knowledge)" [7].

For reference tasks, the knowledge speaker and hearer can be expected to have minimally includes:

Shared Tasks. The speaker and hearer's shared tasks determine what is relevant and important to them, and thus their communication goals as well. Using the pragmatic theory of [8], the information needs of the task constitute its **questions under discussion**, which provide the impetus for communication. From our computational perspective, we take a *referential* question under discussion to be an *unbounded typed variable* in a plan. The question is answered when the variable is bound to a knowledge representation that meets certain type restrictions. Questions under discussion give rise to communication goals, which are fulfilled by communication acts toward these goals (e.g., speaking, gesturing). For reference tasks, the communication goal is at least in part referential: to make the intended referent(s) mutually known to hearer and speaker (i.e., in the proverbial common ground).

Referential Domain. Entities in the **environment**, which are mutually perceived, along with concepts from **background knowledge** constitute potential targets of referring expressions.

Dialogue History. The speaker and hearer can be expected to remember the previous dialogue acts. For reference, this is especially important because after a speaker introduces a referent to discourse, she typically mentions it again—often using abbreviated referring expressions [9–11]. From a computational perspective, the referents in the dialogue history could be thought of as *symbol table* used by compilers and interpreters to map each symbol to its type, scope and value—namely, its location in memory.

Instead of describing these contextual constraints individually, we will introduce an abstraction called the **context set**. It is a construct from theoretical linguistics that represents the "live options"—viable candidates for an interpretation process, which evolves over the course of dialogue [12]. We take this to be the hypothesis space of interpretations. For utterances outside of reference, the concept of "what constitutes an interpretation" is difficult to pin down; however, for reference tasks, we take the **context set** to be a representation of the *referential domain* plus all of their combinatoric possibilities.

1.2   Characterizing the Two Reference Tasks

The referential domain and its valid means of combination are constrained by information from the task, dialogue history, and lexical-semantic knowledge. By constraining each of these elements, then, at least for reference tasks, we can replace the illusive concept of context with a single construct, the context set, which expresses the sum of all contextual constraints on the targets for interpretation. We will now attempt to formalize the broader communication tasks of the speaker and hearer. When referring, the speaker and hearer complete two structurally similar tasks. The speaker completes a **referring expression generation (REG)** task: given an initial *context set* (defined in Section 1.4) and a designated member of it called the *target set*, she produces a *referring expression* which she expects will enable the hearer to infer her intended target set from the rest of the elements in the context set, called *distractors* [13]:

$$\text{REG}(\text{context set}, \text{target set}) \rightarrow \text{referring expression} \tag{1}$$

A hearer completes a **referring expression interpretation (REI)** task: given a referring expression, his goal is to jointly infer the initial context set and the targets that the speaker intended:

$$\text{REI}(\text{referring expression}) \rightarrow \langle\text{context set}, \text{target set}\rangle_1 \dots \langle\text{context set}, \text{target set}\rangle_n \tag{2}$$

Reference tasks do not always succeed. We define a **reference failure** as a mismatch between the speaker's intended target set and the one (or ones) yielded by the hearer's interpretation. If the referring expression leads the hearer to mutually exclusive interpretations (e.g., $n > 1$), we call the referring expression *uncertain*. In the next section, we describe some of the issues that lead to these uncertain referring expressions, which in turn can lead to reference failures.

1.3   Restricting the Discourse Context

Although all of the aforementioned components of context can potentially impact reference interpretation [14, 11, 15], to avoid their influence we can restrict the task setting so that many aspects of context *prior* to an utterance are constrained. This allows us to model how lexical units interact with context. We do this by:

- using a **referential domain** that is co-present [16], which we achieved by using *visual scenes*. The referring expressions described in this paper will be interpreted with respect to one of two referential domains, CIRCLES and KINDLES, which are expressed as visual scenes assumed to be mutually known.
- when using descriptive referring expression (i.e., noun phrases), ensuring that it is purely referential and does not serve ulterior communication goals.
- embedding referring expressions within a consistent and simple task context. Presumably there is always an implicit task context that is motivating the hearer to cooperate, so it is important that at least the local goal be controlled [17, pp. 313]. In psycholinguistic research about reference production, it is routine to give hearer's an imperative sentence requiring them to manipulate physical referents (e.g., *Pass me the green cup*), this provides a neutral task context that is consistent across subjects.
- assuming there is no dialogue history: we have "one-shot referring expressions" [9].

Such one-shot, task-neutral, purely referential referring expressions in co-present visual domains are the focus of the paper. They allow us to investigate out

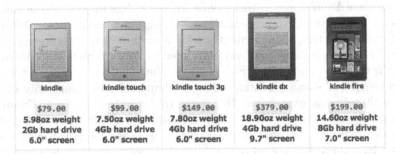

Fig. 1. The Amazon KINDLES referential domain containing 5 referents: k_1, k_2, k_3, k_4 and k_5

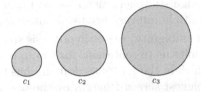

Fig. 2. The CIRCLES referential domain containing referents: c_1, c_2 and c_3

the context set evolves over the course of a single interpretation; and allow us to characterize the discourse context exclusively in terms of the elements in a referential domain (as we do in Section 1.4).

1.4 Formalizing the Context Set: The Hypothesis Space of Interpretations

By restricting our attention to one-shot, purely referential referring expressions, we can represent the context set in explicit detail.

A candidate **interpretation** represents hypothetical constraints on the initial context set and can be viewed *intensionally* as some epistemic data structure or *extensionally* by its **denotation**, denotation($\cdot$),[2] which enumerates the groups of targets that match its intensional description. For example, given the CIRCLES reference domain and the referring expression "the biggest one", the denotation is all of the possible targets that are consistent with its intension (which we represent using belief states): denotation("the biggest one") = $\{c_3\}$. Although the semantic, intensional meaning representations for "the biggest one" and "the blue circle" are presumably very different, their denotations are the same. The denotation of a referring expression provides one means to probe how people represent linguistic meanings—e.g., it is easy enough to ask a subject to "*select the second biggest green one*" from a visual scene.

Under our constrained reference task, we can describe the upper bounds of the context set's *denotational complexity* in terms of the referential domain, R, and the model's expressiveness. Keep in mind that there may be a large

---

[2] Commonly represented by $[\![\cdot]\!]$.

number of varied intensional descriptions for each denotation, whose number depends on the particular representation used (e.g., typically a logical form or attribute-valued matrix). The context set for a system that interprets (or generates) referring expressions that can only refer to *single targets* can maximally contain $|R|$ distinct denotations. For example, the singleton context set for the CIRCLES referential domain contains $|R| = 3$ elements, and would only be able to deal with referring expressions that refer to $\{c_1\}$, $\{c_2\}$ or $\{c_3\}$. Examples: denotation("the blue circle") $= \{c_3\}$ and denotation("the red triangle") $= \emptyset$.

If an interpreter can refer to sets, as do the approaches described in [18–20], it explores a hypothesis space containing $2^{|R|} - 1$ denotations, which is analogous to a **belief state**[3] about the singleton domain, R. An example in the CIRCLES domain: denotation("the green circles") $= \{c_1, c_2\}$.

To handle all of the linguistic phenomena we will describe in Section 2, we will want to represent multiple interpretations about sets (due to unspecific descriptions, vagueness and ambiguity) so our hypothesis space contains $2^{2^{|R|}-1} - 1$ interpretations. This permits us to represent, for example, the lexical ambiguity of the word "biggest", which in the KINDLES domain, has two senses: it can refer to the Kindle with the biggest screen ('big$_1$'), or the one with the biggest hard drive ('big$_2$'): denotation("the biggest kindle") $= \{k_4\} \oplus \{k_5\}$. We treat these two interpretations as mutually exclusive, represented by the $\oplus$ symbol. This state-space grows large quickly, however: for the CIRCLE domain, where $|R| = 3$, there are 127 denotations; while for KINDLE, where $|R| = 5$, there are over two billion. Fortunately, there are many ways to avoid this complexity [21].

2   Context-Sensitive Referring Expressions

2.1   Lexical Ambiguity

Lexical ambiguity is when a *lexical unit* maps to multiple meanings. Determining whether a lexical unit's meanings (*senses*) are truly the same can be challenging, because it is common for the various senses to all be related somehow (e.g., with polysemous words) [22, 23]. In other cases, a lexical unit's different senses are clearly disjoint (e.g., homonyms), as with the canonically ambiguous noun "bank", whose meanings include bank$_1$, *a financial institution*, and bank$_2$, *the land border along of a river*. Upon encountering ambiguity, the reader is confronted with a choice between alternative meanings.

(1.a) Let's go stop by the *bank*
(2.a) Let's go fish by the *bank*

---

[3] In artificial intelligence, the power-set of a set of propositions is commonly used to represent a *belief state*, which characterizes incomplete knowledge about an underlying set. Beliefs are an abstraction of any lower layer, so beliefs can be about beliefs about beliefs. Here, we use second-order belief states that are two layers removed from the referential domain to represent uncertainty about representations of sets of candidate targets.

Lexical ambiguity is also constrained by the initial context set. If (1.a) were uttered in a rural community that did not have any financial institutions but did have accessible rivers, we would expect the meaning of "<u>bank</u>" to only describe bank$_2$ (river); and, because it is singular and definite (i.e., begins with 'the'), it presupposes that the referring expression along with the initial context set is enough for the hearer to arrive at a target set containing a single river bank.

Psycholinguistic studies have given compelling evidence that readers' disambiguation choices are influenced by the referents that are available in the context set, and that readers update their context sets incrementally and frequently while reading. Such research, surveyed in [17], present subjects (or hearers) with a spoken referring expression in a visual scene (ensuring co-presence and common ground), and monitor the subject's eye movements (which tend to focus on the working target interpretation). For compositional theories, this implies that humans incrementally *evaluate* the semantic representation to yield its denotation [24], which implies syntax and semantics are tightly coupled. What this means is that when interpreting the referring expression online, by the time we have arrived at the ambiguous choice point, the interpretation has already updated to reflect the partial information imposed by the verb's selectional constraints and may bias us to favor one particular resolution:

(1.b) Let's go stop by <u>the *bank*</u> → bank$_1$ (finance)
(2.b) Let's go fish by <u>the *bank*</u> → bank$_2$ (river)

For our purpose of modeling human performance in the REG and REI tasks, these issues raise important computational questions, including:

Q1. What kind of interpreter will incrementally perform syntactic and semantic analysis, and allow the denotation to be available at each choice point?
Q2. At what granularity should choice points be represented?
Q3. Are the multiple senses of an ambiguous lexical unit first generated and subsequently filtered when they are incompatible with the initial context set, or generated as a function that operates on a partial interpretation?

2.2   Garden Paths and Incremental Interpretations

To illustrate the highly incremental nature of interpretation, observe that the reader's initial disambiguation choices, which produced the interpretations alluded to in (1.b) and (2.b), can be reversed by adding linguistic context. These examples produce the so-called *garden-path effect*, because they cause the reader to revise his initial ambiguity resolution decision in the face of new conflicting evidence:

(1.c) Let's go stop by <u>the *bank* of the Charles River</u> → bank$_2$ (river)
(2.c) Let's go fish by <u>the *Bank* of Commerce</u> → bank$_1$ (finance)

A reader, despite the fact the text of (1.a/1.b) is a prefix of (1.c), will react to the additional context flexibly by switching from one sense of *bank* to another.

This means the semantic content of her interpretation is *non-monotonic*: the combined meaning up to word w_{i+1} may not have been included in (or entailed from) the meaning up to word w_i; and this implies for the usage of "bank" in this instance that "not all mouths of rivers are financial institutions."

Q4. Are multiple interpretations constructed simultaneously (e.g., by taking all choices in parallel), or just one at a time (e.g., maintaining a single best interpretation and then backtracking when necessary)?

2.3   Vagueness and Gradable Adjectives

Another threat to recovering the speakers' intended reference is **vagueness**. The term "vagueness" itself is lexically ambiguous. Linguists and laypeople typically use it as vagueness₁ (insufficient information), which means (autologically), *insufficiently informative for the current purposes* [25]. An example of vagueness₁ (insufficient information) is:

(3) Let's meet for dinner at a restaurant

when there are more than one restaurants in the referential domain. The other sense, vagueness₂ (borderline cases), is better known to philosophers of language, and connotes something more specific: *predicates with unclear denotations—i.e. denotations containing borderline cases* [26]. This is a symptom found in many *gradable (scalar) adjectives* such as 'tall,' 'big,' and 'short.'

(4) Let's watch a *short* movie → *short for movie: less than 2 hours? 1.5 hours?*

Gradable adjectives impose a *relational constraint* between ordered values of an attribute that varies between referents in the target set and its distractors [27]. They can be problematic when there are referents whose values for that attribute are in the middle of the ordering. For example "expensive restaurants" may definitely include restaurants whose average meal costs $10 or less, definitely exclude those whose average meal price is more than $40, but create discourse confusion and chaos for restaurants whose average price is in between.

Referents that are "in between" are *borderline cases*, and in referring expressions these can cause reference failures [4]. For you to succeed at interpreting (4), "a short movie", you must pick (a) a *comparison class* that defines the set of movies relevant to your comparison, and (b) a *standard of comparison* that delineates $\text{SHORT}(x_i)$ from $\neg\text{SHORT}(x_{i-1})$ for the ordered elements x in the comparison class. Under the constrained reference task we described in 1.4, the comparison class (a) can be assumed to be the referents that are consistent with the current interpretation, leaving the standard, (b), as our main concern. Depending on how you set this standard, the interpreter may arrive at different interpretations.

Q5. How is the *standard of comparison* for gradable meanings chosen?
Q6. What representation allows interpretations to be individuated in a way that distinguishes vagueness₁ (insufficient information), vagueness₂ (borderline cases), and ambiguity?

3   Our Approach: Planning in Belief Space

We have developed a fast belief-state planner, AIGRE,[4] that can generate and interpret simple English referring expressions. In order to represent the combined constraints of all constraints accumulated up to the decision point of an ambiguous or vague lexical unit (i.e., **Q1**), AIGRE avoids traditional pipeline architectures and takes an integrated "lexicalized approach," following [28–31], in which each surface form (lexical unit) and its syntactic, semantic, and (conventional) pragmatic contributions are collectively represented in a *lexical entry* (**Q2**) and come into effect at the same time. This allows us to interleave decisions about *what* to say and *how* to say them [32].

This formulation reduces the entire generation task (REG) to choosing the actions whose effects achieve the speaker's communicational goal and putting them in the correct order, a formulation that bears a strong analogy with **automated planning**. However, instead of changing the state of the world, the actions change *belief-states*, which represent complete interpretations—implicitly representing all possible targets. For REI, we complete a **plan recognition** task of a similarly searching for a plan. Rather than being directed by a communication goal, fore the REI task, the action sequence is constrained to those that can produce the observed utterance and by a language model that enforces syntax constraints. The goal of the belief-state planner using heuristic search is to find a sequence of lexical units that map the initial belief state onto a target belief state (see [21] for more details).

Because belief states are complete interpretations, the planner is incremental and the denotations for all candidate interpretation can be output at any stage. The initial belief state is one of complete uncertainty—all $2^{|R|}$ target sets are possible; only as it accumulates information do the possibilities decrease. As we mentioned in Section 1.4, belief states have a strong connection with *context sets*, which we take to represent all target sets from all combined belief states throughout the interpretation process.

3.1   Representing Context-Sensitive Actions

AIGRE's lexicon is comprised of lexical units, which are belief-changing actions. Currently, AIGRE's lexicon is restricted to nouns and prenominal modifiers. Each action/word is an instantiation of an action class and has (1) a syntactic category (part of speech), (2) a lexical unit, (3) a specific semantic contribution—determined in part by its syntactic category, (4) a fixed lexical cost, and (5) a computed effect cost. Actions are defined by instantiating class instances:

- `GradableAdjective(lexeme='big', attribute='size')`
- `CrispAdjective(lexeme='blue', attribute='color', value='blue')`

---

[4] Automatic interpretation and generation of referring expressions. In French, it means "sour".

When instantiating an action, the first argument is its lexeme in its *root form*; the class' initialization method uses the root lexeme to instantiate variant derivative lexical units (e.g. plural, comparative, superlative, etc). Syntax constraints are expressed in the transitions between states by the *action proposal function*, which is given a state and returns valid actions.

The actions, which generate lexical items, operate on an interpretation and yield successors. Ambiguity and gradable meanings are modeled using non-deterministic actions (see Algorithms 1 and 2): they receive a belief state as input and lazily generate 0 or successors,[5] depending on the contents of the belief state. Thus part of a word's meaning can come from its interaction with the belief state. Not having any effects is analogous to not having its preconditions satisfied. This lends itself to a procedural semantics where the meaning of a given word can interact directly with the contents of a given hypothesis (interpretation, belief state) in the context set (**Q3**).

3.2   Crisp and Graded Adjectives

The semantic contribution of a CRISPADJECTIVE (e.g. *silk, John's, prime, pregnant*), is akin to traditional assignment: an attribute in the intensional representation is assigned a specific value. It is only non-deterministic when the parent state has members with multiple properties with the same attribute name.

Data: Initialized with an attribute name, a, and value, v
Input   : A search node, S, containing a belief state
Output: A successor search node, $\hat{S}$

foreach a *in* $S.getAttributesByName(attributeName)$ **do** breadth-first iteration of referents' attributes $= a$
   | create copy of S, named $\hat{S}$;
   | attempt to merge $\hat{S}.a$ with value v;
   | yield $\hat{S}$
end

Algorithm 1. Effects of a CRISPADJECTIVE. Belief states' properties represent partial information using *ranges* of values; they are updated by `merge` rather than `setter` methods (based on the *cell* datastructure of [33]).

Unlike CRISPADJECTIVE, a GRADABLEADJECTIVE does not require a `value` parameter when initialized, because its value comes from the partial interpretation it is applied to (**Q5**); it adds *intervals* values to the belief state's description rather than atomic values:

Gradable adjectives yield an effect for each same-named attribute (ambiguity) for each value (vagueness$_2$ (borderline cases)). For example, given the action

---

[5] Rather, they generate *effect functions* that operate on states. To simplify the exposition, we pretend our actions are like those of typical planners and generate states.

Data: Initialized attribute, a, and $minimize = False$
Input : A search node, S, containing a belief state
Output: Yields 0 or more search nodes, $\hat{S}$

foreach a *in S.getAttributesByName(attributeName)* **do** breadth-first iteration of referents' attributes $= a$

> **foreach** v *in S.getUniqueValues(a,minimize)* **do** iterate context set's unique, sorted values of a
>
>> create copy of S, named $\hat{S}$;
>> **if** *minimize* **then**
>>> | attempt to merge $\hat{S}.a$ with interval $(-\infty, v]$
>>
>> **else**
>>> | attempt to merge $\hat{S}.a$ with interval $[v, \infty)$
>>
>> **end**
>> yield $\hat{S}$;
>
> **end**

end

Algorithm 2. The lexical entry for a *gradable adjective* action: its job is to lazily yield successors for each sense (ambiguity) for each value (vagueness). Actions act on *belief states*, datastructures that represent an *intensional* description that picks out a subset of the context set.

BIG$_{JJ}$ applied to b_0 (about the KINDLE referential domain) yields a separate effect for each unique value of each unique attribute-path named size, producing 6 effects in total, BIG(b_0) → $e_0, e_1 \ldots e_6$. Three of the effects, when executed, would create target.size properties and the other three create target.hard_drive.size properties. Gradable adjectives' values are represented with an interval. For "big," e_0 would add (if it doesn't already exist) and then attempt to merge the belief state's target.size value with an interval beginning at the largest size value ($\theta = 7$) of a referent consistent with b_0.

3.3 Interpreting "the big ones" in Two Domains

To illustrate how AIGRE interprets a referring expression, "the big ones", which contains both ambiguity and vagueness$_2$ (borderline cases), we interpret it with respect to both domains.

For the KINDLES domain, denotation("the big ones") $= \{k_4, k_5\} \oplus \{k_2, k_3, k_4, k_5\} \oplus \{k_1, k_2, k_3, k_4, k_5\}$. For CIRCLES, denotation("the big ones") $= \{c_2, c_3\} \oplus \{c_1, c_2, c_3\}$. The diamonds correspond to the sum choices from the lexical ambiguity[6] ('big$_1$' versus 'big$_2$'), the ways one can set the standard of comparison for each sense of 'big'—at one extreme value for the standard, only the biggest element is BIG and at the other extreme *all* elements are considered BIG, along with other constraints like number agreement.

---

[6] The lexical ambiguity is only applicable in the KINDLES domain, because each referent has two size properties, whereas in CIRCLES they only have one.

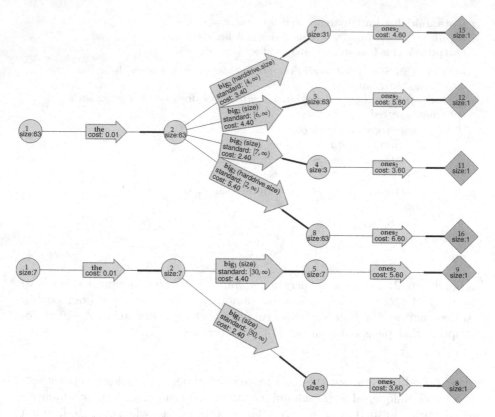

Fig. 3. A side-by-side comparison of the top-to-bottom **search graphs** for interpreting "the big ones" in both the KINDLES (top) and SHAPES (bottom) domains. Each circle represents a belief state, the diamonds are *goal* belief states, and the labeled edges correspond to *choice* about which (sense of a) lexical unit to apply. A single belief state implicitly represents multiple targets (e.g., vagueness and unspecificity), while the two branching belief states represent mutual exclusion (e.g., ambiguity) (**Q6**).

4   Related Work

For REG with ambiguity, [34] described an approach to learning how to predict whether a given referring expression contains a structural ambiguity. For work on vagueness, [18, 35]'s system, VAGUE, generated referring expressions that included gradable adjectives, but managed to do so in a deterministic way. The authors intentionally avoided plural gradable adjectives in their base form because of the arbitrariness of their meanings, so they were required to produce "the two biggest ones" rather than "the biggest ones" when describing multiple items. With AIGRE, we embrace the non-determinism and control the search such that most common standards of comparison are chosen first, while the less common standards remain possibilities through the use of backtracking. In addition, there are different characterizations of gradable adjectives' semantics: [36]

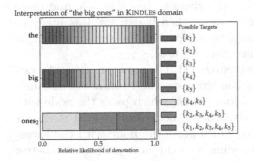

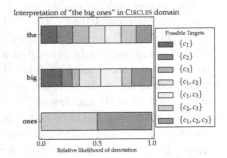

Fig. 4. An alternative view of the same two interpretations, showing the incremental *combined* denotations after each word. Each row corresponds to a column of states in the search graphs in Figure 3, excluding the initial belief state (node 1). For the first row in KINDLES, "the," is node 2 and the last row, "ones," is the denotations of interpretations of nodes 7, 8, 9 and 10 combined. The size of the member indicates its relative likelihood, derived by summing the denotations' inverted costs.

uses probabilities and the fuzzy-logic community does so using gradual membership functions [37, 38].

Finally, we would like to note that [39] presented a different formalization of the context set, in which its elements also contained weights that indicated its *salience*. This view is not incompatible with ours; salience can be viewed as *prior distribution* over the entities in the context set. We make a simplifying assumption that all of the groups of referents are equally salient.

5   Algorithmic Evaluation: The Scalability of the Lexicon

A key bottleneck to scalability is the *number of relevant actions* that need to be considered during generation and interpretation. For interpretation, AIGRE's actions are highly constrained to those that appeared in the referring expression, so search space is constrained enough that it can be generated and entirely explored in less than a second. However for generation, the worse case branching factor is the total number of actions in the lexicon. Worse, in our representation the effects of vague

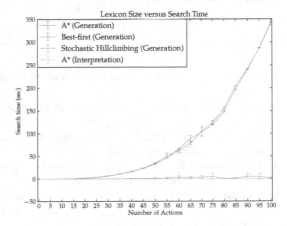

Fig. 5. Each condition had 5 trials

and ambiguous actions proliferate: if the adjective BIG has s senses, and there are r referents compatible with the belief state, then it can yield as many as $s \times r$ successors. To avoid this complexity, ambiguous words' *senses* and vague words' *standards* are only generated when needed (**Q4**).

We compared three methods to control search: (1) A^* *search*, an optimal strategy that picks the node with the lowest combined cost and estimated distance, and expands all of its successors (2) *best-first search*, which picks the node with the lowest estimated distance and expands all of its successors, and (3) *stochastic hill climbing* (or stochastic local search), which picks the node with the lowest estimated distance and then stops expanding as soon as it generates a better successor. As you can see in Figure 4, the stochastic hill-climbing time scaled linearly while the others scaled exponentially.

6 Conclusion

Viewing reference generation and interpretation as a search through belief states allows one to see the tasks through procedural lenses. From this perspective, it was clear that the numerous shades of meaning introduced by ambiguous and vague modifiers should be restricted to only those senses that are *relevant* based on everything we know up to that lexical item. Consequently, we have modeled the possible meanings of ambiguous and vague modifiers using the properties of the items in the context set. With backtracking, we avoided generating every possibly-relevant meaning at once, and instead structured the search space to *make the common senses of lexical units easiest to find, while enabling the less common meanings to still be possible*. For vagueness$_2$ (borderline cases) this seems straightforward: start at the most conservative meaning (i.e., 'big' = 'biggest') and work backward when needed; however, the ordering is not obvious for lexical ambiguity. Our next steps will be to learn these orderings from human behavioral data.

References

1. Wilson, D., Sperber, D.: Meaning and Relevance. Cambridge University Press (2012)
2. Reiter, E., Dale, R.: Building natural language generation systems. Cambridge University Press, New York (2000)
3. Piantadosi, S.T., Tily, H., Gibson, E.: The communicative function of ambiguity in language. Cognition (2012)
4. Van Deemter, K.: Not exactly: In praise of vagueness. OUP, Oxford (2010)
5. Clark, H.H.: Using language (1996)
6. Tomasello, M.: Origins of Human Communication. MIT Press (2008)
7. Cruse, A.: Meaning in Language: An Introduction to Semantics and Pragmatics. Oxford University Press (2010)
8. Roberts, C.: Context in dynamic interpretation. In: The Handbook of Pragmatics (2004)

9. Brennan, S.E., Clark, H.H.: Conceptual pacts and lexical choice in conversation. The Journal of Experimental Psychology (1996)
10. Branigan, H.P., Pickering, M.J., Pearson, J., McLean, J.F.: Linguistic alignment between people and computers. Journal of Pragmatics (2010)
11. Goudbeek, M., Krahmer, E.: Alignment in Interactive Reference Production: Content Planning, Modifier Ordering, and Referential Overspecification. Topics in Cognitive Science (2012)
12. Stalnaker, R.C.: Assertion Revisited: On the Interpretation of Two-Dimensional Modal Semantics. Philosophical Studies (2004)
13. Dale, R., Reiter, E.: Computational interpretations of the Gricean maxims in the generation of referring expressions. Cognitive Science (1995)
14. Clark, H.H., Schreuder, R., Buttrick, S.: Common ground at the understanding of demonstrative reference. Journal of Verbal Learning and Verbal Behavior (1983)
15. Janarthanam, S., Lemon, O.: Learning lexical alignment policies for generating referring expressions for spoken dialogue systems. In: Proceedings of the 12th European Workshop on Natural Language Generation (2009)
16. Clark, H.H., Marshall, C.R.: Definite reference and mutual knowledge. Psycholinguistics: Critical Concepts in Psychology (2002)
17. Tanenhaus, M.K.: Spoken language comprehension: Insights from eye movements. In: Oxford Handbook of Psycholinguistics (2007)
18. Van Deemter, K.: Generating vague descriptions. In: INLG 2000: Proceedings of the First International Conference on Natural Language Generation (2000)
19. Stone, M.: On identifying sets. In: INLG 2000: Proceedings of the First International Conference on Natural Language Generation (2000)
20. Horacek, H.: On Referring to Sets of Objects Naturally. In: Belz, A., Evans, R., Piwek, P. (eds.) INLG 2004. LNCS (LNAI), vol. 3123, pp. 70–79. Springer, Heidelberg (2004)
21. Smith, D., Lieberman, H.: Generating and Interpreting Referring Expressions as Belief State Planning and Plan Recognition. In: Proceedings of the 14th European Workshop on Natural Language Generation (2013)
22. Palmer, M.: Consistent criteria for sense distinctions. Computers and the Humanities (2000)
23. Allen, J.F.: Word Senses, Semantic Roles and Entailment. In: 5th International Conference on Generative Approaches to the Lexicon
24. Altmann, G., Steedman, M.: Interaction with context during human sentence processing. Cognition (1988)
25. Dubois, D.: Have fuzzy sets anything to do with vagueness. This volume (2011)
26. Graff, D.: Shifting sands: An interest-relative theory of vagueness. Philosophical Topics (2002)
27. Sedivy, J.C., Tanenhaus, M.K., Chambers, C.G., Carlson, G.N.: Achieving incremental semantic interpretation through contextual representation. Cognition (1999)
28. Stone, M., Doran, C., Webber, B.L., Bleam, T., Palmer, M.: Microplanning with communicative intentions: The spud system. Computational Intelligence 19(4), 311–381 (2003)
29. Koller, A., Stone, M.: Sentence generation as a planning problem. In: Annual Meeting of the Association of Computational Linguistics (2007)
30. Bauer, D.: Statistical natural language generation as planning. Master's thesis, Department of Computational Linguistics, Saarland University, Saarbrücken, Germany (2009)

31. Koller, A., Gargett, A., Garoufi, K.: A scalable model of planning perlocutionary acts. In: Proceedings of the 14th Workshop on the Semantics and Pragmatics of Dialogue (2010)
32. Appelt, D.E.: Planning English referring expressions. Artificial Intelligence (1985)
33. Radul, A., Sussman, G.: The art of the propagator. Technical Report MIT-CSAIL-TR-2009-002, MIT Computer Science and Artifcial Intelligence Laboratory (2009)
34. Khan, I., van Deemter, K., Ritchie, G.: Managing ambiguity in reference generation: the role of surface structure. Topics in Cognitive Science (2012)
35. van Deemter, K.: Generating Referring Expressions that Involve Gradable Properties. Computational Linguistics (2006)
36. Lassiter, D.: Vagueness as probabilistic linguistic knowledge. In: Nouwen, R., van Rooij, R., Sauerland, U., Schmitz, H.-C. (eds.) ViC 2009. LNCS(LNAI), vol. 6517, pp. 127–150. Springer, Heidelberg (2011)
37. Zadeh, L.A.: Fuzzy logic and approximate reasoning. Synthese (1975)
38. Hersh, H.M., Caramazza, A.: A Fuzzy Set Approach to Modifiers and Vagueness in Natural Language (1976)
39. Krahmer, E., Theune, M.: Context sensitive generation of descriptions (1998)

Evaluation of a Refinement Algorithm
for the Generation of Referring Expressions

Luciana Benotti and Romina Altamirano

LIIS Team, Universidad Nacional de Córdoba, Argentina
{benotti,ialtamir}@famaf.unc.edu.ar
http://cs.famaf.unc.edu.ar/~luciana/,
http://cs.famaf.unc.edu.ar/~romina/

Abstract. In this paper we describe and evaluate an algorithm for generating referring expressions that uses linear regression for learning the probability of using certain properties to describe an object in a given scene. The algorithm we present is an extension of a refinement algorithm modified to take probabilities learnt from corpora into account. As a result, the algorithm is able not only to generate correct referring expressions that uniquely identify the referents but it also generates referring expressions that are considered equal or better than those generated by humans in 92% of the cases by a human judge. We classify and give examples of the referring expressions that humans prefer, and indicate the potential impact of our work for theories of the egocentric use of language.

1 Introduction

A *referring expression* (RE) is an expression that unequivocally identifies the intended target to the interlocutor, from a set of possible distractors, in a given situation. For example, if we intend to identify a certain animal d from a picture of pets, the expression "the dog" will be an RE if d is the only dog in the picture, and if we are confident that our interlocutor will identify d as a dog.

The generation of referring expressions (GRE) is a key task of most natural language generation (NLG) systems [18]. Depending on the information available to the NLG system, certain objects might not be associated with an identifier which can be easily recognized by the user. In those cases, the system will have to generate a, possibly complex, description that contains enough information so that the interlocutor will be able to identify the intended referent. The generation of referring expressions is a well developed field in automated natural language generation building upon GRE foundational work [21,6,7].

Low complexity algorithms for the generation of REs have been proposed [3,2]. These algorithms are based on variations of the partition refinement algorithms of [16]. The information provided by a given scene is interpreted as a relational model whose objects are classified into sets that fit the same description. This classification is successively *refined* till the target is the only element fitting the description of its class. The existence of an RE depends on the information

P. Brézillon, P. Blackburn, and R. Dapoigny (Eds.): CONTEXT 2013, LNAI 8175, pp. 31–44, 2013.
© Springer-Verlag Berlin Heidelberg 2013

available in the input scene, and on the expressive power of the formal language used to describe elements of the different classes in the refinement.

Existing GRE algorithms can effectively compute REs for all individuals in the domain, at the same time. The algorithms always terminate returning a formula of the formal language chosen that uniquely describes the target. However, GRE algorithms require a ranking of the properties that are to be used in the referring expressions, and the naturalness of the generated REs strongly depends on this ranking. [1] show that a refinement algorithm using the description language $\mathcal{EL}$ as formal language is capable of generating 75% of the REs present in the dataset described in [20]. In this paper we perform a human evaluation of the REs generated by this algorithm on two new corpora and show that even when the generated REs do not coincide with those found in corpora, people actually prefer the REs generated by the system in 92% of the cases.

The rest of the paper is structured as follows. In Section 2 we introduce the technical details of the refinement algorithm and explain how it uses the ranking of properties. In this section, we assume that this list is provided as input to the algorithm. In Section 3, we show how to estimate the probability of use of a property from corpora in order to obtain the ranking of properties. Given corpora consisting of pairs (scene, target) together with the REs used to describe the target in each case, we propose a method to compute the probability of use of each property for each scene, and use a machine learning approach to generalize this approach to new targets and scenes not appearing in the corpora. Section 4 presents an automatic evaluation and a human evaluation of the generated REs. In Section 5 we discuss related work and analyze the structure of the refinement algorithm in relation to the work of [12], on the egocentric basis of language generation.

2   The Referring Expression Generation Algorithm

Refinement algorithms for GRE are based on the following basic idea: given a scene S, the objects appearing in S are successively classified according to their properties into finer and finer classes. A description (in some formal language $\mathcal{L}$) of each class is computed every time a class is refined. The procedure always stops when the set of classes stabilizes, i.e., no further refinement is possible with the information available in the scene[1]. If the target element is in a singleton class, then the formal description of that class is a referring expression; otherwise the target cannot be unequivocally described (in $\mathcal{L}$).

We present a modification of the algorithm in [3] where the fixed order of properties in the input scene is replaced by a finite probability distribution. The resulting algorithm (see Figure 3) is now non-deterministic: two runs of the algorithm with the same input might result in different REs for objects in the scene. The input to the algorithm will be a relational model $\mathcal{M} = \langle \Delta, \|\cdot\| \rangle$, where Δ is the non-empty domain of objects in the scene, and $\|\cdot\|$ is an interpretation

---

[1] Of course, if we are only interested in a referring expression for a given target we can stop the procedure as soon as the target is the only element of some of the classes.

function that assigns to all properties in the scene its intended extension. For example, the scene shown in Figure 1 could be represented by the model $\mathcal{M} = \langle \Delta, \| \cdot \| \rangle$ shown in Figure 2. In Figure 2, $\Delta = \{e_1, \ldots, e_7\}$, and for example the extension of blue is $\|blue\| = \{e_5, e_6, e_7\}$ because 3 objects are blue in the scene. In the Figure, xn indicates that the object is in position n with regard to its x-dimension in the grid and yn is interpreted similarly.

Fig. 1. Scene, target *blue chair facing left*   **Fig. 2.** The scene as a relational model

On termination, the algorithm computes what are called the $\mathcal{L}$-similarity classes of the input model $\mathcal{M}$. Intuitively, if two elements in the model belong to the same $\mathcal{L}$-similarity class, then $\mathcal{L}$ is not expressive enough to tell them apart (i.e., no formula in $\mathcal{L}$ can distinguish them). All the objects in Figure 1 are distinguishable, but if, for instance, color and position are not considered then e_2 and e_7 are indistinguishable and, hence, will remain in the same similarity class when the algorithm terminates.

The algorithm we discuss uses formulas of the $\mathcal{EL}$ description logic language [5] to describe refinement classes[2]. For a detailed description of $\mathcal{EL}$, we refer to [5]. The interpretation of the $\mathcal{EL}$ formula $\exists green.\top$ is the set of all the green elements of the model. In Figure 1, $\|\exists green.\top\| = \{e_1, e_2\}$. The interpretation of $\psi \sqcap \varphi$ is the set of all elements that satisfy ψ and φ. In Figure 1, $\|\exists green.\top \sqcap \exists chair.\top\| = \{e_2\}$.

Now that we have an intuitive understanding of $\mathcal{EL}$, we are ready to describe Algorithms 1 and 2.

Algorithm 1 takes as input a model and a list Rs of pairs $(R, R.p_{use})$ that links each relation $R \in$ REL, the set of all relation symbols in the model[3], to some probability of use $R.p_{use}$. For example, *green* and *large* are relations in the model of Figure 2. The set RE contains the formal description of the refinement classes and it is initialized by the most general description $\top$. The formula $\top$ can be intuitively understood as the referring expression *thing* or *thingummy*. For each

---

[2] Notice, though, that the particular formal language used is independent of the main algorithm, and different $add_{\mathcal{L}}(R, \varphi, RE)$ functions can be used depending on the language involved.

[3] We represent each unary relation R as binary, hence $\|\exists R.\top\|$ is the set of all elements in the model that have the property R.

Algorithm 1. Computing $\mathcal{L}$-similarity classes

Input: A model $\mathcal{M}$ and a list $Rs \in (REL \times [0,1])^*$ of relation symbols with
    their p_{use} values, ordered by p_{use}
Output: A set of formulas RE such that $\{\|\varphi\| \mid \varphi \in RE\}$ is the set of
    $\mathcal{L}$-similarity classes of $\mathcal{M}$
$RE \leftarrow \{\top\}$ // the most general description $\top$ applies to all elements
in the scene
for $(R, R.p_{use}) \in Rs$ **do**
   | $R.rnd_{use} = Random(0,1)$ // $R.rnd_{use}$ is the probability of using R
   | $R.inc_{use} = (1 - R.p_{use})$ / MaxIterations
repeat
   | **while** $\exists(\varphi \in RE).(\#\|\varphi\| > 1)$ **do** // while some class has at least two
   | elements
   | | $RE' \leftarrow RE$ // make a copy for future comparison
   | | **for** $(R, R.p_{use}) \in Rs$ **do**
   | | | **if** $R.rnd_{use} \leq R.p_{use}$ **then** // R will be used in the expression
   | | | | **for** $\varphi \in RE$ **do** $add_{\mathcal{EL}}(R, \varphi, RE)$ // refine classes using R
   | | | **if** $RE \neq RE'$ **then**   // the classification has changed
   | | | | exit   // exit for-loop to try again highest $R.p_{use}$
   | | **if** $RE = RE'$ **then**   // the classification has stabilized
   | | | exit   // exit while-loop to increase $R.p_{use}$
   | **for** $(R, R.p_{use}) \in Rs$ **do** $R.p_{use} \leftarrow R.p_{use} + R.inc_{use}$ // increase $R.p_{use}$
until $\forall((R, R.p_{use}) \in Rs).(R.p_{use} \geq 1)$ // $R.p_{use}$ are incremented until 1

Algorithm 2. $add_{\mathcal{EL}}(R, \varphi, RE)$

---

if FirstLoop? **then**   // are we in the first loop?
  | Informative $\leftarrow$ TRUE   // allow overspecification
else Informative $\leftarrow \|\psi \sqcap \exists R.\varphi\| \neq \|\psi\|$;   // informative: smaller than the
original?
for $\psi \in RE$ with $\#\|\psi\| > 1$ **do**
  | **if** $\psi \sqcap \exists R.\varphi$ is not subsumed in RE **and**   // non-redundant: can't be
  | obtained from RE?
  | $\|\psi \sqcap \exists R.\varphi\| \neq \emptyset$ **and**   // non-trivial: has elements?
  | Informative **then**
  | | add $\psi \sqcap \exists R.\varphi$ to RE   // add the new class to the classification
  | | remove subsumed formulas from RE   // remove redundant classes

---

Fig. 3. Refinement algorithm with probabilities for the $\mathcal{EL}$-language

R, we first compute $R.rnd_{use}$, a random number in [0,1]. If $R.rnd_{use} \leq R.p_{use}$ then R is used to refine the set of classes. The value of $R.p_{use}$ will be incremented by $R.inc_{use}$ in each main loop, to ensure that all relations are, at some point, considered by the algorithm. This ensures that a referring expression will be found if it exists; but gives higher probability to expressions using relations with a high $R.p_{use}$. While RE contains descriptions that can be refined (i.e., classes with at least two elements) the refinement function $add_{\mathcal{L}}(R, \varphi, RE)$ is called successively with each relation in Rs. If the model contains binary relations between its elements, a change in one of the classes, can trigger changes in others. For that reason, if RE changes, we exit the **for** loop to start again with the relations of higher $R.p_{use}$. If after trying to refine the set with all relations in Rs, the set RE has not changed, then we have reached a stable state (i.e., the classes described in RE cannot be further refined with the current $R.p_{use}$ values). We will then increment all the $R.p_{use}$ values and start the procedure again.

Algorithm 2 behaves as follows. The **for** loop refines each description in RE using the relation R and the other descriptions already in RE, under certain conditions. The new description should be *non-redundant* (it cannot be obtained from classes already in RE), *non-trivial* (it is not empty), and *informative* (it does not coincide with the original class). If these conditions are met, the new description is added to RE, and redundant descriptions created by the new description are eliminated. The **if** statement at the beginning of Algorithm 2 disregards the informativity test during the first loop of the algorithm allowing overspecification; without this condition the algorithm would generate minimal REs. For example, a minimal RE for e_2 is "the green chair" while an overspecified RE for this element is "the green chair in the top row".

3   Learning to Describe New Objects from Corpora

In the previous section we presented an algorithm that assumes that each relation R used in a referring expression has a known probability of use $R.p_{use}$. Intuitively, the $R.p_{use}$ is the probability of using relation R to describe the target. In Tables 1 and 2 we show the probabilities of use that we are able to learn from corpora and to apply to the models of Figures 1 and 4. In Figure 1, the probability of using *blue* to describe the target is higher than the probability of using *facing left*, although both are properties of the target.

The probability of using *green* is not zero because a green object may be used in a relational description of the target (for example, "the blue chair far from the green fan").

In this section, we describe how to calculate these probabilities from corpora. The general set up is the following: we assume available a corpus of REs associated to different scenes that are prototypical of the domain in which the GRE algorithm has to operate; we call this the training data. We then show how to generalize these values to other scenes in the domain, using a machine learning algorithm. We exemplify the methodology using the TUNA corpus.

The TUNA Corpus [10] is a set of human-produced referring expressions (REs) for entities in visual domains of pictures of furniture and people as exemplified in Figures 1 and 4. The corpus was collected during an online elicitation experiment in which subjects typed descriptions of a target single referent or pair of referents. In each picture there were 5 or 6 other objects. In the experiment, the participation was not controlled, but there was a main condition manipulated the +/-LOC: in +LOC condition, participants were told that they could refer to

Table 1. Probabilities of use learned from corpora and instantiated for Figure 1

Table 2. Probabilities of use learned from corpora and instantiated for Figure 4

Top 10 relations in Figure 1	learned p_{use}	Top 10 relations in Figure 4	learned p_{use}
chair	0.94	person	0.79
blue	0.89	hasGlasses	0.71
y3	0.29	y2	0.20
x5	0.27	x5	0.18
left	0.25	hasHair	0.13
large	0.21	hairDark	0.13
green	0.05	hairLight	0.11
small	0.05	ageOld	0.05
back	0.02	y3	0.03
y1	0.02	x2	0.02

entities using any of their properties (including their location on the screen). In the -LOC condition, they were discouraged from doing so, though not prevented. The attributes for each entity include properties such as an object's color or a person's characteristic such as having dark hair. In this paper we will use the singular part of the TUNA corpus. The corpus contains 780 singular referring expressions divided into 80% training data, 20% test.

In order to collect the corpus, each participant in the elicitation experiment carried out 38 trials, 20 furniture descriptions and 18 people descriptions. For each word in the corpus we train a machine learning model that computes a function of its p_{use}. When this function is instantiated with a set of domain independent features that we define below.

To clarify the computation of R.p_{use} in the training data and the model $\mathcal{M}$ associated to each scene we list the required steps in detail, and discuss how we carried them out in the TUNA corpus:

1. Tokenize the referring expressions and call the set of tokens T. In particular, multi-word expressions like "in the top row" should be matched to a single token like *y1*.
2. Replace hyperonyms from T. E.g., if both *man* and *picture* appear in T, delete *picture*.
3. If the set of tokens obtained in the previous steps contains synonyms normalize them to a representative in the synonym class, and call the resulting set REL; it will be the signature of the model $\mathcal{M}$ used by the algorithm. E.g., the tokens *man* and *guy* are both represented by the token *man*.
4. For each scene, define $\mathcal{M}$ such that the interpretation $\| \cdot \|$ ensures that all REs in the corpus are REs. E.g., the $\mathcal{EL}$ formula $\exists left.\top \sqcap \exists blue.\top \sqcap \exists chair.\top$, which represents the RE "the blue chair facing left" found in the corpus for the scene in Figure 1, is a RE for the target in the model $\mathcal{M}$ depicted in Figure 2.
5. For each $R \in$ REL we assign 1 to R.p_{use} if R occurs in the RE, we assign 0 otherwise. In case that the corpus has more than one RE per scene we calculate the proportion of appearance of each property.

Fig. 4. Scene used during the collection of the TUNA corpus. The referring expression collected has to distinguish the target from the rest of the people. For this scene, the RE was *the man with glasses.*

The learning was done with the machine learning toolkit WEKA [11], learning on the training data of the TUNA corpus. We use linear regression to learn the function of p_{use} for each relation in the signature. For a given scene in the test set, we replace the variables of the obtained function by the values of the features in the scene that we want to describe. We use simple features to obtain the function, all the features can be extracted automatically from the relational model and are listed in Table 3.

Table 3. Features used for learning the p_{use} for each token in the signature of the scenes of the TUNA corpus

target-has	whether the target element has the property
location-has	whether the RE may use the location of the target in the figure
discrimination	1 / the number of objects in the model that have the property
p_{use}	probability of using the property to describe the target

Our feature set is intentionally simplistic in order for it to be domain independent. As a result there are some complex relations between characteristics of the scenes that it is not able to capture.

Starting from the scene in Figure 1 the resulting signature and their associated p_{use} are listed in the Table 1 and for the Figure 4 in Table 2. Notice that even though the TUNA corpus contains only one RE per scene the p_{use} values represent the proportion of use of each property as learned using linear regression.

Notice that the values $R.p_{use}$ obtained in this way should be interpreted as the probability of using R to describe the target in model $\mathcal{M}$, and we could argue that they are correlated to the *saliency* of R in the model.

Using linear regression we are able to learn interesting characteristics of the domain. To start with, it learns known facts such that the saliency of a color depends strongly on whether the target object is of that color, and it does not depend on its discrimination power in the model. Moreover, it learns that size relations (e.g., large and small) are used more frequently when it has a higher discriminative power which confirms a previous finding reported in [20]. Finally, it is able to learn that the orientation properties (e.g., facing left and facing right) are used as a last resource, when it is necessary to identify the target uniquely.

4 Evaluation

In this section we present two different evaluations we performed on our algorithm. Section 4.1 describes an evaluation with respect to the state of the art algorithm GRAPH [13]. GRAPH was the top performer in both editions of the ASGRE, shared task [10]. Due to the limitations of the automatic metrics, in Section 4.2 we perform a human evaluation in which we ask human subjects to compare the output produced by our algorithm to expressions produced by humans.

4.1 Automatic Evaluation

In this section we present the comparison of our algorithm to the state of the art algorithm GRAPH introduced above. The GRAPH algorithm is a deterministic algorithm and hence produces the same referring expression when run with the same target and model. Our algorithm is non deterministic, it may give a different referring expression each time it is run. In order to compare them we run our algorithm k times and we make a ranking of the top 20 produced referring expressions ordered by the frequency they were produced. We use the test part of the TUNA corpus to compare algorithm to the GRAPH algorithm whose results on this dataset are described in [13] and reproduced in the Table 4.

The GRAPH algorithm defines the generation of referring expressions as a graph search problem, which outputs the cheapest distinguishing graph (if one exists) given a particular cost function. We compare to this algorithm using the metrics accuracy, Dice and MASI. Accuracy is defined as the percentage of exact matches between each RE produced by a human and the RE produced by the system for the same scene.

Dice coefficient is a set comparison metric, ranging between 0 and 1, where 1 indicates a perfect match between sets. For two attribute sets A and B, Dice is computed as follows:

$$Dice(A, B) = \frac{2 \times |A \cap B|}{|A| + |B|}$$

The MASI score [17] is an adaptation of the Jaccard coefficient which biases it in favor of similarity where one set is a subset of the other. Like Dice, it ranges between 0 and 1, where 1 indicates a perfect match. It is computed as follows:

$$\text{MASI}(A, B) = \delta \times \frac{|A \cap B|}{|A \cup B|}$$

where δ is a monotonicity coefficient defined as follows:

$$\delta = \begin{cases} 0 & \text{if } A \cap B = \emptyset \\ 1 & \text{if } A = B \\ \frac{2}{3} & \text{if } A \subset B \text{ or } B \subset A \\ \frac{1}{3} & \text{otherwise} \end{cases} \tag{1}$$

Intuitively, this means that those system-produced descriptions are preferred which do not include attributes that are omitted by a human.

In Table 4 we show the automatic metrics and compare the performance of our system with the GRAPH system for the first RE in the ranking and the first 20 REs in the ranking.

Table 4. Comparison of the GRAPH algorithm and our system. We consider the 3 automatic metrics for the top 1 and the top 20 REs produced by our algorithm.

	Dice	MASI	ACCURACY
GRAPH system, Furniture domain	.80	.59	.48
GRAPH system, People domain	.72	.48	.28
Our system, Furniture domain (top 1)	.80	.60	.47
Our system, People domain (top 1)	.65	.37	.19
Our system, Furniture domain (top 20)	.87	.75	.65
Our system, People domain (top 20)	.81	.68	.60

Accuracy, Dice and MASI assess humanlikeness with respect to a corpus of human referring expressions. In the Figure 5 the accuracy for our system and the GRAPH system is compared. The left GRAPH corresponds to the furniture domain and the right GRAPH corresponds to the people domain. We can see that taking the top 1 RE our system accuracy is lower than GRAPH performance for the people domain. However, if we consider the top 20 REs that our algorithm is able to produce we can see that the accuracy for both domains gets higher than 60%. This shows that our algorithm is able to generate REs that are more similar to those produced by humans than the GRAPH algorithm, although these REs are not ranked first.

Another result that we can observe is that the people domain accuracy is much lower for the top 1 RE than for the furniture domain (19 vs 47), but the accuracy stabilizes when REs lower in our ranking are considered. This may be explained by the fact that the training set for the people domain is smaller and less balanced and hence, the probabilities of use inferred do not generalize as well as in the furniture domain.

4.2   Human Evaluation

We asked two native speaker judges of English to evaluate our referring expressions via an experiment on the web. The authors of the paper did not participate during the evaluation. The judges could register to the evaluation system so that they did not have to complete it in one go, the could come back to it later. During the evaluation we showed each judge the scenes and two randomly ordered REs. One RE corresponded to the RE present in the corpus and produced by a person and the other RE corresponded to the top 1 RE produced by our system. We asked the judges to select the RE that would be more useful to identify the target in the scene. That is, to select it from among the other objects in the stimulus pictures.

Our goal is to show that even if the RE generated by our algorithm does not coincide with the RE produced by a human in the corpus collection, it can be judged as good or even better than the REs generated by humans.

In Table 5 we show the results from the human evaluation experiment. The REs produced by the system were considered equal or better by both judges in 60 % of the cases and, by at least one judge in 92% of the cases.

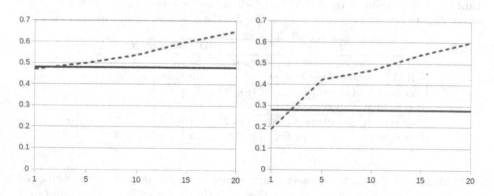

Fig. 5. Comparison of the accuracy of the GRAPH algorithm and our system. The x axis indicates that the accuracy was calculated considering the x first REs in the ranking. The y axis indicates the accuracy. Our system is depicted as a dotted line and the GRAPH system as a continuous line.

Table 5. Percentage of system versus human selected choices

	Furniture domain	People domain	Weighted mean
system equal to human	.46	.19	.33
system better by 2 judges	.29	.24	.27
system better by 1 or 2 judges	.51	.68	.59
system worse by 2 judges	.03	.13	.08
system equal or better by 2 judges	.75	.43	.60
system equal or better by 1 judge	.97	.87	.92

Below, we illustrate the evaluation experiment by showing examples of cases in which the system expression was considered better by both judges, by only one judge or by neither of them.

Figure 6 illustrates a case in which the human generated an underspecified RE while the system produced an RE which unequivocally identifies the target. The RE generated by the system for this figure is "small blue fan" while the RE produced by the human is "blue fan". The human RE fails to uniquely identify the target and is then not preferred by the human judges. Humans are known for producing underspecified REs which may be due to cognitive limitations for not being able to consider the whole referential context at the same time. Our algorithm is able to consider the whole referential context and combine this ability with the probability of use of the REs learned from humans.

Fig. 6. Scene used during the collection of the TUNA corpus. The human RE *blue fan*, and the system *small blue fan*. Judges prefer the system generated.

Fig. 7. Scene used during the collection of the TUNA corpus. The human RE was *blue frontal chair*, and the system *the blue chair in the bottom*. Both human judges prefer the system generated RE.

In Figure 7 the human RE was "blue frontal chair", and the system RE was "the blue chair in the bottom"; both judges selected the system RE. This case can be explained by the fact that, in this domain, the property "bottom" helps more during the identification than the property "frontal" because it concentrates the attention of the interpreter in the lower part of the scene. Our system learns this fact by learning a higher value of p_{use} for "bottom" than for "frontal" from the training data.

Figure 8 is an example for which both judges preferred the human expression. The human RE was "the man with black hair", and the system's "the man wearing glasses in the fourth column". This example makes evident the fact that, in the people domain some properties are more salient in some images than in others because of different shades of colors. Gradable properties such as this ones (in contrast to absolute properties) are still an open problem for GRE algorithms.

Fig. 8. Scene used during the collection of the TUNA corpus. The human RE was *the man with black hair*, and the system *the man wearing glasses in the fourth column*. Judges prefer the human RE.

Fig. 9. Scene used during the collection of the TUNA corpus. The human RE was *man with a beard*, and the system *man with a beard wearing glasses*. Judges did not agree in their preference.

Figure 9 illustrates a case in which the system RE was more overspecified than the human RE; the system included "wearing glasses" while the human did not. In this case one human subject preferred the system RE and the other the human RE. The amount of overspecification is a subjective matter where human themselves disagree. Further evaluation where REs are actually used for a task would be interesting to investigate this issue.

5　Discussion and Conclusions

In this article we presented the evaluation of the algorithm presented in [3] extended to generate REs similar to those produced by humans. The modifications proposed are based on the observation that humans frequently overspecify their REs [8,4]. We tested the proposed algorithm on the TUNA corpus and found that it is able to generate a large proportion of the overspecified REs found in the corpus without generating trivially redundant referring expressions. The expressions generated are preferred by (one or more) human judges 92% of the time for the TUNA corpus.

Different algorithms for the generation of overspecified and distinguishing referring expressions have been proposed in recent years (see, e.g., [14,19]). In this paper we compare ourselves to the Graph algorithm [13] wich has been shown to achieve better accuracy than algorithms describe in [14,19] in the TUNA shared task [10].

An interestesting outcome of our work is that it makes evident the relationship between overspecification and the saliency of properties in the context os a scene.

As we described in Section 2 the generation of overspecified REs is performed in two steps. In the first iteration, the probability of including a property in the RE depends only on its p_{use}. We believe our definition of p_{use} is intended to captures the saliency of the properties for different scenes and targets. The p_{use}

of a property changes according to the scene as we discussed in Section 3. This is in contrast with previous work where the saliency of a property is constant in a domain. In the first iteration, if the p_{use} is high, that is, if the property is very salient, it does not matter whether the property eliminates any distractor, it will probably be used anyway. After all properties had a chance of being included in this way, if the resulting RE is not distinguishing, then the algorithm enters a second phase in which it makes sure that the RE identifies the target uniquely.

Our two-step algorithm is inspired by the work of [12] on egocentrism and natural language production. Keysar et al. put forwards the proposal that when producing language, considering the hearers point of view is not done from the outset but it is rather an afterthought [12]. They argue that adult speakers produce REs egocentrically, just like children do, but then adjust the REs so that the addressee is able to identify the target unequivocally. The egocentric step is a heuristic process based in a model of saliency of the scene that contains the target. As a result, the REs that include salient properties are preferred by our algorithm even if such properties are not necessary to identify the target univocally. Keysar et al. argue that the reason for the generate-and-adjust procedure may have to do with information processing limitations of the mind: if the heuristic that guides the egocentric phase is well tunned, it succeeds with a suitable RE in most cases and seldom requires adjustments. Interestingly, we observe a similar behavior with our algorithm: when p_{use} values learn from the domain are used, the algorithm is not only much more accurate but also much faster.

As future work we plan to evaluate our algorithm to generate referring expressions inside discourse as required by domains like those provided by Open Domain Folksonimies [15]. We also plan to explore corpora obtain from interaction, such as the GIVE Corpus [9] where it is common to observe multi shot REs. Under time pressure subjects will first produce an underspecified expression that includes salient properties of the target (e.g., "the red button"). And then, in a following utterance, they add additional properties (e.g., "to the left of the lamp") to make the expression a proper RE identifying the target uniquely.

References

1. Altamirano, R., Areces, C., Benotti, L.: Probabilistic refinement algorithms for the generation of referring expressions. In: Proceedings of the 24th International Conference on Computational Linguistics, pp. 53–62 (2012)
2. Areces, C., Figueira, S., Gorín, D.: Using logic in the generation of referring expressions. In: Pogodalla, S., Prost, J.-P. (eds.) LACL 2011. LNCS, vol. 6736, pp. 17–32. Springer, Heidelberg (2011)
3. Areces, C., Koller, A., Striegnitz, K.: Referring expressions as formulas of description logic. In: Proceedings of the 5th International Natural Language Generation Conference (INLG 2008), pp. 42–49. Association for Computational Linguistics, Morristown (2008)
4. Arts, A., Maes, A., Noordman, L., Jansen, C.: Overspecification facilitates object identification. Journal of Pragmatics 43(1), 361–374 (2011)

5. Baader, F., McGuiness, D., Nardi, D., Patel-Schneider, P. (eds.): The Description Logic Handbook: Theory, implementation and applications. Cambridge University Press (2003)
6. Dale, R.: Cooking up referring expressions. In: Proceedings of the 27th Annual Meeting on Association for Computational Linguistics, pp. 68–75 (1989)
7. Dale, R., Reiter, E.: Computational interpretations of the Gricean maxims in the generation of referring expressions. Cognitive Science 19(2), 233–263 (1995)
8. Engelhardt, P., Bailey, K., Ferreira, F.: Do speakers and listeners observe the gricean maxim of quantity? Journal of Memory and Language 54(4), 554–573 (2006)
9. Gargett, A., Garoufi, K., Koller, A., Striegnitz, K.: The GIVE-2 corpus of giving instructions in virtual environments. In: Proceedings of the 7th International Conference on Language Resources and Evaluation (LREC), Malta (2010)
10. Gatt, A., Belz, A., Kow, E.: The TUNA challenge 2008: Overview and evaluation results. In: Proceedings of the 5th International Conference on Natural Language Generation, pp. 198–206. Association for Computational Linguistics (2008)
11. Hall, M., Frank, E., Holmes, G., Pfahringer, B., Reutemann, P., Witten, I.H.: The WEKA data mining software: an update. ACM SIGKDD Explorations Newsletter 11(1), 10–18 (2009)
12. Keysar, B., Barr, D.J., Horton, W.S.: The Egocentric Basis of Language Use. Current Directions in Psychological Science 7(2), 46–49 (1998)
13. Krahmer, E.J., Theune, M., Viethen, J., Hendrickx, I.: Graph: The costs of redundancy in referring expressions. In: Proceedings of the 5th International Natural Language Generation Conference, Salt Fork, Ohio, USA, pp. 227–229. The Association for Computational Linguistics, USA (2008)
14. de Lucena, D.J., Paraboni, I.: USP-EACH frequency-based greedy attribute selection for referring expressions generation. In: Proceedings of the 5th International Conference on Natural Language Generation (INLG 2008), pp. 219–220. Association for Computational Linguistics (2008)
15. Pacheco, F., Duboue, P., Domínguez, M.: On the feasibility of open domain referring expression generation using large scale folksonomies. In: Proceedings of the 2012 Conference of the North American Chapter of the Association for Computational Linguistics: Human Language Technologies, pp. 641–645. Association for Computational Linguistics, Montréal (2012)
16. Paige, R., Tarjan, R.: Three partition refinement algorithms. SIAM Journal on Computing 16(6), 973–989 (1987)
17. Passonneau, R.: Measuring agreement on set-valued items (MASI) for semantic and pragmatic annotation. In: Proceedings of the International Conference on Language Resources and Evaluation, LREC (2006)
18. Reiter, E., Dale, R.: Building Natural Language Generation Systems. Cambridge University Press, Cambridge (2000)
19. Ruud, K., Emiel, K., Mariët, T.: Learning preferences for referring expression generation: Effects of domain, language and algorithm. In: INLG 2012 Proceedings of the Seventh International Natural Language Generation Conference, pp. 3–11. Association for Computational Linguistics, Utica (2012)
20. Viethen, H.A.E.: The Generation of Natural Descriptions: Corpus-Based Investigations of Referring Expressions in Visual Domains. Ph.D. thesis, Macquarie University, Sydney, Australia (2011)
21. Winograd, T.: Understanding natural language. Cognitive Psychology 3(1), 1–191 (1972)

Looking for a Synergy between Human and Artificial Cognition

Jeanne E. Parker[1], Debra L. Hollister[2], Avelino J. Gonzalez[1],
Patrick Brézillon[3], and Shane T. Parker[1]

[1] Intelligent Systems Laboratory, Department of EECS- CS Division,
University of Central Florida
jeanne13@knights.ucf.edu, Avelino.Gonzalez@ucf.edu
[2] Valencia College, Lake Nona Campus
dhollister@valenciacollege.edu
[3] LIP6, Université Pierre et Marie Curie (UPMC)
Patrick.Brezillon@lip6.fr

Abstract. Contextually based reasoning is an essential aspect of human cognition, permeating language, memory, and reasoning capabilities. This integral process is developed over the lifetime through experiential learning. Given the goal of artificial intelligence to mimic human intelligence, it is essential to include such contextual considerations in system design and implementation. We compare selected computational architectures and cognitive paradigms on the basis of key elements in human intelligence understanding in order to illustrate the similarities and differences between the two viewpoints and highlight the potential effectiveness of context based computing. In the literature, we discover meaningful parallels between the assessment of context in cognition and computation which have implications for both fields of study.

Keywords: Context, Cognition, Artificial Intelligence.

1   Introduction

The evident goal of today's artificial intelligence agenda is to create a system that can operate on par with human intelligence, if not surpass it. We are reaching for a system that can not only perform calculations and computations, but also reason and discern with a human like propensity. We believe contextual reasoning is a critical element of human intelligence and reasoning, and we claim that to create systems that are human-like in their intelligence requires imbuing them with the ability to process context. Kokinov [24] states that to be effective, Artificial Intelligence systems must be able to provide solutions to problems which are both correct and relevant, they must be able to communicate using natural language with the appropriate level of description, and they must act in an efficient manner. We do not discuss here the new realm of "big data" where only artificial intelligence can process and extract relevant findings thanks to the brute capacity of computational processing of machines.

In light of these necessities, we discuss many aspects of contextual processing in human cognition, offering comparisons with a selection of relevant computational

P. Brézillon, P. Blackburn, and R. Dapoigny (Eds.): CONTEXT 2013, LNAI 8175, pp. 45–58, 2013.

architectures. However, the Artificial Intelligence literature is filled with reports of the implementation of context in AI systems. A full discussion of this cannot be done in the scope of this paper, but we will focus on a few, well-known contextual paradigms that reflect, to a greater or lesser degree, the cognitive context-based processes to be discussed. Finally, we will assess how the human cognitive ability or set of abilities is developed or learned, as we feel that this will offer a more complete view as to how such contextual systems may be further developed computationally.

Before beginning in earnest we feel that it would be advantageous to first take a moment to define exactly what we mean when we use the word, "context," as we will be utilizing this term in traversing both the worlds of cognition and computation. McCarthy [26] pointed out the difficulty in computer science of modeling context because context possesses an infinite dimension. Furthermore, he addresses the difficulty in translating contextual assessment that has been conducted in the psychological or philosophical realm into formal computational logic. He acknowledges the changing complexities of context and even the interrelational properties that can be at work, and even further includes a person's internal mental states as specific types of contexts [26]. It is also essential when considering context to also consider the human ability to analyze the context of a situation and rank the different stimuli of the outside environment. This skill is absolutely essential to the propensity of the human brain for acting and reacting while embedded in the physical world; whether we are speaking, encoding, recalling a memory, or using reasoning capabilities [13]. Therefore, we believe it is necessary to analyze context from a number of different aspects. To this end, Bazire and Brézillon [8] analyzed a corpus of 166 definitions of context found in a number of domains and come to the conclusion that context can be derived from anything that is significant in a given moment and potentially including the environment, an item within that environment, a user, or even an observer. It is this inclusive definition that we will seek to use in this paper and, as such, will be assessing context from many aspects.

Hereafter the paper is organized in the following way. Section 2 briefly discusses how context is developed over the human lifetime. Following, Section 3 will begin the introduction of specific applications of context in human cognition with contextual paradigms in language. This will be followed by Section 4 which assesses contextual paradigms in human memory and reasoning. Sections 3 and 4 will also address computational architectures intermediately in the text following the discussions of the cognitive paradigms to which they are most similar.

2   Development of Human Contextual Reasoning Capability

Given our versatile definition of context, we believe that beginning with an analysis of its development over the course of the lifecycle will highlight the diversity of situations and factors through which contextual understanding is formed in human cognition. The evidence for the learned nature of situational propriety is found in the general definition of learning - that it is considered to be a relatively permanent change in behavior brought about by practice or experience. This experiential learning view of context is where we begin our discussion of how humans obtain contextual processing abilities.

Contextual learning begins as early as the infant stages of human development [1], [31]. Infants learn to navigate ambiguous situations by referring to the experience of social agents such as close caregivers in order to better understand the situation at hand. This concept was illustrated in a visual cliff study, which presents an infant with a threateningly deep chasm to cross which is safely covered by thick clear plastic. The infant cannot tell that it is safe to cross based on visual cues, and in fact views the situation as perilous. The study assessed infant reactions to the affectual displays of his/her mother while the infant was deciding whether or not to cross. When faced with the decision of whether or not to cross the cliff, the expressions of the mother were highly influential on the outcome. Even though the innate visual processing units of the infant indicated an unsafe environment, when the mother showed expressions of joy and encouragement, the majority of the infants crossed the deep side [39]. This study illustrates the power of context from the beginning of human development. Despite innate biological mechanisms warning the infant of danger, the contextual importance of the mother as a role model can override the impression of danger. The infant then learns to rely on the social agent above other contextual cues.

While this type of very closely guided contextual reasoning is effective for a time, it is recognized by many that the ideal state would be for children to develop autonomy and be able to reason through contextual environmental cues and develop preferences and weighting systems on their own. Piaget [30], [31] began conceptualizing this goal. The goal of Piaget's approach was for developing children to be able to think for themselves and not have to be told what it was they were to do. This is accomplished, according to Piaget, through the exchange of points of view. In this model, children do not merely learn through formulaic stimulus response patterns. Instead, they develop ways of thinking for themselves based upon the information imparted by social agents through guided instruction and modeling.

Through this modeling, the child would learn different behaviors and patterns that would be considered acceptable in a particular culture or context. Instead of the explicit mimicry of more experienced social agents, children would begin to be able to understand and apply the guidance they receive to decide for themselves what would be appropriate in a given circumstance [31]. For example, once the child learned a particular way of thinking and interacting with the world from a social agent then she would develop mental schemata, or blueprints, for future decisions. Then, as the child began to experience the world for herself, she could be confronted by discrepancies between these schemata and the events she perceives. This dissonance between what she perceives and her existing schemata would motivate changes in thinking and reorganization of the schemata. New contextual reasoning strategies would then develop as a result. This example illustrates the two parts of the social cognitive approach; the importance of the social agent in modeling behavior and the cognitive representations within the mind of the child to model and understand contextual cues from the social environment.

Humans are not passively absorbing standards of behavior from whatever influences they experience, whether they be respected social agents or otherwise. After an individual begins to recognize their preferences and standards, they select other individuals and activities that share the same standards and preferences, further reinforcing their performances and environments [7], [12], [17], [28]. If an individual does not approve of or internalize a behavioral standard, they will disregard it. This behavioral filter provides for more behavioral regularity and maintains the performance of preferred behaviors [5], [37]. This is to say that while outer context and the environment do play an indispensible role in human cognition, one must also take into account a person's inner context, their sense of self and their making sense of the world. There is not simply one single aspect to human cognition, but rather a complex matrix of systems of which contextual processing is a vital one.

One can, however, assert that context and the environment can have an influence on an individual's sense of self in their preferences and activities. As individuals, we frequently base our actions on our interests, and these interests can change based on experiences and interactions with others. This ongoing development involves not only physical, but emotional and cognitive development as well. This is important because it implies that our cognitive development is undergoing changes that allow one to perceive changes in the context of a situation and the environment that one is then able to manipulate.

This conscious manipulation of the environment based on contextual learning is very important to the development of children. A cycle seems to develop between context and the environment shaping internal preferences, and the agentic action of the child. Agentic action being defined here as behavior that is performed with intentionality, forethought, self-reactiveness, and self-reflection [6]. Essentially, contextual and environmental cues and experiences shape the preferences of individuals. These preferences then guide the agentic actions of the individual, leading to environmental consequences, which then influence the future preferences of the individual. This is not to say that these associations, often called conditioned reactions, are automatically evoked as part of a purely reflexive process. On the contrary, these associations are largely self activated, or agentic, on the basis of learned expectations [4]. The critical factor, therefore, is not that events occur together in time, but that people have learned to predict the events occurring and to summon up the appropriate anticipatory reactions because of the learned memories [4]. Within these memories there exist vast amounts of contextual information assisting our decisions based on how situations have proceeded in the past. This allows us to move forward and make more informed decisions as we discern the most appropriate course of action in any given situation. The development of contextual processing is a lifelong process involving the constant addition of knowledge as we have new experiences and receive new information. This process is ordered and structured in accordance with personal preference and identity.

3   Context in Language

It is widely accepted that humans utilize contextual processing in linguistic comprehension, whether written or spoken [20]. The question we entertain here is how this processing is achieved. In order to better define this goal we take the view that language, to some extent or another, activates representations within the mind that pertain to definitions and connotations of the words used, and processing continues from there. We examine how human mental processes are able to decide which representation and which definition is appropriate for a situation and how irrelevant representations are kept from activation depending on the context.

One of the most widely accepted models of linguistic processing and representation activation is the semantic network, or spreading activation model, proposed by Meyer and Schvaneveldt [27]. In this semantic network, activation of a concept spreads along routes of contextual familiarity. For example, if the word "baseball" is activated, then according to this model, the concepts associated with baseball begin to activate as well in order to provide the appropriate contextual information for processing. The theory was created after a lexical decision test in which subjects were presented with words on a screen and asked to state if they were both, in fact, English words. The results indicated that the time it took the subject to make their decision was significantly reduced if the words were contextually related to each other [27]. These results support the idea that the natural language processing system of the brain relies heavily on contextual connectivity.

Semantic Networks. Such a contextually-based system is highly promising for AI as it underscores the effectiveness of contextual associations in linguistic processing. It is also a parsimonious and elegant way of conceptualizing the representational system of language processing. As such, it is a system that lends itself well to translation into the realm of AI. To elaborate, there is, in fact, a Semantic Network structure in Artificial Intelligence.

Developed and extensively researched by Simmons [38] and Quillian [33], [34], [35] and later further examined by Collins and Quillian [15], as well as by Collins and Loftus [14], this structure, much like the conceptual structure of the cognitive semantic network, works to represent knowledge in a graphical method that connects associated concepts in knowledge. The AI conception of the semantic network proceeds further in that it can be used not only to represent the concepts and knowledge themselves, but it can also be used as a supporting function for other knowledge representation systems Furthermore, there are varying subtypes of semantic networks which lend themselves to differing methods of conceptual relation, such as definitional, assertional, or implicational [41]. According to Sowa [41], these structures are used to assess relations of supertype-subtype, to assert propositions of conceptual relation, and to represent patterns of causality or inference, respectively. Such diversity would be highly useful in contextual linguistic processing, as the semantic network could effectively work in conjunction with other linguistic systems to assess the contextual connectedness of linguistic input.

A related computational paradigm discussed by Sowa [40] is an architecture which is similar to the semantic network called the conceptual graph. Instead of representing language specifically, the conceptual graph represents concepts and their relations to one another. The benefit of this format is that it represents knowledge in a way that can be easily read and understood by humans, but is also directly useful to a computer. This is accomplished by representing knowledge, or a given situation, graphically through the use of formal logic, a language that both humans and computers can understand [40]. By operating in this format, a conceptual graph can both bridge some of the gap between cognitive and computational representation and provide a background context for a computer to operate in conjunction with a computational paradigm such as a semantic network.

Another promising cognitive theory of linguistic contextual processing is the Attenuation Model outlined by Treisman [42]. This model states that there are different attention channels entering into a selective filter in the brain. This filter assigns how much attention should be paid to each channel based on the situation. From the filter, both signals proceed to a dictionary in the brain, which then decides what message is being received by activating the correct words and meanings for the message. This process results in an activation threshold, or the probability of activation and recognition, for words. The level of attention needed to activate recognition of a word is influenced by the context of the situation in which the word is presented. The exception to this phenomenon is the utterance of universally low threshold words, such as a person's name or danger words, such as fire. This theory was developed from a classic dichotomous listening task. Subjects were given headphones and asked to attend to, and repeat, the information in only one channel, even though both channels contained messages. Treisman found that the subjects would repeat the word in the unattended channel if it made more sense for the passage they were shadowing. For example, if the passage in the attended channel said, "I sang a..." the subject was much more likely to repeat the word, "song" from the unattended channel before returning to the repetition of the attended channel. This, according to Treisman's model, would be because the threshold for the word song is lowered by the high transition probability after the previous statement [42].

Hidden Markov Model. Treisman's model describes a vital process in human contextual reasoning; the idea that individuals use context in language to highlight relevant information to make the most sense possible out of the myriad of phrases they hear throughout the day. Attending to everything an individual may hear with equal weight would be an impossibly large amount of information to sort through, thus highlighting the need for a contextual parsing system in the brain. A system in Artificial Intelligence that assists in speech recognition using contextual awareness to narrow down the number of possible options for a statement is the Hidden Markov Model [36]. This system must first be trained by being given correct, rational sentences so that it can construct a probabilistic model from which to work. It can then use this model in a situation to predict what will likely be the next word in a series. This is highly advantageous for linguistic processing as it uses its probabilistic model to parse down from an entire vocabulary to the likely next word in the series based on the previous situations it encountered. It would, however, be prudent to note that the Markov Model has historically had a weakness in the way it processes language; it only assesses the word directly in front of whatever word it is attempting to predict. Thus, if given the sentence, "I sang a..." the system would only assess the probability for words that would come directly after the, "a" and ignore the beginning of the sentence. This is not to say that the Hidden Markov Model is not practical or useful, simply that its ideal and quite important use in speech recognition would be as a contextual support system.

Attention to stimuli is undoubtedly important for our retention of the material. However, the significance of the phonological properties of words and concepts that make a difference in our retention and acceptance of the material at hand should also be noted. This is demonstrated by highlighting a different implication of Treisman's [42] dichotic listening project than previously analyzed; the specific properties of the material in the unattended channel and what it can mean for contextual processing. As long as the material in the unattended ear passed the test of being of sufficient loudness, brightness, and pitch, then the participants did not consciously analyze the material. The exception, of course, being the times when the context of the material was more appropriate. These would be instances such as the unintentional switch from the attended channel to the unattended channel in the aforementioned example of the word, "song" being activated after the subject repeated the statement, "I sang a..." However, even then there was no conscious analysis and the switch was handled subconsciously. This demonstrates that the material analysis was dismissed quickly and no active cognitive resources were wasted on the phonologically unimportant material.

Prosody Model. The above experiment has implications for the application of contextual processing in computer systems. Ananthakrishnan and Narayanan [2] investigated a computational model which analyzed the phonological properties of speech in order to assist in speech recognition. The results produced a 1.3% improvement in the automatic speech recognition's word error rate over the baseline. While this is not completely congruent to the phonological dismissal evident in the Treisman [42] study, it does illustrate the potential utility of a phonological assessment tool in computation. This system could be employed in conjunction with other contextual systems to assess phonological properties and only attend to those which were deemed to meet specified parameters in tone, pitch, and timbre.

Many words in the English language are homophones, with multiple meanings for the same word sound. For example; the car brakes stop a car from moving, but one breaks an egg for an omelet for breakfast. Most individuals are able to understand the meaning of a sentence because of the context of the surrounding words. One answer as to how this might be accomplished is posed by Gernsbacher [19] in a paper analyzing experiments with language comprehension. The Treisman model suggests how related contextual information is activated and retrieved in the brain and how phonologically irrelevant information is filtered out. However, it does not seem to explain how contextually irrelevant information is filtered out in a situation such as a homophone, where there would be no phonological cue. Hearing such a word would seemingly highlight two representations simultaneously, resulting in a bit of confusion as to which meaning is most appropriate.

In the break versus brake example, both meanings of the words would be activated until contextual information more clearly pointed out which meaning was appropriate. We would then have to sift through the extraneous information, slowing down situational comprehension. For truly successful real time comprehension to occur, it is necessary to keep this extraneous information from affecting the other processes at work. To accomplish this goal, we develop a suppression mechanism. This happens as we learn to successfully order schemata and are more and more competent at intuitively understanding contextual cues. To borrow terminology from Treisman [42], this mechanism would increase the activation threshold for the inappropriate homophone, thus decreasing the likelihood of the activation of its mental representation [19].

The aforementioned suppression mechanism plays a pivotal role in appropriate real time contextual understanding in human linguistics. Thus, there are weighty implications for the application of such a mechanism in artificial intelligence. A difficult problem faced by such an AI system is that of inefficient contextual information suppression resulting in a myriad of issues [16]. However, with a contextual suppression mechanism to weed out the irrelevant information, these issues could be avoided, at least in linguistic trials. The application of both these processes could prove to be highly beneficial to an AI system whose function was to perform any sort of linguistic processing.

4   Context in Memory and Reasoning

4.1   Memory

The human memory system is arranged in such a manner as to facilitate the use of contextual processing to augment both encoding and retrieval. For example, a study by Wagner et al [45] used fMRI scanning and demonstrated that there was a context-dependent aspect to memory at the neurological level, as different areas of the brain were activated depending on whether or not the context was familiar to the subject. The processes of encoding and retrieval greatly influence our cognitive behaviors, including perception, attention, learning, and cognition. The associations we form using context will guide how we remember information and what circumstances will trigger its retrieval.

There is evidence that when we encode new information, we also encode the context in which it was presented [21]. This can assist in more accurate recall. This phenomenon is called state dependent learning. The idea is that, since we encode not only the information itself, but also the context in which we learn it, replicating that context when it is time for recall will greatly increase accuracy. The experiment by Godden and Baddeley [21] illustrates this point effectively. They found a sample of SCUBA divers and took half out into the water and had half stay on dry land to learn a set of words. Then, one week later, they took them out again, only this time half of the dry land group went in the water and half of the water group stayed on dry land. When asked to recall the words on the list from one week earlier, the subjects who were in consistent environments were able to accurately recall significantly more words than the subjects who switched environments [21].

The SCUBA experiment illustrates the need for organizing information using context. If an intelligent system were taught to organize information by connecting relevant information based on context, then it would conceivably be much more capable of running in a real time environment. Fast, accurate recall is essential to a number of processes for which intelligent systems are to be used. The use of schemata, or contextual maps, would be invaluable to this goal. They would provide faster routes for recalling the most relevant information for a given function and could assist in filling in any contextual blanks when a situation is unclear, based upon previously ordered knowledge.

The formation of associations and schemata must take into account memory storage and transference from one type of memory system to another [3]. It is widely recognized that for learning to be effective, it is necessary for information to be placed into the long term memory where it can be part of the schemata to be assimilated and built upon. The question then becomes how and when these schemata are updated for new contextual information to be added.

Long term memories can be reactivated and made malleable, then modified with new information, and re-established [23]. When this happens largely depends on context. In a study involving young children Hubach, Gomez, and Nadel [23] found that these long term memories were very rarely activated when the children were in a familiar setting, such as their home. This indicates that when a situation is familiar, human cognition need not trouble itself with assimilating new information and using extra resources on a context which is already learned and familiar. However, there was an observed difference when the children were placed in less familiar contextual situations. In these situations, the context did trigger the reactivation of the older memories, indicating that the children were adding new information to their schemata and learning the contextual information for a new situation [23].

Hubach, Gomez, & Nadel's experiment reinforces the idea that the use of contextual processing in memory can significantly decrease the cognitive load placed on human beings in terms of active processing. The following intuition is then that the employment of a contextual map in an intelligent system would also ideally have the same effect. This, coupled with the previous example of state dependent learning argues for a contextual organization of intelligent systems for more effective information processing and retrieval.

4.2   Reasoning

When given a difficult abstract problem to solve, one of the first, if not the very first questions an individual will likely ask is, "Well, what is the context?" This is because we draw on previous knowledge to help with problem solving. Advanced human reasoning is largely top down, meaning it draws from previous knowledge and situational understanding in order to make sense of a current situation.

The use of contextual facilitation in learning is highlighted in mathematics education where there is a view that mathematics is much easier to understand if, instead of being presented in an abstract manner, it is presented in a contextualized format [44]. This view coordinates well with the previous assertion that the assimilation of information into long term memory is affected by context. Since the student would have a familiar situation in which to process the information, they could focus on the reorganization of the mathematics schemata as facilitated by a previously constructed situational schema.

A study by Pratt et al [32] carries this idea even further by assessing statistical problems, which according to the authors are different from mathematical problems in that they are not simply referenced using contextual information, but are actually about the real world and are therefore even more profoundly affected by context. More specifically, the authors' target for the study is risk assessment, which the authors assert is a highly complex example of statistical assessment and modeling. In this study, test subjects were given a hypothetical situation involving a medical risk and asked to recount how they made their decision of whether or not they would authorize a risky procedure. In making their decision, all the subjects drew heavily on their knowledge of the context of the situation and on personal experience involving such a situation [32].

Another study involving formal decision making was done by Pennycook and Thompson [29]. In this study, subjects were asked to place fictional individuals in one of two categories. They were given base rates for the probability of an individual belonging to a group and a personality profile that was either consistent or at odds with the base rate. The subjects were much more likely to draw upon the personality profile to make their decision, even when it called for the subject to disregard very strong base rate probability [29].

This study provides support for context-based reasoning over other types of information processing among humans. It shows that humans are much more likely to draw upon experience (i.e. context) rather than raw statistical analysis to make a decision. This can be invaluable when dealing with a confounding variable. Statistical modeling can move reasoning only so far, but for truly successful navigation within the real world, contextual weighting and experience must be incorporated.

These studies provide evidence for the use of contextual processing in formal human reasoning; however, it is also valuable to highlight its importance in informal reasoning. A study by Lee and Grace [25] explores the use of informal contextual reasoning in socio-scientific issues. The study incorporated students in two different cultural contexts involving disparities in access to information, adherence to tradition, and materialistic concerns. The assertion is that the disparities in cultural context will lead to disparities in the respective decision making of the students of the two different regions [25]. This assertion was found to be justified, as the students in the two regions studied did have dissimilar conclusions in the reasoning situation that showed to be in line with the expected differences in cultural contextual value systems [25].

4.3 Context Based Reasoning and Contextual Graphs

Given the recently discussed cognitive paradigms at work in contextually involved memory, as well as state dependant learning and reasoning, it would be prudent to discuss two computational architectures which excel in these areas; Context Based Reasoning and Contextual Graphs.

Context Based Reasoning. Context Based Reasoning, or CxBR, has been successfully used to represent tactical knowledge in simulated as well as physical agents [22]. It decomposes the agents' behaviors into contexts and sub-contexts. Each of these contexts contains behavioral information that is relevant to that context. This applies the principles of relevancy and exclusion that we discussed above. Additionally, each context contains environmental information that has to be true for that context to be in control of the agent. As the situation evolves during a tactical event, another context may be more applicable than the currently active one. The CxBR system then transitions the controlling context to the one that better addresses the current situation.

GenCL, or Genetic Context Learning, combines the use of Context Based Reasoning and genetic programming. This architecture was developed by Fernlund and colleagues [18] and strives to incorporate the two concepts of a tactical contextual map and state dependent learning. GenCL begins by initializing a first generation of agents for whom the structure of contexts and sub-contexts has been predefined, but each of which is empty. Then, for each generation, the performance of the agents is compared to that of an observed human expert. The best performing are selected for "breeding" the next generation via crossover and mutation. Specifically the genetic programming aspect of the system evolves not only the functions of each context used within the CxBR system, but also the transition conditions from one context to the next. Successive generations then become increasingly competent at the task presented to the system [18]. While this system does make large strides into the area of state dependent learning and contextual awareness, it would also be prudent to note that all of the contexts must be defined a priori. As of the time of the study by Fernlund et al, new contexts could not be learned.

A related system of note is Turner's Context-Mediated Behaviors or CMB, which is somewhat similar to CxBR, but has some critical differences. For one, the control of the context transition is done centrally in CMB, whereas it is done in a distributed basis in CxBR. Additionally, CMB allows the merging of contexts when a context by itself cannot successfully address the situation [43]. However, this feature was never implemented in practice.

Contextual Graphs. Brézillon [10] proposes a conceptual framework for studying context and a formalism called Contextual Graphs (CxG). He shows that context can only be considered in reference to a focus. According to this focus, a part of the context—the contextual knowledge—is more or less related to the focus, while the rest of context—external knowledge—has nothing to do with the focus at the moment. The contextual knowledge is recorded in a CxG while the external knowledge stays in the head of the actors. This AI approach is closely related to Piaget's work on children.

The specific purpose of this AI system is to utilize contextual information in order to model the human decision making and intuitive process [9]. By representing context at a progressively refined level, the situation can be identified clearly enough so that a decision becomes easy. To elaborate, the CxG is conceptually created to represent not only knowledge, but experience, which is knowledge with the addition of context, in a decision making paradigm that can be continually enriched in order to adapt to changing contexts and requirements. Furthermore, the CxG was designed with the assessment of real world situations as its core function, making it an ideal system to complete tasks such as the statistical questions posed in the study conducted by Pratt and colleagues [32].

5   Conclusion

The literature surveyed above points to the conclusion that contextual processing is a necessary and inextricable part of human cognition. It permeates all aspects, including linguistic processing, memory encoding and retrieval, and reasoning capabilities. In light of this, we further conclude that contextual processing must also be included in artificial intelligence if we are to ultimately succeed in our ambitious goals. Included not just in part as a component, but in totality within a system if it is to be truly successful as a human like, embodied intelligent system.

Moreover, as in the focus of this work, the study of the similarities and differences between human and artificial cognition can shed light onto the mechanisms of the application of contextual reasoning in artificial intelligence. The literature surveyed illustrates the deeper understanding of modeling context that can be obtained through the study of human cognition. The human brain is able to assess the many aspects of context that are relevant in any given situation with superb fluidity. Therefore, the study of the function of the different contextual paradigms at work in human cognition leads to new insights as to how a human like intelligence may be achieved in artificial intelligence. Conversely, there is much that the study of artificial intelligence may bring to our understanding of human intelligence. The innovations in cognitive modeling illustrate the types of mechanisms which could be at work in human cognition. The ability to directly observe theories of cognition at work in a controlled, computationally based way, wherein the data and steps behind a process are visible to the user, offers insight into what may be considered a successful theory of cognition.

References

1. Abravanel, E., Ferguson, S.: Observational learning and the use of retrieval information during the second and third years. Journal of Genetic Psychology 159(4) (1998)
2. Ananthakrishnan, S., Narayanan, S.: Improved speech recognition using acoustic and lexical correlates of pitch accent in a n-best rescoring framework. In: IEEE International Conference on Acoustics, Speech and Signal Processing, ICASSP 2007, vol. 4, p. IV-873. IEEE (2007)
3. Atkinson, R.C., Shriffin, R.M.: The control of short term memory. Scientific American 225, 82–90 (1971)
4. Bandura, A.: Behavior theory and the models of man. American Psychologist 29(12), 859–869 (1974)
5. Bandura, A.: Social learning theory. Prentice-Hall, Englewood Cliffs (1977)

6. Bandura, A.: Social cognitive theory: An agentic perspective. Annual Review of Psychology 52, 1–26 (2001)
7. Bandura, A., Walters, R.H.: Adolescent aggression. Ronald Press, New York (1959)
8. Bazire, M., Brézillon, P.: Understanding context before using it. In: Dey, A.K., Kokinov, B., Leake, D.B., Turner, R. (eds.) CONTEXT 2005. LNCS (LNAI), vol. 3554, pp. 29–40. Springer, Heidelberg (2005)
9. Brézillon, P.: Representation of Procedures and Practices in Contextual Graphs. The Knowledge Engineering Review 18(2), 147–174 (2003)
10. Brézillon, P.: Task-realization models in Contextual Graphs. In: Dey, A.K., Kokinov, B., Leake, D.B., Turner, R. (eds.) CONTEXT 2005. LNCS (LNAI), vol. 3554, pp. 55–68. Springer, Heidelberg (2005)
11. Brézillon, P., Gonzalez, A.J.: Tale of two context-based formalisms for representing human knowledge. In: Ali, M., Dapoigny, R. (eds.) IEA/AIE 2006. LNCS (LNAI), vol. 4031, pp. 137–145. Springer, Heidelberg (2006)
12. Bullock, D., Merrill, L.: The impact of personal preference on consistency through time: The case of childhood aggression. Child Development 51, 808–814 (1980)
13. Butterworth, G., Light, P.: Context and cognition: ways of learning and knowing. L. Erlbaum Associates, Hillsdale (1993)
14. Collins, A.M., Loftus, E.F.: A spreading-activation theory of semantic processing. Psychological Review 82(6), 407–428 (1975)
15. Collins, A.M., Quillian, M.R.: Retrieval time from semantic memory. Journal of Verbal Learning and Verbal Behavior 8(2), 240–247 (1969)
16. Dennett, D.: Cognitive Wheels: The Frame Problem of AI. In: Hookaway, C. (ed.) Minds, Machines, and Evolution. Cambridge University Press, Cambridge (1984)
17. Elkin, F., Westley, W.A.: The myth of adolescent culture. American Sociological Review 20, 680–684 (1955)
18. Fernlund, H.K.G., Gonzalez, A.J., Georgiopoulos, M., DeMara, R.F.: Learning tactical human behavior through observation of human performance. IEEE Transactions on Systems, Man, and Cybernetics 36(1), 128–140 (2006b)
19. Gernsbacher, M.A.: Less skilled readers have less efficient suppression mechanisms. Psychological Science 4(5), 294–298 (1993)
20. Glucksberg, S., Kreuz, R.J., Rho, S.H.: Context can constrain lexical access: Implications for models of language comprehension. Journal of Experimental Psychology: Learning, Memory, and Cognition 12(3) (1986)
21. Godden, D.R., Baddeley, A.D.: Context-dependent memory in two natural environments: On land and underwater. British Journal of Psychology 66(3), 325–331 (1975)
22. Gonzalez, A.J., Stensrud, B.S., Barrett, G.: Formalizing Context-Based Reasoning - A Modeling Paradigm for Representing Tactical Human Behavior. International Journal of Intelligent Systems 23(7), 822–847 (2008)
23. Hupbach, A., Gomez, R., Nadel, L.: Episodic memory updating: The role of context familiarity. Psychonomic Bulletin & Review 18(4), 787–797 (2011)
24. Kokinov, B.: Dynamics and automaticity of context: A cognitive modeling approach. In: Bouquet, P., Serafini, L., Brézillon, P., Benercetti, M., Castellani, F. (eds.) CONTEXT 1999. LNCS (LNAI), vol. 1688, pp. 200–213. Springer, Heidelberg (1999)
25. Lee, Y., Grace, M.: Students' reasoning and decision making about a socioscientific issue: A cross context comparison. Science Education 96(5), 787–807 (2012)
26. McCarthy, J.: Notes on formalizing context (1993)
27. Meyer, D.E., Schvaneveldt, R.W.: Facilitation in recognizing pairs of words: Evidence of a dependence between retrieval operations. Journal of Experimental Psychology 90(2), 227–234 (1971)

28. Mischel, W.: Personality and Assessment. Wiley, New York (1968)
29. Pennycook, G., Thompson, V.A.: Reasoning with base rates is routine, relatively effortless, and context dependent. Psychonomic Bulletin & Review 19(3), 528–534 (2012)
30. Piaget, J.: The Moral Judgement of the Child. Harcourt, Brace, New York (1932)
31. Piaget, J.: The Development of Thought: Equilibration of Cognitive Structures. Viking, New York (1977a)
32. Pratt, D., Ainley, J., Kent, P., Levinson, R., Yogui, C., Kapadia, R.: Role of context in risk-based reasoning. Mathematical Thinking and Learning 13(4), 322–345 (2011)
33. Quillian, M.R.: A notation for representing conceptual information: An application to semantics and mechanical English paraphrasing, SP-1395. System Development Corporation, Santa Monica (1963)
34. Quillian, M.R.: Word concepts: A theory and simulation of some basic semantic capabilities. Behavioral Science 12(5), 410–430 (1967)
35. Quillian, M.R.: The teachable language comprehender: a simulation program and theory of language. Communications of the ACM 12(8), 459–476 (1969)
36. Rabiner, L.R.: A tutorial on hidden Markov models and selected applications in speech recognition. Proceedings of the IEEE 77(2), 257–286 (1989)
37. Raush, H.L., Barry, W.A., Hertel, R.K., Swain, M.A.: Communication, conflict, and marriage. Jossey-Bass, San Francisco (1974)
38. Simmons, R.F.: Synthetic language behavior. System Development Corporation (1963)
39. Sorce, J.F., Emde, R.N., Campos, J.J., Klinnert, M.D.: Maternal emotional signaling: Its effect on the visual cliff behavior of 1-year-olds. Developmental Psychology 21(1), 195–200 (1985)
40. Sowa, J.F.: Conceptual graphs. Information Processing in Mind and Machine (1984)
41. Sowa, J.F.: Semantic Networks. In: Encyclopedia of Cognitive Science (2006)
42. Treisman, A.M.: Contextual Cues in Selective Listening. Quarterly Journal of Experimental Psychology 12(4), 242–248 (1960)
43. Turner, R.M.: A Model of Explicit Context Representation and Use for Intelligent Agents. Springer (1999)
44. van den Heuvel-Panhuizen, M.: The role of contexts in assessment problems in mathematics. For the Learning of Mathematics 25(2), 2–10 (2005)
45. Wagner, A.D., Desmond, J.E., Glover, G.H., Gabrieli, J.D.: Prefrontal cortex and recognition memory. Functional-MRI Evidence for Context-dependent Retrieval Processes. Brain 121(10), 1985–2002 (1998)

The Role of Context in Practice-Based Organizational Learning and Performance Improvement

John Hegarty[1,2], Patrick Brézillon[1], and Frédéric Adam[2]

[1] LIP6, Université Pierre et Marie Curie, Paris, France
jhegarty@groupe-igs.fr,
Patrick.Brezillon@lip6.fr
[2] AFIS, University College Cork, Cork, Ireland
fadam@afis.ucc.ie

Abstract. Using Contextual-Graphs (CxG) to represent organizational activity supports selecting key performance indicators (KPIs) that are free from causality assumptions and measuring practice-based organizational learning as distinct from organizational change. This paper presents four tools developed as part of a research program to extend CxG to *practice-based organizational learning and performance improvement. Aspectual comparison of practices represented in contextual graphs together with a practice-based organizational learning novelty typology*, a *practice maturity model*, and an *organizational-performance-improvement prioritization matrix* operationalize the construct of *practice maturity* that is proposed as a guide for researchers and practitioners in understanding and improving *practice-based activity management*. Results are presented for a transport planning organization that elucidate the role of context in *practice-based organizational learning and performance improvement* in the case of an activity (*light rail route selection*) that involved both political/managerial and engineering decisions.

Keywords: Modeling context in organizational activity, assessing practice maturity, strategic decisions, tactical decisions, using context to leverage lessons learned from experience, contextual graphs.

1 Introduction

This paper investigates the role of context[1] in practice-based organizational learning performance improvement. The case presented concerns the activity of *light rail route selection* in an organization charged with public transport planning in a European capital city. The subject here[2] is the role of context *qua* context in the organization's learning and performance improvement of one of its most complex activities.

---

[1] Here, context is defined as the elements of the environment that bear on an activity without entering directly into the description of the activity [*after* 1, 2]

[2] This paper presents results of research carried out by the first author under the supervision of the co-authors as part of the requirements for dual PhDs of the National University of Ireland and of the University Pierre et Marie Curie in Paris.

P. Brézillon, P. Blackburn, and R. Dapoigny (Eds.): CONTEXT 2013, LNAI 8175, pp. 59–72, 2013.

Learning is essentially a process of contextualization and de-contextualization [1, 2, 3]. Leveraging lessons learned is a priori amenable to context-based intelligent assistant support (CIAS) [4]. This paper extends the CIAS paradigm to *practice-based organizational learning and performance improvement*. There is no prior research (that the authors are aware of) on CIAS in *practice-based organizational learning and performance improvement* of complex activities. A challenging starting point is the real-world problem of leveraging organizational learning in long-cycle complex projects (like route selection in transport planning) where contextualization is particularly challenging for five reasons. First, complex *activity* is hard to isolate from its *environment*. Second, complex projects have both *strategic* and *tactical* levels. Third, *activity* and *artifact* interact recursively. Fourth, project *stakeholders* evolve with the *institutional context*. Fifth, *long-cycle* projects are prone to staff leaving before the organization abstracts *lessons learned* from their experience.

Hereafter, the paper is organized in the following way. Section 2 presents a synthesis of the prior literature on *practice-based organizational learning and performance improvement* in the form of a conceptual framework, highlights the research gaps that motivate the research, and formalizes the research objective. Section 3 presents the methodology used, a context-based intelligent assistant support (CIAS) approach, the tools developed and the research protocol. Section 4 presents the results of the field study that demonstrate the relevance of our context-based approach. Section 5 presents conclusions and implications for future research.

2   Conceptual Framework

This section presents a synthesis of the prior literature on *practice-based organizational learning and performance improvement* in the form of a conceptual framework, highlights the research gaps that motivate the research, and formalizes the research objective.

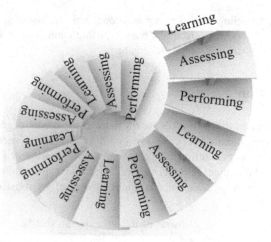

Fig. 1. The spiral of continuous improvement

There is an emerging consensus in both the cognitive and social sciences that the purpose of assessing is to learn from experience [5], and the purpose of learning is to improve performance [6]. This consensus is illustrated in Fig. 1 as a spiral of continuous improvement that draws attention to the embedded nature of performing, assessing, and learning in management activities.

A review, in the light of the context-based intelligent assistant support (CIAS) paradigm, of research literature in organizational learning and performance management is summarized here in a conceptual framework that highlights the role of context in the process of *practice-based organizational learning and performance improvement*. The social and cognitive mechanisms involved in *practice-based organizational learning and performance improvement* are characterized as *contextualizing, de-contextualizing,* and *re-contextualizing management activities*, in which the focus of managerial attention falls successively on *problems, practices, procedures,* and *practice maturity* as shown in Table 1.

Table 1. Conceptual framework

Focus of managerial attention	Contextualizing management activities	De-contextualizing management activities	Re-contextualizing management activity
Problems Practices Procedures Practice maturity	Situation assessment Problem solving Decision making Implementing	Representing practices Abstracting lessons learned	Leveraging lessons learned

The contextualizing activities of Table 1, *situation assessment, problem solving, decision making,* and *implementing* correspond to performing in Fig. 1. The de-contextualizing activities of Table 1, *representing practices,* and *abstracting lessons learned,* correspond to assessing and learning in Fig. 1 and the re-contextualizing activity of *leveraging lessons learned* corresponds to the higher levels of performance in Fig.1. The continuous cycle of contextualization of *problems,* de-contextualization of *practices,* and re-contextualization of *procedures* leads to *practice maturity* as illustrated in Fig. 2.

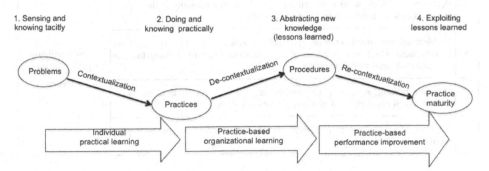

Fig. 2. Practice-based organizational learning and performance improvement

"Practice-based organizational learning occurs when new associations between <u>actions</u> and <u>situations</u> are discovered during <u>performance assessment</u> and are abstracted from the details of the discovery situation as <u>lessons learned</u> codified for future use. Practice-based performance improvement occurs in organizations when exploiting <u>lessons learned</u> from experience in realizing an <u>activity</u> leads to <u>practice maturity</u>."

Problems, practices, procedures, and *practice maturity* are representations of knowledge, reasoning, and context that are the focus of managerial attention. Their transformation in contextualizing, de-contextualizing, and re-contextualizing management activities is subject to *integrity rules* and *inference rules*. The elicitation and elucidation of the rules governing the felicitous use of knowledge, reasoning, and context in the case of *route selection* at ABC is the purpose of the research presented here.

The conceptual framework proposed for researching and understanding *practice-based organizational learning and performance improvement* is underpinned by a number of interpreting propositions that emerged from the review of prior literature and are shown in Table 2.

Table 2. Interpreting propositions

	Prior results (synthesis of literature review)	On
1	Representing practice-based organizational knowledge involves *formalizing* and *interpreting* an organizational activity together with the elements of the environment that bear on its realization in a given situation.	Practice-based Knowledge
2	Transforming practice-based organizational knowledge involves *accommodating* an activity in an organization to a new situation in which it is realized and *assimilating* the new situation to the activity.	Practice-based Learning
3	Using practice-based organizational knowledge involves reasoning about situations and reasoning in situations and is subject to *integrity rules* and *inference rules*.	Practice-based Reasoning
4	Situation assessment: *Analogy* and *enactment* are used in organizations to determine which elements of the environment bear on an activity in the organization's expected, desired, and planned worlds.	Contextualizing management activities
5	Problem solving: *Means-ends analysis* and *heuristics* are used in organizations to determine which *action*, taken in a given situation, would bring the expected and desired worlds together.	
6	Decision making: *Reason* and *rationality* are used in organizations to chose among hypothetical plans of action in a given situation.	
7	Implementing: *Technology* and *practices* are used in organizations to implement chosen plans of action.	

Table 2. (*Continued*)

	Prior results (synthesis of literature review)	On
8	Representing practices: *State descriptions* and *process descriptions* are used in organizations to represent different aspects of their practices. A representation of practice is *eo ipso* a *performance assessment*.	De-contextualizing management activities
9	Abstracting lessons learned: *Measurement* and *evaluation* are used in organizations to abstract *lessons learned* from experience.	
10	Leveraging lessons learned: *Exploitation* of lessons learned is an alternative to *exploration* of new practices and activities used in organizations to improve performance. It leads to *practice maturity*.	Re-contextualizing management activity

Three research gaps suggested by the conceptual framework were pursued in the research presented here. First, selecting practice-based measures of organizational performance. Second, measuring practice-based organizational learning. Third, identifying context-based intelligent assistant support (CIAS) opportunities for *practice-based organizational learning and performance improvement*. The first research gap addresses one of the shortcomings in current theories of organizational performance [7, 8], namely how to free performance indicator selection from assumptions of causality. The second research gap was explicitly evoked by [9] and represents an ongoing challenge to researchers and practitioners of organizational learning since first evoked. The third research gap derives directly from the purpose of the research to extend the CIAS approach to organizational learning and performance improvement.

The research objective is *to understand the role of context in practice-based organizational learning and performance improvement and to identify opportunities for CIAS support for practice-based organizational learning and performance improvement*. The next section presents the methodology used, a CIAS approach, the tools developed, and the research protocol.

3   Methodology

In this Section, the research questions, methods, and tools that operationalize the research are presented and summarized in the research protocol. The section is divided into four parts. First, the research questions are presented. Second, the method of formalizing practice using contextual graphs is explained. Third, the four new tools developed to interpret practice expressed as paths in contextual graphs are presented. Fourth, the research protocol is outlined.

3.1   Research Questions

The research objective is operationalized by breaking it down into three main research questions and associated subsidiary research questions, as shown in Table 3.

Table 3. Research questions and subsidiary research questions

Main Research Questions		Subsidiary Research Questions	
RQ1	How do organizations use experience to improve performance?	RQ1a	How do organizations represent their experience?
		RQ1b	How do organizations abstract lessons learned from their experience?
		RQ1c	How do organizations leverage lessons learned from experience?
RQ2	What issues confront organizations leveraging lessons learned from experience?	RQ2a	How do organizations ensure the relevance of their activities?
		RQ2b	How do organizations ensure the efficiency of their ways and means of realizing their activities?
RQ3	What opportunities exist for context-based intelligent assistant support (CIAS) for practice-based organizational learning and performance improvement?	RQ3a	What opportunities exist for context-based intelligent assistant support (CIAS) for recording relevant organizational experience ?
		RQ3b	What opportunities exist for context-based intelligent assistant support (CIAS) for retrieving relevant experience to improve performance in organizations?

The first research question investigates how *organizations* use experience to improve performance of an *activity*. Experienced organizations by definition have at least one effective way of realizing the activity considered. The first research question focuses on the manner in which practical experience is recorded and made available for future use in the organization.

The second research question investigates issues confronting *learning organizations* and focuses on how they select activities and how they manage performance of those activities. In other words, how organizations ensure they are *doing the right things* and how they ensure they are *doing those things right*.

The third research question applies to responsible organizations i.e. to organizations that already ensure the relevance of their activities and the efficiency of their practices. It looks at opportunities for CIAS support for *practice-based organizational learning and performance improvement*. It focuses on the use of CIAS to record relevant experience and retrieve it to improve future performance.

To answer the three research questions using a CIAS-based approach involves first formalizing the practice in contextual graphs and then interpreting the practice expressed in the Contextual-Graphs representation formalism using tools developed specially for the purpose.

3.2   Formalizing Practice Using Contextual Graphs

There are two difficulties in formalizing practice, one associated with formalizing *situations*, the other with formalizing *activity*. The difficulty with formalizing situations is in *denoting* the elements of the environment perceived as bearing on the activity and *referring* to them with specific values [1,10,11]. The difficulty in formalizing activity, whether *expected, desired, planned, actual,* or *learned* lies in determining the boundary of the active system. Activity separates the world into an inner and outer environment and elements of <u>both</u> environments are used to situate action as shown in Fig. 3.

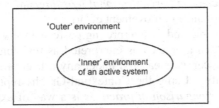

Fig. 3. Inner and outer environments of an active system

Practice in organizations is embodied in the realization of an activity. Four contextualizing management activities convert a problem, perceived as a gap between the desired and expected worlds, into a realization that closes the gap in specific circumstances as shown in Fig. 4.

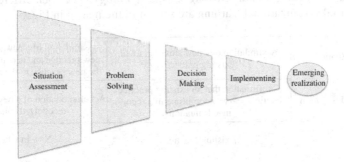

Fig. 4. Contextualizing management activities converging on an emerging realization

To formalize practice is to de-contextualize experience, leaving aside some aspects in favor of others. The CIAS approach followed here, attaches importance only to those elements of the situation that bear on the action as the activity unfolds. The CIAS paradigm suggests an approach to the collection of data summarized in the slogan 'ask about practice not about procedures'. This approach is implemented using the Contextual-Graphs representation formalism, and is very effective in collecting data on the practice of complex activities. The paths in a contextual graph formally represent different ways of realizing an activity; they formally represent practices and express the experience of the organization in the particular circumstances that prevailed at the time of the action.

3.3   Interpreting Practice Using Four New Tools

There are three difficulties in interpreting practice, one associated with interpreting the *performance of a practice*, the second with interpreting the *evolution over time of practices* that realize the same activity, the third with interpreting the *priority of organizational performance improvement effort*. In this section we propose four new tools, *viz.*, a new method for selecting *performance indicators*, new tools for measuring and assessing *practice-based organizational learning*, and a new tool for prioritizing organizational performance improvement effort.

The first tool is a new method of interpreting performance we call *aspectual comparison of practices*. When a practice is interpreted as realizing an activity, the performance of the practice can be measured under any aspect of its representation as a realization of the activity.   Using the Contextual-Graphs representation formalism together with *aspectual comparison of practices* is a way of expressing performance without recourse to assumptions about causality that taint the currently popular methods of selecting performance indicators used by managers, *viz.*, the generic Balanced Scorecard method and the *ad hoc* Tableau de bord method [7, 8].

The second tool is used to interpret practice-based organizational learning. Since the paths in contextual graphs express practical knowledge i.e. knowledge about what works in a given situation, their evolution over time expresses practice-based organizational learning.   The evolution in contextual graphs is interpreted using a *practice-based organizational learning novelty typology*. The four different types of practice-based organizational learning are shown in the matrix in Fig. 5.

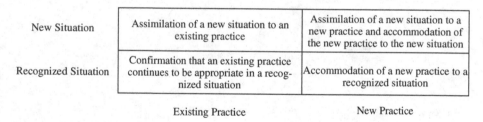

New Situation	Assimilation of a new situation to an existing practice	Assimilation of a new situation to a new practice and accommodation of the new practice to the new situation
Recognized Situation	Confirmation that an existing practice continues to be appropriate in a recognized situation	Accommodation of a new practice to a recognized situation
	Existing Practice	New Practice

Fig. 5. A practice-based organizational learning novelty typology

The appearance over time of new nodes in contextual graphs can be interpreted in terms of new situations and or new practices using the *practice-based organizational learning novelty typology* shown in Fig. 5. New contextual elements or new instances of existing contextual elements in a contextual graph express assimilation whereas the appearance of new actions or activities signals accommodation. Formalizing the evolution over time of practices using contextual graphs and interpreting the graphs using the *practice-based organizational learning novelty typology* effectively *measures* practice-based organizational learning.

The third new tool *assesses* practice-based organizational learning. The *practice maturity model* is shown in Fig. 6. Organizations develop practices over time. Initially there is just one practice, later new ways of realizing the activity are discovered and the number of practices increases. This can be observed in a densification of the contextual graphs used to measure the learning as shown in the previous section. As time goes on best practices displace less effective ones in the process of continuous improvement. And as the activity matures further optimization leads to the one best way. *Practice maturity* is the reflection and measure of activity maturity. The practice maturity model expresses this idea schematically in Fig. 6.

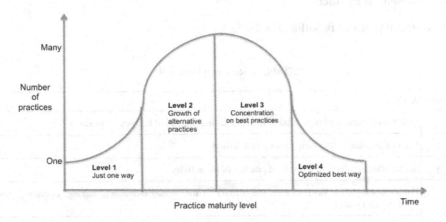

Fig. 6. A practice maturity model

Insofar as the levels of practice maturity are measured by observing the evolution in contextual graphs, the *practice maturity model* represents an extension of the context-based intelligent assistant support (CIAS) paradigm to *practice based activity management*.

The fourth new tool supports the prioritization of managerial improvement efforts. *An organizational-performance-improvement prioritization matrix* combines the characterization of activities by *practice maturity level* with an assessment of the *strategic relevance of the activity*. Whether effort should be invested in *exploration* or *exploitation* [12] depends on *strategic relevance* and *practice maturity* as shown in Fig. 7.

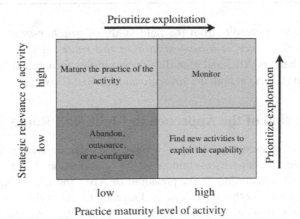

Fig. 7. An organizational-performance-improvement prioritization matrix

The four new tools presented in this section together with the Contextual-Graphs representation formalism were deployed using the research protocol outlined in the next sub-section.

3.4 Research Protocol

The research protocol is outlined in Table 4.

Table 4. Research Protocol

Item	Action
1	Select an experienced organization with procedure-controlled long-cycle projects
2	Select a mission-critical complex project activity
3	Select actual projects that involved practice of the activity
4	For each project, collect data on the activity in the strategic-decision-making, operating, and information systems
5	Analyze the data using contextual graphs, *the method of aspectual comparison of practices, the practice-based organizational learning novelty typology, the practice maturity model,* and *the organizational-performance-improvement prioritization matrix* with the objective of closing the gaps identified in prior research i.e. selecting practice-based measures of organizational performance, measuring practice-based organizational learning and identifying context-based intelligent assistant support (CIAS) opportunities for practice-based organizational learning and performance improvement
6	Present the results to the organization's strategic management for validation
7	Triangulate with expert opinion and public domain information
8	Interpret implications and contributions to theory and practice
9	Identify opportunities for further research

Section 4 presents results from the field study of *practice-based organizational learning and performance improvement* in *light rail route selection* at the organization referred to here as ABC and identifies opportunities for context-based intelligent assistant support (CIAS) at both the *strategic* and *tactical levels.*

4 Application of the Approach to Light Rail Route Selection

In this section, we present the results of a field study demonstrating the relevance of our approach and assessing its usefulness to the organization. *Light rail route selection* is a key process according to the president of ABC and the decisions concerning route selection involve both the *strategic* and *tactical* levels of the organization. Three network extension projects, here called Lines X, Y, and Z , were studied. The evolution of route selection practice at ABC is presented in this section in the form of a cross-case analysis.

In the first case, Line X, route selection practice was represented by ABC as route selection *actions* taken by ABC in response to *situations* that emerged from the environment. Different forms of representation were used for different levels of responsibility. At the top-management level, the representation took the form of a board paper concentrating on the two dozen most important items. At the operation management level, the representation took the form of a project review by function, complemented by a *lessons learned log* with more than a hundred items relating to Line X.

The formal distinction of *actions* and *situations* proposed in the conceptual framework was tested by transposing ABC management representations at both levels into contextual graphs and validating the transposition with the authors of the original representations. This was done in a *contextual graph research workshop* carried out at ABC headquarters and in follow-up communications with the managers involved. ABC represents its route selection practice as a structured relationship between ABC actions and elements of the evolving situation that bear on the action. The context of the action is formally captured on the one hand by the activity designation (here *route selection at top-management level* and *route selection at operational management level),* and on the other hand by the situational elements and their specific values at the time of the action. The Line Y case differs in its *point of view* from that of Line X in its emphasis on *governance and risk management.* ABC embedded risk *control activities* in its practice of route selection in response to *risk situations* perceived as threatening its objectives. Route selection activity on Line Z was intermediated by a consortium in Public Private Partnership (PPP) with ABC and was represented as the practice of *project management* (of route selection).

The focus of management attention moved from describing the substantive activity in Line X to describing how the activity is kept under control in Line Y, to how the activity can be delegated in Line Z. This is evidence of ABC confidence increasing with experience leading to a more sophisticated approach to its route selection activity. In the first extension project, Line X, the practice and performance of route selection was represented as a demonstration of ABC ability to select the best route in spite of well-organized opposition from powerful business interests. In the second extension project, Line Y, the emphasis moved to control of an activity that the organization confidently masters. In the third extension project, Line Z, the delegation by ABC of some important route selection activities to a consortium of developers demonstrates an increasing *practice maturity level.*

In the Line X case, three issues were identified as critical to leveraging lessons learned from experience, *viz.,* recording context at the right level of *granularity,* assessing activity against an *emerging baseline,* and reporting experience in the *right context.* In the Line Y case, additional issues were ensuring *alignment of objectives* with ABC mission and values, and with government policy; and ensuring risk management gave *assurance on expected cash flows,* appropriate to ABC *risk appetite.* In the Line Z case, ABC was confronted with the additional issue of representing route selection activities coordination as an inter-organization project.

Different opportunities for CIAS support emerged at ABC. First, in *practice-based organizational learning and performance improvement,* then in *governance and risk management,* and later in *project management.* This evolution towards more complex forms of support echoes the increasing confidence of the organization and the increasing *practice maturity* of its route selection activity. CIAS support must take account of time- and role-dependency; *reasoning about* a route selection situation is time-dependent and *reasoning in* a route selection situation is role-dependent. Time-dependency can be captured in a route selection contextual graph by recording the evolution of the structure over time[3]. Role-dependency can be captured in a route selection contextual graph by collecting practices that interpret the same role[4]. In order to assess how this might happen at ABC, separate graphs were used to analyze *top-management route selection* and *operations-level route selection*.

Route selection performance assessment is an interpretation of the activity and practice of route selection in particular circumstances. Whether to *exploit* the activity or *search* for new activities depends on the *strategic relevance* and *practice maturity* of the activity [12]. In the case of ABC, route selection is mission-critical and its practice is maturing through the efforts being made to record and exploit lessons learned described in this research.

The considerable effort required by the current ABC approach to *practice-based organizational learning and performance improvement* suggests that an alternative approach is worth investigating and explains the motivation of ABC to participate in the research project presented here. The transposition of ABC documents into contextual graphs (CxG) and their analysis with ABC management in the *CxG research workshops* demonstrated the relevance of the context-based intelligent assistant support (CIAS) approach to *practice-based organizational learning and performance improvement*. The next section presents conclusions and further research.

5   Conclusion

The Contextual-Graphs representation formalism opens up a new approach to the investigation of *practice-based organizational learning and performance improvement*. The use of contextual graphs to represent practices, at both the *political-strategic* and the *tactical-operational* levels, was demonstrated in a field study of *route selection in light rail infrastructure projects* of an organization charged with responsibility for public transport in a European capital city.

Since representations of practices are eo ipso performance assessments, contextual graphs immediately open up a new approach to the selection of Key Performance Indicators (KPI), here called *the aspectual comparison of practices*. The approach is free of the causality assumptions that taint both the Balanced Scorecard and the tableaux de bord approaches to KPI selection [7].

---

[3] A route selection contextual graph is both a snapshot of the activity at a point in time and a film of the unfolding activity. The evolution over time of route selection contextual graphs can be interpreted using the *practice-based organizational learning novelty typology* and monitored using the *practice maturity model*.

[4] Roles correspond to different interpretations of responsibility and different logics. The Contextual-Graphs representation formalism is not bound to any particular logic and as such offers an opportunity to 'explore behavioral logics as complementary rather than assume any dominant logic' [13].

The evolution of contextual graphs over time expresses practice-based organizational learning and can be measured using a *practice-based organizational learning novelty typology*.

This paper proposes *practice maturity* as a new construct, expressing both *practice-based organizational learning* and *performance improvement*, to guide researchers and practitioners in a practice-based approach to activity management. *Practice maturity* is measured using *a practice maturity model* calibrated using *a practice-based organizational learning novelty typology*. Management effort can be directed to activities that exhibit low practice maturity.

This research makes five contributions to the theory and practice of *practice-based organizational learning and performance improvement*. First, it extends context-based intelligent assistant support (CIAS) to *practice-based organizational learning and performance improvement*. Second, it develops a new method for selecting Key Performance Indicators (KPIs) free from causality assumptions, *viz., aspectual comparison of practices* represented as paths in contextual graphs. Third, it develops a new method for measuring practice-based organizational learning *viz., a practice-based organizational learning novelty typology* to interpret the evolution of practices in contextual graphs. Fourth, it develops a new method for assessing practice-based organizational learning using a *practice maturity model*. Fifth, it develops a new method for prioritizing organizational improvement efforts combining *practice maturity* and *strategic relevance* in an *organizational-performance-improvement prioritization matrix* that captures both the effectiveness and efficiency dimensions of performance and orients effort towards exploration or exploitation.

Future research could investigate the effect of social factors on *practice based organizational learning and performance improvement* by holding the technology fixed and doing a cross case study of two organizations involved in the same activity Such a project is under preparation comparing *light rail route selection* in the organization studied in this paper with another organization involved in the same activity but in another European capital city.

References

1. Brézillon, P., Pomerol, J.-C.: Framing Decision Making at Two Levels. In: Respicio, A., et al. (eds.) Bridging the Socio-technical Gap in Decision Support Systems, DSS (2010)
2. Edmonds, B.: The Pragmatic Roots of Contex. In: Bouquet, P., Serafini, L., Brézillon, P., Benercetti, M., Castellani, F. (eds.) CONTEXT 1999. LNCS (LNAI), vol. 1688, pp. 119–132. Springer, Heidelberg (1999)
3. King, W.R.: Knowledge Management and Organizational learning. Annals of Information Systems 4 (2009)
4. Brézillon, P.: From expert systems to context-based intelligent assistant systems a testimony. Knowledge Engineering Review 26(1), 19–24 (2011)
5. Neely, A., Al Najjar, M.: Management Learning Not Management Control, the True Role of Performance Measurement. California Mgt. Review 48(3), 101–114 (2006)
6. Pfeffer, J., Sutton, R.I.: The knowing doing gap. How smart firms turn knowledge into action. Harvard Business Review (2000)
7. Talbot, C.: Theories of Performance: Organizational and Service Improvement in the Public Domain. Oxford University Press (2010)

8. Neely, A.D., Gregory, M.J., Platts, K.W.: Performance measurement system design: A literature review and research agenda. International Journal of Operations and Production Management 25(12), 1228–1263 (2005)
9. Fiol, C.M., Lyles, M.: Organizational learning. Academy of Management Review 10(4), 803–813 (1985)
10. Allwood, J.: Meaning potentials and context: Some consequences for the analysis of variation in meaning. In: Cuyckens, et al. (eds.) Cognitive Approaches to Lexical Semantics, pp. 29–66. Mouton de Gruyter, Berlin (2003)
11. Donnellan, K.: Reference and definite Descriptions. The Philosophical Review 75(3), 281–304 (1966)
12. March, J.G.: Exploration and Exploitation. Organizational Learning, Organizational Science 2(1) (1991)
13. March, J., Olsen, P.: The logic of appropriateness. Arena Centre for European Studies. University of Oslo, Working Papers WP 04/09 (2004)

DCCLA: Automatic Indoor Localization Using Unsupervised Wi-Fi Fingerprinting

Yaqian Xu[1], Sian Lun Lau[2], Rico Kusber[1], and Klaus David[1]

[1] Chair for Communication Technology (ComTec)
Faculty of Electrical Engineering and Computer Science, University of Kassel
Wilhelmshöher Allee 73, 34121 Kassel, Germany
comtec@uni-kassel.de
[2] Department of Computer Science and Networked Systems
Faculty of Science and Technology, Sunway University
5, Jalan Universiti, Bandar Sunway, 46150 Petaling Jaya, Malaysia
sianlunl@sunway.edu.my

Abstract. People spend most of their time in a few significant places and often indoors in a small number of select rooms and locations. Indoor localization in terms of a user's current place, related to a user's daily life, routines or activities, is an important context. We implemented an automatic approach DCCLA (Density-based Clustering Combined Localization Algorithm) to automatically learn the Wi-Fi fingerprints of the significant places based on density based clustering. In order to accommodate the influence of the signal variation, clustering procedure separately works on a list of RSSIs (Received Signal Strength Indicators) from each AP (Access Point). In this paper, the approach is experimentally investigated in a laboratory setup and a real-world scenario in an office area with adjacent rooms, which is a key challenge to distinguish for place learning and recognition approaches. From these experiments, we compare and identify the most suitable parameters for the unsupervised learning.

1 Introduction

The location of a user is an important and useful context for many emerging location-based applications. For outdoor localization, the location information is usually obtained by using the Global Positioning System (GPS) technology and for indoor localization with the help of specialized infrastructure (e.g., infrared device [1] or ultra-wideband (UWB) network [2]), or by utilizing existing infrastructure such as cellular networks or Wi-Fi networks.

Despite the increasing amount of research, indoor localization is still a not completely resolved challenge. Wi-Fi network-based techniques usually rely on explicit pre-deployment effort, such as extensive site survey with data annotation to build a Wi-Fi fingerprint database [3] and/or radio propagation model [4]. These techniques, while providing localization accuracies of about 2-3m, are seen as expensive and time consuming to get running in the first place.

P. Brézillon, P. Blackburn, and R. Dapoigny (Eds.): CONTEXT 2013, LNAI 8175, pp. 73–86, 2013.
© Springer-Verlag Berlin Heidelberg 2013

Provided a technique could learn locations without the need of data annotation, i.e. in an unsupervised manner, one can eliminate the need of the pre-deployment process. As shown in our paper here, to eliminate the purpose-designed site survey for generating a Wi-Fi fingerprint database, the available data can be collected by a user's smartphone in his daily life.

We observed that a user spends most of his time in a few specific places, such as "home", "office", "leader's office", "café" and so on, which are usually significant to him. If a user stays in a place for a while, the received signal strength indicators (RSSIs) from one Wi-Fi access points (APs) are usually similar, presenting a high-density distribution. The specific characteristic offers us the possibility to build the fingerprints in an unsupervised manner by an autonomic approach.

It turns out to be an approach that learns the places a user goes to, and then recognizes them when he returns to these places. The notion of "place" in indoor localization usually provides a representation of locations that relates to a user's daily life, routines or activities. The solution is specifically called "place learning or/and recognition", which is one category of indoor localization.

In this paper, we demonstrate an automatic indoor localization approach called DCCLA (Density-based Clustering Combined Localization Algorithm) [5] to build place fingerprints from Wi-Fi received signal strength indicators (RSSIs) from surrounding access points (APs) in an unsupervised manner, i.e. without explicit pre-deployment effort.

Our unsupervised approach has two advantages. Firstly, a Wi-Fi fingerprint consists of a set of clusters, which belong to different APs observed in one location. Compared to a list of representative or calibrated RSSI values used in most similar approaches, a cluster is an RSSI range with respect to a place, which is more informative than a set of individual values. Secondly, the clustering procedure separately works on a list of RSSIs from each AP, which makes the approach more robust to the unstable presence of APs in the Wi-Fi measurements.

In many cases, learned places are useful context, for example, for a control system which turns on heating and lighting in a room, according to a user's preferences when he returns to this room. Without the need of data annotation, the unsupervised place learning and recognition technique can provide room level recognition, if it is able to learn and recognize two places from two adjacent rooms.

The goal of this paper is to present the algorithm and to investigate the performance in an office environment with adjacent rooms, which is a key challenge to distinguish for unsupervised place learning and recognition approaches. Evaluations will be carried out in a laboratory setup with known APs and also in a real-life environment using all detectable APs. We investigate which combinations of DCCLA parameters provide the best correct recognition probability.

This paper is organized as follows. Section 2 presents related work that utilizes similar approaches and a comparison with our technique. Based upon this, we elaborate the DCCLA algorithm in Section 3. In Section 4, the measurements and evaluations performed are explained. In Section 5, the conclusion is presented.

2   Related Work

2.1   Place Learning

Generally, place learning is the process of analyzing various sensor data to discover or learn the significant places, which relate to a user's daily life, routines or activities. The comMotion system [6] is one of the earliest applications about learning places. It detects and defines the indoor places by comparing the locations where the GPS signals disappear and re-appear later. If two measurements are within a certain distance, the location is considered to be a place.

In recent years, detecting places from the radio environment is regarded as a promising option for place learning. For example, the BeaconPrint algorithm [7] scans the GSM and Wi-Fi information to learn and recognize the places, under the assumption that the user is in a place if the scans remain fairly stable during a pre-defined time window. The basic idea of these radio beacon algorithms is to detect the places from successive scans and applying radius- or time-based clustering.

The approaches using successive scans with time sequences are sensitive to the Wi-Fi signal noise during short times. Density-based clustering [8] is proposed to handle the signal noise. ARIEL [9] incorporates a clustering procedure to partition the collected Wi-Fi scans into clusters, each corresponding to one stationary zone. Dousse et al. apply a density-based clustering algorithm OPTICS [10] directly on the raw Wi-Fi vectors, identifying the representative Wi-Fi clusters for a place [11]. Both of them apply density-based clustering on the Wi-Fi scans, consisting of a list of APs. However, calculating the similarity between scans is complex and sensitive to the signal variation.

In order to eliminate the effect of Wi-Fi signal variation between scans, the DCCLA (Density-based Clustering Combined Localization Algorithm) approach proposed by ComTec performs density-based clustering on the RSSIs from each AP, separately. The clusters from different APs related to the same place are later combined together, generating a Wi-Fi fingerprint. Because the clustering procedure separately works on a list of RSSIs from each AP, the unstable presence of APs and signal variation in Wi-Fi scans has less effect on the clustering results than it usually has in the above-mentioned approaches [9] [11].

2.2   Fingerprinting-Based Technique

Place learning is one category of indoor localization. Most current place learning approaches apply fingerprinting-based technique. The basic idea of the fingerprinting-based technique is to discover the signal characteristics in certain locations to form the "Fingerprint (FP)" of these locations. The localization is then realized when the real-time measurement matches a certain FP. Because of the differences of learned data and learning procedures, FP learning can be implemented with supervised learning or unsupervised learning.

Supervised Learning: For supervised learning, pre-deployment effort is required to build the desired fingerprint database. During the collection phase, explicit input is needed to produce labeled data for the training of localization models. For example, in RADAR [3] from Microsoft, empirical Wi-Fi information was collected at predefined locations to generate a complete Wi-Fi fingerprint database for the selected area.

Such approaches learn the FPs from known locations and respectively collected data with data annotations, mostly in terms of semantic names. In many cases, such explicit pre-deployment effort is seen as costly and not practical. Time and resources are needed to build the required fingerprint database.

Unsupervised Learning: The aim of unsupervised learning is to omit the pre-deployment effort for the generation of FPs in the supervised learning. An example is the Redpin approach [12]. It omits the pre-deployment effort by detecting the stable state when Wi-Fi scans keep stable. Then users are immediately prompted to confirm and correct the FP, when an unknown or a wrong one is detected. This approach is seen as unsupervised, because no pre-deployment effort is required to identify a location. However, it requires users' explicit input to annotate the detected location; otherwise the location database is not updated.

Another popular unsupervised approach is based on a technique "Dead Reckoning (DR)". DR is the process of detecting a location based on previously determined locations and known or estimated speeds [13]. A recent project UnLoc [14], developed by Duke University, bypasses the need of pre-deployment effort by identifying the significant landmark in DR. However, the method still relies on known information of some specific locations, e.g., the location of a door, or staircase, or elevator. The landmarks must be first modeled and identified before the unsupervised Wi-Fi FPs can be created.

A pure unsupervised solution without pre-deployment effort and external landmark information is usually based on radius-based clustering or density-based clustering as we introduced. It is usually applied in place learning applications, e.g. DCCLA works based on the assumption that a significant place is a location where people socially stay for more than a certain time period (e.g. 10 minutes) [15]. The periodically collected Wi-Fi data present a high-density distribution in the significant places, while the data present low-density distribution or vary quickly in the non-significant places. The basic idea of DCCLA is to discover the high-density clusters for each detectable AP. To the best of our knowledge, DCCLA is the first approach to separately apply density-based clustering on the RSSIs from each AP, to eliminate the effect of the signal variation between scans. In the Section 3, we will introduce the DCCLA algorithm in detail.

3   Algorithm Description

The algorithm of DCCLA includes three phases: collection, learning and recognition phase.

Collection Phase: The smartphone periodically scans the surrounding APs. The *scans*, consisting of *RSSI points* from all detectable APs, are stored in a *Wi-Fi database*. To collect RSSI points, smartphones do not need to connect to any APs.

Definition 1: (RSSI point) An *RSSI point* (P_{ik}) is a record, including the timestamp (t_k) of scanning this point, the MAC (Medium Access Control) address (MAC_i) of the Wi-Fi AP (AP_i) and the corresponding RSSI value ($RSSI_{ik}$).

$$P_{ik} = \{t_k; \; MAC_i; \; RSSI_{ik}\} \; (i, k \in \mathbb{N}^*)$$

Definition 2: (scan) For a timestamp t_k, more than one AP may be detected. Thus, a *scan (S_k)* consists of RSSI points from all detectable APs related to a timestamp t_k. The *length* of a scan is the number of the RSSI points in the scan.

$$S_k = \{P_{ik}, \dots , \qquad P_{jk}\} \; (i, j, k \in \mathbb{N}^*, i \leq j)$$

Definition 3: (Wi-Fi database) A *Wi-Fi database (WD)* is a list of scans collected during a time period $[t_k, t_m]$.

$$WD = \{S_k, \dots , \qquad S_m\} \; (k, m \in \mathbb{N}^*, k \leq m)$$

Learning Phase: The RSSI points are automatically learned to be the Wi-Fi FPs of the significant places. In our work, we separately perform density-based clustering on a set of RSSI points from each Wi-Fi AP in a WD. Then we combine clusters related to the same place together, generating a Wi-Fi FP. Details of the two sub-phase algorithms, cluster learning algorithm and fingerprint learning algorithm, are described in Section 3.1 and 3.2.

Recognition Phase: As the user visits a place, a snapshot of the momentary scan S_k will be compared to the Wi-Fi FPs in the fingerprint database obtained from the learning phase. If there is a matching Wi-Fi FP, the recognition algorithm returns the matched result. This indicates that the user returns to a place related to this Wi-Fi FP. The user is located. Details of the Wi-Fi fingerprint recognition algorithm are described in Section 3.3.

3.1   DCCLA Cluster Learning Algorithm

As we observed in previous work [5], the collected RSSI points from one Wi-Fi AP perform a high-density distribution in a significant place. The density-based clustering algorithm in [8] is modified to learn the high-density range for each AP.

Definition 4: (neighborhood of P_{ik}) An RSSI point (P_{im}) with the same MAC address as P_{ik} within a neighborhood range (NR) is a *neighbor of P_{ik}*, denoted by $n(P_{ik})$. The collection of all neighbors of P_{ik} is called *neighborhood of P_{ik}*, denoted by $N\,(P_{ik})$. Here we define P_{ik} itself belongs to $N\,(P_{ik})$ as well.

$$N\,(P_{ik}) = \{P_{im} \in D \mid 0 \leq RSSI_{im} - RSSI_{ik} \leq NR\} \; (i, k, m \in \mathbb{N}^*)$$

The *neighborhood range (NR)* is one parameter, used to delimit the range of the neighborhood starting from the RSSI point (P_{ik}). The unit of NR is dB.

Definition 5: (neighborhood density) *Neighborhood density of P_{ik} ($\rho(P_{ik})$)* is the number of neighbors of P_{ik} the NR.

$$\rho(P_{ik}) = \sum_{RSSI_{ik}}^{RSSI_{ik}+NR} P_{ik} \; (i, k \in \mathbb{N}^*) \tag{1}$$

We take ($NR=2dB$) as an example. For an RSSI point P_{ik} with RSSI value ($RSSI_{ik}$=-62dB), all the RSSI points, who have the same MAC address (MAC_i) and

RSSI values [*-62dB,-61dB,-60dB*], are the neighbors of P_{ik}. The number of the RSSI points in the neighborhood range [*-62dB, -60dB*] is the neighborhood density of P_{ik}.

Two parameters are introduced to determine the criterion of high neighborhood density. One is the *neighborhood range (NR)* as we introduced above. Another is the *minimum number of RSSI points (MinPts)*. It is a natural number which is introduced to determine if the Neighborhood density of P_{ik} is high enough to create a cluster.

For an RSSI point (P_{ik}), its neighborhood density is high enough to create a cluster if the following requirement is satisfied:

$$\rho(P_{ik}) \geq MinPts \ (i, k \in \mathbb{N}^*) \tag{2}$$

Definition 6: (cluster) A cluster (C_i^o) is a collection of RSSI points. Its representative form is a consecutive RSSI range with high RSSI density, associated with MAC_i, which can be indicated by:

$$C_i^o = \{MAC_i, RSSI_{ib}, RSSI_{ie}\} \ (o, i, b, e \in \mathbb{N}^*, RSSI_{ib} \geq RSSI_{ie})$$

$RSSI_{ib}$ represents the beginning and $RSSI_{ie}$ represents the end RSSI value of the high-density range (e.g. $C_i^o = \{00: aa: 00: 62: c6: 00, -56dB, -62dB\}$). We extract the cluster with a consecutive RSSI range because it is more informative than a set of individual RSSI values. A set of RSSI points with one MAC address may be grouped into several clusters (e.g. $\{C_i^o, ..., C_i^p\}$) without overlapping. C_i^o is the oth cluster related to the MAC address MAC_i.

After a cluster is created, the algorithm check if this cluster can be extended by checking if the requirement of cluster-extension is satisfied.

Definition 7: (cluster-extension) A cluster (C_i^o) can be extended if the following two conditions are met:

- $P_{im} \in C_i^o$

- $\rho(P_{im}) \geq MinPts$

The neighborhood of P_{im} is merged into the cluster (C_i^o), as the cluster is extended.

The basic idea to generate a cluster is the following. For each RSSI point P_{ik}, the algorithm calculates its neighborhood Density ($\rho(P_{ik})$). If $\rho(P_{ik})$ is lower than *MinPts*, the algorithm continues to check the next unchecked RSSI point. Otherwise, the neighborhood of P_{ik} is either used to create a new cluster if P_{ik} does not belong to any existing cluster, or merged to an existing cluster if P_{ik} belongs to the existing cluster. The set of RSSI points not belonging to any cluster is defined as *noise*. The pseudo code of the DCCLA cluster learning algorithm is described as follows.

```
Input: a Wi-Fi database (WD).
Output: a set of all learned clusters {C_i^o,…, C_j^q}.
1) Separate the WD into datasets, each dataset with a
   unique MAC address MAC_i.
2) Order each dataset to form a list L_i with increasing
   RSSI values.
3) Label each RSSI point (P_ik) on each L_i as unchecked
```

```
4) for each ordered Lᵢ, do
     1) while there exist an unchecked Pᵢₖ, do
          1) Calculate the neighborhood density of Pᵢₖ
             (ρ(Pᵢₖ))
          2) if ρ(Pᵢₖ) is smaller than MinPts , then
               1) Label Pᵢₖ as checked.
               2) continue the while loop
          3) else if Pᵢₖ belongs to an existing cluster Cᵢᵒ,
             then
               1) Merge neighborhood of Pᵢₖ to Cᵢᵒ.
          4) else
               1) Create a new cluster Cᵢᵖ.
          5) end if
          6) Label Pᵢₖ as checked.
     2) end while
5) end for
```

As indicated above, the range of a cluster is not restricted by the parameter neighborhood range (*NR*). The cluster range is automatically adapted to the high-density distribution of RSSI points in the Wi-Fi database. Consequently, the density-based clustering algorithm is suitable for indoor localization where signal variations in different scenarios are mostly not the same.

3.2   DCCLA Fingerprint Learning Algorithm

After the clustering process, the algorithm learns the Wi-Fi fingerprints.

Definition 8: (Wi-Fi fingerprint) A *Wi-Fi fingerprint* (FP_k) is a set of clusters, which belong to different APs related to a scan S_k collected at the time t_k.

$$FP_k = \{C_i^p, \dots, C_j^q\} \, (k, i, j, p, q \in \mathbb{N}^*)$$

In most offices or residential areas, more than one AP can be detected. The RSSI points in a scan S_k with the same timestamp t_k and different MAC addresses are collected in the same place. We develop the fingerprint learning algorithm based on the above fact. In the fingerprint learning sub-phase, the algorithm compares all scans in the WD with the learned clusters. For each scan $S_k = \{P_{ik}, \dots, P_{jk}\}$ with the timestamp t_k, if they respectively belong to a set of clusters $\{C_i^p, \dots, C_j^q\}$, the algorithm combines these clusters to generate a Wi-Fi fingerprint FP_k, corresponding to a significant place where this scan is collected. The pseudo code of the DCCLA fingerprint learning algorithm is described as follows.

```
Input: a Wi-Fi database (WD) and a set of clusters
{Cᵢᵒ,…, Cⱼq} learned from this WD.
Output: a fingerprint database (FD).
```

```
1) for each scan S_k in the WD, do
   1) Label all learned clusters {C_i^o, ..., C_j^q} as
      unmatched.
   2) for each RSSI point (P_ik) in S_k, do
      1) Compare with {C_i^o, ..., C_j^q}.
      2) if P_ik belongs to a learned cluster (C_i^p), then
         1) Label C_i^p as matched.
      3) else
         1) break the for loop.
   3) end for
   4) if the number of matched clusters equals to the
      length of S_k, then
      1) Combine the set of matched clusters {C_i^p ..., C_j^q}
         together as a fingerprint FP_k.
      2) if FP_k does not exist in a FD, then
         1) Add FP_k to FD.
      3) else
         1) continue the for loop.
   5) else
      1) continue the for loop.
2) end for
```

One place may have more than one corresponding set of fingerprints because of the variation of detectable APs. Ideally, the fingerprints in each distinguishable place are unique, so as to be able to separate places from one another. All Wi-Fi fingerprints are stored in the *fingerprint database (FD)*. In the update phase, the learning phase is repeated on a newly collected Wi-Fi database. But only new Wi-Fi fingerprints are added to the *FD*.

3.3 DCCLA Fingerprint Recognition Algorithm

As the user visits a place, a snapshot of the momentary scan $S_m = \{P_{im}, ..., P_{jm}\}$ is compared to the Wi-Fi fingerprints in the fingerprint database (*FD*). If, and only if, each RSSI point in S_m belongs to each cluster of a Wi-Fi fingerprint (FP_k), the recognition algorithm returns the matched result. The pseudo code of the DCCLA cluster learning algorithm is described as follows.

```
Input: a momentary scan S_m = {P_im, ..., P_jm} and a
fingerprint database (FD).
Output: a matched Wi-Fi fingerprint (FP_k).
1) for a momentary scan S_m = {P_im, ..., P_jm}, do
   1) Label each fingerprint (FP_k) in the FD as
      unchecked
```

  2) **while** there exists an unchecked FP_k in FD, **do**
    1) **if** the length of S_m equals to the number of clusters in FP_k, **do**
      1) **if** each RSSI point (P_{im}) in S_m falls into each cluster in FP_k, **do**
        1) Return FP_k.
      2) **else**
        1) **continue** the while loop.
    2) **else**
      1) **continue** the while loop.
    3) **end while**
  2) **end for**

This is known as 100% degree of matching. For example, if there are three RSSI points measured in a scan, $\{t_k, MAC_1, -45dB\}$, $\{t_k, MAC_2, -50dB\}$, $\{t_k, MAC_3, -57dB\}$, a 100% matched fingerprint contains three clusters with respective MAC address and cluster range where the RSSI value of each RSSI point belongs to.

A matched scan indicates that the user has returned to a place corresponding to this fingerprint. The user's current place is recognized. Currently, in order to reduce the localization errors, we utilize the 100% degree of matching to recognize the matched Wi-Fi fingerprint.

4   Experimental Evaluation

We select two scenarios in an office area with adjacent rooms for the intended investigations. The decision to select a small-scale office area is that it is generally a challenge to distinguish adjacent rooms in an unsupervised manner. In the first scenario, we use four APs with known locations to investigate the influence of the number of APs. For the second scenario, all detectable APs (up to 17 APs) in reality are included. The office area is located on the second floor of a three-story building. The area consists of five office rooms next to each other. Room 2408 has an area of $38.32m^2$, and each of rooms 2410, 2411, 2412, and 2414 has an area of $18.41m^2$. The layout is shown in Fig. 1.

Five Motorola Milestones smartphones with Android version 2.2.1 are used as measuring devices. The collection locations are shown in Fig. 1. These smartphones are placed at the height of a table (about 70cm). We assume that most users are used to putting their smartphones on the table (meaning a similar height).

The RSSIs are collected at a collection interval of 5 seconds. In contrast to the previous investigation [15], we now allow the presence of people throughout the measurements. In this way, possible influence on signal variation due to occupancy, which will be the case in a real life scenario, is included in the collected data.

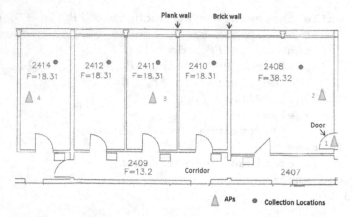

Fig. 1. The office area, and the collection locations, i.e. the positions of the APs as well as smartphones used for the evaluation

For the evaluations, training and test data are extracted from the collected data. Training data from each room are used to generate fingerprints of respective rooms. Test data from each room are used to evaluate the recognition performance of the DCCLA approach. We define an evaluation metric for the recognition phase. "*Correct*" means a smartphone is in a place and the algorithm recognizes it is in this place. "*False*" means a smartphone is in a place but the algorithm recognizes it is in a different place. "*Correct Recognition Probability (CRP)*" is defined as the number of the "*Correct*"s divided by the number of the "*Correct*"'s and the "*False*"'s.

$$CRP = \frac{\sum Correct}{\sum Correct + \sum False} \times 100\% \tag{3}$$

The *CRP* metric indicates how well the DCCLA can recognize a place correctly without having it mistaken as another place.

4.1   Influence of the Number of APs

From our previous investigation [15], we know that the *CRP* of two locations from two adjacent rooms using Wi-Fi RSSI from a single AP was 76%. In this evaluation, we investigate the *CRP* of the DCCLA in an environment with more than one AP. Fig. 1 presents the placement of the APs used in our investigation.

We use the first 30 minutes of the collected Wi-Fi RSSIs as training data and the subsequent 30 minutes of Wi-Fi RSSIs as test data. Measurements are repeated by increasing the number of AP from one to four APs. Based on the results in [15], *NR*=2 and *MinPts*=120 are used as parameters for the DCCLA learning process. The arithmetic average *CRP* is then calculated for all rooms. The results are listed in Fig. 2.

The increase of APs uses for localization results in an improvement in the *CRP*. From the *CRP* of 59.17% (only one AP), the *CRP* with three and four APs increases to 97.63% and 99.25% respectively. The *CRP* using one AP in this paper is lower than the result from our previous paper (76%) [15]. This is due to possible interference caused by occupancy and changes in the environment during the

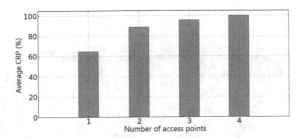

Fig. 2. Average *CRP* using one to four APs

measurement period. In our previous investigation, the measurements were performed without disturbance of surrounding people. From this result, it is shown that the increase of the number of APs improved the *CRP* of the DCCLA approach.

4.2   Parameters for the Generation of Fingerprints Using the DCCLA

In the previous paper [15], we identified parameters based on the use of a single AP. Furthermore, the selected environment had minimal disturbance such as interference and signal variation due to people movements and environment changes. In reality, these factors cannot be neglected. In this subsection, we compare the *CRP* obtained with different combinations of parameters to build the fingerprint database using the DCCLA learning algorithm. The parameters to be investigated are: neighborhood range (*NR*) and the minimum number of RSSI points (*MinPts*).

We use the data collected from three APs with known locations (AP$_2$, AP$_3$, and AP$_4$ in Fig. 1). The values of *NR* and *MinPts* are changed in each repetition of the learning phase. Selected *NR* values are 1, 2, 3, 4, 5, 6, 7, 8, 9, and 10 *dB*. Selected *MinPts* values range from 10 to 240 with an increment of 10. For each repetition, the test data from every room are tested with the generated fingerprints from each room to produce the *CRP*. Fig. 3 shows the results of the comparison. The values *NR*=3 and *MinPts*=110 are the parameters with the best *CRP*. The *CRP* declines if *NR* is more than 4. This is because when the *NR* was too large, the generated clusters have the tendency to overlap locations from two adjacent rooms. This causes the DCCLA approach to fail to differentiate these places. Based on these results, we repeat the evaluation for a range of *NR* values (from 1 to 10) and number of APs (from 1 to 4 APs) to see whether the optimal values (*NR* and number of APs) from the previous evaluations were still valid. The value of *MinPts* is kept as 110. The results show that the best *CRP* is obtained for three APs and an *NR* between 3 and 7. As observed earlier, a lower number of APs produces a lower number of clusters for recognizing locations in adjacent rooms. By increasing the number of APs, it is possible to generate clusters and fingerprints that can distinguish these adjacent rooms. However, the physical location of the AP should also be taken into consideration. As shown in Fig. 4, a total of 4 APs does not provide higher recognition as 3 APs if the value of *NR* is lower than 7. This is due to the additional AP$_2$ being close to AP$_1$ (see Fig. 1).

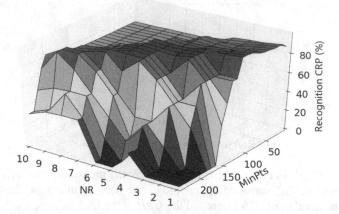

Fig. 3. Comparison of different DCCLA learning parameters, *NR* (x-axis) and *MinPts* (y-axis)

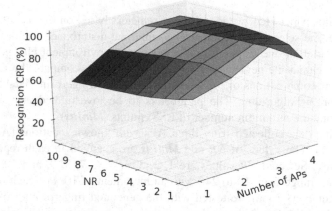

Fig. 4. The *CRP* for different *NR* (x-axis) and numbers of APs (y-axis)

4.3   Inclusion of All Detectable Wi-Fi Access Points from the Surroundings

Besides the four APs used in the previous evaluation, there are also other detectable APs from neighboring departments. From the collected data, the number of detectable existing APs is from 2 to 17. We investigate the performance of the DCCLA approach when Wi-Fi RSSIs from all available APs are to be used.

We repeat the evaluation in the previous subsection, and use collected RSSIs from all existing APs to build the fingerprint dataset. Test data from each room are used to evaluate fingerprint dataset of each room. The *CRP* for each combination of *NR* and *MinPts* are computed for comparison. The result is shown in Fig. 5.

As compared to the result in Section 4.2, the *CRP* has increased (see Fig. 3). The *CRP* is 100% for all values of *NR* if we keep the *MinPts* lower than 100. Similarly, the highest *MinPts* with 100% *CRP* is 180, when the value of *NR* is kept between 7 and 10. In other words, the selection of *NR* and *MinPts* within these ranges enables the DCCLA approach to recognize the selected places in the office area without false recognition.

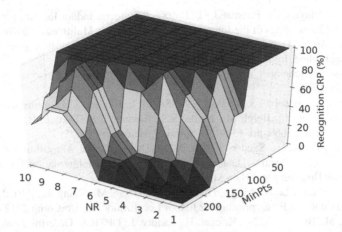

Fig. 5. The *CRP* using all available APs for different values *NR* (x-axis) and *MinPts* (y-axis)

5 Conclusion

In this paper, we have presented the DCCLA (Density-based Clustering Combined Localization Algorithm) approach in detail. It is an unsupervised indoor localization approach that is designed to automatically generate Wi-Fi RSSI-based fingerprints without any explicit user input or control. The performance of the approach is experimentally investigated in a laboratory setup and a real-world scenario. From the experiments, we have identified the ideal parameters suitable for the small-scale office area with adjacent rooms. It is shown that even in a small-scale office area, adjacent rooms can be correctly distinguished and recognized with a *CRP* (Correct Recognition Probability) between 97% and 100% with at least 3 APs. The results have given us promising techniques that can improve and optimize the DCCLA approach. Index Expanded.

Acknowledgments. This paper is funded by the German "Bundesministerium fr Wirtschaft und Technologie by funding the project" pinta (Pervasive Energie durch internetbasierte Telekommunikationsdienste), reference number 01ME11027. The authors are responsible for the content of this publication and would like to acknowledge the contributions of their colleagues.

References

1. Want, R., Hopper, A., Falcao, V., Gibbons, J.: The active badge location system. ACM Transactions on Information Systems 10(1), 91–102 (1992)
2. Mahfouz, M.R., Zhang, C., Merkl, B.C., Kuhn, M.J., Fathy, A.E.: Investigation of High-Accuracy Indoor 3-D Positioning Using UWB Technology. IEEE Transactions on Microwave Theory and Techniques (2008)
3. Bahl, P., Padmanabhan, V.N.: RADAR: An in-building rf-based user location and tracking system. In: INFOCOM (2000)

4. Martin, E., Vinyals, O., Friedland, G., Bajcsy, R.: Precise indoor localization using smart phones. In: Proceedings of the International Conference on Multimedia (2010)
5. Lau, S.L., Xu, Y., David, K.: Novel indoor localisation using an unsupervised Wi-Fi signal clustering method. In: Future Network & Mobile Summit (2011)
6. Marmasse, N., Schmandt, C.: A user-centered location model. In: Personal and Ubiquitous Computing (2002)
7. Hightower, J., Consolvo, S., LaMarca, A., Smith, I., Hughes, J.: Learning and recognizing the places we go. In: Beigl, M., Intille, S.S., Rekimoto, J., Tokuda, H. (eds.) UbiComp 2005. LNCS, vol. 3660, pp. 159–176. Springer, Heidelberg (2005)
8. Ester, E., Kriegel, H., Sander, J., Xu, X.: A Density-Based Algorithm for Discovering Clusters in Large Spatial Databases with Noise. In: 2nd International Conference on Knowledge Discovery and Data Mining (1996)
9. Jiang, Y., Pan, X., Li, K., Lv, Q., Dick, R.P., Hannigan, M., Shang, L.: ARIEL: Automatic Wi-Fi based Room Fingerprinting for Indoor Localization. In: UbiComp 2012 (2012)
10. Ankerst, M., Breunig, M.M., Kriegel, H., Sander, J.: OPTICS: Ordering Points to Identify the Clustering Structure. In: ACM SIGMOD International Conference on Management of Data (1999)
11. Dousse, O., Eberle, J., Mertens, M.: Place learning via direct WiFi fingerprint clustering. In: IEEE 13th International Conference on Mobile Data Management (2012)
12. Bolliger, P.: Redpin - adaptive, zero-configuration indoor localization through user collaboration. In: The 1st ACM International Workshop on Mobile Entity Localization and Tracking in GPS-less Environments (2008)
13. Mautz, R.: Indoor Positioning Technologies, ETH Zurich, Department of Civil, Environmental and Geomatic Engineering, Institute of Geodesy and Photogrammetry (2012)
14. Wang, H., Sen, S., Elgohary, A., Farid, M., Youssef, M., Choudhury, R.R.: No need to war-drive: unsupervised indoor localization. In: MobiSys 2012 (2012)
15. Xu, Y., Lau, S.L., Kusber, R., David, K.: An Experimental Investigation of Indoor Localization by Unsupervised Wi-Fi Signal Clustering. In: Future Network and Mobile Summit (2012)

Context-Based Development of Experience Bases

Patrick Brézillon

University Pierre and Marie Curie (UPMC), Paris, France
Patrick.Brezillon@lip6.fr

Abstract. The experience of experts relies on the process of decision-making jointly with the progressive elaboration of a context-specific model. However, context modeling generally stays implicit because only the result of the decision-making process matters. Modeling context within a decision-making process supposes a uniform representation of knowledge, reasoning and contexts. In the Contextual-Graphs formalism, a decision-making episode is represented as a contextual graph where each path represents a practice developed by actors for making this decision in a specific working context. By incremental accumulation of the practices developed by experts, a contextual graph becomes an experience base with the decision-making process. Such an experience base may be used by humans for training future experts how to behave in the different ways to make a decision according to the variants of the working context. An intelligent assistant system exploiting such an experience base will be able to propose a more effective support to users than previous knowledge-based systems. This work is realized in the framework of a project in medicine for supporting experts in breast cancer diagnosis.

Keywords: Contextual Graphs, decision-making process, experience base, working context, intelligent assistant system.

1 Introduction

Experts rely on a highly compiled experience because they are few, and generally act under temporal pressure. They are very concerned by the consequences of their decision. Expert knowledge is more than domain knowledge because expert knowledge emerges from a contextualization process and expertise appears as chunks of contextual knowledge. The two challenges for designing an efficient support system based on expert knowledge then are: (1) modeling the contextualization process, and (2) exploiting bases of experiences rather than usual bases of knowledge.

Experience never can be reused directly because each context of a decision-making is unique. Thus, any experience must be adapted to be efficient in another context. This presupposes (1) identifying how the initial experience was contextualized, (2) isolating the reusable part of the experience, and (3) applying the process of contextualization in the new working context [6]. Conversely, procedures are developed by the executive board of an enterprise by decontextualizing practices that are accumulated in a flat way (e.g. like in reports on incident solving). A procedure

P. Brézillon, P. Blackburn, and R. Dapoigny (Eds.): CONTEXT 2013, LNAI 8175, pp. 87–100, 2013.

tries to cover a class of problems, while an actor develops a practice by adapting the procedure to the specific working context in which the actor makes a decision. Procedures are described in pairs {problem, solution}, while practices suppose a triple {problem, context, solution} representation.

Thus, experience reuse implies a management of the process of contextualization, decontextualization and recontextualization. This supposes a formalism providing a uniform representation of elements of knowledge, reasoning and contexts. This also requires having a support system with powerful functions—like simulation and learning—for processing such a representation.

Hereafter, the paper is organized as follows. Section 2 discusses the need to make context explicit for representing experience and the specificity of the Contextual-Graphs formalism. Section 3 presents the specificity of simulating experiences. Section 4 relates our approach with other works. Section 5 ends this paper with a conclusion.

2   Representing Experience in Context

2.1   Need of Context in the Representation

A practice represents how work actually gets done, not what is supposed to happen (i.e. the procedure). Contextual cues in a practice rely on actors' preferences, the particularities of the task realization, the situation where the task is realized and the local environment where resources are available. As a consequence, there are as many practices (or activities) as actors and contexts.

Context depends on the actor's focus, but, conversely, the focus determines what is contextual knowledge and external knowledge at a given moment. At each step of the decision-making process, a sub-set of the contextual knowledge is proceduralized for addressing the current focus. This "proceduralized context" is built from elements of the contextual knowledge that are invoked, assembled, organized, structured and situated according to the given focus.

A contextual element corresponds to an element of the nature that must be analyzed. The value taken by the contextual element when the focus is on it, its instantiation, is taken into account as long as the situation is under the analysis. The distinction between contextual elements and instances is important for the reuse of experience because a difference between a past context and the working context can be a difference either on a contextual element (e.g. a contextual element only exists in one of the contexts) or on an instance (e.g. a given contextual element takes different instances in the two contexts). For example, most of car accidents occur on the way from home to work, a well-known way that leads the driver to rely on past experience, say, for crossing an intersection. The accident occurs when the driver does not pay attention to the specificity of the driving context at hand where there is a new contextual element (e.g. oil poured from a truck on the pavement) or a change in the instantiation of a contextual element (e.g. the traffic light is off). Experience management supposes to consider explicitly the working context as well as the decision-making process.

2.2   A Transdisciplinary Problem

The difference between procedure and practice appears in different approaches for modeling human behaviors: procedures and practices [4], task and activity [13; 9], logic of functioning and logic of use [16]. Indeed, one perspective (procedure, task, logic of functioning) focuses on the task, while the other perspective considers the actor realizing the task in a working context [6]. Procedure represents a task realization and the constraints imposed by the logic of functioning. Conversely, a practice represents actors' activities in a logic of use. Modeling experience must be discussed in terms of activities and concretely represented in terms of practices.

The problem of decision-making reuses can be explained in the light of these different units of analysis (different perspectives) for modeling human behaviors. In one perspective (procedure, task, logic of functioning), one considers only the task, while according to the other perspective one considers the actor, the task, the situation in which the actor realizes the task, and the local environment with its resources available. Brézillon [6] proposes an interpretation of this dichotomy in terms of {decisional levels (policy, strategy, tactics, operation), contexts} as illustrated in Table 1. Links with the decisional levels are discussed in [6] and results are applied in [10]. This paper discusses the dichotomy in terms of context and the consequence for experience modeling.

Table 1. A classification of opposed terms

Level \ Context	Decontextualized	Contextualized
Strategic	Logic of functioning	Logic of use
Tactical	Task	Activity
Operational	Procedure	Practice

Procedure is the (formal) translation of a task realization at operational level. The translation takes into account task realization and the constraints imposed by the logic of functioning at the strategic level. Conversely, a practice is the expression of an activity led by an actor accomplishing a task in a particular situation with the available resources in the local environment. An actor's experience appears as an accumulation of practices based on activities developed in logic of use. Thus, experience can be discussed in terms of activities and, concretely represented in terms of practices.

A decision-making episode is an activity that starts with the analysis of the working context (identification of the relevant contextual elements and their instantiations) to have a picture of the problem as complete as possible before any action. Brézillon [6] speaks of a two-step decision-making. The instantiated contextual elements are then assembled, organized and structured in a proceduralized context that allows the actor to make his decision and continue his activity. Then, making a decision consists of the assembling and execution of actions in a sequence. Indeed, these steps constitute a unique process.

2.3   The Contextual Graph Approach

Brézillon [4] introduces the Contextual-Graphs (CxG) formalism for giving a uniform representation of elements of knowledge, reasoning and context. Contextual graphs are acyclic due to the time-directed representation and warranty of algorithm termination. Each contextual graph has exactly one root and one end node because the decision-making process starts in a state of affairs and ends in another state of affairs (generally with different solutions on the different paths) and the branches express only different contextually-dependent ways to achieve this goal. A contextual graph represents a task realization, and paths correspond to the different practices developed by actors for realizing the task. An actor's experience correspond to the sum of all the practices developped and accumulated by the actor and represented in a contextual graph. Thus a contextual graph is a kind of experience base for the task realization.

Our context modeling is different of other models that propose, for instance, context as a layer between data and applications or as a middleware or ontology found in the literature. In the CxG formalism, contextual elements structure experiences differently, on the one hand, of knowledge bases of expert systems represented in a flat way where context is not represented explicitly, and, on the other hand, of knowledge organization in an ontology where links between concepts depend only on the domain (is-a, kind-of, etc.) while contextual elements concern the actor, the task, the situation and the local environment. Moreover, contextual elements have a heterogeneous nature not necessarily linked to the domain (e.g. a choice may be made because the actor is in a hurry). This implies that for using an experience base, a support system must have some specific functions.

The CxG formalism allows the incremental enrichment of experience by the refinement of existing practices. The introduction of a new practice corresponds to a new contextual element where (at least) two values are discriminated (the one implicitly used up to now and the new one) and the action(s) corresponding to the new instantiation of the contextual element.

The notion of chunk of knowledge proposed by Schank [17] has a clear implementation in contextual graphs as an ordered series of instantiated contextual elements (the proceduralized context). This illustrates the two steps in the decision-making process by looking for, first, relevant contextual elements, and, second, their current instantiations. The proceduralized context evolves dynamically during practice development by addition (at the contextual node) or removal (at the recombination node) of a contextual element.

The CxG_Platform [6] contains an editor with the usual functions for managing a contextual graph. The piece of software is available at cxg.fr under GNU license. As illustrated on Figure 1, it is an interface used by an actor wishing to edit a contextual graph, reading practices for selecting the best one in his working context, browsing alternatives of a practice, exploring a contextual graph at a different granularity (by representing an activity by an item or by the contextual graph representing this activity), analyzing contextual information attached to each item (date of creation, comments, etc.). The software is written in Java, and contextual graphs are stored as XML files to be reused by other software. Note that an activity, being itself represented in a contextual graph, also is stored as an independent XML file. Design and development of the software is user-centered for an easy use by non-specialists in

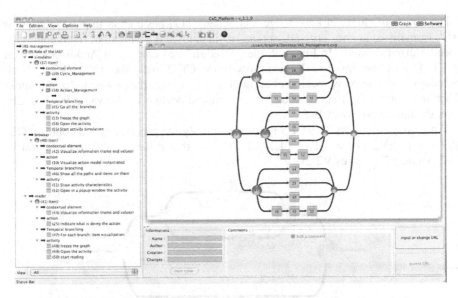

Fig. 1. A CxG_representation of the IAS management

computer science and mathematics. The two specific functions are the incremental knowledge acquisition and the possibility to link an item in the CxG to an external document (Word, PDF, etc.), to run an external piece of software, etc.

2.4   Discussion

Our context model is different of other models that propose, for instance, context as a layer between data and applications or as a middleware or an ontology found in the literature. In our model, context is intimately linked to knowledge and reasoning. Contextual elements structure experiences differently, on the one hand, of knowledge bases of expert systems represented in a flat way because context is not represented explicitly, and, on the other hand, of knowledge organization in an ontology where links between concepts depend only on the domain (is-a, kind-of, etc.) while elements in our context model concern the actor, the task, the situation and the local environment. Moreover, contextual elements have a heterogeneous nature not linked to the domain (e.g. a choice may be made because the actor is in a hurry). This implies that for using an experience base, a support system must have specific functions.

A contextual graph allows the incremental enrichment of experiences by the refinement of existing practices. The introduction of a new practice generally corresponds to a contextual element that was not considered explicitly up to now because always having the same value, but that has a different value in the working context at hand. Thus, this contextual element is introduced in the contextual graph with the value implicitly considered up to now, and the value taken in the working context with the action(s) corresponding to this new instantiation.

The notion of chunk of knowledge a la Schank [17] has a clear implementation in CxG formalism as an ordered series of instantiated contextual elements (the proceduralized context). In Figure 2, the proceduralized context of Action 3 is given by CE-1 with the instance V1.1 followed by CE-2 with the value V2.1. Each proceduralized context is specific of an item. For example, the proceduralized context of actions 3 and 4-5 differs from the proceduralized context by the value V2.2 of CE-2, i.e. the instantiation of CE-2.

For example, actions 3 and 4-5 have respectively the proceduralized contexts CE-1(V1.1)-CE-2(V2.1) and CE-1(V1.1)-CE-2(V2.2) that differ by the instantiation of CE-2 (value V2.1 versus V2.2).

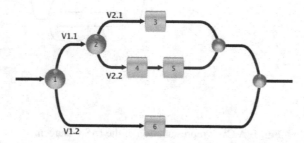

Fig. 2. Representation of a task realization as a contextual graph

Note that a particular action (or an activity) that would exist on two different paths will have different proceduralized contexts. Brézillon and Brézillon [4] give the example of a driver that brakes strongly arriving at an intersection because a car arrives on the right side. It is a context of correct driving if nobody is behind the driver, and a dangerous context if there is another car just behind. Thus, the proceduralized context specifies the quality of an action or activity.

The proceduralized context of a practice evolves dynamically during its development by entering contextual nodes and leaving at recombination nodes of contextual elements. The CxG formalism provides a representation of actors' experience such as a graph of practices structured by contextual elements.

3   Specificity of Experience-Based Simulation

3.1   Introduction

Previously, expert systems used a flat base of rules (atoms of human reasoning) and a base of facts, and their reasoning was represented as a series of rules (the reasoning trace) that fired according to heuristics not always clearly stated and control knowledge often implicitly coded in the inference engine (e.g. check the "less expensive rule" first). Nevertheless, expert systems were considered as "model based" and introduced a means of modeling processes qualitatively [8].

Conversely, the CxG formalism provides a structured base of experiences. Each path in a contextual graph (i.e. a series of independent rules in an expert system, but here connected by contextual elements) corresponds to a practice effectively developed by a human actor in a working context. Thus, if the expert system builds its own reasoning by assembling a sequence of fired rules (i.e. the reasoning trace of the system often not understandable by users), a system using an experience base develops practices effectively built by human actors. The latter is called an "Intelligent Assistant Systems" (IAS) with tools such as a simulator, a learning module, an explaination module.

3.2   Model-Based versus CxG-Based Simulation

Usually, a simulation describes the evolution of a (formal) model, starting from a set of initial conditions. The model expresses a statement about a real system that is based on formalized concepts and hypothesis about the functioning of the real system. Such a model is given by a structure that is specified by parameters that appear in the relationships between variables (a usual formalism of representation is differential equations). A model-based simulation gives a description of the evolution of the variables with respect to an independent variable, generally time, given a set of values for the parameters and a set of initial conditions for the variables. The evolution of some variables is then compared to temporal observations of the real system. (We will not discuss here the aspect time-based or real time of the representation).

In a formal model, time appears through the evolution of the variables from the model structure and relationships between variables (e.g. $y(t)$ in a model expressed in the formalism of differential equations like $dy/dt = -a.y + b$). The working context in a model-based simulation (initial conditions and parameter values) is constant during all the simulation: The initial conditions $y(0)$ specify the initial state of the model and the parameter values generally are not modified during the simulation. There is no "unpredicted event" during an experiment.

At a qualitative level, the (formal) model represents a statement in a formal language of hypothesis and formalized concepts about observations of the real system. "Browsing" a model is exploiting its mathematical properties for predicting variables' evolution (number and stability of steady states, self-oscillations, exponential decreasing curve, etc.) for different sets of parameter values that verify some constraints such as the conditions to have an unstable steady state.

At a quantitative level, model-based simulation is used to find the best set of parameter values and initial conditions describing a set of real-world observations (generally by optimization methods). Here, the formal model is used for the prediction of any behavior of the real system in other contexts, assimilating this context to constraints and initial conditions. In a model-based simulation, the working context describes the initial state only, variables evolving during the whole model-based simulation.

Formal models address the evolution of a system, and the corresponding trajectory is unique because the model structure is unique (parameter values are constant during the entire simulation). Thus, a model-based simulation relies on {model structure, parameters, initial conditions on variables} where model structure, parameter values and initial conditions are fixed during all the simulation.

In the CxG approach, the practice (i.e. the equivalent of the model structure) is build jointly with its development. Then, a contextual graph appears as a structure of practices organized by context-specific models that correspond to all the working contexts already faced by actors.

At the quantitative level, the IAS needs to know only the instanciations of the contextual elements that will be used in a simulation (i.e. the contextual elements belonging to the developed practice), and the effects of action execution. The execution of an action may modify the instantiation of a contextual element. The change of working context (i.e. the change of instantiation of a contextual element) leads the IAS to consider another practice with different consequences: the stop of the simulation (e.g. the required resource is no more available), the simulation must be restarted in the new working context, a routine action in the practice development must be executed several times, and a contextual element not yet met during the current practice development. In the last situation, the simulation can be pursued because there is no divergence because the change of context does not impact the practice development.

Table 2 gives a comparison of model-based simulation and CxG-based simulation according to seven characteristics.

Table 2. Comparison of model- and CxG-based simulations

	Model-based	CxG-based
Goal	Represent a real system	Represent a task realization on the real system (a level above the real system)
Real system	An internal viewpoint	An external viewpoint
Tactical level	A model structure	A graph of model structures (practices)
Operational level	Simulation from an initial state	Simulation and building of a context-specific model
Working context	Initial values of variables and parameters (constant during the simulation)	Contextual elements and instantiations (may vary during the simulation)
Simulation	Evolution of the variables in the model	Building and use of a model specific of the working context with practice development
Type of support	Prediction, interpretation of deviation (real-system centered)	Task realization on the real system (use-centered)

3.3   Simulation Management

A practice that is developed in the working context is the "best practice" because the practice is built at the same time it is used, thus taking into account all that occurs during this process. For example, action execution may modify the instantiation of a contextual element due, say, to a lack of availability of a resource. This change of the working context is visible if we consider the activity represented by the practice development, not the task realization.

The working context has two parts. First, a static part contains the list of the contextual elements in the contextual graph and their known values. Second, a dynamic part gives the list of the known instances, i.e. the value taken by contextual elements at simulation time.

A contextual element allows the management of context-dependent methods for a part of the task realization. The choice of an alternative corresponds to the value taken by the contextual element in the working context (i.e. its instantiation). The instantiation can be known prior to the practice development or is provided by the actor to the system during the practice development or found by the IAS in the local environment.

During a CxG-based simulation, the instantiation of contextual elements may be altered by either an external event or an internal event. The external event corresponds to an unpredicted event, i.e. not represented in the contextual graph. For example, an external resource stops to be available.

An internal event occurs as the result of an action execution. A contextual graph represents the task realization at a tactical level because the contextual graph contains all the practices used for the task realization at the operational level. An action (or an activity) is executed at the operational level (e.g. execution of an external program or a service). The way in which an action is executed does not matter at the tactical level, but there are some consequences that may impact the practice development as a side-effect at the tactical level. The most obvious consequence is the duration of the action execution that may delay the practice development. Other consequences may be indirect like a change of the instantiation of a contextual element.

The alteration of an instantiation implies a change of the working context. The first type of change may concern a contextual element already crossed. Then, the IAS must decide (1) to stop the development of the current practice and re-start the simulation in the new working context; (2) to redo the part of the part of the practice that is concerned (e.g. for a routine action); or (3) to finish the development of the practice at hand and then analyze the need for a new simulation in the new working context. The IAS will have to interact with the actor to make a decision on the strategy to apply. The second type of change concerns a contextual element not yet crossed by the focus, and the IAS can continue its simulation to progress in the contextual graph because this change of instantiation does not affect the part of the practice already built. The lesson here is that the working context is intimately associated with the simulation.

3.4   Related Functions

Learning Management. Conversely to the old image of an expert system as an oracle and the user as a novice [11], our users are experts in their domain. Thus, the IAS must follow (as a "novice") what the expert (the "oracle") is doing, and benefits of the opportunity to learn incrementally new practices developed by experts during their interaction (and stored in the base of experience). Controling a representation of actors' experience, the IAS may learn when it does not know the practice that the expert is developing. Generally, it is often a problem of missing knowledge to discriminate between two methods (i.e. two practices).

However, there is an eventual more drastic change of the experience base when the expert decides that it is not a simple action that is concerned but a sub graph. For example, consider in Fig. 3a the action 1 "Take water" in coffee preparation. Implicitly, the actor considers that he is speaking of running water, i.e. this contextual element "Type of water" does not appear in the representation. Now, suppose that the same actor is in a hurry one morning and decides to use "hot (running) water" to make his coffee more rapidly. An IAS that will observe the actor's behavior will fail to follow the actor reasoning because it does not know the difference between the choices "cold water" and "hot water". Then, the actor will have to provide the IAS (see Fig. 3b) with the contextual element CE1 "In a hurry?" with the two values, namely "No" for the previous action 1 "Take (cold) water" and the value "Yes" for the new action 2 "Take hot water".

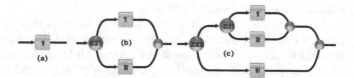

Fig. 3. The two types of learning in coffee preparation

Now, suppose that the IAS helps another actor in the same task of coffee preparation, and that this new actor only uses mineral water instead of running water to prepare his coffee. Then, when the IAS will ask him "Are you in a hurry?", and the actor will have to explain that this question may be relevant for running water, but not for mineral water in a bottle. The IAS will need to add a new contextual element CE2 "Type of water?" with the value "running water" for the previous practices (toward CE1 in Fig. 3c) and the value "mineral water" for a new action 3 "Take your bottle of water".

The example presents two types of learning for the IAS. In the first learning, the IAS learns by assimilation of a new practice (refinement of an existing practice). It is a practice-based learning. In the second learning, the structure of the experience base is modified for integrating a new method for preparing coffee (i.e. use of mineral water versus running water). It is a procedure-based learning and the IAS must learn by accommodation.

The IAS also may be a trainer for actors not quite familiar with practices for realizing a task as described in a contextual graph. The training here consists of explaining the elements used during a practice development, especially contextual elements and their possible instantiations in a chunk of contextual knowledge (i.e. the proceduralized context). Note that a contextual element corresponds to a piece of "surface knowledge" (e.g. take hot water) representing a more complex "deep knowledge" (e.g. the goal of the coffee machine is to make hot the water before to pour it on the coffee, and using hot water will speed up this long process).

Explanation Generation. More than twenty years ago, Artificial Intelligence was considered as the science of explanation [12], but few concrete results were obtained at that time (e.g. see [15] in French).

The explicit representation of context at the same level of knowledge and reasoning provides now a new insight on explanation generation. Previously, we showed that a proceduralized context is attached to each item in a contextual graph. A proceduralized context is a subset of contextual knowledge that is assembled, organized and structured to be used in the current focus. Its representation in the CxG formalism is an ordered sequence of instantiated contextual elements that can be used for explanation generation.

A contextual graph represents a base of experiences. The IAS applies a human expert's reasoning, and not an "automated reasoning" constrained by control knowledge hidden in the inference engine (e.g. fire the first rule f the list).

The uniform representation of elements of knowledge, reasoning and contexts in a contextual graph allows the generation of different types of expressive context-based explanations [5], like visual explanations, dynamic explanations, user-based explanations, context-based explanations, micro- and macro-explanations, real-time explanations. These different types of explanation can be combined in different ways such as visual and dynamic explanations for presenting future alternatives and abandoned options.

3.5   Discussion

The contextual-graph representation puts in the front stage different interesting findings for working on an experience base.

First, a contextual graph is the representation of a task realization by one or different actors. The realization of a task by actors having different roles must be represented in different contextual graphs because they do not use the same methods. For example, a physician and a computer engineer analyze bioimages differently. This implies a new step for representing collaboration of actors through CxG interaction.

Second, a contextual graph gives a representation of a task realization at a given level of granularity at which actions are the building block of the representation. Thus, requirements for action execution do not matter. However, some aspects may have some effects on the representation. For example, time for an action execution may modify the instantiation of a contextual element and thus the practice development. This means that for developing a practice in the contextual graph like in a simulation, we need to consider it within the working context.

Three, for interacting intelligently with an actor that is an expert in his domain, the IAS, on the one hand, adheres to expert's viewpoint, and, on the other hand, makes explicit the needed tools for the management of context, actions, the contextual graph, learning, explanations, etc. We are working on such an architecture for IAS [7]. The key point here is that domain knowledge and expertise are only in the experience base. The IAS architecture may be reused in a domain-independent way. Globally, a contextal graph (i.e. "optimal" practices in their working contexts) is a better solution than the "best practice" that is generally consider with the few contextual elements found in a large number of practices.

4   Related Works

In a classical case-based reasoning (CBR) scenario, a case consists of a problem description and a solution. A case contains a set of (structured) information entities, and optional artifacts. Structured information is represented as attribute – value pairs, while the optional meta-information contains unstructured textual information.

Atzmueller [2] uses stored cases (experiences) for selecting an appropriate task and method, reusing those stored task-configurations that are similar to a (partially) defined characterization. The process of capturing and reusing complex task-experiences is lead in four main steps: Experience Retrieval, Task Instantiation, Task Evaluation and Deployment, and Experience Maintenance. Thus, a case is recalled as a whole and its characterization is then adapted to the context at hand. There are now extensions of this formalism towards process-oriented CBR[1] and trace-based reasoning [14]. In the CxG formalism, the practice, the equivalent of the case, is identified jointly with its use. The main difference here is that cases generally are represented in a flat way (logic of functioning), while practices are organized in a Contextual-Graphs representation (logic of use). In the CBR, the approach is "result-oriented" while in Contextual-Graphs, the approach is "reasoning-oriented".

Clancey [9] proposed that solving a particular problem (e.g. diagnosing a patient) involves creating situation-specific models. "Situation-specific" refers to a particular case, setting, or scenario. "Situation-specific" is not "situated cognition" that refers to how people are conceiving and thus coordinating their identity, values, and activities in an ongoing process enabled by high order consciousness. In the CxG approach, context concerns an actor accomplishing a task in a particular situation in a specific local environment. A practice development is associated with the progressive building of a "context-specific model". For Clancey, the "situation-specific model" is embedded in the problem solving as a static description fixed initially and filled progressively during the problem solving. Conversely, the context-specific model (i.e. the proceduralized context) is built in parallel with the practice development with the movement of contextual elements entering and leaving the proceduralized context. Note that we consider also situation as a part of the context.

A model-based simulation is a top-down (deductive) modeling, while a CxG-based simulation corresponds to a bottom-up (inductive) modeling. In a model-based simulation, the whole working context is defined at the start of the simulation and stays constant during the simulation, while in a CxG-based simulation, the working context evolves during practice development. A formal model is given initially (its structure is confronted to observations), while a practice (the contextualized model of a task realization) is built progressively from the contextual graph and evolves with its working context. In that sense CxG-based simulation is a partiular type of simulation. The behavior of a CxG simulator is comparable with the usual model-based simulator's behavior, supposing that (1) contextual elements in the contextual graph can be compared to the parameters in the formal model (a change of parameter values impacts the model behavior as a change of instantiation modifies the practice developed), and (2) variables in a model-based simulation are related to the result of the progressive building of the practice corresponding to the working context.

These approaches also can be discussed with respect to decisional levels: Case-based reasoning approach is at an operational level and model-based simulation at a tactical level. An IAS, which uses an experience base, plays the role of a CxG Browser at the tactical (qualitative) level and of a CxG Simulator at the operational (quantitative) level. The CxG Browser allows working on the experience base. The CxG Simulator is a tool at the tactic level or the operational level because it takes into account the specificity of the working context to find the best practice.

---

[1] www.iccbr.org/iccbr12/ICCBR-12_WS_proc.pdf

5   Conclusion

Our goal is to develop an IAS for users that have a high level of expertise in a domain not well known or too complex. Their expertise is highly compiled, like chunks of contextual knowledge built mainly by incremental enrichment of their experience. Such an expertise is generally used in a decision-making process leading to a critical and definitive decision. In the MICO project, the expert is an anatomo-cyto-pathologist that analyzes digital slides (coming from biopsies) to diagnose if a patient in a surgery has or not breast cancer.

The consequences are:

(1)   An IAS follows what the expert is doing, how he is doing it, and anticipates potential needs. This supposes that the IAS possesses a representation of the experts' reasoning, may fix alone all the simple problems, and prepare a complete folder on complex situations letting experts make their decision. It is the role of an experience base.

(2)   The IAS must work from practices developed by experts in different working contexts. The line of reasoning of the system is drawn from lines of experts' reasoning described in the experience base, which gives a user-centered representation of the task realization.

(3)   The IAS must be able to develop the decision-making process in real time to analyze the association diagnosis and action built by experts during their reasoning. Indeed, the IAS simultaneously develops the decision-making process and its context-specific model like experts.

(4)   The decision-making process being highly contextual, the IAS must benefit of its interaction with the expert to learn new practices by acquiring incrementally the missing knowledge, and thus enriching its experience base.

(5)   Making context explicit in the experience base leads to the possibility to generate relevant explanations for presenting the rationale behind a practice with alternatives abandoned; training (future) experts on the different practices developed; facilitating experience sharing among experts in a kind of dynamic corporate memory; allowing a first step towards the certification of their protocol. An example in anatomo-cyto pathology is given in [1].

(6)   The main tool of an IAS is the CxG simulator. Its originality is to build and apply at the same time the practice. Indeed the CxG simulator is the key element of a real-time decision making because it is possible to account for unpredicted events, thank to an explicit modeling of context as contextual elements covering, the user, the task realization, the working situation, the local environment with its available resources [7]. All the items are interdependent and also time-dependent. Thus, IASs cover a more general problematic than context-aware applications. This seems to us also the key point for mobile decision making because the instantiations of contextual elements are taken into account at the moment it is necessary.

Acknowledgments. This work is supported by grants from ANR TecSan for the MICO project (ANR-10-TECS-015), and we thank partners (IPAL, TRIBVN, UIMAP of Service d'Anatomie Cytologie Pathologie at La Pitié, Thalès, Agfa) for fruitful discussions, and from the TACTIC project funded by the ASTRID program of Délégation Générale aux Armées.

References

1. Attieh, E., Calvo, J., Brezillon, P., Capron, F.: Modélisation informatisée des étapes d'un examen anatomo-cyto-pathologique: "Graphes contextuels". 36es Assises de Pathologie Versailles, Mai 23-24 (2013)
2. Atzmueller, M.: Experience Management with Task-Configurations and Task-Patterns for Descriptive Data Mining. KESE (2007), http://ceur-ws.org/Vol-282/02-AtzmuellerM-KESE-Paper-CRC.pdf
3. Brézillon, J., Brézillon, P.: Context modeling: Context as a dressing of a focus. In: Kokinov, B., Richardson, D.C., Roth-Berghofer, T.R., Vieu, L. (eds.) CONTEXT 2007. LNCS (LNAI), vol. 4635, pp. 136–149. Springer, Heidelberg (2007)
4. Brézillon, P.: Context modeling: Task model and practice model. In: Kokinov, B., Richardson, D.C., Roth-Berghofer, T.R., Vieu, L. (eds.) CONTEXT 2007. LNCS (LNAI), vol. 4635, pp. 122–135. Springer, Heidelberg (2007)
5. Brézillon, P.: Explaining for Contextualizing and Contextualizing for Explaining. In: Proc. of 3rd International Workshop on Explanation-aware Computing ExaCt 2008. CEUR Workshop Proceedings (2008) ISSN 1613-0073, http://CEUR-WS.org/Vol-391/00010001.pdf
6. Brezillon, P.: Contextualization of scientific workflows. In: Beigl, M., Christiansen, H., Roth-Berghofer, T.R., Kofod-Petersen, A., Coventry, K.R., Schmidtke, H.R. (eds.) CONTEXT 2011. LNCS, vol. 6967, pp. 40–53. Springer, Heidelberg (2011)
7. Brézillon, P.: A context-centered architecture for intelligent assistant systems. In: Faucher, C., Jain, L. (eds.) Recent Advances in Knowledge Engineering: Paradigms and Applications. SCI, vol. 514. Springer (to appear, 2013)
8. Clancey, W.J.: Viewing knowledge bases as qualitative models. IEEE Expert: Intelligent Systems and Their Applications 4(2), 9–23 (1989)
9. Clancey, W.J.: Simulating Activities: Relating Motives, Deliberation, and Attentive Coordination. Cognitive Systems Research 3(3), 471–499 (2002)
10. Fan, X.: Context-oriented scientific worlflow and its application in medicine. Ph.D. Thesis, University Pierre and Marie Curie, Paris, France (2011)
11. Karsenty, L., Brézillon, P.: Cooperative problem solving and explanation. Expert Systems with Applications 8(4), 445–462 (1995)
12. Kodratoff, Y.: Is artificial intelligence a subfield of computer science or is artificial intelligence the science of explanation? In: Bratko, I., Lavrac, N. (eds.) Progress in Machine Learning, pp. 91–106. Sigma Press, Cheshire (1987)
13. Leplat, J., Hoc, J.M.: Tâche et activité dans l'analyse psychologique des situations. Cahiers de Psychologie Cognitive 3, 49–63 (1983)
14. Mille, A.: From case-based reasoning to traces-based reasoning. Annual Reviews in Control 30, 223–232 (2006)
15. PRC-GDR. Actes des 3e journées nationales PRC-GDR IA organisées par le CNRS (1989)
16. Richard, J.F.: Logique du fonctionnement et logique de l'utilisation. Rapport de Recherche INRIA no 202 (1983)
17. Schank, R.C.: Dynamic memory, a theory of learning in computers and people. University Press, Cambridge (1983)

A Context-Aware Approach to Selecting Adaptations for Case-Based Reasoning

Vahid Jalali and David Leake

School of Informatics and Computing, Indiana University
Bloomington IN 47408, USA
{vjalalib,leake}@cs.indiana.edu

Abstract. Case-based reasoning solves new problems by retrieving cases of similar previously-solved problems and adapting their solutions to fit new circumstances. The case adaptation step is often done by applying context-independent adaptation rules. A substantial body of research has studied generating these rules automatically from comparisons of prior pairs of cases. This paper presents a method for increasing the context-awareness of case adaptation using these rules, by exploiting contextual information about the prior problems from which the rules were generated to predict their applicability to the context of the new problem, in order to select the most relevant rules. The paper tests the approach for the task of case-based prediction of numerical values (case-based regression). It evaluates performance on standard machine learning data sets to assess the method's performance benefits, and also tests it on synthetic domains to study how performance is affected by different problem space characteristics. The results show the proposed method for context-awareness brings significant gains in solution accuracy.

1 Introduction

Problem solving by case-based reasoning (CBR) retrieves cases capturing the solutions of similar past problems and adapts their solutions to fit new circumstances [1]. How to generate knowledge to guide the case adaptation process is a classic challenge for case-based reasoning. Often, case-based reasoning systems adapt cases based on a limited set of context-independent rules hand coded by domain experts [2]. Given the cost and difficulty of generating case adaptation knowledge, the CBR community has investigated using more knowledge-light approaches to acquire case adaptation rules by machine learning, and especially learning by comparing cases in collection of prior cases (the "case base") and inferring how differences in problem descriptions suggest solution differences— which in turn show how solutions should be adapted to address the differences between new problems and retrieved cases [3,4]. Such methods are highly promising. However, they can result in a large set of possible rules for adapting any particular difference, which raises the question of how to select the adaptation rules to apply. Traditionally, selection of adaptation rules has been based only on the feature differences between old and new situations, with little attention to

P. Brézillon, P. Blackburn, and R. Dapoigny (Eds.): CONTEXT 2013, LNAI 8175, pp. 101–114, 2013.

the context in which the differences appear. This paper presents a new method for making case adaptation more context-aware, by favoring rules which were generated for not only similar differences, but for differences which arose in similar contexts.

This paper provides both a general perspective on the role of context in case adaptation for CBR and a specific method for context-aware adaptation rule selection when CBR is applied to the task of numeric regression, for which the goal is to estimate a numeric value associated with a set of input parameters. When case-based reasoning is applied to the regression task, the set of inputs is considered the "problem" to solve, and the "solution"—the output value—is estimated by retrieving similar past problems from the case base and building a solution based on the solution values of those similar cases. The prior solution values are "adapted" according to the differences between the problems they solved and the new problem. For example, a real-world application of case-based regression is real estate appraisal [5], for which the task is to predict the value of a property, based on the values of similar properties. If the most similar prior case is a smaller house, a new house's price should be predicted by adjusting the prior house's price to reflect the size difference.

Obviously, when rules are generated automatically from case comparison, many overlapping and inconsistent rules might be generated. Consequently, how to select the adaptation rules to apply to a particular problem becomes an important question. This paper presents a case study of a new context-based approach to selecting adaptation rules for case-based regression, for adaptation rules generated automatically based on case differences. It tests performance of the approach compared to five alternative methods, on six standard machine learning data sets and on synthetically generated domains designed to study how particular domain characteristics affect performance of the approach.

The paper is organized as follows. Section 2 presents an overview of case-based regression and previous work on using knowledge-light approaches to generate case adaptation rules for case-based regression, focusing on a popular method for generating adaptation rules, the *case difference heuristic* approach [3]. Section 3 explains our method for context-aware application of case adaptation rules, which has been implemented in the system CAAR (Context-Aware Adaptation Retrieval). Section 4 discusses the motivations for the design of the synthetic data sets, provides details about the synthetic and standard data set characteristics and reports the results of empirical evaluation of the candidate methods on a set of synthetic and real world data sets analyzing and comparing the performance of the methods under different circumstances. Section 5 presents conclusions and future research directions.

2   Applying Case-Based Reasoning to Regression Tasks

2.1   Overview of Case-Based Regression

Case-based regression computes the solution value of a new problem based on the values of k "nearest neighbor" cases (for some predefined integer k) retrieved

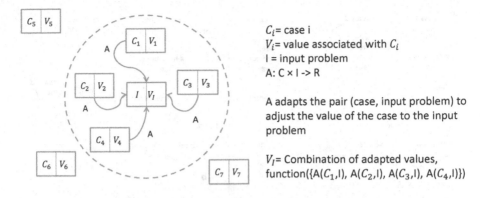

C_i = case i
V_i = value associated with C_i
I = input problem
A: C × I -> R

A adapts the pair (case, input problem) to adjust the value of the case to the input problem

V_I = Combination of adapted values,
function({A(C_1,I), A(C_2,I), A(C_3,I), A(C_4,I)})

Fig. 1. Illustration of the generic case-based regression process

from the case base. Given an input problem description (generally in the form of a vector of feature values), the nearest neighbor cases are those whose problem descriptions are most similar to the input problem, according to a predefined similarity metric. To calculate the solution value, the values of the nearest neighbor cases may be adapted, based on the differences between the problems they addressed and the new problem. The values are then combined by a combination function (e.g., into a weighted average in which the contributions of each case are weighted by the similarity of their problem to the input problem). Figure 1 illustrates 4-*NN*, with *A* designating the adaptation function.

2.2 Generating Adaptation Rules by the Case Difference Heuristic

Given the potential difficulty and cost of generating case adaptation rules by hand, it is desirable to generate them automatically. A highly influential approach to automatically generating case adaptation rules for case-based regression is the *case difference heuristic* method, introduced by Hanney and Keane [3]. This approach generates adaptation rules from prior cases, by comparing pairs of cases in the case base. For each pair, the approach compares the problem specifications of the two cases, generating a description of their differences which we refer to as "case difference vector". Often, this vector simply records the numerical differences between the case features. This vector is used as the applicability condition for the new rule; the new rule will be applied when a new input problem and a retrieved case have similar differences in each of their features.

For each pair, the approach also compares the solutions, generating a description of their solution differences. The observed difference becomes the adaptation part of the new rule; the rule adjusts the value of the prior case by this difference when the rule applies. For example, for real estate price prediction, if two

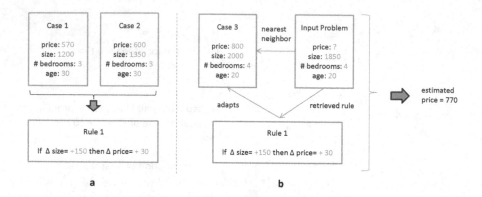

Fig. 2. illustration of problem differences and solution differences

apartments' descriptions differ only in that one is 150 square feet larger than the other, and the larger apartment's rent is $30 more per month, this suggests the rule that a 150 square foot size increase should increase the rent by $30. Part a of Fig. 2 depicts the generation of this rule (rule 1) from two cases, case 1 and case 2; part b depicts the application of rule 1 to a new case, case 3.

We note that the previous example rule is extremely simplified, and that many alternative rules might apply. For example, the adjustments might depend on percent changes, or correspond to a more complicated formula; how to address these issues is beyond the scope of this paper but is addressed elsewhere in the literature (e.g., [6]). Other case adaptation approaches for regression include alternative work on case difference heuristics [7], using linear regression for adapting the solutions [8], using a committee of machine learning methods [9].

2.3   Characterizing Context for the Case Adaptation

The importance of context is becoming widely recognized in artificial intelligence, but how to precisely define and characterize context in particular areas remains challenging. Dey [10] proposes that context is "any information that can be used to characterize the situation of an entity;" Brézillon [11] defines it as "what constrains a problem solving without intervening in it explicitly" and observes that context provides guidance for focusing attention in different tasks and that sometimes the "contextual reasoning is local reasoning."

In case-based reasoning research, adaptation rules have generally reflected only case differences, not the context in which those differences were observed. However, in some domains, the needed adaptations may vary substantially with context (e.g., in the real estate domain, the effect of the size of a lot on price may vary strongly based on whether the property being sold is in a city or a rural area, so adaptations should be sensitive to the location of the property).

Table 1. Comparison of Related Approaches

Method	Context Representation	Limited set of base cases	Focus of context
McDonnell [12]	Gradient Vector	False	Input query
Jalali [13]	Covariance Vector	True	Case to adapt
CAAR	Gradient Vector	True	Input query and case to adapt

Some previous research on case-based reasoning for regression has attempted to consider context in case adaptation. McDonnell and Cunningham [12] define the context of a point in problem space by approximating the rate of change (i.e., the gradient) of the regression system's target value function at that point. We note that their approach only considers the context for the input problem and for the corresponding case used to generate the adaptation rule.

Our own previous work [13] introduced EAR (Ensembles of Adaptations for Regression), in which the context of adaptation problems is characterized in terms of covariance vectors for the case to adapt and the corresponding case used to generate an adaptation rule. EAR selects adaptation rules to apply by doing a pair-wise multiplication of each component of two vectors. The first is the context vector which represents the covariance between the input features and the cases' values. The second is the case difference vector which represents the differences in the problem specification of the pair of input problem and case to adapt and pair of generating cases of the rule to apply. The distance between the vector calculated for the pair (input problem, case to adapt), and for the pair of the two cases used to generate the adaptation rule, is considered to measure their contextual similarities.

In addition to the contextual similarities, the similarities between the input problem and previous problems are calculated as the distance between the case difference vectors of the rule to apply (i.e. the case difference vector of the pair of cases used to generate the rule) and the pair of input problem and the case to adapt. The final rank score for an adaptation rule is generated by combining its case-based and contextual similarities to the pair of input problem-case to adapt by using a weighted average.

This paper presents a characterization of context for selecting learned adaptation rules that considers both the local situation of the problem to be adapted and the local situation of the cases from which the rules were generated, considering the changes that the gradient predicts in the case solutions, based on their feature differences. Table 1 summarizes the major differences between the two previous methods and the one proposed in this paper, implemented in CAAR. In addition, CAAR includes methods for refining adaptation rule retrieval and generation methods to make both more local, as well as for reducing computational cost by fixing the cases to adapt and focusing on the context-aware retrieval of adaptations for the selected set of cases to adapt.

3   CAAR

We hypothesize that performance of case adaptation can be improved by refining the treatment of adaptation context in two ways:

1. *Maximizing locality of data used in rule generation:* By restricting the cases used to generate adaptation rules to nearby cases, this aims to draw both cases from the same context, so that the relationship between the cases will give rise to meaningful rules.
2. *Enriching the context description:* By using context information to characterize both the similarity of the input problem and case to adapt, and the similarity of the case pair to the case pair used to generate the adaptation rule, this aims to select more relevant cases to adapt and rules to apply.

CAAR's algorithm respects the first condition by

1. First fixing the cases to adapt, choosing them to be the top nearest neighbors of the input problem, and then
2. Generating the adaptation rules to apply to the cases to adapt on demand, by comparing each case to adapt with its top nearest neighbors, and favoring rules addressing similar contexts.

The main focus of this paper is the second point, enriching the context description, which is described below.

3.1   CAAR's Adaptation Selection

CAAR selects adaptations to apply by ranking the candidate adaptations based on the similarity of the current adaptation context to the adaptation context in which the rule was generated, as follows. Let Q represent the input problem and C_b a case whose solution must be adapted to provide a solution to Q. Let C_i and C_j be the composing cases of the adaptation rule $R_{i,j}$ and $R_{j,i}$, where $R_{i,j}$ is a candidate for adjusting the value of case C_b to provide a value for Q. CAAR ranks candidate adaptations based on the similarity of two contexts: The context of the input problem and the corresponding composing case of an adaptation rule with regard to their differences with the case to adapt and its corresponding composing case of the adaptation and the context of the case to adapt and the corresponding composing case of the adaptation rule with regard to same changes respectively.

The ranking score is calculated by the function $score : rules \times cases \times problems \rightarrow R^+$, calculated by:

$$score((C_i, C_j, C_b, Q)) = contextSim((C_i, C_j, C_b, Q)) + contextSim((C_j, C_i, Q, C_b)) \tag{1}$$

As input, *score* takes the two cases used to generate the adaptation rule being assessed, the case to be adapted, and the input problem. It calls the function *contextSim* twice, once to determine the appropriateness of the adaptation rule $R_{i,j}$ to adapt C_b to the query Q (based on the similarity of the context in which the rule was generated to the adaptation context defined by the relationship between C_b and Q), and once to assess context-based appropriateness of the reverse rule $(R_{j,i})$, applied to adapt Q to C_b. By considering both directions, the computation takes into account both the context at the query (via the first term) and at the case to be adapted (via the second term). The final score is the sum of both terms.

The function *contextSim* is defined as follows. Like *score*, *contextSim* takes four arguments, the two cases used to generate the adaptation rule $R_{i,j}$, a case to adapt, and a query. Let $\nabla(C)$ represent the gradient vector around the case C, $Diff((C_i, C_j))$ represent the feature differences of the ordered pair of cases C_i and C_j, $\cdot$ be the dot product, and K be a function for tuning the range of results. The *contextSim* function is calculated as:

$$contextSim((C_i, C_j, C_k, C_l)) = K(\mid Diff(C_i, C_j) cdot \nabla(C_i) - Diff(C_k, C_l) \cdot \nabla(C_k) \mid) \tag{2}$$

For example, if it is desired that the ranking score of Eq. 1 generate a higher score given one very high and one very low underlying similarity than given two medium level underlying similarities, K could be set to an exponential function, to scale the raw values such that extremal values have more weight.

3.2 Applying the Selected Adaptation Rules

Let Q represent the input problem and R_i represent the ith adaptation rule in the ranked list generated using Eq. 1. Then CAAR's case adaptation adjusts the value of the case to adapt, C_b, by the average of the solution changes proposed by the top r adaptations, as follows:

$$adjustedVal(C_b, Q) = \sum_{i=1,r} \frac{1}{r} \times proposedAdjustment(R_i) \tag{3}$$

For k the number of selected cases to adapt to generate the solution, we use the algorithm we introduced in [13] to estimate the final solution, as follows:

$$finalEstimate(C_b, Q) = \sum_{i=1,k} \frac{1}{k} \times adjustedVal(C_{b,i}, Q) \tag{4}$$

Algorithm 1 summarizes the entire process.

4 Evaluation

Our evaluation addressed four questions:

1. How does the accuracy of CAAR compare to that of the baseline methods locally weighted linear regression, k-NN, and EAR?

Algorithm 1. Case-based regression with context-aware adaptation retrieval's basic algorithm [13]

Input:
Q: input problem
k: number of base cases to adapt to solve query
r: number of rules to be applied per base case
CB: case base
R: set of existing adaptations
Output: Estimated solution value for Q

> $CasesToAdapt \leftarrow$ NeighborhoodSelection(Q,k,CB)
> **for** c in $CasesToAdapt$ **do**
> $\qquad$ RankedRules $\leftarrow$ RankRules(R,c,Q)
> $\qquad$ $ValEstimate(c) \leftarrow$ CombineAdaptations($RankedRules, c, r$)
> **end for**
> return CombineVals($\cup_{c \in CasesToAdapt} ValEstimate(c)$)

---

2. How does CAAR's consideration of context at both the input case and the case to adapt affect performance, compared to considering context only at one or the other?
3. How is the accuracy of the candidate methods affected by increasing the density of case base coverage of the problem space? (Density will normally be correlated to case base size.)
4. How do changes in domain regularity (i.e., the lack of value fluctuations associate with different contexts) affect the accuracies of the candidate methods?

We expect that either increasing case base size or increased regularity will improve performance of all methods, because increased case base size increases the likelihood of finding cases to adapt from regions with similar characteristics. On the other hand, we expect increasing the rate of fluctuations in the context to make it harder for all methods to generate accurate estimations. However, we expect this to affect locally weighted learning more drastically than CAAR, especially for sparser case bases: We predict that when there is a shift in the changes of the target function (e.g. descending and then ascending), taking the average of the training data will be more accurate than fitting a locally learned linear model. Therefore, we expect to see an increase in the accuracy of CAAR compared to that of locally weighted linear regression for higher frequencies.

4.1   Data Sets

We tested CAAR's method on both synthetic and real world data sets. Synthetic data sets were used to enable precise control over the data characteristics, for addressing questions 3 and 4. Real world data sets were used to assess performance of CAAR's method compared to other candidate methods under more realistic scenarios in domains with more features.

Standard data sets: The standard data sets included four from the UCI repository [14]:Automobile (A), Auto MPG (AM), Housing (H), Computer Hardware (HW) and two from Luis Torgo's Regression data sets [15]: Stock (S) and CPU. For all data sets, records with unknown values were removed. To enable comparison with linear regression, only numeric features were used in the experiments. For each feature, values were standardized by subtracting that feature's mean value from each individual feature value and dividing the result by the standard deviation of that feature.

Synthetic data sets: The synthetic data sets were generated by a sinusoidal model. This model was chosen for two reasons: First, because its behavior in different regions corresponds to different contexts (given our treatment of context in terms of gradient and the changes in the gradient of the sine function over the X axis), and second, because it provides a repetitive pattern of context changes, so that rules generated from different parts of the domain space can still have similar contexts. Cases in the synthetic datasets all have a single input feature, which during data generation is associated to the value given by $sin(\frac{f}{2\pi}x)$, where f is a frequency value held constant for a given data set. Case input feature values are in the range [0,100], selected randomly with a uniform distribution. Data sets were generated for all combinations of 20 case base sizes (from 50 to 525 cases, step size 25) and 10 frequencies (from 0.021 to 0.083, which gave rise to sine waves covering from approximately 2-8 complete periods as x varied from 0 to 100). This gave rise to a total of 200 synthetic data sets.

4.2   Experimental Design

The experiments estimate the target value for an input query. In all cases Mean Absolute Error is used for assessing accuracy. Leave-one-out testing and ten fold cross validation are used for conducting the experiments on the synthetic and real world data sets respectively. Candidate methods tested for generating estimations are k-NN, locally weighted linear regression (LWLR), EAR and CAAR.

For the Auto, MPG, Housing, Hardware, Stock and CPU data sets the respective values to estimate are price (the reported values are the actual prices divided by 1000), mpg, MEDV (median value of owner-occupied homes in $1000's), PRP (published relative performance), the company stock price and portion of time that cpu runs in user mode respectively. For the synthetic data sets, the value to predict is assigned to the cases based on their feature value, as explained in section 4.1.

The k-NN procedure and locally weighted linear regression were implemented using WEKA's [16] IBk and locally weighted learning (using the linear regression class as the base learner) classes. EAR is the method "EAR4" introduced in [13].

For each method and data set, parameters for each regression method were tuned using hill climbing and leave-one-out testing on the training data. The tuned parameter for the k-NN is k, the number of cases to consider; the tuned parameter for LWLR methods is the number of neighbor cases for building the estimation. For EAR and CAAR, tuning set the number of cases to adapt for

Table 2. MAE of EAR, k-NN, LWLR and LR for the sample domains

Method	Domains					
	Auto (A)	MPG (AM)	Housing (H)	Hardware (HW)	Stock (S)	CPU
k-NN	1.6	2.1	2.72	31.5	0.47	2.1
LWLR	1.64	1.87	2.22	26.4	0.51	1.9
EAR	1.43	1.93	2.14	25.64	**0.43**	1.93
CAAR1	1.44	1.78	2.01	26.4	0.53	1.98
CAAR2	1.58	1.82	1.98	28.2	0.54	2
CAAR	**1.35**	**1.77**	**1.91**	**25.24**	**0.43**	**1.87**

each problem and the number of adaptations to apply. When k-NN and LWLR were tuned, there was no limit on the number of cases to be used for building the estimations and models. The number of base cases for EAR was limited to the minimum of ten or top 2.5 % cases in the case base and the maximum number of adaptations to be applied per case is respectively limited to the number of adaptation rules generated from those base cases (following the rationale of [13], omitted here for reasons of space). The number of base cases for CAAR is also limited to the minimum of ten and the top 2.5% cases in the case base and the number of applied adaptations per base case is limited to 150. The scaling function K in Eq. 1 was set to the identity function.

4.3   Experimental Results

Standard Data Sets: Experiments on standard data sets were used to address evaluation question 1, how the accuracy of CAAR compares to that of the baseline methods locally weighted linear regression, k-NN, and EAR, and question 2, how the consideration of context of both input query and case to adapt affects performance, versus only considering context at one or the other, as in previous work. Table 2 lists the mean absolute error of the methods for the six methods and six data sets. CAAR1 and CAAR2 are ablated versions of CAAR, respectively considering only the context of the input problem or only the context of the case to adapt.

CAAR has the highest accuracy in all data sets, and outperforms its ablated versions, demonstrating the value of CAAR's more extensive consideration of context. k-NN has the lowest accuracy in four of the six domains. For four of the six data sets EAR outperforms locally weighted linear regression.

Figure 3 shows the percent of improvement in MAE for CAAR, EAR and LWLR over k-NN. Improvement of CAAR over k-NN ranges from 9% to 30%. Using a one side paired t-test with 95% confidence interval, and null hypothesis that the MAE of LWLR is less than that of CAAR, in the Auto domain p<.001, in the MPG domain p<.038, in the Housing domain p<.001, in the Hardware domain p<.3 (not significant), in the Stock domain p<.001 and in the CPU domain p<.001.

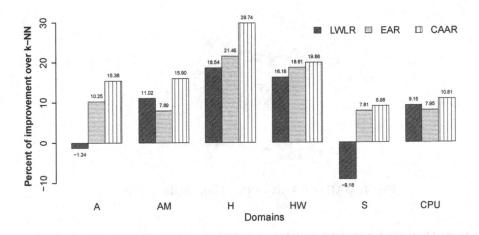

Fig. 3. Percent improvement in MAE of CAAR, EAR and LWLR over k-NN for the real world data sets

Synthetic Data Sets: Tests on synthetic data sets were used to explore Question 3, how the accuracy of the candidate methods is affected by increasing the density of case base coverage of the problem space, and Question 4, how changes in domain regularity (i.e., the level of fluctuations across different contexts) affect the accuracies of the candidate methods. Figure 4 shows the MAE of CAAR's estimates for the synthetic domains as a function of the frequency of domain changes and case base size. To show the whole spectrum of MAEs, a logarithmic scale is used. Figure 4 shows that increasing case density decreases MAE, and increasing frequency increases MAE. The explanation is that increased case base coverage increases the likelihood of CAAR being able to select prior cases within a similar context, and that higher frequencies decrease the size of regions with similar context, increasing likelihood of generating new adaptation rules from cases in different contexts.

Fig. 5 provides some representative examples from tests on the synthetic data. Part a of Fig. 5 fixes a representative synthetic data set frequency (0.049) and shows how the number of cases in the case base affects relative performance at that frequency of EAR, LWLR and CAAR compared to k-NN (lines have been added between points for visibility only). Increasing case-base size increases accuracy of all methods compared to k-NN, but CAAR always shows the best performance followed by LWLR and EAR.

Part b of Fig. 5 fixes case base size at a representative size, 150 cases, and illustrates performance as a function of frequency. Increasing frequency causes the relative advantage of EAR, LWLR and CAAR over k-NN to decrease,

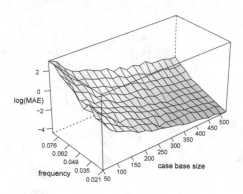

Fig. 4. MAE of CAAR on the synthetic data sets

Table 3. MAEs of k-NN, LWLR, EAR and CAAR methods for different synthetic data sets with 150 cases

Method	frequency									
	0.0208	0.0278	0.0347	0.0417	0.0486	0.0556	0.0625	0.0694	0.0764	0.0833
k-NN	1.87	2.43	2.41	2.53	3.42	3.45	3.87	4.61	6.27	7.91
LWLR	0.18	0.2	0.22	0.36	0.43	0.59	0.62	1.25	2.21	3.59
EAR	0.70	0.78	1.00	1.10	1.54	1.57	2.12	2.77	4.60	5.74
CAAR	**0.16**	**0.17**	**0.16**	**0.33**	**0.33**	**0.47**	**0.48**	**0.86**	**1.56**	**2.36**

but the loss for CAAR is less than for the other two methods. Table 3 shows the actual mean absolute errors for these results.

Part c of Fig. 5 shows the percent of improvement of CAAR compared to LWLR for frequency 0.049. CAAR shows an improvement ranging from 7% to 35%, for different case base sizes. However, there is no clear pattern. Part d of Fig. 5 shows relative improvement of CAAR compared to LWLR for a a case base of 150 cases. Here increasing the frequency increases the relative benefit of CAAR, with up to 34% improvement over LWLR when the frequency is maximum. We hypothesize that this is because higher frequencies result in higher fluctuations in the values of cases in local neighborhoods, which can make the locally fitted linear model inaccurate, but CAAR's reuse of the differences derived from similar contexts in the case base mitigates this problem to a certain degree.

Parts b and d show that on the synthetic data, CAAR's use of regularities with previous problems enables it to make more accurate estimations compared to LWLR, which supports its approach for regression tasks in domains with fairly regular patterns of past problem-solution pairs. Using a one-side paired t-test with 95% confidence interval, and null hypothesis that the MAE of LWLR and k-NN is less than that of CAAR, in all synthetic domains p<.001.

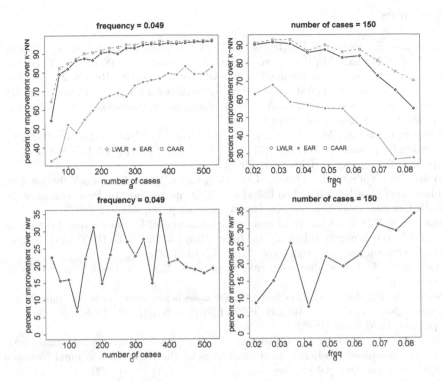

Fig. 5. comparison of the candidate methods performance on synthetic data sets

5   Conclusion and Future Research

This paper has introduced a method for using contextual information to improve the accuracy of case-based regression. The approach considers two types of context, the context of the input problem, and the context in which candidate case adaptation rules were generated, and uses these types of context to select cases to adapt to solve problems and to select automatically-generated adaptation rules to adapt those cases. Context is based on the gradient of the locally weighted fitted linear model at each point of the domain space.

An experimental evaluation of the new method compared to four baseline methods and two ablations, in 200 synthetic and six real-world domains showed that the approach can improve the estimation accuracies, and that considering both problem context and adaptation context is more beneficial than considering either alone.

Future work includes exploration of whether also considering the level of confidence in particular solutions can be used to improve context calculations (cf. [17]). Long term goals include extending this general approach to apply to domains with symbolic features, as well as to develop methods for defining and using adaptation context in tasks such as classification, and eventually for more knowledge-rich tasks such as case-based planning.

References

1. Mantaras, R., McSherry, D., Bridge, D., Leake, D., Smyth, B., Craw, S., Faltings, B., Maher, M., Cox, M., Forbus, K., Keane, M., Aamodt, A., Watson, I.: Retrieval, reuse, revision, and retention in CBR. Knowledge Engineering Review 20(3) (2005)
2. Leake, D.: Learning adaptation strategies by introspective reasoning about memory search. In: Proceedings of the AAAI 1993 Workshop on Case-Based Reasoning, pp. 57–63. AAAI Press, Menlo Park (1993)
3. Hanney, K., Keane, M.: The adaptation knowledge bottleneck: How to ease it by learning from cases. In: Leake, D.B., Plaza, E. (eds.) ICCBR 1997. LNCS, vol. 1266, pp. 359–370. Springer, Heidelberg (1997)
4. Wilke, W., Vollrath, I., Althoff, K.D., Bergmann, R.: A framework for learning adaptation knowledge based on knowledge light approaches. In: Proceedings of the Fifth German Workshop on Case-Based Reasoning, pp. 235–242 (1997)
5. Bonissone, P., Cheetham, W.: Financial applications of fuzzy case-based reasoning to residential property valuation. In: Proceedings of the Sixth IEEE International Conference on Fuzzy Systems, vol. 1, pp. 37–44 (1997)
6. Hanney, K.: Learning adaptation rules from cases. Master's thesis, Trinity College, Dublin (1997)
7. McSherry, D.: An adaptation heuristic for case-based estimation. In: Smyth, B., Cunningham, P. (eds.) EWCBR 1998. LNCS (LNAI), vol. 1488, pp. 184–195. Springer, Heidelberg (1998)
8. Patterson, D., Rooney, N., Galushka, M.: A regression based adaptation strategy for case-based reasoning. In: Proceedings of the Eighteenth Annual National Conference on Artificial Intelligence, pp. 87–92. AAAI Press (2002)
9. Policastro, C.A., Carvalho, A.C., Delbem, A.C.: A hybrid case adaptation approach for case-based reasoning. Applied Intelligence 28(2), 101–119 (2008)
10. Dey, A.: Understanding and using context. Personal Ubiquitous Computing 5(1), 4–7 (2001)
11. Brézillon, P.: Context in problem solving: A survey. The Knowledge Engineering Review 14(1), 1–34 (1999)
12. McDonnell, N., Cunningham, P.: A knowledge-light approach to regression using case-based reasoning. In: Roth-Berghofer, T.R., Göker, M.H., Güvenir, H.A. (eds.) ECCBR 2006. LNCS (LNAI), vol. 4106, pp. 91–105. Springer, Heidelberg (2006)
13. Jalali, V., Leake, D.: Extending case adaptation with automatically-generated ensembles of adaptation rules. In: Delany, S.J., Ontañón, S. (eds.) ICCBR 2013. LNCS, vol. 7969, pp. 188–202. Springer, Heidelberg (2013)
14. Frank, A., Asuncion, A.: UCI machine learning repository (2010), http://archive.ics.uci.edu/ml
15. Torgo, L.: Lus torgo - regression data sets, http://www.dcc.fc.up.pt/~ltorgo/Regression/DataSets.html
16. Hall, M., Frank, E., Holmes, G., Pfahringer, B., Reutemann, P., Witten, I.H.: The WEKA data mining software: an update. SIGKDD Explor. Newsl. 11(1), 10–18 (2009)
17. Jalali, V., Leake, D.: On deriving adaptation rule confidence from the rule generation process. In: Delany, S.J., Ontañón, S. (eds.) ICCBR 2013. LNCS, vol. 7969, pp. 179–187. Springer, Heidelberg (2013)

A Context-Sensitive Intervention Approach
for Collaboration in Dynamic Environments

Stefan Werner Knoll and Stephan G. Lukosch

Delft University of Technology,
Faculty of Technology, Policy and Management, The Netherlands
{s.w.knoll,s.g.lukosch}@tudelft.nl

Abstract. Complex design and engineering processes are characterized by dynamic requirements, like changing process goals or group constellations. To deal with these dynamics, a context-sensitive approach is needed to consider a changing environment and provides teams with the support they need. This paper describes research about a context-sensitive intervention approach to support collaboration in dynamic environments. Based on a review of existing approaches for context modeling in collaboration, a semantic model is presented to describe a collaboration process design as well as contextual process information. Using existing theories on collaboration performance, the paper discusses how the semantic model can be used to monitor group performance during collaboration. Thereby, a rule concept is introduced to derive interventions for dynamic collaboration processes and discusses their application to build new context-sensitive collaboration support systems.

Keywords: Context model, collaboration, dynamic environment, intervention.

1   Introduction

Nowadays, profit and non-profit organizations operate in a rapid changing world, which is characterized by changing technologies, customer demands and unexpected events. To remain competitive, organizations combine their knowledge resources in a collaborative process to improve the adaptation of their working processes and structures to new market situations. Over the years, organizations started to operate in inter-organizational networks to pool or exchange their knowledge resources, and jointly develop new ideas and skills. In this context, collaboration in organizations has changed from local teams to virtual teams, whose members are geographically distributed and use technological support to work across space, time, cultural and organizational boundaries.

Today, virtual teams are an important component of many multinational organizations to lower cost factors like travel and facility costs. However, collaboration in virtual teams faces new challenges that make it more difficult to manage them than face-to-face collaboration [1]. Besides the loss of non-verbal clues, different work processes and cultures between the team members, the dynamics of the collaboration

P. Brézillon, P. Blackburn, and R. Dapoigny (Eds.): CONTEXT 2013, LNAI 8175, pp. 115–128, 2013.
© Springer-Verlag Berlin Heidelberg 2013

processes represents a challenge for the design of technological support. For example, in complex design and engineering processes, a change in the collaboration context, like a changing process goal or the reduction of time available to achieve a collaborative goal, can lead to a need for a process adaptation during runtime.

In face-to-face collaboration, a team leader can provide process support by monitoring the collaboration process and redefining the goals and objectives of the team as well as to outline the procedures, activities, and tasks to accomplish these goals [2]. To deal with these types of dynamics in a virtual environment, teams need technological support that provide flexible features to monitor the context of a collaboration process as well as to adapt the process to the new situation. Depending on the expertise of the team members for the collaboration process, such support can range from prescribed collaboration processes and tools for inexperienced teams to flexible collaboration support in which the support system just gives recommendations on how to improve the process or on which tools to use.

Current context-aware systems for collaboration make use of contextual information to provide awareness support [3-4] or to adapt the collaborative workspace [5]. However, less research has focused on the relationship between group performance of a collaboration process and the need for process adaptation. In this paper, it is assumed that contextual information of a collaboration processes can be used to monitor the performance of a group in prescribed as well as flexible collaboration support environments. An analysis of existing approaches for modeling context of dynamic collaboration processes shows that given modeling approaches only provide limited support to define prescribed and emergent collaboration processes as well as to express their contextual process information. To overcome this situation, a new semantic model for collaboration processes is introduced and its application to derive interventions for context-aware systems for collaboration is discussed.

The paper is structured in the following way. Section 2 introduces a framework of group performance in dynamic collaboration processes and discusses the concept of interventions. In section 3, related work on context modeling in collaboration is analyzed. Section 4 introduces a semantic model for collaboration processes and discusses how context for prescribed and emergent collaboration processes can be described. In section 5 the application of this contextual information is illustrated by a rule concept for context-sensitive intervention, whereas section 6 summarizes the paper and closes with a discussion on future work.

2   Background

Different approaches exist to define the concept of collaboration. A general definition is given by the Oxford dictionary, where collaboration is defined as the *"the act of working with another person or group of people to create or produce something"*. From a computer science perspective, collaboration can involve humans as well as computational agents, who use technological support in *"a process in which two or more agents work together to achieve a shared goal"* [6]. A more specific definition is given in behavioral science, where collaboration *"occurs when a group of autonomous stakeholders of a problem domain engage in an interactive process, using shared rules, norms, and structures, to act or decide on issues related to that domain"* [7].

In this paper, the focus is on collaboration as *"an interactive process in which a group of individual group members uses shared rules, norms, and structures to create or share knowledge in order to perform a collaborative task"*. Thereby, collaboration can make use of technological support to provide an environment that supports the shared rules, norms, and structures of an organization. In the context of virtual teams and cross-organizational collaboration, it is further assumed that collaboration takes place in a dynamic environment, which is characterized by changing requirements and resources such as a changing process goal, available time or group constellation. As a result, technological support needs to be aware of a collaboration context to provide groups with the support they need. Such technological support can be a context-aware system, which *"uses context to provide relevant information and/or services to the user, where relevancy depends on the user's task"* [8]. Thereby, context-aware applications can support the presentation of information and services to a user, the automatic execution of a service for a user or the tagging of context information to support later retrieval [8].

Several context-aware systems focus on physical context elements such as user's location, time and activity [3-4]. However, less research has been done on using context to predict group performance during collaboration. Research on groupware systems [9-10] still indicates that a collaboration process and its outcome are affected by different contextual factors like group characteristics, task complexity, technology used or organizational culture. Today, different social psychological theories [11-15] describe and predict the influence of such contextual factors on group behavior and performance. As result, in this paper is assumed that by monitoring group performance during collaboration, a context-aware systems can provide new services to handle negative group behaviors such as groupthink [11] or social loafing [12] and thereby improve group performance.

2.1   Group Performance in Dynamic Collaboration Processes

This section introduces a framework for group performance in dynamic collaboration processes. Based on the input-process-output framework for analyzing group behavior and performance by Hackman [16], the framework consists of the elements *collaboration task, individual group member, collaboration process, collaboration outcome and collaboration context* (see Fig. 1).

Similar to Hackman [16], in this paper it is assumed that performance in collaboration can be observed from an individual and group level. In the center of Fig. 1 individual group members form a group for collaboration and represent the individual level. The composition of the group is influenced by the collaborative task, which defines the necessary resources to complete a task. These resources can represent knowledge, skills, and abilities (KSAs) of individual group members as well as their motives, emotions and personality.

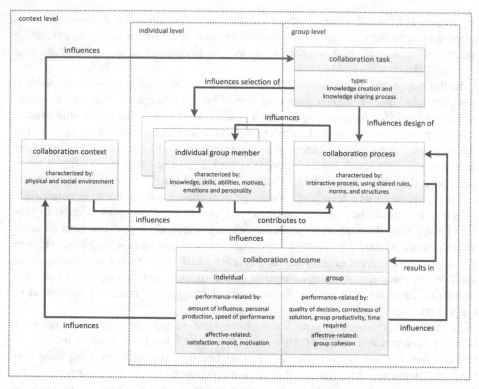

Fig. 1. A general framework of group performance in dynamic collaboration processes (adapted from Hackman [16])

During the collaboration process, individual group members interact with the organizational context by making use of external resources such as task related information or technological support. From a group level perspective, individual group members contribute different resources in an interactive process to the group. The design of the interactive process is influenced by the collaborative task, which defines the shared rules, norms, and structures to generate a group outcome. During the interactive process, individual group members can influence each other's work by sharing contributions.

The outcome of a collaboration process can be classified into the dimensions performance and affective. On the individual level, performance of an individual group member can be represented in different ways such as the amount of influence of an individual during a decision-making process, the number of contributions in a discussion or the personal speed of performance. The affective-related outcome can be defined by psychological factors like satisfaction, mood or motivation of an individual group member. On the group level, performance of a group can be represented by factors like the quality of a decision, the correctness of a solution, the group productivity or the time required to achieve a shared goal. The affective-related outcome can be group cohesion.

The context of a collaboration process is defined by its physical and social environment. The group composition is influenced if an individual group member is instructed to leave or join the group. The group performance is influenced by the provided resources of the physical environment. A possible negative effect is described as the production blocking effect [13], where individual group members are hindered by the technological support or process design to contribute at any given time. The social environment may further effect group members motivation and mood and as a result the performance of the collaboration process. For example, the fear of negative evaluation may cause individual group members to withhold their contributions during the collaboration process (evaluation apprehension [14]). Further, individual group members expend less effort when they believe their contributions to be dispensable and not needed for group success (social loafing [15]).

2.2   Concept of Interventions

A change in the collaboration context can lead to a need to adapt the collaboration process to the new situation. However, for inexperienced groups it can be difficult to overcome typical challenges of collaboration (social loafing, groupthink etc.). In face-to-face collaboration, a facilitator can monitor the collaboration process and perform interventions to help the group and solve its problem. A key skill for a facilitator is to make effective interventions to ensure that the collaboration process fits to a given collaboration context. An intervention can take place in three stages [17]:

- *Stage 1: to recognize symptoms of a process problem* - The recognition process is characterized by analyzing the behavior of the individual group members. In face-to-face collaboration, this can be done by analyzing the contributions, the body language as well as the interaction of the group.
- *Stage 2: to interpret the syndromes* - To identify the underlying pattern of given syndromes, the facilitator needs knowledge about theories on group behaviors as well as expertise with group dynamics. During this identification process, a list of generic problem syndromes could support a facilitator (for example the generic meeting problem syndromes by Westley [17]) .
- *Stage 3: to make an intervention* - To deal with a process problem, a facilitator can choose between action and interpretation interventions. Action interventions directly manipulate the collaboration process (for example: to change the group constellation if expert knowledge is needed; or to prevent interruptions of an individual group member). By using an interpretation intervention, a facilitator communicates the observed patterns to the group to improve awareness and help the group to solve the problem on their own.

Compared face-to-face collaboration, virtual teams face the challenge that the used technology often reduces or eliminates visual communication channels such as facial expressions or body language. To make use of the concept of interventions, a support technology needs to provide services to monitor and analyze content-related as well as interaction-related data. Highly dynamic processes, such as complex design and engineering processes, requires elastic collaboration support [18]. Elastic collaboration support ranges from prescribed collaboration to emergent forms of collaboration [18]. On the one extreme, prescribed collaboration supports a group with less expertise in collaboration by predefining process as well as support tools. Here, a support technology can provide support by monitoring the collaboration process performance and providing interventions based on predefined rules. On the other extreme, emergent collaboration supports expert groups that do not need guidance and coordination during collaboration. Here, the group monitors the collaboration process performance and coordinates the use of support tools. During a collaboration process, the support can move between these extremes. Thus, making the support elastic.

A context-aware system can support such elastic collaboration by providing a service to monitor the group performance of a collaboration process. Based on a rule concept, such a system can further provide services that provide action as well as interpretation interventions. However, to make this possible, first a semantic model is needed to describe the context of a dynamic collaboration process. Such a model needs to address the following requirements:

- *R1:* to recognize symptoms of a process problem, a semantic model needs to capture data about prescribed as well as emergent collaboration processes.
- *R2*: to provide interventions in prescribed collaboration, a semantic model needs to express the underlying process logic of the process. This data can be used by a context-aware system to provide a service to detect for deviation of a process plan currently being used.
- *R3*: to provide interventions in emergent collaboration, a semantic model needs to log all activities of a prescribed and emergent collaboration process. This data can be used by a context-aware system to provide a service to recognize symptoms of a process problem by comparing the current process context with historic context data.

3   Analysis of Context Modeling Approaches

The following section analyzes existing context modeling approaches with respect to their feasibility to express contextual information of a dynamic collaboration process. In the context of business process management, Reiter et al. [19] introduce a conceptual context approach that uses data from a business process model to describe the communication context of an individual group member during collaboration. This approach characterizes the communication context by the dimensions: *task* (the activity in a process model), *location* (the workplace of an activity), *presence* (the availability of an individual for communication in relation to a location or task), and *relation* (the relationship between the individuals). The authors argue that data for each of these dimensions can be determined by the components of a business process management system. However, they also indicate that a process activity in the context of a business process model is usually not designed in such granularity to relate every activity to a specific task.

Haake et al. [5] introduce a generic context framework for context-based adaptation that uses the layers: *knowledge layer, state layer, contextualization layer* and *adaptation layer*. The knowledge layer is used to represent an application domain model as well as situation-independent contextual information. Based on the knowledge layer, the state layer provides information about the current state in a collaboration process. The contextualization layer provides rules that define, which subset of the state is relevant for a given focus. Finally, the adaptation layer defines a set of adaptation rules on how to change properties of the collaborative environment according to the contextual state. Haake et al. [5] discuss the application of their framework along a domain model for collaborative workspaces.

Vieira et al. [20] introduce an ontology-based approach to formally represent context in groupware systems. This approach divides context into three subclasses: *physical context, organizational context* and *interaction context*. Thereby, the physical context characterizes the situation of an individual group member at a specific time of a collaboration process. Organizational context defines the individual group member, the group and the related project of a collaboration process. The interaction context characterizes the interaction process by the concepts application and artifact that are used during a process step. Vieira et al. [20] discuss the application of the ontology to define inference rules for communication tools recommendation based on the current context of each individual group member.

Another ontology-based approach is given by the Ontology for Contextual Collaborative Applications (OCCA) by Wang et al. [21]. OCCA classifies the contextual information into context related to *person, task, interaction, artifact, tool, collaboration control, environment* and *history*. For example, the context of a person is represented by the FOAF ontology [22], which is used to describe the individual group members and their relationships. Similar to a business process model, OCCA describes the context of a task as an abstract activity of a collaboration process. The interaction context consists of information that represents the action, which takes place during the task running. Thereby, the artifact context describes objects produced or consumed during collaboration. Information about the used collaboration tools are described by the concept tool. Wang et al. [21] discuss the possible application of their context model for different context-aware application like a context matching service and collaboration control mechanism.

The above approaches seem to be feasible to express collaboration situations. Resulting contextual information can be used to define process adaptations for specific situations [5], to recommend services and tools [21], [20] or to represent awareness information [19]. Reiter et al. [19] uses a business process model to describe the logical order of activities in a collaboration process. Here, a process activity is defined as an abstract concept that does not provide detailed information about the individual group members or the services that will be used during collaboration. However, such detailed information is necessary to monitor the performance of a collaboration process at runtime. The discussed ontological approaches [20-21] and the domain model [5] express more contextual information about collaboration. However, they do not provide a concept to describe the process workflow, which is needed to prescribe a collaboration process. Therefore, a new modeling approach is necessary to define a collaboration process as well as to express contextual process information. The next section introduces a semantic model that combines properties of a process definition language to express the workflow of a collaboration process with given ontology-based approaches to capture contextual process information.

4   A Semantic Model for Dynamic Collaboration Processes

The semantic model in this section is built using methodologies for ontology engineering [23-24]. These methodologies suggest the following steps to design and evaluate a semantic model: to define purpose and scope of a model; to capture and formalize key concepts and relationships; and to evaluate and document the model.

The purpose of the semantic model is to describe a collaboration process as well as to capture and analyze contextual information about this process in dynamic environments. As discussed, dynamic environments require different forms of collaboration which can range from prescribed to emergent forms of collaboration. As a result, the semantic model needs to be able to describe the workflow of a predefined collaboration process as well to log the process of an emergent collaboration process. To define the workflow of a process, modeling languages for business processes use the entities: *process*, *activity*, *component*, *data* and *flow connector* [25]. To account for the human interaction in dynamic collaboration processes, an additional entity *participant* is added to these entities.

Based on these entities a set of competency questions that a semantic model should be able to answer is classified and defined. The competency question are used to identify abstract entities (key concepts), to name important properties and to define relationships between the entities.

4.1   Concepts of the Semantic Model

Fig. 2 illustrates a first approach for a semantic model for dynamic collaboration processes. Fig. 2 shows the key concepts and their relations. In this model, the concept *participant* describes an individual group member who participates in a collaboration process. The concept participant has certain skills that can be a prerequisite of a role in a process. Similar to Haake et al. [5], the concept *role* is used to denote abstractly a set of behaviors, rights and obligation of a process participant. A participant can be assigned to a group in a specific role. Besides the concept role, the concept *skill* is used to distinguish different participants and thus to be able to define requirements for the participants of a process. The entity *process* describes a collaboration process in which a group uses shared rules, norms, and structures to create or share knowledge. Similar to Oliveira et al. [26], a process has an *objective*, defining its main purpose or collaborative task. How a group moves through this process to create an intended state in the process can be prescribed by work tactics of a group, similar to the concept of a collaboration pattern [27]. The semantic model in Fig. 2 represents these stages in a process by the concept *phase* and relating this concept to a *group*. During a phase, a group of participants moves through a sequence of activities.

Similar to concepts like participation [26] or action [5], the concept *activity* represents an atomic activity that is executed by a participant using a software tool represented by the concept *component*. To control the collaboration process and allow the representation of parallel phases, the concept *gateway* is used to implement given workflow patterns such as parallel split, exclusive choice or simple merge [28].

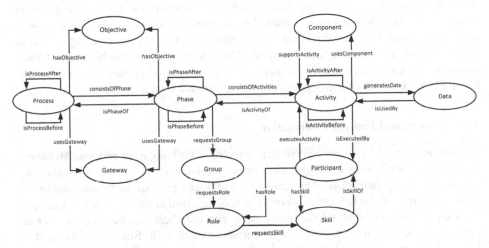

Fig. 2. A semantic model for dynamic collaboration processes

4.2   Collaborative Process Definition

The semantic model can be used to define the workflow of prescribed as well as emergent collaboration processes. A prescribed collaboration process is represented by the concept process, which is defined by its properties (for example process:name, process:type or process:description). As a process can be structured into different stages, the concept process is related to different phases. For example, a problem solving process can involve the phases: problem definition, solution search, solution generation, solution evaluation and solution implementation [29]. Each phase represents a specific collaborative tasks, which is defined by the concept objective. As each phase could require a different group composition, a phase is related to a group, which requires participants with a specific role. The role itself is related to the concept skills. Thereby, the selection of participants with different expertise for a phase can be influenced. Each phase itself defines a sequence of activities which are related to predefined components. For example, the activity to generate a solution for a problem can be implemented by a brainstorming component. An activity sequence defines the possible interaction of the participant with a component. For example, a component brainstorming could provide support for the activity sequences AS_1:{to view; to create} and AS_2:{to view, to create, to comment}. Here, the activity sequence AS_1 represents a common brainstorming process, whereas the activity sequence AS_2 allows brainstorming participants to comment existing contributions.

An emergent collaboration process can be reviewed by creating a process log. As it cannot be known before process start, through which phases a group passes, the process log can be initialized as a process which related a phase to a group. During the collaboration process the group uses a set of components. The relation between a component and an activity defines the supported activities of a component. As a result, the process log can describe executed activities in the process as a relation between the concepts phase, participant, component, activity and data. As a group is related to a phase, a new phase is started if the group constellation is changing over time. The process log can be refined by searching for patterns or comparing a process log to a predefined collaboration process. Thereby, a specific combination of used components or a specific activity sequence over a time period could give some indicators for a work tactics of a group that can be represented by a new phase.

4.3   Contextual Process Information

The semantic model can be used to define or log a collaboration process. However, besides the workflow of a collaboration process, contextual information is necessary to monitor group behaviors. The semantic model can provide such information by using properties of the key concepts or by connecting further ontologies. For example, contextual information about the individual group members can be described by the properties and relations of the concepts participant and skill. Similar to Wang et al. [21], this information can be improved by connecting the FOAF ontology to the concept participant.

Contextual information about a collaborative task is given by the concept objective, which defines the goal for a phase or the whole collaboration process. This information can be improved by relating the concept process to an ontology such as the organization ontology [30] that described organizational structures of an organization in which the collaboration process is executed. Contextual information about the interaction process is provided by the concepts component, activity, data and participant. Here, the relation between the concepts component, activity and data defines the possible activities as well as the used or generated data that is supported by a component. Further, the process model of a prescribed collaboration process provides information on how to perform a collaborative task. In this context, a process log represents contextual information about the history of a group, an individual group member and the executed collaboration process.

5   A Context-Sensitive Intervention Approach

This section discusses the application of the semantic model to define context-sensitive intervention for context-aware systems that support collaboration in dynamic environments. Assuming that contextual information of a collaboration processes can be used to monitor the performance of a group during collaboration, such information can be used to define interventions in relation to a specific collaboration situation by means of event-condition-action (ECA) rules [31]. The semantics of an ECA rule (ON event IF condition DO actions) is defined as follows:

- **Event**: specifies the situation in which a rule is used to coordinate the use of possible interventions that are related to this situation.
- **Condition**: defines a logical test that, if satisfied or evaluated to be true, causes the action to be carried out. The concept of a condition combines the stages of an intervention to recognize and interpret symptoms of a process problem. The expression of such a condition can make use of given logical operations and can refer to the concepts of the semantic model. As a result, a condition could combine workflow as well as contextual information about a collaboration process. For example, a condition could use information about the process workflow to check if the intended components of a prescribed phase have been activated by the participant. Otherwise, contextual information could be used to define conditions which check for syndromes that could indicate negative group behaviors. Such information could be given by the relationship between the participants, their hierarchical structure in an organization, or by contextual information about the history of a participant in similar collaboration processes.
- **Action:** defines a change or update in a collaboration process by means of an intervention. With regard to the concept of interventions, these interventions can be action and interpretation interventions. As a result, the concept of action can support collaboration by adapting the collaboration process or by providing awareness information to the individual group members.

A possible application of the ECA rule approach is the design of an interpretational intervention for the social loafing theory [13]. This theory describes the tendency of participants to expend less effort when they believe their contributions are dispensable and not needed for group success. The effect increases with increasing group size and can be reduced when participants believe that they are being evaluated as individuals rather than collectively as a group. As group size affects this group behavior, an intervention rule can be related to the number of individual group members in a process. During the collaboration process, indicators such as the number of contributions or the time between two contributions can be monitored. A possible condition for an intervention can be the situation that a group has a stable contribution rate instead of one individual group member with a declining contribution rate over time. At a certain discrepancy level between individual contribution rate and average group contribution rate, an interpretation intervention can inform the group about this situation and suggest approaches to overcome this situation.

In contrast, an action intervention can be designed for the evaluation apprehension theory [14]. The evaluation apprehension theory describes the effect that the fear to be criticized for a contribution causes participants to withhold their contributions during the collaboration process. This effect is likely to occur for low-status participants of a group that includes dominant, high-status participants. A possible intervention rule can target the group constellation by using the contextual information on the organizational role of the participants. During the collaboration process, the contribution rate of a low-status participant can be monitored as an indicator. A possible condition for such an intervention can be a declining contribution rate of a low-status participant after a high-status participant submitted a contribution in relation to a contribution of the low-status participant. At a certain level, an action intervention is made by making the contributions of the whole group anonymous or by hiding the contributions of the low-status participant from the high-status participant.

In conclusion, the introduced context-sensitive intervention approach uses process as well as contextual information. As a result, more data can be used to monitor the performance of a collaboration process. A context-aware system can use this information to provide new services to handle negative group behaviors. To improve interventions over time, rules can be seen as a part of a collaboration process model. By analyzing the process log of an executed collaboration process, existing interventions can be evaluated and adapted to new identified pattern in a process.

6   Summary and Discussion

The paper described research about a context-sensitive approach to support collaboration in dynamic environments. Complex design and engineering processes are characterized by dynamic requirements, like changing process goals or group constellations. To deal with these dynamics, a context-sensitive approach is needed to consider a changing environment and provides teams with the support they need. The paper introduced a framework of group performance in dynamic collaboration processes and discusses the concept of interventions as an approach to support collaboration.

Based on the assumption that by monitoring group performance a context-aware system can provide new services to handle negative group behaviors, existing approaches for context modeling in collaboration with respect to their feasibility to describe the context of dynamic collaboration processes were analyzed. The analysis showed that the discussed modeling approaches only provide limited support to define prescribed and emergent collaboration processes as well as to express their contextual process information. The paper presented a first approach of a semantic model that can be used to capture, share and reuse information about a process definition and contextual information. An application of the semantic model is discussed to define context-sensitive intervention for collaboration processes. Here, the ECA rules concept is used to describe the relation between an intervention and a specific collaborative situation.

In the current form, the context-sensitive intervention approach can be used to monitor common performance indicators like the number of contributions or the number of responses to contributions. Finally, more research is needed to understand the relation between these indicators and the performance of a group in a specific situation. Currently, the semantic model is deployed in a context-aware systems for collaboration [32] to evaluate the semantic model and possible intervention rules. Resulting knowledge can then be used to improve the existing semantic model and to provide new services to handle negative group behaviors in collaboration processes.

Acknowledgments. This work has been partially supported by the FP7 EU Large-scale Integrating Project SMART VORTEX (Scalable Semantic Product Data Stream Management for Collaboration and Decision Making in Engineering) co-financed by the European Union. For more details, visit http://www.smartvortex.eu/.

References

1. Nunamaker Jr., J.F., Reinig, B.A., Briggs, R.O.: Principles for Effective Virtual Teamwork. Communications of the ACM 52(4), 113–117 (2009)
2. Sarin, S., McDermott, C.: The Effect of Team Leader Characteristics on Learning, Knowledge Application, and Performance of Cross-Functional New Product Development Teams. Decision Sciences 34(4), 707–739 (2003)
3. Ardissono, L., Bosio, G.: Context-dependent Awareness Support in Open Collaboration Environments. User Modeling and User-Adapted Interaction 22(3), 223–254 (2012)
4. Ferscha, A., Holzmann, C., Oppl, S.: Context Awareness for Group Interaction Support. In: 2nd International Workshop on Mobility Management Wireless Access Protocols, New York, pp. 88–97 (2004)
5. Haake, J.M., Hussein, T., Joop, B., Lukosch, S.G., Veiel, D., Ziegler, J.: Modeling and Exploiting Context for Adaptive Collaboration. International Journal of Cooperative Information Systems 19(1&2), 71–120 (2010)
6. Terveen, L.G.: An Overview of Human-Computer Collaboration. Knowledge-Based Systems 8(2-3), 67–81 (1995)
7. Wood, D.J., Gray, B.: Toward a Comprehensive Theory of Collaboration. Journal of Applied Behavioral Science 27(2), 139–162 (1991)
8. Dey, A.K.: Understanding and Using Context. Personal and Ubiquitous Computing 5, 4–7 (2001)
9. Dennis, A.R., George, J.F., Jessup, L.M., Nunamaker Jr., J.F., Vogel, D.R.: Information Technology to Support Electronic Meetings. Management Information Systems Quarterly 12(4), 591–624 (1988)
10. Nunamaker Jr., J.F., Dennis, A.R., Valacich, J.S., Vogel, D., George, J.F.: Electronic Meeting Systems to Support Group Work. Communications of the ACM 34(7), 40–61 (1991)
11. Janis, I.L.: Victims of Groupthink. Houghton-Mifflin, Boston (1982)
12. Karau, S.J., Williams, K.D.: Social Loafing: A Meta-Analytic Review and Theoretical Integration. Journal of Personality and Social Psychology 65(4), 681–706 (1993)
13. Diehl, M., Stroebe, W.: Productivity Loss in Idea-Generating Groups: Tracking Down the Blocking Effect. Journal of Personality and Social Psychology 61(3), 392–403 (1991)
14. Gallupe, R.B., Dennis, A.R., Cooper, W.H., Valacich, J.S., Bastianutti, L.M., Nunamaker Jr., J.F.: Electronic Brainstorming and Group Size. The Academy of Management Journal 35(2), 350–369 (1992)
15. Tajfel, H.: Social Identity and Intergroup Behaviour. Social Science Information 13(2), 65–93 (1974)
16. Hackman, J.R.: The Design of Work Teams. In: Lorsch, J.L. (ed.) Handbook of Organizational Behavior, pp. 315–342. Prentice Hall, Englewood Cliffs (1987)
17. Westley, F., Waters, J.A.: Group Facilitation Skills for Managers. Management Learning 19(2), 134–143 (1988)
18. Janeiro, J., Lukosch, S.G., Brazier, F.M.T.: Elastic Collaboration Support: from Workflow-based to Emergent Collaboration. In: 17th ACM International Conference on Supporting Group Work, pp. 317–320 (2012)

19. Reiter, M., Houy, C., Fettke, P., Loos, P.: Context-Sensitive Collaboration in Service Processes through the Integration of Telecommunication Technology and Business Process Management. In: 46th Hawaii International Conference on System Sciences, Hawaii, pp. 491–500 (2013)
20. Vieira, V., Tedesco, P., Salgado, A.C.: Towards an Ontology for Context Representation in Groupware. In: Fukś, H., Lukosch, S., Salgado, A.C. (eds.) CRIWG 2005. LNCS, vol. 3706, pp. 367–375. Springer, Heidelberg (2005)
21. Wang, G., Jiang, J., Shi, M.: A Context Model for Collaborative Environment. In: 10th International Conference on Computer Supported Cooperative Work in Design (2006)
22. FOAF Vocabulary Specification, http://www.foaf-project.org
23. Grueninger, M., Fox, M.S.: Methodology for the Design and Evaluation of Ontologies. In: Proceedings of the International Joint Conference on Artificial Intelligence, Workshop on Basic Ontological Issues in Knowledge Sharing (1995)
24. Pinto, H.S., Martins, J.P.: Ontologies: How Can They Be Built? Knowledge and Information Systems 6, 441–464 (2004)
25. zur Muehlen, M., Indulska, M.: Modeling Languages for Business Processes and Business Rules: A Representational Analysis. Information Systems 35(4), 379–390 (2010)
26. Oliveira, F.F., Antunes, J.C.P., Guizzardi, R.S.S.: Towards a Collaboration Ontology. In: 2nd Workshop on Ontologies and Metamodeling in Software and Data Engineering, pp. 97–108 (2007)
27. Pattberg, J., Fluegge, M.: Towards an Ontology of Collaboration Patterns. In: Proceedings of the International Workshop on Challenges in Collaborative Engineering (2007)
28. van der Aalst, W.M.P., ter Hofstede, A.H.M., Kiepuszewski, B., Barros, A.P.: Workflow Patterns. Distributed and Parallel Databases 14(1), 5–51 (2003)
29. Knoll, S.W., Janeiro, J., Lukosch, S.G., Kolfschoten, G.L.: A Semantic Model for Adaptive Collaboration Support Systems. In: Hussein, T., Paulheim, H., Lukosch, S.G., Ziegler, J., Calvary, G. (eds.) Semantic Models for Adaptive Interactive Systems, pp. 59–81. Springer, London (2013)
30. The Organization Ontology, http://www.w3.org/TR/vocab-org/
31. Goh, A., Koh, Y.K., Domazet, D.S.: ECA Rule-Based Support for Workflows. Artificial Intelligence in Engineering 15(1), 37–46 (2001)
32. Janeiro, J., Lukosch, S.G., Radomski, S., Johanson, M., Mecella, M.: Supporting Elastic Collaboration: Integration of Collaboration Components in Dynamic Contexts. In: ACM SIGCHI Symposium on Engineering Interactive Computing Systems, pp. 127–132 (2013)

Rationality in Context: An Analogical Perspective

Tarek R. Besold

Institute of Cognitive Science
University of Osnabrück
49069 Osnabrück, Germany

Abstract. At times, human behavior seems erratic and irrational. Therefore, when modeling human decision-making, it seems reasonable to take the remarkable abilities of humans into account with respect to rational behavior, but also their apparent deviations from the normative standards of rationality shining up in certain rationality tasks. Based on well-known challenges for human rationality, together with results from psychological studies on decision-making and from previous work in the field of computational modeling of analogy-making, I argue that the analysis and modeling of rational belief and behavior should also consider context-related cognitive mechanisms like analogy-making and coherence maximization of the background theory. Subsequently, I conceptually outline a high-level algorithmic approach for a Heuristic Driven Theory Projection-based system for simulating context-dependent human-style rational behavior. Finally, I show and elaborate on the close connections, but also on the significant differences, of this approach to notions of "ecological rationality".

1 Introduction

At times, human behavior seems erratic and irrational. Still, it is widely undoubted that humans can act rational and, in fact, appear to act rational most of the time. In explaining behavior, we use terms like beliefs and desires. If an agent's behavior makes sense to us, then we interpret it as a reasonable way to achieve the agent's goals given his beliefs. I take this as indication that some concept of rationality does play a crucial role when describing and explaining human behavior in a large variety of situations.

Based on ideas from vernacular psychology, in many cases rational beliefs are interpreted as a foundation of rational behavior. Therefore, in what follows, I will mostly be concerned with beliefs and knowledge, i.e. the epistemic aspects of rationality. Combining and further developing work separately presented in [1,2], I want to shed light on some aspects of situated rationality (i.e., rationality and rational behavior as it happens in given situations and contexts, as opposed to purely theoretical and abstract notions of rationality) from a mostly computational cognitive science point of view. Although, even in psychology or economics there is no generally accepted formal framework for rationality, I will argue for a model that links rationality to the ability of humans to establish analogical relations based on contextual and situational clues. This is an attempt for further developing a non-classical perspective and framework for rationality implementing principles of the "subject-centered rationality" meta-framework [3]. Furthermore, in the course of a mostly overview-like presentation, I want to give some hints

P. Brézillon, P. Blackburn, and R. Dapoigny (Eds.): CONTEXT 2013, LNAI 8175, pp. 129–142, 2013.

at how already existing frameworks for computational analogy-making integrate some aspects considered characteristic for human decision making, and how the proposed view connects to the better known high-level framework of "ecological rationality" [4].

2 Rationality Concepts and Challenges

2.1 Rationality

Many quite distinct frameworks for modeling rationality have been proposed, and an attempt at clustering these frameworks to the best of our knowledge results in at least four classes: logic-based models (cf. e.g. [5]), probability-based models (cf. e.g. [6]), heuristic-based models (cf. e.g. [7]), and game-theoretically based models (cf. e.g. [8]).

Several of these models have been considered for establishing a normative theory of rationality, not only trying to model "rational behavior", but also to offer predictive power for determining whether a certain belief, action, or behavior may be considered rational or not. Also, every of these theories specifies some sort of *definition* of rationality. Unfortunately, when comparing the distinct frameworks, it shows that these definitions are in many cases almost orthogonal to each other (as are the frameworks). Therefore, in this paper, I will propose certain cognitive mechanisms for explaining and specifying rationality in an integrated, more homogeneous way.

2.2 Well-Known Challenges

Although the aforementioned frameworks have gained merit in modeling certain aspects of human intelligence, the generality of each such class of frameworks has at the same time been challenged by psychological experiments. For example, as described in detail below, in the famous Wason-selection task [9] human subjects fail at a seemingly simple logical task (cf. Table 1). Also, experiments by Byrne on human reasoning with conditionals [10] indicated severe deviations from classical logic (cf. Table 1). Similarly, Tversky and Kahneman's Linda problem [11] illustrates a striking violation of the rules of probability theory (cf. Table 1). Heuristic approaches to judgment and reasoning [12] are often seen as approximations to a rational ideal and in some cases could work in practice, but often lack formal transparency and explanatory power. Game-based frameworks are questioned due to the lack of a unique concept of optimality in game-theory that can support different "rational behaviors" for one and the same situations (e.g. Pareto optimality vs. Nash equilibrium vs. Hick's optimality etc., [13]).

Wason Selection Task: This task shows that a large majority of subjects are seemingly unable to verify or to falsify a simple logical implication: "If on one side of the card there is a D, then on the other there is the number 3". In order to check this rule, subjects need to turn D and 7, i.e. subjects need to check the direct rule application and the contrapositive implication. After a slight modification of the content of the rule (content-change), while keeping the structure of the problem isomorphic, subjects perform significantly better: In [14], the authors show that a change of the abstract rule "$p \rightarrow q$" to a problem accommodated in a more natural and familiar context than the mere card checking setup significantly increases correct answers of subjects.

Table 1. The Wason-selection task questions whether humans reason in such situations according to the laws of classical logic. Byrne's experiments on how humans handle conditionals also shed doubt on a logic-based model. Tversky and Kahneman's Linda problem questions the ability of humans to reason according to the laws of probability theory.

Wason-Selection Task [15]:
Subjects are given the rule "Every card which has a D on one side has a 3 on the other side." and are told that each card has a letter on one side and a number on the other side. Then they are presented with four cards showing respectively D, K, 3, 7, and asked to turn the minimal number of cards to determine the truth of the sentence.

Inferences and Conditionals [10]:
1. If Marian has an essay to write, she will study late in the library. She does not have an essay to write.
2. If Marian has an essay to write, she will study late in the library. She has an essay to write.
3. If Marian has an essay to write, she will study late in the library. She has an essay to write. If the library stays open, she will study late in the library.

Linda-Problem [11]:
Linda is 31 years old, single, outspoken and very bright. She majored in philosophy. As a student, she was deeply concerned with issues of discrimination and social justice, and also participated in anti-nuclear demonstrations.
Linda is a teacher in elementary school.
Linda works in a bookstore and takes Yoga classes.
Linda is active in the feminist movement. (F)
Linda is a psychiatric social worker.
Linda is a member of the League of Women Voters.
Linda is a bank teller. (T)
Linda is an insurance salesperson.
Linda is a bank teller and is active in the feminist movement. (T&F)

The authors use the rule "If a person is drinking beer, then he must be over 20 years old." The cards used in the task were "drinking beer", "drinking coke", "25 years old", and "16 years old". Solving this task according to the rules of classical logic comes down to turning "drinking beer" and "16 years old".

Inferences and Conditionals: Also Byrne's observations question whether human reasoning can be covered by a classical logic-based framework. Presented with the information given in Table 1, from 1. 46% of subjects conclude that Marian will not study late in the library, erring with respect to classical logic (as denial of the antecedent does not validate a negation of the consequent). Also, from 2. 96% of subjects conclude that Marian will study late in the library, whilst only 38% of subjects reach the same conclusion from 3. Thus an introduction of another antecedent (without any indication that the antecedent should not hold) dramatically reduced the number of subjects applying a simple modus ponens in their process of forming a conclusion.

Linda Problem: With respect to the Linda problem it seems to be the case that subjects are amenable to the so-called conjunction fallacy: subjects are told a story specifying a particular profile about the bank teller Linda. Then, eight statements about Linda are shown and subjects are asked to order them according to their probability (cf. Table 1).

85% of subjects decide to rank the eighth statements "Linda is a bank teller and active in the feminist movement" (T & F) as more probable than the sixth statement "Linda is a bank teller" (T). This ranking contradicts basic laws of probability theory, as the joint probability of two events (T & F) is less or at most equal to the probability of each individual event.

Classical Resolution Strategies: Strategies that have been proposed to address the mentioned challenges include non-classical logics for modeling subjects' behavior in the Wason-Selection task [16], or a switch from (syntactic) deductions to reasoning in semantic models [17]. Still, these are only individual case-based solutions, which do not (or only hardly) generalize, and thus do not provide a basis for a unified theory or the genesis of a generally accepted broad concept of rationality.

3   Non-standard Interpretations of Challenges for Rationality

An immediate reaction to the challenges for rationality depicted above may be to deny that humans are always able to correctly reason according to the laws of classical logic or the laws of probability theory. Still, concluding that human behavior therefore is irrational in general does not seem convincing. The most that can be concluded from the experiments is that human agents are neither deduction machines nor probability estimators, but perform their indisputable reasoning capabilities with other means. From our point of view, subjects' behavior in the described tasks is connected to certain situation-sensitive cognitive mechanisms that are used by humans in such reasoning tasks, giving rise to the emergence of behavior commonly described as rational.

3.1   Interlude: Analogy and Analogical Reasoning

Analogy-making refers to the human ability of perceiving dissimilar domains as similar with respect to certain aspects based on shared commonalities in relational structure or appearance. Analogy and analogy-making research has received growing attention during the last decades, changing the perception of analogy from interpreting it as a special and rarely applied case of reasoning to placing it in the center of human cognition itself [18]. The literature on analogies knows a distinction between two subcategories of analogical mapping: attribute mappings (surface mappings) and relational mappings [19]. Whilst both mapping types are standardly assumed to be one-to-one, attribute mappings are based on attributes or surface properties, such as shape or color (i.e., two objects can be said to be similar with respect to a particular attribute or set of attributes), whilst relational mappings are based on relations between objects, such as having the same role or the same effect (i.e., two objects can then be said to be similar with respect to some relation to one or more other objects). Once such an analogical bridge has been established between two domains, analogical reasoning now allows for carrying over inferences from the base to the target domain in order to extend knowledge about the latter, i.e., an inference which holds between elements in the base domain is also assumed to analogically hold between the corresponding elements of the target domain. Formalizing different situations and accompanying contexts in a natural way as distinct domains, analogical reasoning thus offers a by now well-developed framework for modeling cross-situational and cross-contextual reasoning processes.

3.2   How Analogy-Making Enters the Rational Picture

In a short reply to Colman's article *"Cooperation, psychological game theory, and limitations of rationality in social interaction"* [20], Kokinov challenges traditional views on rationality [21]. Taking an initial stance similar to Colman's, agreeing on that rationality fails as both, descriptive theory of human-decision making and normative theory for good decision-making, Kokinov reaches a different, more radical conclusion than Colman did before. Instead of trying to fix the concept of rationality by redefining it, adding formerly unconsidered criteria for optimization of some kind, he proposes to replace the concept of rationality as a theory in its own right by a multilevel theory based on cognitive processes involved in decision-making. Where Colman proposes a collection of ad-hoc strategies for explaining the deviations from rationality which people exhibit in their behavior, Kokinov proposes analogy as means of unifying the different, formerly unconnected parts of Colman's attempt at describing the mechanisms of decision-making. In Kokinov's view, the classical concept of utility making has to be rendered as an emergent property, which will emerge in most, but not all, cases, converting rationality itself in an emergent phenomenon, assigning rational rules the status of approximate explanations of human behavior.

Also psychological studies on decision-making and choice processes provide evidence for a crucial role of analogy. An overview by Markman and Moreau [22], based on experiments and observations from psychological studies, amongst others on consumer behavior and political decision-making, reaches the conclusion that there are at least two central ways how analogy-making influences choice processes. Analogies to other domains can provide means of representation for a choice situation, as generally speaking the making of a decision relies on a certain degree of familiarity with the choice setting. In many cases of this kind, analogy plays a crucial role in structuring the representation of the choice situation, and thus may strongly influence the outcome of a decision. Also, structural alignment (a key process of analogy-making) plays a role when comparing the different possible options offered by a decision situation, with new options being learned by comparison to already known ones. An experimental study by Kokinov [23] demonstrated that people use analogies in the process of decision-making, with significant benefit already if only one case is found to be analogous to the choice situation under consideration. Furthermore, evidence has been found that there is no significant difference between close and remote analogies in this process, and that people are not limited to relying only on analogous cases from their own experience, but that also cases which were only witnessed passively (e.g., by being a bystander, or learning about a situation from reports in the media) may have beneficial influence.

Taking all this together, I strongly argue in favor of taking into account cognitive mechanisms centered around the concept of analogy and their situation- and context-dependent nature when analyzing and modeling rational belief and behavior in humans. In the following, I want to provide an analogy-inspired point of view on the aforementioned well-known challenges for rationality.

3.3   The Wason-Selection Task and Cognitive Mechanisms

As mentioned above, according to [14] subjects perform better (in the sense of more according to the laws of classical logic) in the Wason-Selection task, if content-change to a more natural situational framing makes the task easier to access for subjects. In our reading, subjects' performance is tightly connected to establishing appropriate analogies. Subjects perform badly in the classical version of the Wason-Selection task, simply because they fail to establish a fitting analogy with an already known situation. In the "beer drinking" version mentioned above, i.e. the re-contextualized version of the task, the situation changes substantially, because subjects can do what they would do in an everyday analogous situation: they need to check whether someone younger than 20 years is drinking beer in a bar. This is to check the age of someone who is drinking beer and conversely to check someone who is younger that 20 years whether he is drinking beer or not. In short, the success or failure of managing the task is crucially dependent on the possibility to establish a meaningful analogy, which in turn intrinsically is tightly linked to the provided situational and contextual clues.

3.4   The Inferences and Conditionals Problem and Cognitive Mechanisms

The results concerning conclusions drawn by the subjects in Byrne's experiments can also be explained through analogy-making and context dependence. People faced with the information given in 1. will recall similar conversations they had before, using these known situations as basis for their decision on what to conclude. According to Grice [24], in conversations speakers are supposed to provide the hearer with as much information as is needed for exchanging the necessary information, a rule which goes in accordance with our everyday observation. Thus, when being given the additional information that "Marian does not have to write an essay.", the set of candidate situations for establishing an analogy is re-oriented towards situations in which this information had an impact on the outcome, resulting in the conclusion that Marian would not study late in the library either. Regarding 2. and 3., a similar conjecture seems likely to hold: By additionally mentioning the library, similar situations in which the library might actually have played a crucial role (e.g., by being closed) will be taken into account as possible base domains of the analogy, causing the change in conclusions made.

3.5   The Linda Problem and Cognitive Mechanisms

For Tversky and Kahneman's Linda problem, a natural explanation of subjects' behavior is that people find a lower degree of coherence between Linda's profile (i.e., the context) and the statement "Linda is a bank teller", than they do with the expanded "Linda is a bank teller and is active in the feminist movement". In the latter case, at least one conjunct of the statement fits quite well to Linda's profile. In short, subjects prefer situations that seem to have a stronger inner coherence. Coherence is important for the successful establishment of an analogical relation, as it facilitates the finding of a source domain for an analogy. I conjecture that in order to make sense of the task, humans rate statements with a higher probability where facts are arranged in a contextual theory with a higher degree of coherence. Now, seeing coherence as a means for facilitating situated analogy-making, and taking into account that analogy has been identified as a core element of human cognition, the decision for the coherence-maximizing option is not surprising anymore, but fits neatly into the contextualized analogy-based framework, and can, thus, also be predicted (providing inductive support for our general claim).[1]

4 Rationality, Decision-Making and Analogy-Making Systems

In the following I want to give an overview-like sketch of how computational analogy-making systems can be related to some of the discussed challenges for rationality, as well as to context-sensitive decision-making and choice in general, demonstrating their value as models also in this domain. This prepares the ground for the presentation of a high-level algorithmic approach to simulating context-dependent human-style rational behavior (based on the Heuristic-Driven Theory Projection framework for computational analogy-making) in the following section.

4.1 Heuristic-Driven Theory Projection

Heuristic-Driven Theory Projection (HDTP) is a symbolic framework for computing analogical relations between two domains (formalizing different situations or contexts) that are axiomatized in a many-sorted first order logic language [25]. HDTP, after being given the logic representations of the two domains, by means of anti-unification [26] computes a common generalization of both, and uses this resulting theory as basis for establishing an analogy, also involving analogical transfer of knowledge between the domains (i.e., the system provides an explicit generalization of the two domains as a by-product of the analogy-making process). Thus, conceptually, HDTP proceeds in two phases: in the *mapping phase*, the formal representations of source and target domain are compared to find structural commonalities, and a generalized description is created, which subsumes the matching parts of both domains. In the *transfer phase*, unmatched knowledge in the source domain can be transferred to the target domain to establish new hypotheses in an analogical way (cf. Fig. 1).

As an example for cross-contextual reasoning in HDTP think about the Rutherford-Bohr planetary model of the atom in analogy to a model of the solar system: HDTP, after finding commonalities in the logical representation of the solar system as base domain, and the atom model as target domain (for example, that in both cases less massive objects are somehow related to a more massive central object, or that always a positive distance and a positive force between these lighter objects and the heavier core can be found), a generalization is computed, via which known laws from the base can be re-instantiated in the target (e.g., that a lighter object revolves around a heavier

---

[1] Tversky and Kahneman [11] proposed the representativeness heuristic for explaining their findings, hypothesizing for the probability of an event to be evaluated by the degree to which the event is representative of a corresponding mental model. Although this notion superficially seems almost identical to a coherence-based account certain distinctions have to be noted, most prominently a difference in basic perspective: Whilst representativeness takes into account, e.g., notions of typicality, similarity in essential characteristics, but also puts significant emphasis on different degrees of salience between elements, coherence targets a maximization of achieved homogeneity and seamless integration (at first leaving levels of salience and similar aspects out of consideration).

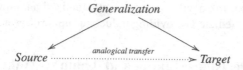

Fig. 1. HDTP's overall approach to creating analogies

one when there is negative centrifugal force between the lighter and the heavier one, yielding the revolution of the electrons around the nucleus, or that the centrifugal force between two spatially separated objects with positive gravitational force between both is equal to the negative value of that gravity, resulting in stable orbits of the electrons in the model).

HDTP implements a principle (by using heuristics) that maximizes the coverage of the involved domains [25]. Intuitively, this means that the sub-theory of the source (or the target) that can be generated by re-instantiating the generalization is maximized. Putting it the other way round, the original domain-specific information and structure shall implicitly be preserved as far as possible. The higher the coverage the better, because more support for the analogy is provided by the generalization (in a way, the higher the achieved degree of coverage, the more firmly the analogy is rooted in the underlying domains, used for creating the generalization). A further heuristic in HDTP is the minimization of substitution lengths in the analogical relation, i.e. the simpler the analogy the better [27]. The motivation for this heuristic is to prevent arbitrary associations. Clearly there is a trade-off between high coverage and simplicity of substitutions: An appropriate analogy should intuitively be as simple as possible, but also as general and broad as necessary in order to be non-trivial. Unfortunately, high coverage normally comes with higher complexity of substitutions (as a more complex generalization allows for a higher degree of re-representation of domain-specific structures and information), whilst the simplicity constraint is trying to steer the analogy-making process in exactly the opposite direction. This kind of trade-off is similar to the kind of trade-off that is usually the topic of model selection in machine learning and statistics.

4.2   The Wason-Selection Task Revisited

A modeling of the Wason-Selection task with HDTP is quite simple as long as appropriate background knowledge is available, in case an analogy should be established, or the lack of appropriate background knowledge prevents analogy-making, in case no analogy should be established: On the one hand, if background knowledge for an analogous case is missing (i.e., in the case of HDTP, no domain representation which offers sufficient commonalities to the target domain as to serve as a base for the analogy process can be retrieved from memory), then there is no chance to establish an analogical relation. Hence, subjects have to apply other auxiliary strategies, possibly deviating from the expected "right" answer. If there is a source theory with sufficient structural commonalities on the other hand, then the establishment of an analogical relation is straightforward, resulting in a smooth solution process of the task.

4.3   Analogy in Choice

Coming back to Markman and Moreau's meta-study of the role analogy and analogical comparison play in the process of human choice, presented in [22], I want to show some connections of their findings to computational systems for analogy-making.

It is without doubt that the choice of options taken into account when making a decision is of crucial importance for the entire process of decision-making. Markman and Moreau present the formation of consideration sets (i.e., the set of options taken into account by a decision maker) as one of the places at which the influence of analogy on decision-making clearly shines up. An analogical reasoning process is involved when deciding on which scenarios are likely to happen, and thus have to be considered (also see [28] for related results). According to their findings, there are different factors influencing which analogies will be used in a choice situation, resulting in a set of analogies which are considered similar or familiar to the current situation. Close analogs have the advantage of probably allowing the transfer of more lower-order relations than distant analogs would, i.e., closer concepts are more likely to be considered as an option due to an easier and more fruitful analogy-making process. This goes in accordance with characteristics exhibited by many computational models of analogy-making, where again I want to use HDTP as prototypical example: As pointed out in [25], although HDTP basically aligns any entity, function or predicate, it clearly prefers literally-matching alignments over non-literally ones, and equivalent structures to structural mismatches, thus reconstructing a preference and behavior also shown by humans.

Also, experiments indicate that commonly shared surface elements of domains are more useful as retrieval cues than are connected relational systems. Also this carries over to the principles underlying HDTP, with the system trying to minimize the complexity of analogical relations whilst maximizing the degree of coverage: Connected relational systems have the strong tendency of reaching higher-order stages, whilst direct surface correspondences stay on a low level, allowing for a direct matching of features. Thus, handling common surface elements allows for a certain degree of coverage without having to escalate complexity, probably also making HDTP prefer surface elements for supporting an analogy over relational ones (if both types are equally available).

Finally, it shows that elements related to a person's individual history of experiences influence the way decisions are taken. These elements have the advantage of being (mostly) highly accessible, with base domains which form part of someone's past being more likely to have richly connected relational structures, providing good ground for eventual analogical inference. When searching for a way of computationally modeling this phenomenon, it comes to mind that a similar effect can already be found in AMBR, Kokinov's hybrid analogy-making system [29]. This system exhibits signs of priming effects in the retrieval process of a fitting base domain for an analogy's given target domain, together with a general influence of earlier memory states on later ones.

5   Cornerstones of an Architecture for Human-Style Rationality

In this section, I outline how solving a rationality puzzle can mechanistically be modeled in terms of HDTP, by this also pointing towards principles for a HDTP-based architecture for a cognitive rationality system. The described model naturally connects to previous foundational work in the field of decision theory and economics. Almost two decades ago, [30] developed an (at least partly) case-based theory and model for decision-making under uncertainty. In their model, cases are primitive and provide a simple axiomatization of a decision rule that selects an act to be performed based on the act's past performance in similar cases. Each act is evaluated by the sum of the utility levels that resulted from using this act in past cases, where the degree of (dis)similarity between the past cases and the problem at hand is accounted for by weighting the respective utility by the value of a similarity measure between both situations. Remarkably, this formal approach in a natural way gives rise to (amongst others) the notions of satisficing decisions and aspiration levels (cf. [31] for a detailed account).

The subsequently proposed general architecture, on a very abstract level, can functionally be subdivided into four steps (adding a framing pre- and post-processing step to the original HDTP setting described above): Given a problem description and domain, select and retrieve analogical situations (and embedding contexts) from memory (*retrieval*). Use the problem as target domain for an analogy, the retrieved situation as source domain, and establish an analogy between both (*mapping*). Transfer solution-relevant knowledge from the source domain to the target domain via the analogical mapping (*transfer*). Apply the newly obtained knowledge in the target domain (i.e. the problem domain) for solving the problem (*application*).

As already stated before, in HDTP, source and target domains for analogy-making are represented as theories in a many-sorted first-order logical language. In the following, I additionally assume that the system has access to a library of previously formalized situations and scenes (i.e., domains that had already initially been pre-compiled, or that have been learned and acquired during runtime up to the present moment in time), corresponding to a human's (episodic) memory of previously seen and experienced happenings and events (here, constraints on human memory could e.g. be modeled by limiting the number of domains available to the system).

Given the (rationality) problem at hand as target domain for the analogy, the *retrieval* problem within HDTP comes down to selecting a fitting domain from memory as source domain. This can be done in different ways, for example by means of a separate module (similar to the MAC stage in the MAC/FAC analogy model [32]), or by forcing HDTP to construct analogies between all possible pairings of the target domain with a candidate source domain, subsequently taking the heuristic value HDTP computed when constructing the analogy as a measure for analogical distance between domains and proceeding e.g. with the analogically closest domain as source domain for the analogy. By now additionally assuming that candidate source domains had been labeled with overall satisfaction levels, a mechanism similar in output to the utility-based approach of [30] arises: Weighted by the respective analogical distance, the satisfaction level can serve as parameter for the domain selection. Also, the outcome of the retrieval process of course does not have to be unique, and always strongly depends on the heuristics or distance measures used, thereby introducing a degree of uncertainty into the system (matching the uncertainty and irregularities in human rational behavior).

Once a source and target domain have been identified, HDTP constructs an analogical relation between both, *mapping* between elements from source and target domain. The construction of this mapping is based on the previously outlined generalization mechanism, guided by a heuristic which tries to keep the analogy as simple (i.e. less general) as possible, whilst still maximizing the sub-theories of the sources which can be re-instantiated from the generalization (a trade off close in spirit to the precision/recall problem in pattern recognition and information retrieval). Also here, in most cases the mappings between elements of the respective domains do not have to be unique (e.g. different elements of the source could be mapped to one certain element of the target domain), again introducing a source of uncertainty.

In the transfer phase, knowledge from the (with respect to problem solutions richer) source domain is transferred to the target domain (i.e. the problem at hand). Making use of the mappings established in the previous step, the concepts from the source domain are re-instantiated from the generalized theory into the target domain, enriching the latter and giving additional information needed for computing a solution to the problem.

In the last step, the newly added knowledge is *applied* in the target domain (e.g. used for reasoning and inference), in most cases yielding a solution to the problem (sometimes, although additional knowledge has been provided via the analogical process, the problem solving process still will fail, a phenomenon reminiscent of human failure in seemingly familiar, in the past already mastered problem situations). This step also includes a consolidation process, integrating the transferred knowledge into the target domain, giving an expanded or richer domain.

Of course, this type of architecture leaves ample space for uncertainty and deviating behavior: Apart of the already mentioned systemic influences, a certain chance of deviation from HDTP's predicted outcome for a certain problem situation is automatically introduced by the use of logical theories as descriptive framework for contexts, situations and problems. As with every symbolic formalization, decisive information might accidentally be left out of considerations when formulating the domain descriptions. Nonetheless, I do not see this as a major drawback, but rather as a natural constraint every system trying to predict a phenomenon as complex as human rational behavior has to face, and which even holds in the case where humans try to predict each other.

6   On the Relation of Analogical and Ecological Rationality

Over the last years, "ecological rationality" [4] has become one of the most prominent new, non-classical notions of rationality. Within this framework, human reasoning and behavior are considered rational if they are adapted to the environment in which humans act: One cannot understand human cognition by studying either the environment or cognition alone, and peoples reasoning has to be seen as the result of an adaptation of the individual to his or her environment.

This approach at first glance seems almost identical to the contextualized analogy approach presented in this paper. But, although there indeed are close conceptual ties and many underlying intuitions and first assumptions are shared, there still are significant differences. The insight that in order to understand cognition one also needs to explore the characteristics of the environment upon which cognition is based and within which it is happening is common to both views, but the conclusions drawn from this observation differ in their focus: Ecological rationality on the one hand mostly emphasizes the impact the environment has on the reasoner and the reasoning process in that, e.g., reasoning mechanisms have to be adaptive to the environment and that the environment imposes certain ways of reasoning on the reasoner via resource constraints and efficiency optimization. The contextualized analogy approach on the other hand is based on a certain type of mechanism which is assumed to play a crucial role in the reasoner's cognitive setup in the first place, independent of the particular environment. Clearly, at the moment of reasoning the situation and the context the reasoner currently is situated in play an important and fundamental role in providing additional clues and, thus, allowing for efficient and resource adequate reasoning. Nonetheless, the perspective stays subject-centered in that the reasoner and his or her cognitive capacities are the determining elements (placing it under the conceptual umbrella of "subject-centered rationality" [3]). Under the advocated paradigm, given an environment, it is not said that the reasoner would always (almost automatically) prefer a theoretically more efficient reasoning mechanism (as it would be the case under the ecological rationality assumption). Instead, properties and preferences specific to the situationally and contextutally situated subject have to be taken into account — where a strong bias towards analogy as core cognitive capacity is assumed.

7   Concluding Remarks

The evidence for a crucial role of analogy-making and context-sensitive forms of reasoning presented over the last pages falls far from being complete. Yet another example can be given in form of well-known studies on human decision-making under time pressure, which show a change in the applied inference procedure. In [33], the authors report that, whilst the best predicting model of human inference for decision making in an unstressed conditions was a weighted linear model integrating all available information, when time pressure was induced, best predictions were obtained by using a simple lexicographic heuristic [34]. This presumed change from a more complex strategy using complex relational structures to a simple single-attribute-based procedure also can be found in research on analogy-making: In [35], it is reported that anxiety made participants of an analogical-reasoning experiment switch from a preference for complex relational mappings to simple attribute-based mappings. Still, whilst not claiming completeness of the given overview of evidence, I am convinced that the examples and indications are sufficient as not to allow for leaving analogy and cognitive processes out of consideration.

A criticism with respect to the analogy-making approach might be a seeming lack of normativity as a theory. Although work on this topic is still in a very early stage, I am confident that this objection is partially conceptually mistaken and partially grasps at nothing: First of all it has to be noticed that the presented ideas clearly aim at a positive theory and predictive notion of situated rationality rather than at an a priori normative conception (also see [3] for further details). Secondly, normativity can a posteriori be introduced in several different ways on distinct levels, for instance in a subject-independent fashion by considering the reasonableness (or unreasonableness) of made analogies. Roughly speaking, it is obvious that different analogies may have different degrees of reasonableness, e.g., based on the level to which they result in coherent beliefs and to which they encompass both, the source and the target domain of the analogy (again see [3] for a sketch of an alternate, subject-centered proposal).

In this paper, I argued in favor of the concept of analogy and for a strengthened awareness for the importance of situation dependence and context effects in conceptual research on rationality and decision-making on a foundational level. Based on a review of some basic concepts and existing work within the fields of analogy research and research on decision-making and choice, together with an exemplifying proposal of new resolution strategies for classical rationality puzzles and a high-level conceptual sketch of an algorithmic approach for an analogy-based computational model, I advocated that the usage of frameworks for establishing analogical relations and the usage of frameworks that can maximize the situational and contextual coherence of a theory necessarily have to be taken into account when modeling (and possibly implementing) what is commonly considered rational belief in a not overly simplified manner.

Acknowledgements. I owe a debt of gratitude to the (present and former) members of the AI Research Group at the *Institute of Cognitive Science of the University of Osnabrück*, namely K.-U. Kühnberger, M. Martinez (now: *Universidad de los Andes, Bogotá*), M. Schmidt, H. Gust, A. Abdel Fattah, and U. Krumnack for valuable feedback, ideas and suggestions they provided me with in numerous conversations and discussions we had concerning this line of work.

References

1. Besold, T.R., Gust, H., Krumnack, U., Abdel-Fattah, A., Schmidt, M., Kühnberger, K.U.: An Argument for an Analogical Perspective on Rationality & Decision-Making. In: Proc. of the Workshop on Reasoning About Other Minds (RAOM 2011). CEUR Workshop Proceedings, vol. 751, pp. 20–31, CEUR-WS.org (2011)
2. Besold, T.R., Schmidt, M., Gust, H., Krumnack, U., Abdel-Fattah, A., Kühnberger, K.U.: Rationality Through Analogy: On HDTP and Human-Style Rationality. In: Proc. of SAMAI: Similarity and Analogy-based Methods in AI, Workshop at ECAI 2012 (2012)
3. Besold, T.R., Kühnberger, K.U.: E Pluribus Multa In Unum: The Rationality Multiverse. In: Proc. of the 34th Annual Conference of the Cognitive Science Society. Cognitive Science Society, Austin (2012)
4. Rieskamp, J., Reimer, T.: Ecological rationality. In: Baumeister, R., Vohs, K. (eds.) Encyclopedia of Social Psychology, pp. 273–275. Sage (2007)
5. Evans, J.: Logic and human reasoning: An assessment of the deduction paradigm. Psychological Bulletin 128, 978–996 (2002)
6. Griffiths, T., Kemp, C., Tenenbaum, J.: Bayesian models of cognition. In: Sun, R. (ed.) The Cambridge Handbook of Computational Cognitive Modeling. Cambridge University Press (2008)
7. Gigerenzer, G., Hertwig, R., Pachur, T. (eds.): Heuristics: The Foundation of Adaptive Behavior. Oxford University Press (2011)
8. Osborne, M., Rubinstein, A.: A Course in Game Theory. MIT Press (1994)
9. Wason, P.C.: New Horizons in psychology. Penguin (1966)
10. Byrne, R.: Suppressing valid inferences with conditionals. Cognition 31(1), 61–83 (1989)
11. Tversky, A., Kahneman, D.: Extensional versus intuitive reasoning: The conjunction fallacy in probability judgement. Psychological Review 90(4), 293–315 (1983)
12. Gigerenzer, G.: Rationality for Mortals: How People Cope with Uncertainty. Oxford University Press (2008)

13. Chinchuluun, A., Pardalos, P., Migdalas, A., Pitsoulis, L. (eds.): Pareto Optimality, Game Theory and Equilibria. Springer (2008)
14. Cosmides, L., Tooby, J.: Cognitive Adaptions for Social Exchange. Oxford University Press (1992)
15. Wason, P.C., Shapiro, D.: Natural and contrived experience in a reasoning problem. The Quarterly Journal of Experimental Psychology 23(1), 63–71 (1971)
16. Stenning, K., van Lambalgen, M.: Human Reasoning and Cognitive Science. MIT Press (2008)
17. Johnson-Laird, P.: Mental Models. Harvard University Press (1983)
18. Holyoak, K., Gentner, D., Kokinov, B.: Introduction: The place of analogy in cognition. In: Gentner, D., Holyoak, K., Kokinov, B. (eds.) The Analogical Mind: Perspectives from Cognitive Science, pp. 1–19. MIT Press (2001)
19. Gentner, D.: Structure mapping: A theoretical framework for analogy. Cognitive Science 7, 155–170 (1983)
20. Colman, A.M.: Cooperation, psychological game theory, and limitations of rationality in social interaction. Behavioral and Brain Sciences 26(2), 139–198 (2003)
21. Kokinov, B.: Analogy in decision-making, social interaction, and emergent rationality. Behavioral and Braind Sciences 26(2), 167–169 (2003)
22. Markman, A., Moreau, C.: Analogy and analogical comparison in choice. In: Gentner, D., Holyoak, K., Kokinov, B. (eds.) The Analogical Mind: Perspectives from Cognitive Science, pp. 363–399. MIT Press (2001)
23. Kokinov, B.: Can a Single Episode or a Single Story Change our Willingness to Risk? The Role of Analogies in Decision-Making. In: Kokinov, B. (ed.) Advances in Cognitive Economics. NBU Press (2005)
24. Grice, H.P.: Logic and conversations. In: Cole, P., Morgan, J.L. (eds.) Syntax and Semantics. Speech Acts, vol. 3, pp. 41–58. Academic Press (1975)
25. Schwering, A., Krumnack, U., Kühnberger, K., Gust, H.: Syntactic principles of heuristic-driven theory projection. Cognitive Systems Research 10(3), 251–269 (2009)
26. Plotkin, G.D.: A note on inductive generalization. Machine Intelligence 5, 153–163 (1970)
27. Gust, H., Kühnberger, K., Schmid, U.: Metaphors and heuristic-driven theory projection (hdtp). Theoretical Computer Science 354, 98–117 (2006)
28. Schwenk, C.: Cognitive simplification processes in strategic decision-making. Strategic Management Journal 5(2), 111–128 (1984)
29. Kokinov, B., Petrov, A.: Integrating memory and reasoning in analogy-making: The AMBR model. In: Gentner, D., Holyoak, K., Kokinov, B. (eds.) The Analogical Mind: Perspectives from Cognitive Science, pp. 59–124. MIT Press (2001)
30. Gilboa, I., Schmeidler, D.: Case-Based Decision Theory. The Quarterly Journal of Economics 110, 605–639 (1995)
31. Gilboa, I., Schmeidler, D.: A Theory of Case-Based Decisions. Cambridge University Press (2001)
32. Forbus, K., Gentner, D., Law, K.: MAC/FAC: A model of Similarity-based Retrieval. Cognitive Science 19(2), 141–205 (1995)
33. Rieskamp, J., Hoffrage, U.: Inferences under time pressure: How opportunity costs affect strategy selection. Acta Psychologica 127, 258–276 (2008)
34. Fishburn, P.: Lexicographics orders, utilities and decision rules: A survey. Management Science 20, 1442–1471 (1974)
35. Tohill, J., Holyoak, K.: The impact of anxiety on analogical reasoning. Thinking & Reasoning 6(1), 27–40 (2000)

Context Meets Culture

Anneli Heimbürger

University of Jyväskylä, Finland
Department of Mathematical Information Technology
anneli.a.heimburger@jyu.fi

Abstract. Culture is embodied in how people interact with other individuals and with their environment. It is a way of life formed under specific historical, natural and social conditions. Cross-cultural communication consists of human-to-human, human-to-machine, and human-to-environment communication in cross-cultural environments. The environment can be physical, virtual or hybrid. In our research, context is defined as a situation a user has at hand. *Cross-cultural communication environment – user – situation* is the key triplet in our context research. We introduce a context model for cross-cultural communication environments, and we give two examples of how we have applied it to the design of cross-cultural environments. Our case cultures are those of Japan and Finland.

Keywords: Cross-cultural communication environment, context, cultural models, user Japan, Finland.

1 Introduction

Globalization is one of the main trends in our world. Increasingly, eastern and western cultures meet each other through business, governmental and environmental issues, research, education and tourism. Professionals, including business executives, project managers and project team members, are finding themselves in uncertain situations due to culturally dependent differences in the communication protocol, language and value systems. Cross-cultural communication is a current topic in many multicultural organizations and companies. In cross-cultural world, many collaborative activities take place in virtual and physical environments: teleconferences and workshops, web meetings, virtual spaces, face-to-face meetings and email, among others. Some of the differences between Eastern and Western cultures that we may come across are related to various meeting protocols, formality and rituals, orientation to time, communication style and decision-making process [1-2].

Cultural competence has become an important dimension for success in today's international business and research. Cultural computing is an emerging, multidisciplinary computer science field, as discussed by Fei-Yue Wang in his Letter from the Editor in IEEE Intelligent Systems Special Issue for AI and Cultural Heritage [3]. In the near future, cultural computing will have several important applications in our

P. Brézillon, P. Blackburn, and R. Dapoigny (Eds.): CONTEXT 2013, LNAI 8175, pp. 143–156, 2013.

knowledge societies in the fields of business, environment, health care, education and research, for example.

What is culture? Culture is embodied in how people interact with other individuals and with their environment; it is a way of life formed under specific historical, natural and social conditions [3]. Culture can be considered as one example of context and cultural computing as a subset of context computing. A computational method, a computer system, or an application is context-sensitive if it includes context-based functions and if it uses context to provide relevant information and services to the user, their relevancy depending on the user's situation. The essential concepts used in our paper are summarized in Table 1.

Context-sensitive applications have to adapt not only to the device, the connection state and the user environment but also to the user's circumstances. These parameters partially characterize a contextual situation. For example, a project manager can monitor a project's forthcoming milestones by means of a project management system and also use the same system to prepare for the next day's advisory board meeting. In the first case the contextual situation is a long-term project monitoring undertaking with more general content, whereas in the second case the contextual situation is a short-term project monitoring task with detailed content.

Table 1. The essential concepts used in our paper

Concept	Definition
Culture	Culture is embodied in how people interact with other individuals and with their environment; it is a way of life formed under specific historical, natural and social conditions [3]. Other cultural levels also exist, such as organization and team cultures.
Cross-cultural	Considers studies and knowledge between two cultures [4].
Cross-cultural communication	Consists of human-to-human, human-to-machine and human-to-environment communication in cross-cultural environments. The environment can be physical, virtual or hybrid. [5]
Cultural computing	Research, development, design and implementation of computational models, methods, functions and algorithms for cultural applications [5].
Context	Situation and/or task at hand. Cross-cultural situation can be considered as one example of context. [6-7]
Context-sensitive	A computational method, a computer system, or an application is context-sensitive if it includes context-based functions and if it uses context to provide relevant information and services to the user, their relevancy depending on the user's situation [6].
Context computing	Context computing can be defined as the use of context in software applications, where the applications adapt to discovered contexts by changing their behavior. A context-sensitive application presents the following features: context sensing, presentation of information and services to a user, automatic execution of a service, and tagging of context to information for later retrieval. [5]

A variety of context models have been subject of research. Many of them model only the physical environment, i.e. location, identity, and time [8-9]. The focus of our context modeling is on users' situations at hand in cross-cultural communication environments. We introduce a context model for cross-cultural communication environments, and we give two examples of how we have applied it to the design of cross-cultural environments. Our case cultures are those of Japan and Finland. Cultural competence might help us achieve project goals and avoid potential risks in multicultural or cross-cultural project environments. It would also support projects by promoting creativity and motivation through flexible leadership and "teamship".

The remainder of the paper is organized as follows. In Section 2, we discuss cultural models. In Section 3, we introduce our context model for cross-cultural communication environments. Section 4 describes two case studies on applying our model to design cross-cultural communication environments. Section 5 is reserved for conclusions and issues for further research.

2   Cultural Models

When we talk about the concept of culture, it is very important to understand its different levels. According to King [10], cultures can be considered at four levels: national cultures, organizational cultures, organizational subcultures and subunit cultures. Here we extend the King's categorization to team cultures. Related to national cultures, two of the most widely cited studies are Hofstede's framework for cultural dimensions [11-13] and Lewis' cultural model for communication [14]. Organizational culture is characterized by consistency across individuals and units in terms of assumptions, values and artefacts. These assumptions are formed over time, as the members of an organization make decisions, cope with problems and take advantage of opportunities. Values are a set of social norms. Artefacts, for example a knowledge repository system, are visible aspects of an organizational culture. Organizational subcultures may reflect organizational structure, professional occupations, task assignments, rank in a hierarchy or technologies used. Subunit cultures are created within the boundaries of particular subunits of an organization. Team cultures are mechanisms for individuals with diverse specialized knowledge to work towards a common goal. Teams are typically focused on a single objective, and they are temporary. If all team members are from the same organization, the team culture reflects the organizational culture. In multi-organizational projects, many team cultures may collide or softly meet, depending on the cultural competence of the team manager, team members and the ICT systems they are using.

Cultural knowledge, cultural awareness and cultural sensitivity all convey the idea of improving cross-cultural capacity. Cultural knowledge results from familiarization with selected cultural characteristics, history, values, belief systems, and behaviours of the members of another ethnic group. Cultural awareness means developing sensitivity and understanding towards another ethnic group. This usually requires internal changes in terms of attitudes and values. Awareness and sensitivity also refer to the qualities of openness and flexibility that people develop in relation to others. Cultural awareness must be supplemented with cultural knowledge. Cultural sensitivity means knowing that cultural differences as well as similarities exist, without assigning values, i.e., better or worse, right or wrong, to those cultural differences. Cultural competence has become one important dimension for the success in today's international business and research arena. It is defined as a set of congruent behaviours, attitudes, and policies that come together in a system and/or among professionals and enables the system and/or professionals to work effectively in cross-cultural situations.

Cross-cultural knowledge can be considered at three main levels:

1. Explicit knowledge, for example temporal facts (holidays, festivals, business hours, academic terms) and geographical facts (cities, climate, people, language, etc.)
2. Reported knowledge based on cultural models, survey data and/or field studies, for example related to meeting protocol, formality and rituals, orientation to time, communication style and decision-making process.
3. Tacit knowledge, for example knowledge specific to an organization, project or team. Tacit knowledge is often classified.

How do cultures relate to knowledge management? Culture shapes assumptions about which knowledge is important. Culture mediates the relationships between organizational and individual knowledge. Culture creates a context for social interaction. Culture also shapes processes for the creation and adoption of new knowledge.

We share our view of culture with that of Fei-Yue Wang [3]. However, several viewpoints on culture exist in literature, culture being a subject that has a long research history. Many challenges remain, however, and the ambiguity in the definition of culture is one of them. In 1952, Kroeber and Kluckhohn [15] found over 164 definitions, and Lonner [16] found over 200 definitions in 1994. Hoft [17] has categorized culture into four meta models: the onion, pyramid, iceberg, and objective and subjective models. These models help to categorize and understand theories and models of different kinds related to culture.

Two of the most referenced researchers who have researched national cultures and communication styles are Geert Hofstede [11-13] and Richard D. Lewis [14]. Hofstede has defined five cultural dimensions, and Lewis has defined three cultural types.

2.1   Cultural Dimensions

The definitions of Hofstede's cultural dimensions are based on the surveys conducted by the IBM (International Business Machines) company in almost 80 countries [11]. These cultural dimensions reflect relative cultural differences between nations, and they give us a macro level framework to study cultures:

- Power distance (PDI) is perceived in how people think about equality and relationships with superiors and subordinates. Individuals with a high power-distance index accept decisions and opinions of their supervisors more easily. Those with low power index believe that inequity should be minimized in the organization.
- Uncertainty avoidance (UAI) indicates the degree to which people feel either uncomfortable or comfortable in ambiguous situations. People with a high uncertainty avoidance index attempt to avoid uncertainty in all forms and situations.

- Masculinity (MAS) in this context means "toughness" needed in taking care of business versus softer values of taking care of people and being concerned with quality of life, which is defined as femininity.
- Individualism/Collectivism (IND) indicates how a person sees her/himself as an individual rather than a member of a group. In individualistic cultures, people are expected to have their own opinions, and they are concerned with personal achievements. In collectivistic cultures, people see themselves first as a part of a group.
- Long-term/short-term orientation (LTO/STO). This dimension indicates the difference between Western and East Asian cultures. A large difference can be seen between the western "here and now thinking" versus the eastern "future and long-term thinking".

Hofstede's approach proposes a set of cultural dimensions along which dominant value systems can be ordered. All the dimensions are generalizations, and individuals may differ from their society's descriptors. However, these dimensions provide interesting information because they show differences in answers between groups of respondents. Different value systems affect human thinking, feeling, and acting, the behaviour of teams and organizations and the temporal dimensions of research projects and negotiations. Hofstede's cultural dimensions for Finland and Japan are presented in Table 2 (scale 1-100) [13]. In Table 3, as an example, we have summarized implications of cross-cultural differences for meetings and negotiations, in accordance with Hofstede's dimensions of culture [1].

Table 2. Cultural dimensions for Finland and for Japan

Dimensions	Finland	Japan
PDI	33	54
UAI	59	92
MAS	26	95
IDV	63	46
LTO/STO	41	80

Table 3. Implications of cross-cultural differences for meetings and negotiations

Dimension	Implication
Individualism/ Collectivism	Negotiators from a collectivistic society are likely to spend more time on long-term goals, are more likely to make realistic offers, and are more likely to be cooperative. Conversely, negotiators from individualistic societies are more likely to focus on the short-term, make extreme offers, view negotiations from a fixed perspective and be competitive.
Power distance	Negotiators from low power-distance cultures may be frustrated by the need of negotiators from high power-distance cultures to seek approvals from higher authority. On the other hand, negotiators from high power-distance cultures may feel pressured by the pace imposed by negotiators from low power-distance cultures. *Table continues...*

Table 3. *(continued)*

Masculinity/ Femininity	When negotiating, individuals from masculine cultures are more likely to be competitive (win-lose) and those from feminine cultures more empathic and compromise-seeking (win-win). This means that negotiators from masculine cultures are likely to view the feminine negotiator as an "avoider", while the feminine negotiator is likely to view their masculine negotiator as a "contender."
Uncertainty avoidance	Negotiators from high risk-avoidance cultures are likely to view those from low risk-avoidance cultures as unfocused. Those from low risk-avoidance cultures are likely to view negotiators from high risk-avoidance cultures as rigid.
Long-term/short-term orientation	Long-term/short-term orientation refers to the extent to which a culture programs its members to accept delayed gratification of their material, social, and emotional needs. Business people in long-term oriented cultures are accustomed to working toward building strong positions in their markets and do not expect immediate results. In short-term oriented cultures the results of the past month, quarter, or year are a major concern. Time is seen in a different way by eastern and western cultures, and even within these groupings temporal culture differs from country to country. Also, temporal identities of different organizations and teams in organizations may vary.

2.2   Cultural Types

Richard D. Lewis has studied cultural characteristics of over 70 of the world's major countries and regions. He has described, e.g., what is typical in meetings with people from certain nations. He has also developed a cultural model in which different nations are classified in a simple way. However, it must be noted that the model is a simplification, and within one nation there may be several cultures. Lewis has divided the world's cultures into three types [14]:

- Linear-active cultures. These cultures plan, schedule, organize, pursue action chains, and do one thing at a time. For example, Germans and Swiss belong to this category.
- Multi-active cultures. Cultures of lively, loquacious people who do many things at once, planning their priorities not according to a time schedule, but in accordance with the relative thrill or importance that each appointment brings with it. For example, Italians, Latin Americans and Arabs belong to this category.
- Reactive cultures. These cultures prioritize courtesy high, and they respect listening quietly and calmly to their interlocutors and react carefully to the other side's proposals. For example, Chinese and Japanese are typical representatives of this category.

In the following, we discuss, from the viewpoint of the Lewis's culture types, management and leadership, motivating people, team building issues and meetings.

Management and leadership: Managers in linear-active cultures will generally demonstrate task orientation. They look for technical competence, place facts before sentiments and logic before emotion and are deal-oriented. They are orderly, stick to agendas and inspire staff with their careful planning. Multi-active managers are much more extroverted, rely on their eloquence and ability to persuade and use human force as an inspirational factor. They are also usually more oriented to networking. Leaders in reactive cultures are equally people-oriented but dominate with knowledge, patience and quiet control. They display modesty and courtesy, despite their accepted seniority. They are good at creating a harmonious atmosphere for teamwork.

Motivating people: A multicultural team manager should know that motivating people from different cultures is a challenging task because motivating factors can vary enormously even between close neighbours. Linear-active individuals are motivated by access to high-level technology, generous funding for research and increased opportunities for individual flair. They are also motivated by achievement rather than words. Multi-active people are motivated by words more than deeds. They get inspiration from people or circumstances that are conductive to boosting their self-confidence. Nurture and security are also important for this cultural category. Reactive people are motivated by collective goals and action, common loyalty to respectable organization and unswerving diligence in preserving integrity and face amongst family, friends and colleagues.

Team building issues: Agility is a very important issue in every software team nowadays, but all team members are not equally disposed towards change and innovation. For example, whilst Americans are the drivers of change, Arabs are more interested in the status quo and Russians fear change. Common sense, self-awareness and a modicum of unhurried thought are all useful resources for avoiding behaviour that might prove irritable to some team members. If it is accepted that certain cultural traits are not going to disappear, we may come to a realization that these very differing traits can make a positive contribution to team efforts. For example, American enthusiasm connected to German planning and supervision can be very effective. So manager in an international team should be skilled at choosing the right person for each environment and task.

Meetings: A successful meeting can be difficult to achieve in a multicultural environment because the purpose of the meeting depends on where one is coming from. For example, Britons and Americans see a meeting as an opportunity for decision-making and getting things done, whilst Frenchmen see it as a forum where a briefing can be delivered to cover all aspects of a problem. Linear-active members need relatively little preamble or small talk before getting to business. They like to introduce bullet points that can serve as an agenda. Multi-active members are not happy with the bullet-point approach, which they see as premature conclusions reached by their linear colleagues. They prefer to take points in random order and discuss them for hours. When they see topics listed at the beginning, they feel they have been manipulated. Reactive people do not have the linear obsession with agendas, neither are they wooed by multi-active arguments. They see arguments and ideas as points converging and ultimately merging.

According to Lewis model, Finland (reactive/linear-active) and Japan (reactive) are quite near to each other. There are many similarities between Japan and Finnish communication styles. These similarities include introversion, modesty, quietness, thinking in silence, not interrupting, distrusting big talkers, using silence, using body language meagerly (Authors' comment: both nations have a rich body language, but it is unnoticed by persons who cannot interpret it). One difference is in the way that diplomacy and truth are handled: Japanese put diplomacy or harmony before truth, while Finnish put truth before diplomacy. This is, however, understandable if we think about the history, geography and population of both nations.

When we are a guest in another country, we notice that things don't work exactly the same way as they do at home. No matter how well we have prepared ourselves, we won't be prepared for every situation. Practical experiences within research organizations in our joint projects between Japan and Finland have been extremely valuable, as they have greatly educated us about cross-cultural communication. These projects are an important mirror, reflecting our styles of communication. Based on our own experiences during joint cross-cultural research projects, we can summarize the key concepts of Japanese culture and communication styles as group orientation, politeness, harmony, and indirectness, the key concepts of Finnish culture being equality, individualism, pragmatism and directness. These concepts are discussed in more detail in [18].

3   Context Meets Culture

Culture is embodied in how we interact with other individuals and with our environment in different situations; it is a way of life formed under specific historical, natural and social conditions [3]. Cultural computing is an emerging, multidisciplinary computer science field as discussed in [5]. We are living in many different cultural spaces. For example, Japanese are living in Japanese cultural space and Finns in Finnish cultural space. The question is how our different cultural spaces could effectively communicate with each other. Broadly speaking, the question concerns all aspects of human life: technological, environmental and social, among others. We need a common language to create, discover and share cross-cultural knowledge as well as to exchange experiences about our environments.

Cross-cultural communication consists of human-to-human (for example, Finnish to Japanese), human-to-machine (for example, Japanese to a train ticket machine in Finland), and human-to-environment (for example, Finnish at a train station in Japan) communication. The environment can be physical, virtual or hybrid, such as a train station, groupware and Skype, respectively. In these environments, we face different kinds of situations in our everyday life.

When dealing with a context meeting a culture, we are talking about two concepts with a number of definitions. In the literature, several definitions of the term context can be found [6-7], [9], [19-22]. We have summarized these definitions and context modeling approaches in [23]. The concept of context is still a matter of discussion, and through the years several different definitions have been proposed. Coppola et al. 2009 in [24] divide the definitions into extensional and intensional definitions. Extensional definitions present the context through a list of possible context dimensions and their associated values. The context is represented by the location of the user, the surrounding objects, proximity to other people, temperature, computing devices, user profile, and physical conditions and time. Intensional definitions present the concept of context more formally. Extensional definitions seem to be useful in practical applications, where the abstract concept of context has to be made concrete. However, from a theoretical point of view, these definitions are not quite correct, as the context cannot be outlined just by some of its aspects. On the other hand, intensional definitions are of little use in practice, despite being theoretically satisfying. Context is a multi-dimensional concept.

In our research, generally speaking, context is understood as a situation at user's hand. The focus in our study is on modeling cross-cultural communication contexts, i.e. user in cross-cultural environments. Cross-cultural communication environment – user/actor – situation is the key triplet in our context research.

In a cross-cultural environment, the user can communicate with (a) another user/actor (or users/actors), (b) a machine or (c) a physical, virtual or hybrid environment. Our first objective is to model cross-cultural communication contexts. Our approach is extensional and ontology-based. We illustrate this by Figure 1 in which we introduce context processing architecture for cross-cultural communication environments. The system has two main input modes: a situation/task-specific input mode and an explicit/tacit knowledge input mode. The explicit/tacit knowledge input mode can be used to store the actor's own experiences in everyday life or as a feedback from using the context-sensitive service system. By means of the situation/task-specific interface, the actor inputs static or dynamic contexts. The context can be divided into low and high level contexts. The inputted low level contexts can be mapped to high level contexts (for example the mapping function transforms geographical coordinates to a street address or a series of geographical coordinates into a route). The high level contexts are transferred to the context integrator and manager module.

The contexts, i.e. the situation the actor has at hand, can be mapped to the cross-cultural communication context ontology structure by the context manager. The mapping function transforms the inputted context for reasoning and decisions. The reasoning engine creates decisions which are inferred by means of a relation and rule database. The context logs database includes context history for more detailed situation analysis and for learning of user's intentions. The reasoning and decision procedures create knowledge.

4   Examples of Implementations in Cross-Cultural Contexts

In this section, we describe two examples of our implementations in cross-cultural communication contexts. The examples are: (a) e-Assistant for supporting cross-cultural communication and (b) cross-cultural icons in musical context.

4.1   e-Assistant

As a first example, we introduce the Context-based e-Assistant for Supporting Cross-Cultural Communication [19]. The core idea is to support the user/actor in a cross-cultural situation. The situation can consist of, for example, a research or business meeting or travelling. An input to e-Assistant is a context, i.e., situation. An output from the system for the user/actor determines how to interpret a given context and behave in it. Let's study an example where the user is in Japan for the first time and is trying to travel from Tsukuba to Shonandai by train during the rush hour. He/she needs information on the train routes and fares as well as information on how to behave correctly in stations and trains.

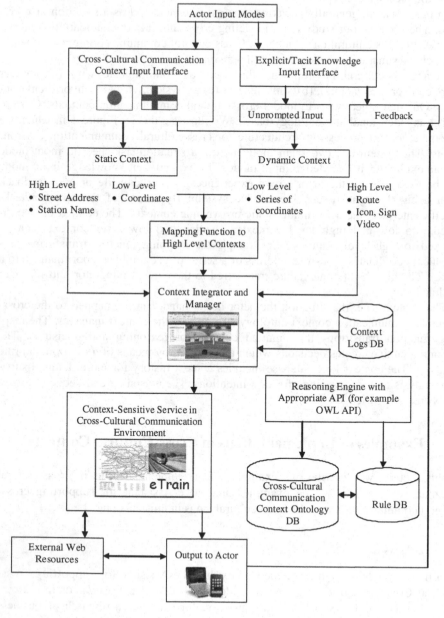

Fig. 1. Context processing architecture for cross-cultural communication environments

The user can use a free browsing feature to get information on various situations and on timetables, ticket prices, etc. However, it may be tedious to search all the information items individually. The user could instead try to find the situation (travelling from Tsukuba to Shonandai) listed in guided tours and thus get all the related information more easily. If the situation is not listed in the guided tours, the user can find information by using the search methods available. The situation can be entered in natural language, for example: "travelling from Tsukuba to Shonandai during rush hour". Also a map-based search can be used. The user can first select a Tokyo district train map and then select the stations to receive all the necessary information. The user can indicate two (or more) points in the map along with some additional preferences, like the shortest, quickest or cheapest route.

In the e-Assistant, we also sketched a new information search concept, a situation recognition functionality that analyses a user-provided pictorial file (an image, an icon, a sign or a symbol) of the situation. A situation recognition mode could function as in the following example:

- Cross-cultural situation: A train station in Japan, an unknown symbol for the actor (nationality: for example Finnish – first time in Japan).
- Activity: When encountering an unknown sign or symbol in the train station, the actor can take a picture of it with her/his mobile device and use e-Assistant's image recognition feature to help interpret the sign or symbol.
- Service: The actor submits the image by her/his mobile device to the e-Assistant pictorial database. The actor can also give additional information in order to help the interpretation of the content of the image such as "to focus on a certain part of the image" or "omit something from the image". The image service sends the picture to e-Assistant's pictorial database.
- Function: A pictorial recognition service identifies the symbol and associated description of its meaning.
- Service: The image service sends the symbol description and action guidelines to the actor.
- Activity: The actor knows how to interpret the symbol and how to behave in the situation at hand (= context).

4.2   Cross-Cultural Icons in Musical Context

In the second example depicted in Figure 2, the cross-cultural context is traditional music and the sub-contexts are traditional musical instruments and national icons [25-26]. The demonstration has a Finnish area and a Japanese area, which both include symbols in a form of icons. There is also a cross-cultural area symbolized by flags of both countries

The pictorial symbols have both horizontal and vertical dimensions for information browsing and deeper knowledge mining in the Web, respectively. For example, selecting the icon of kantele, a traditional Finnish instrument, will give a picture of koto, a corresponding traditional Japanese instrument. The demonstration offers links to Wikipedia articles (seen as thumbnails in the picture) about both instruments as horizontal knowledge. As vertical (deeper) knowledge, the demo also offers links to an article about a cross-cultural group of musicians from Finland and Japan, who play these instruments together, and to another article in which the tones of these instruments are compared. The vertical dimension can employ a more advanced calculus related to semantic knowledge mining, for example finding similarities between the instruments' sounds [2, 27-28].

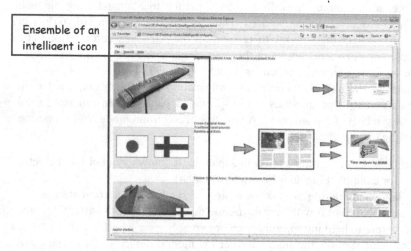

Fig. 2. An example of cross-cultural icons in musical context

5   Conclusions and Issues for Further Research

Culture is embodied in how people interact with other individuals and with their environment. It is a way of life formed under specific historical, natural and social conditions. Cross-cultural communication consists of human-to-human, human-to-machine, and human-to-environment communication in cross-cultural environments. The environment can be physical, virtual or hybrid. In our research, context is understood as a situation a user has at hand. In our paper, we introduced a context model for cross-cultural communication environments, and we described two examples of how we have applied it to the design of cross-cultural environments.

Our interest for further research is deeper study and understanding on implications for cross-cultural interpretations of context for example based on Handy's cultures [29] and Morgan's nine organizational perspectives [30]. We are also interested in developing contextual icons for cross-cultural communication.

References

1. Heimbürger, A.: Temporal Entities in the Context of Cross-Cultural Meetings and Negotiations. In: Kiyoki, Y., Tokuda, T., Jaakkola, H. (eds.) Information Modelling and Knowledge Bases XX. Frontiers in Artificial Intelligence and Applications, vol. 190, pp. 290–308. IOS Press, Amsterdam (2009)

2. Heimbürger, A., Jaakkola, H., Sasaki, S., Yoshida, N., Kiyoki, Y.: Context-Based Knowledge Creation and Sharing in Cross-Cultural Collaborative Communities. In: Kiyoki, Y., Tokuda, T., Jaakkola, H. (eds.) Information Modelling and Knowledge Bases XXI. Frontiers in Artificial Intelligence and Applications, vol. 206, pp. 76–88. IOS Press, Amsterdam (2010)

3. Wang, F.-Y.: Is Culture Computable? A Letter from the Editors, Special Issue: AI and Cultural Heritage. IEEE Intelligent Systems 24, 2–3 (2009)

4. Samovar, L.A., Porter, R.E., McDaniel, E.R.: Communication between Cultures. Thomson Wadsworth, Belmont (2007)

5. Heimbürger, A., Sasaki, S., Yoshida, N., Venäläinen, T., Linna, P., Welzer, T.: Cross-Cultural Collaborative Systems: Towards Cultural Computing. In: Kiyoki, Y., Tokuda, T., Jaakkola, H. (eds.) Information Modelling and Knowledge Bases XXI. Frontiers in Artificial Intelligence and Applications, vol. 206, pp. 403–417. IOS Press, Amsterdam (2010)

6. Bazire, M., Brézillon, P.: Understanding Context before Using It. In: Dey, A., Kokinov, B., Leake, D., Turner, R. (eds.) CONTEXT 2005. LNCS (LNAI), vol. 3554, pp. 29–40. Springer, Heidelberg (2005)

7. Dey, A., Kokinov, B., Leake, D., Turner, R. (eds.): CONTEXT 2005. LNCS (LNAI), vol. 3554. Springer, Heidelberg (2005)

8. Chaari, T., Ejigu, D., Laforest, F., Scuturici, V.-M.: A Comprehensive Approach to Model and Use Context for Adapting Applications in Pervasive Environments. Journal of Systems and Software 80, 1973–1992 (2007)

9. Strang, T., Linnhoff-Popien, C.: A Context Modeling Survey. In: Workshop on Advanced Context Modelling, Reasoning and Management. UbiComp 2004 – The Sixth International Conference on Ubiquitous Computing, Nottingham, England (2004)

10. King, W.R.: A Research Agenda for the Relationships between Culture and Knowledge Management. Knowledge and Process Management 14, 226–236 (2007)

11. Hofstede, G.: Culture's Consequences, Comparing Values, Behaviors, Institutions, and Organizations Across Nations. Sage Publications, Thousand Oaks (2001)

12. Hofstede, G., Hofstede, G.J.: Cultures and Organizations: Software of the Mind: Intercultural Cooperation and Its Importance for Survival. McGraw-Hill, New York (2004)

13. Hofstede, G.: Geert Hofstede™ Cultural Dimensions (referred July 11, 2013), http://geert-hofstede.com/

14. Lewis, R.D.: When Cultures Collide. Managing Successfully Across Cultures. Nicholas Brealey Publishing, London (1999)

15. Kroeber, A.L., Kluckhohn, C.: Culture: A Critical Review of Concepts and Definitions, The Museum (1952)

16. Lonner, W.J.: Psychology and Culture. Allyn & Bacon, Incorporated (1994)

17. Hoft, N.: Developing a Cultural Model. In: Galdo, D., Nielson, J. (eds.) International User Interfaces. John Wiley & Sons, New York (1996)

18. Heimburger, A., Kiyoki, Y., Ylikotila, T.: Communication Across Cultures in the Context of Multicultural, Software Development. Reports of the Department of Mathematical Information Technology. Series C. Software and Computational Engineering (C1) (2011)

19. Coutaz, J., Crowley, J., Dobson, S., Garlan, D.: Context is key. Communications of the ACM 48, 49–53 (2005)

20. Leppänen, M.: An Ontological Framework and a Methodical Skeleton for Method Engineering – A Contextual Approach. Jyväskylä Studies in Computing, vol. 52, 702 p. University Press, Jyväskylä (2005)

21. Winograd, T.: Architectures for Context. Human–Computer Interaction 16, 401–419 (2001)

22. Zhou, M.X., Houck, K., Pan, S., Shaw, J., Aggarwal, V., Wen, Z.: Enabling Context-Sensitive Information Seeking. In: Proceedings of the 11th International Conference on Intelligent User Interfaces, Sydney, Australia, pp. 116–123 (2006)

23. Heimbürger, A., Nurminen, M., Venäläinen, T., Kinnunen, S.: Modelling Contexts in Cross-Cultural Communication Environments. In: Heimbürger, A., Kiyoki, Y., Tokuda, T., Jaakkola, H., Yoshida, N. (eds.) Information Modelling and Knowledge Bases XXII. Frontiers in Artificial Intelligence and Applications, vol. 225, pp. 301–311. IOS Press, Amsterdam (2011)

24. Coppola, P., Della Mea, V., Di Gaspero, L., Lomuscio, R., Mischis, D., Mizzaro, S., Nazzi, E., Scagnetto, I., Vassena, L.: AI Techniques in a Context-Aware Ubiquitous Environment. In: Hassanien, A.-E., Abawajy, J.H., Akraham, A., Hagras, H. (eds.) Pervasive Computing, Innovation in Intelligent Multimedia and Applications, pp. 157–180. Springer, London (2009)

25. Heimburger, A., Kiyoki, Y., Kohtala, S.: Intelligent Icons for Cross-Cultural Knowledge Searching. In: Henno, J., Kiyoki, Y., Tokuda, T., Jaakkola, H., Yoshida, N. (eds.) Information Modelling and Knowledge Bases XXII. Frontiers in Artificial Intelligence and Applications, vol. 237, pp. 77–89. IOS Press, Amsterdam (2012)

26. Heimbürger, A., Kiyoki, Y.: Pictorial Symbols in Context - A Means for Visual Communication in Cross-Cultural Environments. In: Xiao, Y., Muffoletto, R., Amon, T. (eds.) Proceedings of the IADIS International Conferences: (a) Computer Graphics, Visualization, Computer Vision and Image Processing 2010, (b) Web Virtual Reality and Three-Dimensional Worlds, (c) Visual Communication: Creative Industries, Photography and Culture, pp. 463–467. IADIS Press (2010)

27. Barakbah, A.R., Kiyoki, Y.: An Emotion-Oriented Image Search System with Cluster based Similarity Measurement using Pillar-Kmeans Algorithm. In: Heimbürger, A., Kiyoki, Y., Tokuda, T., Jaakkola, H., Yoshida, N. (eds.) Information Modelling and Knowledge Bases XXII. Frontiers in Artificial Intelligence and Applications, vol. 225, pp. 117–136. IOS Press, Amsterdam (2011)

28. Kiyoki, Y., Kitagawa, T., Hayama, T.: A Metadatabase System for Semantic Image Search by a Mathematical Model of Meaning. ACM SIGMOD Record 23, 34–41 (1994)

29. Handy, C.: Understanding Organizations, 4th edn. Penguin Books (1993)

30. Morgan, G.: Images of Organization. SAGE (2006)

Notes on Synthesis of Context between Engineering and Social Science

Ziyad Alshaikh[1] and Clive Boughton[2]

[1] King Abdulaziz City for Science and Technology, Riyadh, Saudi Arabia
zshiakh@kacst.edu.sa
[2] The Australian National University, Canberra 0200, Australia
clive.boughton@anu.edu.au

Abstract. The term 'context,' in software engineering, has been typically associated to mean the act of setting boundaries and setting system scope. In this paper, we revisit the concept of 'context' and draw ideas from other areas of engineering and the social sciences to suggest that context is a much richer concept that requires a systematic approach to model all of its relative aspects. It constitutes more complex phenomena concerning how a system interacts with its surroundings or even the world. Therefore, we outline a synthesised view of context to be used as a foundation for any approach that intends to apply 'context' effectively within a process or a modelling framework for software engineering. The synthesis is identified from five combined themes for any model to use context effectively.

Keywords: Context modelling, Context analysis, Software methods.

1 Introduction

The word *context* originates from the Latin verb *contexere* that means literally means "together (con) weave (textere)" or in more modern terms "to weave together." Weaving together directs the attention to an important aspect of the meaning of context, and that is is likely to consist of several elements that can be combined in many different ways to present differently depending on what/who is being affected. So, context can be considered to be dynamic, especially when considering terms like moving/being in/out of context. Other related terms are typically used: environment, circumstances, conditions, state of affairs, setting, frame of reference, and factors. But how do things move from being *in* context to be *out* of context?

Scharfstein [1] proposes a solution to the problem of context when he defines it as: *"that which environs the object of our interest and helps by its relevance to explain it."* Scharfstein's definition distinguishes three elements of any context: an object, relevance, and purpose (to explain); where elements move in and out of context in relation to each other. Therefore, context is relational concerning a specific purpose: to explain, to describe, to design, and so on. But by using the

P. Brézillon, P. Blackburn, and R. Dapoigny (Eds.): CONTEXT 2013, LNAI 8175, pp. 157–170, 2013.

word 'environ,' the definition does not limit context to specific types of elements, either tangible or abstract. Context, then, is still open to being wide range of possible elements.

Similarly, Christopher Alexander [2] recognises that the context of an ensemble is an element of design that cannot be fully described, because attempting to produce a full description of context is an endless task. But he approaches the problem of describing context by using the concept of *force*. Force, accordingly, becomes the only relevant element within a design problem. The result of this 'force' is undesired outcomes, or what he calls misfits. Alexander and similarly Wittgenstein [3], is not concerned with the definition of context. So, instead of asking what context means, he asks how to use it.

To compare Alexander's approach to Scharfstein's, they both agree that context has to be limited for analysis. To Alexander, what is relevant to 'form' is context and its force causing stress on the ensemble; to Scharfstein, context should be limited by what it explains. Both definitions, however, create serious difficulties in approaching the concept of context. Through the term 'force,' Alexander ties context closely to 'form,' thereby creating a duality between context and form—Alexander refers to it as context-form. Scharfstein's definition, on the other hand, leads to relativism, which at its extreme, does not help to explain anything [1].

Other approaches have recognised the importance to limit context, but they have tended to apply very stringent limits. In context-aware systems, for example, context is limited to information [4]. In linguistics, Halliday[5] for example, divides context into three elements: field (e.g., activities), tenor in the form of the relation between participants, and mode (e.g., written or spoken). Based on Halliday's work the *Systematic Functional Linguistics (SFM)* approach to semantic analysis was founded. A sociocultural definition of context is given by Fetzer [6], which argues that context is comprised of individuals' physical, physiological placement, knowledge, and intention. A similar approach in anthropology[7] is followed, where context is divided into elements: the setting or the physical world, knowledge, language, and non-verbal signs. Context in all of these approaches is a reflection of the concerns of the discipline (linguistics, anthropology, and so on). Work has been also directed to identify a common understanding of context by a study of how its defined across disciplines. Bezire and Brzillon [8], for example, studied 150 definitions of context. As a result, they identified that context is formed by six components: constraints, influence, behaviour, systems, nature, and structure. But Bezire and Brzillon report that there is no consensus about answers to questions such as: Is context static or dynamic? Is context internal or external? Is context whole or a set of connected element?

To combine different views of context we propose to synthesise context through five themes. A model that aims to capture context, we believe, should be able to combine the five themes identified from literature. The themes show how different disciplines have approached context, and at certain points have shared similar views. A model that combines the five themes represents, to a large degree, a combination that straddles multiple disciplines, mainly social science and engineering. Thus serving the view that context is a cross-discipline concept. The thematic approach presented here, was first applied on analysing/modelling requirements [9], later to be extended in [10].

In Section 2 we present how context is used in software engineering. In Section 3 we present how context is viewed by the different disciplines of social science and engineering. In Section 4 we show how the concepts drawn from literature are synthesised into five themes. Finally, we present summary and conclusion in Section 5.

2   Context in Software Engineering

In software engineering, little attention is directed to provide a formal definition of context beyond the synonyms introduced earlier. Thus the discipline's approach to context may be interpreted by examining how modelling approaches *use* context to solve system problems. By examining modelling approaches, two themes can be identified: context as the boundary of the system, and context as common-sense. Therefore, following Wittgenstein's [3] advice, to ask about the use not the meaning; a survey is presented on the use of context in current approaches to software development, on the level of requirements, architecture and design.

2.1   Context in Requirements

Context in early requirements approaches is typically associated with the task of setting system boundaries, but in later approaches context became identified through the narrative of scenario-based requirements. In setting system boundaries, the term 'context' is used explicitly to develop context diagrams in structured analysis approaches, for example. Later, with the emergence of object orientated analysis approaches, the use of the term 'context' became less common. But context as a concept continued to be used implicitly within the scenario-based requirements, or what could be identified as a common-sense approach to context.

In what follows, a review of the early uses of the term 'context' in structured analysis as part of setting system boundaries, followed by a review of the common-sense approach to context that became popular in the last two decades.

Context as Boundaries: DeMarco [11] is perhaps the first to use 'context' in software requirements explicitly. By setting the boundary of the system as its context, DeMarco's approach abstracts data inputs and outputs, and represents data flow going through a series of processes/transformations, which ultimately forms a Data Flow Diagram (DFD). The set of data, data flows, and data processes, help to understand the interconnected processes at different levels within a system. The approach depicts a high level view of the system in the context diagram—representing level zero—by identifying the scope and boundary of the

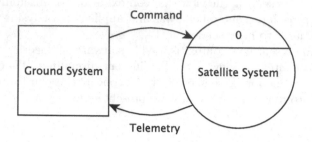

Fig. 1. A DFD context-diagram of a satellite system

system, in addition to the system's interaction with external entities. Figure 1 shows an example of a DFD context-diagram of a satellite system interacting with the ground system as its external entity. The process of identifying boundaries and managing scope is a difficult task that demands a series of refinements and revisions with the involvement of stakeholders [12]. It is the purpose of the context diagram to show relevant system terminators or external entities that interact with the system, and show data flow between the system and its external entities.

But the use of context diagrams is not limited to representing data flow. Context diagrams are used to describe the relationship between the 'machine' (system) and the 'world' or the application domain [13]. In representing the machine and the world, unlike DeMarco's context diagram, the diagram does not show any description of the interaction between the system and other elements within the application domain. But beyond the representation of context as boundaries in the simple sense, the machine-world view may express the understanding of context using examples outside the software domain, such as the context of building a bridge. The example of the bridge points out that the context is not the problem, but rather what surrounds the problem. However, the machine-world view does not discuss what should be considered as part of the context and what should be excluded. Alternatively, the machine-world view extends the context diagram using problem frames [13]. Problem frames, here, are similar to extending the context diagram by processes in the DFD approach. The use of frames, is also common as another term used to mean context in sociology [14], for example. Accordingly, the machine-world view starts from the problem domain to recognise the context as a whole, then begins to limit the context by using frames, capturing relevant elements concerning the problem and application.

In Object Oriented Analysis (OOA), use-cases describe a sequence of interactions between the system and external entities as actors [15]. They are perhaps 'specified' contexts that help focus on a particular aspect of a system's overall context. Even when the term 'context' is not used, as in context diagrams, a use-case represents an interaction between the system, as an internal entity, and its context, as an external entity. The interaction between internal and external system elements underlies most approaches to system analysis. For example, Executable UML [16] uses a similar approach in sequence diagrams and collaboration diagrams. Unlike the (DFD) context diagram, however, sequence diagrams and collaboration diagrams are not used in the early stages of analysis, but rather in conjunction with the more detailed system and class state models [16]. The driving force to adapt use-cases, and other similar methods, is the need to understand what the user intends to do with the system, rather than asking for what the user wants the system to do [15]. Thus, focusing on the user is part of the user centred design approach [17]. Unlike focusing on the world and the machine as the context, user centred design shifts the context to the user. The analyst is no longer interested only in the external world, but also in the internal world of users, their intensions, their emotions [18], and mainly their mental model [17].

Context as Common-Sense. The common-sense approach to context emerged due to the focus on the user. Within such an approach requirements are described in a narrative that focuses on the user's interaction with the system. In such a narrative, context is not identified explicitly, but through the user's situation, to which the analyst is able to relate.

For example, organisational goals using are linked to the user's intention through scenarios [19]. Thus, a scenario's narrative captures user's intentions within individual tasks to achieve the system aim. Each scenario has a description of a single instance of an interaction with the system [15]. Describing user aims and intentions, rather than what is needed from the system, is a response to the need for designing software to enhance usability [15]. Similar to the bridge analogy, in which the engineer imagines the bridge to be part of the scene, the analyst using scenarios can also imagine the user's situation following a similar approach.

The scenario-based technique is used also to describe non-functional requirements, where the concern about the user's actions is replaced by the concern about quality attributes. For example, quality requirements are described using general and concrete scenarios [20]. In a general scenario the narrative does not relate to a specific system. For instance, a general scenario may be to secure data from unauthorised users. To make the scenario concrete, the scenario must specify which data and which level of security. For example, a general scenario might state that 'financial transactions must be fully secured,' a concrete scenario, however, would state that 'credit card details must be secured from all users no less than 99% of the time'. When analysts move from a general to a concrete scenario they have to provide additional information about the specific context in which a function or a task is performed. The implications of such information, with other similar statements, is left to the analyst's judgement to decide how it may influence system decisions.

Although several approaches adapt some form of a scenario-based technique [21–24], they still address narrow system concerns, and lack uniformity.

For example, adapting one scenario approach is not enough, and its recommended to integrate multiple scenario-based methods to enhance their ability to represent multiple concerns [25]. Choices between scenario-based techniques should not be taken without a careful consideration of the system being developed [26].

2.2   Context in Architecture

Software architecture approaches often realise context, but without necessarily adopting the term. Approaches such as: Architecture Tradeoff Analysis Method (ATAM) [22] and Attribute Driven Design (ADD) [27], among others. For the purpose of reviewing context in software architecture, it is possible to classify the use of context into two forms: 'context as state,' and 'context as boundaries.'

'Context as state' in software architecture is realised when an architecture is either already decided or exists in a running system. Thus the context of an architecture is derived from three elements: organisational goals, the system state, and constraints [26]. In the review of software architecture analysis approaches [26], context is stressed as the first criteria for choosing a software architecture analysis method. Although not identified as such, the context of an architecture is derived as a state, formed by an amalgamation of the three elements. Thus, an analyst must examine the state of the context of the system's architecture before choosing an analysis method. For example, if an architecture is chosen as a result of a specific constraint, the state of the context changes as the constraint is removed.

Context as boundaries are identified in the traditional sense, similar to what is defined by the structured analysis approach, or by defining what is relevant to the architecture in general by setting a conceptual boundary. Context is recognised as boundaries [28], where the context is identified in the form of interfaces between internal and external entities, thus play a role in defining functional and non-functional requirements for each architecture interface. The use of interfaces is similar to context-diagrams, in which the system is defined by a boundary in relation to external entities. Another approach is to define what is relevant to the architecture by setting conceptual boundaries. For example, the context of software architecture requirements is set according to quality. The context is recognised only through requirements that have an impact on quality [29]. Choosing what impacts quality, sets a boundary based on the concept that what is relevant to architecture is to achieve quality. As a result, the concept is used to decide what to include and exclude as part of the analysis. An architect then uses the concept of quality to select from requirements what elements fit a predefined classification drawn from specific quality measures. It is not clear, however, how to determine when a requirement is or is not significant except by using experience and judgment [29].

2.3   Context in Design Patterns and Pattern Language

Design patterns are based on building patterns introduced by Christopher Alexander [30]. Building patterns represent a language for design from common designs of houses and cities. The concept of context and its relation to patterns in the software design community is borrowed largely from the work of Alexander. But software patterns have not matured enough to form a complete pattern language that developers can use to design software systems completely based on patterns [31].

Alexander addressed the patterns community in a speech [32] where he mentioned that design patterns of software lack two attributes: they do not work together to solve multiple design problems, and they do not aim to improve human life. While the latter is improved by the recent developments in the use of patterns in usability [33], the former remains a challenging issue [34].

Although Alexander [30] describes each architecture pattern before introducing a pattern, and identifies architecture descriptions as its context, software patterns were not described in a similar manner. The term 'context' in patterns of software is either replaced by intent and motivation [31], or introduced through a short description of where to use the pattern[35]. For example, in the pipe-and-filter pattern [35], the pattern's context is summarised in a single sentence as: '*processing data streams*,' followed by an example. Both approaches are goal oriented, in that a pattern's context is manifested in the way a software designer intends to use it.

Recently more attention is given to rethinking the role of context in patterns. Two issues are raised in how context is identified in relation to patterns. First, context descriptions are criticised for being short and too general, context descriptions should be precise, and avoid general descriptions that can be easily ignored [36]. One example of such general descriptions is the example of the BRIDGE pattern [30]. Because the BRIDGE pattern's description is imprecise, the pattern may be applied in the wrong context [36]. Second, when trying to be precise about a pattern's context, a context-pattern boundary dilemma arises: Is the context part of the pattern or not? [36]. The discussion becomes similar to what analysts would have when they draw a context-diagram, the question then becomes: What is part of the system and what is not?

3 Context in Other Disciplines

Although the concept of context demonstrated an important role in the development of several fields of study, embracing the concept itself, as will be shown in sections to follow, comes with difficulties of its own. Therefore, a discussion is presented from a number of disciplines that focus primarily on context as a course of study. The discussion first starts by exploring *context* as a problem, then *context* as a solution, and finally *context* as form.

3.1 Context as a Problem

Context is a problem because its' includes elements endlessly by one form of association or another. Context becomes overloaded with related elements, and instead of enhancing understanding it destroys it [1]. Context's difficulty is a result of three aspects: the regression of context, the shell problem, and the problem of relevance.

Regression is the results of elements being defined or understood by other elements. These other elements may also be understood through further elements. To proceed in this manner yields a contextualisation process that continues indefinitely. For example, Harvey [37] explains that discourse analysis in a bilingual culture is difficult because one language implicitly stands as the context for the other, forming an *implicit* context, leading to context regression. In social science, three approaches to the regression of meaning [38] are identified: external context, internal context, and mental context. External context regresses outwardly, where meaning is obtained from the external world. Internal context is based on language or text being the source of meaning, and that nothing exists outside of text. Mental context exists in the mind, as part of an internal intention or a psychological state.

The shell problem is the result of attempting to be thorough in understanding context. Thereby leading to total contextualisation, where everything becomes the context of everything else. Thus a twist of context occurs, in which the parameters of the problem are turned inside out [1]. This issue is referred to as the shell problem. The shell problem results from the context becoming the new problem, while the old problem, or its contents, become the new shell or context [38]. In interpreting text, for instance, a similar problem occurs—in what is known, according to Ricoeur [38], as the hermeneutic circle—where starting from the text to understand the context leads to using the context to understand the text. Text is bounded by meaning and meaning is bounded by context, yet context is boundless. Whereby any definition of context can itself be contextualised by means of a new context, and the process is open to infinite regression [38].

The problem of relevance is summarised by Scharfstein [1]. Scharfstein draws our attention to the issue of relativism, that makes context difficult to relay on. The difficulty comes because context is a kind of limited relativism, whereas relativism itself is hard to limit [38]. Failing to limit context leads to extreme relativity, which consequently leads to extreme individualism [1]. With extreme individualism, where each individual case has a unique context, it is possible to justify anything.

The problem, then, becomes how to identify what is *significantly* relevant from what is not. For one, deconstruction allows choosing relevance within the text as part of a critical reading process where the text is turned against itself. But Foucault [39] argues that what is relevant—or what is believed to be relevant— changes according to the change of knowledge. Knowledge then directs relevance even in the closed system of language presented by deconstructionists.

3.2 Context as a Solution

Context may cause an analytical problem, but context is also an intuitive solution. Scharfstein [1] observes that we are more aware of context in practice than in theory—Scharfstein's observation relates to what is previously identified as the common-sense approach to context in software engineering.

One possible approach to demarcate context, or the domains indicated by it, is to represent context in terms of connections. Interpretation either form connections or disconnections [38, 40]. Such an approach relates the system to its surroundings, it is a result of an interpretation, and by itself, yields an explanation [38]. Therefore context can be analysed only interactively and not disconnected from its application [37].

Wittgenstein [3] observes that people play a language game using context. The game is defined based on how to agree on the meaning and the use of a word. Therefore, Wittgenstein prefers to ask how context is used, rather than to ask what its meaning is [3]. Malinowski [5], derived the term 'context of situation,' referring to the meaning of words that relate to the culture in which those words are used, a platform, perhaps, in which the language game can be played. An example of how the language game and the context of the situation play an important role in any technical discourse is presented in a conversation by an analyst and a stakeholder given by Ozkaya et, al.[41].

When two people start to identify what is meant by a word by referring to its use, a platform is established where the word becomes a *focal event* [7]. A focal event demonstrates a contextualisation act of a term. A focal event, or a phenomenon when investigated, can be contextualised through four parameters: social and spatial framework, behavioural environment (represented in gestures or behaviour), language (as context), and the extra situational context (background knowledge and frame of relevance) [7]. Two extra parameters may be added: the historical and psychological context [38]. But in order to make effective use of contextual parameters in any analysis, especially given the complexity involved in accounting for such diverse interrelationships, an interpretive conceptual framework of reality must be formulated [38]. Thus, framing context as an object of investigation [3].

3.3 Context as Form

According to Alexander [2], 'form' is the manifestation of context. On one hand, form is required to respond to the needs of a context, but when form is implemented as a solution, it becomes part of the context. Thus context, in general, is made of an ensemble of forms, inevitably becoming a context for yet another form [2].

To illustrate how 'form' relates to 'context,' take the example of a meeting room. In a meeting room, the room has to interface with the floor plan shaped relative to other forms: the office across the hall, the hall itself, the height of the roof, and so on. After the form of the meeting room is finalised, the meeting room becomes the new context for items to be fitted within the room: the meeting table, chairs, etc. It is possible to notice how form and context regress with the physical boundaries.

But the context-form regression is a cause and a result of several interrelated form based and non-form based patterns. The pattern of crowd movement may influence the way a road is designed between a point of departure and a point of destination. Therefore, a pattern is to be found, or looked for, in the earliest

Table 1. Summary of themes that appeared in the literature on the use of context

Theme	Related Sources
Context is a set of connections	Contextualisation is an act of making connections [40], while DeMarco [11] uses data flow to connect processes.
Relevance is directed by knowledge	A system of signs is directed by knowledge [39]. Similarly, the knowledge of a language directs reference [44, 45].
Context regresses endlessly	Extending context beyond boundaries produces new insights [46]. Similarly, contextual moves transforms understanding and meaning [38]. Context-diagrams, according to DeMarco [11], sets the boundary for a system.
Context has states	Goals, the concept of architecture state, and constraints combined, form the state of the architecture [26]. Connections have states as well: connected or disconnected [40].
Context has influence	A misfit is identified as any stress on an ensemble resulting from the interaction between context and form [2]. Similarly, a system of patterns has an influence on individual patterns [34].

functional origins of a problem [2]. Where patterns of form are deeply rooted in patterns of life.

What is particularly relevant to form is the demands placed by the context, recognised for example [42, 43] as forces. According to [2], form achieves fit by resolving contextual forces. Accordingly, it is possible to replace context by the term 'force.' A force then becomes recognised as a result of its effect, or misfit. For example, if a new tool is first used, say a Swiss army knife, the user takes notice of signs of irregularities: failing to cut a string because the knife is not sharp enough, the handle is too small or too large, and so on.

4   Synthesis of Context

From the ideas reviewed in the literature on the use of context in software systems and other views from other disciplines, it is possible to identify some key themes on context. These themes summarise the different ways context is used in various disciplines, and suggest key concepts that any model should consider when it attempts to represent context.

The main themes identified from literature are derived from software and other disciplines that suggest that these themes apply beyond the concern of analysing software systems. Each theme confirms the notion that context in reality is more sophisticated and more complex than realised in theory. This assumption is reinforced by software engineering examples presented earlier, in particular, the acceptance and use of the common-sense approach to context. Table 4 gives a summary of the main themes presented here.

Theme 1: context is a set of connections. Connections characterise the process of contextualising and interpreting as a process of making connections and disconnections [40]. Connections are derived also from realising context not as objects, but as the result of the interaction between elements. Then such interaction is captured in the form of connections. Context is expressed also in terms of connections in the context-diagram and DFDs at large, as defined by DeMarco [11]. But compared to connections in DFDs, which refer to connections in terms of data flow, context connections and disconnections are more abstract [40].

Theme 2: relevance is directed by knowledge. relevance is directed within a system of signs through knowledge [39]. Therefore, contextualisation must be guided by a knowledge framework. Directing relevance relates also to how to direct a connection in a process of making connections [40]. Other indications surrounding the use of knowledge to direct relevance could be found in the use of models following [44]: semantic, pragmatic, and indexical models; and the AI context model [45].

Theme 3: context regresses endlessly. Context requires a guiding process that enables a natural regression from one context element to another. But regression must be limited at some point by a *rational* decision that postulates the absence of relevance based on knowledge. Extending context beyond traditional boundaries provides opportunities for redefining the context of the problem, hence producing new insights [46]. Redefining boundaries is referred to as contextual moves [38]. Therefore, context-diagrams represent mainly the act of limiting context, as an analyst sets the boundary to limit context from extending endlessly.

Theme 4: context has states. three elements for the context of software architectures are listed: goals, architecture state, and constraint [26]. Thus, different architectures may have different context states based on a certain combination of these three elements. Accordingly, it is possible to generalise the notion of context states to levels of software and system development other than architecture.

The concept of states for context is implied also through connections and disconnections [40]. If context is the act of making connections, disconnections is an act of identifying elements that are not part of the context. As a result, the system may be formed by a set of connections and disconnection, whereby an element could be either in a state of connection with another element, or a state of disconnection.

Theme 5: context has influence. Alexander [2] identifies the role of context as the main source of influence on elements of design through what he identifies as force. This phenomenon is observed also by the influence of the architecture on how structure patterns are to be integrated within a larger context [34]. The concept of context and force have been used by software patterns as the main source of influence on design decisions [36]. Both observations are in line with the observation made on the satellite system thought experiment, on the existence of influencing factors that shape requirements and architecture. But what these ideas do not mention are that context has different degrees of influence, and how these influences change over time.

5   Summary and Conclusion

Answering the question 'What is context?,' by reviewing different disciplines that approached the question, has led us to the conclusion that context lies in the interaction between two or more elements, not in the elements themselves. Furthermore, literature shows that it is of more use to present an answer to the question of how to use context rather than answering what it means.

A review of how software engineers use 'context' showed different uses of the term. Two main approaches are identified: first, context is used as part of setting system boundaries, exemplified in the context-diagrams as part of structured modelling such as DFDs. The second, is the common-sense approach to context manifested in the use of requirement scenarios.

Extending the review of context to literature in other disciplines, showed that context is discussed conceptually as a separate issue. Aspects of the discussion either focus on context as a problem, a solution, or as form. Context as a problem is manifested in three problems: the problem of regression, the shell problem, and the problem of relevance. Context as a solution is summarised by the Wittgenstein [3] observation that its more useful to ask how context is used, rather then ask what is the context. Other more formal approaches to context are identified, either modelling context itself through certain parameters in anthropology [7], in the study of semantics by using semantic models [44], or contextual frameworks in Artificial Intelligence [45]. In context as form, form is the result of its context [2]. Context becomes consumed as form and is recognised through its effect. Context in design places demands on the form recognised by Alexander [2] as force. The role of form is to resolve the demands placed by context to achieve a fit between the form and its context.

Comparing how context is viewed by different disciplines allowed us to draw five themes that summarise how to make use of the concept. To be able to use context more effectively we propose that any model of context must be able to achieve a synthesis based on the five themes presented. Without the five themes, we believe, a model of context is incomplete, and so, cannot be utilised context as a concept, fully.

References

1. Scharfstein, B.A.: The Dilemma of Context. NYU Press (1989)
2. Alexander, C.: Notes on the Synthesis of Form. Harvard University Press (1964)
3. Wittgenstein, L.: Philosophical investigations. Blackwell, Oxford (1974)

 4. Dey, A.K.: Understanding and using context. Personal and Ubiquitous Computing 5, 4–7 (2001)
 5. Halliday, M.: Explorations in the functions of language. In: Explorations in Language Study. Elsevier, North-Holland (1977)
 6. Fetzer, A.: Recontextualizing context: grammaticality meets appropriateness. John Benjamins Publishing Company, Amsterdam (2004)
 7. Goodwin, C., Duranti, A.: Rethinking context: an introduction. In: Rethinking Context: Language as an Interactive Phenomenon. Cambridge University Press (1992)
 8. Bazire, M., Brézillon, P.: Understanding context before using it. In: Dey, A., Kokinov, B., Leake, D., Turner, R. (eds.) CONTEXT 2005. LNCS (LNAI), vol. 3554, pp. 29–40. Springer, Heidelberg (2005)
 9. Alshaikh, Z., Boughton, C.: The Context Dynamics Matrix (CDM): An Approach to Modelling Context. In: 16th Asia Pecific Software Engineering Conference, APSEC 2009 (2009)
10. Alshaikh, Z.: Notes on the Synthesis of Context: A Noval Approach to Model Context in Software Engineering, Ph.D. thesis, National Australian University, Canberra, Australia (February 2011)
11. DeMarco, T.: Structured Analysis and System Specification. Yourdon Press, Upper Saddle River (1979)
12. Yourdon, E.: Modern Structured Analysis. Prentice-Hall International Editions (1989)
13. Jackson, M.: Software Requirements and Specifications: A Lexicon of Practice, Principles and Prejudices. ACM Press (1995)
14. Goffman, E.: Frame analysis: an essay on the organization of experience. Penguin, Harmondsworth (1975)
15. Wiegers, K.E.: Software Requirements. Microsoft Press (2003)
16. Mellor, S.J., Balcer, M.J.: Executable UML A foundation for Model-Driven Architecture. The Addison-Wesley Object Technology Series (2002)
17. Norman, D.A.: The psychology of everyday things. Basic Books (1988)
18. Norman, D.A.: Emotional design: why we love (or hate) everyday things. Basic Books (2005)
19. Potts, C.: Using schematic scenarios to understand user needs. In: DIS 1995: Proceedings of the 1st Conference on Designing Interactive Systems, pp. 247–256. ACM, New York (1995), doi:http://doi.acm.org/10.1145/225434.225462
20. Bass, L., Clements, P., Kazman, R.: Software architecture in practice, 2nd edn. Addison-Wesley, MA (2003)
21. Gheorghita, S.V., Palkovic, M., Hamers, J., Vandecappelle, A., Mamagkakis, S., Basten, T., Eeckhout, L., Corporaal, H., Catthoor, F., Vandeputte, F., Bosschere, K.D.: System-scenario-based design of dynamic embedded systems. ACM Trans. Des. Autom. Electron. Syst. 14(1), 1–45 (2009), doi:http://doi.acm.org/10.1145/1455229.1455232
22. Kazman, R., Klein, M., Clements, P.: ATAM: Method for Architecture Evaluation. Tech. Rep. CMU/SEI-2000-TR-004, The Software Engineering Institute, Carnegie Mellon University, Pittsburgh, PA 15213 (August 2000)
23. Bengtsson, P., Bosch, J.: Scenario-based software architecture reengineering. In: ICSR 1998: Proceedings of the 5th International Conference on Software Reuse, p. 308. IEEE Computer Society, Washington, DC (1998)
24. Kazman, R., Bass, L., Webb, M., Abowd, G.: SAAM: a method for analyzing the properties of software architectures. In: ICSE 1994: Proceedings of the 16th International Conference on Software Engineering, pp. 81–90. IEEE Computer Society Press, Los Alamitos (1994)

25. Ralyté, J., Rolland, C., Plihon, V.: Method enhancement with scenario based techniques. In: Jarke, M., Oberweis, A. (eds.) CAiSE 1999. LNCS, vol. 1626, pp. 103–118. Springer, Heidelberg (1999)
26. Kazman, R., Bass, L., Klein, M., Lattanze, T., Northrop, L.: A basis for analyzing software architecture analysis methods. Software Quality Journal 13, 329–355 (2005)
27. Wojcik, R., Bachmann, F., Bass, L., Clements, P., Merson, P., Nord, R., Wood, B.: Attribute-driven design (ADD), version 2.0. Tech. Rep. CMU/SEI-2006-TR-023, Software Engineering Institute, Carnegie Mellon University (November 2006)
28. Bosch, J.: Design & use of software architectures. Addison-Wesley, London (2000)
29. Bass, L., Bergey, J., Clements, P., Merson, P., Ozkaya, I., Sangwan, R.: A comparison of requirements specification methods from a software architecture perspective. Tech. rep., Software Engineering Institute, Carnegie Mellon (2006)
30. Alexander, C., Ishikawa, S., Silverstein, M., Jacobson, M., Fiksdahl-King, I., Angel, S.: A pattern language: towns, buildings, construction. Oxford University Press (1977)
31. Gamma, E., Helm, R., Johnson, R., Vlissides, J.: Design Patterns Elements of Reusable Object-Oriented Software. Addison Wesley (1994)
32. Alexander, C.: The origins of pattern theory: The future of the theory, and the generation of a living world. IEEE Software, 71–82 (1999)
33. Dearden, A., Finlay, J.: Pattern Languages in HCI: A Critical Review. Human-Computer Interaction 21(1), 49–102 (2006)
34. John, B.E., Bass, L., Golden, E., Stoll, P.: A Responsibility-Based Pattern Language for Usability-Supporting Architectural Patterns. In: EICS 2009: Proceedings of the 1st ACM SIGCHI Symposium on Engineering Interactive Computing Systems, pp. 3–12. ACM, New York (2009)
35. Buschmann, F., Meunier, R., Rohnert, H., Sommerlad, P., Stal, M.: Pattern-Oriented Software Architecture A System of Patterns. John Wiley & Sons (1996)
36. Buschmann, F., Henney, K., Schmidt, D.C.: Software-Oriented Software Architecture on Patterns and Pattern Languages, vol. 5. John Wiley & Sons, Ltd. (2007)
37. Harvey, P.: Culture and context: The effects of visibilty. In: The Problem of Context. Berghan Books (1999)
38. Dilley, R.: The Problem of Context. Berghan Books (1999)
39. Foucault, M.: Archaeology of knowledge. Routledge classics, Routledge (2002)
40. Kristeva, J.: Psychoanalysis and the polis. In: Ormiston, G.L., Schrift, A.D. (eds.) Transforming the Hermeneutic Context, ch. 4, pp. 89–105. State University of New York Press (1990)
41. Ozkaya, I., Bass, L., Nord, R.L., Sangwan, R.S.: Making practical use of quality attribute information. IEEE Software 25, 25–33 (2008)
42. Skjeltorp, A., Belushkin, A.V.: Forces, Growth and Form in Soft Condensed Matter: At the Interface between Physics and Biology. Springer (2004)
43. Thompson, D.W.: On growth and form. Cambridge University Press (1966)
44. Cappelen, H.: Semantics and pragmatics: Some central issues. In: Preyer, G., Peter, G. (eds.) Context-Sensitivity and Semantic Minimalism: New Essays on Semantics and Pragmatics, pp. 3–22. Oxford University Press (2007)
45. Guha, R., McCarthy, J.: Varieties of contexts. In: Blackburn, P., Ghidini, C., Turner, R.M., Giunchiglia, F. (eds.) CONTEXT 2003. LNCS, vol. 2680, pp. 164–177. Springer, Heidelberg (2003)
46. Culler, J.: Literary Theory, A Brief Insight, Sterling (2009)

A Constraint-Based Approach to Context

Arlette van Wissen[1], Bart Kamphorst[2], and Rob van Eijk[3]

[1] VU University Amsterdam, De Boelelaan 1081a,
1081 HV Amsterdam, The Netherlands
a.van.wissen@vu.nl
[2] Utrecht University, Janskerkhof 13A,
3512 BL Utrecht, The Netherlands
b.a.kamphorst@uu.nl
[3] Leiden University, Faculty Campus Den Haag,
Postbus 13228, 2501 EE Den Haag, The Netherlands
r.j.van.eijk@umail.leidenuniv.nl

Abstract. Finding a shared understanding of context that is both theoretically coherent and operationalizable — e.g., for application in robotics, intelligent agent systems, or e-coaching products — is a significant challenge currently present in context research. This paper tries to capture the myriad of factors that together shape the multifaceted notion of context by conceptualizing the boundaries of contexts as a multitude of constraints within which actors operate. Within this 'constraint-based approach', context is broken down into different types, distinguishing between external and internal, as well as individual and shared contexts. In addition, it introduces vocabulary to differentiate between types of context transitions. This vocabulary is used to explain misinterpretations of context and misunderstandings between actors about the current context. Finally, the paper proposes a way of understanding context synchronization (or, context conflict resolution) between actors through context negotiation.

Keywords: context, constraints, transitions, negotiation.

1 Introduction

Contexts are related to, but different from, situations (Edmonds, 2012; Gero and Smith, 2009) and the environment (Zimmermann et al., 2007). However, even with this distinction in place, the notion of context still means (sometimes radically) different things to different people.[1] Finding a shared understanding of context that is theoretically coherent and can also be operationalized for application in robotics, intelligent (e-coaching, agent) systems, and other fields, is a significant challenge currently present in context research.

---

[1] Just consider how intuitions differ about what context is exactly between those researchers studying social norms, those who use context to explain cognitive phenomena such as learning, and those who design ambient systems.

P. Brézillon, P. Blackburn, and R. Dapoigny (Eds.): CONTEXT 2013, LNAI 8175, pp. 171–184, 2013.
© Springer-Verlag Berlin Heidelberg 2013

This paper proposes a conceptual model for context. The paper has three distinct aims. First, it tries to capture the myriad of factors that together shape the multifaceted notion of context by conceptualizing the boundaries of contexts as a series of constraints within which actors operate.[2] Within this 'constraint-based approach', context is broken down into different types, distinguishing between external and internal, as well as individual and shared contexts. Secondly, it aims to differentiate between types of context transitions. To do so, a vocabulary is introduced to explain misinterpretations of context and misunderstandings between actors about the current context. Thirdly, the paper proposes a way of understanding context synchronization (or, context conflict resolution) between actors through *context negotiation*.

The structure of the paper is as follows. Section 2 discusses related work on (operationalizations of) context. Section 3 explains the constraint-based approach in detail. Section 4 is concerned with transitions in context (Section 4.1) and the process of context negotiation (Section 4.2). In Section 5 four distinct cases are analyzed using the constraint-based approach. These cases are chosen to represent one specific dimension of constraints (e.g., case 1 is primarily concerned with legal constraints). Finally, Section 6 discusses possibilities for operationalizing the constraint-based approach and other ideas for future research.

2 Related Work

One of the main concerns in context research is how to define context such that it is general enough to avoid coping with unnecessary details and complexity, yet at the same time specific enough that it allows for a meaningful interpretation of behavior and appropriate responses:

> The key challenge in developing contextual theories is to identify from among the myriad of potentially relevant situational factors those that are most crucial for understanding the form and occurrence of the target phenomenon. I will refer to that subset of influential situational factors as the effective context of the target phenomenon. (Stokols, 1987, p. 144)

The study of context spans a broad range of disciplines and many works address this challenge. In this section we focus on the ones that inspired our approach.

Clitheroe, Stokols, and Zmuidzinas aim to find a conceptualization of context that is able to explain and accommodate desired behavior in the world (Clitheroe et al., 1998). In their work they differentiate between context, environment, behavior setting, and situation. They argue that a contextual approach requires clear delineation of: (1) the prompts that initiate behaviors; (2) the behaviors, which are the focus of the context; (3) all relevant personal factors; (4) all formal social factors; (5) all informal social factors; (6) the physical factors relevant to the context; (7) the time period of responding to the prompt occurs;

---

[2] In this paper, human beings are distinguished from computer agents (hereinafter, agents). The term 'actor' can refer to both.

and (8) the effect of outcomes of the process. Although many authors distinguish between contexts, situations and environments, it often remains unclear how these constructs and their relations with one another can be defined more precisely. A formal approach can shed light on the exact definitions of, and relations between such constructs.

McCarthy was one of the first to attempt a formal approach to context, by considering contexts as formal objects. Such objects could be used to provide logic-based artificial intelligence (AI) programs capabilities such as human fact representation and reasoning processes (McCarthy, 1986). The main building block is the relation *ist(c,p)* that asserts that proposition *p* is true in the context *c*. McCarthy does not offer a definition of context, but rather specifies how context can be used and applied in reasoning. McCarthy's proposal was used as a basis for a formal context model of natural language, proposed by Akman and Surav (1996). Their model is based on situation theory, which uses the notion of *constraints* to indicate how information in language can be inferred from situations (Devlin, 1991). Although their approach does incorporate constraints, it is nevertheless very different from the one we propose here, which uses constraints to reason about the limits of context.

Gero and Smith approach context with the design of intelligent systems (agents) in mind (Gero and Smith, 2009). They provide a distinction between contexts and *situations*, describing the external world of an agent as the aggregation of all entities that the agent can sense or affect, and context as that part of the external world that the agent interacts with and is *aware* of. Gero and Smith also define 'common ground', which is the interpretation of the world according to memories of past experiences and interpretation of the current situation. Their work suggests relations between context, situations, and common grounds. Similar relations are presupposed in the literature addressed in this section. However, few works address the specific nature of such relations or discuss under which circumstances contexts are altered.

In Clitheroe et al. (1998), the authors do discuss contextual changes and refine the term 'contextual change' to *contextual shifts* and *contextual transformations*. Shifts are incremental changes in predictable or understandable ways that do not significantly disrupt the context (i.e. the same behaviors remain appropriate), while transformations constitute a fundamental change in behavior of the participants (Clitheroe et al., 1998).

Zimmermann, Lorenz, and Oppermann also examine several context transitions. They provide a context definition that comprises three parts: a definition in general terms, a (semi-)formal definition, and an operational definition (Zimmermann et al., 2007). The operational extension suggests that something is in a context because of the way it is used in interpretation, not due to its inherent properties. Several context transitions are examined: variation of approximation, change of focus and shift of attention. Furthermore, they state that parts of the context information can be shared by different processes such as establishing relations, adjusting shared contexts and exploiting relations.

It is clear that as of yet there is no general consensus about the correct use and definition of context. Nevertheless, it is useful to distinguish between the types of factors that make up context. In the above-mentioned works, several factors are discussed. Two factors that are not yet discussed but that are often mentioned in relation to context are social environment and *social norms*. Social norms — rules of custom governing group behavior — play an important role in understanding human behavior on a group or organizational level. As such, social norms are an important area of study in the social sciences (e.g., Coleman (1990); Parsons (1951)). With the emergence of game theory and social choice, as well as agent-based and organization-based modeling techniques, norms have received increasing attention from other fields as well, most notably (behavioral) economics (e.g., Ostrom (2000); Young (1998)) and computer science (e.g., Dignum et al. (2000)). This literature suggests a strong link between social norms and context.

Legal norms and policies are also identified as factors of influence with respect to context. For example, **Nissenbaum** discusses the tension between technology, policy and the integrity of social life (Nissenbaum, 2010). Nissenbaum discusses privacy in context, where context is defined as a structural social setting characterized by canonical activities, roles, relationships, power structures, norms, and internal values (Nissenbaum, 2010, 132,181-182). Nissenbaum's approach consists of 9 steps to determine the contextual integrity of a situation.

The present work aims to integrate several intuitions and ideas from the literature as discussed in this section, in an attempt to conceptualize context in a way that is intuitive and has explanatory power in different disciplines. In particular, it proposes that the factors mentioned above can be viewed as different (types of) constraints, which together make up the boundaries of context. In the following section this approach will be explained in more detail.

3   The Constraint-Based Approach

One of the main contributions of this work is that it provides a vocabulary with which to intuitively but precisely describe context, transitions in context, and conflicts between actors about context. We propose a constraint-based approach with several dimensions of constraints to identify and delimit the context of an actor. The main assumption of the approach is that all external context is constrained. Four types of constraints have thus far been identified: *legal, physical, socio-cultural*, and *technical* constraints. Each of these constraint types captures multiple factors.[3] For example, legal constraints are comprised by rules resulting from legislation, such as contracts and statutes. The physical constraints include the physical structures in the environment of actors (e.g., buildings, materials, room dimensions) but also the biological constraints of the body. The socio-cultural constraints include all social relations between actors (e.g., family, friends, spouses), as well as the properties of the structure of such relations

---

[3] The factors mentioned in the following are not an exhaustive list, but serve illustrative purposes.

(hierarchy, authority, leadership) or the role that people have within these relationships. Finally, the technical constraints identify limits imposed by software technology, such as constraints on data use or access (in which they differ from physical limits imposed by hardware, for example). Each constraint type will be illustrated in a use case in Section 5.

Together, the constraints make up the *constraint space* (CS). This CS provides the boundaries of the *external context*. Each individual actor is constrained by a personal external context (PEC_A) within the absolute limits that hold for everyone. That is, within the CS, there can be individual differences in the external context (e.g., someone may have a restraining order against him). The intersection of the personal external contexts of actors is considered *shared external context* (SEC), which for example is relevant when actors are at the same location (cf. Zimmermann et al. (2007)). The shared context between actor α and β can be defined as $SEC_{\alpha\beta} = PEC_\alpha \cap PEC_\beta$.

In addition to an external context each actor has a personal, internal context (PIC_A). PIC_A is constituted by two components. First, it is an *interpretation* of external context. As such, it is a partial representation of the PEC_A as it is fed by observations from the agent's external context. Secondly, PIC_A is constituted by cognitive states, such as relevant beliefs that were learned in other contexts (for instance about traditions or etiquette), motivations or intentions. The personal context of actor α, PC_α, can then be denoted as $PIC_\alpha \cup PEC_\alpha$. Similar to external context, internal contexts can also be shared. The shared internal context (SIC) is composed as $SIC_{\alpha\beta} = PIC_\alpha \cap PIC_\beta$. This relates to the notion of common ground by Goro and Smith (2009), as referred to in Section 2. Comparing the current approach to that of Stokols (1987), it should be noted that the proposed definition of CS can include context that is not directly relevant to the actor. That is, the *effective context* — as used by Stokols — entails only part of the constraint space. Specifically, in the current approach it is the personal context of an actor (PC) that corresponds to Stokols' notion of effective context.

Using the constraints, the behavior of the actors can be identified as *appropriate*, i.e. not violating any of the constraints, or *inappropriate*, i.e. violating one or more constraints. As mentioned above, such interpretation of the constraints is part of the internal context. By interpretation an actor gives meaning to the context, deriving implications for the behaviors that are acceptable in this context. For example, in certain social contexts it is appropriate behavior to make fun of your boss, in others it is not. Note that although the internal context is not delimited by the CS (since it is also constituted by cognitive states), the set of appropriate behaviors (P) is. However, one can accidentally or intentionally violate one of the constraints. In case of accidental violation, there has been a misinterpretation of the PEC, resulting in a set of appropriate behaviors that does not match the context. In case of intentional violation however, an actor chooses to execute behavior b, where $b \notin P$.

Figure 1 presents the contexts of actors α and β. It shows that α and β both have personal external and internal contexts and that they share some, but not all of their context. The arrows indicate the different ways in which elements

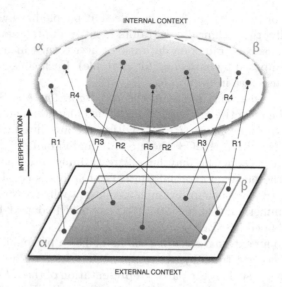

Fig. 1. A visualization of internal and external context for persons α and β

from external context can relate to internal context. The figure also illustrates that PIC is not a perfect reflection of PEC. For instance, the R2 relations show how actors can be constrained by external context without taking this into account (in their PIC). It can also be that there exists a difference between the PICs of two actors who are constrained by the same external constraint. Consider how the point in $SEC_{\alpha\beta}$ for R4 corresponds to PIC_{β} but not to PIC_{α}. Actor α may simply not have taken note of this aspect of PEC_{α}. The relations are represented in Table 1, each with an (informal) example.

The process of identifying and evaluating context can be done from different perspectives: from an observer's perspective an actor might be in one context, whilst from a first person perspective, the actor is in another. Determining which context one is in is a continuous process of reevaluation of the internal context against the external context. For example, consider a scenario where two people in a designated 'quiet car' of a train start having a conversation, to the displeasure of the other passengers. What happens next can be best described as a type of context

Table 1. Relations between internal and external contexts

ID	Relation	Example
R1	$R(PEC_{\alpha}, PIC_{\alpha})$	A playful cat turns α's work context into a play context.
R2	$R(PEC_{\alpha}, PIC_{\beta,\alpha\neq\beta})$	α's friend β learns about the restraining order that α's ex-girlfriend took out against α.
R3	$R(PEC_{\alpha}, SIC_{\alpha\beta})$	α confides to friend β his fear of cats.
R4	$R(SEC_{\alpha\beta}, PIC_{\beta})$	A playful cat turns person β's work context into one of fear while owner α continues working.
R5	$R(SEC_{\alpha\beta}, SIC_{\alpha\beta})$	A loud noise distracts friends α and β from a discussion they were having.

negotiation between actors: will the other passengers adjust their context and corresponding behavior (i.e. accept the noise in the car and exchange reading books for making phone calls) or can they persuade the speakers to be quiet, for instance by pointing towards the sign that indicates a quiet area?

In the next section, we take a closer look at different types of context transitions (Section 4.1) and expand on the idea of context negotiation (Section 4.2).

4   Context Transitions and Conflicts

Contexts are constantly changing (Stokols, 1987). Those changes can be initiated by prompts from the environment, by an individual's or a group's own behavior, or by the outcomes of that behavior (Clitheroe et al., 1998). However, in order to identify such changes and to understand their implications for the extent to which context is shared, it is necessary to further specify the concepts that govern context dynamics.

4.1   Shifts, Transformations, Changes and Switches

This section introduces four terms that capture different levels of modifications to internal and external context: *shifts, transformations, changes* and *switches*. We borrow the notions of contextual shift and contextual transformation from Clitheroe et al. (1998) to refer to modifications of internal contexts. A contextual *shift* is defined as "the subtle evolutionary contextual change that occurs when personal, social, or physical contextual factors incrementally change in predictable or understandable ways that do not significantly disrupt the context (the relationships between focal variables and contextual factors) under consideration" (Clitheroe et al., 1998, p. 106). Importantly, "[d]uring contextual shifts, the same or very similar behaviors remain appropriate responses to the prompts that initiated individual or collective action" (Clitheroe et al., 1998, p. 107). That is, the set of appropriate behaviors does not (or very minimally) change due to a contextual shift. This is different in case of a transformation. A *transformation* is a "sudden and/or dramatic contextual change, [which] is the result of significant change in one or more personal, social or physical factors comprising the context, or in the individual's or group's behavior" (Stokols (1988), as cited by Clitheroe et al. (1998, p. 107)). A transformation — which can be either self-initiated or in reaction to cues in the environment (Clitheroe et al., 1998, p. 108) — results in a significantly different or 'new' context and as such entails a fundamental change in the set of appropriate behaviors.

While Clitheroe et al. use shifts and transformations to talk about contextual modifications in general, we propose to use it solely to refer to modifications of the internal context. However, the definitions of shifts and transformations demonstrate a close relation with events in the external context. We propose to use two different but related concepts to refer to such events, namely contextual *changes* and *switches*. See Table 2 for an overview. Contextual *changes* relate to external context in the same way contextual shifts relate to the internal

Table 2. Shifts, transformations, changes and switches

Name	Int/Ext	Example
Shift	Internal	Person A adjusts his context slightly when person C joins a conversation A was having with friend B.
Transformation	Internal	Person A's context is transformed from a work context to a play context by his cat.
Change	External	Colleague B enters the conference room person A is in.
Switch	External	Person A enters his office building.

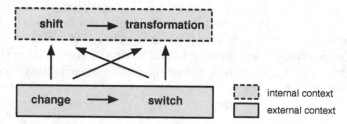

Fig. 2. Relations between different types of alterations in internal and external context

context, in the sense that they are minor, gradual changes that are predictable or understandable in the current context. More precisely, they refer to small, non-significant alterations in one of the constraints in the CS. Context *switches* on the other hand are sudden and significant alterations to the external context, caused by many or large alterations in the CS. Accumulations of contextual changes/shifts can also result in a switch/transformation. Figure 2 shows how the modifications in internal and external context relate to each other. It seems plausible that the degree to which the external context changes is reflected by the degree to which the internal context changes. As such, one expects an external change to result in an internal shift, and an external switch in an internal transformation. However, one can imagine that a change can result in a transformation (see case 3 in Section 5.3), or a switch in a shift (e.g., changing from indoor tennis to outdoor tennis).

4.2   Appropriate Behaviors and Context Negotiation

Actors constantly reevaluate their internal context by contrasting observations from their external environment with their internal context. The set of appropriate behaviors for a particular context is tested against the happenings in the world. Any observation that deviates from what is expected should be resolved. Minor discrepancies between internal and external contexts are often smoothed over automatically by making minor *shifts*. However, under certain circumstances, mostly when the discrepancies are large, a more significant modification of the context would be justified.[4] First, there is an evaluation of whether

---

[4] In this process of detecting changes in context, attention will play an important role (see, e.g., Rensink et al. (1997)).

the new, observed behavior is compatible with the set of appropriate behaviors. If so, PIC should be modified with a *shift*. An example of this is when one learns an unspoken rule in a gentleman's club (e.g., never ask a man about his salary) that is consistent with other rules about topics that are better left undiscussed. If the new behavior seems incompatible with the appropriate behaviors, however, an actor can actively probe the environment for clues about the current context. For instance, are there any signs that a *switch* happened without the actor knowing? If so, a *transformation* is in order. If not, then it might be time to negotiate context.

In social settings, it is not always clear what the context is. Yet, because different contexts bring along different sets of appropriate behavior, it is important for actors to 'synchronize' contexts. We propose that this synchronization process is a type of negotiation between actors where the shared goal is to resolve any (major) conflicts about the context. Of course, actors can have other goals and motivations (pure selfishness could be one) for wanting the other actors to adjust to their context instead of vice versa. Context negotiations will involve trading information about the current context. Actor α will try to a) justify PIC_α by giving the reasons for assuming this context, b) convince β by offering information from $SEC_{\alpha,\beta}$ that α assumes is not part of PIC_β, and c) incorporate all the information that β presents in return. In step b) of the negotiation, both actors look for information for which a R2-type relation holds, so that sharing that information will lead to R1. For example, actor α may have observed that actor β did not register the specific change that caused a transformation of α's context. It will be α's hope that notifying β of that change may lead to a similar transformation for β. If, however, α was mistaken about that change being part of PIC_β, than sharing the information changes nothing (cf. R5).

There are two things to take note of. The first is that the environment can provide additional reasons in a negotiation for a particular reading of the context. For instance, in a negotiation between actors whether something is a learning context or a play context, the deciding reason for seeing it as a learning context can be that the current location is specifically designed for it (e.g., a class room). The second is that negotiations are not always rational and reason-based. Sometimes, people make emotional pleas instead. Consider for example a negotiation between α and a group of α's friends Γ about whether something is a learning context or a play context and assume that a) the environmental signs point towards it being a learning context (they are in a class room) and b) the people who are in group Γ all agree that it is a learning context. However, it is perfectly conceivable that if α starts crying and exclaims 'But it's my birthday!' that the people in Γ will transform their context into a play context to accommodate α. The constraint-based approach can explain this outcome because it considers other agents to be part of an agent's external context, making it that the wants and needs of others can also make up some of the constraints of the context. In this way, emotional pleas can be considered on a par with other negotiations: it is α trying to convey part of $SEC_{\alpha,\Gamma}$ to $SIC_{\alpha,\Gamma}$.

5 Case Analyses

This section presents four cases in which context plays an important role. We show that the constraint-based approach can adequately analyze these cases. While the cases are neither stereotypical, nor in any way exhaustive, the scope of the cases demonstrates the promise of the approach.

5.1 Case 1 (Legal Constraint): The Civilian Police Officer

Consider the following scene. Two men are having a row in the middle of a shopping area. It looks as if the argument could be developing into a physical fight. Bystanders are watching from a safe distance, hesitant to interfere. One of the bystanders happens to be an off-duty police officer. Initially, he goes unnoticed by the bystanders and the arguing men. After assessing the situation, the officer takes off his overcoat to reveal his police uniform. Suddenly, things change: nearby bystanders, noticing the uniform, clear out a path, and people start to whisper. When the officer approaches the two arguing men, they need only a split second to realize that they had better cool down, so they do.

   Looking at the context of this scenario from a broader perspective, it might seem hard to explain these events. The external context was one of a beginning fight, with a police officer on scene. The fact that the police officer took off his overcoat does not change this, so why would it have an effect? To give a proper analysis of this scenario, the individual's contexts have to be taken into account.

Officer. The officer's internal context (PIC_o) was modified only slightly with a *shift*. He had anticipated that showing his uniform would bring about a *transformation* in context for others, but not his own. His external context (PEC_o) did *change* because of the altered attitude from the surrounding people.

Man_1. The external context of Man_1 (PEC_{m1}) *changed* only slightly when the police officer presented himself. However, seeing the police uniform caused a *transformation* of Man_1's internal context (PIC_{m1}) because it made salient (i.e. brought to his attention) the constraints imposed by the law. For example, Man_1 was suddenly more aware of the possible consequences of the argument turning violent.

Man_2. The story of Man_2 is in many respects similar to that of Man_1. A slight *change* in his external context (PEC_{m2}) — which he shared for a large part with Man_1 $(SEC_{m1,m2})$ — triggered a *transformation* of his internal context. Notice, however, that the internal constraints of Man_2 are more strict assuming he recalled that he had been convicted for two prior offenses. Because a third offense would land him in jail, his internal context was more constrained than that of Man_1.

Bystander X. From the bystander's perspective (bystander b_X from the group of bystanders B), the internal context (PIC_{b_X}) *shifted* because of a slight *change* in the external context, namely the police officer revealing himself.

Finally, to complete the analysis, the shared external context $SEC_{m1,m2,o,B}$ was extended after the police officer showed his uniform because everyone became aware that a police officer was present at the scene.

5.2   Case 2 (Physical Constraint): The Ineffective e-Coach

Suggestion technology is about *kairos*: "providing the right information at the best time" (Andrew et al., 2007, p. 259). What should be considered 'the best time', is highly context-dependent. Consider an e-coaching system designed to support overeater Amy in her aim of making healthy food choices. Suppose that the system's strategy is to send motivational messages to Amy in order to prevent her from buying unhealthy foods. Such messages would be particularly relevant when she is indeed in a position to buy unhealthy foods. However, one's current mindset is also crucial: suggesting to Amy not to buy candy when she in a supermarket might have the adverse effect if buying candy had not even crossed her mind at the time of the intervention. Bringing candy to Amy's attention might just cause her to pick some up!

Now assume that Amy did in fact buy candy, after having specifically been instructed not to. How should this case be analyzed in terms of context? Referring to Figure 1, take Amy to be α and the e-coach to be β. With regard to the external context $SEC_{\alpha,\beta}$, α was indeed in a context in which candy could easily be purchased. So, given that α is an overeater with sweets being a particular weakness, solely on the basis of this information, β would be right to try and steer α away from buying candy. So why did the intervention fail? Because the temptations that were present in PEC_α — and in $SEC_{\alpha,\beta}$ — were not included in PIC_α. Only when β's message made α aware of the lurking temptations, did α's internal context *shift* to include the tempting treats in PIC_α. The temptations were however clearly present in PIC_β, corresponding to R4 of Table 1. The 'coaching error' stems from β assuming incorrectly that because the temptations were in $SEC_{\alpha,\beta}$ and also in PIC_β, that they would also be present in PIC_α.

5.3   Case 3 (Socio-cultural Constraint): The Patriotic Kids

This third case shows how social and cultural norms play a role in determining context. Consider an English child who goes to an American Boy Scouts camp for the summer. On day 1, the child, speaking the same language (albeit with a different accent) as the other kids, has no problem fitting in. Just like he does back home, he interacts with his peers in a natural manner and collaborates without a problem when the situation (or the Scout Leader!) demands it (e.g., setting up tents, building fires, etc.). So, it can be assumed that there is no inherent problem for the child to navigate between contexts.

On day 2, the scouts are asked to gather around the flag pole. The atmosphere is light and the boys are a little rowdy. That is, until the national flag is brought out. All of a sudden, the American boys fall silent, they stand up straight, facing the flag-bearer, waiting for him to present the colors. When he does, the boys perform a hand-to-forehead salute and recite the pledge of allegiance.

This whole episode leaves the English boy baffled. The reason for this is not that he is ill-adapted socially, but that he did not know the proper response to a culturally significant event. The boy witnessed the exact same *change* (the flag being brought in), but it did not lead to a *transformation*, as apparently it did for the American boys (judging from the modified (appropriate) behavior matching a ceremonial rather than an informal context).

5.4   Case 4 (Technical Constraint): Interest-Based Advertising

The fourth case shows how technical constraints play a role in determining contextual integrity. Similar to the application of the framework proposed by Nissenbaum, the contextual integrity can be determined using the constraint-based approach we propose.

Today's digital ad ecosystem is a complex network of different parties. Ads are no longer static images served directly from the website a user is visiting. When a user visits a web page, a request is generated that spins out to a number of parties that trade in real time in ad exchanges for the advertisement space available on the web page.[5] Parties looking to bid may augment user data with information from users' browsing history previously collected on the Internet. Data brokers may add information about the user such that a rich profile motivates the decision to bid on a chance to show an ad to the user.

Consider Bob, who on Sunday visits the sports page of his favorite news site. The page contains an ad for an expensive sports watch. The ad doesn't stand out, as Bob is reading all kinds of sports-related content. He is not interested in the ad, and continues to visit other websites. On some of these sites the sports watch ad is also displayed, which Bob notices. On Monday, the ad shows up again, this time when Bob is surfing online for work. Suddenly, the fact that the ad is shown outside of the original sports page makes him ill at ease and concerned for his browsing privacy. Why is Bob's reaction to the ad suddenly different? Because Bob's internal context has transformed from a leisure context to a work-related context and he now judges the ad as inappropriate.

6   Discussion and Conclusion

Some points for discussion remain. One concern is the normative status of the set of appropriate behaviors P that an actor considers. As discussed, P is influenced by social norms, which in the constraint-based approach are taken to be part of the socio-cultural constraints.[6] Social norms carry some normativity in that they function as 'social guidelines' by prescribing appropriate group

---

[5] See for example an animation on behavioural advertising by **CM Summit (2013)** 'Behind the banner', URL: http://cmsummit.com/behindthebanner/, and a description of Real Time Bidding by **Natasha Singer (2012)**, 'You for sale. Your Attention, Bought in an Instant', NY Times, Online edition 17 Nov. 2012, URL: http://www.nytimes.com/2012/11/18/technology/ your-online-attention-bought-in-an-instant-by-advertisers.html

[6] This should by no means be seen as downplaying the importance of social norms. A good theory of social norms is crucial to understanding group dynamics.

behavior. Because of this, we contend that P also carries some normativity, for if an actor's intention is to act appropriately within a context, P limits his options for action. Given that social norms are constraints in the external context, some norms can be lost in the translation to an actor's internal context. Also, actors can actively try to influence other actors' P, as they can negotiate context.

A second point relates to the citation of Stokols from Section 2, where he points out the importance of identifying those factors that are *most crucial* for understanding a phenomenon. The constraint-based approach does identify different types of context determinants but does not specify whether and to what extent they are significant. In Section 3 it was mentioned that the PEC corresponds to the *effective context*, as the constraints that are not relevant to an actor's context are not part of that context. It remains an open question how this relevance can be determined. This is also connected with the process of the *extension or reduction* of the PEC to include or exclude constraints. As hinted at in Sections 4.2, 5.1 and 5.2, we suspect that attention plays a key role in this process (in line with Zimmermann et al., 2007).

The present work is a step towards developing a shared vocabulary for the different disciplines that study context. This vocabulary can be used to describe why actors sometimes misunderstand contexts and why they can have conflicts about context. It also introduces context negotiation as a way of resolving these conflicts. The constraint-based approach is however not a complete theory. Many interesting directions for future research remain. For example, future work should provide a detailed account of the sets of appropriate behaviors, explaining for instance how these sets relate to action selection. Furthermore, the conceptual model presented here can serve as a starting point for constraint-based formal and computational models of context. In this work, we have not not stipulated any negotiation protocols or strategies for successful negotiation. Future work could explore different protocols and strategies, both in agent-based social simulations (e.g., concerning decision making in emergency situations, cf. Bosse et al. (2013)), and in settings where humans and agents interact in teams (such as team trainings in virtual environments, cf. Traum et al. (2003)). Particularly interesting would be to examine whether constraint-based reasoning is a good mechanism for designing effective strategies. Finding effective strategies is especially important for the design of ambient coaching systems that use intervention techniques to suggest appropriate actions. Such systems need to reason about the actions of a user as well as their own, and therefore need a model that includes the context of both, and use this to identify and resolve possible conflicts.

Acknowlegdements. The foundation for this paper was laid during the Lorentz Center 'Workshop on Formal methods for the Informal World' (http://www.lorentzcenter.nl/lc/web/2013/531/info.php3?wsid=531). Our gratitude goes out to the scientific organizers of the workshop, as well as the participants who contributed to the 'context group', especially Bruce Edmonds. This contribution was supported by Philips and Technology Foundation STW, Nationaal Initiatief Hersenen en Cognitie NIHC under the Partnership programme Healthy Lifestyle Solutions.

References

Akman, V., Surav, M.: The use of situation theory in context modeling. Computational Intelligence 13(3), 427–438 (1996)

Andrew, A., Borriello, G., Fogarty, J.: Toward a systematic understanding of suggestion tactics in persuasive technologies. In: de Kort, Y., IJsselsteijn, W.A., Midden, C., Eggen, B., Fogg, B.J. (eds.) PERSUASIVE 2007. LNCS, vol. 4744, pp. 259–270. Springer, Heidelberg (2007)

Bosse, T., Hoogendoorn, M., Klein, M., Treur, J., van der Wal, C.N., van Wissen, A.: Modelling collective decision making in groups and crowds: Integrating social contagion and interacting emotions, beliefs and intentions. Autonomous Agents and Multi-Agent Systems Journal (JAAMAS) 27(1), 52–84 (2013)

Clitheroe Jr., H., Stokols, D., Zmuidzinas, M.: Conceptualizing the context of environment and behavior. Journal of Environmental Psychology (1998)

Coleman, J.: Foundations of Social Theory. Belknap, Cambridge (1990)

Devlin, K.: Logic and information. Cambridge UP, New York (1991)

Dignum, F., Morley, D., Sonenberg, E., Cavedon, L.: Towards socially sophisticated bdi agents. In: Proc. of 4th International Conference on MultiAgent Systems, pp. 111–118 (2000)

Edmonds, B.: Complexity and context-dependency. In: Foundations of Science. Springer (2012)

Gero, J., Smith, G.: Context, situations, and design agents. Knowledge-Based Systems 22(8), 600–609 (2009)

McCarthy, J.: Notes on formalizing context. In: Kehler, T., Rosenschein, S. (eds.) Proc. of the Fifth National Conference on Artificial Intelligence, pp. 555–560. Morgan Kaufmann (1986)

Nissenbaum, H.: Technology, Policy, and the Integrity of Social Life. Stanford UP, Stanford (2010)

Ostrom, E.: Collective action and the evolution of social norms. The Journal of Economic Perspectives 14(3), 137–158 (2000)

Parsons, T.: The Social System. Routledge, New York (1951)

Rensink, R., O'Regan, J., Clark, J.: To see or not to see: The need for attention to perceive changes in scenes. Psychological Science 8, 368–373 (1997)

Stokols, D.: Conceptual strategies of environmental psychology. John Wiley & Sons, New York (1987)

Stokols, D.: Transformational process in people-environment relations, pp. 233–252. Sage Publications, Beverly Hills (1988)

Traum, D., Rickel, J., Gratch, J., Marsella, S.: Negotiation over tasks in hybrid human-agent teams for simulation-based training. In: Proceedings of the Second International Joint Conference on Autonomous Agents and Multiagent Systems, AAMAS 2003, pp. 441–448. ACM, New York (2003)

Young, H.: Social norms and economic welfare. European Economic Review 42, 821–830 (1998)

Zimmermann, A., Lorenz, A., Oppermann, R.: An operational definition of context. In: Kokinov, B., Richardson, D.C., Roth-Berghofer, T.R., Vieu, L. (eds.) CONTEXT 2007. LNCS (LNAI), vol. 4635, pp. 558–571. Springer, Heidelberg (2007)

Contextual Validity in Hybrid Logic

Patrick Blackburn and Klaus Frovin Jørgensen

Department for Philosophy and Science Studies
Roskilde University

Abstract. Hybrid tense logic is an extension of Priorean tense logic in which it is possible to refer to times using special propositional symbols called nominals. Temporal indexicals are expressions such as *now*, *yesterday*, *today*, *tomorrow* and *four days ago* that have highly context-dependent interpretations. Moreover, such indexicals give rise to a special kind of validity—*contextual validity*—that interacts with ordinary logical validity in interesting and often unexpected ways. In this paper we model these interactions by combining standard techniques from hybrid logic with insights from the work of Hans Kamp and David Kaplan. We introduce a simple proof rule, which we call the Kamp Rule, and first we show that it is all we need to take us from logical validities involving *now* to contextual validities involving *now* too. We then go on to show that this deductive bridge is strong enough to carry us to contextual validities involving *yesterday*, *today* and *tomorrow* as well.

1   Introduction

Hybrid tense logic is an extension of Priorean tense logic in which it is possible to refer to times using special propositional symbols called nominals. Temporal indexicals are expressions such as *now*, *yesterday*, *today*, *tomorrow* and *four days ago*. The most obvious fact about temporal indexicals (and indeed, other indexicals such as *I*, *you*, and *here*) is that their interpretation is highly context-dependent. A less obvious fact about them is that they give rise to a new kind of validity—*contextual validity*—that interacts in interesting (and tricky) ways with logical validity. Modelling these interactions is a challenging task.

The logical study of temporal indexicals was initiated by Hans Kamp in his paper "Formal properties of 'now'" [8]. This introduced several ideas—most notably, *two-dimensional semantics*—which have since become widely used in a number of fields. Kamp's work was refined and generalized to other indexicals by David Kaplan [9], who introduced the concept of *character*. The character of an indexical expression is a function specifying how the indexical exploits the context of utterance. For example, the character of *I* is a function which maps this indexical to the speaker in a given context, whereas the character of *you* maps this indexical to the person or people being addressed. We will specify characters for *now*, *yesterday*, *today*, and *tomorrow* later in this paper.

Both Kamp and Kaplan worked with ordinary tense logics. But, as has already been mentioned, there is a referential extension of tense logic called hybrid

P. Brézillon, P. Blackburn, and R. Dapoigny (Eds.): CONTEXT 2013, LNAI 8175, pp. 185–198, 2013.
© Springer-Verlag Berlin Heidelberg 2013

logic. Because hybrid logic allows reference to times, it seems natural to use it as the base logic for explorations of indexicals in the spirit of Kamp and Kaplan. After all, expressions such as *now, yesterday, today,* and *tomorrow* clearly do refer to certain (contextually selected) times, so why not work with a logic in which temporal reference is built in? The idea of using hybrid logic in this way dates back to Blackburn [1], and was explored in more depth by Blackburn and Jørgensen [3]. The latter paper gave complete tableau systems for hybrid reasoning with *now, yesterday, today,* and *tomorrow,* but it did something else which we think is more important: it showed that the indexical *now* acts as a sort of 'deductive bridge' between ordinary logical validity and contextual validity. This is rather surprising. It has been known ever since Kamp's pioneering work that the operator associated with 'now' is in a sense expressively weak. Nonetheless, in spite of its expressive weakness, 'now' is deductively important.

The present paper explores and clarifies this idea. We do so in two ways. First, we change the underlying semantics. In our previous paper, we used Kamp's original two-dimensional semantics for Now; here we shall use an (equivalent) semantics called *designated time semantics*. This is closer to the standard semantics of hybrid logic and is (we believe) more perspicuous. Second, we move from tableau-based deduction, to Hilbert-style axiomatic deduction. This may seem strange. Aren't tableaus easier to use than axiom systems? They certainly are—but in this paper we are not particularly interested in actually doing deductions. Rather, our goal is to clarify the inferential architecture, and axiom systems are a good way of doing that.

We proceed as follows. In Section 2 we introduce the basics of hybrid tense logic. In Section 3 we make an (almost invisible) extension, adding a new nominal *now* to the language. In Section 4 we introduce a standard axiomatization for hybrid tense logic and show that it is complete for the *now*-enriched language. At least, it's complete as far a *logical* validity is concerned, but what about *contextual* validity? Section 5 provides the answer. We introduce one more (very simple) rule which we call the Kamp Rule. The rule is unusual in that it can only be used once in any proof, and only as the very last step. Nonetheless, this rule is the bridge from the world of logical validity to the world of contextual validity. Moreover, as Section 6 shows, if we walk across this narrow bridge we will find the contextual logics of *yesterday, today,* and *tomorrow* waiting on the other side, as the Kamp Rule feeds a crucial piece of contextual information to the character functions of these indexicals. Section 7 concludes.

2   Hybrid Tense Logic

As already said, hybrid tense logic is a simple extension of ordinary Priorean tense logic in which it is possible to refer to times. It can do this because it contains a collection of special propositional symbols called *nominals*. Nominals are true at one and only one time: they 'name' the time they are true at. This is the framework we will use to explore temporal indexicals, so to get the ball rolling, let's define its syntax and semantics.

Let $\mathcal{L}$ be a standard minimal hybrid tense language: a set Nom of nominals, a set Prop of ordinary propositional symbols, boolean operators $\neg$ and $\wedge$, an $@_i$-operator for each nominal i, and two (existential) tense operators P and F. Formulas of $\mathcal{L}$ are built as follows:

$$\varphi ::= i \mid p \mid \neg\varphi \mid \varphi \wedge \psi \mid P\varphi \mid F\varphi \mid @_i\varphi.$$

We define $G\varphi$ to be $\neg F\neg\varphi$ and $H\varphi$ to be $\neg P\neg\varphi$ and say that G and F, and H and P, are dual operator pairs. Likewise, boolean symbols such as $\vee$, $\rightarrow$, $\leftrightarrow$ and $\bot$ are defined in the usual way. Note that a nominal i can occur syntactically in two distinct ways: in *formula position* as the atomic symbol i, or in *operator position* as in $@_i\varphi$. Finally, if a formula contains no ordinary propositional symbols, but only nominals as atomic symbols, it is a *pure formula*.

Models $\mathfrak{m}$ are based on frames (T, R). We think of T as a set of times and R as the earlier-later relation. What properties should R have? Well, we typically think of R as an irreflexive and transitive relation. But sometimes we think of it as a linear relation, and sometimes we think of it as branching towards the future. Moreover, for some applications we may want to think of R as dense, whereas for others we may need a discrete temporal order. And sometimes we want a first (or last) point of time, and sometimes we don't. Fortunately, we don't need to make such choices here: they are easy to specify axiomatically in hybrid logic (we'll discuss this later) so we don't need to hardwire them into the semantics. Thus we are free to work with an arbitrary relation R.

But to fully specify a model we also need an *information distribution* together with a *specification of names* for times of interest. Both tasks are performed by a valuation function V, which takes propositional symbols and nominals to subsets of points of T. Ordinary propositional symbols are unrestricted in their interpretation: they encode ordinary information, such as when it is raining, or when the printer was enabled, or when Felicity had her disastrous relationship with Brad. But we place an important restriction on the valuation $V(i)$ of any nominal i: this must be a *singleton* subset of T. This means (as we said above) that nominals enable us to specify names for times in T.

Given a model $\mathfrak{m} = (T, R, V)$ we define *satisfaction* as follows:

$$\mathfrak{m}, t \models a \qquad \text{iff} \quad a \text{ is atomic and } t \in V(a)$$
$$\mathfrak{m}, t \models \neg\varphi \qquad \text{iff} \quad \mathfrak{m}, t \not\models \varphi$$
$$\mathfrak{m}, t \models \varphi \wedge \psi \qquad \text{iff} \quad \mathfrak{m}, t \models \varphi \text{ and } \mathfrak{m}, t \models \psi$$
$$\mathfrak{m}, t \models P\varphi \qquad \text{iff} \quad \text{for some } t', t'Rt \text{ and } \mathfrak{m}, t' \models \varphi$$
$$\mathfrak{m}, t \models F\varphi \qquad \text{iff} \quad \text{for some } t', tRt' \text{ and } \mathfrak{m}, t' \models \varphi$$
$$\mathfrak{m}, t \models @_i\varphi \qquad \text{iff} \quad \mathfrak{m}, t' \models \varphi \text{ and } t' \in V(i).$$

Most of this is familiar from ordinary Priorean tense logic. In particular, $F\varphi$ scans the future looking for a time where φ is true (thus it makes an existential claim about the future) while its dual form, $G\varphi$, claims that φ is going to be true at all future times (a universal claim). Analogously, $P\varphi$ scans the past looking for a φ-verifying time, while $H\varphi$ claims that φ has always been true in the past.

What is new is the role played by the nominals and the @-operators. First, note that an atom a can be either a nominal or a propositional symbol, so the first clause of the definition handles both types of symbol in a uniform way. It also means that our fundamental restriction on the interpretation of nominals is built right into the heart of the satisfaction definition. Next, note that $@_i\varphi$ is satisfied at a time in a model $\mathfrak{M}$ if and only if φ is satisfied at the time that i names in $\mathfrak{M}$. So to speak, $@_i\varphi$ peeks at the time named i (and there *must* be such a time because of the restriction imposed on the interpretation of nominals) and checks whether φ is satisfied then or not. Note also that a formula of the form $@_i\varphi$ is satisfied at the time named i in $\mathfrak{M}$ if and only if it is satisfied at *all* times in $\mathfrak{M}$; this is because all that is relevant for formulas of this form is whether φ is satisfied at the point named i or not.

We say that a formula φ is *true in a model* $\mathfrak{M}$ if and only if it is satisfied at all times in $\mathfrak{M}$, and we say that φ is *logically valid* if and only if it is true in all models. Some examples of logical validity may be helpful: the propositional tautology $p \vee \neg p$ is (obviously) logically valid, as is the ordinary Priorean tense logical formula $Fp \vee Fq \rightarrow F(p \vee q)$, which simply says that if p is true in the future or q is true in the future then $p \vee q$ is true in the future. More interestingly, here's a genuinely *hybrid* tense logical validity: it contains an ordinary propositional symbol p and a nominal i in both formula and operator position:

$$Fi \wedge @_ip \rightarrow Fp.$$

This says that if the point named i lies in the future, and p is true at the point named i, then p will be true in the future. Intuitively, this should be logically valid, and indeed its validity follows from the definitions just given.

That's all we need to know about hybrid tense logic for the moment, so let's turn to the central task of the paper: the modelling of temporal indexicality.

3   Adding *now*

For a start, we will just add the temporal indexical *now* to our language. This will be the most straightforward addition we shall make—we're pretty much going to treat *now* as a nominal—but it will turn out to be the most fundamental. As we shall see, *now* is a key that will let us unlock the contextual semantics of the temporal indexicals *yesterday*, *today*, and *tomorrow*. By the end of the paper it will be clear that although *now* is a nominal, it is not 'just another' nominal.

And so to work. We first add the new atomic symbol *now* to $\mathcal{L}$, thus obtaining the language $\mathcal{L}(now)$. Syntactically, *now* is simply a nominal. Like ordinary nominals, *now* can occur in formula position as the atomic symbol *now*, and in operator position, as in $@_{now}\varphi$. Indeed, this latter expression is simply our hybrid-logical reconstruction of Hans Kamp's [8] celebrated Now operator.

But what is its semantics? The idea we shall use here is simplicity itself: take an ordinary model $\mathfrak{M} = (T, R, V)$ for hybrid tense logic and choose one of its times (that is, an element of T) as the *designated time*. Later in the paper, when we model other temporal indexicals and introduce character functions, we shall think of the designated time as the "utterance time of the context associated with the model". But here we just think of the designated time as the now of the model, and insist that our new atomic symbol *now* names now.

Spelling this out precisely, a *designated time model* $\mathfrak{M} = (T, R, V, t_0)$ is an ordinary model $\mathfrak{M}' = (T, R, V')$, together with a designated time $t_0 \in T$, where V is V' extended in the following way:

$$V(a) = \begin{cases} \{t_0\}, & \text{if } a \text{ is } now, \\ V'(a), & \text{otherwise.} \end{cases}$$

So the fact that *now* denotes the designated time—that is, that *now* really does mean now—is hardwired into the definition of what valuations are.[1]

Given the concept of a designated time model $\mathfrak{M} = (T, R, V, t_0)$, the satisfaction definition for $\mathcal{L}(now)$ is a straightforward extension of the one given earlier for hybrid tense logic. Indeed, to the earlier given clauses we simply add:

$$\mathfrak{M}, t \models now \qquad \text{iff} \quad t \in V(now)$$
$$\mathfrak{M}, t \models @_{now}\varphi \quad \text{iff} \quad \mathfrak{M}, t' \models \varphi \text{ and } t' \in V(now).$$

Because the special role played by the designated time t_0 is built into the definition of the valuation V, these clauses (which have exactly the same form as the clauses for ordinary nominals) guarantee that *now* really is a name for t_0, and that $@_{now}$ really is a hybrid-logical reconstruction of Kamp's Now operator.

We are ready for an idea that has underpinned the study of indexical expressions since the pioneering work of Hans Kamp and David Kaplan: *indexicals are interesting because they give rise to a new species of validity*. As before, we have the familiar notion of logical validity, and indeed this is defined for $\mathcal{L}(now)$ in the same manner as it was for $\mathcal{L}$. That is, a formula φ is *true in a designated time model* $\mathfrak{M}$ if and only if it is satisfied at all times in $\mathfrak{M}$, and φ is *logically valid* when it is true in all designated time models.

But indexicals introduce a second notion of validity, which we call contextual validity. A formula φ is *contextually true* in a designated time model $\mathfrak{M}$ if and only if it is satisfied *at the designated point* t_0 *of* $\mathfrak{M}$. That is, contextual truth in $\mathfrak{M}$ means that $\mathfrak{M}, t_0 \models \varphi$. And now for the crucial definition: a formula φ is *contextually valid* when it is contextually true in all designated time models. In words: a contextual validity is a formula that is true at the now of every model.

---

[1] Kamp's classic "Formal properties of 'now'" [8] uses a different semantics: it uses (indeed it introduced) the idea of *two-dimensional semantics* in which formulas are evaluated at *pairs* of times. But the approach we are using in this paper, which is sometimes called *pointed semantics*, also has a long history; for example, it was used by John Burgess [6] in his 1984 survey of tense logic when discussing Kamp's work. Moreover, pointed semantics is generally the preferred option in contemporary discussions of the Actuality operator, a modal operator that picks out the actual world in much the same way that the Now operator selects the utterance time; see Blackburn and Marx [4] for discussion and results. It would be a mistake to exaggerate the differences between the two approaches (for the simple propositional systems discussed here they are equivalent) and indeed our earlier work on temporal indexicals (see Blackburn and Jørgensen [3]) used Kaplan's generalisation of Kamp's original two-dimensional semantics. Nonetheless, we find the approach used here more perspicuous, both technically and conceptually.

Contextual validity is central to this paper, so let's consider some examples. As discussed earlier, propositional tautologies like $p \vee \neg p$, are logically valid, as are more complex formulas like $Fp \vee Fq \rightarrow F(p \vee q)$ and $Fi \wedge @_i p \rightarrow Fp$. To the point, *logically* valid formulas are *contextually* valid too. Why? Well, logical valid means "satisfied at *all* points in *all* designated time models"—hence any logical validity must be satisfied at the designated time in any designated model. In short, the set of logical validities is a subset of the set of contextual validities.

But it is a *proper* subset. That is, there are contextual validities that are not logical validities. To give the simplest example, *now* is not logically valid, but it is contextually valid: given any $\mathfrak{M}$ we have that *now* is satisfied at the designated point t_0. This is for the obvious reason that *now* is hardwired to denote the designated point, and so for all models $\mathfrak{M}$ we have $\mathfrak{M}, t_0 \models now$.

Here's another example, one that will play a suggestive role in our later work: the formula-schema $\varphi \leftrightarrow @_{now}\varphi$ is not logically valid, but it is contextually valid. Why is it not logically valid? Well, suppose we are working in a model in which *now* denotes the time you are reading these words (yes, right now, here in the 21st century!) and p means "Jane Austin is writing the last words of *Persuasion*". Well, if we look back in time to the moment in the early 19th century when Ms Austin finished her masterpiece, p certainly was true. But at that historic moment, $@_{now}p$ was clearly false: after all, this formula says she finished her masterpiece right now, that is, in the 21st century! Hence $p \leftrightarrow @_{now}p$ was false at an important moment of English literary history. So we have falsified an instance of the schema, and hence it is not logically valid.

But it *is* contextually valid. For suppose we evaluate any given φ at the designated time of some model $\mathfrak{M}$. Regardless what proposition φ is, it will be either true or false then. But then $@_{now}\varphi$ will have the same truth value as φ, for the simple reason that that *now* picks out the designated point, and $@_{now}\varphi$ reports the truth value of φ at that special time. To put it another way: when evaluating any formula φ *at* the designated point of any model, φ and $@_{now}\varphi$ stand or fall together. But this means that $\varphi \leftrightarrow @_{now}\varphi$ is a contextual validity.

4   Axiomatizing Logical Validity

In the previous section we defined the syntax and semantics of the language $\mathcal{L}(now)$. We defined two notions of validity for the language, and saw they were distinct. And this leads to some obvious questions. Can we characterize these two different logics? In particular, can we axiomatize them? And can we axiomatize them in a simple fashion that show the connection between them?

We are going to do this, and we are going to do it in two steps. In this section, we shall show that logical validity for $\mathcal{L}(now)$ can be reduced to ordinary hybrid tense logical validity, and hence that standard hybrid axiom systems successfully capture this notion. We postpone till the following section the trickier issue of capturing contextual validity axiomatically.

Here's the axiom system we shall work with. When working with $\mathcal{L}(now)$ we call it $K_h^t(now)$, and then a and b in the axioms listed in Figure 1 range over both ordinary nominals and the *now* nominal. When working with $\mathcal{L}$, we call this system K_h^t, and then a and b range over ordinary nominals.[2] That is, $K_h^t(now)$ and K_h^t differ only in whether *now* is in the language or not.

The system $K_h^t(now)$

Axioms

CT	All classical tautologies	
Duality	$\vdash Pp \leftrightarrow \neg H \neg p$	$\vdash Fp \leftrightarrow \neg G \neg p$
K$_\square$	$\vdash H(p \to q) \to (Hp \to Hq)$	$\vdash G(p \to q) \to (Gp \to Gq)$
K$_@$	$\vdash @_a(p \to q) \to (@_a p \to @_a q)$	
Selfdual$_@$	$\vdash @_a p \leftrightarrow \neg @_a \neg p$	
Ref$_@$	$\vdash @_a a$	
Agree	$\vdash @_a @_b p \leftrightarrow @_b p$	
Intro	$\vdash a \to (p \leftrightarrow @_a p)$	
Back$_{P,F}$	$\vdash P@_a p \to @_a p$	$\vdash F@_a p \to @_a p$
Interact	$\vdash @_a Pb \leftrightarrow @_b Fa$	

Rules

MP	If $\vdash \psi \to \varphi$ and $\vdash \psi$ then $\vdash \varphi$	
Subst	If $\vdash \varphi$ then $\vdash \varphi^\sigma$	
Gen$_{H,G}$	If $\vdash \varphi$ then $\vdash H\varphi$	If $\vdash \varphi$ then $\vdash G\varphi$
Gen$_@$	If $\vdash \varphi$ then $\vdash @_a \varphi$	
Name	If $\vdash @_a \varphi$ and a does not occur in φ then $\vdash \varphi$	
BG$_P$	If $\vdash @_a Pb \to @_b \varphi$ and $b \neq a$ does not occur in φ then $\vdash @_a H\varphi$	
BG$_F$	If $\vdash @_a Fb \to @_b \varphi$ and $b \neq a$ does not occur in φ then $\vdash @_a G\varphi$	

Fig. 1.

Two general remarks are in order. First, when it comes to dealing with *now*, there is nothing particularly special about the axiomatization that we have chosen. Indeed, the whole point of the (essentially semantic) argument we shall soon give is that logical validity for $\mathcal{L}(now)$ is reducible to logical validity for $\mathcal{L}$, that is, to ordinary hybrid tense logical validity. In effect, we show that *any* sound and complete axiomatization of logical validity in $\mathcal{L}$ captures logical validity for $\mathcal{L}(now)$ as well. We chose this axiomatization because we know it and like it.

---

[2] In fact, K_h^t is just the tense-logical version of a complete axiomatization of the minimal hybrid modal logic given in Blackburn and ten Cate [2]. While the details of K_h^t and $K_h^t(now)$ don't play an important role in this paper, we would like to make a remark about the substitution rule being used: σ is any substitution that uniformly substitutes formulas in Nom $\cup$ {*now*} by formulas in Nom $\cup$ {*now*}, and uniformly substitutes ordinary propositional symbols by arbitrary formulas.

Second, to return to a remark made earlier, when working with real applications, we often want to put restrictions on the properties possessed by the relation R. For example, we may wish to work with branching time or linear time, with dense time or discrete time. We remarked that hybrid logic made it easy to impose restrictions on the flow of time axiomatically, and this was no idle boast. One of the most useful aspects of hybrid logic is its deductive modularity.

Here's a simple example. Consider the following three axioms. A little thought shows that they correspond to irreflexivity, transitivity and linearity respectively:

$$@_i \neg F i \qquad FFi \to Fi \qquad @_i Fj \vee @_i j \vee @_j Fi$$

For example, the formula on the left says that if you are at the point named i, you cannot look into the future and see i, which is a way of describing irreflexivity. Adding these three axioms gives us a sound and complete proof system when time possesses these three properties, and this example is only the tip of a very large iceberg. Recall that a pure formula is a formula that only contains nominals as atoms. A fundamental result of hybrid logic tells us that when we add additional pure axioms (note that the three axioms in our example above are pure) then the resulting system is guaranteed to be complete with respect to models the axioms describe.[3] And because of our strategy of reducing $\mathcal{L}(now)$ logical validity to $\mathcal{L}$ logical validity, this deductive modularity will be inherited by all our indexical logics. This is one of the reasons we feel that hybrid logic is a particularly good logical setting for exploring temporal indexicals.

Time to return to our axiomatic work. First we check soundness:

Theorem 1 (Soundness). *The axioms and rules denoted by $K_h^t(now)$ are sound with respect to designated time models.*

Proof. The proof is a straightforward variant of the ordinary inductive soundness proof for hybrid tense logics.

Now for the key lemma. That the axiom system $K_h^t(now)$ characterises the logically valid formulas follows from the observation that satisfiability of formulas in $\mathcal{L}(now)$ can be reduced to satisfiability of formulas in $\mathcal{L}$. We'll use the following notation: if in φ we uniformly substitute ρ for ψ we obtain $\varphi[\psi \leftarrow \rho]$.

Lemma 1 (Reduction to Basic Hybrid Tense Logic). *Let φ be a formula in $\mathcal{L}(now)$ and j a nominal not occurring in φ, then $\varphi[now \leftarrow j]$ is satisfiable in an ordinary model iff φ satisfiable is in a designated time model.*

Proof. Suppose some φ in $\mathcal{L}(now)$ is given with j not occurring in φ. We prove by induction on φ a slightly stronger version of the lemma, namely that $\varphi[now \leftarrow j]$

---

[3] It would take us too far from the concerns of this paper to discuss why hybrid logic is deductively modular, but the two more complex rules, BG_P and BG_F, play a central role here. For a discussion of the role of such rules, see Chapter 7, Section 3 of Blackburn, De Rijke and Venema [5] and Blackburn and ten Cate [2]. For detailed model-theoretic results on what can be achieved using pure axioms, see ten Cate [7].

is satisfied at t in the ordinary model $\mathfrak{M} = (T, R, V)$ iff φ is satisfied at t in the designated time model $\mathfrak{M}' = (T, R, V', V'(j))$. Here V' is identical with V on all nominals and propositional symbols and $V'(now) = V(j)$. Note our abuse of notation: we actually mean the unique element of $V'(j)$ when we write the fourth element of the designated time model tuple—we use this conflation systematically in the proof below. Also, note that $V'(j) = V(j)$. So $V'(now)$, $V'(j)$, and $V(j)$ are alternative ways of picking out the designated time.

First, the three base cases. Suppose φ is i (which is the same as $\varphi[now \leftarrow j]$) and that it is satisfied at t in $\mathfrak{M} = (T, R, V)$. Let $\mathfrak{M}' = (T, R, V', V'(j))$ be the designated time model defined as just described. Clearly $\mathfrak{M}, t \models i$ iff $V(i) = t$ iff $V'(i) = t$ iff $\mathfrak{M}', t \models i$. This completes the argument for ordinary nominals. And clearly, if φ is p, then an analogous argument also works. So we only need to check the case when φ is now. So suppose that $\varphi[now \leftarrow j]$, which is j, is satisfied at t in $\mathfrak{M} = (T, R, V)$. Then for the designated time model $\mathfrak{M}' = (T, R, V', V'(j))$, we have $\mathfrak{M}', t \models now$. As for the other direction, if t is the denotation of both j and now in $\mathfrak{M}'$, then t is the denotation of j under V in $\mathfrak{M}$. This completes the three base cases.

We shall prove one case of the inductive step of the argument. Let φ be $@_{now}\psi$. Then $\varphi[now \leftarrow j]$ is $@_j\psi[now \leftarrow j]$. Suppose this is satisfied at t in $\mathfrak{M} = (T, R, V)$. If t' is the unique element of $V(j)$, then $\mathfrak{M}, t' \models \psi[now \leftarrow j]$. For $\mathfrak{M}' = (T, R, V', V'(j))$ as defined above, the induction hypothesis gives us that $\mathfrak{M}', t' \models \psi$, and as t' is the denotation of now under V' we have that $\mathfrak{M}', t \models @_{now}\psi$. The other direction is similar, as are the rest of the inductive cases. This completes the proof.

Theorem 2. (Logical Completeness) $K_h^t(now)$ *is complete with respect to designated time models. Moreover, when pure formulas are added as additional axioms, it is complete with respect to the class of models they define.*

Proof. Recall that K_h^t is a complete axiomatisation of hybrid tense logic in the now-free language $\mathcal{L}$. Let φ be a formula of $\mathcal{L}(now)$ that is $K_h^t(now)$-consistent, and let j be a nominal not occurring in φ. Then $\varphi[now \leftarrow j]$ is a formula in $\mathcal{L}$, and it must be K_h^t-consistent—for if it wasn't, we could prove the inconsistency of φ in $\mathcal{L}(now)$, as now functions syntactically like any other nominal. Therefore, by the completeness of K_h^t, we know that $\varphi[now \leftarrow j]$ has a model. By our reduction to hybrid tense logic (Lemma 1) this means that φ has a designated time model, which means that $K_h^t(now)$ is complete with respect to the designated model semantics, as claimed. That adding pure formulas as additional axioms yields additional completeness results is standard in hybrid logic (recall the discussion of deductive modularity).

5   Axiomatizing Contextual Validity

Now we want to axiomatize *contextual* validity, and indeed, to axiomatize it as an extension of our previous axiomatisation, $K_h^t(now)$, which captured *logical* validity in $\mathcal{L}(now)$. How are we to do this? The answer is both surprisingly simple and rather subtle. First the simplicity: all we have to do is extend $K_h^t(now)$ with the following rule, which we have called the Kamp Rule:[4]

Kamp Rule: If we have proved $@_{now}\varphi$, then we have a proof of φ. That is:

If $\vdash @_{now}\varphi$ then $\vdash \varphi$.

Restriction: Can only be used once in a proof and only as the very last step.

This rule is *contextually sound*. For let any $\mathfrak{M} = (T, R, V, t_0)$ be given, and suppose $@_{now}\varphi$ is satisfied at the designated time. That is, suppose we have $\mathfrak{M}, t_0 \models @_{now}\varphi$. This means that $\mathfrak{M}, t_0 \models \varphi$. So the conclusion of the Kamp Rule is satisfied in the same model at the same (designated) time, and thus the rule is contextually sound.

Here's a simple example of the rule at work: a two-step proof of *now*:

1.	$@_{now}\,now$	(Standard axiom, instance of $@_i i$)
2.	now	(Kamp Rule)

This makes good sense. As we saw earlier, *now* is the simplest example of a contextual validity, and so it should be provable in any complete system for contextual validity.

But now for the subtlety. Why did we impose the restriction that the rule can only be used once, and only as the very last step of the proof? Well, for the simple reason that without this restriction the system would collapse! Why is this? Because, as we mentioned at the start of the paper, logical and contextual validity interact in tricky ways. Let's think this through.

Suppose φ is logically valid. That is, by the previous completeness result, φ is provable in $K_h^t(now)$. So we have $\vdash \varphi$, hence by using the Gen_G rule we can obtain $\vdash G\varphi$. And this makes perfect sense: if φ is *logically* valid then of course it is going to be true at all future times, hence $G\varphi$ is also a logical validity, and thus it should be provable. No problem here. It's exactly what we want.

But now suppose we add the Kamp Rule *without* the restriction. Well, we have just given a two line proof of *now*, so we have $\vdash now$. And here comes the collapse: we now use Gen_G to prove that $\vdash Gnow$, which means that it is always going to be the case that *now*. In terms of our models this means that all future points are identical to the designated time, and that is not what we want at all. Therefore, we can only apply the Kamp Rule once in a proof—and then stop!

But then, what about completeness? With such a drastic restriction in place, surely the rule is too weak to yield contextual completeness? But it's not: with

---

[4] As far as we are aware, this rule has not been proposed before. We call it the Kamp Rule because it trades on ideas similar to those Kamp used in his proof that his Now operator is, in certain sense, eliminable in standard propositional tense logic. For Kamp's original proof of the elimination result, see [8], and for a hybrid logic generalization, see Blackburn and Jørgensen [3].

the help of the following lemma we shall prove the contextual completeness of $K_h^t(now) + \text{KR}$.

Lemma 2. *For $\varphi \in \mathcal{L}(now)$, $@_{now}\varphi$ is logically valid iff φ is contextually valid.*

Proof. Suppose $@_{now}\varphi$ is logically valid. Let $\mathfrak{M} = (T, R, V, t_0)$ be given. We need to show that φ is contextually true in $\mathfrak{M}$, that is, that it is satisfied at the designated point t_0. As $@_{now}\varphi$ is logically valid, for all times t in T we have that $\mathfrak{M}, t \models @_{now}\varphi$. But this means that $\mathfrak{M}, t_0 \models \varphi$. For the other direction, suppose φ is contextually valid, that is, satisfied in any model at the designated point. Given any $\mathfrak{M} = (T, R, V, t_0)$ we need to show that $@_{now}\varphi$ is satisfied at any $t \in T$. But this is clear: by assumption we have that $\mathfrak{M}, t_0 \models \varphi$. This means, for all $t \in T$ we have that $\mathfrak{M}, t \models @_{now}\varphi$.

Theorem 3 (Contextual Completeness). $K_h^t(now) + \text{KR}$ *is contextually complete with respect to designated time models. Moreover, when pure formulas are added as additional axioms, it is contextually complete with respect to the class of models they define*

Proof. If φ is contextually valid, then, by the previous lemma, $@_{now}\varphi$ is logically valid. Hence, by our previous completeness theorem, we have that $@_{now}\varphi$ is provable in $K_h^t(now)$. Simply take this proof and apply the Kamp Rule to the end formula: this gives us the required proof of φ. The result about the effect of additional pure axioms is standard in hybrid logic

The moral of the story is this. Yes, logical and contextual validity interact in tricky ways. But these effects can be unravelled, even in a Hilbert system. In particular, this completeness result tells us is that any axiomatic proof of a contextually valid formula φ can be broken down into a (possibly very lengthy) proof of $@_{now}\varphi$, followed by a one step application of the Kamp Rule which strips off the outermost operator.

There is an important point of contact between the use of the the Kamp Rule and the tableau system for contextual validity developed in Blackburn and Jørgensen [3]. In our earlier paper, logical validity was captured using a standard hybrid tableau system. Contextual validity was captured by building tableaus for the input formula in which the root node of the tableau was labelled *now*. In other words, capturing contextual validity tableau-style means that instead of trying to falsify the input formula at an *arbitrary* time, you have to try to falsify it at the time where *now* is true. Labeling the root node of the tableau with *now*, which happens as the very *first* step of tableau construction, corresponds to the use of the Kamp Rule as the very *last* step of a Hilbert-style proof.

6   Crossing to *yesterday*, *today* and *tomorrow*

It is time to consider other temporal indexicals. Accordingly, we enrich $\mathcal{L}(now)$ with three new propositional symbols: *yesterday*, *today* and *tomorrow*. Like *now*, all three symbols can occur in formula position. Unlike *now*, they cannot occur in operator position. This is because they are not nominals, and @ requires nominals as subscripts.

Well, if they are not nominals, then what are they? Simply three special propositional symbols mutually constrained in their interpretation, but not constrained (as nominals are) to be true at a single time. Intuitively (and unsurprisingly) each of these symbols represents a day. The following diagram illustrates how to envisage the mutual constraints on their interpretations:

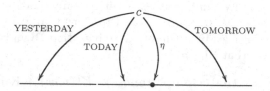

That is, each of our three new symbols denotes a "daylike" set of times, each correctly positioned in the model with respect to the others, and with respect to the designated time t_0, which is marked in the diagram as a black dot.

In fact, the above diagram is essentially a pictorial representation of the *characters* of the indexicals *yesterday*, *today*, *tomorrow* and *now*. As we said earlier, a character function stipulates how an indexical exploits the context. In this diagram we see a context c and its image under four character functions, YESTERDAY, TODAY, TOMORROW and η. Intuitively, η is the most fundamental: $\eta(c)$ is the utterance time of c, the time that *now* names. The sets of points picked out by the other indexicals group naturally around this central time.

Models for our expanded language simply build in this extra structure. First, instead of designated time models, we now work with *designated context models*. These are simply 4-tuples $\mathfrak{M} = (T, R, V, c)$ where $\mathfrak{M} = (T, R, V)$ is a model for hybrid tense logic, and c is the designated context.

It only remains to specify the valuation functions for our three new symbols and for *now* in this new setting. And (by this stage) the reasons for the following stipulations should be clear. If V' is a valuation for hybrid tense logic on a model $\mathfrak{M}$, and c is a context in $\mathfrak{M}$, then we extend V' to a valuation V for our enriched language as follows:

$$
V(a) = \begin{cases}
\{\eta(c)\}, \text{ if } a \text{ is } now, \\
\text{YESTERDAY}(c), \text{ if } a \text{ is } yesterday, \\
\text{TODAY}(c), \text{ if } a \text{ is } today, \\
\text{TOMORROW}(c), \text{ if } a \text{ is } tomorrow, \\
V'(a), \text{ otherwise.}
\end{cases}
$$

Once more, we have hardwired the meaning of our special symbols at the atomic level, and because of this we can simply interpret the language as before.

But we are not yet finished. The previous diagram shows a well-behaved context, with well-behaved character functions. That is, everything lines up in the expected way. But if we want a complete logic for working with our new symbols, we must pin down what it is about the previous diagram that we like. And this is easy to do. We simply stipulate that we will only work with models in which the following axioms are true at all times:

Now Placement	**Disjointness**
$now \rightarrow today$	$today \rightarrow \neg tomorrow$
$yesterday \rightarrow F\,now$	$today \rightarrow \neg yesterday$
$tomorrow \rightarrow P\,now$	$yesterday \rightarrow \neg tomorrow$
One Step Alignment	**Two Step Alignment**
$today \rightarrow G\neg yesterday$	
$tomorrow \rightarrow G\neg today$	$tomorrow \rightarrow G\neg yesterday$
Convexity	**No Gaps**
$P\,yesterday \wedge F\,yesterday \rightarrow yesterday$	$P\,yesterday \wedge F\,today \rightarrow yesterday \vee today$
$P\,today \wedge F\,today \rightarrow today$	$P\,today \wedge F\,tomorrow \rightarrow today \vee tomorrow$
$P\,tomorrow \wedge F\,tomorrow \rightarrow tomorrow$	

Suppose all these axioms are true in some designated context model $\mathfrak{M}$ (that is, true at all times t in $\mathfrak{M}$). Then it is easy to see that at $\eta(c)$—the utterance time—there will be a yesterday, a today, and a tomorrow, and that these will be grouped around $\eta(c)$ exactly as in our picture.

But are they complete? Well, logical completeness is clear. By definition, we are only going to work with models that make the above axioms globally true. Hence (by definition) these axioms are complete with respect to the desired class of models. It's when we get to *contextual* completeness that things become more interesting. That's when we start bridge building.

Look at the *form* of these axioms. Imagine you are in the context of utterance. Here, of course, *now* is true. But this means modus ponens fires, making *today* true (this is due to the first Now Placement axiom). And indeed, *all* the logical consequences of *now* are going to hold, and all the logical consequences of these axioms will hold, and the familiar properties of our four indexicals just drop into place. Basically, the axioms given above record general properties of the four character functions. And when this information is relevant—that is, when we are reasoning about the utterance time—we access it by contextual reasoning.

And this is exactly what the Kamp Rule lets us do proof-theoretically. Consider the following (simplified) Hilbert proof:

$$\dfrac{@_{now}now \quad \dfrac{\dfrac{now \rightarrow today}{@_{now}(now \rightarrow today)}\ (\text{Gen}_@)}{}}{\dfrac{@_{now}today}{today}\ (\text{KR})}\ (\text{MP})$$

The second-to-last line of the proof is a logical truth, namely $@_{now}\,today$. If we make use of the Kamp Rule at this point—that is, if we walk across the bridge and say: *I really am here now!*—then we strip of the outer operator and realize that (right then and there!) we are in the day called today. As we said at the start of the paper: the Kamp Rule feeds a crucial piece of information to the other indexicals. And that information is simply: *Now!*

7　Conclusion

In this paper we argued that hybrid logic was a good setting for exploring temporal indexicality. The technical arguments in favour of hybrid logic are strong: it is deductively modular, well understood, and the fact that temporal reference is built into its very core makes it a natural candidate for this application.

But the heart of this paper was conceptual, not technical. We wanted to show that (at least for temporal indexicals) the path from logical validity to contextual validity is unexpectedly simple: the indexical *now* provides a bridge to the contextual validity of other indexicals. And this leads to our our next question: what happens when we move beyond temporal indexicals to the full range of indexicals considered by David Kaplan? We don't expect *now* to provide a bridge to non-temporal indexicals such as *you* and *here*, but are there other bridge indexicals? And are there analogs of the Kamp Rule? And can hybrid logic yield perspicuous analyses in these richer setting? We hope to find out.

References

1. Blackburn, P.: Tense, Temporal Reference and Tense Logic. Journal of Semantics 11, 83–101 (1994)
2. Blackburn, P., Cate, B.T.: Pure Extensions, Proof Rules, and Hybrid Axiomatics. Studia Logica 84, 277–322 (2006)
3. Blackburn, P., Jørgensen, K.F.: Indexical Hybrid Tense Logic. In: Bolander, T., Bräuner, T., Ghilardi, S., Moss, L. (eds.) Advances in Modal Logic, vol. 9, pp. 144–160 (2012)
4. Blackburn, P., Marx, M.: Remarks on Gregory's actuality operator. Journal of Philosophical Logic 31(3), 281–288 (2002)
5. Blackburn, P., de Rijke, M., Venema, Y.: Modal Logic. Cambridge University Press, Cambridge (2001)
6. Burgess, J.: Basic tense logic. In: Gabbay, Guenthner (eds.) Handbook of Philosophical Logic, vol. 2, pp. 89–133, Reidel (1984)
7. Cate, B.: Model theory for extended modal languages. Ph.D. thesis, University of Amsterdam, ILLC Dissertation Series DS-2005-01 (2005)
8. Kamp, H.: Formal Properties of 'Now'. Theoria 37, 237–273 (1971)
9. Kaplan, D.: Demonstratives: An Essay on the Semantics, Logic, Metaphysics, and Epistemology of Demonstratives and Other Indexicals. In: Almog, J., Perry, J., Wettstein, H. (eds.) Themes from Kaplan, pp. 481–564. Oxford University Press, Oxford (1989)

ExpTime Tableaux Algorithm for Contextualized $\mathcal{ALC}$

Loris Bozzato[1], Martin Homola[2], and Luciano Serafini[1]

[1] Fondazione Bruno Kessler, Via Sommarive 18, 38123 Trento, Italy
[2] FMFI, Comenius University, Mlynská dolina, 84248 Bratislava, Slovakia
{bozzato,serafini}@fbk.eu, homola@fmph.uniba.sk

Abstract. Contextualized Knowledge Repository (CKR) is a DL-based framework for representation and reasoning with context dependent knowledge. It addresses the widely recognized need for contextualization of the Semantic Web data sources. Reasoning with CKR is possible thanks to a reduction to standard DL, and more recently a NExpTime tableaux algorithm was introduced for $\mathcal{ALC}$-based CKR. In this paper we present an ExpTime tableaux algorithm for $\mathcal{ALC}$-based CKR. The algorithm not only formally defines a tableaux decision procedure with optimal complexity, it is also presented in a form that can be effectively applied in practice employing a suitable rule application strategy together with node caching.

1 Introduction

The enormous amount of semantic resources available in the Web in form of data sets and ontologies brings unforeseen opportunities for their reuse in different applications. It is becoming more and more clear that most of the knowledge represented in these resources is not universally valid, but it rather holds under certain circumstances, such as within a given time, location, or specific domain of interest. However, in many cases, information about this validity scope is completely missing from resource meta data.

Thus, the development of formal frameworks enabling specification and principled interpretation of such contextual meta data is an important issue for the Semantic Web and Linked Open Data communities. A number of such formalisms have been proposed, e.g. [2,9]. Contextualized Knowledge Repository (CKR) [11] is one of them. CKR is a logical framework that allows for encapsulation of description logic (DL) knowledge bases (KB) into contexts, and for specification of the contextual structure in a formal meta language. CKR KB can be built on $\mathcal{SROIQ}$ DL (corresponding to OWL 2) or on any of its fragments.

The only decision procedure known for $\mathcal{SROIQ}$-based CKR is based on translation [11] into a single $\mathcal{SROIQ}$ KB. This translation showed decidability of CKR, but for actual reasoning it is not very practical, since it introduces a significant blowup in the KB size. This approach is especially unpractical for any of the more effective fragments of $\mathcal{SROIQ}$: regardless of the initial fragment, the translation in [11] produces a KB that uses constructs strictly in $\mathcal{SROIQ}$ and complexity of $\mathcal{SROIQ}$ is very high (2NExpTime). For realistic reasoning with DL, tableau algorithms are typically employed. The first known direct tableaux algorithm was devised for $\mathcal{ALC}$-based

P. Brézillon, P. Blackburn, and R. Dapoigny (Eds.): CONTEXT 2013, LNAI 8175, pp. 199–212, 2013.

CKR [4]. It extends the well known tableau algorithm for $\mathcal{ALC}$ [1] and its complexity is NExpTime. However, $\mathcal{ALC}$ is ExpTime-complete [1] and ExpTime decision procedures for $\mathcal{ALC}$ are known [5,6].

In this paper we describe an ExpTime-tableau algorithm for $\mathcal{ALC}$-based CKR. We build on the ideas of Goré and Nguyen [6]. In order to eliminate non-determinism, the completion trees are replaced with structures called and-or graphs. In such structure, both branches of a non-deterministic choice introduced by disjunction ($\sqcup$) are explicitly represented. Satisfiability of the branches is propagated bottom-up and if it reaches an initial node, we can be sure that a model exists. To guarantee the exponential bound on the size of the graph, a global caching of nodes is used, enabled by a proper rule-application strategy. In order to reason with contexts, the algorithm of [6] was extended in multiple respects. Multiple node labels were introduced and a number of new expansion rules were added in order to implement the CKR semantics. We have also extended the algorithm with ABoxes, to be able to decide satisfiability of realistic CKR knowledge bases. We have thus reached an optimized ExpTime decision procedure for $\mathcal{ALC}$-based CKR.

2   Contextualized Knowledge Repositories

Throughout this section we will recall some of the needed definitions for DL and $\mathcal{ALC}$: for precise semantics and other details please refer to [1]. A DL vocabulary $\Sigma = N_C \uplus N_R \uplus N_I$ is composed of the three mutually disjoint subsets N_C of atomic concepts, N_R of roles, and N_I of individuals. In $\mathcal{ALC}$ [10], concepts are inductively defined from atomic concepts and the constructors $\neg, \sqcap$ and $\exists$. A TBox $\mathcal{T}$ is a finite set of general concept inclusions (GCI) of the form $C \sqsubseteq D$. An ABox $\mathcal{A}$ is a finite set of axioms of the form $C(a)$ or $R(a, b)$. A knowledge base is a pair $\mathcal{K} = \langle \mathcal{T}, \mathcal{A} \rangle$.

We briefly introduce the basic definition of CKR, for all details see [11]. A *meta vocabulary* Γ is used to state information about contexts. It contains contextual attributes (called dimensions), their possible values and coverage relations between these values. Formally, it is a DL vocabulary that contains: (a) a finite set of individuals called *context identifiers*; (b) a finite set of roles $\mathbf{A}$ called *dimensions*; (c) for every dimension $A \in \mathbf{A}$, a finite set of individuals D_A, called *dimensional values*, and a role $\prec_A$, called *coverage relation*. The number of dimensions $k = |\mathbf{A}|$ is assumed to be a fixed constant.

Dimensional vectors are used to identify each context with a specific set of dimensional values. Given a meta-vocabulary Γ with dimensions $\mathbf{A} = \{A_1, \ldots, A_k\}$, a *dimensional vector* $\mathbf{d} = \{A_{i_1}{:=}d_1, \ldots, A_{i_m}{:=}d_m\}$ is a (possibly empty) set of assignments such that for every j, h, with $1 \leq j \leq h \leq m$, $d_j \in D_{A_{i_j}}$, and $j \neq h$ implies $i_j \neq i_h$. A dimensional vector $\mathbf{d}$ is *full* if it assigns values to all dimensions (i.e., $|\mathbf{d}| = k$), otherwise it is *partial*. If it is apparent which value belongs to which dimension, we simply write $\{d_1, \ldots, d_m\}$. By d_A (e_A, etc.) we denote the actual value that $\mathbf{d}$ (e, etc.) assigns to the dimension A. The *dimensional space* $\mathfrak{D}_\Gamma$ of Γ is the set of all full dimensional vectors of Γ.

An *object-vocabulary* encodes knowledge inside contexts: it is a standard DL vocabulary Σ closed w.r.t. *concept/role qualification*. That is, for every concept or role symbol X of Σ and every (possibly partial) dimensional vector $\mathbf{d}$, a new symbol $X_\mathbf{d}$

is added to Σ, called the *qualification* of X w.r.t. **d**. If **d** is partial then $X_\mathbf{d}$ is *partially qualified*, if **d** is full, it is *fully qualified*. Qualified symbols are used inside contexts to refer to the meaning of symbols w.r.t. some other context.

Contexts and CKR knowledge bases are formally defined as follows.

Definition 1 (Context). *Given a pair of meta and object vocabularies $\langle \Gamma, \Sigma \rangle$, a context is a triple $\langle \mathcal{C}, \dim(\mathcal{C}), \mathrm{K}(\mathcal{C}) \rangle$ where: (a) $\mathcal{C}$ is a context identifier of Γ; (b) $\dim(\mathcal{C})$ is a full dimensional vector of $\mathfrak{D}_\Gamma$; (c) $\mathrm{K}(\mathcal{C})$ is an $\mathcal{ALC}$ knowledge base over Σ.*

Definition 2 (Contextualized Knowledge Repository). *Given a pair of meta and object vocabularies $\langle \Gamma, \Sigma \rangle$, a CKR knowledge base (CKR) is a pair $\mathfrak{K} = \langle \mathfrak{M}, \mathfrak{C} \rangle$ where $\mathfrak{C}$ is a set of contexts on $\langle \Gamma, \Sigma \rangle$ and $\mathfrak{M}$, called* meta knowledge, *is a DL knowledge base over Γ such that:*

(a) for $A \in \mathbf{A}$ and $d, d' \in D_A$, if $\mathfrak{M} \models A(\mathcal{C}, d)$ and $\mathfrak{M} \models A(\mathcal{C}, d')$ then $\mathfrak{M} \models d = d'$;
(b) for $\mathcal{C} \in \mathfrak{C}$ with $\dim(\mathcal{C}) = \mathbf{d}$ and for $A \in \mathbf{A}$, we have $\mathfrak{M} \models A(\mathcal{C}, d_A)$;
(c) the relation $\{ \langle d, d' \rangle \mid \mathfrak{M} \models d \prec_A d' \}$ is a strict partial order on D_A.

Note that in CKR built over more expressive logics, conditions *(a)–(c)* can be assured directly in the meta knowledge with respective axioms: each $A \in \mathbf{A}$ is declared functional, and each $\prec_A$ is declared irreflexive and transitive. In $\mathcal{ALC}$ we do not have this option, however, since the number of dimensions and contexts is assumed to be finite, the conditions can be verified even without a reasoner (e.g., by some script) once the meta knowledge is modeled. These conditions are needed to assure reasonable properties of contextual space, i.e., acyclicity, dimensional values uniquely determined [11].

In the rest of the paper we assume that CKR knowledge bases are defined over some suitable vocabulary $\langle \Gamma, \Sigma \rangle$, and all concepts are in negation normal form (NNF). We also assume the unique name assumption (UNA) for the meta knowledge (i.e., if $a \neq b$ are two different symbols then $\mathfrak{M} \not\models a = b$). This is just to avoid the confusing possibility of two contexts located as the same place in the dimensional space.

For a CKR $\mathfrak{K}$, we will denote by $\mathcal{C}_\mathbf{d}$ a context with $\dim(\mathcal{C}) = \mathbf{d}$. For $\mathbf{d}, \mathbf{e} \in \mathfrak{D}_\Gamma$ and $\mathbf{B}, \mathbf{C} \subseteq \mathbf{A}$, $\mathbf{d}_\mathbf{B} := \{ (A{:=}d) \in \mathbf{d} \mid A \in \mathbf{B} \}$ is the projection of **d** w.r.t. **B**; and $\mathbf{d}_\mathbf{B} + \mathbf{e}_\mathbf{C} := \mathbf{d}_\mathbf{B} \cup \{ (A{:=}d) \in \mathbf{e}_\mathbf{C} \mid A \notin \mathbf{B} \}$ is the completion of $\mathbf{d}_\mathbf{B}$ w.r.t. $\mathbf{e}_\mathbf{C}$.

We define strict ($\prec$) and non-strict ($\preceq$) coverage between dimensional values: for $d, d' \in D_A$, $d \prec d'$ if $\mathfrak{M} \models d \prec_A d'$; and $d \preceq d'$ if either $d \prec d'$ or $\mathfrak{M} \models d = d'$. Similarly, for dimensional vectors: $\mathbf{d} \preceq_\mathbf{B} \mathbf{e}$ for some $\mathbf{B} \subseteq \mathbf{A}$ if $d_B \preceq e_B$ for each $B \in \mathbf{B}$; and $\mathbf{d} \prec_\mathbf{B} \mathbf{e}$ if $\mathbf{d} \preceq_\mathbf{B} \mathbf{e}$ and $d_B \prec e_B$ for at least one $B \in \mathbf{B}$. Also, $\mathbf{d} \preceq \mathbf{e}$ if $\mathbf{d} \preceq_\mathbf{A} \mathbf{e}$, and $\mathbf{d} \prec \mathbf{e}$ if $\mathbf{d} \prec_\mathbf{A} \mathbf{e}$. Finally, for contexts: $\mathcal{C}_\mathbf{d} \preceq \mathcal{C}_\mathbf{e}$ if $\mathbf{d} \preceq \mathbf{e}$, and $\mathcal{C}_\mathbf{d} \prec \mathcal{C}_\mathbf{e}$ if $\mathbf{d} \prec \mathbf{e}$. Intuitively, if $\mathcal{C}_\mathbf{d} \prec \mathcal{C}_\mathbf{e}$, then $\mathcal{C}_\mathbf{d}$ is the narrower and $\mathcal{C}_\mathbf{e}$ is the broader context.

Example 1. We explain the possibilities in representation and reasoning of the CKR framework with a simple running example. In this example, we want to model the football domain and related competitions: each of these football events can be thus represented as a separate context, defining the situation of each particular competition. An example CKR $\mathfrak{K}_{fb}$ instantiating this scenario is shown in Fig. 1. This CKR uses three dimensions time, location, and topic. It shows three contexts representing the general football context and two particular competitions. The contexts are identified by dimensional vectors **fb** (general context of football in 2010), **wc10** (FIFA World Cup

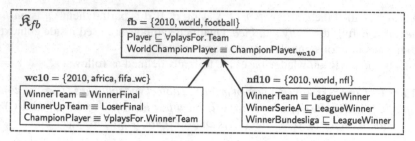

Fig. 1. Example CKR knowledge base $\mathfrak{K}_{fb}$

2010), and **nfl10** (national football leagues in 2010). Axioms are placed inside each context while the associated vector is placed above it. The coverage relation $\prec$ is visualized with arrows. Note that, for instance, it is evident that the interpretation of concept WinnerTeam depends on the particular context of reference: while in the situation of the World Cup the winner team is defined as "the winner of the final match", in the context of national leagues a winner team is "a winner of a national league". Note also that, by using the qualified symbol ChampionPlayer$_{wc10}$, we can refer to the interpretation of the symbol in the World Cup context from the general football context.   ◇

CKR uses DL semantics inside each context combined with some additional semantic restrictions that ensure proper meaning of qualified symbols.

Definition 3. *A partial DL interpretation of a vocabulary Σ is a pair $\mathcal{I} = \langle \Delta^{\mathcal{I}}, \cdot^{\mathcal{I}} \rangle$, where $\Delta^{\mathcal{I}}$ is a possibly empty set, and $\cdot^{\mathcal{I}}$ is a partial function, that is totally defined on N_C and N_R, with $C^{\mathcal{I}} \subseteq \Delta^{\mathcal{I}}$ for $C \in N_C$ and $R^{\mathcal{I}} \subseteq \Delta^{\mathcal{I}} \times \Delta^{\mathcal{I}}$ for $R \in N_R$, and it is partially defined on N_I, with $a^{\mathcal{I}} \in \Delta^{\mathcal{I}}$ for $a \in N_I$ on which $\mathcal{I}$ is defined.*

Note that the definition asks for some exceptions to the standard DL semantics [1]. Partial interpretations need not necessarily provide denotations for all individuals of Σ. This is needed for technical reasons: intuitively, all contexts rely on the same object vocabulary Σ, but some element of Σ may not be meaningful in all contexts. Also, interpretations with empty domains are useful to treat inconsistency among contexts [11].

Semantics of non-atomic concepts is defined from the usual interpretation of $\mathcal{ALC}$ constructors [1]. Notice that for each concept C, if $\mathcal{I}$ is the interpretation on the empty set $\Delta_{\mathcal{I}}$, then $C^{\mathcal{I}} = \emptyset$. An interpretation $\mathcal{I}$ *satisfies* an axiom α (denoted $\mathcal{I} \models \alpha$) if it is defined on all the symbols occurring in α and the following holds: $\mathcal{I} \models C \sqsubseteq D$ iff $C^{\mathcal{I}} \subseteq D^{\mathcal{I}}$; $\mathcal{I} \models C(a)$ iff $a^{\mathcal{I}} \in C^{\mathcal{I}}$; and $\mathcal{I} \models R(a, b)$ iff $\langle a^{\mathcal{I}}, b^{\mathcal{I}} \rangle \in R^{\mathcal{I}}$. $\mathcal{I}$ is a *model* of $\mathcal{K} = \langle \mathcal{T}, \mathcal{A} \rangle$ (denoted $\mathcal{I} \models \mathcal{K}$) iff it satisfies all axioms in $\mathcal{T} \cup \mathcal{A}$; $\mathcal{K}$ is satisfiable if it has a model. Notice that, if $\mathcal{I}$ is the interpretation on the empty domain we have that $\mathcal{I} \models C \sqsubseteq D$ for every pair of $\mathcal{ALC}$ concepts C and D, and $\mathcal{I} \not\models \alpha$ for every assertion α of the form $C(a)$ and $R(a, b)$. A concept C is *satisfiable* w.r.t. an $\mathcal{ALC}$ KB $\mathcal{K}$ iff there exists a model $\mathcal{I}$ of $\mathcal{K}$ s.t. $C^{\mathcal{I}}$ is non-empty. A subsumption formula $C \sqsubseteq D$ is *entailed* by an $\mathcal{ALC}$ KB $\mathcal{K}$ iff $C^{\mathcal{I}} \subseteq D^{\mathcal{I}}$ in all models $\mathcal{I}$ of $\mathfrak{K}$. It is well known that these two problems are inter-reducible [1].

Definition 4 (CKR-Model). *A model of a CKR $\mathfrak{K}$ is a collection $\mathfrak{I} = \{\mathcal{I}_{\mathbf{d}}\}_{\mathbf{d} \in \mathfrak{D}_\Gamma}$ of partial DL interpretations (local interpretations) s.t. for all $\mathbf{d}, \mathbf{e}, \mathbf{f} \in \mathfrak{D}_\Gamma$, $\mathbf{B} \subseteq \mathbf{A}$, $A \in N_C$, $R \in N_R$, $X \in N_C \cup N_R$, $a \in N_I$:*

1. $(\top_{\mathbf{d}})^{\mathcal{I}_{\mathbf{f}}} \subseteq (\top_{\mathbf{e}})^{\mathcal{I}_{\mathbf{f}}}$ *if* $\mathbf{d} \prec \mathbf{e}$
2. $(A_{\mathbf{f}})^{\mathcal{I}_{\mathbf{d}}} \subseteq (\top_{\mathbf{f}})^{\mathcal{I}_{\mathbf{d}}}$
3. $(R_{\mathbf{f}})^{\mathcal{I}_{\mathbf{d}}} \subseteq (\top_{\mathbf{f}})^{\mathcal{I}_{\mathbf{d}}} \times (\top_{\mathbf{f}})^{\mathcal{I}_{\mathbf{d}}}$
4. $a^{\mathcal{I}_{\mathbf{e}}} = a^{\mathcal{I}_{\mathbf{d}}}$ *if* $\mathbf{d} \prec \mathbf{e}$ *and*
   - $a^{\mathcal{I}_{\mathbf{d}}}$ *is defined or,*
   - $a^{\mathcal{I}_{\mathbf{e}}}$ *is defined and* $a^{\mathcal{I}_{\mathbf{e}}} \in \Delta_{\mathbf{d}}$

5. $(X_{\mathbf{d_B}})^{\mathcal{I}_{\mathbf{e}}} = (X_{\mathbf{d_B}+\mathbf{e}})^{\mathcal{I}_{\mathbf{e}}}$
6. $(X_{\mathbf{d}})^{\mathcal{I}_{\mathbf{e}}} = (X_{\mathbf{d}})^{\mathcal{I}_{\mathbf{d}}}$ *if* $\mathbf{d} \prec \mathbf{e}$
7. $(A_{\mathbf{f}})^{\mathcal{I}_{\mathbf{d}}} = (A_{\mathbf{f}})^{\mathcal{I}_{\mathbf{e}}} \cap \Delta_{\mathbf{d}}$ *if* $\mathbf{d} \prec \mathbf{e}$
8. $(R_{\mathbf{f}})^{\mathcal{I}_{\mathbf{d}}} = (R_{\mathbf{f}})^{\mathcal{I}_{\mathbf{e}}} \cap (\Delta_{\mathbf{d}} \times \Delta_{\mathbf{d}})$ *if* $\mathbf{d} \prec \mathbf{e}$
9. $\mathcal{I}_{\mathbf{d}} \models \mathrm{K}(\mathcal{C}_{\mathbf{d}})$

The semantics takes care that local domains respect the coverage hierarchy (condition 1). Note that $\top_{\mathbf{d}}$ represents the domain of $\mathcal{I}_{\mathbf{d}}$ in the context where it appears. Individuals have a rigid meaning: however, the meaning of an individual in a super-context is independent if its meaning in a sub-context is undefined (condition 4). The interpretation of $X_{\mathbf{f}}$ in any context $\mathcal{C}_{\mathbf{d}}$ is roofed under $(\top_{\mathbf{f}})^{\mathcal{I}_{\mathbf{d}}}$ (conditions 2, 3). The meaning of $X_{\mathbf{f}}$ in some context $\mathcal{C}_{\mathbf{e}}$ is based on its context of origin $\mathcal{C}_{\mathbf{f}}$ if this context is less specific than $\mathcal{C}_{\mathbf{e}}$ (condition 6); otherwise, at least, any $X_{\mathbf{f}}$ in $\mathcal{C}_{\mathbf{d}}$ and $\mathcal{C}_{\mathbf{e}}$ must be equal on the shared part of their domains (conditions 7,8). Each $\mathcal{I}_{\mathbf{d}}$ is a DL-model of $\mathcal{C}_{\mathbf{d}}$ (condition 9). Condition 5 provides the meaning of partially qualified symbols: values for attributes not specified are taken from the dimensions of the context in which the symbol appears. From this reading, we can show that, albeit useful for modeling, partially qualified vectors are a kind of syntactic sugar [11].

Given a CKR $\mathfrak{K}$ and $\mathbf{d} \in \mathfrak{D}_\Gamma$, a concept C is $\mathbf{d}$-*satisfiable* w.r.t. $\mathfrak{K}$ if there exists a CKR model $\mathfrak{I} = \{\mathcal{I}_{\mathbf{e}}\}_{\mathbf{e} \in \mathfrak{D}_\Gamma}$ of $\mathfrak{K}$ such that $C^{\mathcal{I}_{\mathbf{d}}} \neq \emptyset$; $\mathfrak{K}$ is $\mathbf{d}$-satisfiable if it has a CKR model $\mathfrak{I} = \{\mathcal{I}_{\mathbf{e}}\}_{\mathbf{e} \in \mathfrak{D}_\Gamma}$ such that $\Delta_{\mathbf{d}} \neq \emptyset$; $\mathfrak{K}$ is *globally satisfiable* if it has a CKR model $\mathfrak{I} = \{\mathcal{I}_{\mathbf{e}}\}_{\mathbf{e} \in \mathfrak{D}_\Gamma}$ such that $\Delta_{\mathbf{e}} \neq \emptyset$ for every $\mathbf{e} \in \mathfrak{D}_\Gamma$. An axiom α is $\mathbf{d}$-*entailed* by $\mathfrak{K}$ (denoted $\mathfrak{K} \vdash \mathbf{d} . \alpha$) if for every model $\mathfrak{I} = \{\mathcal{I}_{\mathbf{e}}\}_{\mathbf{e} \in \mathfrak{D}_\Gamma}$ of $\mathfrak{K}$ it holds $\mathcal{I}_{\mathbf{d}} \models \alpha$. As usual, $\mathbf{d}$-entailment can be reduced to $\mathbf{d}$-satisfiability: in particular $\mathfrak{K} \vdash \mathbf{d} : C \sqsubseteq D$ iff $C \sqcap \neg D$ is not $\mathbf{d}$-satisfiable w.r.t. $\mathfrak{K}$. Also, C is $\mathbf{d}$-satisfiable w.r.t. $\mathfrak{K}$ iff $\mathfrak{K}'$ is $\mathbf{d}$-satisfiable, where $\mathfrak{K}'$ is obtained from $\mathfrak{K}$ by adding the axiom $C(s_0)$ to $\mathcal{C}_{\mathbf{d}}$ and s_0 is a new constant not used elsewhere in $\mathfrak{K}$.

In the rest of the paper we will assume that all symbols are fully qualified. Given a $\mathfrak{K}$ with partially qualified symbols, it can be replaced by an equivalent KB $\mathfrak{K}'$ in which any partially qualified symbol $X_{\mathbf{d_B}}$ appearing in some context $\mathcal{C}_{\mathbf{e}}$ is replaced by $X_{\mathbf{d_B}+\mathbf{e}}$ (see [11]), however for sake of legibility we will occasionally use partially qualified symbols as syntactic sugar in the examples.

Given a concept C and a CKR $\mathfrak{K} = \langle \mathfrak{M}, \mathfrak{C} \rangle$, we will denote $\mathrm{clos}(C)$ the set of all syntactically correct atomic and complex concepts that occur in C. We will denote by $\mathrm{clos}_{\mathfrak{K}}(C)$ the set of all syntactically correct atomic and complex concepts that occur in C or in any axiom of the contexts in $\mathfrak{C}$. We denote by $\mathcal{R}_{\mathfrak{K},C}$ the set of roles appearing in C or some or in any axiom of the contexts in $\mathfrak{C}$.

3 EXPTIME Tableaux Algorithm for CKR

The known tableaux algorithm for $\mathcal{ALC}$-based CKR takes at most exponentially many steps before it decides if the input concept/CKR is satisfiable. To deal with disjunction ($\sqcup$) the algorithm makes non-deterministic choices, and therefore it is NEXPTIME. This is similar to the classic tableaux algorithm for $\mathcal{ALC}$. To obtain an EXPTIME algorithm for $\mathcal{ALC}$ the non-determinism has to be eliminated [5,6].

Similarly to Goré and Nguyen [6] we will employ and-or graphs to eliminate non-determinism. This is obtained by explicitly representing both possibilities resulting from a disjunctive choice.

Definition 5 (And-or graph). *Given a CKR $\mathfrak{K}$ and a concept C in NNF and $\mathbf{d} \in \mathfrak{D}_\Gamma$, an* and-or graph *is a quadruple $G = \langle V, E, \mathcal{L}, \{\mathcal{L}_\mathbf{e}\}_{\mathbf{e} \in \mathfrak{D}_\Gamma} \rangle$ where:*

(a) V is a set of structured nodes s.t. for every $x \in V$:
- *x.type $\subseteq \{\mathsf{TOP}, \mathsf{AND}, \mathsf{OR}\}$,*
- *x.status $\in \{\mathsf{EXP}, \mathsf{UNEXP}, \mathsf{SAT}, \mathsf{UNSAT}\}$,*
- *for each $\mathbf{e} \in \mathfrak{D}_\Gamma$, $V_\mathbf{e} \subseteq V$ is a distinguished subset of V;*

(b) $E \subseteq V \times V$ is a set of edges;

(c) $\mathcal{L}$ is a partial labeling function from E to $2^{\mathcal{R}_{\mathfrak{K}, C}}$;

(d) for each $\mathbf{e} \in \mathfrak{D}_\Gamma$, $\mathcal{L}_\mathbf{e}$ is a labeling function from $V_\mathbf{e}$ to $2^{\mathrm{clos}_{\mathfrak{K}}(C)}$.

And-or graphs are similar to completion trees which are often used by tableaux algorithms [4,6] in that they are composed of nodes with labels[1]. There are multiple types of nodes: if AND (OR, TOP) belongs to x.type then x is called an *and-node (or-node, top-node)*. And-nodes are similar to nodes in a completion tree: their successors represent other nodes related by some role. Or-nodes represent choices: their successors can be understood as alternative versions. And- and or-nodes are mutually exclusive. Top-nodes represent ABox individuals and they can also be and- or or-nodes.

If $\langle x, y \rangle \in E$, then y is a *predecessor* of x and conversely y is a *successor* of x. If in addition $R \in \mathcal{L}(\langle x, y \rangle)$, then y is an *R-predecessor* of x and conversely y is an *R-successor* of x. If y is a successor of an or-node x, then y is an *or-successor* of x and x is an *or-predecessor* of y. Ancestors, R-ancestors, or-ancestors and descendants, R-descendants, or-descendants are defined as transitive closure on the respective type of predecessors and successors as usual.

The algorithm iteratively expands the nodes of the and-or graph using a set of tableaux expansion rules. The status of each node x is tracked in x.status. First the status is UNEXP. If all of the nodes labels are fully expanded, the status is EXP and the node is evaluated. A node x contains a *clash* if for some $\mathbf{d} \in \mathfrak{D}_\Gamma$ and some concept C both $C \in \mathcal{L}_\mathbf{d}(x)$ and $\neg C \in \mathcal{L}_\mathbf{d}(x)$ or if $\bot \in \mathcal{L}_\mathbf{d}(x)$. In such a case the status is set to UNSAT. Otherwise the node is *clash-free* and its status is set to SAT.

In order to limit the size of the generated and-or graph (and in turn the time complexity) node caching [6] will be employed (see also blocking condition in [4]). If two nodes have all labels equal, we only store one of them and use it as representation of both. A node $x \in V$ is a *witness* for another node $y \in V$ if $\mathcal{L}_\mathbf{e}(x) = \mathcal{L}_\mathbf{e}(y)$ for all $\mathbf{e} \in \mathfrak{D}_\Gamma$. If a witness is found, the node y is removed and the witness x is used in its place by redirecting to x all of the incoming edges of y.

In order to deal with the ABox, the ABox individuals are encoded into the and-or graph during the initialization. This technique is well known for logics like $\mathcal{ALC}$ [1].

---

[1] Note that, differently from the previous version of the algorithm [4], the labels for edges are not distinguished by dimensional vector, as in the case of node labels. This allow us to simplify the completion rules (namely, by removing the R-rule used by [4]), but special care must be observed when proving the correctness of the algorithm.

However in CKR same individuals appearing in different contexts may possibly have different meanings. In the graph, individuals will be represented by nodes with status TOP of the form a^g where $a \in N_I$ and $g \in \mathfrak{D}_\Gamma$ identifies the context in which the individual was first introduced. To implement condition 4 of CKR-models we will merge nodes when needed using a $\mathrm{merge}(x, y)$ procedure.

Definition 6 (Merging). *Executing* $\mathrm{merge}(x, y)$ *on* $G = \langle V, E, \mathcal{L}, \{\mathcal{L}_e\}_{e \in \mathfrak{D}_\Gamma}\rangle$, *with* $x, y \in V$, *transforms* G *as follows: a) node* x *is added into* V_e *for all* $e \in \mathfrak{D}_\Gamma$ *s.t.* $y \in V_e$; *b) all concepts from* $\mathcal{L}_e(y)$ *are added into* $\mathcal{L}_e(x)$, *for all* $e \in \mathfrak{D}_\Gamma$; *c) all edges directed into/from* y *are redirected into/from* x; *d) node* y *is removed from* V.

The algorithm uses tableau expansion rules from Table 1. We say that a tableaux rule is *applicable* on some node $x \in V$ if all of its preconditions (the if-part of the rule) are satisfied for x. The and-or graph is *complete* if none of the rules is applicable. The rules can be split into two groups: $\sqcup$- and $\exists$-rules are *generating* because they generate new nodes; the remaining rules are *expanding* because they do not generate new nodes but instead expand the labels within existing nodes. For reasoning inside each context the well known $\mathcal{ALC}$ tableaux rules [1] are used (the left hand side of Table 1) with some notable modifications. The $\sqcup$-rule is adapted for and-or graphs, instead of an non-deterministic choice it generates or-successors. The perspective of the $\forall$-rule is altered in order to unify it with other expanding rules: it is applicable on a node x which has a predecessor y which has a value restriction in its label. The $\exists$-rule implements part of the CKR semantics because it also adds $\top_f$ to the label of the generated R_f-successor. Similarly the A-rule propagates concepts between labels. The $\top_A$- and $\top_\exists$-rules ensure conditions 2-3 of the CKR models (and partly the $\exists$-rule is also instrumental in this).

Table 1. CKR tableaux completion rules

$\sqcap$-rule:	**if** $x \in V_d$, $C_1 \sqcap C_2 \in \mathcal{L}_d(x)$, $\{C_1, C_2\} \not\subseteq \mathcal{L}_d(x)$ **then** $\mathcal{L}_d(x) := \mathcal{L}_d(x) \cup \{C_1, C_2\}$
$\sqcup$-rule:	**if** $x \in V_d$, $C_1 \sqcup C_2 \in \mathcal{L}_d(x)$, $\{C_1, C_2\} \cap \mathcal{L}_d(x) = \emptyset$ **then** $V_d := V_d \cup \{y, z\}$ with y, z new $E := E \cup \{\langle x, y\rangle, \langle x, z\rangle\}$, $\mathcal{L}_d(y) := \mathcal{L}_d(x) \cup \{C_1\}$, $\mathcal{L}_d(z) := \mathcal{L}_d(x) \cup \{C_2\}$
$\exists$-rule:	**if** $x \in V_d$, $\exists R_f.C \in \mathcal{L}_d(x)$, and there is no R_f-successor $y \in V_d$ of x s.t. $C \in \mathcal{L}_d(y)$ **then** $V_d := V_d \cup \{z\}$ with z new, $E := E \cup \{\langle x, z\rangle\}$, $\mathcal{L}(\langle x, z\rangle) := \{R_f\}$, $\mathcal{L}_d(z) := \{C, \top_f\}$
$\forall$-rule:	**if** $x \in V_d$, $\forall R_f.C \in \mathcal{L}_d(y)$, $C \notin \mathcal{L}_d(x)$, $y \in V_d$ is an R_f-predecessor of x **then** $\mathcal{L}_d(x) := \mathcal{L}_d(x) \cup \{C\}$
$\mathcal{T}$-rule:	**if** $x \in V_d$, $C \sqsubseteq D \in K(\mathcal{C}_d)$, $\mathrm{nnf}(\neg C \sqcup D) \notin \mathcal{L}_d(x)$ **then** $\mathcal{L}_d(x) := \mathcal{L}_d(x) \cup \{\mathrm{nnf}(\neg C \sqcup D)\}$

$\triangle\uparrow$-rule:	**if** $x \in V_d$, $d \prec e$, $x \notin V_e$ **then** $V_e := V_e \cup \{x\}$
$\triangle\downarrow$-rule:	**if** $x \in V_e$, $d \prec e$, $x \notin V_d$ $\top_d \in \mathcal{L}_e(x)$ **then** $V_d = V_d \cup \{x\}$
A-rule:	**if** $x \in V_d \cap V_e$, $d \prec e$ or $d \succ e$, $A_f \in \mathcal{L}_d(x)$, $A_f \notin \mathcal{L}_e(x)$ **then** $\mathcal{L}_e(x) := \mathcal{L}_e(x) \cup \{A_f\}$
$\top_\exists$-rule:	**if** $x \in V_d$, $\exists R_f.C \in \mathcal{L}_d(x)$, $\top_f \notin \mathcal{L}_d(x)$ **then** $\mathcal{L}_d(x) := \mathcal{L}_d(x) \cup \{\top_f\}$
$\top_A$-rule:	**if** $x \in V_e$, $A_d \in \mathcal{L}_e(x)$, $\top_d \notin \mathcal{L}_e(x)$ **then** $\mathcal{L}_e(x) := \mathcal{L}_e(x) \cup \{\top_d\}$
$\top_\sqsubseteq$-rule:	**if** $x \in V_d$, $e \prec f$, $\neg \top_e \sqcup \top_f \notin \mathcal{L}_d(x)$ **then** $\mathcal{L}_d(x) := \mathcal{L}_d(x) \cup \{\neg \top_e \sqcup \top_f\}$
M-rule:	**if** $a^g \in V_d$, $a^h \in V_e$, and $d \preceq e$ **then** $\mathrm{merge}(a^g, a^h)$

Rules on the right of Table 1 are largely responsible for maintaining the CKR semantics. The $\Delta\downarrow$- and $\Delta\uparrow$-rules propagate nodes across contexts. Finally the $\top_{\sqsubseteq}$ is responsible to maintain the hierarchy of tops within each contexts, and the M-rule is responsible for note merging. These rules are adapted from the existing NEXPTIME algorithm for $\mathcal{ALC}$-based CKR: refer to [4] for further details. Necessary adaptations include especially implementing the so called *never look behind* strategy [6] under which all nodes are fully expanded before any generating rule is applied. The previously used $\top_R$-rule [4] violated this strategy: its function is now divided between $\exists$- and $\top_\exists$-rules.

The algorithm itself is presented in Fig. 2. It takes as input a CKR $\mathfrak{K}$ and generates an and-or graph. If eventually all top-nodes have status SAT the algorithm concludes that $\mathfrak{K}$ is d-satisfiable. If one of the top-nodes reaches status UNSAT the algorithm concludes the contrary. The and-or graph G is initialized in the first for each loop. All of the original ABox individuals are represented as nodes and marked as TOP.

In the main loop that follows G is expanded until all the TOP elements have a defined status SAT or UNSAT. In each iteration, an unexpanded node x is picked and processed. First, all of the expanding rules are applied on x; in this process the node is fully expanded. Consecutively the cache is queried and if the node was generated before, it is discarded and represented by its cached version. If there is a clash, the node is marked as UNSAT. Otherwise the algorithm proceeds with generating the successors of x. Following the never look behind strategy, or-successors are generated first so that we generate all the alternative versions of x which are further expanded in the future iterations of the loop. Only if the $\sqcup$-rule is no longer applicable, the $\exists$-rule is finally applied. Finally the node is pronounced satisfiable if its a leaf node (at this point there is no clash due to the preceding unsatisfiability check). If the rule has successors, its status is set to EXP and its satisfiability will be verified later by propagation from its successors. If the status SAT or UNSAT is already known, it is propagated to the node predecessors by calling the $\mathrm{propagate}(G, x)$ procedure shown in Fig. 3.

Special care must be observed when top-nodes (or their or-successors) are processed. Occasionally some of these nodes have to be merged using the M-rule: labels of such nodes and also incoming and outgoing edges are combined. Also, if the $\sqcup$-rule is applied on such a node x resulting into successors y and z, all ABox relations need to be propagated to y and z. Note also that after merging and or-branching of top-nodes or their or-successors the neighboring nodes are affected because further expansions may be triggered by the $\forall$-rule; hence these nodes are reset to status UNEXP.

Before discussing correctness of the procedure, we present an example of deduction.

Example 2. We revise the deduction example from [4]. Using the algorithm and our example CKR $\mathfrak{K}_{fb}$, we can show a proof for the following subsumption:

$$\mathfrak{K}_{fb} \models \mathbf{nfl10} : \mathsf{WorldChampionPlayer}_{fb} \sqsubseteq \forall\mathsf{playsFor}_{wc10}.\mathsf{WinnerTeam}_{wc10}$$

Intuitively, we are asking to verify whether, in the context of **nfl10**, "all of the world champion players play in a winner team in the World Cup". In the initialization step, since $\mathfrak{K}_{fb}$ does not contain ABoxes, we have $V_{\mathbf{nfl10}} = \{s_0^{\mathbf{nfl10}}\}$, $\mathcal{L}_{\mathbf{nfl10}}(s_0^{\mathbf{nfl10}}) = \{\mathsf{WorldChampionPlayer}_{fb} \sqcap \exists\mathsf{playsFor}_{wc10}.\neg\mathsf{WinnerTeam}_{wc10}\}$, and $s_0^{\mathbf{nfl10}}.\mathrm{type} = \mathsf{TOP}$, $s_0^{\mathbf{nfl10}}.\mathrm{status} = \mathsf{UNEXP}$. Since $\mathcal{C}_{\mathbf{nfl10}}$ is the only initialized context, we write s_0 in place of $s_0^{\mathbf{nfl10}}$ for simplicity of presentation. The expansion starts from s_0 with the following steps:

Input: CKR $\mathfrak{K}$, $\mathbf{d} \in \mathfrak{D}_\Gamma$
Output: And-or graph $G = \langle V, E, \mathcal{L}, \{\mathcal{L}_\mathbf{e}\}_{\mathbf{e} \in \mathfrak{D}_\Gamma} \rangle$ s.t. $\mathfrak{K}$ is $\mathbf{d}$-satisfiable iff,
for all $x \in V$ with TOP $\in$ x.type, x.status $=$ SAT

```
begin
  for each e ∈ 𝔇_Γ initialize V_e, ℒ_e, E, and ℒ:
```
$\quad\quad V_\mathbf{e} := \{a^\mathbf{e} \mid C(a) \in \mathrm{K}(\mathcal{C}_\mathbf{e})\} \cup \{a^\mathbf{e}, b^\mathbf{e} \mid R(a, b) \in \mathrm{K}(\mathcal{C}_\mathbf{e})\}$;
$\quad\quad E := \{\langle a^\mathbf{e}, b^\mathbf{e}\rangle \mid R(a, b) \in \mathrm{K}(\mathcal{C}_\mathbf{e}), \mathbf{e} \in \mathfrak{D}_\Gamma\}$;
$\quad\quad \mathcal{L}_\mathbf{e}(a^\mathbf{e}) := \{C \mid C(a) \in \mathrm{K}(\mathcal{C}_\mathbf{e})\}$, for all $a^\mathbf{e} \in V$;
$\quad\quad \mathcal{L}(\langle a^\mathbf{e}, b^\mathbf{e}\rangle) := \{R \mid R(a, b) \in \mathrm{K}(\mathcal{C}_\mathbf{e})\}$, for all $\langle a^\mathbf{e}, b^\mathbf{e}\rangle \in E$;
$\quad\quad x$.type $:= \{\text{TOP}\}$, x.status $:=$ UNEXP, for all $x \in V$;

```
  while (y.status ∉ {SAT, UNSAT} for some y ∈ V s.t. TOP ∈ y.type and
         there is x ∈ V s.t. x.status = UNEXP)
```

$\quad\quad$ // Node expansion
$\quad\quad$ **while** (one of $\sqcap$, $\forall$, $\mathcal{T}$, $\Delta_\uparrow$, $\Delta_\downarrow$, A, $\mathsf{T}_\exists$, T_A, $\mathsf{T}_\sqsubseteq$, M-rules is applicable on x)
$\quad\quad\quad$ **if** (M-rule is applicable on x and some y)
$\quad\quad\quad\quad$ apply M-rule on x and y yielding z; z.type $:= \{\text{TOP}\}$;
$\quad\quad\quad\quad$ z.status $:=$ UNEXP; w.status $:=$ UNEXP for all successors w of z;
$\quad\quad\quad$ **else** apply one of $\sqcap$, $\forall$, $\mathcal{T}$, $\Delta_\uparrow$, $\Delta_\downarrow$, A, $\mathsf{T}_\exists$, T_A, $\mathsf{T}_\sqsubseteq$-rules to x;
$\quad\quad\quad$ **end if**;
$\quad\quad$ **end while**;

$\quad\quad$ // Caching (the node is now fully expanded)
$\quad\quad$ **if** (there is a witness $x' \in V$ of x and TOP $\notin x$.type and TOP $\notin y$.type for all or-ancestors y of x)
$\quad\quad\quad$ **for** each $(y \in V$; y predecessor of $x)$
$\quad\quad\quad\quad$ add $\langle y, x'\rangle$ to E; $\mathcal{L}(\langle y, x'\rangle) := \mathcal{L}(\langle y, x\rangle)$; remove $\langle y, x\rangle$ from E;
$\quad\quad\quad$ **end for each**;
$\quad\quad\quad$ remove x from V;

$\quad\quad$ // Unsatisfiability check
$\quad\quad$ **else if** (x contains a clash) x.status $:=$ UNSAT;

$\quad\quad$ // Or-branching
$\quad\quad$ **else if** ($\sqcup$-rule is applicable on x)
$\quad\quad\quad$ apply $\sqcup$-rule to x yielding new nodes y, z;
$\quad\quad\quad$ **if** (TOP $\in x$.type)
$\quad\quad\quad\quad$ double all edges from/to x including labels and redirect to both y and z;
$\quad\quad\quad\quad$ w.status $:=$ UNEXP for all successors w of y and z;
$\quad\quad\quad$ **end if**;
$\quad\quad\quad$ y.type $:= z$.type $:= \{\}$; y.status $:= z$.status $:=$ UNEXP;
$\quad\quad\quad$ x.type $:= x$.type $\cup \{\text{OR}\}$; x.status $:=$ EXP;

$\quad\quad$ // And-branching
$\quad\quad$ **else if** ($\exists$-rule is applicable on x)
$\quad\quad\quad$ **while** ($\exists$-rule is applicable on x)
$\quad\quad\quad\quad$ apply $\exists$-rule to x yielding a new node y;
$\quad\quad\quad\quad$ y.type $:= \{\}$; y.status $:=$ UNEXP;
$\quad\quad\quad$ **end while**;
$\quad\quad\quad$ x.type $:= x$.type $\cup \{\text{AND}\}$; x.status $:=$ EXP;

$\quad\quad$ // Now x is a leaf node, fully expanded and satisfiable
$\quad\quad$ **else** x.status $:=$ SAT;
$\quad\quad$ **end if**;

$\quad\quad$ // Propagation check
$\quad\quad$ **if** (x.status $\in \{\text{SAT}, \text{UNSAT}\}$) propagate$(G, x)$; **end if**;
$\quad$ **end while**;
end.

Fig. 2. EXPTIME procedure for $\mathcal{ALC}$ CKR

Input: and-or graph $G = \langle V, E, \mathcal{L}, \{\mathcal{L}_\mathbf{e}\}_{\mathbf{e} \in \mathfrak{D}_\Gamma} \rangle$ and $y \in V$ with $y.\text{status} \in \{\text{SAT}, \text{UNSAT}\}$
Output: modified and-or graph G

```
begin
  queue := {y};
    while (queue not empty)
      extract x from queue;
      for each u ∈ V with (u, x) ∈ E and u.status = EXP
        if (u.type ∈ OR and one of its successors has status SAT)
        or (u.type ∈ AND and all of its successors have status SAT)
            u.status := SAT; queue := queue ∪ {u};
          if (u.type ∈ AND and one of its successors has status UNSAT)
          or (u.type ∈ OR and all of its successors have status UNSAT)
              u.status := UNSAT; queue := queue ∪ {u};
      end for each;
  end while;
end.
```

Fig. 3. $\texttt{propagate}(G, y)$ procedure

- $\mathcal{L}_{\mathbf{nfl10}}(s_0) := \mathcal{L}_{\mathbf{nfl10}}(s_0) \cup \{\text{WorldChampionPlayer}_{\mathbf{fb}},$
  $\exists \text{playsFor}_{\mathbf{wc10}}.\neg \text{WinnerTeam}_{\mathbf{wc10}}\}$ by $\sqcap$-rule;
- $V_{\mathbf{fb}} := \{s_0\}, \mathcal{L}_{\mathbf{fb}}(s_0) := \{\text{WorldChampionPlayer}\}$ by $\Delta\uparrow$ and A-rule;
- $\mathcal{L}_{\mathbf{nfl10}}(s_0) := \mathcal{L}_{\mathbf{nfl10}}(s_0) \cup \{\top_{\mathbf{wc10}}\}$ by $\top_\exists$-rule;
- $\mathcal{L}_{\mathbf{fb}}(s_0) := \mathcal{L}_{\mathbf{fb}}(s_0) \cup \{\top_{\mathbf{wc10}}\}, V_{\mathbf{wc10}} := \{s_0\}$ by A and $\Delta\downarrow$-rule;
- $\mathcal{L}_{\mathbf{fb}}(s_0) := \mathcal{L}_{\mathbf{fb}}(s_0) \cup \{\neg \text{WorldChampionPlayer} \sqcup \text{ChampionPlayer}_{\mathbf{wc10}}\},$
  $\mathcal{L}_{\mathbf{wc10}}(s_0) := \mathcal{L}_{\mathbf{fb}}(s_0) \cup \{\neg \text{ChampionPlayer} \sqcup \forall \text{playsFor.WinnerTeam}\}$ by $\mathcal{T}$-rule;
- The local expansion on s_0 terminates here: a pair of or-successors s_0^0 and s_0^1 are generated by the application of $\sqcup$-rule;
- $\{\neg \text{WorldChampionPlayer}, \text{WorldChampionPlayer}\} \subseteq \mathcal{L}_{\mathbf{fb}}(s_0^0)$, thus this node is recognized as clashing and $s_0^0.\text{status} := \text{UNSAT}$; $\mathcal{L}_{\mathbf{fb}}(s_0^1) := \mathcal{L}_{\mathbf{fb}}(s_0) \cup \{\text{ChampionPlayer}_{\mathbf{wc10}}\}$;
- $\mathcal{L}_{\mathbf{wc10}}(s_0^1) := \mathcal{L}_{\mathbf{wc10}}(s_0^1) \cup \{\text{ChampionPlayer}\}$ by A-rule;
- The local expansion on s_0^1 terminates here: a pair of or-successors s_0^2 and s_0^3 are generated by the application of $\sqcup$-rule;
- $\{\neg \text{ChampionPlayer}, \text{ChampionPlayer}\} \subseteq \mathcal{L}_{\mathbf{wc10}}(s_0^2)$, thus this node is recognized as clashing and $s_0^2.\text{status} := \text{UNSAT}$; $\mathcal{L}_{\mathbf{wc10}}(s_0^3) := \mathcal{L}_{\mathbf{wc10}}(s_0^1) \cup \{\forall \text{playsFor.WinnerTeam}\}$;
- The local expansion on s_0^3 terminates here: a successor $s_1 \in V_{\mathbf{nfl10}}$ is generated by the application of $\exists$-rule with $\mathcal{L}(\langle s_0^3, s_1 \rangle) = \{\text{playsFor}_{\mathbf{wc10}}\}, \mathcal{L}_{\mathbf{nfl10}}(s_1) := \{\neg \text{WinnerTeam}, \top_{\mathbf{wc10}}\}$;
- $V_{\mathbf{fb}} := V_{\mathbf{fb}} \cup \{s_1\}, \mathcal{L}_{\mathbf{fb}}(s_1) := \{\top_{\mathbf{wc10}}\}, V_{\mathbf{wc10}} := V_{\mathbf{wc10}} \cup \{s_1\}$ by $\Delta\uparrow$, A and $\Delta\downarrow$-rules;
- $\mathcal{L}_{\mathbf{wc10}}(s_1) := \mathcal{L}_{\mathbf{wc10}}(s_1) \cup \{\text{WinnerTeam}\}$ by $\forall$-rule;
- $\mathcal{L}_{\mathbf{fb}}(s_1) := \mathcal{L}_{\mathbf{fb}}(s_1) \cup \{\text{WinnerTeam}\}, \mathcal{L}_{\mathbf{nfl10}}(s_1) := \mathcal{L}_{\mathbf{nfl10}}(s_1) \cup \{\text{WinnerTeam}\}$ by A-rule;

Last rule application on s_1 leads to a clash, since $\{\neg \text{WinnerTeam}, \text{WinnerTeam}\} \subseteq \mathcal{L}_{\mathbf{nfl10}}(s_1)$. This causes the propagation of UNSAT status to s_0^3 and its predecessors until $s_0.\text{status}$ is assigned UNSAT, closing the deduction. The resulting and-or graph is depicted in Fig. 4: links from OR nodes are represented by dotted arrows, while solid arrows represent links from AND nodes. $\diamond$

3.1 Algorithm Correctness

We now prove that the presented algorithm is terminating, sound and complete w.r.t. CKR semantics. This is showed by a correspondence between the generated and-or graph and a CKR model. For space reasons, we provide only a sketch of the main steps.

Theorem 1 (Correctness). *Given a CKR $\mathfrak{K}$ and $\mathbf{d} \in \mathfrak{D}_\Gamma$ on the input, the tableaux algorithm always terminates and $\mathfrak{K}$ is $\mathbf{d}$-satisfiable iff it generates an and-or graph $G = \langle V, E, \mathcal{L}, \{\mathcal{L}_\mathbf{e}\}_{\mathbf{e} \in \mathfrak{D}_\Gamma}\rangle$ s.t. for all $x \in V$ with $\mathsf{TOP} \in x.\mathrm{type}$, $x.\mathrm{status} = \mathsf{SAT}$.*

Proof (Sketch.). **Termination.** Follows from Theorem 2 (see below).

Soundness. Assume that the algorithm constructs an and-or graph G such that $x.\mathrm{status} = \mathsf{SAT}$ for all $x \in V$ with $\mathsf{TOP} \in x.\mathrm{type}$. We show that $\mathfrak{K}$ is $\mathbf{d}$-satisfiable by constructing a model $\mathfrak{J} = \{\mathcal{I}_\mathbf{e}\}_{\mathbf{e} \in \mathfrak{D}_\Gamma}$ from G s.t. $\Delta_\mathbf{d} \neq \emptyset$ as follows:

- let $S := \emptyset$; for $x = a^{\mathbf{g}} \in V$, $\mathsf{TOP} \in x.\mathrm{type}$: if $\mathsf{OR} \notin x.\mathrm{type}$, define $S := S \cup \{x\}$ and $a^{\mathcal{I}_\mathbf{e}} = x$ for $\mathbf{e} \in \mathfrak{D}_\Gamma$ s.t. $a^{\mathbf{g}} \in V_\mathbf{e}$. Otherwise, if $\mathsf{OR} \in x.\mathrm{type}$, let $S := S \cup \{y\}$ and $a^{\mathcal{I}_\mathbf{e}} = y$ for y an or-successor of x s.t. $y.\mathrm{status} = \mathsf{SAT}$ and $\mathsf{OR} \notin y.\mathrm{type}$.
- for $x \in S$, let $\Delta_\mathbf{e} := \Delta_\mathbf{e} \cup \{x\}$ if $\mathbf{e} \in \mathfrak{D}_\Gamma$ s.t. $x \in V_\mathbf{e}$.
- for $x \in S$, let $A^{\mathcal{I}_\mathbf{e}} := A^{\mathcal{I}_\mathbf{e}} \cup \{x\}$ for all $A \in \mathcal{L}_\mathbf{e}(x)$ for $\mathbf{e} \in \mathfrak{D}_\Gamma$ s.t. $x \in V_\mathbf{e}$.
- for $x \in S$, if y is a R-successor of x: if y is not an OR node, $R^{\mathcal{I}_\mathbf{e}} := R^{\mathcal{I}_\mathbf{e}} \cup \{\langle x, y\rangle\}$, for all $R \in \mathcal{L}(\langle x, y\rangle)$ and $\mathbf{e} \in \mathfrak{D}_\Gamma$ s.t. $x, y \in V_\mathbf{e}$; add y to S if it has not been visited yet. Otherwise, if y is an OR node and z is an or-successor of y s.t. $z.\mathrm{status} = \mathsf{SAT}$ and $\mathsf{OR} \notin z.\mathrm{type}$, $R^{\mathcal{I}_\mathbf{e}} := R^{\mathcal{I}_\mathbf{e}} \cup \{\langle x, z\rangle\}$, for all $R \in \mathcal{L}(\langle x, y\rangle)$ and $\mathbf{e} \in \mathfrak{D}_\Gamma$ s.t. $x, y \in V_\mathbf{e}$; add z to S if it has not been visited yet.

From this model definition, we can show that if $C \in \mathcal{L}_\mathbf{e}(x)$ then $x \in C^{\mathcal{I}_\mathbf{e}}$.

Moreover we can show that $\mathfrak{J}$ satisfies conditions (1–9) of Definition 4. In particular, we note that condition 8 is satisfied: To prove the $\sqsubseteq$ inclusion, assume $\langle x, y\rangle \in R_\mathbf{f}^{\mathcal{I}_\mathbf{d}}$. Then by the construction $\langle x, y\rangle \in (\Delta_\mathbf{d} \times \Delta_\mathbf{d})$. Now we need to distinguish two cases. If $\langle x, y\rangle \in E$, then by application of the $\Delta\uparrow$-rule we obtain $x, y \in V_\mathbf{e}$ thus proving that also $\langle x, y\rangle \in R_\mathbf{f}^{\mathcal{I}_\mathbf{e}}$. The other case, when $\langle x, y\rangle \notin E$ is proven similarly, by showing the property for a $\langle x, y'\rangle \in E$ with y' an or-predecessor of y. On the other hand, to prove the $\sqsupseteq$ inclusion, we assume that $\langle x, y\rangle \in R_\mathbf{f}^{\mathcal{I}_\mathbf{e}} \cap (\Delta_\mathbf{d} \times \Delta_\mathbf{d})$. We can now show that $\langle x, y\rangle \in R_\mathbf{f}^{\mathcal{I}_\mathbf{d}}$ by the application of the $\Delta\downarrow$-rule.

Thus, $\mathfrak{J}$ is indeed a CKR model for $\mathfrak{K}$ and by construction $\Delta_\mathbf{d} \neq \emptyset$.

Completeness. Let $\mathfrak{J}$ be a model of $\mathfrak{K}$ s.t. $\mathfrak{K}$ is $\mathbf{d}$-satisfiable w.r.t. $\mathfrak{J}$. The proof is by bi-simulation: we simulate the run of the algorithm on the given input following the

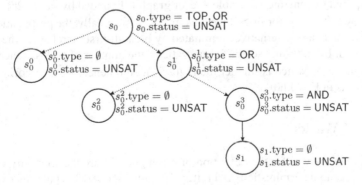

Fig. 4. And-or graph for Example 2

branch identified by $\mathfrak{J}$ and inductively construct a partial mapping $\pi : V \to \bigcup_{e \in \mathfrak{D}_\Gamma} \Delta_e$ for which we will show the following property ($*$):

For each node $x \in V$ and for each $e \in \mathfrak{D}_\Gamma$: (a) if $x \in V_e$ then $\pi(x) \in \Delta_e$; (b) if $C \in \mathcal{L}_e(x)$ then $\pi(x) \in C^{\mathcal{I}_e}$; (c) if $R \in \mathcal{L}(\langle x, y \rangle)$ with $x, y \in V_e$ then $\langle \pi(x), \pi(y) \rangle \in R^{\mathcal{I}_e}$; (d) if $a^g \in V_e$ then $a^{\mathcal{I}_e} = \pi(a^g)$.

The proof proceeds by showing that ($*$) is verified on every node $x \in V$ after each rule application and algorithm step. For example, in the application of the $\sqcup$-rule, with TOP $\notin x.\text{type}$: if the rule is applicable, $C_1 \sqcup C_2 \in \mathcal{L}_e(x)$. As ($*$) was satisfied before the rule was applied, we have either $\pi(x) \in C_1^{\mathcal{I}_e}$ or $\pi(x) \in C_2^{\mathcal{I}_e}$. After the rule is applied, let us define $\pi(y) := \pi(x)$ in the case $\pi(x) \in C_1^{\mathcal{I}_e}$ and $\pi(z) := \pi(x)$ otherwise. Hence ($*$) is still satisfied after the rule was applied: basically, in the definition of π we follow a branch that is consistent with the interpretation $\mathfrak{J}$.

At the end of the run, we can show by contradiction that no node mapped by π contains a clash: suppose that for $x \in V$ (in the domain of π), $e \in \mathfrak{D}_\Gamma$ and some concept D, we have both $D \in \mathcal{L}_e(x)$ and $\neg D \in \mathcal{L}_e(x)$. However, from ($*$) this would imply that $\pi(x) \in D^{\mathcal{I}_e} \cap \neg D^{\mathcal{I}_e}$, contradicting the fact that $\mathfrak{J}$ is a CKR interpretation.   □

3.2   Computational Complexity

Theorem 2 (Complexity). *The algorithm always terminates and runs in* EXPTIME.

Proof (Sketch.). The size of the input KB will be denoted by $|\mathfrak{K}| = |\mathfrak{M}| + \sum_{\mathcal{C} \in \mathfrak{C}} |K(\mathcal{C})| = m$. Observe that for the number n of contexts in $\mathfrak{K}$ we have $n \le m$ as adding a context into $\mathfrak{C}$ requires to add a number of axioms into $\mathfrak{M}$. There are at most m^2 possible concepts that can possibly appear in one of the labels. There are at most n labels, therefore the number of concepts in all node's labels is bounded by m^3. Therefore there are at most 2^{m^3} different nodes. For the nodes that are subject to caching this is a firm bound. However, the initial nodes and their or-descendant are not cached. Under each initial node, the binary tree of or-descendants has the depth at most m^3 because with each or-branching at least one label is expanded. Hence the maximum number of these nodes altogether is $m \times 2^{m^3}$. By analysing the main loop and each of the rules we are able to estimate the maximum number of steps required to generate one node by m^6. Hence the total number of steps required to generate the whole and-or graph is bounded by $m^7 \times 2^{m^3}$ and this is bounded by $O(2^{m^5})$ as for $m > 4$ we have $m^7 \le 2^{m^2}$. Finally, the propagation of the status bottom-up can be alternatively emulated by breadth-first search once the graph is fully generated. Breadth-first search is quadratic in the number of nodes, hence it takes at most $(m \times 2^{m^3})^2$ which is smaller then $O(2^{m^5})$. And hence, as the algorithm is deterministic, it is in EXPTIME.   □

4   Related Works

The principal references for the definition of our algorithm are the works by Goré and Nguyen proposing deterministic EXPTIME procedures for $\mathcal{ALC}$ [6] and its extensions (e.g. for $\mathcal{SHI}$ in [7]). For our goals, we only adapted the non optimized version of the algorithm from [6]. However, also by the fact that we follow the same *never look behind* approach in our rules and we work on a similar and-or structure, we could easily adopt some of the optimizations from [6]. For example, we can *avoid redundant computations* by noting that, if x is an AND node we can mark it as UNSAT as soon as an UNSAT successor is found (and similarly for OR nodes and SAT successors). We can also investigate *different search strategies* and *cutoffs* for our algorithm, to possibly prune unuseful branches on the base of node statuses.

The main complexity result for CKR has been described in [11]. Through a polynomial reduction to $\mathcal{SROIQ}$, it is proved that reasoning in $\mathcal{SROIQ}$-based CKR is 2NExpTime-complete. Thus, the contextualization of knowledge provided by CKR does not imply a complexity jump in reasoning. This "non-jumping property", however, can not be guaranteed for weaker languages by reusing the same translation: given that it introduces role chain axioms in the target, the resulting KB is strictly in $\mathcal{SROIQ}$. This property has been verified for $\mathcal{ALC}$-based CKR by proposing a different reduction in [3]. In order to stay in ExpTime, the reduction has been adapted to produce an $\mathcal{ALCO}(\sqcup)$ KB. However, using this reduction for reasoning is not practically efficient: the translation adds a large (cubic) number of axioms in order to track complex relations between qualified symbols in a single KB. Thus, while the presented ExpTime procedure may not add novelty to the complexity result, it clearly allows for more effective reasoning: local reasoning is executed on single node labels and only relevant consequences are propagated to other contexts.

A related proposal for the contextualization of the $\mathcal{ALC}$ is $\mathcal{ALC}_{\mathcal{ALC}}$ [9], a multimodal extension of $\mathcal{ALC}$ which shares with CKR the possibility to formalize the contextual structure in a distinct meta language. The two frameworks differ from the expressivity of the contextual assertions: for instance, in $\mathcal{ALC}_{\mathcal{ALC}}$ it is also possible to qualify knowledge with respect to classes of contexts. Complexity of reasoning in $\mathcal{ALC}_{\mathcal{ALC}}$ jumps to 2ExpTime: on the other hand, the result presented for CKR proves that contextualization of $\mathcal{ALC}$ can be obtained without such a complexity jump.

5 Conclusions

Contextualized Knowledge Repository (CKR) is a DL-based representation framework providing a contextual layer for Semantic Web knowledge resources. CKR knowledge bases can be built on top of $\mathcal{SROIQ}$ or any of its fragments: one relevant fragment is the $\mathcal{ALC}$ DL, for which reasoning is known to be ExpTime-complete. In this paper we presented a sound and complete ExpTime tableaux algorithm for $\mathcal{ALC}$ based CKR. While it was already known that reasoning in $\mathcal{ALC}$ based CKR is ExpTime-complete [3], this is the first direct tableaux procedure for this fragment meeting the complexity bound. The algorithm has been defined starting from a NExpTime tableaux algorithm [4,8] by adopting the approach introduced for $\mathcal{ALC}$ in [6]. Our procedure is extended to manage CKR contextual semantics and to include ABox reasoning.

As for future directions, we would like to extend the procedure to more expressive DL (e.g. $\mathcal{SROIQ}$) and study its optimizations, possibly by adapting some of the ideas in [6], in view of an implementation. Moreover, the fact that contexts are compatible but, to a certain extent, also independent, may be exploited [4] to study parallelization and distribution of reasoning.

References

1. Baader, F., Calvanese, D., McGuinness, D.L., Nardi, D., Patel-Schneider, P.F. (eds.): The Description Logic Handbook. Cambridge University Press (2003)
2. Bao, J., Tao, J., McGuinness, D.L.: Context representation for the semantic web. In: WebSci 2010 (2010)
3. Bozzato, L., Homola, M., Serafini, L.: ExpTime reasoning for contextualized $\mathcal{ALC}$. Tech. Rep. TR-FBK-DKM-2012-1, Fondazione Bruno Kessler, Trento, Italy (2012), http://dkm.fbk.eu/index.php/Resources
4. Bozzato, L., Homola, M., Serafini, L.: Towards More Effective Tableaux Reasoning for CKR. In: DL 2012. CEUR-WP, vol. 824, pp. 114–124. CEUR-WS.org (2012)
5. Donini, F.M., Massacci, F.: EXPTIME tableaux for $\mathcal{ALC}$. Artif. Intell. 124(1), 87–138 (2000)
6. Goré, R., Nguyen, L.: EXPTIME tableaux for $\mathcal{ALC}$ using sound global caching. In: DL 2007. CEUR-WP, vol. 250, pp. 299–306. CEUR-WS.org (2007)
7. Goré, R., Nguyen, L.A.: EXPTIME Tableaux with Global Caching for Description Logics with Transitive Roles, Inverse Roles and Role Hierarchies. In: Olivetti, N. (ed.) TABLEAUX 2007. LNCS (LNAI), vol. 4548, pp. 133–148. Springer, Heidelberg (2007)
8. Homola, M., Bozzato, L., Serafini, L.: Tableaux algorithm for reasoning with contextualized knowledge. Tech. Rep. TR-FBK-DKM-2011-1, Fondazione Bruno Kessler, Trento, Italy (2012), http://dkm.fbk.eu/index.php/Resources
9. Klarman, S., Gutiérrez-Basulto, V.: Two-dimensional description logics for context-based semantic interoperability. In: AAAI 2011. AAAI Press (2011)
10. Schmidt-Schauß, M., Smolka, G.: Attributive concept descriptions with complements. Artificial Intelligence 48(1), 1–26 (1991)
11. Serafini, L., Homola, M.: Contextualized knowledge repositories for the semantic web. J. of Web Sem., Special Issue: Reasoning with Context in the Semantic Web 12 (2012)

An Extended Turing Test: A Context Based Approach Designed to Educate Youth in Computing

James Hollister, Shane T. Parker, Avelino J. Gonzalez, and Ron DeMara

Intelligent Systems Lab (ISL), University of Central Florida, Orlando, FL, USA
{JHollister,Shane}@isl.ucf.edu,
{Avelino.Gonzalez,Ronald.Demara}@ucf.edu

Abstract. In a Science Museum / Center setting, a context based approach to an exhibit could provide the best results when trying to encourage young teens to pursue a career in a STEM (Science, Technology, Engineering, and Mathematics) field. An overview of our new context based exhibit that is currently being developed along with some preliminary test results indicate that the methods used in this exhibit have drawn young teens into exploring STEM careers.

Keywords: Context Based Reasoning, Turing Test, STEM, Avatar, Virtual Humans.

1 Introduction

Science Museums / Centers provide a great location to reach technology minded young teens and to encourage them to pursue a career in a STEM (Science, Technology, Engineering, and Mathematics) field. Several projects have already tried to take advantage of this fact by placing exhibits in Science Centers across the world. The exhibits have taken on a variety of forms. For example, the TOUr-guide RoBOT (TOURBOT) is a physical robot that moves around the environment where it is located. [1] "Ada and Grace" are at the Museum of Science in Boston and are avatars that inhabit a large screen in a fixed location. [2] Both of these exhibits act as museum guides or docents for visitors. The TOURBOT, having a physical presence, can guide guests through the different exhibits. Whereas "Ada and Grace" can only tell guests about different exhibits. A drawback with these particular AI embodiments, is a basic lack of understanding on the part of the guide and its ability to adapt to the context of the current situation. The context of the current situation plays an important role in understanding what a guest is asking. For example, if a guest simply asks the question "How far is it?" without knowing the current context, these AI guides would have no way of understanding what "it" refers to, however, if there was an awareness that the guest has been inquiring about the planet Mars, that gives the proper context of the question. We proposed a context based exhibit that would not only understand the current context but change contexts as needed. During this new exhibit, the user will be taught about the Turing Test through the creation of their own avatars. The use of contexts is further exploited when the guest is allowed to ask questions of their

P. Brézillon, P. Blackburn, and R. Dapoigny (Eds.): CONTEXT 2013, LNAI 8175, pp. 213–221, 2013.

created avatar. An overview of our new context based exhibit that is currently being developed along with some preliminary test results that lead us to believe we are on the right path is presented. Our exhibit and test results are based upon the American School System as the exhibit will be deployed in Orlando, Florida.

This paper is arranged in the following manner. Section two contains a brief overview of the exhibit setup and a description of the storyboard. The context based methods used within the exhibit are described and discussed in section three. The testing procedure and results are found in sections four and five, followed by conclusions in section six.

2   Overview

The goal of this exhibit is to present American middle school students (ages 11 - 14) with computer science and engineering topics and hopefully encourage them to pursue a career in a STEM (Science, Technology, Engineering, and Mathematics) field. Research has shown that students have already determined what field they want explore by the time they reach high school. [3] This reinforces the need to reach middle school students to influence them to pursue a career in a STEM field. In the exhibit, a display of a virtual representation of Dr. Alan Turing guides the user through the creation of their own virtual human (an avatar) and educates them about the Turing Test by putting their avatar through a modified Turing Test. The Turing Test was designed by Dr. Turing as a test for machine intelligence. [4] During the test, an individual submits a question to a machine and a secondary person and receives and answer from both. If the questioner cannot distinguish between a machine and the person from the responses, then the machine was said to be intelligent. During the creation of the user's virtual human, the user is able to customize what the avatar will look like, sound like, and know simply by selecting a face, a text to speech (TTS) voice, and selecting one of the provided knowledge bases. The ten provided faces are a diverse group mostly made up from people who work within our lab. There are a total of four TTS voices (two male and two female) for the user to make their selection and five different knowledge bases. The knowledge bases are: Planets, Science Center Information, Dinosaurs, Natural Disasters, and Mythical Creatures. Each knowledge base contains basic information about that particular topic. The exhibit booth is still in the development stages but will house the computer, speakers, microphone, web camera, Microsoft Kinect, a 23" LCD display screen positioned at sitting eye level, and a large touch screen positioned below the other display and angled so that the user can use it like a keyboard during the interaction. The display positioned at sitting eye level is the main display and used to display a virtual representation of Dr Alan Turing, the host of the exhibit and father of computer science and artificial intelligence. The touch screen is used to display pictures and videos to help the user understand concepts that the virtual representation of Dr. Alan Turing is presenting and provides the user with a secondary way of providing input into the system.

The exhibit begins with virtual representation of Dr Alan Turing standing in front of Colossus, the world's first programmable, electronic digital computer. [5] A large, green button with the words "Touch Here to Begin" is displayed on the touch screen. The user must touch the button on the touch screen to start the exhibit. Turing begins by giving the user a quick explanation of what they will be doing during the exhibit and give them information about the Turing Test. Dr. Turing then presents a small bit of information about Eliza, one of the first interactive intelligent programs, and allows the user a chance to interact with her. At this point, the user is presented with ten faces from which to select. The selected face will become the face of their virtual human that the user is creating. After the face has been selected, Turing walks the user through the process converting a picture into an avatar by narrating a video of the process on the touch screen. The user's avatar then joins Turing on the main display. An image of Turing and a user created avatar on the screen together can be seen in figure 1. At this point, the user is able to make a decision as to what part of their avatar to work on next: the voice, the brain, or the eyes.

Fig. 1. Dr. Turing on screen with an user created avatar

During the voice information, Turing explains the basics of how speech recognition functions and how a text to speech (TTS) system works. After the explanation, the user is able test four different TTS voices (two male and two female) for their avatar. When the user selects the brain topic, Turing provides the user with general information about knowledge bases. After Turing finishes giving the information, the user is able to select from five different pre-built knowledge bases to give to their avatar. Four of the five knowledge bases contain basic information about science topics including: Planets, Science Center Information, Dinosaurs, and Natural Disasters. The fifth knowledge base, Mythical Creatures, was designed to be a fun topic for the user. In the third option, the eyes, Turing uses the touch screen to show the user a live video feed of the user with boxes drawn around the all of the faces that are around the screen as Turing explains the need of knowing where to look. After the user completes all three modules, Turing gives the user a chance to interact with the avatar they created and ask questions related to the knowledge base they picked during the brain module. A list of known topics within the selected knowledge base are displayed on the touch screen in order to give the user a better idea of what to ask their avatar. The user can also ask their avatar questions by touching the topic on the touch screen. After the user has received three answers from their avatar, Turing moves the exhibit along by purposing the question "Could you be fooled into thinking your avatar is a real person?" This is our modified Turing Test. Turing provides some information to the user based upon how they answer the modified Turing Test and then tries to convince the user that they should pursue a career in computer science or engineering. At this point, Turing says goodbye to the user and the system resets by having the created avatar walk off screen.

3   Context Based Methods

The exhibit uses two separate context based systems in order to make the exhibit function as designed. The first context based system is a slightly modified version of Dr. Brézillon's Contextual Graph (CxG). [6] In a normal CxG, there are four basic components placed within a decision tree. A CxG can be seen in figure 2, a sample CxG that contains all of the possible elements of a CxG. The numbers located on each element is use only to identify the particular component. The first component is an Element Contextual, represented by the blue circle in the CxG below. The Element Contextual represents a decision that must be made during the processing of a decision tree. The response to the decision purposed within each Element Contextual dictates which branch to take in the decision tree. The second component of a CxG is an Action node, which is denoted by the green square.

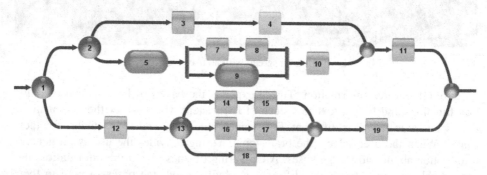

Fig. 2. An Example of a Contextual Graph

The Action node represents an action that must be completed in order to have the desired outcome from the decision tree. The Activity node, which is the third component, is represented by the purple oval. An Activity node is a contextual graph within a contextual graph. The one node representing an entire contextual graph within the current CxG. The fourth and final component of a CxG is a Gap, which is denoted by the red lines. A Gap signifies that all of the paths must be taken, however, the order of which paths is up to the person using the decision tree.

Our exhibit framework uses two of the four components of a contextual graph and introduces a new component. The framework reads in a CxG file and the controls the exhibit. The Element Contextual and Action node components are used from the original work. In our version, the Action nodes contains just about everything that is said, shown, or done on both of the screens. For example, everything that Turing could say during the exhibit and all of the different videos displayed on the touch screen is stored in several different Action nodes throughout the CxG. The Action nodes also allows certain internal variables to be set at the beginning of the exhibit and accessed later. Decisions based upon the internal variables and responses from the users are handled by the Element Contextual component in the CxG. This allows the exhibit to know and use the current context. For example, the user's avatar should not speak until the user has given it a voice and a newly created avatar should be trying out its new face by making "faces". We know exactly what the user has done in the exhibit and can adapt accordingly. The third component used in a CxG in our exhibit framework is a Goto node, which is represented by the orange box in the CxG above. The added Goto node allows the exhibit to amend the current context and move quickly into different context when required by being able to jump anywhere in the CxG. These three components are used in the CxG for our exhibit framework.

The second context based system used within the exhibit is contained in the section where the user interacts with their created avatar. This yet unnamed system is based upon the Hung's CONtext-centric Corpus-based Utterance Robustness (CONCUR). [7] CONCUR is designed to overcome poor automatic speech recognition (ASR). The quality of an ASR system can be determined by the word error rate (WER), which can vary between the speaker and the ambient noise. The WER is a percentage of errors found by dividing the number of errors by the number of words. In testing CONCUR, it was found that the ASR system had a WER of 60-70%. CONCUR uses a lightly annotated corpus / knowledge base that is contextually organized. This organization allows the system to quickly process corpus and categorize the knowledge into different contexts. When a user's input is received during a typical interaction, the text is analyzed and the keywords are extracted. After the text analysis, CONCUR performs two separate searches on the knowledge base. The first search is an exact search. Does what the user said match a contextual topic word for word? The exact search is extremely fast and has the potential of finding a suitable context but has a low success rate, as most users tend not to describe the contextual topic word for word. The second search compensates for the variation of speech patterns of the user along with the any errors introduced by the speech recognition. This is done though use of the keywords. During this search, each extracted keyword is evaluated to the different contextual topics. If a match is confirmed to a contextual topic, then that topic is added to a list of possible topics. After all the contextual topics in the knowledge base have been evaluated, the system analyzes the list of possible topics. If this list only contains one item, that topic is presented to the user. However, if the list contains multiple possible items, the list of topics is presented to the user and asks them to refine what was asked. The drawback with CONCUR is the lack of the ability to refine the answer. CONCUR randomly pulls several different sentences from the desired topic and hopes these sentences will answer the question. This hindrance means CONCUR can only answer general questions and not specific questions.

In our modification of CONCUR, we used a contextual graph with the Element Contextual and Action node components as the knowledge base instead of a lightly annotated corpus. All of the possible responses are stored within their own individual Action node and each path through the CxG will only contain one Action node. This allows the system to stop processing as soon as an Action node is located on a path. The Element Contextual components are used to refine the context of each of the responses. For example, the knowledge base includes information about the different planets. The first level, node 1 in figure 3, (or the context) would contain the broad topic of the names of the planets along with any other information that does not belong in any other contexts.

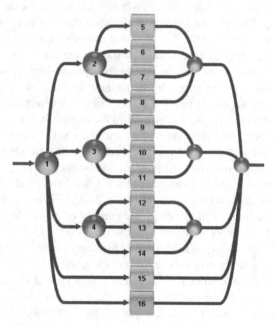

Fig. 3. An Example of the knowledge base format

The second level, nodes 2, 3, and 4 in figure 3, (or the sub-context) contains keywords that help the system refine the context in order to find the correct response for the question asked. In our example, the second level would contain items such as: life, water, and general information along with any common synonyms for those sub-contexts. The knowledge base format is not the only change we made to CONCUR.

Another modification we made to CONCUR, is the way the searches are conducted. We eliminated the exact search as it was atypical for this search to find a context let alone the correct sub-context. We begin with the original keyword search from CONCUR. In the improbable event that the search fails to find the context of what the user asked, we added a secondary search. In this secondary search, the system looks for keywords within words to help identify the proper context. For example, if the only keyword listed to end the conversation was "bye" and the speech recognition detected "goodbye," then the contains search would recognize that "goodbye" contains "bye" and select that context. For this search, we disqualify words with two letters or less. This disqualification prevents the system from matching common words such as "is" and "a" to the improper context. The "contains search" ensures that if there is any possibility of finding the correct context, we should be able to find it unless the speech recognition completely failed.

In order to understand how this functions, we walk through a plausible interaction using the planets knowledge base. Before the interaction occurs, the system reads into memory the selected knowledge base, in this case "Planets." This section of the exhibit begins with the user's created avatar asking "What would you like to know about" the selected knowledge base. A list of five possible contexts are randomly selected and displayed on the other screen in order to give the user a better idea of what to ask. For this example, let's say the speech recognition only detects the word "Mars." After completing the keyword search, the system will have found several matches, which causes the system to skip the "contains search". The system analyzes the several matches and determines that most of the possible matches are within the Mars context. All the possible matches that are not within the Mars context are removed from the list of possible matches. The user's created avatar inquires what the user would like to know about Mars. On the touch screen, the user is shown five or less, if the list is smaller, of the possible matches. The user's next input is compared against all of the sub-contexts within the Mars context, as that is the current conversational context, using the keyword search. If a match is found, the found response is returned and the whole process starts from the beginning all over again. If no matches can be found within the current context, the system assumes that the user may want to change the current context and commences the original search process from the beginning. This is how our exhibit framework uses context to answer the user's questions.

The reason behind the use of two different context based system is portability. We have the ability to immediately use the exhibit framework on an entirely new project with different needs and goals without requiring many changes. The question and answer component was designed to backwards compatible with our previous system, Project Lifelike. By keeping the two systems separate, we are able to maintain the portability of the different components.

4   Testing

In order to make the framework function as designed, the exhibit has undergone two rounds of testing at the Orlando Science Center, the final destination of the exhibit. The goal of the first round of testing was to make sure all of the user's interfaces were intuitive and easy to use. The exhibit was setup in a backroom at the Orlando Science Center and over the course of a weekend at least 40 guests were asked to try out the exhibit. The guests were only told that they were testing out a new exhibit and the Center would like their feedback on it. They were not given any direction on how to operate the exhibit. After they had finished running through the exhibit, the guests were asked to fill out a short survey about their experience and any issues they may have had. The guests were observed throughout the testing. All of the issues found during this round of testing were repaired and we performed a second round of testing. The goal of the second round of testing was to collect data on the guest overall experience with the exhibit. For example, was the length of the exhibit appropriate, did the exhibit flow smoothly, was the exhibit easy to follow, did the exhibit increase their interest in engineering, and did they enjoy the exhibit. They second round of testing was conducted in same manner as the first round with a focus on the surveys.

5   Results

Each response to the survey questions was answered on a scale from "strongly disagree" (1) to "strongly agree" (5). A response of 3 indicated a neutral stance on the question. On average, everyone had no opinion on the length of the exhibit, which had an average runtime of 6 minutes and 15 seconds. We had an overall positive response about the exhibit being easy to follow and flowed smoothly from one selection into another. The question about whether the exhibit increased the guest's interest in engineering provided some interesting results.

Table 1. Average for each question across the different age groups

	Length	Easy to Follow	Flowed Smoothly	Interest	Enjoyment
Elementary School (n=5)	3.00	4.30	4.60	4.80	5.00
Middle School (n=11)	3.00	4.36	5.00	4.18	4.91
High School (n=25)	3.17	4.22	4.04	3.61	4.35
Post College (n=15)	2.73	3.60	3.70	3.07	4.07
Overall (n=56)	3.11	4.24	4.2	3.82	4.45

Although the sample size was not large enough for all age groups, it appeared that the exhibit provoked a far greater interest in Elementary aged children than any other group. The Post College and our target age group (Middle school) had a slightly greater interest in engineering after the exhibit. The High school age remained, for the most part neutral. This could be due to the fact that they have already decided what field they would like to study. The question about whether the guest enjoyed the exhibit also showed an interesting trend. Elementary and Middle school aged children both provided overwhelmingly positive feedback about enjoying the exhibit. The High school and Post college age group provided a slightly positive feedback. The feedback across all of the age groups for the enjoyment level was a 4.45, which was close to our goal of 4.5. The averages for each age group including the overall group for each category can be seen in table 1.

6   Conclusions

The context of the situation and the conversional context both play an important role with conveying information. Based upon the results of the surveys (Easy to Follow and Flowed Smoothly), the framework appears to be able to correctly identify the current context and properly switch to the next one and make a smooth change that the user does not notice. The primary results lead us to believe that the modification of CONCUR may outperform our other dialog management systems in the question and answering domain. [8] The exhibit is currently being prepared for a third round of testing at the Orlando Science Center. This time the exhibit will not be in a backroom but placed on the main floor. This will allow us to gain a better understanding of how the user will interact with the exhibit during normal hours and use. By incorporating the context into the exhibit framework, we are able to quickly adjust to the desires of the users which will allow us to provide them with an enjoyable experience and provoke a young guest's interest in engineering.

Acknowledgements. A special thanks to Roger Thacher who provided the voice for Dr. Alan Turing.

References

1. Reitelmann, A., Niehaus, A., Trahanias, P.: TOURBOT: Interactive Museum Tele-presence Through Robotic Avatars Project Deliverable D12: TOURBOT Validation (2001)
2. Swartout, W., et al.: Ada and Grace: Toward Realistic and Engaging Virtual Museum Guides. In: Safonova, A. (ed.) IVA 2010. LNCS (LNAI), vol. 6356, pp. 286–300. Springer, Heidelberg (2010)
3. Tai, R.H., Qi Liu, C., Maltese, A.V., et al.: Planning Early for Careers in Science. Science 312, 1143–1144 (2006)
4. Turing, A.: Computing Machinery and Intelligence. In: Epstein, R., Roberts, G., Beber, G. (eds.) Parsing the Turing Test, pp. 23–65. Springer, Netherlands (2009)
5. Copeland, B.J.: Colossus: The First Electronic Computer: The secrets of Bletchley Park's code-breaking computers. OUP, Oxford (2006)
6. Brezillon, P., Pasquier, L., Pomerol, J.-C.: Reasoning with contextual graphs. European Journal of Operational Research 136, 290–298 (2002)
7. Hung, V.C.: Robust Dialog Management Through a Context-centric Architecture. University of Central Florida, Orlando, Florida (2010)
8. Hollister, J., Parker, S., Gonzalez, A., et al.: Who says it best? A Comparison of Four Different Dialog Management Systems. In: Society, B. (ed.) 21st Behavior Representation in Modeling & Simulation (BRIMS) Conference, Amelia Island, FL (2012)

Toward Distributed Context-Mediated Behavior for Multiagent Systems

Roy M. Turner[1], Sonia Rode[1], and David Gagne[2]

[1] School of Computing, University of Maine, Orono, ME 04444 USA
{rturner,sonia.rode}@maine.edu
[2] Department of Computer Science,
University of Southern Maine, Portland
ME 04104 USA
david.gagne1@maine.edu

Abstract. Although much attention has been devoted to modeling and using context in intelligent agents, relatively little has been given to the problem for multiagent systems (MASs). Yet, just as with an individual agent, context affects how a MAS should behave. In this paper, we discuss an approach to distributed context management for multiagent systems. The approach is based on earlier work on context-mediated behavior (CMB) for single agents, which explicitly represents contexts as c-schemas that contain knowledge about how to behave in the contexts represented. We are distributing CMB for use in advanced multiagent systems. This work is just beginning, and so the paper discusses issues and potential approaches to distributing CMB.

Keywords: Context-mediated behavior, multiagent systems, context assessment.

1 Introduction

Modeling context and the use of contextual knowledge has been the subject of intense interest in recent years, not only in the interdisciplinary context community (as represented, e.g., in the CONTEXT conference series), but also in natural language understanding, ubiquitous computing, and context-aware applications. With the exception of work in natural language understanding, most work has focused on understanding the role of context and contextual knowledge in the decision processes of single agents. The literature is far too broad to synopsize here, but our own past work (e.g., [1,2]) is somewhat representative, focusing on explicitly representing contexts as first-class objects, having agents assess their current situation in terms of known contexts, and then using the resulting contextual knowledge to guide the agent to behave appropriately.

Context is also important for multiagent systems (MAS), however. In the simplest case, a context-aware agent will know how best to behave within the structure and environment of a MAS. But the role of context in a MAS goes beyond this. One can also think of the context of the MAS as a whole. If the

P. Brézillon, P. Blackburn, and R. Dapoigny (Eds.): CONTEXT 2013, LNAI 8175, pp. 222–234, 2013.

MAS' agents can, together, recognize this *global context* (joint context, shared context), then potentially they can all behave more appropriately and effectively as members of the MAS, and, consequently, the MAS as an entity will behave appropriately for its context.

As an example, consider a complex scenario: using a MAS composed of autonomous underwater vehicles (AUVs) to respond to a plane going down in the North Atlantic. The MAS will need to characterize the debris field, search for any survivors, and find the airplane's black boxes. Using a MAS for this is ideal in many respects, since the area is remote, the environment is hostile, and the task may take a long time, all things that argue against a human presence. However, such a MAS faces many practical problems. First, the AUVs must somehow arrive at the site of the crash. This means that either they must travel there under their own power, be delivered by ship or submarine, or be dropped from an airplane, so it is likely some of the AUVs may not survive, or may arrive very late. Second, since the frequency of crashes is low and the cost of AUVs is very high, it would likely not make sense to have a dedicated set of vehicles for this task. Rather, the MAS should be able to use any AUVs that can be made available by governments, industry, or academia. Thus the resulting MAS will be heterogeneous, and, due also to the delivery problem, its composition and capabilities may not be predictable ahead of time. This means that an organization for the MAS cannot be devised ahead of time, but rather must be designed by the MAS itself, on-site. Third, agents by their nature will occasionally fail, need to refuel/recharge, or be needed elsewhere; others may become available. Consequently, the composition of the MAS will change over time, which, coupled with the fact that the environment will be dynamic, the sensors uncertain, and the agents' knowledge uncertain and incomplete, means that the MAS will need to be able to reorganize itself as needed.

Attention to context comes into play in several ways for such a MAS. Individual agents that are aware of the global context can make better decisions about how to behave within the MAS by matching their local behavior to the needs and constraints of the MAS as a whole. They can interpret their sensory information better by making use of knowledge about the global context, for instance, and they can focus their attention on goals that are most supportive of the goals of the MAS, either those explicitly known or those inferred from the context. They can choose actions to take to achieve goals that are appropriate for the MAS' context.

Beyond the local behavior of individual agents, however, knowledge about the global context can directly benefit the MAS as a whole. This is most apparent for the kind of MAS just described. The problem of designing an organization for such a MAS is context-dependent. Different organizations (e.g., hierarchies, teams, etc.) have different strengths and weaknesses depending on properties of the environment (e.g., uncertainty and change), communication (e.g., bandwidth, type of communication channel, whether or not the mission is covert), and the MAS itself (e.g., how many agents are present, their intelligence level, etc.). Identifying the global context that is implied by such properties of the current situation can help the MAS decide which organization or organizations (if it can merge several) are best.

In past work, we have concentrated on single-agent context assessment and use, and we have considered the problem of extending this to the multiagent case by having a single agent design the organization based on its view of the global context [3]. However, a much better approach, and the one we consider in this paper, is decentralizing the context assessment process. This removes a potential single point of failure, offloads from a single agent some of the burden of context assessment, and makes use of different agents' viewpoints and contextual knowledge.

The work presented in this paper is preliminary. We first discuss our overall approach, called *context-mediated behavior* (CMB) [1]. We then discuss issues relating to distributing this process across a subset of agents of a MAS and some directions we are exploring to address these issues.

2   Context-Mediated Behavior

In context-mediated behavior, an agent's contextual knowledge is stored in knowledge structures called *contextual schemas* (c-schemas).[1] Each is a frame-like structure representing a *context*, which in our approach is a class of similar situations, each of which has similar or the same implications for the agent's behavior. C-schemas are usually stored in a content-addressable memory (e.g., [5]) to allow features of the situation to be used to retrieve c-schemas that are similar to the current situation.

A given situation can be a member of more than one context. For example, if an AUV is taking data samples under sea ice while its batteries are low, then this situation can be viewed as an instance of each of the contexts "data collection mission", "under ice", and "low power", depending on which contexts the agent knows about before hand. If this situation turned out to have different implications about behavior than could be derived from combining information in the c-schemas, then a new c-schema would be learned for this context and stored appropriately by relating it to the other contexts.

The process of context-mediated behavior for an individual agent is shown in Figure 1. We call the part of the agent that does context assessment the *context manager* (ConMan). ConMan contains functionality to assess the context as well as interface with the rest of the agent to distribute the contextual knowledge as needed.

The overall process of assessing the context is a diagnostic process analogous to medical diagnosis, where features of the situation (cf. "signs and symptoms" of medical diagnosis) are used to diagnose the context (i.e., select a context that can explain the features). We use a differential diagnosis process based on work in the artificial intelligence in medicine program INTERNIST-I [6] that allows

---

[1] The name was chosen to differentiate these schemas from others used in the original work for procedural and strategic knowledge, p-schemas and s-schemas, respectively [4].

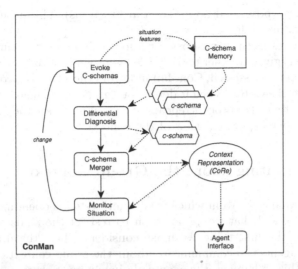

Fig. 1. The context-mediated behavior process. For clarity, lines representing information flow about situation features into the context manager (ConMan) are not shown.

multiple context hypotheses to be played off against one another to find the best one(s) that fit the situation.

The process starts when ConMan uses features of the situation to probe its c-schema memory. This will elicit, or *evoke*, one or more c-schemas, each of which is a candidate to represent some facet of the current situation; we can think of this as ConMan being "reminded" of these c-schemas based on the situation (cf. [7]).

The next step is to more closely examine and compare the c-schemas to find those that truly represent aspects of the current context. This is done by comparing the c-schemas with respect to the features they predict that are present and those that are not, and those that are present they do not predict. To do this, c-schemas are grouped into *logical competitor sets* [8], each element of which is a c-schema that can basically explain the same set of situational features. The hypotheses are scored, and then ConMan attempts to *solve* the set by increasing confidence in one hypothesis relative to the others by some given amount. This is done using various strategies based on those described by Miller *et al.* [6]. This is done for each competitor set until ConMan is left one or more c-schemas, each of which represents part of the context.[2]

The c-schemas remaining are then merged to create an overall picture of the context called the *context representation*, or (CoRe). This is not a simple problem, since the elements of each c-schema can have various relationships with each other, such as compatible, overlapping, superseding, conflicting, and so forth. Note that our approach differs from, e.g., that of [9], who use a simple

---

[2] The process is not quite this simple, since the act of trying to solve a competitor set can cause the sets to need to be recomputed.

algebra for this purpose (and no differential diagnosis). This aspect of CMB is an area of active research.

The CoRe serves as the repository for knowledge about the current context. This knowledge is given to other parts of the agent via ConMan's agent interface.

After the context is assessed, ConMan monitors the situation, comparing it to predictions from the CoRe. When it detects a significant change (which depends partly on the context), the process repeats so that at all times, the agent attempts to maintain a coherent, current view of the context.

3   Communicating about the Group Context

Given that the kind of MAS in which we are interested is open, meaning agents can come and go, and that we do not wish to restrict the kinds of agents that can participate, the first thing we must consider is how the different, likely heterogeneous, agents can communicate about the group context.

In order for this to happen, the agents obviously must share a common communication language. There are many existing agent communication languages, and our approach is agnostic as to which to use, as long as all agents have access to it and the language is sufficiently expressive to carry the knowledge needed. Second, along with the language, the agents also need to be able to express their own knowledge, regardless of their internal knowledge representation, in a common representation that can be transmitted via the language. In our work, we have used a frame-based representation, and we are now considering augmenting or replacing this with a description logic. Mastrogiovanni *et al.* [10] has made a start toward a situation description language. However, our approach is agnostic as to this shared representation language as well.

The third thing that is needed is a common ontology for context and contextual knowledge. There has been some work on ontologies for context (e.g., [11,12,13]). However, many of these approaches take a simplistic view of context (e.g., context is location or user task), have a shallow ontology, or both. What is needed is not only an ontology for contexts per se, but also one that includes the kinds of things that comprise contextual knowledge for open MASs.

Unfortunately, an ontology of contexts is somewhat difficult to specify a priori given our approach to context representation. Contextual schemas grew out of work in case-based reasoning: they are essentially generalized cases. Our approach relies on an agent being able to update its contextual knowledge based on its own experience, including modifying existing c-schemas, learning new relationships between them, and learning new ones. This is supported by the kind of schema memory we use (e.g., [5]). One can view the c-schema memory as an evolving, changing ontology.

We can, however, provide agents with a basic ontology for contexts to serve as the basis for their (ultimately) idiosyncratic ontologies. A start toward such an ontology is shown in Figure 2. To the extent that the agents do not modify this "upper ontology", they will have at least some basis for communication. Idiosyncratic contexts derived from the agents' own experiences will need to be

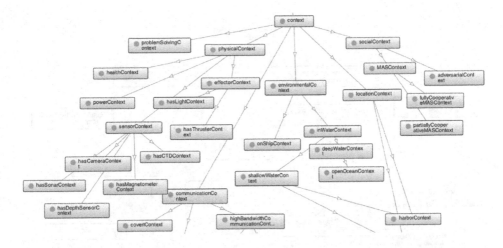

Fig. 2. A starting point for an ontology of contexts. (Figure produced by OntoGraf.)

discussed in relation to a shared upper ontology. Work on how this is to be done is ongoing.

With respect to the contents of contextual schemas, a shared ontology is more feasible and straightforward. The classes in the ontology reflect the kinds of knowledge useful in our c-schemas (and, we believe, for contextual reasoning in general), as shown in Figure 3. This includes knowledge about predicted features of the situation, context-dependent meaning of concepts (e.g., [14]), event-handling knowledge, knowledge about goal priority (attention focusing knowledge), knowledge of how to achieve goals, and various behavioral settings ("standing orders") that should automatically come into effect in the context.

A key problem for an agent during context assessment is deciding if others are referring to the same context it is. This is a variant of the reference problem from natural language processing [e.g., E. Turner and Matthias, 1998]. There are three possibilities here, if agent A believes the context is represented by c-schema C_A and agent B is believes it is represented by its c-schema C_B. First, C_A and C_B could actually refer to the same context. Determining this seems at first glance straightforward, but it is not. The context may be labeled differently by A and B, for example, if the c-schemas have been learned from their own experience (and hence, were not part of the common context ontology). Even if they are labeled the same, the knowledge contained in each may differ, even about the same context, again due to the differences in the agent's experiences. However, if the agents can recognize that their c-schemas represent the same context, they may be able to synchronize their knowledge.

A second case is when C_A and C_B are not identical, but each represent variants of the same context. For example, C_A may refer to "in Boston Harbor on a weekend" while C_B is "in Boston Harbor on a holiday". Here, the agents may be able to use their ontologies to identify a common ancestor of the c-schemas (e.g., "in Boston Harbor") as a basis to begin reasoning about the context.

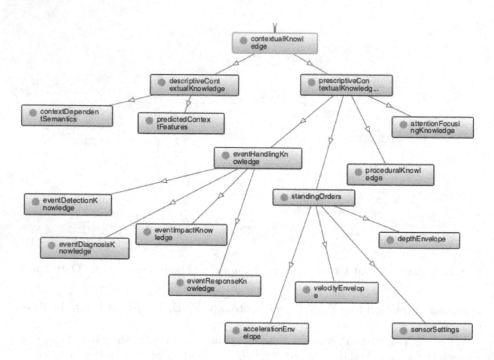

Fig. 3. A portion of the ontology for contextual knowledge. (Figure produced by On-toGraf.)

Finally, C_A and C_B may represent entirely different, possibly incommensurate, contexts. In this case, the agents will need to negotiate to attempt to resolve the conflict.

This problem, as well as the related problem of ensuring that contextual knowledge stored in c-schemas is mutually commensurate, is an active area of research.

4   Deciding How to Distribute the Process

The problem of distributed context assessment is, itself, context-dependent. The appropriate way to distribute the task is determined by such things as the number of agents capable of participating, the communication characteristics (bandwidth, speed of channel, broadcast versus point-to-point channel, etc.), and the degree of time pressure. For example, if there are many agents, reasonable bandwidth, and no significant time pressure, then distributing the process over all agents may make sense; if there are only a very few agents capable of participating, very low bandwidth, or very high time pressure, then it may make sense to allow one agent to assess the context for everyone.

The first step, then, in distributing context assessment is for each agent to "pre-assess" the context.[3] Depending on the assessment, the agents may have to seek agreement from others, or the outcome may be so clear that no further communication is needed. This will depend on the cooperation protocols in use by the MAS.[4]

The distribution mechanism may vary as well, depending on the context. For example, there are four basic tasks for context assessment in CMB: evoke hypotheses, form competitor sets, solve competitor sets, and merge the results. Any or all of these could be distributed, depending on the context pre-assessment. For example, to reduce communication, the process could be distributed as follows: agents all evoke hypotheses based on their local context and communicate the hypotheses to everyone; competitor sets are formed by each agent, with the (possibly fallacious) assumption that agents will all create the same sets; agents select which set(s) they will attempt to solve based on some a priori convention (e.g., an agent might select a set if it was the first to evoke its top hypothesis); and then the final set of hypotheses would be used for distributed context merger to create a context representation. In a different context, it might be better to distribute each of the parts.

At present, we are concentrating on the case in which all parts of the CMB process will be distributed. Future work will look more closely at this issue of pre-assessment and context-dependent selection of distribution strategy.

5   Distributed Context Hypothesis Evocation

The first step of context assessment is finding candidate context hypotheses by determining which c-schemas are *evoked* from memory based on the situation. This could be done by a single agent if necessary, but the different viewpoints, agent knowledge, and c-schema repertoires all argue for having each agent perform this task.

Each agent's evocation of some candidate hypotheses for the global context is a natural consequence of its own context assessment. (Here, we assume that distributed context assessment is restricted to context-aware agents.) The problem is determining which c-schemas have global rather than purely local scope. This is somewhat harder than it seems. For example, if a local hypothesis is that the agent is in the context of operating on low power, this would seem to be a purely local context; however, it may be the case that the global context is affected by this, as well, since the MAS may need to take into account that some of its assets (e.g., this agent) may have to leave the system before the mission is done.

A question also arises of which of the locally-evoked c-schemas should be shared. While the most general solution would be to share all of them, this may

---

[3] The c-schemas representing this "meta-context" likely will be similar to our earlier strategic schemas that determined the style of problem solving [4].

[4] See [16] for an example of protocols where individual decisions can be followed with little need for communication.

not be the most efficient, both from the standpoint of communication bandwidth and computational load on the overall system. It may be best to share only those that have gone through the local agent's differential diagnosis process to become part of its own CoRE; however, this may cause the MAS to miss some reasonable candidates that were ruled out by the local agent because it lacked global knowledge that would have included it.

Although the set of agents' c-schemas evoked this way will be a good source of global context hypotheses, it may not be sufficient. Some c-schemas might have been evoked locally by an agent if only it had access to information another agent has about the environment or other situational features. For example, suppose agent A has knowledge about operating in a context in which a thermocline (a temperature/density discontinuity which affects acoustic communication) is present, but does not observe one from its location, and agent B observes a thermocline, but does not have any knowledge about such a context. In this case, the information about the environmental feature should be communicated from B to A. In general, though, it is a difficult to determine what should be communicated: too much, and the communication channel will possibly be saturated; too little, and some c-schemas will not be evoked that should be.

It may be that some kinds of information can be identified as generally evocative, for example, particular environmental features, or the properties of an agent's schema memory may predict the value of asking others for particular information. For example, in a dynamic conceptual memory as we have used in the past [5,4], an agent could during memory search identify salient features that, if it knew their value, would allow it to retrieve important c-schemas. Addressing this problem in general will be an active area of future research.

6   Competitor Set Formation

The next step is to create logical competitor sets from the evoked hypotheses by grouping them according to what they explain. As part of this process, the hypotheses are scored and ranked according to what they do and do not explain. The issues involved in distributing this process are determining who makes the decision about which hypothesis belongs in which set and determining which situational features each hypothesis does/does not explain.

The entire MAS (or rather, the context-aware members) could decide on the composition of the sets. This could be done by all agents reaching common knowledge (by communication and possibly negotiation) about the set of evoked c-schemas, then negotiating about set membership. Alternatively, this process could progress in a general sense like the process of partial global plan formation [17]. Agents could each decide on the set of competitor sets, then share this with their neighbors (by location, e.g., to reduce communication lag time), which then critique the set based on their own sets and knowledge of what each hypothesis explains. Over time, a (partial) global set of competitor sets could evolve via negotiation. Or, finally, the problem of competitor set creation could be divided amongst the agents by negotiation or convention, as mentioned above. The best way to do this has yet to be determined.

7   Solving Competitor Sets

Differential diagnosis is used to "solve" the competitor sets to arrive at a final set of c-schemas. It involves comparing hypotheses within each competitor set based on what they each explain or fail to explain about the current situation and gathering new information until one hypothesis exceeds some threshold value beyond the nearest competitor.

Similarly to the above discussion about distributing context evocation, this process can be fully distributed or done largely by individual agents. In a fully-distributed version, the agents would all have common knowledge of the competitor sets and their composition, and they would exchange information about situational features and negotiate to come to agreement about the scores of the hypotheses. The agents would also need to gather additional information to solve the sets, either by eliciting information already known by some agent(s) in the system or by taking actions (e.g., using a sensor) to gather new information. With agents having common knowledge about the set being worked on, some communication might be avoided: an agent that had the requisite information could just supply it rather than having to be asked.

Another possibility is for the competitor sets to be parceled out to individual agents for them to solve. This could be done by convention, for example, based on which agent suggested the topmost hypothesis in a set (with ties also being broken by convention). Or a more sophisticated distribution could be done, with the kinds of information needed to solve the set being matched to what knowledge particular agents have. Responsibility for solving a set could even be shifted among the agents over time based on what information is currently needed to make progress on the solution.

Regardless of the distribution, the agents will likely disagree on some aspects of the process, in particular, which situational features are or are not explained by a given c-schema. Consequently, there will need to be negotiation mechanisms in place to allow the agents to arrive at some consensus on such issues.

8   Merging Contextual Knowledge

Once all the competitor sets have been solved, the MAS will be left with a set of c-schemas, each of which represents some part of the current context. The next step is to merge the knowledge from these to form the overall context representation (CoRe). Context merger could be handed off to a single agent, but to make use of all agents' different knowledge and viewpoints, it should be distributed. Merger can be done proactively, with all knowledge merged immediately, or more lazily, with knowledge merged only when needed, e.g., to make a decision about an aspect of organization design.

Merging contextual knowledge is difficult, especially in the distributed case. Not only can different c-schemas provide conflicting knowledge (e.g., the predicted impact of an unanticipated event), but different agents can have different beliefs about it as well.

We have looked at the former problem to some extent and have some idea about how to merge knowledge from different c-schemas. For example, if the knowledge is numerical, depending on the context, it may be reasonable to abstract the information to a range of values or a set of possible values; ranges can be intersected or unioned, as can fuzzy sets; and symbolic values can sometimes be merged by appeal to the ontology (e.g., by abstracting to a common ancestor). Others, for example, Bikakis and Antoniou [18], have looked at this problem of conflict resolution in the multiagent case, but the strategies for merger tend to be much simpler than what we feel is needed. In addition, getting different agents to agree on which features a c-schema does/does not explain will also be difficult and will likely involve negotiation.

All agents could participate in all aspects of the merger process. Alternatively, an agent or a small set of agents could be identified for different elements of the c-schemas, for example, for event-handling knowledge. It would then be responsible for merging that portion of the CoRe. The CoRe might itself be distributed this way, with no agent having knowledge of the whole thing; instead, the agents that merged portions of the CoRe could be responsible for that portion. Although this is attractive from the standpoint of reducing any particular agent's need to store the CoRE, drawbacks include having possible single points of failure for some parts of the CoRe as well increasing message traffic to access parts of the CoRe that an agent does not have.

9   Using the Contextual Knowledge

Once the MAS has assessed the context and has a CoRe available, the contextual knowledge it contains needs to be made available to the agents as they require it. If the CoRe is disseminated in its entirety to all agents, then this problem is trivial. However, if not, then an agent needing, say, organizational design knowledge, would first have to determine where such knowledge resides, then obtain it. Finding the knowledge could be done easily by giving all agents common knowledge of which agents are responsible for which parts of the CoRe. However, since we are interested in an open MAS, that may change over time. A better approach might be either to have a broker (e.g., [19]) for the information or to have agents broadcast requests for contextual knowledge, depending on the communication constraints (which are, of course, context-dependent).

10   Continuous Context Assessment

Creating the CoRe is only one phase of the overall process of context management. As the situation changes, the MAS will have to assess the context in response. Thus, in addition to carrying out the tasks assigned to the MLO, the MLO will also have to devote effort and communication bandwidth to monitoring and assessing the context. For example, in our work on multiagent systems, a *meta-level organization* (MLO) first self-organizes in order to design an efficient *task-level organization* (TLO) to carry out the mission [16]. In past work, the

MLO disappeared as the system transitioned to the TLO. To add decentralized context assessment to this approach, the MLO will need to continue in some capacity as an entity that can continuously assess the context.

11   Conclusions and Future Work

In this paper, we have discussed some issues related to distributed context assessment for multiagent systems, in particular for distributing our context-mediated behavior approach. As should be apparent, although we have identified important issues and some mechanisms to address them, this work is still in an early stage.

We are currently working to integrate a distributed version of CMB into our CoDA (Cooperative Distributed AOSN[5] control) approach to multiagent organization/reorganization [16]. Work is currently focusing on developing an ontology for context and a representation language to allow communication between the agents and developing the distributed CMB approach described above.

We anticipate that adding contextual reasoning abilities to multiagent systems will dramatically improve the performance of individual agents as well as that of the MAS as a whole, in particular by improving the speed and quality of organization design. Whether or not this improvement is outweighed by the overhead of distributed context assessment, which may entail adding ConMan modules to non-context-aware agents, is an open question, although we believe that it will be worth it. As our work matures, we intend to test this hypothesis via simulation experiments and experiments using our autonomous land robots.

References

1. Turner, R.M.: Context-mediated behavior for intelligent agents. International Journal of Human–Computer Studies 48(3), 307–330 (1998)
2. Turner, R.M.: A model of explicit context representation and use for intelligent agents. In: Bouquet, P., Serafini, L., Brézillon, P., Benercetti, M., Castellani, F. (eds.) CONTEXT 1999. LNCS (LNAI), vol. 1688, pp. 375–388. Springer, Heidelberg (1999)
3. Gagne, D., Rode, S., Turner, R.M.: Distributed, context-based organization and reorganization of multi-AUV systems. In: Proceedings of the 18th International Symposium on Unmanned, Untethered Submersible Technology (UUST), Portsmouth, NH (August to appear)
4. Turner, R.M.: Adaptive Reasoning for Real-World Problems: A Schema-Based Approach. Lawrence Erlbaum Associates, Hillsdale (1994)
5. Lawton, J.H., Turner, R.M., Turner, E.H.: A unified long-term memory system. In: Althoff, K.-D., Bergmann, R., Branting, L.K. (eds.) ICCBR 1999. LNCS (LNAI), vol. 1650, pp. 188–202. Springer, Heidelberg (1999)
6. Miller, R.A., Pople, H.E., Myers, J.D.: INTERNIST–1, an experimental computer-based diagnostic consultant for general internal medicine. New England Journal of Medicine 307, 468–476 (1982)

---

[5] Autonomous oceanographic sampling networks [20].

7. Kolodner, J.L.: Retrieval and Organizational Strategies in Conceptual Memory. Lawrence Erlbaum Associates, Hillsdale (1984)
8. Feltovich, P.J., Johnson, P.E., Moller, J.A., Swanson, D.B.: LCS: The role and development of medical knowledge and diagnostic expertise. In: Clancey, W.J., Shortliffe, E.H. (eds.) Readings in Medical Artificial Intelligence, pp. 275–319. Addison–Wesley Publishing Company, Reading (1984)
9. Padovitz, A., Loke, S.W., Zaslavsky, A.: Multiple-agent perspectives in reasoning about situations for context-aware pervasive computing systems. IEEE Transactions on Systems, Man and Cybernetics, Part A: Systems and Humans 38(4), 729–742 (2008)
10. Mastrogiovanni, F., Scalmato, A., Sgorbissa, A., Zaccaria, R.: Robots and Intelligent Environments: Knowledge Representation and Distributed Context Assessment. Automatika–Journal for Control, Measurement, Electronics, Computing and Communications 52(3) (2011)
11. Wang, X.H., Zhang, D.Q., Gu, T., Pung, H.K.: Ontology based context modeling and reasoning using OWL. In: Proceedings of the Second IEEE Annual Conference on Pervasive Computing and Communications, pp. 18–22 (2004)
12. Bucur, O., Beaune, P., Boissier, O.: Representing context in an agent architecture for context-based decision making. In: Proceedings of the Workshop on Context Representation and Reasoning (CRR 2005), Paris, France (2005); Co-located with CONTEXT 2005
13. Chen, H., Finin, T., Joshi, A.: An ontology for context-aware pervasive computing environments. The Knowledge Engineering Review 18(03), 197–207 (2003)
14. Turner, R.M.: Determining the context-dependent meaning of fuzzy subsets. In: Proceedings of the 1997 International and Interdisciplinary Conference on Modeling and Using Context (CONTEXT 1997), Rio de Janeiro (1997)
15. Turner, E.H., Matthias, C.: Understanding pronomial references to quantified expressions. Journal of Natural Language Engineering 4(4), 345–361 (1998)
16. Turner, R.M., Turner, E.H.: A two-level, protocol-based approach to controlling autonomous oceanographic sampling networks. IEEE Journal of Oceanic Engineering 26(4) (October 2001)
17. Durfee, E.H., Lesser, V.R.: Using partial global plans to coordinate distributed problem solvers. In: Proceedings of the 1987 International Joint Conference on Artificial Intelligence, pp. 875–883 (1987)
18. Bikakis, A., Antoniou, G.: Distributed Defeasible Reasoning in Multi-Context Systems. NMR (2008)
19. Decker, K., Williamson, M., Sycara, K.: Matchmaking and brokering. In: Proceedings of the Second International Conference on Multi-Agent Systems (ICMAS 1996), p. 432 (1996)
20. Curtin, T., Bellingham, J., Catipovic, J., Webb, D.: Autonomous oceanographic sampling networks. Oceanography 6(3) (1993)

Context-Based Modeling of an Anatomo-Cyto-Pathology Department Workflow for Quality Control

Elham Attieh[1,2], Frédérique Capron[2], and Patrick Brézillon[1]

[1] LIP6, University Pierre & Marie Curie (UPMC)
[2] UIMAP, Department of Pathology, Groupe Hospitalier Pitié-Salpêtrière, APHP
`elhamattieh@hotmail.com, patrick.brezillon@lip6.fr,`
`frederique.capron@psl.aphp.fr`

Abstract. The paper presents the contextualization of the Anatomical pathology (AP) workflow focusing on nonconformity during the reception and registration steps. Context is described by contextual elements related to heterogeneous sources such as the actor, the task, the situation and the local environment. The objective of this work is the application of contextual graph to the "workflow" of an AP exam, limited to the steps of reception and registration. The main point is the context-based representation of practices developed by actors instead of an object-centered view on the workflow to identify and ultimately avoid risky practices leading to nonconformity and prejudice. Therefore contextual graphs can be considered as a tool for monitoring the quality of work in an AP department, the actions, detection and correction of nonconformities as well as a base for intelligent software creation that links different modules in medical care.

Keywords: Workflow, contextual graphs, contextual element, nonconformity, reception, registration, anatomical pathology, medicine, quality control.

1 Introduction

Anatomical Pathology (AP), named in France Anatomical and Cytological Pathology (ACP) is a medical specialty unknown to the public but essential in oncology [1]. AP aims to examine macroscopically, but also microscopically, patients' tissue samples and cells in order to establish the diagnosis and the factors of severity of the disease, contributing thus to medical care [1], [2]. AP physicians follow procedures that include a gross examination (visual examination of organs), dissection and sampling of surgical specimens according to standardized protocols and then a microscopic examination of stained tissue sections. AP is a medical activity based on normal anatomy, histology and cytology to identify, by analogy, macroscopic and microscopic morphological abnormalities. It performs several techniques such as immunohistochemistry, cytogenetic and molecular to identify abnormalities in cells or tissues [2]. The process begins with a request form associated to a sample. All over the workflow each action and information collected is integrated in the laboratory information management system (LIS) file related to the AP exam. The latter is a part of

P. Brézillon, P. Blackburn, and R. Dapoigny (Eds.): CONTEXT 2013, LNAI 8175, pp. 235–247, 2013.

the patient's medical data conditioning his medical chart. Therefore the Pathology Advisory Committee, formed in 2008 by the *direction de la lutte contre le cancer*, aims to identify key issues in pathology and suggest specific interventions for the ongoing improvement of quality in accordance with the principles of evidence-based medicine [3]. While conformity is the fulfillment of a requirement, nonconformity is defined as "the failure to fulfill the requirements of a standard, in whole or in part" which may be prejudicial to the patient. We distinguish two categories of nonconformities: critical nonconformity and non-critical nonconformity. A critical nonconformity is "the failure to fulfill the requirements blocking the process of the sample examination", while a non-critical nonconformity does not lead to a sample rejection [2].

Beyond this large spectrum of data, information and knowledge about the problem, external events intervene such as the type of task to accomplish, the actor realizing the task (technician, pathologist...), the situation in which the task is realized and the available resources in the immediate environment. Such contextual elements may impact the task realization. If they are not integrated in the reasoning, this could lead to nonconformity. Thus, this work aims to (a) represent exams in AP as a workflow, and (b) identify the practical limits of this representation.

Focusing on nonconformity during the steps of the process, we look for risky points at each step. Any bad decision at one step may cause a cascade of undesirable events, or even be visible only at a late step. For example, during an examination, a pathologist may refer or not to immunohistochemistry or special techniques or stains to make a diagnosis. The degree of variation may be inconsequential, and more important, create a nonconformity. Therefore task automation in the AP department is limited because it depends largely on human decision-making, especially in the reception/registration area where actors rely implicitly or explicitly on many contextual elements to decide which actions must be done. The decision-making process includes assembling, organizing, structuring a large number of heterogeneous contextual elements, and finally builds an action sequence.

The complete trace of an AP's examination (mainly the reasons on which is based on a decision or an action at the different steps of the process) is rarely recorded. The focus is on the result (or the conclusion), not on the process leading to it, the latter relying heavily on the working context. Thus, when a nonconformity situation occurs, it is difficult to identify the reason of nonconformity, to correct the problem and to learn how to avoid it again.

Making the contextualization process explicit supposes to use a formalism providing a uniform representation of elements of knowledge, reasoning and context. Contextual Graphs are such a context-based formalism of representation [4] that is implemented in a piece of software called CxG_Platform [5]. Thus, the representation of the task realization in an AP Department as a contextual graph becomes a contextualized workflow. Each path in this graph represents a practice as sequences of contextual elements and actions. Thus, the task is represented as an organization of practices structured by contextual elements (i.e. the contextual graph). Such a representation is well adapted for modeling AP's examination workflow.

In this paper Section 2 introduces the sample orientation in AP department and the quality in AP. Section 3 discusses Contextual elements and Contextual-Graphs formalism for representing the modeling of AP's examination. The results with the contextual graph that we have obtained are detailed in section 4. Section 5 offers a discussion of these results while section 6 proposes some new challenges to address.

2   Dispatching of Sample Examination in AP Department

Our work is based on the workflow in the AP Department of the Pitié-Salpêtrière Hospital (APHP, France) from the arrival of the sample and request form at the reception bench to the AP report sent to the referent physician (Figure 1).

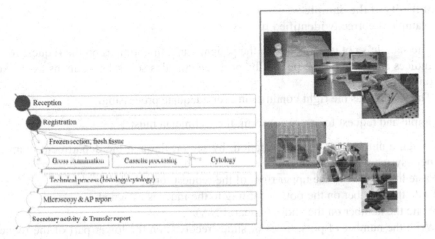

Fig. 1. AP Examination workflow at the Pitié-Salpêtrière AP department

In this paper we discuss the two first steps, namely the reception area and the registration area as presented Table 1, the procedures of the department and the different actors doing their daily work. Our study concerns the different contextual elements that influence actions in the reception and registration activities.

2.1   Sample and Request Form at the Reception and Registration Bench

Samples and request forms reach our AP department by two possible paths:

- Received by the pneumatic system, from the clinical wards, operating rooms or from the sorting center; and
- Carried by a messenger from the sorting center or operating rooms: delivery of large surgical specimens and samples from other services not connected to the pneumatic.

A request form is attached to each sample, which is a paper document and therefore not yet computerized. The technician takes in charge the sample and the request form.

The technician stamps the date and the time of the reception on the request form and checks the conformity of both the sample and the request form.

Conformity of the Request Form.
The conformity of a request form is warranted if all the following fields are filled:

1. The identification label of the patient (first and last name),
2. The date and time of completion of the sampling,
3. The time of fixation of the sample if known,
4. The nature of the samples or slides (marked when multiple samples are sent),
5. The clinical diagnosis (known or suspected),
6. Identification (Stamp and / or signature) of the responsible physician who made the sample or the doctor who asked for it.

Conformity of the Sample.
The sample is correctly identified if:

1. The sample's pot is labeled with the patient's identification as on the request form,
2. Indices are noted on the pots if the package contains several specimens as marked on the request form,
3. The sample has the right conditioning for adequate processing.

If sample and request form are conform, the technician must:

- Assign a number for the examination, by sector, through the department management system,
- Paste the number in the upper right of the request form,
- Paste this number on the pots according to the indexes assigned,
- Write the number on the slides (smear, FNA),
- Write the number of pots, tubes or slides received on the lower part of the request form, in the section reserved to the laboratory,
- For samples oriented to the gross examination, put the stamp where the medical sector will appear after registration,
- When an application contains jointly cytology and surgical specimens or biopsies, renumber bottles and reindex the request form giving cellular samples (Fluid) letters and tissue samples numbers. Then, photocopy the request form (or give the double) and transmit to the Cytology section,
- Sign the request form at the bottom left,
- Note a fresh sample on the request form and prevent the duty doctor.

Nonconformity at the Reception and Registration Steps.
Nonconformity (NC) concerns the request form and the sample. The NC that does not block the completion of the examination must be declared to the sender department, and involved anomalies are recorded through a keyword entered in the computer file. NC that blocks the completion of the examination requires that a form is filled to explain the reasons and the technician must accomplish the following actions:

- Alert the sender department and the responsible physician who should come to correct the nonconformity,

- Assign a number "N" on nonconformity sheet and request form (top left),
- Fill the nonconformity form completely and legibly,
- Save in LIS "Registering of a nonconformity",
- Scan and file the form,
- Final decision taken by the Head of the Pathology department.

Once the reception part completed, the same technician that has taken in charge the sample initially will proceed with the registration task. The technician now must:

- Select the medical sector, corresponding to the medical dispatching of the duty,
- Enter the barcode number of the examination,
- Enter the patient identification number (PIN) and confirm the patient's identity,
- Enter the source of the sample; therefore refer to the label on the request form. In the absence of the latter, do a search on Gilda (AP-HP patient's identity management system),
- Put a X unless a prescriber is already pre-recorded,
- Date the request form; if no date is specified, put the actual date of the day,
- Enter the code of the pathology exam (referring to a table of AP acts affected to APHP AP structures),
- Specify the exact nature of the sample and the number of slides or pots in the tab "*further examination*",
- Select the Medical Sector Activity (MSA),
- Check the sheet bench (for printing) for cytology tests or complex examination (multiple pots) for the gross section,
- Check the anteriority in the AP department,
- Confirm with the OK box at the bottom of the screen,
- Note the MSA on the request form for samples dispatched to gross examination room,
- Carry samples and request forms to: cytology, frozen section or fresh tissue, gross examination, cassette processing room, and
- Scan the request form.

Actions in the reception/registration step depend on human made decision, which is based on training, competence and experience.

2.2   Workflow Information in a Table Representation

According to WHO [6], and concerning health institutions, a quality process guarantees to each patient an assortment of diagnostic and therapeutic acts, which ensures the best result in terms of health. This supposes that all actors adhere to rules and standards to find out who did what, how and why. Therefore, it is required to elaborate recommendations, written procedures and protocols, to guide the workflow and for the quality control.

Table 1. Workflow table at reception and registration areas of Pitié-salpêtrière AP Dpt.

Room	Tasks and subtasks	Actors	LIS and connections	Constraints
Reception Registration	• To receive (sample and request form): - Stamp date and time - Assign an examination number - Check the conformity - Contact the pathologist or technician concerned - Check the conditioning and the fixing fluid volume • To register immediately or later: - Identity verification on GILDA, origin of the examination - Protocols - Assign to the proper benches: cytology, Frozen section/fresh tissue, gross examination, cassette processing	Reception's technician	SGL Gilda Printers labels	Nonconformity Emergency situations' management Decision making and choices

First, the components of the AP department's workflow were identified. Table 1 presents a part of the initial workflow in terms of location, task to realize, actors that are concerned, laboratory identification system (LIS) and connection systems with the hospital information system and constraints. This table is an important tool that highlights and identifies the different key elements in the reception/registration step, for instance, to identify the task and who is doing it.

3   Contextual Elements in the Workflow of the AP Department

Contextual elements come from heterogeneous sources: the actor, the task, the situation and the local environment [7]. In this study, contextual elements concern the functioning of an AP Department, focusing mainly on nonconformity and related domain knowledge. The reception and registration areas are crucial steps in the workflow of sample examination because it is the first step in the chain of actions of actors. Occurrence of nonconformity at this level could lead to a whole series of inadequate actions. Thus, there is an important challenge to limit as much as possible these risky situations by detecting them at the source (information meetings, observation and controls…). Such measures are necessary conditions, but they are not sufficient because they don't make explicit at which particular level the error did happen and which contextual(s) element(s) could be controlled to avoid it next time hence the need of the Contextual Graphs (CxG) formalism [8].

• The Actor

Technicians (actors) at reception and registration desks constitute a highly qualified staff trained to accomplish their tasks under control of the medical staff. Non-habilitated actors (with different skills) will generate a risk of nonconformity. Even with technicians working routinely, there are risks of NC because they may rely too much on their experience and be less attentive to the task realization (e.g. emergency situation, noncompliance with instructions, trying to help another actor, etc).

Several samples may arrive simultaneously, the technician normally handles them one by one. Nevertheless, an error may occur during task execution, especially if samples have the same nature. Another risk is the mixing or confusion in examinations if the technician tries to deal multiple samples simultaneously.

The responsible of any action is clearly identified (signed initials, IT code) otherwise, the responsibility of the mistake cannot be allocated to a specific actor, which could affect the follow-up and the management of nonconformity. In addition, signing the request form provides written evidence and thus a trail to explore if any error occurs. Cultural and organizational diversity of actors also is an important element that could be considered as well as the age and experience of the technicians.

• The Task

The task is modeled in a workflow as a multi-step process. Each step (a component of the workflow) is a (sub) process. The different parts of the process at reception/registration steps are presented in Table 1. Checking the conformity of the request form is made in eight items. The technician controls them in an order or another depending on the way he prefers to do the control (and other contextual factors). A similar procedure is applied for checking the conformity of the sample.

The conformity of the move from one step to the next one also must be checked (e.g. transfer context may be incompatible with step contexts). This move may concern a unique technician or a transfer of tasks between technicians, and thus context switching plays an important role (contextual dimension of the task).

The nature of the task is an important contextual element like for instance deciding if everything is compliant to norms or not, if the conformity blocks the sample processing, choosing the medical and technical sectors, evaluating the emergency of the situation, etc. Moreover, decision-making depends on multiple factors [9]. For example, the non-respect of the (implicit) rule "What I touch, I treat" (i.e. any transfer of work responsibility from one person to another) is a risk of error. Responsibility transfer supposes a transfer of information, an assessment of the situation to manage with all necessary details, especially with a new technician.

• The Situation

The actor selects a method among different ones on the basis of training and contextual information such as "the patient is known", "the surgeon is waiting the answer". Such information (and others like "it is vacation time and the team is reduced" or "the device X is busy") is characteristic of the situation.

The simultaneous deposit of several samples may lead to errors by mixing examinations. The emergency of the exam and work overload generate stress, implicitly or explicitly, on actors in their actions. This stress is handled differently from one actor to another. NC is a situation requiring specific actions different from the usual process. The working context must be replaced by a specific and independent NC context for problem solving before to return to the working context.

• The Local Environment

The environment includes all the entities (objects, space rooms, people and events) that are external to the current task but having a potential impact on task realization [10]. The environment of interest is all that may modify the normal status of the task (e.g. software crash following an overvoltage, an intranet problem, the pot containing the sample is broken, the glove box is empty or missing), of the actor (the physician on duty having problems and thus he is unable to concentrate), of the situation (e.g. power supply failure, poor conditioning of a sample). Thus, any problem in the ventilation or cooling systems is unfavorable, as well as personal discussions during working hours. A major risk is a failure in the pneumatic system generating either delay to the reception or the possible loss of the samples. Fortunately degraded procedures are implemented for emergency situations to do not interrupt or interfere with the work.

4   Contextual-Graph Modeling of the Examination Process

Figures 2-6 represents the integration of the Table 1 of Section 2 and the contextual elements identified in Section 3. The contextual graph contains a series of activities representing the workflow components. Each activity is a contextual graph itself.

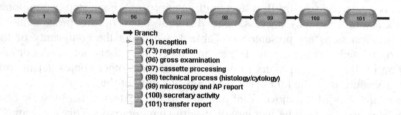

➡ Branch
○─ ▣ (1) reception
   ▣ (73) registration
   ▣ (96) gross examination
   ▣ (97) cassette processing
   ▣ (98) technical process (histology/cytology)
   ▣ (99) microscopy and AP report
   ▣ (100) secretary activity
   ▣ (101) transfer report

Fig. 2. AP Examination processing in AP department represented as a contextualized workflow The activity in the reception room is described by the following contextual graph.

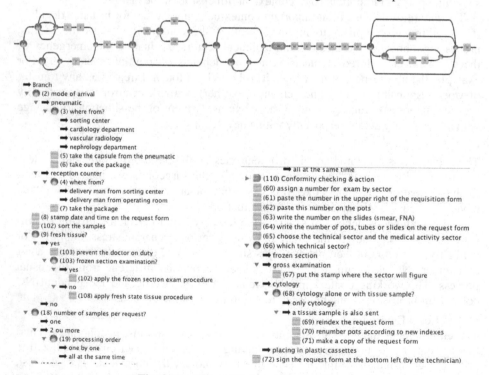

➡ Branch
▼ ◐ (2) mode of arrival
  ▼ ➡ pneumatic
    ▼ ◐ (3) where from?
      ➡ sorting center
      ➡ cardiology department
      ➡ vascular radiology
      ➡ nephrology department
    ▣ (5) take the capsule from the pneumatic
    ▣ (6) take out the package
  ▼ ➡ reception counter
    ▼ ◐ (4) where from?
      ➡ delivery man from sorting center
      ➡ delivery man from operating room
    ▣ (7) take the package
▣ (8) stamp date and time on the request form
▣ (102) sort the samples
▼ ◐ (9) fresh tissue?
  ▼ ➡ yes
    ▣ (103) prevent the doctor on duty
    ▼ ◐ (103) frozen section examination?
      ▼ ➡ yes
        ▣ (102) apply the frozen section exam procedure
      ▼ ➡ no
        ▣ (108) apply fresh state tissue procedure
  ➡ no
▼ ◐ (18) number of samples per request?
  ➡ one
  ▼ ➡ 2 ou more
    ▼ ◐ (19) processing order
      ➡ one by one
      ➡ all at the same time

      ➡ all at the same time
▶ ▣ (110) Conformity checking & action
▣ (60) assign a number for exam by sector
▣ (61) paste the number in the upper right of the requisition form
▣ (62) paste this number on the pots
▣ (63) write the number on the slides (smear, FNA)
▣ (64) write the number of pots, tubes or slides on the request form
▣ (65) choose the technical sector and the medical activity sector
▼ ◐ (66) which technical sector?
  ➡ frozen section
  ▼ ➡ gross examination
    ▣ (67) put the stamp where the sector will figure
  ▼ ➡ cytology
    ▼ ◐ (68) cytology alone or with tissue sample?
      ➡ only cytology
      ▼ ➡ a tissue sample is also sent
        ▣ (69) reindex the request form
        ▣ (70) renumber pots according to new indexes
        ▣ (71) make a copy of the request form
➡ placing in plastic cassettes
▣ (72) sign the request form at the bottom left (by the technician)

Fig. 3. Modeling of the reception workflow

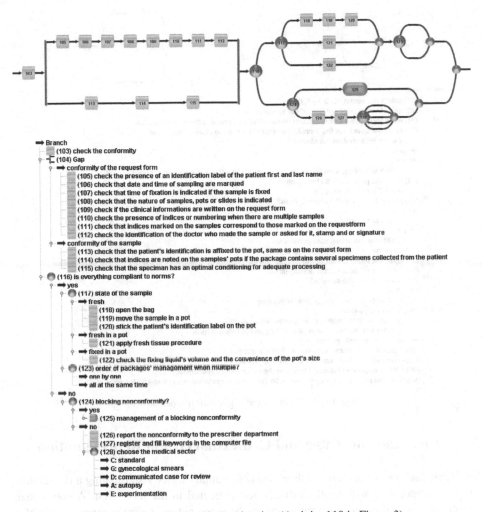

Fig. 4. Conformity checking and action (Activity 110 in Figure 3)

The management of a blocking nonconformity (Activity 125 in Figure 4) is obtained by a sequence of actions (see Figure 5).

Fig. 5. Management of a blocking nonconformity

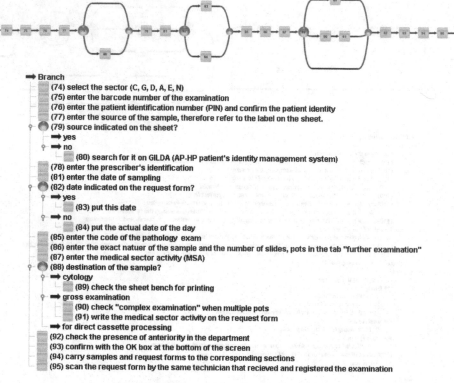

➡ Branch
    (74) select the sector (C, G, D, A, E, N)
    (75) enter the barcode number of the examination
    (76) enter the patient identification number (PIN) and confirm the patient identity
    (77) enter the source of the sample, therefore refer to the label on the sheet.
    (79) source indicated on the sheet?
      ➡ yes
      ➡ no
        (80) search for it on GILDA (AP-HP patient's identity management system)
    (78) enter the prescriber's identification
    (81) enter the date of sampling
    (82) date indicated on the request form?
      ➡ yes
        (83) put this date
      ➡ no
        (84) put the actual date of the day
    (85) enter the code of the pathology exam
    (86) enter the exact natuer of the sample and the number of slides, pots in the tab "further examination"
    (87) enter the medical sector activity (MSA)
    (88) destination of the sample?
      ➡ cytology
        (89) check the sheet bench for printing
      ➡ gross examination
        (90) check "complex examination" when multiple pots
        (91) write the medical sector activity on the request form
    ➡ for direct cassette processing
    (92) check the presence of anteriority in the department
    (93) confirm with the OK box at the bottom of the screen
    (94) carry samples and request forms to the corresponding sections
    (95) scan the request form by the same technician that recieved and registered the examination

Fig. 6. Modeling of the registration workflow

5   Discussion on Table and Contextual Graph Representation

The table and the contextual graph are complementary tools. Establishing a contextual graph is impossible without the information collected in the table first. A contextual graph gives a unified view on relationships between actors, tasks, documents or links to a specific action, by taking into consideration the working context, adding new situations thanks to its dynamic and incremental characteristic and finally allowing the analysis. Moreover, the contextualized workflow may evolve dynamically, thanks to the incremental knowledge acquisition that enriches the contextual graph by adding a new practice as the refinement of an existing one.

From this graph we can make a tool for practice analysis at different moments. The graph will reveal the deficiency of the standard practices document, the necessity to improve the practices and quality control. In other words, a contextual graph is a way to objectify events influencing the AP examination process [11]. Therefore it can be considered as a monitoring tool on the quality of the work.

6   Perspectives

We propose a new method for quality control at both medical and technical levels. This approach aims to tackle nonconformity situations and therefore prevent a medical error and an eventual prejudice. This supposes to trace the origin and the cause of the nonconformity to correct the problem and avoid it the next time. For realizing such a progress it would be wise to do regular reports on nonconformity met, and to improve the communication between the different actors internal and external to the AP Department.

A contextual graph contains the practices effectively developed by doctors and technicians, and not procedures as decontextualized average over practices. It is possible to follow step-by-step the real practice developed by an actor and to compare it directly to known practices included in the contextual graph in order to detect a discrepancy that could lead to noncompliance. Because all the paths in a contextual graph correspond to real practices developed for a task realization, a contextual graph is, by itself, a kind of "base of experiences" [9], [12].

In addition, an actor may identify a "new practice" (good or bad) and thus enriches the base of shared experiences. The CXG formalism provides the ability to incrementally add this new practice that will avoid later another technician to repeat it.

An assessment and an effective monitoring of nonconformity are possible, thanks to the installation of software that allows to track, manage, and prevent nonconformity and to monitor ongoing or delayed actions or activities [9]. It provides in few clicks all the statistics we need: nonconformity source, cause, examination number and description, the correlation with the day, the sample sender, the technician at the reception, etc., the goal being to allow an incremental revision of the contextual graph. It is also a way to keep technicians aware of their work and let them to react immediately to correct a degrading situation.

Improving communication between actors would be possible with 2.0-collaborative tools, secure and easy to use. Complete information could then be provided in a "patient record" in preset files, where the prescriber has to fill in the boxes and whose access is limited to persons involved and protected by passwords.

7   Conclusion

The Contextual-Graphs formalism relies on the fact that past contexts can be remembered and adapted to solve problems in the current context. The main point here is to obtain a context-based representation of practices developed by actors that is richer than the procedures and recommendations generally proposed, which always need to be adapted to the working context. We note that the engineering domain where the domain is better understood, people try, when possible, to replace procedures by "best practices", although only a part of the context is taken into account.

In the Contextual-Graphs representation, the organization of the practices developed by all actors is structured by contextual elements. The interest of representing technicians' practices at the AP Department is: (1) to identify risky practices, (2) to understand how a mistake has been made, (3) to train new technicians, and (4) to know how to manage nonconformity. The main finding here is that nonconformity is related to a contextual element that was left implicit or forgotten (e.g. between two examinations, a woman gets married and come the second time with a new name, and the physician does not find the results of the previous examination) or the change of instantiation of a contextual element (e.g. status of the sample, number of request arriving at the same time, number of samples per request, proceeding order, qualification of the technician that does the task).

A risk may become a prejudice because context is not considered, underestimated or among too numerous other contextual elements. Thus, the modeling of tasks and context and its interaction with data, information and knowledge are essential in order to anticipate, control and avoid possible risks. This is particularly important when the workflow consists of a sequence of interrelated actions where an error at a particular step of the process leads to a cascade of wrong events or may be identified at the final step of the sample processing.

Modeling the context of a workflow in a pathology department and the representation of the different steps in a contextual graph leads to a structure of the relevant practices (actual work) instead of the official procedure (the prescribed task) in a kind of contextualized procedure more powerful than the generally proposed "best practices".

The contextual graph can be designed as a tool for monitoring the quality of work, the actions, detection and correction of nonconformities. It can integrate the AP department procedures and be used as a quality control and training tool for technicians and doctors. It can also be considered as a base for IT software creation and a link between IT modules or systems in medical care.

Acknowledgments. This work is supported by grants from ANR TecSan for the MICO project (ANR-10-TECS-015), and we thank partners of IPAL and TRIBVN for fruitful discussions and from the TACTIC project funded bt the ASTRID program of Délégation Générale aux Armées.

References

1. Société Française de Pathologie, http://www.sfpathol.org (last visit: May 29, 2013)
2. Association Française d'Assurance Qualité en Anatomie et Cytologie Pathologiques, http://www.afaqap.org (last visit: May 29, 2013)
3. Guide sur l'assurance qualité en anatomopathologie, Phases pré-analytique et analytique, Comité consultatif en anatomopathologie (Novembre 2011), http://www.msss.gouv.qc.ca/cancer (last visit: May 29, 2013)
4. Brézillon, P.: Task-Realization Models in Contextual Graphs. In: Dey, A., Kokinov, B., Leake, D., Turner, R. (eds.) CONTEXT 2005. LNCS (LNAI), vol. 3554, pp. 55–68. Springer, Heidelberg (2005)
5. Brézillon, P.: Context modeling: Task model and practice model. In: Kokinov, B., Richardson, D.C., Roth-Berghofer, T.R., Vieu, L. (eds.) CONTEXT 2007. LNCS (LNAI), vol. 4635, pp. 122–135. Springer, Heidelberg (2007)

6. Quality of care: A process for making strategic choices in health systems, WHO 2006 (2006), http://www.who.int/management/quality/assurance/QualityCare_B.Def.pdf (last visit: May 29, 2013)
7. Brezillon, P.: Contextualization of scientific workflows. In: Beigl, M., Christiansen, H., Roth-Berghofer, T.R., Kofod-Petersen, A., Coventry, K.R., Schmidtke, H.R. (eds.) CONTEXT 2011. LNCS (LNAI), vol. 6967, pp. 40–53. Springer, Heidelberg (2011)
8. Brézillon, P.: Context Dynamic and Explanation in Contextual Graphs. In: Blackburn, P., Ghidini, C., Turner, R.M., Giunchiglia, F. (eds.) CONTEXT 2003. LNCS (LNAI), vol. 2680, pp. 94–106. Springer, Heidelberg (2003)
9. Brézillon, P., Aroua, A.: Real-time decision making in contextual-graphs based simulation. Journal of Decision Systems 22(1), 28–42 (2013)
10. Thevenin, D., Coutaz, J.: Plasticity of User Interfaces: Framework and Research Agenda. In: Proceedings of INTERACT 1999, pp. 110–117 (1999)
11. Brézillon, P.: Modeling activity management instead of task realization. In: Recipio, A., Burstien, F. (eds.) Fusing DSS into the Fabric of the Context, pp. 51–62. IOS Press, Amsterdam (2012)

Production-Contextual Clinical Information

Gert Galster

Medical Informatics Group, Department of Health Science and Technology,
Aalborg University, Aalborg, Denmark

Abstract. There is a widespread health informatics vision of unlimited exchange, understanding and reuse of clinical information. However, it has also been pointed out that to understand clinical information it is to some extent necessary to know the circumstances of its production - the production-contextual clinical information.

The purpose of this study was to investigate the nature and significance of production-contextual clinical information in doctors' everyday clinical work in order to asses whether standardization is necessary and possible. The study was performed through observation and focus group interviews at a cardiology department in a midsize Danish hospital.

It was found that production-contextual clinical information is complex, extensive, non-quantitative, and that it has an elusive structure. It is concluded that while it may be possible to standardise a limited amount of production-contextual clinical information, a general standardisation may very well be impossible.

Keywords: Medical informatics, Electronic health records, Clinical information, Context.

1   Introduction

Over several years, there has throughout the health informatics community been a widespread common vision of universal interoperability. The vision has been described numerous times, e.g. in the Semantic Health Report[1] which sketches a scenario where health-related information can be shared seamlessly across national boundaries, where clinical information can be exchanged and reused for both clinical and non-clinical purposes, and where any health actor can understand and integrate the information in a collaborative manner as if the information was generated locally. A key element towards this vision is the systematic standardisation of information that is essential to everyday clinical work.

On the other hand, it has been pointed out that both primary and secondary utilisation of health information can be critically dependent on production-contextual clinical information, i.e. the description of the circumstances of obtaining clinical information[2][3]. It has also been described that standardisation of contextual information poses several problems - not the least to delimit context, and to formalise it[4][5][6][7]. Thus, the need for standardisation of production-contextual information

P. Brézillon, P. Blackburn, and R. Dapoigny (Eds.): CONTEXT 2013, LNAI 8175, pp. 248–258, 2013.

has the potential to be a major obstacle to the realisation of the envisioned degree of interoperability.

The objective of this study was to investigate the nature and significance of production-contextual clinical information in the everyday clinical work of physicians in order to assess whether standardisation is necessary and possible. Thus, the study should answer these three questions:

- What constitutes production-contextual clinical information?
- What is production-contextual clinical information used for, and to what extent does it impact on everyday clinical work?
- How can production-contextual clinical information be operationalized in order to support clinical reasoning?

1.1   The Perception and Significance of Context

This study's overall perception of 'context' is based on the definition given in ISO/TR 17119:2005 Health informatics profiling framework:

> *related conditions and situations that provide a useful understanding and meaning of a subject[8]*

As pointed out by Winograd[5] and Dourish[6], context can be viewed as fixed and pre-determined, or as variable and situational. In this project, context is perceived as highly situational. As expressed by Winograd:

> *Context is an operational term: Something is context because of the way it is used in interpretation, not due to its inherent properties[5].*

Thus, rather than perceiving context as something which can be designated in advance, this study is based on the perception that context is what a given actor in a given situation considers of relevance. Furthermore, contextual information is perceived as a description of context for the purpose of communication.

But even though information is described as relevant, it may be more or less significant. It has been exemplified that contextual clinical information may be of crucial importance[2][3][9], but it is not clear to what extent this is true in everyday clinical work. For the sake of operationality, this study perceives contextual clinical information as essential, if it by inference leads to explicit reconsideration of existing information.

1.2   Contextual Clinical Information

Communication based on documented clinical information (e.g. progress notes, lab results) is one-way, and not real-time. It is thus possible to view communication through a simple model with a sender and an unknown number of receivers where sender has a very limited knowledge, if any, of the receiver(s).

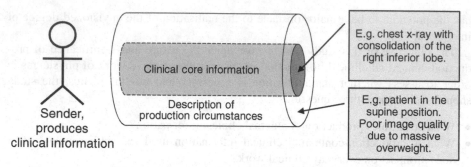

Fig. 1. Production-contextual clinical information

With reference to Fig. 1: Health information is produced under some circumstances and documented by the sender as a core of clinical information. A description of the circumstances may be documented along with the core. E.g. a radiologist describes a chest x-ray with (as core information) consolidation of the right inferior lobe. He mentions (as a description of production circumstances) that the patient was in the supine position, and that the image quality is poor due to massive overweight.

At a later time, a receiver reads the documentation. In order to achieve a useful understanding and meaning of the message core, the receiver needs to understand the former circumstances.

Thus, production-contextual information is not a description of what the sender considered relevant in the situation, but of those details of the sender's situation which the receiver finds of current relevance.

2   Materials and Methods

Doctors' use of production-contextual clinical information was studied through observations and focus group interviews. The basic question posed was which supplementary information the doctors requested, and whether the requested information concerned the circumstances of obtaining information - i.e. whether production-contextual information was requested.

2.1   Observations and Interviews

The observations and interviews were done in the Cardiology Department of Bispebjerg Hospital in Copenhagen - a mid-size hospital in the capital region of Denmark.

Observations were performed at five random morning conferences for doctors. The conferences included two types of scenario: the reporting of yesterday's patients and the collective analysis of selected case stories. The focus of observation was the recurring requests for additional information, and whether the requested information was production-contextual.

The interviews were carried out as five sessions of focus group interviews[10] with three to six doctors in each. As preparation for the interviews, different pieces of clinical information were collected from random cardiology health records. A total of 63 pieces of information were collected. In order to ensure a fair coverage of health-care activities, the below mentioned analytical framework was used as a guide for selection. Thus, all information types were represented, e.g.

- "Pt. has consented to angioplasty" (Observation)
- "Peripheral venous access was obtained" (Action)
- "Diagnosis: fever with no known cause" (Opinion-Diagnosis)
- "Pt. should lose at least 10 kg" (Opinion-Goal)
- "Plan: observation in telemetry for the next 24 hours" (Instruction)

Table 1. Healthcare activities and their resulting information types

Healthcare activity	Basic information type	Information subtypes
Observation	Observation information created by an act of observation, meas-urement, questioning, or testing of the patient or related substance, in short, the entire stream of in-formation captured by the investigator, used to characterise the patient system.	
Action	Action a record of intervention actions that have occurred, due to instructions or otherwise.	
Evaluation	Opinion inferences of the investigator using the personal and published knowledge base about what the observa-tions mean, and what to do about them; includes all diagnoses, assessments, plans, goals.	Diagnosis Risk Prognosis Scenario Goal Recommendation
Instruction	Instruction opinion-based instructions sufficiently detailed so as to be directly executable by investigator agents, in order to effect a desired intervention.	Investigation request Intervention request

The collected pieces of information were printed out as cards, and used as basis for the interviews as follows: the participants would draw a card at random and use this single piece of information as their focus for discussion. Their objective was to spec-ify which supplementary information they would require, and the significance thereof.

As the need for supplementary information depends on the specific situation, and in order to keep focus on the piece of information at hand, it was decided to avoid any indication of situational context. Hence, the participants had to discuss the signifi-cance of requested information for varying situations.

2.2   Analytical Framework

In the present study the generation and usage of clinical information was analysed on the basis of the model described by Beale & Heard[11]. This model describes four kinds of healthcare activities (by implication) and ten corresponding clinical information types, as shown in Table 1.

This framework was used for the collection of information from health records and for the analysis of observations and interviews.

3   Results

3.1   Observations

When observing the flow of information at the doctors morning conferences, it was noticed that every presentation of a new patient began with a "starter package" consisting of the basic observations of age and gender, the diagnoses which were the reason for the current encounter, any relevant co-morbidity, and a statement regarding the status in relation to the current encounter. E.g. "63-year-old female with no history of serious illness is admitted with suspected AMI. Non-specific ECG changes. Coronar enzymes are under way."

Then supplementary information was presented in a dialogue of questions and answers until some kind of decision or collective perception was reached. The case stories followed the same path, except that the initial narrative was more fluent, and the questions more pointed.

During the five conferences, a total of 206 instances of supplementary clinical information were recorded. Of these were 54 (26%) found to concern the circumstances of obtaining information, i.e. to be production-contextual information. Examples of the requests for production-contextual information are shown in Table 2.

It was repeatedly observed how a question about some detail regarding a healthcare activity led on to further questions with the obvious purpose to perform source criticism, and assess the credibility of information obtained from the healthcare activity. E.g. a question about when an observation was done, led to further questioning about whether the observation was done spontaneously, and what was the reason for the observer to be there at the time, and was the observed event actually foreseeable. Another example: a question about where an examination was performed, led to a discussion about another hospital's reputation, and whether the examination result should be trusted.

Thus, production-contextual information was through this process of source criticism repeatedly causing reconsideration of clinical information, as illustrated in Table 2. It seemed to be a continuous and integral part of the overall information flow between the doctors.

Table 2. Examples of essential production-contextual information

Information type	was reconsidered due to production-contextual information, e.g.
Observation	Doctor-patient interaction - "He seemed not at ease so I am not sure whether he told me the truth about his medication." Organisational location - "The examination wasn't done here, so we can't use the results as basis for a risky intervention." Topicality (information shelf life) - "But this ECG is more than a week old!"
Action	Competence - "This echocardiography should have been performed by a specialist." Method - "Are you sure she was informed according to our guidelines?"
Opinion	Quality - "Did she mention her confidence in the diagnosis?" Competence - "If the dietician says so, it's true."
Instruction	Logistics - "I would have prescribed sotalol tablets, but we only had sotalol for injection." Consent - "I would have ordered a PCI, but the patient didn't want it."

Table 2 illustrates types of clinical information which were reconsidered as a result of production-contextual information. E.g. (observation): A junior doctor questioned a patient about his medication and was told that the patient took his medication as prescribed. However, this information was later reconsidered in the light of the patient's condition at the time of questioning.

3.2   Interviews

As mentioned, the interviews were performed with a single piece of clinical information as focus and without any kind of situational framing. The absence of situational context repeatedly raised some discussion about which situations would constitute a relevant context for the current piece of information. These discussions gave rise to a broad palette of contextual information related to the current piece of information. A few participants, however, noted that they would have preferred real case stories and expressed frustration over the absent situational context which made it difficult to relate to the given piece of information.

During the five interviews, the participants requested a total of 67 instances of supplementary clinical information. Of these, 40 instances were found to be production-contextual.

The question on information credibility was a major topic, and even more so than during the observed conferences. The participants repeatedly requested supplementary information in order to perform source criticism, i.e. for balancing of likelihood, credibility, and overall weight of the given information.

From the discussions between the participants on what could be context for a given piece of clinical information, it was evident that they perceived contextuality as highly situational. In addition, the discussions repeatedly touched on significance being situational. Thus, it was again and again pointed out that even if a piece of contextual information, e.g. the description of an operation, in the majority of cases were only of interest as an outline of what had happened, there could be situations where the precise details, e.g. the use of certain materials or implants, would be crucial.

3.3   Data Processing

The outcome of observations and interviews were coded according to the above mentioned analytical framework. It was thus possible to group the (54 + 40=) 94 instances of production-contextual information according to their related type of healthcare activity, i.e. groups concerning clinical information obtained by observation, action, evaluation, and instruction, see Table 1.

In an attempt to organize the contents of each of the four groups, it became clear that there is no obvious connection between healthcare activity and contextualized clinical information. Hence, it was only possible to make a very general categorisation. Table 3 shows an overall view on the collected production-contextual information organised with the healthcare activity as key and according to the "Kipling method" (5W1H).

Table 3. Overall view on the production-contextual information

Who
Patient
e.g. supine vs. upright position; exercise vs. at rest
e.g. mental capacity
Healthcare professional(s)
e.g. nurse vs. doctor
e.g. senior vs. junior doctor; specialist vs. generalist
Where
e.g. reputation of this vs. that hospital
e.g. admitted vs. at home
When
e.g. relevance of (older) observations
e.g. information availability
Why
e.g. implicit or explicit grounds
e.g. reported evidence
e.g. consent
What
e.g. level of detail; (missing) partial results (Observation)
e.g. reported likelihood; reported evidence (Opinion)
How
e.g. utensils, tools, drugs; conformance to instruction
e.g. uncertainty of measurements (Observation)
e.g. planned or spontaneous

4   Discussion

4.1   The Use of Production-Contextual Clinical Information

Several authors, e.g. [12], [2], [3], [9], have from examples of production-contextual clinical information deduced that knowledge of the healthcare activities that produce clinical information is essential for the clinical use of this information. It was an objective of this study two investigate whether these examples are rule or exception. In order to operationalize the importance of contextual information, it was assessed against whether it led to explicit reconsideration of existing information. This delimitation, while seemingly arbitrary, reflects a pragmatic choice: firstly, the delimitation is based on actual relevance; secondly, the condition is directly observable.

The observations of doctors' morning conference demonstrated that the participating doctors, based on the clinical information, repeatedly requested information about how the clinical information was produced - i.e. production-contextual clinical information.

Observations for this study were performed at a single department, and it cannot be ruled out that doctors in other circumstances have access to more consistent and unambiguous clinical information. However, the observed amount of significant production-contextual information, and the ease with which the doctors changed plans as a consequence of it, leaves the impression that handling of essential production-contextual information is a continuous and integral part of clinical everyday work.

During the observations, it was noticed that production-contextual clinical information to a great extent was used for source criticism, i.e. for balancing of likelihood, credibility, and overall weight of information concerning the patient. This is consistent with the findings by Kassirer & Gorry[12] who in detail describe several of the underlying mechanisms for critically gathering of clinical information, including the need for, and the comprehensive use of, source criticism in doctor's problem solving.

4.2   The Nature of Production-Contextual Clinical Information

The sample of observed instances of production-contextual clinical information was too small to give an in-depth understanding of what this kind of information consists of. This in itself could explain why the collected production-contextual clinical information was so difficult to categorise, cf. Table 3 . However, from the collected instances it is obvious that they include in considerable degree information that is complex (e.g. education, experience) and qualitative (e.g. mental capacity, intensity of treatment). Besides, several authors, e.g. [4], [5], [6], [7], have pointed out the difficulty of defining and modelling context. As stated by Bricon-Souf&Newman:

> One difficulty is, as yet, the research community has not reached a consensus as to the best way to model context and architectures to support its use[7].

Furthermore, it has been pointed out that the interpretation of a single piece of clinical information must take into account

> ... an in principle interminable list of context attributes, each with a weight determined both by the context in which the piece of information is currently to be used and the context in which it was originally recorded [13].

Basically, production-contextual clinical information is information related to a healthcare activity, and it is therefore not surprising that the description of the activity itself - the who, what, when, where, why, and how - is an essential part of the collected production-contextual clinical information. The material from this study, however, demonstrates that production-contextual clinical information includes far more than just a description of the healthcare activities; e.g. not only the simple "who?", meaning "which patient and which healthcare professionals?", but in addition a diverse amount of derivative information like the patient's spatial orientation, mental capacity, and whether on leave, and the healthcare professionals' education, organizational affiliations and experience. So while the basic who, where, when, and what may be easily obtained from existing structured sources, the basic why and how will probably need some human registration. And the real challenge lies in the need for an ascending order of derivative information like the doctor's experience with this procedure, with this procedure under these circumstances, with this procedure under these circumstances using this technique, and so on.

In this context it should also be noted that while this study registered 94 instances of production-contextual clinical information the actual incidence is necessarily greater. Thus, it was often a matter exactly who had provided the clinical information (e.g. by performing an examination), and since the staff know each other the naming of a person is also an indication of a number of personal characteristics which can be used in balancing the weight and importance of the clinical information. Likewise, the doctors' common knowledge of work flows, procedures and guidelines constitutes a significant amount of production-contextual clinical information.

It is, without doubt, possible to express some amount of production-contextual clinical information in a structured way, but as an overall concept it seems so extensive, so complex, and with such an elusive structure that an exhaustive structuring of production-contextual clinical information seems to be impossible.

4.3   How to Operationalize Production-Contextual Clinical Information

Production-contextual clinical information can be essential to clinical reasoning and its documentation thus is of importance to supporting of clinical work. This applies in particular if the level of ambition is as outlined in the Semantic Health Report where

> ... any health actor can understand and integrate the information in a collaborative manner as if the information was generated locally[1].

However, achieving this kind of documentation of production-contextual clinical information is problematic for three reasons:

First, production-contextual clinical information is complex, extensive, non-quantitative, and has an elusive structure. As mentioned above it seems unlikely to develop a model that permits a comprehensive expression.

Second, regardless of model, the amount of production-contextual clinical information needed to meet every health actor's needs is enormous, even compared to the already huge amounts of clinical core information. The amount of information raises several logistic questions, not the least of how the information should be obtained. Since the production-contextual clinical information largely consists of complex and qualitative information it would require manual registration, and as pointed out by Berg & Goorman, the disadvantages of this registration easily exceeds the benefits [2].

Third, even if the level of ambition is reduced it is challenging to bring about the necessary amount of production-contextual clinical information. As stated in the introduction, production-context is not what the sender considered relevant in the situation, but those details of the sender's situation which the receiver finds of current relevance. So unless the sender is told what contextual information to register, there is no guarantee that the existing production-contextual information will suffice.

On this basis, the operationalization of production-contextual clinical information can include standards and agreements which, in consideration of the registration burden, specify what is to be documented and in what detail. Registration of production-contextual clinical information in an amount that satisfies the vision of the Semantic Health Report [1] seems to be an illusion.

5   Conclusion

Production-contextual clinical information is the description of the circumstances of obtaining clinical information. In this paper the nature of production-contextual clinical information and the implications of its use were studied through observations and focus group interviews at a cardiology department in a mid-size hospital.

The circumstances under which clinical information is obtained can be many and very diverse. Accordingly, it was found that production-contextual clinical information is very extensive, complex, and with an elusive structure. It was also demonstrated that production-contextual clinical information is an integral part of doctors' daily work and that it can be crucial for balancing of likelihood, credibility, and overall weight of the given clinical information. Thus, access to production-contextual clinical information is an essential part of supporting the doctors' clinical work.

The potential volume, the complexity and the elusive structure, however, pose a significant barrier to making production-contextual clinical information available on a large scale. It is recommended that the operationalization of production-contextual clinical information is performed through standards and agreements which, in consideration of the registration burden, specify what is to be documented and in what detail.

References

1. Stroetmann, V., Kalra, D., Lewalle, P., Rector, A., Rodrigues, J.M., Stroetmann, K.A., Surjan, G., Ustun, B., Virtanen, M., Zanstra, P.E.: Semantic interoperability for better health and safer healthcare. European Commission, Luxembourg (2009)

2. Berg, M., Goorman, E.: The Contextual Nature of Medical Information. Int. J. Med. Inf. 56, 51–60 (1999)
3. Weiner, S.J.: Contextualizing Medical Decisions to Individualize Care. J. Gen. Intern. Med. 19, 281–285 (2004)
4. Brézillon, P., Pomerol, J.C.: Contextual Knowledge Sharing and Cooperation in Intelligent Assistant Systems. Travail Humain 62, 36 (1999)
5. Winograd, T.: Architectures for Context. Hum.-Comput. Interact. 16, 401–419 (2001)
6. Dourish, P.: What we Talk about when we Talk about Context. Pers. Ubiquit. Comput. 8, 19–30 (2004)
7. Bricon-Souf, N., Newman, C.R.: Context Awareness in Health Care: A Review. Int. J. Med. Inform. 76, 2–12 (2007)
8. ISO: ISO/TR 17119:2005 health informatics - health informatics profiling framework. ISO/TR (2005)
9. Galster, G.: Why is Clinical Information Not Reused? Stud. Health Technol. Inform. 180, 624–628 (2012)
10. Kitzinger, J.: Qualitative Research: Introducing Focus Groups. BMJ 311, 299–302 (1995)
11. Beale, T., Heard, S.: An Ontology-Based Model of Clinical Information. Stud. Health Technol. Inform. 129, 760–764 (2007)
12. Kassirer, J.P., Gorry, G.A.: Clinical Problem Solving: A Behavioral Analysis. Ann. Intern. Med. 89, 245–255 (1978)
13. Galster, G.: How to Distinguish Double Documentation from Documentation of Distinct Data. In: Fensli, R., Dale, J.G. (eds.) SHI 2011 Proceedings: 9th Scandinavian Conference on Health Informatics, August 30, pp. 16–20. TAPIR Akademisk Forlag, Oslo (2011)

Contextual Graphs Platform as a Basis for Designing a Context-Based Intelligent Assistant System

Hassane Tahir and Patrick Brézillon

LIP6, University Pierre & Marie Curie (UPMC),
4 Place Jussieu, 75005, Paris, France
{Hassane.Tahir,Patrick.Brezillon}@lip6.fr

Abstract. The complexity of tasks and problems in the management of databases requires the development of tools for supporting database experts. For instance, in the database administration area, when problems occur, the database administrator (DBA) is frequently the first person blamed. Most DBAs work in a fire-fighting mode and have little opportunity to plan ahead or be proactive. They must be constantly ready to analyze and correct failures based on a large set of procedures. In addition, they are continually readjusting these procedures and developing practices to manage a multitude of specific situations that differ from the generic situation by some few contextual elements. These practices have to deal with these contextual elements in order to solve the problem at hand. This paper proposes to use "Contextual Graphs" formalism to improve existing procedures used in database administration. Up to now, this improvement is achieved by a DBA through practices that adapt procedures to the context in which tasks should be performed and the incidents appear. This work present a new version of the contextual graph platform as a basis for designing and implementing a context-based intelligent assistant system for supporting database administrators.

1 Introduction

Nowadays, with the rapidly increasing evolution of information technology and internet applications (i.e. e-commerce and social networking), the decision-making in most organizations is becoming increasingly complex. As a consequence, decision makers have been obliged to make the best decisions in the shortest possible time. In the area of database administration, support is needed for experts to make decisions regarding complex activities such as tuning problems and managing the continuous changes in databases.

The Database administration area is typically concerned with many of the policies set by data designers. For Mullins [16], the DBA is the person responsible for carrying out these policies and to ensure the ongoing operational functionality and efficiency of an organization's databases and the applications that access those databases. The DBA carries out different tasks such as database design, performance monitoring and tuning, database availability, security, backup and recovery, data integrity, release migration. In addition, he must be constantly available to deal with

P. Brézillon, P. Blackburn, and R. Dapoigny (Eds.): CONTEXT 2013, LNAI 8175, pp. 259–273, 2013.

the variety of failures and to analyze and correct serious incidents using a large set of standard procedures. He is continually readjusting these procedures to deal with the specific situations that differ from the generic situation by some contextual elements. Contextual elements are relevant at a given time (e.g. memory size, hard drives), and the values taken by these contextual elements at that moment: (memory size: 70%, full, hard drives: HP-1, IBM-23). The DBA often developed practices to manage these contextual elements in order to solve the problem at hand. Practices encompass what the users do with procedures. Sometimes when one critical problem, suddenly appears, companies may lose large amounts of money for each hour of downtime. In such situations, the life of database administrators may become stressful because of the excessive pressure to solve problems quickly.

We can point two categories of problems: technical and social. Technical problems can impact the performance of the entire information system of the company. This includes problems due to the database, the server, the network and/or the application. For instance, one of the most important database problems is when users are unable to connect to the database because of a locked account, slow time response or bad performance, and sometimes because the database is down. Social problems are mainly due to bad communications and collaborations with other users. One of the mysterious messages that users often see on their terminal "A database is going down". This is frequently due to some DBA procedures programmed to run automatically and to reboot the database (or a database server) in order to perform upgrades, critical patches, or any other task on a database server. How about if the boss is using the application at that moment? Other situations and contexts may be much more critical like medical applications treating a patient (collecting sensitive data from database in real-time). We cannot state all situations and contexts, the list may be long. Another example that we can give concerns some collaboration problems due to the bad collaboration between DBA and other actors. In some cases, developers do not cooperate with a DBA to solve database errors due to a bad application coding. The reason for this is that developers may not feel comfortable while their code is being reviewed if their managers are invited.

This work relies on the Contextual-Graphs formalism [5] for implementing the different DBA activities and actions according to the different contextual elements. The main advantage of Contextual Graphs is the possibility to enrich incrementally the system with new knowledge and practice learning capability when needed. Moreover, a contextual graph is a good communication tool for helping the DBAs and actors of the organization to exchange their experiences and viewpoints.

The paper begins by the description of a case study illustrating performance problems in an ETL process in a data migration project in order to give the reason why an intelligent assistant system is needed to support database administrators in such stressful and similar situations and contexts. After, we present related works in the literature. Then we present the main features of the used approach followed by a presentation of contextual graph platform. Finally we conclude and evaluate our work.

2   A Case Study

This case study is about one of the important processes in data migration and data warehouses. This process is called ETL (Extraction, Transformation and Loading). The ETL functionality includes (a) Identifying relevant data in the source systems, (b) Extracting the required relevant data, (c) Customizing and integrating data coming from multiple sources into a common format, (d) Cleaning the resulting data set according to the database and business rules, and (e) Propagating and loading of the data into a target system.

The ETL process can involve a great complexity, and critical operational problems that can appear with bad and improperly design. Each ETL system depends on a Database Management System (DBMS), which is composed of a set of subsystems executing specific tasks and compete for system resources allocated by the DBMS. In some of the ETL tools, the whole process to be optimized is composed of set of workflows. Each workflow is composed of a set of sessions. A session corresponds to a task to perform a set of actions such as truncate a database table, execute an Oracle PL SQL stored procedure, load data into a table, etc. During this process, the DBA can perform a variety of tasks. In this case study, we focus on performance monitoring and tuning problems. There are two important tasks in DBMS performance tuning. The first task concerns "diagnosis" to determine which resources are responsible for the performance problem. The second task is about "resource adjustment" (or "tuning") and it involves altering resource allocations to reach better performance.

The main problems are about. (1) A potential impact on the whole data loading due to the slow and long running ETL processes; (2) Long hours at work both by project and production team members (i.e. a real wasting time risk especially in fire-fighting impacting even other related applications); and (3) Some process failures due to different process dependencies and timing conflicts. In this case study, the DBA is asked to decrease the total ETL process execution time by at least 50%. The main challenge is to improve the ETL performance by satisfying constraints such as minimal change of ETL code, no change and impact in existing IT operations and no additional hardware and other software tools to minimize costs.

Many questions may be asked by actors involved in the ETL process. They concern some of the different contextual elements that intervene in the different phases of the ETL process (with their known values). The following are some examples:

- What is the response time? (i.e. excellent, good or bad)
- Are all parts of the ETL system causing bad performance identified? (i.e. code of the ETL Software or data injection programs, database, or network infrastructure)
- Are database backups rescheduled to support and take into account the new ETL workflow jobs durations and planning?
- Should indexes be dropped and recreated, respectively before and after each data loading and how (i.e. manually, automatically)?
- Is the DBA aware of the new ETL process constraints? (i.e. long durations of the new ETL jobs, fast growing data)

For sharing contextual elements, the DBA and actors interacting with him must make explicit their viewpoints. Response time is a crucial problem of ETL process in this case study, because data should be transferred in the new system in a period that should not be longer than the brief cutover period where the production environment is taken offline. The typical procedure used by the DBA to solve the tuning problem is shown in Fig. 1. In the performance diagnosis, the DBA have to explore one of the three choices. The first one is based on tuning database parameters. The second one is to examine the application code to identify major time-consuming operations. The third choice is to diagnose network. Notice that other choices are not explored by the DBA in this case study.

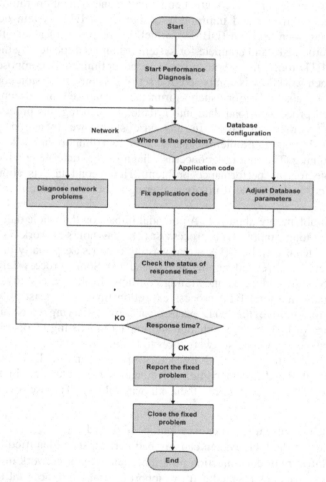

Fig. 1. A typical DBA procedure for diagnosis performance in ETL processes

The above discussion shows a great need for an intelligent tool not to replace the DBA but to help him in such stressful situations to solve expected new critical incidents as is the case of tuning problems. The following section discusses some of the commonly used approaches to intelligent assistance for database management.

3   Related Work

Intelligent assistance is one of the important active research fields within Artificial Intelligence (AI). The machine should assist humans to make decision, to search for information, to control complex objects, and finally to understand the meaning of words. Many solutions have been proposed to implement the notion of intelligent assistance (in different domains) over the years. The following lists some examples in the domain of database management:

- Expert systems: Generalized Expert System for Database Design (GESDD) by Dogac et al. [8];
- Decision Support Systems: An interactive DSS tool to support the database designer by Palvia [17];
- Case-Based Reasoning Systems: CABSYDD (Case-Based System for Database Design) by Choobineh & Lo [7].
- Intelligent Tutoring Systems (ITS): (1) Mitrovic et al. [13] and Mitrovic et al. [14] proposed DB-suite which consists of three web-based intelligent tutoring systems (SQL Tutor, NORMIT for data normalization, KERMIT for teaching conceptual database modeling using the ER model); and (2) Risco and Reye [20] presented a Personal Access Tutor (PAT), an Intelligent Tutoring System (ITS) for Learning Rapid Application Development (RAD) in a database environment.
- Intelligent Agents and multi-agents systems: (1) Carneiro et al. [6] proposed DBSitter, a tool for monitoring database environment; (2) Moraes et al. [15] proposed a software tool called AutonomousDB that supports the task of schema evolution in heterogeneous multi-database environments where there are replicated schemas; (3) Elfayoumy and Patel [9] proposed an intelligent agent assistant (IAA) to aid DBAs in performance monitoring tasks and the automation of resolution actions.; and (4) Oracle [19] provides a database "Grid Control Agent" which can help DBAs to monitor and maintain Oracle databases.

The above solutions cannot always successfully handle all the DBA tasks and problems encountered in multitude of specific new situations and contexts that differ from the procedures set for performing the same tasks and problems happened in other situations and contexts. Up to now, the improvement of the existing procedures is achieved through DBA practices that adapt these procedures to the context in which the incidents appear and where tasks should be performed. Another important problem is that IT tools do not provide proper support for the collaborative tasks performed by system administrators as seen in the research in ethnographic studies of system administrators carried out by Barrett et al. [1] and Haber and Bailey [11]. Kandogan et al. [10] and Haber et al. [12] concluded that improved tools for system administrator collaboration have great potential to significantly impact system administration work.

For these reasons, we are interested to take context into consideration and incorporate it in the database administration procedures. The following section presents features of the proposed approach for representing DBA practices as contextualization of procedures and the requirements of an intelligent assistant system. Our approach focuses on a support to the DBA. Thus, interactions with the other actors are "DBA centered". For this reason, we consider shared context and collaboration from the viewpoint of one of the actors (i.e. DBA) instead of observing actors collaborating together to accomplish a given task.

4   Main Features of the Proposed Approach

The notion of context can be used to address dynamic change and requirements in database administration procedures. Brézillon and Pomerol [5] consider that context is "what constrains something without intervening in it explicitly." An important consequence is that we must speak of context in relationships with a focus [5] and thus distinguish three types of context (see Fig. 2), namely, external knowledge, contextual knowledge, and proceduralized context. The external knowledge is the knowledge that has nothing to do with the current focus. The contextual knowledge is the knowledge that is more or less related to the current focus. The actor proceduralizes a part of the contextual knowledge for addressing the current focus (the proceduralized context). Our study focuses both on technical and user (or human) contexts. The technical context is related to the knowledge about changes in environment, upgrades of the database, upgrades of applications, incidents related to database recovery, etc. The user context is about human knowledge and specific conditions to consider when performing database management tasks.

In the area of incident management for subway lines, Pomerol and Brézillon [18] identified two parts in a context-based reasoning, namely diagnosis and action. The diagnosis part analyzes the situation at hand and its context in order to extract the essential facts for the actions. The actions are undertaken in a predictable order to realize the desired task. Sometimes, actions are undertaken even if the situation is not completely analyzed (or even not analyzed at all). For example, a driver puts a vehicle into gear before any action or situation analysis. Diagnosis and actions constitute a continuous twofold process, not two successive phases in context-based reasoning. Moreover, actions introduce changes in the situation or in knowledge about the situation, and imply a revision of the diagnosis, and thus of the decision making process itself. As a consequence, context must be considered explicitly with knowledge and reasoning. This is the role of the Contextual-Graphs formalism on which intelligent assistant systems (IASs) rely. According to Brézillon [2], an IAS must present different properties like:

- Providing users with a first approximation of environmental trends and events;
- Pointing out useful information implicit in large volumes of data to alert users to sudden changes;
- Developing multiple scenarios and perspectives on a given line of action;
- Attracting user attention to existing and emerging strategic issues;
- Supporting users in sharing and communicating their views and perspectives;
- Guiding user attention to specific data and their interpretation in particular issues.

An Intelligent Assistant system must be designed and developed in a formalism providing a uniform representation of knowledge, reasoning, and contextual elements. The contextual graph formalism can provide the incremental knowledge acquisition and practice learning. Context is the key factor of intelligent assistant systems. Making context explicit allows us to use knowledge in its context of use, to capture variants in the reasoning (e.g. recording practices effectively developed by operators), to generate relevant explanations. The following section presents the adopted conceptual framework.

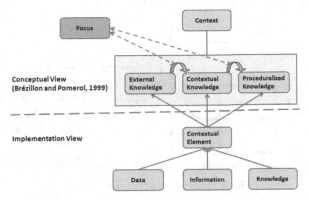

Fig. 2. Context, data, information and knowledge

5   Contextual-Graphs Platform

5.1   Brief Description of Contextual Graphs

A contextual graph (CxG) allows the representation of the different ways to solve a problem. It is a directed graph, acyclic with one input and one output and a general structure of spindle [3]. Each path in a CxG corresponds to a practice, a way to fix the problem. Fig. 3 provides the definition of the four elements in a contextual graph. A more detailed presentation of this formalism and its implementation can be found in [3].

A contextual graph is composed of the following elements: actions, contextual elements, activities and temporal branching.

An **action** is the building block of contextual graphs at the chosen granularity. An action can appear on several paths but it will be in different contexts.

A **contextual element** is a couple of nodes, a contextual node and a recombination node. A contextual node has one input and N branches [1, N] corresponding to the N instantiations of the contextual element already encountered. The recombination node is [N, 1] and shows that, once items on the branch between the contextual and recombination nodes has been processed, it does not matter to know which branch was followed. Contextual elements are used to represent and implement context about the different events occurring in a given situation.

An **activity** is a contextual graph by itself that is identified by participants because it appears on different paths and/or in several contextual graphs. This recurring substructure is generally considered as a complex action. An activity is a kind a contextualized task that can be aggregated in a unit or expanded in a sub graph according to the needs [21].

A **temporal branching** expresses the fact (and reduces the complexity of the representation) that several groups of actions must be accomplished but that the order in which action groups must be considered is not important, or even could be done in parallel, but all actions must be accomplished before continuing the practice development. The temporal branching is the expression of a complex contextual element at a lower granularity of the representation.

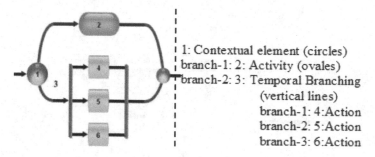

1: Contextual element (circles)
branch-1: 2: Activity (ovales)
branch-2: 3: Temporal Branching
            (vertical lines)
        branch-1: 4:Action
        branch-2: 5:Action
        branch-3: 6:Action

Fig. 3. Elements of a contextual graph

The following section describes the Contextual Graphs Platform on which the intelligent assistant system for DBAs will be based.

5.2   Proceduralized and Shared Contexts

A proceduralized context (PC) is an ordered series of instantiated contextual elements (CEs). It explains how the different items along a practice were introduced. The difference between two practices is explained through the divergence between their proceduralized contexts. Two PCs have at least a different CE or a same CE with different instantiations.

We distinguish the collaborative and the individual proceduralized contexts. The collaborative proceduralized context emerges from the interaction between actors, the introduction of each CE in the PC by one actor is the result of other actors' agreement. This constitutes the shared context associated with the current focus at hand. The individual proceduralized context corresponds to an actor's interpretation of the cooperative PC and contains the collaborative way in which the focus is addressed.

Sharing context means that actors' contexts have a non empty intersection. In a collaborative-design process, the shared context corresponds to the validity context of the design focus. It is built from contextual elements coming from the different experts' contexts. The shared-context building results from an incremental enrichment of contextual elements coming from individual contexts of experts. Thus, a contextual element proposed by an expert will enter the shared context if accepted (validated) by other experts. Individual contexts are mental representations of the design focus and of its validity context (the shared context). A contextual element provided by an expert must be integrated in other experts' mental representation, i.e. each expert must find a translation of this shared contextual element in his mental representation.

Thus, the collaborative-design process results by making the different views among experts compatible, not necessarily identical because all mental representations are different.

5.3   Contextual Graph Platform Architecture

The Contextual graphs Platform (or CxG Platfom) contains the building blocks of an experience base on which the context-based intelligent assistant system can reason and accompany a user in the realization of his tasks. At the implementation level, it is built using Java Software and XML database.

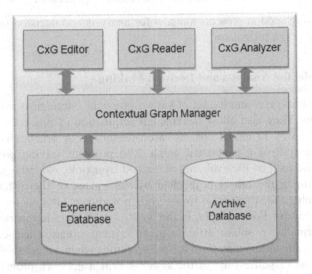

Fig. 4. Architecture of the Contextual Graphs Platform

The architecture of the CxG platform is shown in Fig. 4. It is composed of the following components:

CxG Editor: This component enables authorized users to manage their corresponding contextual graphs representing the main procedures and the significant changes added by them (i.e. practices). All operations such as creating, updating or deleting contextual graphs objects are allowed by the CxG Editor.

CxG Reader: This component allows only reading a desired contextual graph to execute one or more practices already created by different experts to performs a given task or activity. He can run only one practice a time. The reading and analysis process is described in the following.

CxG Analyzer: This component helps and support users in adopting the best strategies and practices when performing complex tasks to reach a given goal. It can be used with both the CxG Reader and the CxG Editor. The CxG Analyzer communicates with experience data warehouse to get the necessary information about the past user practices such as the number of users who have already run a given practice, how users have evaluated the practice, total time needed when adopting a given strategy, number of generated errors, etc.

CxG Manager: The CxG Manager controls and communicates with the different components of the CxG Platform and with the user.

Operational experience database: The CxG Manager uses this component to record and store users' practices. This database stores all information about the contextual graphs objects.

Archive database: This component manages copies of executed contextual graphs.

The following section presents a model for analysis and decision making based on the contextual graph formalism.

5.4   A Model for Analysis and Decision Making

Contextual graphs represent the set of known practices (strategies) in order to solve a given problem. They also allow incremental acquisition of practices and provide an understandable way to model context-based reasoning. A practice is the path from input to the output of a contextual graph. The problem solving process is guided throw a specific path by the evolution of context over time. Adopting a given practice or strategy among the others is dictated by the values of the different contextual elements forming the situation. However, it is not always obvious for a user to select one of these values. For example, in the area of database administration, to solve a serious performance problem within a given critical situation and context, a DBA (Database Administrator) may have different options when asking this question: what causes the slow response time of the system? Is it a network problem? Is it a bad database configuration? Is it a bad query in the application programs? Etc.

User practices are added and stored in an experience database. They may differ from each other because of their contexts that are slightly different where users used different actions at a step of the problem solving. The process of practice acquisition by the CxG system concerns the new action to integrate and the contextual element that discriminates that action with the previous one. The integration of the new practice requires either adding a new branch on an existing contextual node, or introducing of a new contextual node to distinguish the alternatives. The phase of incremental acquisition of practices relies on interaction between the CxG system and the users in order to acquire their expertise, which consists of a context-based strategy and its evolution along the process of the problem solving. We can distinguish two types of practices: (1) Practices created by experts using CxG editor (Design mode) (2) Practices followed by users using CxG Reader (Running mode).

Three phases are required to complete the process for analysis and decision making when reading a contextual graph as shown in the model in Fig. 5. In the pre-decision phase, the user browses the contextual graph about tasks to be performed to reach a given goal. When the graph is loaded, the user enables the CxG reader to start the running of a practice. Then the system enters the analysis and decision phase where different options and choices are presented to the user who may be interested to know what is the most selected option is in a similar context and situation. Once the user validates a given context, he makes his decision about which branch of the contextual element to select and continue reading or running other CxG objects. The process of reading, analyzing and validating context will continue until completing all the steps of the given task. At that moment, the complete decision-making process terminates to enter a post-decision phase where the analysis and evaluation of the practice will be started. The user may also be interested for the statistics about the path he selected (if it already exists in the experience database), number of errors generated when following that path   but also the most used path for solving a critical problem within a context similar to that of his current situation.

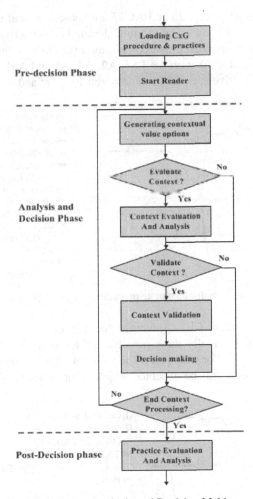

Fig. 5. Model for Analysis and Decision Making

5.5   Example of Contextual Graphs for DBA Procedures

Fig. 6 gives the standard view of contextual graphs (CxG) representation of the procedure for performance troubleshooting presented in the case study (in Fig. 1). This CxG is composed of the following:

- Two contextual elements (circles CE8 and CE17) representing respectively nodes numbered 8 and 17;
- Four square boxes (A9, A18, A19 and A20) representing DBA actions numbered 1, 20, 21 and 22;
- Three oval boxes (AC24, AC25 and AC27) representing DBA activities numbered 24, 25 and 27.

Notice that activities AC24, AC25 and AC27 are sub-contextual graphs. Each activity can contain other sub activities. For example detailed of the activity AC24 is shown in Fig. 7. A24 is a sub-contextual graph containing a set of one contextual element CE= {CE3} and a set of actions A with A= {A1, A2, A4, A5 and A6}. A1, A2, A4, A5 and A6 correspond, respectively, to actions numbered 1, 2, 4, 5and 6.

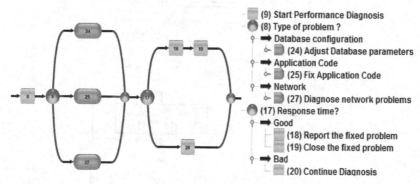

Fig. 6. Contextual graph of a simple procedure for performance troubleshooting

The contextual element CE3 "Database connection status?" numbered 3 (in the contextual graph) has initially three possible values or CE3= {'DB Cache','Block size','Target memory'}. For example, if the value of CE3 is 'DB Cache' or Val (CE3) ='DB Cache', action 4 will be executed. Fig. 7 represents the contextual graph for activity A24.

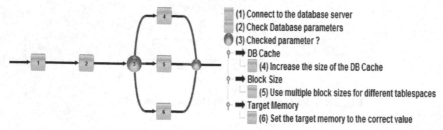

Fig. 7. Sub Contextual graph representing the detailed of an activity

The procedure in Fig. 7 can be adapted if the DBA explore new choices and alternatives when diagnosing the problem as shown in Fig. 8. Notice that a contextual graph represents a task execution at given time. This can correspond to "Try to connect again later", in which case the working context of the application has been changed. As a result, the graph should be re-executed again to deal with the new context. In this example, we have illustrated that contextual graphs are easy to use for representing both the initial DBA procedure and new practices. Other examples about applying context graphs in database administration can be found in [22] and [23].

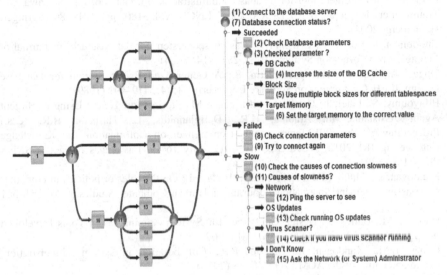

Fig. 8. Contextual graph to represent a procedure and DBA practices.

6   Conclusion

This paper has presented how to contextualize database administration procedures to perform DBA complex tasks. We have illustrated how it is easy to represent different DBA activities, viewpoints and practices by using contextual graphs. The architecture of the contextual graphs platform has also been presented. Our study is in the framework of designing a context-based intelligent assistant system for DBAs. It can also be extended to several other computing areas such as monitoring systems, computer security and network management.

References

1. Barrett, R., Kandogan, E., et al.: Field Studies of Computer System Administrators: Analysis of System Management Tools and Practices. In: Proceedings of CSCW (2004)
2. Brézillon, P.: From expert systems to context-based intelligent assistant systems: a testimony. The Knowledge Engineering Review 26(1), 19–24 (2011)

3. Brézillon, P.: Task-realization models in Contextual Graphs. In: Dey, A., Kokinov, B., Leake, D., Turner, R. (eds.) CONTEXT 2005. LNCS (LNAI), vol. 3554, pp. 55–68. Springer, Heidelberg (2005)
4. Brézillon, P., Pasquier, L., Pomerol, J.-C.: Reasoning with contextual graphs. European Journal of Operational Research 136(2), 290–298 (2002)
5. Brézillon, P., Pomerol, J.-C.: Contextual knowledge and proceduralized context. In: Proceedings of the AAAI 1999 Workshop on Modeling Context in AI Applications, Orlando, Florida, USA, AAAI Technical Report (July 1999)
6. Carneiro, A., Passos, R., Belian, R., Costa, T., Azevedo Tedesco, P., Salgado, A.C.: DBSitter: An intelligent tool for database administration. In: Galindo, F., Takizawa, M., Traunmüller, R., et al. (eds.) DEXA 2004. LNCS, vol. 3180, pp. 171–180. Springer, Heidelberg (2004)
7. Choobineh, J., Lo, A.W.: CABSYDD: Case-based system for database design. Journal of Management Information Systems 21(3), 281–314 (2004)
8. Dogac, A., Yürüten, B., Spaccapietra, S.: A Generalized Expert System for Database Design. IEEE Transactions on Software Engineering 15(4), 479–491 (1989)
9. Elfayoumy, S., Patel, J.: Database Performance Monitoring and Tuning Using Intelligent Agent Assistants. In: Arabnia, H.R., Deligiannidis, L., Hashemi, R.R. (eds.) Proceedings of the 2012 International Conference on Information & Knowledge Engineering, IKE 2012, WORLDCOMP 2012, July 16-19, Las Vegas Nevada. CSREA Press, USA (2012)
10. Kandogan, E., Maglio, P.P., Haber, E.M., Bailey, J.: On the roles of policies in computer systems management. International Journal of Human-Computer Studies 69(6), 351–361 (2011)
11. Haber, E.M., Bailey, J.: Design Guidelines for System Administration Tools Developed through Ethnographic Field Studies. ACM (2007)
12. Haber, E.M., Kandogan, E., Maglio, P.P.: Collaboration in system administration. Communications of the ACM 54(1), 46–53 (2011)
13. Mitrovic, A., Suraweera, P., Martin, B.: Db-suite: Experiences with three intelligent, web-based database tutors. Journal of Interactive Learning Research 15, 409–432 (2004)
14. Mitrovic, A., Team, T.I.: Constraint based tutors. In: Woolf, B.P., Aimeur, E., Nkambou, R., Lajoie, S. (eds.) 9th International Conference on Intelligent Tutoring Systems. LNCS, vol. 5091, pp. 29–32. Springer, Montreal (2008)
15. Moraes, A.C., Salgado, A.C., Tedesco, P.A.: AutonomousDB: a Tool for Autonomic Propagation of Schema Updates in Heterogeneous Multi-Database Environments. In: Fifth International Conference on Autonomic and Autonomous Systems, April 20-25, pp. 251–256. IEEE (2009)
16. Mullins, C.S.: Database Administration. The Complete Guide to Practices and Procedures. Addison Wesley (2012)
17. Palvia, P.: An Interactive DSS Tool for Physical Database Design. Information Sciences 54(3), 239–262 (1991)
18. Pomerol, J.-C., Brézillon, P.: Context proceduralization in decision making. In: Blackburn, P., Ghidini, C., Turner, R.M., Giunchiglia, F. (eds.) CONTEXT 2003. LNCS (LNAI), vol. 2680, pp. 491–498. Springer, Heidelberg (2003)
19. Oracle. Enterprise Manager Agent Downloads, http://www.oracle.com/technetwork/oem/grid-control/downloads/agentsoft-090381.html
20. Risco, S., Reye, J.: Evaluation of an Intelligent Tutoring System used for teaching RAD in a Database Environment. In: Proceedings of the Fourteenth Australasian Computing Education Conference, Melbourne, Australia (2012)

21. Sowa, J.F.: Knowledge Representation: Logical, Philosophical, and Computational Foundations. Brooks Cole Publishing Co., Pacific Grove (2000)
22. Tahir, H., Brézillon, P.: Procedure contextualization for collaborative database administration. In: Proceedings of the 15th International Conference on Computer Supported Cooperative Work in Design, Lausanne, Switzerland, June 8-10 (2011)
23. Tahir, H., Brézillon, P.: Shared context for improving collaboration in database administration. International Journal of Database Management Systems

Situational Awareness in Context

Odd Erik Gundersen[1,2]

[1] Verdande Technology
Stiklestadveien 1, NO-7041 Trondheim, Norway
odderik@verdandetechnology.com
http://www.verdandetechnology.com
[2] Department of Computer and Information Science
Norwegian University of Science and Technology
Sem Sælands vei 7-9, NO-7491 Trondheim, Norway
http://www.idi.ntnu.no

Abstract. In this paper we analyze the relationship between context and situational awareness with the aim to get a better understanding of how context information influences situation assessment. The analysis is based on previous research on situational awareness, context and situations. We show how situation assessment could be specified more detailed with regards to sub-processes through investigating the components of a situation. Events are introduced as situational elements in themselves. The role of context in situation assessment is also analyzed and so is the information that can be treated as contextual. A case study is presented that relates the findings to the monitoring of oil well drilling. Our main contribution is an analysis of the situation assessment process and how it operates on and manipulates the components of the situation. Another contribution is the case study of how the findings apply in monitoring of the oil well drilling situation.

Keywords: Context, Situational Awareness, Situation Assessment.

1 Introduction

Stuational awareness is about how aware someone is about a situation. Although situational awareness has been termed "ill defined" [25], lately, the research community has more or less adopted Mica Endsley's view on situational awareness [6]. Another concept that is ill defined is *context*. One of the reasons that a definition of context is hard to nail down is that *what context is changes with its context*. Thus, the concept of context is more easily analyzed in relation to something else. In this paper, context will be studied in relation to situational awareness, and the aim is to inform the understanding of how they relate.

The motivation for understanding how these two terms relate stems from our work with developing decision support software for drilling engineers that monitor oil well drilling operations [13,12]. Drilling oil wells is a highly complex and risky task that costs huge amounts of money. Because of this, monitoring the drilling process is extremely important.The software we have developed seeks

P. Brézillon, P. Blackburn, and R. Dapoigny (Eds.): CONTEXT 2013, LNAI 8175, pp. 274–287, 2013.

to enhance the situational awareness of drilling engineers that monitor drilling operations. It does so by automatically identifying the elements that the situation is composed of and comparing the current situation with situations stored in a data base of past experiences. In this way, the software system helps the drilling engineers to comprehend the current situation by identifying situational elements and projecting the future.

In this paper we will investigate the relationship between context and situational awareness based on previous research on situational awareness, situations and context. The aim is to get a better understanding of how context information influences the situation assessment. Our main contribution is an analysis of the situation assessment process and how it operates on and manipulates the components of a situation. Another contribution is a case study of how the findings apply in monitoring of an oil well drilling situation.

The rest of this paper is structured as follows: The main ideas that this work is based on will be presented in section 2. Then, our interpretation on how these concepts relate will be presented in section 3. In section 4, a case study is presented that exemplifies the findings in the previous section. Finally in section 5, we conclude and present some future work.

2   Foundations

The main concepts and ideas that the research presented here is based on are Endsley's model for situational awareness [9], situation semantics [8] and the knowledge level context model developed by Öztürk and Aamodt [22,21].

2.1   Situational Awareness

Several models of situational awareness exist, and Rousseau et al. [23] distinguish between descriptive and prescriptive models. Descriptive models describe the cognitive processes related to situational awareness, and prescriptive models are used to simulate situational awareness. Salmon et al. [24] did a systematic review of situational awareness models, and their focus was on the three most cited ones. Apart from Endsley's model, these are models proposed by Smith and Hancock [26] and Bedny and Meister [5], which both are descriptive. Smith and Hancock take an ecological approach to defining situational awareness while Bedny and Meister use activity theory to describe situational awareness.

Endsley's three level information processing model [9] has received most attention and is a descriptive model that seeks to capture how humans become aware of situations. She defines situational awareness as *the perception of the elements in the environment within a volume of time and space, the comprehension of their meaning, and the projection of their status in the near future.* Despite emphasizing that situational awareness is a state of knowledge, the definition focus on how this state is achieved rather than specifying the state of situational awareness itself. However, the definition implicitly specifies what the state contains, which is information of elements relevant for the situation, i.e.

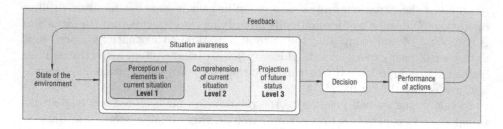

Fig. 1. The three levels of situational awareness [10]

elements in the environment within a volume of time and space, their meaning for the situation and how they can affect the situation in the near future.

The process of achieving this state of knowledge is comprised of three sub-processes, called levels, which are illustrated in figure 1. Level 1 concerns perception of situational elements, while level 2 concerns comprehension of the current situation. Finally, when the situational elements are perceived and the situation is comprehended, one can project the future state of the elements constituting the situation. The model reflects that the three levels are not executed consecutively, but non-sequentially and in parallel. In addition, the different levels interact in a more complex fashion than bottom-up processing of the information when becoming aware of a situation An example that is given is that subjects observe a situational element, which feeds the comprehension, and as part of the comprehension process the subject starts actively looking for situational elements that will support the current comprehension. In addition to the model of situational awareness, a complete theory of situational awareness is presented.

The main strength of the model is its intuitive description of situational awareness, as also is noted by Salmon et al. [24], and the three layers that specify the main processes for how to achieve situational awareness. Decision making and performance of actions are not part of the model. Both the process of assessing the situation and the knowledge of the situation are mental, and thus the performance of actions, which intrinsically is physical, is not part of these concepts. Furthermore, decision making has other input than the knowledge about the situation and the elements in it. For example, a person can be fully aware of all the situational elements, comprehend their meaning perfectly and project their future state completely, and still decide not to perform the actions that will avoid an unwanted situation. This may be because of rules or regulations that must be obliged or the inability to perform the action. Conversely, decisions can be made without any awareness of the situation at all. However, the more informed decision maker that has the better situational awareness will be able to make the better decision. Thus, the degree of situational awareness that a person has can lead to better decisions, but decision making itself is not part of the situational awareness. Still, performing actions can increase the situational awareness, as their effect might impact the situation that is perceived.

2.2   Situations

Situation semantics is a theory for natural language semantics based on a mathematical framework, situation theory, which was developed in parallel. It is a formal way of analyzing situations, and it has a clearly specified definition of what a situation is. Thus, it is a natural starting point when modeling situations. The following quote from [8], which quotes [4], describes the situation semantics view on situations:

> "The world consists not just of objects, or of objects, properties and relations, but of objects having properties and standing in relations to one another. And there are parts of the world, clearly recognized (although not precisely individuated) in common sense and human language. These parts of the world are called situations."

According to this definition, a situation describes a part of the world consisting of objects, their properties and the relations between them. McCarthy and Hayes [20], on the other hand, define a situation as *"the complete state of the universe at an instant of time"*. However, this definition is not commonly accepted, as open systems are not fixed and possibly not completely available, which is noted by Baclawski et al. [3]. Changes and events are described by Barwise in the following manner [4]:

> "Events and episodes are situations in time, scenes are visually perceived situations, changes are sequences of situations, and facts are situations enriched (or polluted) by language."

Events are described as situations in time, and change is a sequence of situations or, as sequences of situations are separated by time, a sequence of events. A situation is thus a static state, and any change in state is another situation. This definition of events is controversial, as it defies the common understanding [1] of an event as well as the definition used in event processing systems. *Event processing* is defined by Etzion and Niblett [11] as "computing that performs operations on events", while complex event processing (CEP) systems combine events into situations [17]. In this regard, *"an event is something that happens"* [7]. Kim [14] represents events as objects described with some attribute that happens over a given timeframe: [(Brutus, Cesar, t), stabs] where t designates a timeframe. From this follows that events represent change.

Baclawski et al. [3] note, in their formalization of situational awareness, that events are used to represent evolution of objects and relations instead of series of ordered situations. In the core ontology for situational awareness described by Matheus et al. [19], they use *event notices* to represent changes. Event notices are not situational elements themselves, but entities that describe changing relations and attributes. Kokar et al. [15] present a thorough analysis of the relationship between situations and situational awareness in which they argue that a situation is not what is perceived in the first level, perception of situational elements, of Endsley's model for situation awareness. The argument is based on the definition of situation found in Merriam Webster's Dictionary, which states that relations between objects are essential parts of situations, similar to the definition of situation in situation theory. Thus, the situation is what is represented in the second level, comprehension of the situation, in which the relations between the situational elements are inferred. Another implication of this interpretation is that situational elements can be immaterial as well as physical, which opens up for comprehending situations in which dreams and hopes are reified and represented as situational elements. This is in line with Kolodner's observations. She observes that the theory underlying case-based reasoning is to reason about, understanding and remembering what she calls *intentional situations* [16]. Intentional situations are situations containing agents and their environments, but also their goals and intentions. Hence, in order to fully reason about and comprehend situations, immaterial objects have to be represented as well. However, events are not first class citizens of Kokar et al.'s work as they capture situation theory as a ontology [15]. In our previous work, we have found that describing situations through events can be very powerful, and we have introduced them as first class citizens of a situation description in which events are treated as situational elements in the same way as physical objects. Events are not "just" changes that affect physical objects, such as *event notices* in [19], but can be described by properties in the same way as objects and have relations to other situational elements.

2.3   Context in Situation Assessment

There is a distinction between the *role* and the *elements* of context according to the knowedge level model of context developed by Öztürk and Aamodt [22,21]. The context elements can belong to the generic context ontology or the domain knowledge. The generic context ontology distinguishes between the problem solver and the external situation, and it is defined from the point of view and emphasizes the active role of the problem solver. Hence, context can be divided into internal and external context, where internal relates to the problem solver and external relates to the external situation. The external context can be related to the target of the problem solving task or the environment of this target. Furthermore, all context elements can be *interactive* or *independent*. Independent context elements do not affect the reasoning process, but are recalled with the material, while interactive context elements are active parts in the reasoning process. The role of context is mainly about relevance and focus, where relevance means choosing the most relevant solution and focus is related to ensuring the efficiency of the problem solving process.

When considering situational awareness, there is a distinction between the context of a situational element and the situation. The context of a situational element can be other situational elements, which Manilla and Moen [18] use when they decide the similarity of event types in event sequences. Hence, an integral part of the context of a situational element is the situation it appears in. The context of the situation itself is another matter. For example, a situation might exist as part of a simulation, a training exercise or a real-world scenario.

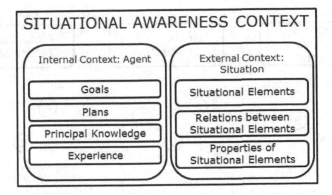

Fig. 2. Components of the situation assessment context divided into internal and external

Which one of these that applies is a highly important bit of information when making a decision. The distinction between the context of a situational element and the situation is not made by Day and Abowd. They define context as *any information that can be used to characterize the situation of an entity* [2], of which a relation is a good example.

Based on the above observations about context and situation assessment, the role of context is focusing the assessment while identifying the most relevant actions to ensure that the best possible decision is made. In the context of training, the *relevancy* of an action can be affected by the how much is learned from performing it. Thus, exploring new actions that are too risky to perform in a real-world scenario is an option in a training scenario.

Context can be either internal or external to the agent assessing the situation. Internal context is the goals, the plans, the experiences and the principal knowledge the agent has. The internal-interactive context decides the perspective on which the agent views the situation. Although the external context is tied to the target situation and its environment, it is described and represented internally in the agent.The external context can be relations, some of the situational elements and some of the properties describing situational elements. Relations describe how situational elements relate to each other, and thus they are context information, while color is a property of a situational element that can be an example of an independent external context. Some elements part of the situation might not play an important role in the situation, such as bystanders of an accident. Figure 2 illustrates the components that form the situation assessment context.

3   Situation Assessment: An Analysis of the Process

To sum up, situation assessment is the process of becoming aware of the situation, which is composed of situational elements, relations and their properties.

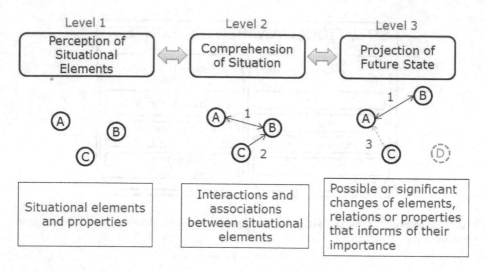

Fig. 3. Situation assessment and high level description of the levels

Situational elements can be both physical and immaterial, as well as events. Relations connect one or more situational elements or relations. Situation assessment has three sub-processes, which are perception of situational elements, comprehension of situation and projection of future state.

New situational elements are perceived, as well as their properties and classes, as part of the first level of situational awareness. However, not all situational elements can be perceived. Only elements that have representations in the physical world can be, which exclude dreams and intentions that have not been communicated. Thus, events, physical objects and information can be perceived in the first level. Immaterial objects, such as dreams and intentions can only be identified through comprehending the situation and the relationships between objects. Comprehending the situation is mapping out relations between objects and identifying immaterial objects that influence the situation. The result of projecting the future state of the situation is the identification of the most relevant and important relations, elements and properties that are part of the situation. These can be found by forwarding the current situation or introducing new situational elements, properties or relations and see how they affect the current situation. By performing this projection, the importance of the different situational elements, properties and relations will become apparent. This result feeds the comprehension of the situation. Thus, the second level is the central process keeping track of the comprehension of the current situation by using the services of the two other processes.

In contrast to Endsley's model, we restrict the information to only flow between neighboring levels. Endsley's model explicitly state that the levels are not processed sequentially, but in parallel, and information flows between them. We agree that the levels are executed in parallel, but we argue that there is a structure to the information flow between them. There can be both top-down and bottom-up processing, where bottom up means that information flows from the lowest level and top down means that information flows from level three to level one. In bottom-up processing, a new situational element is perceived, and the element and its properties inform the second level. The second level analyzes the relations between the new situational element and the existing ones. The situational elements and their relations are the input to the third level, which identify relevant relations through projecting the future. Top-down processing is when the projections of future state make more sense for the comprehension of the current situaion if some other situational element was present. Thus, because the current situation would make more sense if another situational element was present, one starts to look for evidence of this element. Information does not flow directly from level 1 to 3 or the other way, but through level two which can use the information to either look for new elements or analyze future implications.

Figure 3 illustrates the three levels, their roles and how information flows between them. The figure shows how three elements, A, B and C, are identified in level one. Two relations, 1 and 2, are identified in level two and level three analyze a future state in which one relation is removed (relation 2), a new relation is found, relation 3, and a new situational element is projected, element D.

In figure 4, the sub-processes of situation assessment as related to the components of situations are presented. Perception of situational elements is identifying situational elements, observe their properties and classify them. Comprehension of situation is comprised of conception of immaterial situational elements, identifying their properties and classify them, identifying new relations and changes in old, and classifying the situation. Projection of the future is to identify relevant changes to situational elements, properties and relations, play forward the situation (with or without changes), and identify important elements, properties and relations. Based on this, the future situation can be classified.

4   Case Study: Monitoring Oil Well Drilling Operations

This section presents a case study of how the situational awareness of a drilling engineer is developed. First, the process itself is discussed, and then we explain which situational elements and relations the situation consists of. Finally, an example of how the drilling engineer assesses the situation is given.

4.1   Manual Monitoring of Drilling Operations

Oil well drilling is done by crews operating drilling rigs, and the wells they drill are not necessarily vertical holes, but can have S-shaped trajectories and be up to 10 km deep. The drill bit is attached to the end of the drill string, and drilling is performed by, typically, rotating the complete drill string. Drill strings are hollow steel pipes that transport drilling fluid down into the hole on the inside. On its way back, the drilling fluid transports products generated by the drilling process

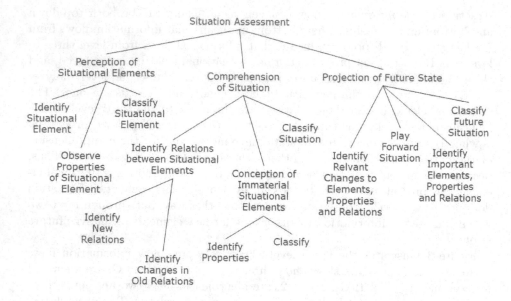

Fig. 4. Decomposition of sub-processes of situation assessment

on the outside of the drill string. The drilling fluid also controls the pressure in the wellbore so that the wellbore does not fracture or fluid from the surrounding formations does not seep into the wellbore. Different parameters relevant for the drilling process are measured both on the rig and down in the hole.

The crew on the rig is responsible for drilling the wellbore, but as they always are taking care of the continuously ongoing drilling processes and immediate problems, they rarely have time to actually look at long term trends, which can lead to severe problems. Therefore, drilling engineers that have participated in planning the drilling operation and are experts on the drilling process monitor the drilling operations remotely in real-time operation centers. The monitoring is done through drilling engineers staring at real-time measurements visualized as graphs. Based on the behaviors of the different measurements, the current situation can be interpreted. From the measurements, the rig activity, the drill bit's location in the well (is it on bottom or close to the top?), formation changes, symptoms and problematic situations can be observed. Typically, more severe situations are preceded by several less severe symptoms, and thus drilling engineers that focus on long term trends can warn the rig crew in advance of the problematic situations. Figure 5 illustrate how drilling engineers assess the drilling situation through graphs visualizing measurements performed on the rig.

However, even though the drilling operations are monitored, problems occur. The drilling engineers can work in 12 hours shifts, and the task is both tiring and boring. Also, maintaining an up to date mental model of the situation is hard. Because of limitations on the working memory of humans, important bits of information can be lost.

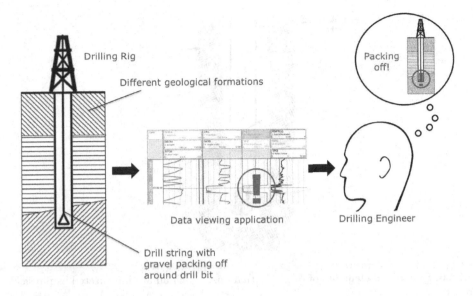

Fig. 5. Drilling engineers monitor drilling operations remotely through viewing real-time measurements visualized as graphs. Based on the behaviors of the different measurements, the current situation can be interpreted and symptoms of problematic situations can be detected.

4.2 The Drilling Situation and Its Context

The drilling engineer is the agent that assesses the situation, as presented in the previous section, and the situation that is assessed is the drilling of an oil well. The situational elements are tools of the drilling process, the mud, the wellbore and the products of the process among others. Figure 6 illustrates some situational elements of the drilling situation. The drill string, its stabilizers, and the drill bit are clear examples of physical situational elements. Another situational element is the wellbore itself even though it is a hole (and thus the negation of something!) The wellbore has a dimension and a surface, which is the surrounding formations. A restriction in the wellbore, such as a formation that is swelling and thus decrease the hole size, is also interpreted as a situational element. Often, the swelling formation, shale in our example, restricts the movement of the drill string when the swelling is so excessive that stabilizers cannot move past it. The restriction can be observed in the measurements when the stabilizers hit it, and it can be removed by proper treatment. As it is a physical entity with a location and volume, it is interpreted as a physical situational element and not a property of the wellbore, as it certainly can be treated as too. Similarly, fractions in the wellbore and holes in the drill string are treated as physical situational elements too, as they also have locations as well as other properties.

An overpull is an increase of the weight of the drill string when pulling it out of the hole, and it is an example of an event. It indicates that the drill string met a restriction on its way out of the hole, such as a swelling formation, but can

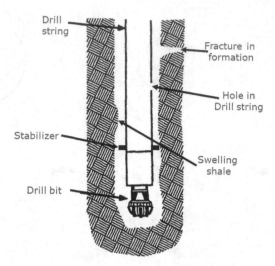

Fig. 6. Situational elements of drilling situations, which all are interpreted as physical objects

also be an indication of a stabilizer being trapped in a ledge. Thus, an overpull event can be both related to ledges in the well bore and swelling formations. Which one of these two situational elements that caused the overpull can be explained by context information, such as the formation type and the form of the products produced when this section of the well was drilled. The degree of increase in weight of the drill string will indicate the severity property of the event. A highly severe overpull can weaken the drill string so that it might be torn in two next time an overpull happen. Other events include pack off, which indicates gravel packing off around the drill bit and thus an increased standpipe pressure, and pressure loss, which can indicate a hole in the drill string. Hence, events can be treated as situational elements in themselves in this domain.

The external context of a drilling situation is specified by situational elements, properties of situational elements and relations between situational elements. The formation layers are examples of a property of the well bore which can focus and make the search for a solution more efficient. These cannot be observed directly in the real-time graphs, but are typically found by measurements done on beforehand and reported elsewhere. Other context information that is related to the condition of the wellbore is chemical and mechanical exposition. Chemical exposition tells how long different parts of the wellbore have been exposed to the drilling fluid, as it can react with the formation and this affect the condition of the wellbore, while mechanical exposition provides information about the amount of wear the drill bit has exposed the well bore to. Both are properties of the wellbore at a given location. Typical examples of relations are the ones between events and the physical objects they are an indication of. An overpull indicates a restriction, so there is a *indicated by* relation between swelling shale and an overpull. Furthermore, a pack off event indicates gravel that packs off around the drill bit, and thus there is an *indicated by* relation between gravel and the pack off event.

The internal context focuses the assessment of the situation and controls the relevancy of the root cause analysis. Goals focus the attention, and a switch from the goal *monitor the drilling situation* to *eat lunch* will probably affect the situational awareness of the drilling engineer. The changing of goals will activate different plans, so might also observation of new situational elements, as it might change the type of the current situation, which will make the drilling engineer look for other indications of a situation type switch. A pack off event can indicate that the situation has changed from *all is well* to *hole cleaning problems*. Understanding of the physics of drilling is principal knowledge and is internal context that is related to each individual and will affect perception of situational elements, comprehension of the situation and projection of the future state. The same applies to experiences, as they also are individual and will focus the attention on what the drilling engineers will concentrate on and increase the relevance of the prediction of the future. For example, drilling engineers with more experience will not stress when observing some pack off events, as they are expected when drilling the current formation and will not lead to problems in the future. Less experienced drilling engineers might want to take immediate action, as they might not be aware that pack off events are less risky in the current situation than generally.

4.3 Drilling Situation Assessment

The following example illustrates how the situation assessment process flows and how situational elements are perceived and the comprehension of the situation evolves. A drilling engineer monitors the drilling and observes that the process continues without any major problems. They are drilling as the drill bit is on the bottom of the well, and the drilling crew is making steady progress. Some tendencies of pressure spikes indicating that gravel has been packing off around the drill bit are observed. This is expected in the formation that they are drilling right now. However, slowly, the pack off events increase in frequency, but the crew on the rig does not notice and continues the drilling. The bit is pulled out a couple of meters, as part of regular operations, and the drilling engineer observes a slight overpull. The overpull indicates that the gravel that has been packing around the drill bit has not been cleaned out of the hole. Thus, the drilling engineer calls the rig and ask them to clean the hole better. After the hole has been cleaned, the amount of pack off events decrease and no more overpull events are noticed.

The drilling engineer identifies events and classify them as pack off with low severity as they are expected. They are related to the formation they are drilling in, and the situation is classified as low risk. Then, a new event of class overpull is identified, and the severity is low as it is barely noticeable. However, now new relations are being made between the overpull and gravel in the hole. The increase in pack off events also point in this direction. The drilling engineer project the future situation by playing it forward, and sees that if this continues the hole can be so full of gravel that the drill string get stuck. Getting stuck is a severe situation, and thus remedying actions must be made. The projection of the future state has indicated that the relation between the overpull and gravel is the cause of the problem, and thus it is deemed more important than the relation between the pack off and expected in this formation. Cleaning the wellbore removes the situational element gravel from the wellbore.

5   Conclusion and Future Work

We have shown how situation assessment could be specified more detailed in regards to sub-processes through investigating the components of a situation. Events were introduced as situational elements in themselves, and it was discussed how they have both properties and relate to other situational elements. The role of context in situation assessment was also analyzed and so was the information that can be treated as contextual. A case study was presented that related the findings to the monitoring of oil well drilling.

In our current software system [13,12], situational elements are the only components of the situation that are modeled explicitly. Relations between situational elements are only modeled through their closeness in time and depth. This has advantages as comparing situations is simpler than if relations are introduced. However, some relations are identified by the system, but this information is not used in the situation description. Future work will include an investigation on how to introduce relations between the situational elements in the situation description.

References

1. Merriam Webster's Dictionary (June 2013), http://www.merriam-webster.com
2. Abowd, G.D., Dey, A.K.: Towards a Better Understanding of Context and Context-awareness. In: Gellersen, H.-W. (ed.) HUC 1999. LNCS, vol. 1707, pp. 304–307. Springer, Heidelberg (1999)
3. Baclawski, K., Kokar, M., Letkowski, J., Matheus, C., Malczewski, M.: Formalization of situation awareness. In: Proceedings of the Eleventh OOPSLA Workshop on Behavioral Semantics, pp. 1–15 (2002)
4. Barwise, J., Perry, J.: The Situation Underground. Stanford Working Papers in Semantics 1, 1–55 (1980)
5. Bedny, G., Meister, D.: Theory of Activity and Situation Awareness. International Journal of Cognitive Ergonomics 3(1), 63–72 (1999)
6. Breton, R., Rousseau, R.: Situational Awareness: A Review of the Concept and Its Measurement. Tech. rep. (2003)
7. Chandy, K.M., Schulte, W.R.: Event Processing - Designing IT Systems for Agile Companies. McGraw-Hill (2010)
8. Devlin, K.: Situation theory and situation semantics. In: Handbook of the History of Logic, vol. 7, pp. 601–664 (2006)
9. Endsley, M.R.: Toward a Theory of Situation Awareness in Dynamic Systems. Human Factors: The Journal of the Human Factors and Ergonomics Society 37, 32–64 (1995)

10. Endsley, M.R., Hoffman, R.R.: The Sacagawea Principle. IEEE Intelligent Systems 17(6), 80–85 (2002)
11. Etzion, O., Niblett, P.: Event Processing in Action. Manning Publications Company (2010)
12. Gundersen, O.E., Sørmo, F.: An Architecture for Multi-Dimensional Temporal Abstraction Supporting Decision Making in Oil-Well Drilling. In: Hatzilygeroudis, I., Palade, V. (eds.) Combinations of Intelligent Methods and Applications. SIST, vol. 23, pp. 21–40. Springer, Heidelberg (2013)
13. Gundersen, O.E., Sørmo, F., Aamodt, A., Skalle, P.: A Real-Time Decision Support System for High Cost Oil-Well Drilling Operations. AI Magazine 34(1), 21–32 (2013)
14. Kim, J.: Causation, Nomic Subsumption, and the Concept of Event. The Journal of Philosophy, 217–236 (1973)
15. Kokar, M.M., Matheus, C.J., Baclawski, K.: Ontology-based Situation Awareness. Information Fusion 10(1), 83–98 (2009)
16. Kolodner, J.L.: Case-Based Reasoning. Morgan Kaufmann Series in Representation and Reasoning Series. Morgan Kaufmann Publishers (1993)
17. Luckham, D.C., Frasca, B.: Complex Event Processing in Distributed Systems. Tech. rep., Stanford University (1998)
18. Mannila, H., Moen, P.: Similarity between event types in sequences. In: Mohania, M., Tjoa, A.M. (eds.) DaWaK 1999. LNCS, vol. 1676, pp. 271–280. Springer, Heidelberg (1999)
19. Matheus, C.J., Kokar, M.M., Baclawski, K.: A core ontology for situation awareness. In: Proceedings of the Sixth International Conference on Information Fusion, pp. 545–552 (2003)
20. McCarthy, J., Hayes, P.J.: Some philosophical problems from the standpoint of artificial intelligence. In: Meltzer, B., Michie, D. (eds.) Machine Intelligence 4, pp. 463–502. Edinburgh University Press (1969); reprinted in McC90
21. Öztürk, P.: Towards a knowledge-level model of context and context use in diagnostic problems. Applied Intelligence 10(2-3), 123–137 (1999)
22. Öztürk, P., Aamodt, A.: Towards a Model of Context for Case-Based Diagnostic Problem Solving. In: Proceedings of the Interdisciplinary Conference on Modeling and Using Context (CONTEXT 1997), pp. 198–208 (1997)
23. Rousseau, R., Tremblay, S., Breton, R.: Defining and Modelling Situation Awareness: A Critical Review. In: Banbury, S., Tremblay, S. (eds.) A Cognitive Approach to Situation Awareness: Theory and Application, pp. 3–21. Ashgate (2004)
24. Salmon, P.M., Stanton, N.A., Walker, G.H., Baber, C., Jenkins, D.P., McMaster, R., Young, M.S.: What Really Is Going on? Review of Situation Awareness Models for Individuals and Teams. Theoretical Issues in Ergonomics Science 9(4), 297–323 (2008)
25. Sarter, N., Woods, D.: Situation Awareness: A Critical But Ill-Defined Phenomenon. International Journal of Aviation Psychology 1, 45–57 (1991)
26. Smith, K., Hancock, P.: Situation awareness is adaptive, externally directed consciousness. Human Factors 37(1), 137–148 (1995)

Context-Assisted Test Cases Reduction
for Cloud Validation

Feras A. Batarseh[1], Avelino J. Gonzalez[1], and Rainer Knauf[2]

[1] Intelligent Systems Lab (ISL), Department of Electrical Engineering and Computer Science,
University of Central Florida, 4000 Central Florida Blvd., Orlando, FL 32816, USA
fbatarseh@knights.ucf.edu,
Avelino.Gonzalez@ucf.edu
[2] Department of Computer Science and Automation, Ilmenau University of Technology,
P.O. Box 100565, Ilmenau, Germany 98684
rainer.knauf@tu-ilmenau.de

Abstract. Cloud computing is currently receiving much attention from the industry, government, and academia. It has changed the way computation is performed and how services are delivered to customers. Most importantly, cloud services change the way software is designed, how data is handled, and how testing is performed. In cloud computing, testing is delivered as a service (TaaS). For instance, case testing (one of the most common validation approaches) could be used. However, executing test cases on a cloud system could be expensive and time consuming. Therefore, test case reduction is performed to minimize the number of test cases to be executed on the system. In this paper, we introduce a validation method called Context-Assisted Test Case Reduction (CATCR) for systems that are deployed on the cloud. In CATCR, test cases are reduced based on the context of the validation process. The results of previous test cases are used to select test cases for the next iteration. The minimized set of test cases needs to have effective coverage of the system on the cloud. To evaluate CATCR, an experimental evaluation is performed through Amazon's Cloud and a Java validation tool. Experimental results are recorded and presented.

Keywords: Cloud Validation, Context, Test Case Reduction, Testing.

1   Introduction and Background

There has been much confusion regarding the term *cloud computing*, mostly because of the novelty of this branch of computer science. In this paper, we choose the following definition for cloud by Foster [1]: "a system that coordinates resources that are not subject to centralized control using standard, open, general-purpose protocols and interfaces to deliver nontrivial qualities of service" [1]. This paper focuses on the quality of software systems running on the cloud and their validation. In the cloud, testing is often referred to as Testing as a Service (TaaS).

P. Brézillon, P. Blackburn, and R. Dapoigny (Eds.): CONTEXT 2013, LNAI 8175, pp. 288–301, 2013.

TaaS provides a pay-per-use type of service that eliminates upfront investments in many cases. Validation tools and services on the cloud are no exception. Although cloud computing provides new opportunities, it also introduces new problems and challenges such as the lack of standards for cloud environments. Currently, there is no standard to validate or incorporate cloud computing resources with a company's data sources, as its vendors may have different models underlying their clouds, and its customers may face interoperability issues if they decide to switch vendors. Other challenges include security, performance, the need for a resilient infrastructure, managing big data, connectivity, and geographical distribution of sites. To tackle such problems, significant cloud testing is required. This paper introduces a testing method that addresses the constant context changes in a cloud environment. More specifically, it tests systems that include multiple users in different locations. We focus on the challenge of cloud testing across different multiple geographical regions and providing TaaS within that context. Besides the fact that TaaS is increasingly gaining attention, it nonetheless begs the question of why perform testing on the cloud? The main reason is that it offers the opportunity to access test tools and test environments from anywhere around the world without the need to own these assets. Testing on the cloud however, is similar in many ways to conventional testing. The effectiveness of any validation method depends on how well the process can identify defects, errors and faults before releasing the system to the customer. This depends on the quality and quantity of the generated test cases used in validation. The steps of validating a system using test cases start with *test case generation* & *test case reduction* - two key steps that we treat in this paper. Reduction happens when a subset of test cases is selected from the universal set to be executed on the system. After that, the test cases inputs are executed on the system and the results are evaluated. The last step is *system refinement*, where actions toward fixing the errors and presenting the solutions are defined and carried out [2 and 3]. Context validation (among other validation methods) is presented next.

1.1 Context Validation and Test Case Reduction

The cloud is dynamic and the context of software running on it is constantly changing; therefore, testing needs to consider the context in which it is running. This paper discusses the ongoing context changes and defines a validation method used to reduce test cases based on the results of previous iterations. Many methods have been proposed for test case reduction [4], [5], [6] and [7], and they vary between random, formal and informal. The idea of testing every input to the system is impossible to design (or implement) in most cases. It is not feasible to run all possible test cases on the system – the exhaustive set of test cases (EST) – especially when some of these test cases may not even be physically possible in the real world. Therefore, Knauf et al [2] and [3] presented a formal method to validate systems using structural knowledge. They used formal approaches to reduce the exhaustive set of test cases in their validation method [4]. They did this by creating a *functionally exhaustive set of test cases*

(FEST), and from there built a *quasi-exhaustive set of test cases* (QUEST). This last set of test cases is meant to have the equivalent effect of testing all possible system cases, but in a reduced number of test cases. In the *quasi-exhaustive set of test cases*, it is sufficient to assume that if a specially selected subset of the test cases (*T*) is valid, then the whole set (*S*) is valid too. After test case sets are defined, for each set, a sub-set of test cases (*T*) will be executed. A set of mathematical classifiers is used to categorize the data into sets where an object can belong to one or more sets. The authors used statistical and formal means to show this [4]. Abel et al [7] and Smith et. al [8] subsequently criticized the *quasi-exhaustive set of test cases* as still being impractical because of its large cardinality. The former [7] introduced another method to further reduce the number of test cases. Their method uses a criteria-driven reduction of test cases to generate a *reasonable set of test cases* (ReST). In ReST, all test cases need to be evaluated by the validation engineers. During the test case selection stage, a criterion is defined by answering the question: how well should the system being validated perform for it to be considered valid? Answering this question requires looking at different criteria: domain related, user related, and expert related. This method reduces the set of test cases to a number much less than the *quasi-exhaustive set of test cases*. Next section focuses on cloud's context-driven testing.

1.2   Context-Driven Testing for the Cloud

Context driven-testing (CDT) is a rapidly growing testing paradigm. It is part of the Agile development school of software development. It is based on the idea that the value of a practice depends on its context, and that projects unfold over time in unpredictable ways that need to be handled in real time. In this paper, we introduce a method that takes use of CDT's philosophy. Ultimately, CDT is about not accepting a specific pre-defined set of best practices but that the best practice is what the recent context entails. Figure 1 below illustrates how context influences testing. In the Figure, testing is defined as a mission that motivates the choices. The seven basic principles of CDT are introduced in reference [9].

Because the cloud is highly flexible and interactive, we believe that context testing and cloud testing could work together very well. We aim to establish that association. No testing method has been found that is solely based on context to validate software deployed on the cloud.

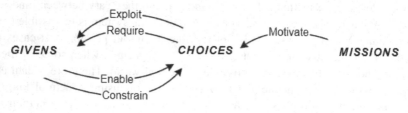

Fig. 1. Context Testing Philosophy [9]

Most methods are based on the conventional performance testing (such as SOASTA CloudTest, CloudTestGo), Integration testing (such as PushToTest and uTest) automated testing (such as IBM cloud, Sauce Labs, Zephyr and STaaS) and load testing (such as GCLOAD, Clap, LoadStorm and BlazeMeter) [10, 11 & 12]. Although there have been efforts in introducing different cloud deployments, there is still a crucial need for a testing method that could be applied to the cloud. Moreover, no method or testing tool was found that provides a dynamic, context-based testing for a cloud framework. We hope to fill that gap with the work described in this paper.

This paper is organized as follows: the cloud infrastructure that we use in this paper is discussed next; then the variables and the procedure of the method are presented. The subsequent section presents the experimental evaluation, and finally, we summarize the paper and draw conclusions.

2   Context-Assisted Test Case Reduction (CATCR)

Our work seeks to reduce the number of test cases to be executed. It seeks to find the *just right* number of test cases to execute that provide ideal coverage with no redundancy. Other test case reduction methods [11, [12], [13] and [14] reduce the set of test cases a priori, and then begin the testing process. Inspired by the CBTCR method in [13], our approach is based on the context of the validation at any point in time. It is a dynamic reduction process that requires several passes for executing a number of subsets of test cases (rather than *one* big set of test cases). In problem solving, the *context* would inherently contain much knowledge about the context of the situation in which the problem is to be solved or that serves as the environment of the problem [4 & 14]. In validation, there is also a context based upon what parts of the code has failed the most in the previous testing cycle. In other words, the test cases executed at each iteration depend on the *current* context. Context is defined by the state of the validation process. Before we introduce the process, it is important to clearly state the cloud model that we assume for this method.

2.1   Cloud Deployment

The deployment architecture of the cloud can have a large impact on its validation process. In this work, we aim to model the cloud architecture in order to represent the variations among different setups. For that, we introduce the basic modeling constructs that are used in our framework.

1) A set VM of Virtual Machines and their associated parameters, VMP (i.e. availability, state, available memory...etc).
2) A set of S of Sites and their associated parameters SP (i.e. number of VMs in the site, geographical location...etc)
3) A set C of clients (such as users, PDAs, computers, and cell phones connecting to the cloud) and their parameters CP (i.e. location, criticality...etc)

4) A set of *SC* software components (such as monitoring, collaboration, and communication applications) and their parameters *SCP* (memory requested, client originating from...etc) - in the experiment presented in this paper, a Knowledge-Based System is used as *SC*.

Figure 2 below represents the cloud layers within the model that we assume for our method and the one we used for our experimentation. It includes 3 main layers, software applications layer, virtual machines layer and the sites layer (shown below).

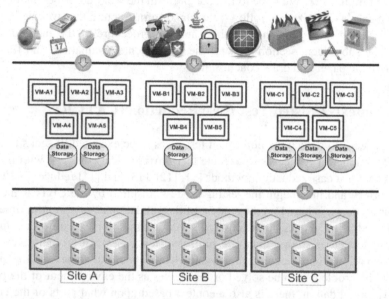

Fig. 2. Cloud Infrastructure

Other related cloud variables include: 1) State of the *VM*: *idle, busy* or empty queue (*EQ*): *SVM* and 2) Number of *idle* or *EQ* machines in a site *S*: *NIS*. The presented variables are used in our method in this paper. Test case reduction variables are presented next.

2.2   Variables Used in Context-Assisted Test case Reduction

Reducing the test cases in CATCR is partly based on a number of variables. At any iteration of development, the values of variables need to be modified while the system undergoes refinement (refer to [13] for more information). Context-assisted test case reduction is controlled by certain variables. The most important ones are *local VM importance* and *N*. More about the process and the variables is discussed in the following four sections/subsections.

Local VM Importance. *Local VM Importance (LVMI)* represents the importance of a test case within its own geographical site (*S*). Each test case is assigned a local importance variable that falls between one and five. *Local importance = Average of (dependency + domain importance + criticality + occurrence).* Local importance is a factor of dependency (Value assigned from 1-5), domain importance (Value assigned from 1-5), criticality (Value assigned from 1-5) and occurrence (Value assigned from 1-5). The values of these four variables are set by the cloud engineer for each test case.

1) **Dependency:** In a cloud design, different virtual machines (*VM*) and software components (*SC*) are dependent upon each other, thus, test cases extracted inherit this relation. Test cases are dependent on each other. Therefore, dependency is defined for each test case by the cloud engineer as part of the test case importance.

2) **Domain importance:** Any test case represents a certain function in the system; some test cases have high importance because of their high representation of certain important functionality within the domain. Other test cases with less importance represent functions that are not strongly related to the domain.

3) **Criticality:** In any organization, some tasks are more important than are others. Any test case is defined to partially or fully evaluate certain functionality. Tasks (and thus, test cases) with more criticality to the overall process have higher importance.

4) **Occurrence:** In a process, some procedures occur more frequently than are others. This variable reflects the level of a procedure occurrence in the system and how often is a certain software component (*SC*) used by a client (*C*).

Number of Test Cases Selected for Each Iteration (N). The value for N could be chosen by the cloud engineer. Nevertheless, CATCR recommends N through the CATCR tool (presented in the next section) for each iteration. In most cases, the number of required test cases (N) increases with the size of the system. The value of N is based on three factors:

1) *The size of a software component (objects to test) within idle machines (NIS)*: In most situations, the number of test cases is greater than the number of objects (building blocks) in any project because any object needs one or more test case to validate it.

2) *The number of test cases generated*: this reflects the amount of testing required for the system.

3) *Project Size (PS)*: The size of the project could be measured in many ways. Common methods for this include counting the number of lines of code in the system or the number of cases in a use case diagram. In this method, we recommend using the average number of *VMs* per site, multiplied by the number of sites (Avg. #*VM* ▢ #*S*).

The formula for N is: *Number of test cases-Number of objects to be tested/PS*.

To utilize LVMI and N within all the sites, and for all VMs, we need to introduce variables at the cloud level, Cloud Site Weight and Global Importance.

Cloud Site Weight (CSW). In CATCR, every model is assigned a weight after each iteration of development. Initially, all the sites have the same weight (CSW is set to 5), and same significance. However, when the development starts, cloud site weights will constantly change based on the outcomes of the test cases. The cloud site weight values fall between one and ten. CSW could be set to any value before the first iteration, 5 is the midpoint from 0 to 10 and therefore it was selected as the initial value.

After the first validation iteration the cloud engineer has no control over the CSW, it is controlled by the results of previous validation results. Cloud site weight reflects the assurance level of the model. When the assurance of all models reaches 10 (100%) and implementation is done, validation stops. Another very important variable is *Global Importance (GI)*. GI is used to define the importance of any test case within the global set of test cases, across all cloud sites. *Global Importance = Local VM Importance * CSW*. Putting all these variables into perspective, we introduce the CATCR steps in the next section.

2.3   The Process

The steps of Context-assisted test case reduction that compose the validation of a system are discussed in this section. This algorithm is built into the CATCR tool (presented in the next section). The iterative process is applied on the software level (SaaS) of a cloud and not on the infrastructure or platform; different applications could be tested using this method. Context testing is applied on the cloud as a service for multiple clients (*C*) running the validation process. For every CATCR step in process, it is indicated as to whether the step is manual or automated within the Java tool. The 12 steps of CATCR for the cloud are:

---

1.   Assign *local VM importance* for each test case. (Semi automated)
2.   Set the size of a subset: *N* based on the criteria discussed above. (Automated)
3.   Set all site *weights/assurance* to 5 as indicated above   (Automated)
4.   Calculate *global importance* = local importance * model weight. Order test cases according to global importance (Automated)
5.   Start iterative implementation, deployment of software on the cloud (Manual)
6.   At the end of the first deployment iteration, select N number of test cases. From the ordered list select test cases 1 to N (Automated)
7.   Execute the test cases on the system, and record the results (Manual)
8.   Based on results for each model test cases, re-assign assurance for each site. Ex: if 30% of the test cases in a certain site are incorrect, that site's assurance will be 7 using the following formula: *100 - (% of successful test case)/10* (Automated)
9.   Recalculate global importance for all test cases and reorder (Automated) In CATCR, if a test case failed, the site from which this test case is from will have a very high importance site in the next iteration.
10. Refine the system. This step includes refining the deployment of software within the cloud. This might lead to adding or deleting new test cases. This step is performed by the cloud engineer in a manual fashion. (Manual)
11. *Flag* test cases with a positive outcome (not to be picked again unless a change to their status was made). *Flag* test cases with unexpected outcomes (this is used to make sure that the test case is reselected before end of validation). *Flag* test cases that are affected by the refinements (to be selected again). Select different test cases and go to the next iteration (Automated)
12. Stop when assurance of all sites is equal to 10 (Automated)

The next section introduces the evaluation of CATCR. The experimentation is performed on the Amazon cloud and a Java tool that we developed in-house.

3   Experimental Evaluation

Since we used the Amazon cloud for the experiments in this paper, we need to discuss the Amazon Cloud before introducing the experiment. Amazon has established itself as an industry leader when it comes to cloud computing. A useful definition that was found on Amazon's Cloud website: "Amazon Cloud provides monitoring for cloud resources and the applications customers run on the cloud. Developers and system administrators can use it to collect and track metrics, gain insight, and react immediately to keep their applications and businesses running smoothly. Amazon *CloudWatch* monitors AWS resources such as Amazon EC2." [15]. Figure 3 below shows that Amazon's Cloud is a leader in terms of execution and the completeness of vision.

Fig. 3. Amazon Cloud Establishing Itself as an Industry Leader [16]

3.1   The Context-Assisted Test Case Reduction Tool

A tool was built to assist in the testing process. This tool also provides support for the context-assisted test case reduction. Test cases are entered into the tool's spread sheet with the following fields: *Test case ID* (an incremental integer that starts from zero and is incremented by one for every test case), *Local VM Importance* (an integer number from 1-5), *Number of Runs* (is set to zero, every time the test case is executed this number is incremented by one), *Site's Weight* (first is set to 5 for all sites then it is modified every iteration), *Global Importance* (the multiplication outcome of local importance and site weight), *Result* (all test cases are set to two because none of the test cases is executed. When a test case is executed with success, the GI value will be set to 1, if it failed, value will change to 0), *Input Variables, Execution Steps, Expected Solution, System Result* (outcome displayed by the system) and an *Informal Description*. Based on the algorithm presented, when the iterative development starts, the tool will recommend certain test cases for every iteration. The main five panels in the Java-based tool are shown below:

Panel 1 displays the selected test cases in a list where the cloud engineer can indicate the outcome of the test case, whether it is success or failure. This panel also displays the iteration number and the value of N. This is the main panel for the cloud engineer, where the test cases could be monitored and the results of the test cases after every iteration could be modified.

Panel 2 has two functionalities; it displays the algorithm's steps and explains how the tool works. Additionally, it is the panel to calculate the recommended N value. The cloud engineer enters the number of test cases, the number of rules in the project and the project size to get N.

Panel 3 displays all the test cases, each with its importance, execution results and the number of test cases in the database. In this panel, all the test cases changing statuses can be observed in real time, after every test case execution.

Panel 4 shows the validation percentage/assurance for the system. This is calculated by averaging of all the sites' assurances. A progress bar displays this percentage.

Panel 5 displays the console showing all the steps and all the actions performed. The console serves as a good documentation tool; it keeps all the test cases as well as all the models and their changing status. Everything is saved and displayed here, then saved to a file on the hard disk.

3.2   Experimental Setup

In this experiment, a knowledge-based system is deployed on the cloud. The KBS is a housing application used by the government of the Netherlands to assign apartments to applicants. The housing application has 3 users, the applicant, the Dutch government and a moderator. The applicant submits a request for an apartment, the moderator assigns him/her one based on the his/her demographics, and the government approves the assignment. This housing KBS aims to replace the manual process of the moderator, and assign apartments based on the moderator's knowledge. The housing KBS is a midsize project described in more detail under reference [13]. For any software system, the users, administrators and vendors have different preferences in regards to which QoS factor is more important. In this paper, we try to leverage these factors, and create a fair tradeoff for different scenarios. While it is often very challenging to provide complete high quality for all parameters (simply because they usually contradict each other), in the context of the cloud, users and vendors focus on two main aspects, the speed of the cloud (latency), and the cost. We configure the model based on scenarios that involve the following QoS factors:

1) **Time**: elapsed between deploying a cloud and reaching a conclusion regarding its validity (testing time).

2) **Cost**: it is the money spent per user, customer or institution.

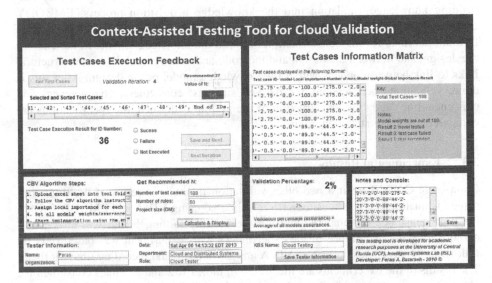

Fig. 4. Context-Assisted Test Case Reduction tool [13]

In this experiment, and because it is rather difficult to calculate the cost of a cloud deployment without a real cloud system with **actual** users, we present this experiment that focuses on the QoS parameter of *Time*. We present a comparison of the time spent to validate a cloud system using CATCR and two other methods that use other testing philosophies. The three methods were deployed on the cloud using Amazon's cloud. The Context-Assisted Test Case Reduction tool was used to select test cases for every validation iteration for CATCR. Test cases are manually executed on the system to detect theses errors. Each test case includes an "expected result" and a "system result". After executing any test case, if the system's result is different from the expected result, this indicates to an existence of an error in the system.

This experiment is only qualitative. We chose two methods (VIVA and Embody) [16 and 17] to compare against CATCR; they are used to validate a knowledge-based system (KBS) on the cloud and their consumption of resources (time) is recorded and compared to CATCR's validation results. After inspecting multiple validation methods and considering many candidates, we found that many of the methods were impossible to use because of different reasons. For example, some of the methods strictly required their development tools to be used and these tools were not readily available. Other methods provided no useful guidance on how to implement the validation method on a knowledge-based system. Yet other methods were only useable within a specific domain, such as validation methods for military or medical applications. Therefore, all these methods were ruled out from consideration. Two methods, however, were found suitable and had no constraints for using them in this validation experiment. These two methods claimed and reported positive outcomes for validation of KBS. They use two different validation approaches that could be applied on the cloud. These two methods are VIVA [16] and EMBODY [17]. VIVA is a life-cycle-independent validation method while EMBODY validates the system by embedding knowledge validation into the knowledge acquisition process. EMBODY uses diagram-based validation and VIVA is based on traceability. VIVA uses transformational links for the transformation between the knowledge model to the code or the design, and between the design and the code and vice versa. VIVA uses structural links to link between objects within the knowledge model or the design. After this is done, validation specifications are derived such as: correctness, completeness and existence. For validation, the structure of the system is defined, the specifications are compared and mismatches are revised.

3.3   Experimental Results

Comparing CATCR against two other validation methods in terms of the time consumed is qualitative. The housing KBS is validated using VIVA and EMBODY. Only the time consumed is compared and not the validity (although that was also considered during the occurrence of the experiment). This experiment was based only on following the processes defined in VIVA and EMBODY and recording time for them. The results of the experiments are illustrated in tables 1, 2 and 3. Times consumed for validation in the three methods are introduced by summing their steps. First, the steps for CATCR are presented in Table 1, VIVA is in Table 2 and EMBODY is in Table 3. Results are in Figure 5.

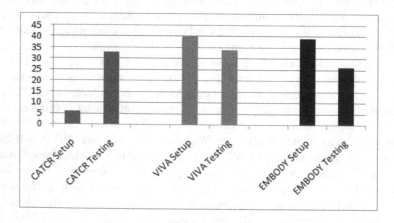

Fig. 5. Experimental Results for CATCR

Table 1. Time consumed using Cloud Context Testing (CATCR)

Stage name/ description	Time consumed
Cloud model deployment	6 hours
Test Cases Extraction/definition	4 hours
Assign local importance for each test case	4 hours
Fill test cases into the sheet of the CATCR tool	11 hours
Set all models' weights/assurance to 5	0 hours (Autonomous process)
Calculate global importance and re-order	0 hours (Autonomous process)
Defining the cloud variables, starting the VMs across different locations, and cloning required VMs.	32 hours (Total)- On Amazon Cloud
Select N number of test cases	0 hours (Autonomous process)
Execute test cases on the system	6 hours (Total for all iterations)
Recalculate global importance	0 hours (Autonomous process)
Flag test cases based on results	0 hours (Autonomous process)
Refine system and go to next iteration	8 hours (Total for all iterations)
Total # hours	**71 hours**

Table 2. Time consumed using EMBODY

Stage name/ description	Time consumed
Knowledge acquisition and organization	10 hours (Manual process)
Defining the cloud variables, Starting the VMs among different locations, and cloning the appropriate machines.	32 hours (Total)- On Amazon Cloud
Using EMBODY flow charts	17 hours (Manual process)
Representing the cloud in EMBODY's tabular format	12 hours (Manual process)
Validating the system	18 hours (Manual process)
Refine system	8 hours (Manual process)
Total # hours	**97 hours**

Table 3. Time consumed using VIVA

Stage name/ description	Time consumed
Knowledge acquisition and organization	17 hours (Manual process)
Defining the cloud variables, Starting the VMs among different locations, and cloning the appropriate machines.	32 hours (Total)- On Amazon Cloud
Using VIVA defined methods	15 hours (Manual process)
Performing the VIVA link types for the cloud system	8 hours (Manual process)
Derivation of validation specification	10 hours (Manual process)
Validating the system	16 hours (Manual process)
Refine system	8 hours (Manual process)
Total # hours	**106 hours**

Figure 5 above illustrates the results (compares setup vs. testing time spent for all three methods). Total for validating the housing KBS on the cloud using VIVA = **106 hours**. Total for validating the housing KBS on the cloud using EMBODY = **97 hours**. Total for validating the same KBS on the cloud using CATCR = **71 hours**. Although CATCR has the least total validation time, what we think is very important to note here, is that CATCR has an obvious difference in terms of setup. The setup time is very low when compared to the other two methods. Based on the projected results, CATCR consumes less time than the two other compared methods. Because time is an essential variable of quality in the cloud, and because customers, users, and vendors pay close attention to the cost of time, we believe that CATCR is a strong candidate for cloud validation.

4   Summary and Conclusions

This paper introduced a context-based approach towards reducing the number of test cases for validation of a cloud system. The method is called CATCR, and it is based on a specific cloud infrastructure presented in this paper. The method was evaluated, and had positive results in terms of resource consumption (*time*) when compared to other validation methods. CATCR has three main advantages. 1) Flexibility: the initial values of the weights and the models could be modified by the cloud engineer. This gives the engineer full control. 2) Usage-oriented: this approach is based on the user needs and a real time testing feedback based on context. It is not a static function, rather a resilient one. 3) Effort and time reduction: reducing the number of test cases reduces effort and time. We plan to evaluate this method further in the future, compare it with more validation methods (such as the ones in [19]), execute it with actual users, and test it with other multiple cloud scenarios and infrastructures.

Acknowledgments. A special thank you goes out to Dr. Sam Malek from the Volgenau School of Engineering at George Mason University (Fairfax, VA) for the support he provided in the field of Cloud Computing.

References

1. Foster, I.: What is the grid? A three point checklist. The Grid-Today (July 2002)
2. Knauf, R., Gonzalez, A.J., Abel, T.: A Framework for Validation of Rule-Based Systems. IEEE Transactions on Systems, Man and Cybernetics 32(3), 181–196 (2002)
3. Knauf, R., Tsuruta, S., Gonzalez, A.J.: Toward Reducing Human Involvement in Validation of Knowledge-Based Systems. Proceedings of the IEEE Transaction on Systems, Man and Cybernetics 37, 120–131 (2007)
4. Gonzalez, A.J., Gupta, U., Chianese, R.: Performance Evaluation of a Large Diagnostic Expert System Using a Heuristic Test Case Generator. Proceedings of the Engineering Applications for Artificial Intelligence 9, 275–284
5. Shreiber, G., Akkermans, H., Anjewierden, A., De Hoog, R., Shadbolt, N., Van De Velde, W., Wielinga, B.: Knowledge Engineering and Management-The CommonKADS Methodology. The MIT Press (2000)

6. Herrmann, J., Jantke, K., Knauf, R.: Using Structural Knowledge for System Validation. In: Proceedings of the 10th FLAIRS Conference, pp. 82–86 (1997)
7. Abel, T., Gonzalez, A.J.: Utilizing Criteria to Reduce a Set of Test Cases for Expert System Validation. In: Proceedings of the 10th FLAIRS Conference, pp. 402–406 (1997)
8. Smith, S., Kandel, A.: Validation of Expert Systems. In: Proceedings of the Third Florida Artificial Intelligence Research Symposium, FLAIRS (1990)
9. Kaner, C.: The Context-Driven Approach to Software Testing. Notes from the Florida Institute of Technology (2002)
10. Bach, J.: Heuristic Test Planning: Context Model. Satisfice, Inc. (2013)
11. Rao, R.: 10 Cloud Based Testing Tools, A report published under: `http://www.toolsjournal.com/testing-lists/item/404-10-cloud-based-testing-tools`
12. Kalliosaari, L., Taipale, O., Smolander, K.: Testing in the Cloud: Exploring the Practice. Paper Published at the IEEE Software Magazine (September 2012)
13. Batarseh, F.A.: Incremental Lifecycle Validation of Knowledge-Based Systems through CommonKADS. A Doctoral Dissertation published at the University of Central Florida (May 2011)
14. Gonzalez, A.J., Stensrud, B., Barrett, G.: Formalizing context-based reasoning: A modeling paradigm for representing tactical human behavior. Proceedings of the International Journal of Intelligent Systems (2008)
15. Amazon Cloud: http://www.amazon.com/cloud
16. Gartner Magic Quadrant for Public Cloud Infrastructure as a service, A report by Gartner Research (2012)
17. Wells, S.: The VIVA Method: A Life Cycle Independent Approach to KBS Validation. In: Proceedings of the IEEE AAAI Conference, pp. 102–106 (1993)
18. Lockwood, S., Chen, Z.: Knowledge Validation of Engineering Expert Systems. Proceedings of the Journal of Advances in Software Engineering (1995)
19. Gill, A.Q., Bunker, D.: Towards the development of a Cloud-Based Communication Technologies Assessment Tool: An Analysis of Practitioners' Perspectives. VINE - Emerald Group 43(1), 57–77 (2013)

QoCIM: A Meta-model for Quality of Context

Pierrick Marie[1], Thierry Desprats[1], Sophie Chabridon[2], and Michelle Sibilla[1]

[1] IRIT UMR 5505 Université Paul Sabatier, 31062 Toulouse, France
<prenom>.<nom>@irit.fr
[2] Institut Mines-Télécom/Télécom SudParis, CNRS UMR 5157, 91011 Évry, France
Sophie.Chabridon@telecom-sudparis.eu

Abstract. In the last decade, several works proposed their own list of quality of context (QoC) criteria. This article relates a comparative study of these successive propositions. The result is that no consensus has been reached about the semantic and the comprehensiveness of QoC criteria. Facing this situation, the QoCIM meta-model offers a generic, computable and expressive solution to handle and to exploit any QoC criterion within distributed context managers and context-aware applications. For validation purposes, QoCIM is successfully applied to the modelling of a set of simple and composite QoC criteria.

Keywords: Quality of context, Quality criterion, Context management, Meta-modelling, Information model.

1 Introduction

The expansion of the Internet of Things (the extension of the Internet to objects of the real world), cloud computing, big data and mobile technologies foster the development of new ubiquitous, context- and situation-aware applications. These situations are computed from ambient data, profiles of users and information collected from heterogeneous and spatially distributed sources. Context-aware applications become more and more usual. These applications require a fine and efficient management of the quality of the context information (QoC) they rely on. QoC is related to any information that describes the quality of context data as stated by the seminal definition of the QoC proposed by [4]. QoC specializes the general notion of Quality of Information (QoI) for context information.

A relevant behaviour of these applications strongly depends on the QoC provided. However, according to the business objectives of these applications, some QoC criteria may appear more important than others. Sometimes the freshness criterion is sufficient, sometimes it is the precision criterion and other times both are necessary. A solution to handle this need is to use context managers. They support context information throughout their life cycle. The life cycle of a piece of context information begins at its creation by a sensor and ends at its consumption by a context-aware application. Between these two events, context information are aggregated, filtered, deduced or transformed many

P. Brézillon, P. Blackburn, and R. Dapoigny (Eds.): CONTEXT 2013, LNAI 8175, pp. 302–315, 2013.

times [3]. But these information are intrinsically incomplete and inaccurate [8]. A bad quality of context information could lead to wrong decisions and irrelevant reactions. That is why context managers must take into account QoC at each step of the context information life cycle. This challenge logically remains in the case of the next generation of multi-scale distributed context managers.

Several solutions have already been proposed. In 2007, the AWARENESS project [15] proposed a middleware to manage context information and offered a way to manipulate the QoC. In 2009, the COSMOS project [1] proposed mechanisms for the efficient management of QoC. Finally, one of the objectives of the INCOME project [2], started in 2012, is to provide context management solutions able to handle QoC as well as to preserve privacy.

Our objective is to provide future context managers with a *generic, computable* and *expressive* way to manipulate and exploit QoC simply and efficiently. *Generic,* because our solution has to model complex and heterogeneous QoC criteria. *Computable,* because the estimation of a quality level of a context information is based on treatments and operations on QoC criteria. Lastly, *expressive,* because context-aware applications must be able to express their QoC requirements to different context managers.

This paper is organized as follows. Section 2 compares the lists of QoC criteria that have been proposed over the last decade. After finding no standard list of criteria to measure QoC, we analyse in Section 3 different models able to bring a *generic, computable* and *expressive* solution to manipulate and exploit QoC. This led us to propose the QoCIM meta-model that we introduce in Section 4. Finally, Section 5 shows an instantiation of our meta-model, at design time, for a geolocation application and Section 6 concludes this paper.

2   Comparative Study on Proposed QoC Criteria Lists

We study in this section the existing works about QoC measurement. QoC measurement is based on a list of QoC criteria. Many authors have already established their own list of QoC criteria to measure QoC. We first enumerate the main proposals published over the last decade, and finally we compare the proposed criteria in terms of their semantic. The study highlights the existing variations in terms of denomination and meaning of QoC criteria. Different authors define a same meaning but associate it with a different denomination. On the contrary, a same denomination defined by different authors may correspond to different meanings.

2.1   Overview of QoC Criteria Lists

BUCHHOLZ 2003 [4] proposed in 2003 the first list of QoC criteria. This list is composed of five criteria : *precision, probability of correctness, trust-worthiness, resolution* and *up-to-dateness.* All of them are defined by a textual description. No computation method is formulated for their estimation, but BUCHHOLZ provides examples to illustrate each of them.

KIM 2006 [10] proposed in 2006 a new list of QoC criteria to measure the QoC. This list was built by confronting QoC criteria listed in [4] to generic criteria to measure quality. [10] provided five criteria associated to a definition from the point of view of the end users of the context information. The end user is the last entity which consumes context information. The proposed criteria are *accuracy, completeness, representation consistency, access security* and *up-to-dateness*. Then, [10] defined a mathematical formula to estimate the value of their first two criteria : *accuracy* and *completeness*.

SHEIKH 2007 [15] for the AWARENESS project, formulated in 2007 its own list of QoC criteria. These criteria are *precision, freshness, temporal resolution, spatial resolution*, and *probability of correctness*. Although these criteria are fully described verbatim, no method is provided to estimate their value. Like [4], [15] gave examples to illustrate the definitions of their criteria. The descriptions of the criteria adopt successively the points of view of the consumer and of the producer of the context information. Producers are entities that create and provide context information as sensors, while consumers are context-aware applications.

FILHO 2010 [7] studied the lists of QoC criteria that had been previously proposed by [4], [10] and [15] and imagined a new list of QoC criteria. FILHO redefined *up-to-dateness, sensitiveness, access security, completeness, precision* and *resolution* criteria. For each criterion, FILHO offered an example to illustrate the notion which is measured. FILHO also provided a mathematical formula or a sample of Java program that he used to estimate these criteria.

NEISSE 2012 [12] suggested in 2012 to adapt the ISO standard used in metrology to define QoC criteria. He established that the concepts of *accuracy* and *precision* used as QoC criteria are just an approximative definition of the precision criterion used in metrology. In the same way, NEISSE estimated that the concepts of *spatial resolution* and *temporal resolution* defined by [15] are just a redefinition of the ISO standard of precision applied to spatial and temporal information. NEISSE suggested to measure the QoC with only two criteria: the *age* and the *precision* of the context information. The *age* is the elapsed time since the production of the information. The *precision* criterion applies the ISO standard of precision on other kind of information depending the needs of the application. So, this *precision* criterion could be applied to the location of the source of the information, for example.

MANZOOR 2012 [11] offered the most complete list of QoC criteria in 2012. They defined seven high level QoC criteria. All of them depend, for their computation, on other low level QoC criteria. For each of these high level QoC criteria, a mathematical formula is associated. The proposed criteria are *reliability, timeliness, completeness, significance, usability, access right, representation consistency*. The definition of some criteria adopts the point of view of the producer of the context information like the precision criterion provided by sensors. Whereas the definition of other criteria adopts the point of view of the consumer of the context information like context-aware applications which define the maximum allowed freshness of the received information.

2.2   Discussion

The study of the semantics of the QoC criteria listed above shows divergences. A same denomination of criterion appears in several lists with a different meaning. Conversely, a same meaning appears in many lists with different denominations. There are also meanings associated with denominations which appear only once into all the lists. Table 1 groups together the studied criteria by author and highlights the differences that exist between all of these criteria.

The different lists of QoC criteria are represented vertically. The name and the year of the first author of each list are mentioned on the first line of the table. The lists are sorted by publication date from left to right. Each criterion has a number, which is indicated in the first column of the table. The second column summarizes the meaning of each criterion. The cells of the table which contain a name, are criteria proposed by the authors registered on the top of the column of the cells. An empty cell indicates that the author did not propose the criterion referenced by the line of this cell. A cell with a check-mark represents a criterion implicitly used by the corresponding author but not clearly defined in its list of QoC criteria. Grey cells represent criteria defined by only one author. The lightgrey color indicates that there is one common meaning used by all authors. The criteria written in italic are names used only once. The criteria written in bold are names used by at least two different authors with different meanings. Some name of criterion are followed by numbers. For example, on line 15, the reliability criterion defined by MANZOOR [11] is followed by the numbers 1, 2, 3 and 4. These numbers reference the numbers in the first column and indicate that this criterion is composed of other criteria. For example, MANZOOR's reliability criterion [11] is computed using the first four criteria listed in this table.

Lastly, QoC criteria are sorted in the table by following a specific order. Criteria extracted directly from raw sensor data and which do not need computation or statistical analysis are placed on the top of the table. Whereas criteria at the bottom of the table require historical analysis or data from many sensors to be estimated. The more a criterion requires computations and lots of data, the lower it is placed in the table. MANZOOR [11] classifies criteria into two categories, objective and subjective criteria; an objective criterion does not depend on the final application whereas a subjective criterion depends on the purpose of the final application. Table 1 rather orders criteria as a function of the effort that is required to estimate them.

Table 1 highlights that there is no consensus about which QoC criteria have to be used to measure the QoC of context information. This supports the idea of [3] indicating that a consensus about the definition of a common list of QoC criteria is still an open problem. Also the table provides a way to compare different lists of QoC criteria. This makes it possible to compare new specific lists between them. Indeed, with the development of context-aware applications, if a new high level criteria appear, Table 1 offers a method to classify lists of QoC criteria relatively to one another.

Table 1. Comparison of different lists of QoC criteria

		BUCHHOLZ 2003 [4]	KIM 2006 [10]	SHEIKH 2007 [15]	FILHO 2010 [7]	MANZOOR 2012 [11]	NEISSE 2012 [12]
1	Probability context is free of errors	Correctness	Accuracy		**Precision**	Accuracy	**Precision**
2	Max. distance to get context					*Sensor range*	
3	Location of the real world entity					*Entity location*	
4	Location of the sensor					*Sensor location*	
5	Time between production of contexts			*Temporal resolution*	✓	*Time period*	
6	Date of collection of context	✓	✓	✓	✓	*Measurement time*	*Timestamps*
7	Granularity location of context			*Spatial resolution*	**Resolution**		
8	Rate the confidence of the provider	*Trust worthiness*					
9	Critical value of context					*Significance*	
10	Granularity (detail level) of context	**Precision**		**Precision**	*Sensitiveness*	*Usability*	
11	Context consumer have access to context		✓			*Access right*	
12	Context transfers restricted, secured		Access security (11)		Access security		
13	Format respects consumer needs		Consistency			Consistency	
14	All aspects of entity are available	**Resolution**	Completeness		Completeness	Completeness	
15	Validity of context based on freshness	**Up to dateness (6)**	**Up to dateness (6)**	*Freshness (6)*	**Up to dateness (5, 6)**	*Timeliness (5, 6)*	
16	Believe in the correctness of context			**Correctness**		*Reliability (1, 2, 3, 4)*	

Meaning   Meaning used by all authors   *Name* Name only defined by one author

Name   Criterion (name + meaning) only defined by one author

Name   Name defined by different authors for different meanings

Name   Name defined by different authors for the same meaning

Name (X)   The definition of this criterion depends on the X criterion

✓   Criterion not defined by author but another criterion depends on it

3   Study of Candidate Modelling Frameworks

Our objective is to provide a *generic, computable* and *expressive* modelling solution. Since no consensus can be reached about the list of QoC criteria that has to be used, the genericity of our solution cannot be based on a unique and exhaustive QoC criteria list. An alternative has to be found for enabling at least the cohabitation and ideally the integration of different lists of QoC criteria whose denominations, meanings and computation methods may differ. A solution to fulfil the genericity property is to provide either a common information model or a meta-model dedicated to quality of context. As far as we know, no such solution exists. Nevertheless, we decided to study several existing models, even if they address only partly our objective, in order to identify and possibly reuse some interesting concepts or modelling patterns they propose. Next sections discuss models of: the Open Geospatial Consortium, the IoT-A project, the COSMOS project, the DMTF and the Open Management Group.

3.1   Frameworks Study Overview

The Open Geospatial Consortium (OGC) model [14] represents observations made by sensors. It models the creation of context information when sensors observe and measure the real world. The model considers the process which is used to produce the result of an observation. It also associates a string with the result. This string contains the quality level of the result. However, the previous section shows that a quality level of a context information is based on a list of QoC criteria. A criterion is at least composed of a denomination, a meaning and a value. And a string is not enough to represent that. So, this model is not generic and expressive enough for our needs.

The IoT-A meta-model [9] provides methods and generic solutions to design applications based on the Internet of Things. The proposed meta-model defines the notion of attributes associated with meta-data. With this notion, meta-data could be considered as QoC criteria and fulfil our objective of a generic solution. However, the model does not include neither notion of context information or QoC criteria. It requires too much effort to extend and to exploit it correctly. The expressiveness and computability objectives are not fulfilled with this solution.

The COSMOS meta-model [5] expresses QoC management contracts. COSMOS is a context manager used for context-aware applications. It manages the QoC levels received by applications with a framework based on contracts. The meta-model proposed by COSMOS is used to establish very detailed quality contracts between a context-aware application and a context information provider. A contract defines the quality level that is required by an application. Such a level is defined for quality parameters, for a kind of context information. Through the definition of contracts, this meta-model fulfils our objective of providing an expressive solution. However, the computability property that we expect is not totally covered by this meta-model. The properties of a criterion are not clearly defined and prevent to build a generic and computable solution.

The DMTF CIM Metrics model [6] is one of the standards developed by the DMTF that is devoted to the management of metrics. It gives a way to express metrics that are used to qualify the state and the behaviour of managed system components (named a managed element) and how their respective values are obtained. In this sense, an analogy could be found with the qualification of context information. Context information are considered as managed elements. In this way, CIM Metrics are comparable to QoC criteria. The abstract class `ManagedElement` could represent context information which has to be qualified. The class `BaseMetricDefinition` that characterizes some metrics, could express a QoC criterion. The class `BaseMetricValue` that provides information on the valuation of an associated metric, could describe an estimation of a QoC criterion. Other subclass specialises metrics: the model proposes different computation patterns for metrics evaluation such as aggregation or discrete value selection. The genericity and computability aspects that we looking for could be fulfilled with the modelling technique used by CIM. It separates the definition of metric and the value of metric. The link between a QoC metric definition and its value is an association. It is a separation of concerns between, meanings and computation methods of QoC metric, and their values. This separation could be an early solution to obtain a generic and computable model of QoC criteria. However, this model does not cover the expressiveness aspect, there is no means for applications to express their requirements.

The Object Management Group (OMG) QoS meta-model [13] does not focus on the QoC domain but on the quality of service (QoS) domain. In this section, we highlight some common points between QoS and QoC management. Like for the CIM Metrics [6], the OMG approach really separates the definition of a criterion from its value. It organises the definitions of QoS criteria into categories to easily manipulate them. A lot of attributes are defined, among which the attribute `direction` compares different values of a same criterion from the point of view of the users of a service. For example, a service measures its response time; when this time increases, it means that the quality of this service decreases for the point of view of users. The attribute `unit` specifies the unit of a criterion, for instance using the units of the International System. The attribute `statisticalQualifier` specifies which statistical method is used to provide a value of a criterion. Another class is used to establish QoS contracts. QoS contracts are based on criteria represented by the class `QoSDimension`. The meta-model of the OMG offers at the same time the quality contracts just like COSMOS [5] and the separation of concerns between meanings and values used by the CIM [6] metrics. These two aspects cover our objective to provide a computable and expressive solution. However, the model does not supports the creation of new composite criteria depending on simple criteria.

3.2   Discussion

Among the studied models, none of them can easily provide without adaptation the three aspects of expressiveness, genericity and computability that we have identified as necessary. Table 2 summarizes the conclusions of our study of these

Table 2. Summary of the studied models

Wished property / Model	OGC	IoT-A	COSMOS	CIM	OMG
Expressiveness			✓		✓
Computability	✓			✓	✓
Genericity		✓		✓	

models. The closest models to our needs are the CIM Metrics model [6] and the QoS meta-model [13]. The next section introduces our proposed meta-model, QoCIM (QoC Information Model), which is inspired of these two models.

4   QoCIM : A New QoC Meta-model

QoCIM is our proposed meta-model able to design and to represent the QoC. It is not dependent on any QoC criterion. It offers a unified solution to model, at design time, heterogeneous QoC criteria. Then, models based on QoCIM could be used, at runtime, by both context managers and context-aware applications, for dynamic valuation of the QoC. This section describes the QoCIM meta-model.

4.1   Presentation of QoCIM

Figure 1 presents the QoCIM meta-model. QoCIM qualifies context information represented with the class **ContextInformation**. The quality of context

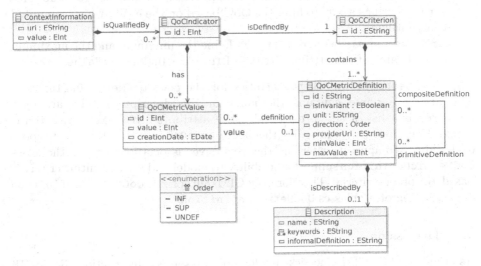

Fig. 1. QoCIM : QoC Information Model

information is designed with the `QoCIndicator`. An indicator is defined by one criterion, with the class `QoCCriterion`. Indicators and criteria are identified with the attribute `id`. At runtime, a valuation of the QoC is available with instances of the class `QoCMetricValue`. This class is identified with the attribute `id`. Its attribute, `value`, provides a valuation of the QoC. The date of creation of a value is contained into the attribute `creationDate`. The attributes of the class `QoCMetricDefinition` define the production of instances of `QoCMetricValues`:

- `isInvariant` indicates if the produced value is a constant, not editable, or dynamically computed.
- `unit` represents the unit of the produced value. It could be one of the units of the International System.
- `direction` compares different `QoCMetricValues` based on its attribute `value` from the point of view of the consumer of context information. The possible values of this attribute are INF, SUP and $UNDEF$:
  - INF means that a high `value` induces a better QoC level. For example, the freshness of a context information is usually computed with the following formula: $freshness = current\ date - date\ of\ the\ production\ of\ the\ context$ The result of this operation increases with the time whereas the quality of the information decreases.
  - SUP means that a high `value` induces a worth QoC level. For example, the precision of a context information computed with the following formula: $precision = 1 - \dfrac{distance\ between\ the\ sensor\ and\ the\ context}{maximum\ distance\ for\ the\ sensor\ to\ get\ context}$ More the sensor is close to the context, more the result of this operation and the quality of context increases.
  - $UNDEF$ is used when neither INF nor SUP can be expressed.
- `providerUri` identifies the resource that provides the `QoCMetricValue`. This attribute brings a way to filter the QoC based on the entity which computed it at runtime.
- `minValue` and `maxValue` respectively define the minimum and the maximum allowed value of the attribute `value` of the class `QoCMetricValue`.

The class `Description` brings semantics for the class `QoCMetricDefinition`. The attribute `name` contains the `name` of the description. The attribute `keywords` is a list of keywords. Finally, the attribute `informalDefinition` is a text that informally describes the `QoCMetricDefinition`. For the purpose of building composite criterion, the recursive association set on the class `QoCMetricDefinition` supports the ability to model and use a resulting criterion based on other criteria. Therefore, QoCIM authorizes `QoCMetricDefinition` depending on other classes `QoCMetricDefinition`.

4.2   Discussion

As the DMTF CIM metrics model [6] presented in Section 3, QoCIM separates the metric definition, `QoCMetricDefinition`, and the metric value,

QoCMetricValue. QoCIM reuses a few attributes of the OMG QoS meta-model presented in Section 3 like isInvariant, direction and unit. QoCIM completes the attributes with providerUri and the class Description which are not specified in the OMG QoS meta-model. The DMTF CIM metrics model and the OMG QoS meta-model build higher level complex definitions of metric based on other definitions of metric. With the same objective, QoCIM also gives to designers of context-aware applications the ability to specify, new composite QoC criterion thanks to the recursive link set on the class QoCMetricDefinition. The next section presents an experimentation of QoCIM which is used at design time for defining three QoC criteria for a geolocation application

5   Experimentations

QoCIM is based on the EMF[1] technology. We used the EMF representation of QoCIM and the Obeo Designer[2] software tool to build a "QoCIM models editor". Obeo Designer is a tool that allows to quickly and easily develop editors of any instances of EMF meta-model. Thanks to the QoCIM models editor, we designed three QoC criteria for a geolocation application. The models of these criteria provide a definition of the QoC used for this application. These models are UML[3] class diagrams. Then, they could be exploited at runtime, to evaluate the QoC. Modelling these three QoC criteria followed two steps. The first step consisted in modelling two QoC primitive criteria. The first primitive criterion is the temporal resolution, the 5th criterion in Table 1. The second primitive criterion is the precision, the 1st criterion in Table 1. The second step consisted to represent a composite criterion based on the two criteria designed during the first step. This composite criterion is based on the temporal resolution and precision criterion.

5.1   Modelling the Temporal Resolution Criterion

The class diagram of Figure 2 shows the definition of the temporal resolution criterion. The value of the attribute id of the class TempResDefinition is "5.1", that is means TempResDefinition is the first definition of the fifth criterion of the Table 1. In this diagram, the default value of the attributes minValue is 0 and maxValue is 60 of the class TempResDefinition. The definition of this criterion is completed with the value of the attributes unit and direction which are respectively set to "minute" and INF. This criterion represents the elapsed time between the production of two context information. It means that more the value of this criterion increases more the quality of the context information decreases. The default values of the attributes of the class TemporalResolution present an informal description of this criterion.

---

[1] Eclipse Modeling Framework: www.eclipse.org/modeling/emf
[2] Obeo Designer: www.obeodesigner.com
[3] Unified Modeling Language: www.uml.org

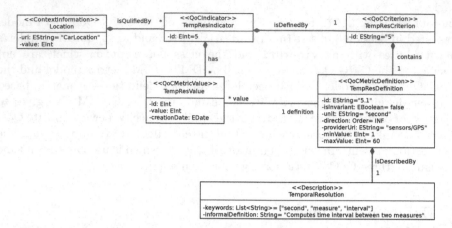

Fig. 2. QoCIM-based model of the QoC temporal resolution criterion

5.2   Modelling the Precision Criterion

The class diagram of Figure 3 shows the definition of the precision criterion. The value of the attribute `id` of the class `PerCentPrecDefinition` is "1.1", that is means `PerCentPrecDefinition` is the first definition of the first criterion of the Table 1. In this diagram, the default value of the attributes `minValue` is 0 and `maxValue` is 100 of the class `PerCentPrecDefinition`. The definition of this criterion is completed with the default value of the attributes `unit` and `direction` which are respectively set to "percent" and *SUP*. This criterion represents the estimation of the accuracy of the location. It means that more the value of this criterion increases more the quality of the context information increases. The default value of the attributes of the class `PerCentPrecision` presents an informal description of this criterion.

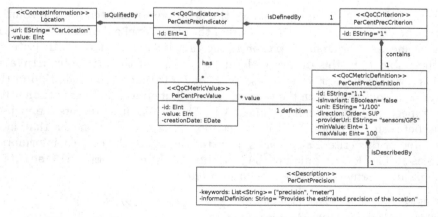

Fig. 3. QoCIM-based model of the QoC precision criterion

5.3   Modelling a Composite Criterion

Figure 4 presents the definition of a composite criterion. The composite criterion depends on the classes `PerCentPrecDefinition` and `TempResDefinition` designed previously. The `id` of this criterion is 17 because it could be classified into Table 1 as a new criterion, that is to say the seventeenth criterion. The value of the attribute `id` of the class `CompositeCriterion` is "5.1 − 1.1". This value refers to the value of the attribute `id` of the classes `TempResDefinition` which is "5.1" and `PerCentPrecDefinition` which is "1.1". The value of the attribute `id` of the class `CompositeDefinition` is "17.1", that is means `CompositeDefinition` is the first definition of the seventeenth criterion. This high level criterion may take three different `QoCMetricValues`: `HighValue`, `MediumValue` and `LowValue`. These `QoCMetricValues` are respectively associated to a default value: 1, 2 and 3. The production of these values are specified with OCL constraints. As an example, listing 1.1 shows the mandatory constraints to product an `HighValue`. As for the precision criterion, the value of the attributes `direction` of the class `CompositeDefinition` is SUP. It means that more the value of this criterion increases more the quality of the context information increase. The production of these values depends on the combined evaluation of the primitive criteria, precision and temporal resolution.

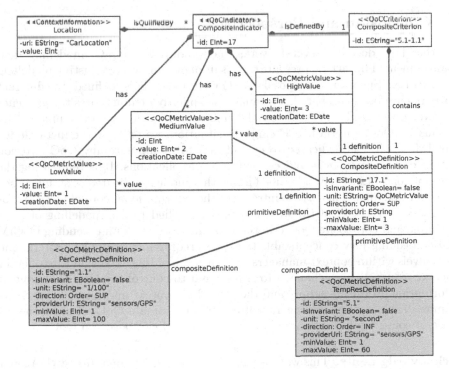

Fig. 4. QoCIM-based model of a QoC composite criterion

```
context  CompositeDefinition :: value ():  HighValue
pre:  self . PerCentPrecDefinition . QoCMetricValue . value >=
      90 % self . PerCentPrecDefinition . maxValue
pre:  self . TempResDefinition . QoCMetricValue . value <=
      15 % self . TempResDefinition . maxValue
```

Listing 1.1. OCL constraints to define HighValue for the composite criteria

5.4   Discussion

The first step of the experimentation of QoCIM on the two primitive criteria of temporal resolution and precision, demonstrates that QoCIM is able to model low level criteria. We have also shown that QoCIM is able to model high level criteria derived from low level criteria. This can be applied to design more complex criteria like the granularity of a location context information, the 7th criterion of Table 1, or the trustworthiness of the provider, the 8th criterion. Figures 2 to 4 show that QoCIM can be used to model, at design time, in an unified way, the definition of any basic or composite QoC criterion. QoCIM is the same conceptual construct used to build those produced models. The processing at runtime any of these QoCIM-based models is then easier for context managers and context-aware applications when they have to deal with QoC criteria evaluation.

6   Conclusion and Perspectives

In the last decade, several works have addressed QoC modelling and management. This article presents the result of our analysis of existing modelling frameworks. Successive proposals of QoC criteria lists defined by different authors have been compared. The analysis explicitly demonstrates the existence of divergences and concludes on the difficulty to converge to a unique and exhaustive QoC criteria list. Facing this situation, we propose the meta-model, QoCIM. QoCIM is dedicated to exploit and to manipulate any QoC criterion within context managers and context-aware applications. It is built using the relevant concepts we have identified from other models dedicated or standardised for other domains. This article introduces the informational core of QoCIM. For validation purpose, QoCIM was successfully applied to the modelling of a set of simple and composite QoC criteria. Currently, we work on extending QoCIM and embedding new concepts able to express requirements on QoC criteria and QoC levels within context managers. The purpose of this extension is to offer for context managers a mechanism to specify and to control the QoC that context information producers supply and the QoC that context information consumers require. Thus, context managers will be able to evaluate QoC all along the life cycle of context information and apply filtering policies based on QoC.

Acknowledgments. This work is part of the French National Research Agency (ANR) project INCOME (ANR-11-INFR-009, 2012-2015).

References

1. Abid, Z., Chabridon, S., Conan, D.: A framework for quality of context management. In: Rothermel, K., Fritsch, D., Blochinger, W., Dürr, F. (eds.) QuaCon 2009. LNCS, vol. 5786, pp. 120–131. Springer, Heidelberg (2009)
2. Arcangeli, J.-P., et al.: INCOME – multi-scale context management for the internet of things. In: Paternò, F., de Ruyter, B., Markopoulos, P., Santoro, C., van Loenen, E., Luyten, K. (eds.) AmI 2012. LNCS, vol. 7683, pp. 338–347. Springer, Heidelberg (2012)
3. Bellavista, P., Corradi, A., Fanelli, M., Foschini, L.: A survey of context data distribution for mobile ubiquitous systems (2012)
4. Buchholz, T., Schiffers, M.: Quality of context: What it is and why we need it. In: Proceedings of the 10th Workshop of the OpenView University Association (2003)
5. Chabridon, S., Conan, D., Abid, Z., Taconet, C.: Building ubiquitous qoc-aware applications through model-driven software engineering. Science of Computer Programming (2012)
6. Distributed Management Task Force: Base Metric Profile (2009)
7. Filho, J.d.R.: A Family of Context-Based Access Control Models for Pervasive Environments. Ph.D. thesis, University of Grenoble Joseph Fourier (2010)
8. Henricksen, K., Indulska, J.: Modelling and using imperfect context information. In: Proc. 1st PerCom Workshop CoMoRea (2004)
9. Internet of Thing Architecture: Deliverable 1.3 (2012), http://www.iot-a.eu/arm/d1.3 (last access May 2013)
10. Kim, Y., Lee, K.: A quality measurement method of context information in ubiquitous environments. In: Proceedings of the International Conference on Hybrid Information Technology (2006)
11. Manzoor, A., Truong, H.L., Dustdar, S.: Quality of context models and applications for context-aware systems in pervasive environments. Knowledge Engineering Review Special Issue on Web and Mobile Information Services (2012)
12. Neisse, R.: Trust and Privacy Management Support for Context-Aware Service Platforms. Ph.D. thesis, University of Twente, Enschede (2012)
13. Object Management Group: UML Profile for Modeling Quality of Service and Fault Tolerance Characteristics and Mechanisms Specification (2008), http://www.omg.org/spec/QFTP/1.1/PDF (last access May 2013)
14. Open Geospatial Consortium: Topic 20: Observations and Measurements (2007), http://portal.opengeospatial.org/files/?artifact_id=41579 (last access May 2013)
15. Sheikh, K., Wegdam, M., Van Sinderen, M.: Middleware support for quality of context in pervasive context-aware systems. In: Pervasive Computing and Communications Workshops (2007)

Petri Nets Context Modeling for the Pervasive Human-Computer Interfaces

Ines Riahi, Faouzi Moussa, and Meriem Riahi

Laboratoire Cristal, Ecole Nationale des Sciences de l'Informatique de Tunis,
Campus Universitaire de la Manouba, 2010 Manouba, Tunisia
ines.riahi@yahoo.fr, faouzimoussa@gmail.com,
meriem.riahi@insat.rnu.tn

Abstract. Nowadays, generation of user interfaces adapted to the context becomes very important in a world where technology and technical adaptations interfaces continue to increase. This paper presents an approach for the automatic and real time generation of user interface adapted to the context of use. We are particularly interested by modeling the data of context as well as the user's task using Petri nets. The Petri nets are used for its simplicity to generate XML files, which will present the specification and generation of the human-computer interfaces adapted to the context. This approach will be illustrated with a case study that presents a diabetic patient suffering from hypoglycemia in a "smart hospital".

Keywords: modeling context, Petri Nets, Human-Computer Interaction, pervasive computing, mobile HCI.

1 Introduction

Pervasive computing seamlessly integrates computers in daily life in response to information provided by sensors in the environment with the direct or indirect intervention of the user. It involves a number of computer entities that interact both with the users and the environment in which they operate. Using these entities, a ubiquitous computing system is able to provide personalized services to users in a context-aware manner when they interact and exchange information with their environment.

The concept of context-awareness has been gaining momentum in the field of distributed systems since the 90s, as it seemed to be a promising solution to many problems related to the use of mobile devices in changing environments. The context, according to Dey [9], is a set of information that characterizes the situation of an entity. The entity can be a person, a place or an object that is considered relevant to the interaction between a user and an application. In 2004, Calvary et al.,[7] substituted the term of context by context of use, and presented the adaptation of user interfaces to their context of use. They therefore proposed a new triplet entitled < user, platform, environment>.

P. Brézillon, P. Blackburn, and R. Dapoigny (Eds.): CONTEXT 2013, LNAI 8175, pp. 316–329, 2013.

Each entity in the ubiquitous computing is equipped with sensors. Sensor data present a high complexity (i.e. different modalities and enormous volumes), an important dynamism (i.e. real-time updated), a problem of accuracy, precision and speed.

To address these problems a number of context modeling approaches have been developed in recent years. Researches models have been accompanied by the development of systems management of context which are able to collect, manage, evaluate and disseminate information on the context. Many of context-aware applications have been developed for a variety of applications to test the efficiency of those models.

In this paper we study different related works in the literature of modeling context. Then we introduce our approach to context modeling based on Petri nets. Finally, this approach will be illustrated by a case study on the monitoring of diabetic patients in a smart hospital.

2   Related Work

Researchers in adaptation to the context area have not introduced a generic and pragmatic definition of the notion of context, and more precisely the parameters constituting the context. After studying the main definitions proposed in the literature, we found that the majority agree on the definition proposed by Dey. For our research work, we will consider the definitions of Dey [9] and Calvary et al., [7] which define the context as the triplet of <user, platform, environment>. These definitions help to clarify the notion of context in Human Computer Systems (HCS). Also, they identify a precise contextual feature that can be considered to support the actions of the user effectively. The question that arises at this point is how to model the context information?

Over the years, several researches targeted the modeling of the context problem [28], [5], [23]. Several approaches to solve the problem were developed such us: (i) The Key-Value pairs [20], (ii) The Markup Schema language (Composite Capabilities/Preference Profile CC/PP [16], User Agent Profile (UAProf) [25]), (iii) The object oriented models ("cues" developed within the TEA project [21], Active Object Model of the GUIDE project and the Context Model Language CML based on the Object Role Model ORM [13]]), (iv) Logic based models [3], (v) Ontology based models [27] [8] and (vi) Hybrid models witch attempt to integrate different models to obtain more flexible and general systems [15], [2].

Indeed, the contextual data captured, must be represented in a suitable form to be analyzed and implemented.

Graphical Models: Petri Nets (PN). Several graphical modeling approaches to context-aware services have been proposed to implement an effective model that specifies the acquisition and management of the various components of the environment such as Unified Modeling Language UML [4], ORM Object Role Modeling [14] and Petri Nets. In this section, we will focus on Petri Nets.

Recently, many approaches to modeling context-aware systems based on PN have been proposed and have been recognized as promising and effective models for the representation of context [12] [24].

Approaches to modeling the context using PN differ depending on the purpose of modeling. Some authors are primarily interested in modeling the behavior of context-aware application; others try to solve the problem of time and resources in applications. There are several extensions of Petri nets such as:

- Synchronized PN: *Reignier et al.,* [19] introduce an approach to the representation of the context and the behavior of the application. They used the concept of situation on places and events on transitions. An event indicates a change of state of the activity, role or relationship describing the situation;
- Colored PN (CPN): *Silva et al.,* [22] proposed to combine 3D modeling tools with CPN for modeling 3D environments. In this model, the place is used to indicate the current state of the user and components such as PDAs and screen. The token identifies the user and its position, and the transition is used to deduce the movement of the user and the behavior of the components. *Kwon* [17] extended CPN to describe context-aware systems. They decompose the system into several major subsystems. They separate the contexts from the global model to produce models of independent context. The CPN have been widely used for modeling and analysis of large and complex systems. In a timed CPN, the color of the token carries synchronization information called "timestamp". It allows modeling and validation of real-time systems where the accuracy depends on the right timing of events. In addition, it offers flexibility in defining and manipulating contextual data [26] [6].

Han et al., proposed a modeling methodology that focuses on the transition contexts [10] [11]. This allows the evaluation of the accessibility and speed of the system. It is able to check whether the system can provide service in a specific time when the context changes.

The constraints of time and resources are essential elements in context-aware environments. However, modeling approaches consider both the time and resource constraints as unusual. Recently, Achilleos et al., proposed a modeling methodology to solve the constraints of time and resources problem [1]. Indeed, the time is set with an upper and lower limit as the duration of typical operations is not constant but variable in dynamic environments. The resource must be clearly identified as being exclusive, busy or shared, depending on the activity. Wang et al., proposed a modeling methodology to estimate the minimum and maximum duration of each activity when the model is built. In addition, it includes the resource constraints that must be set for the performance of services [26].

Evaluation. Several approaches for context modeling have been proposed over the years. At this point, it becomes necessary to choose the most suitable modeling technique. The first objective of our research work was to describe the context. The approaches based on PN inherit all its characteristics. Indeed, the use of Petri nets for modeling aims to prepare the ground for formal verification and validation of the interfaces.

This saves considerable time in the mobile HCI development cycle. Indeed, Petri nets have a formal definition; they offer a great ability to express such aspects as timing, concurrency, etc... They have many techniques for an automatic verification of properties (boundedness, liveness, resettability, etc.). They offer, in addition, an unconstrained graphic representation.

Our choice was naturally oriented towards "small granularity" PN ensuring the accuracy of our model. The context is decomposed in small granularity. However, the PN has a major disadvantage in the modeling of dynamics of a ubiquitous environment. As the context varies from one moment to another, model based on the PN must consider this property. The following section presents our approach to solve this problem.

3   Approach of Context Modeling Based on Petri Nets

The overall objective of our research is to generate a HCI adapted to the current context of use. For that, it's necessary to conduct, first, an analysis of the Human-Computer System (HCS), then to model it. The specifications of HCS must consider the context modeling. As we mentioned in the previous section, the captured context data will be modeled using PN. As the context is defined by the triplet <user, platform, environment>, each component will have its own PN:

- User's PN: this Petri net will aim to model the different users that can use the application;
- Platform's PN: this PN will present the different platforms that can be hosted on our application;
- Environment's PN: it describes the different information of the environment (i.e. geographical location, time etc...).

Since each component of the context is modeled by its own network, the marking of all these networks determines the current state of context at any given time. The marked places in the three networks simultaneously model the current context, and determine the values of the triplet <user, platform, environment>.

Furthermore, according to the context in which the user operates, the user's task may vary. Indeed, each user task is specific to a given context. Our global HCS's model will be composed of a set of pairs "context, task". User tasks will also be modeled using PN. Each task will be decomposed into elementary tasks to be modeled using elementary PN.

We consider that a user task and the components of context are composed by sets of sorted elementary actions. The modeling of an elementary structure is illustrated by Figure 1. The validation of the condition i (transition T1) models the fact that the user will start the execution of the action relative to that condition. After the event, the "end action" (transition T2) expresses the fact that the user action was performed and ended. The place P2 represents a waiting state for the end of the action's execution, while the places P1 and P3 model the state of the user before and after the execution of his action. For example, P1 models the user's mental intention in order to act. The place P3 expresses his state at the end of the action's execution.

All the user's actions and components context behavior (elementary or composed) are arranged according to typical compositions: sequential, parallel, alternative, choice, iterative or of-closure. We present below the principle of parallel, alternative and closure compositions.

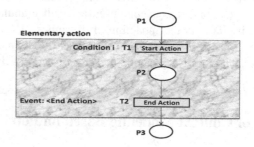

Fig. 1. Structure of an elementary action

Parallel Composition. The parallel composition expresses the possibility of simultaneous execution. The parallelism is ensured thanks to an input synchronization place. This place activates at the same time all the places of initialization of the parallel actions to be executed. Note that the effective parallelism can only be done if the actions to be executed do not use the same resources. Otherwise, a partial or complete sequencing would be necessary. Obviously, the number of places Pn must be equal to the number of parallel actions Ai. Thus, to ensure the parallel composition of actions, it is necessary to synchronize the places of entry and those of exit of those actions (Figure 2).

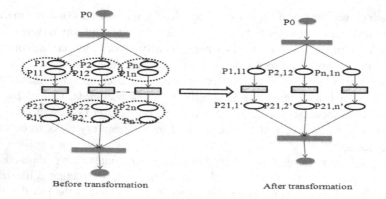

Fig. 2. Parallel composition

Alternative Composition. The alternative composition of n actions reflected a performance always exclusive of these actions. To avoid an actual conflict, conditions are associated with transitions to unambiguously determine which action should be executed. The alternative composition of n networks is realized by composing them sequentially with an ALT structure and merging all the *end* places of these networks. ALT structure allows the validation of a single condition at a time. ALT structure comprises a set of transitions equal to the number of networks to be composed alternately. These transitions are from the same input place P0. They allow, through the conditions associated with them, without ambiguity to initialize a single PN from the n modeled, which guarantees the absence of actual conflict (Figure 3).

The conditions C_i, i varying from 1 to n, depend on the current status of the context.

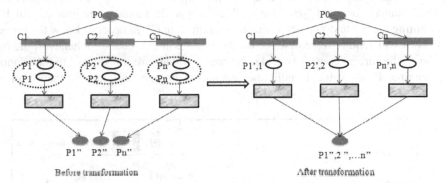

Fig. 3. Alternative composition

Closure Composition. The closure composition of a PN translates the looping of this PN. The closure composition of a PN is achieved by including the network in a structure CF of closure (Figure 4). The closure composition will be used to build the global model of context. More details are presented in Moussa et al., [18]. All elementary and composition structure are stored in the database of PN.

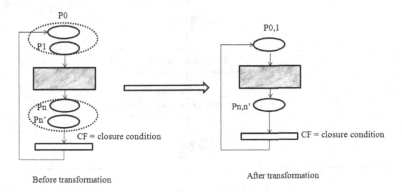

Fig. 4. Iterative composition

At a given moment, the marking of the three PN constituting the current context and the PN of the user task, give the state of our HCS in our ubiquitous environment. The values of these markings are previously stored in a database. Therefore, this database will contain the pairs "context, task". At any times, if the values of PN marking describing the current context are already included in this database, then this will be considered as a normal situation and the user task will be identified, otherwise it will be considered as an unexpected event. Managing this situation will be the subject of our future research.

Figure 5 illustrates our approach stating that once the data is collected from the sensor layer, it will be modeled and decomposed using PN in a user model, a platform model and an environment model. The task of the user will also be modeled using PN. This modeling is realized using the database of PN which contains its elementary structures and compositions. All couples "context, task" will be previously stored in another database denoted "database CT". In a specific moment, the marking of PN constituting the context will determine its current state C_i. In order to know the proper task T_i, it will require to browse the database of "context, task". Whenever, the detection of the current context is made, the couple values are transmitted to the adaptation engine. If its value is null, the adaptation engine will launch the script of

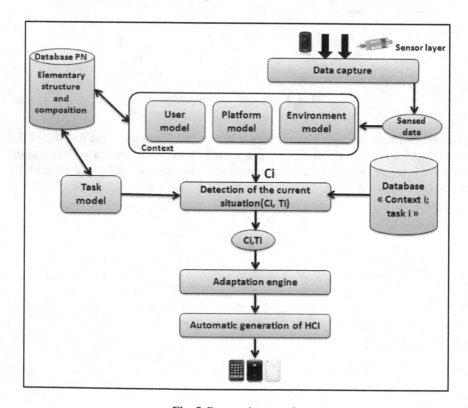

Fig. 5. Proposed approach

adaptation related to unanticipated situations. Otherwise it will trigger scripts to adapt to "normal" situations. Finally, the adaptation engine will trigger the automatic generation of HCI adapted to the current context.

The originality of our approach lies in the decomposition and modeling of the context data. The decomposition of the context data in three models facilitates the detection of any changes in the environment. The construction of these models is made from elementary structures and compositions, which guarantee the validity of these networks. We noticed through our research that the tasks of the user depends of the environment in which he progresses, this justifies the choice of the couple "context, task". The storing of these couples in a database aims to make automatic the detection of unexpected situations.

In order to validate our approach, a case study on the monitoring of a diabetic patient in a medical system, has been applied. The following section presents this example.

4   Case Study: Monitoring of a Diabetic Patient

As a first experiment of our approach, we conducted a case study of a medical system for monitoring of a diabetic patient. This example is designed to monitor at a realtime the evolution status of diabetic patients in a smart hospital. This monitoring is made possible by biological sensors implanted under the skin of patient, which periodically controls the patient's glucose levels. The ubiquitous system must continuously verify the changing state of each patient, saving and guiding any medical interventions.

One of the problems that can arise from such a case study is to know how to notify the medical team (doctor / nurse) for an urgent and immediate intervention, and how should we proceed to carry on. This intervention should take into account the status of the patient and the location of the medical team, nurse or doctor.

The ubiquitous system will therefore generate real-time user interfaces adapted to their preferences, profiles, activities and geographical location. It will guide the user to best accomplish its task while taking into account the various constraints of the system.

Context Modeling. According to the definition of the context given in the previous section, we consider the context as the triplet <user, platform, environment>. Each component of this triplet is modeled by an independent PN. Those components are:

- User's PN (Figure 6): it aims to identify the profile of the user (doctor or nurse). The marking of the network at a given time defines the type of the connected user. For clarity, we considered in our example the green color to represent an elementary action, the blue color for the alternative composition, the red color for closure composition and brown color for parallel composition.

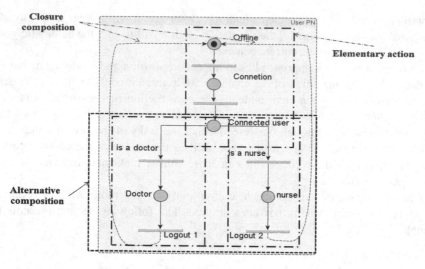

Fig. 6. User's PN

- Platform's PN: Figure 7 describes the different platforms that can be used by users. HCI can be hosted on various platforms. For our case study, we consider that a user can connect using a tablet, a PC or a mobile phone.

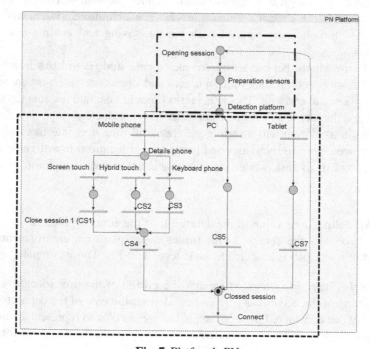

Fig. 7. Platform's PN

- Environment's PN (Figure 8): it describes the different values of our environment. For our example, after the opening of the session, various sensors intercept in parallel, the glucose level (GL) of the patient, the geographical coordinates of the user and the time. Concerning the geographical data, a user can be in the hospital, in the cabinet, at home or outside (i.e. in a restaurant or on the road ...). Concerning the time, it can have three different values: morning, afternoon or evening. Tokens present in different places, will describe the state of the environment by specifying the value of time, geographical data and glucose level.

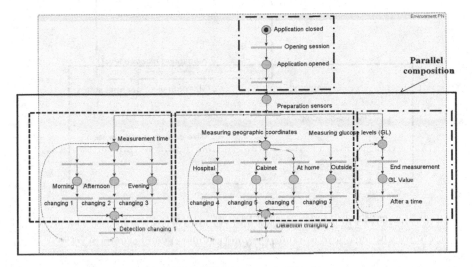

Fig. 8. Environment's PN

The environment's PN must stay attentive to any changes that may happen to the environment. This action is possible by transitions "changing detection 1 and 2", which will monitor the possible changes in the environment. If any change occurs, then the new data will be caught by our sensors measuring.

After modeling the different components of the context, we are interested at this stage in the modeling task.

Modeling the User's Task. As we mentioned in the previous section, the task of the user will also be modeled using Petri nets. The overall HCS will be decomposed into basic tasks. Each task will be executed in a particular context.

For our example, considering that the patient is hypoglycemic, two tasks: T1 and T2 are then occurred. Task 1 (T1), sketched in Figure 9, is assigned to a particular context and can only be executed by a doctor who is in the hospital. The doctor must then, first, check the status of the patient and measure its glucose level:

- If the rate of GL <= 4 mmol, then we must give the patient her/his medicines, wait 15 minutes and repeat the measurement of glucose;

- If the rate of GL> 4 mmol, then she/he must receive food containing carbohydrate and protein;
- If the status is normal, then the patient state should be followed-up for a possible change.

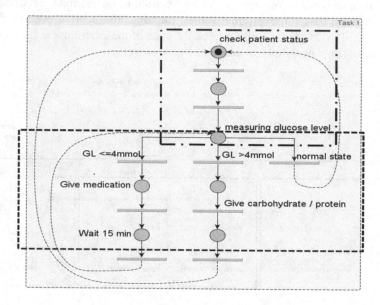

Fig. 9. Task 1

Task 2 (T2), represented in Figure 10, is assigned in the case where the user is a nurse and she/he is in the hospital. In this case, the nurse should at the same time, call the doctor, perform task 1 and consult the state of the patient for a possible change.

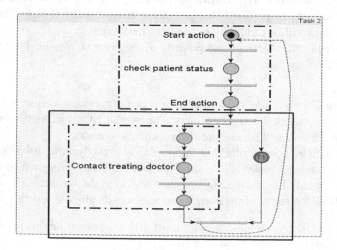

Fig. 10. Task 2

After modeling the context and the user task, we will now deal with the development of the database containing all couples "context, task".

Elaboration of the Database: "Context, Task". This database stores all couples "context, task". At any given time, the execution of the three PN (user's PN, environment's PN and platform's PN) determines the values of context. In each context, a task is assigned. These pairs are stored in the database. If the value of "context, task" is in the database, then this is a known and modeled situation. If this value is not in our database, then this will be considered as an unexpected situation. Table 1 shown below, defines the database relating to our case study.

Table 1. Database "Context, Task"

([doctor, screen touch, morning, hospital, GL<=4mmol] ; T1)	([nurse, screen touch, morning, hospital, GL<=4mmol] ; T2)
([doctor, screen touch, afternoon, hospital, GL<=4mmol] ; T1)	([nurse, screen touch, afternoon, hospital, GL<=4mmol] ; T2)
([doctor, screen touch, evening, hospital, GL<=4mmol] ; T1)	([nurse, screen touch, evening, hospital, GL<=4mmol] ; T2)
([doctor, hybrid touch, morning, hospital, GL<=4mmol] ; T1)	([nurse, hybrid touch, morning, hospital, GL<=4mmol] ; T2)
([doctor, hybrid touch, afternoon, hospital, GL<=4mmol] ; T1)	([nurse, hybrid touch, afternoon, hospital, GL<=4mmol] ; T2)
([doctor, hybrid touch, evening, hospital, GL<=4mmol] ; T1)	([nurse, hybrid touch, evening, hospital, GL<=4mmol] ; T2)
([doctor, keyboard phone, morning, hospital, GL<=4mmol] ; T1)	([nurse, keyboard phone, morning, hospital, GL<=4mmol] ; T2)
([doctor, keyboard phone, afternoon, hospital, GL<=4mmol] ; T1)	([nurse, keyboard phone, afternoon, hospital, GL<=4mmol] ; T2)
([doctor, keyboard phone, evening, hospital, GL<=4mmol] ; T1)	([nurse, keyboard phone, evening, hospital, GL<=4mmol] ; T2)
([doctor, PC, morning, hospital, GL<=4mmol] ; T1)	([nurse, PC, morning, hospital, GL<=4mmol] ; T2)
([doctor, PC, afternoon, hospital, GL<=4mmol] ; T1)	([nurse, PC, afternoon, hospital, GL<=4mmol] ; T2)
([doctor, PC, evening, hospital, GL<=4mmol] ; T1)	([nurse, PC, evening, hospital, GL<=4mmol] ; T2)
([doctor, tablet, morning, hospital, GL<=4mmol] ; T1)	([nurse, tablet, morning, hospital, GL<=4mmol] ; T2)
([doctor, tablet, afternoon, hospital, GL<=4mmol] ; T1)	([nurse, tablet, afternoon, hospital, GL<=4mmol] ; T2)
([doctor, tablet, evening, hospital, GL<=4mmol] ; T1)	([nurse, tablet, evening, hospital, GL<=4mmol] ; T2)

At this stage, all couples "context, task" are identified. They will be forwarded to the adaptation engine that will run the appropriate script for the automatic generation of HCI adapting to the context of use. This part will be discussed in our future work.

5   Conclusion and Future Work

This paper presents an approach for context modeling based on Petri Nets. We model the HCS using a composing process of elementary PN in order to subsequently verify the relevant properties of the system before the generation of the interfaces.

This approach is illustrated with a simple case study on the monitoring of diabetic patients in a smart hospital. There are several issues not discussed in this paper. They will be addressed in our future work. For instance, we will detail the construction of the database "context, task" and we will explain the specification of the adaptation's engine.

References

1. Achilleos, A., Yang, K., Georgalas, N.: Context modeling and a context-aware framework for pervasive service creation: a model-driven approach. Pervasive Mobile Comput. 6, 281–296 (2010)
2. Agostini, A., Bettini, C., Riboni, D.: Hybrid Reasoning in the CARE Middleware for Context-Awareness. International Journal of Web Engineering and Technology 5(1), 3–23 (2009)
3. Akman, V., Surav, M.: The use of situation theory in context modeling. Computational Intelligence 13, 427–438 (1997)
4. Bauer, J.: Identification and Modeling of Contexts for Different Information Scenarios in Air Traffic, Diplomarbeit (March 2003)
5. Bettini, C., Brdiczka, O., Henricksen, K., Indulska, J., Nicklas, D., Ranganathan, A., Riboni, D.: A survey of context modeling and reasoning techniques. Pervasive and Mobile Computing 6, 161–180 (2010)
6. Boucheneb, H.: Interval timed coloured petri net: efficient construction of its state class space preserving linear properties. Formal Aspects Comput. 20(2), 225–238 (2008)
7. Calvary, G., Demeure, A., Coutaz, J., Dâassi, O.: Adaptation des Interfaces Homme-Machine à leur contexte d'usage. Revue d'intelligence Artificielle 18(4), 577–606 (2004)
8. Chen, L., Nugent, C., Mulvenna, M., Finlay, D., Hong, X.: Semantic smart homes: Towards knowledge rich assisted living environments. In: McClean, S., Millard, P., El-Darzi, E., Nugent, C. (eds.) Intelligent Patient Management. SCI, vol. 189, pp. 279–296. Springer, Heidelberg (2009)
9. Dey, A.K., Salber, D., Futakawa, M., Abowd G.D.: An Architecture to Support Context-Aware Applications. GVU Technical Reports (1999)
10. Han, S., Song, S.K., Youn, H.Y.: Modeling and analysis of time critical context aware service using extended interval timed colored Petri nets. Tech. rep., The school of information and communication engineering. Sungkyunkwan University, Seoul (2010)
11. Han, S., Song, S.K., Youn, H.Y.: Modeling and verification of context-awareness service for time critical applications using colored petri-net. In: IEEE/WIC/ACM International Conference on Web Intelligence and Intelligent Agent Technology, WI-IAT 2008, vol. 2, pp. 71–74. IEEE (2009)

12. Han, S., Youn, H.Y.: Petri net-based context modeling for context-aware systems. Artificial Intelligence Review 37, 43–67 (2011)
13. Henricksen, K., Indulska, J.: Modelling and using imperfect context information. In: 1st Workshop on Context Modeling and Reasoning (CoMoRea), PerCom 2004 Workshop Proceedings. IEEE Computer Society (2004)
14. Henricksen, K., Indulska, J., Rakotonirainy, A.: Generating Context Management Infrastructure from High-Level Context Models. In: Industrial Track Proceedings of the 4th International Conference on Mobile Data Management (MDM 2003), pp. 1–6 (2003)
15. Henricksen, K., Livingstone, S., Indulska, J.: Towards a hybrid approach to context modelling, reasoning and interoperation. In: Indulska, J., Roure, D.D. (eds.) Proceedings of the First International Workshop on Advanced Context Modelling, Reasoning and Management, University of Southampton, Nottingham, England (2004)
16. Kiss, C.: Composite Capability/Preference Profiles (CC/PP): Structure and Vocabularies 2.0 - W3C Working Draft (April 30, 2007), http://www.w3.org/TR/2007/WD-CCPP-struct-vocab2-20070430/ (last consultation April 2011)
17. Kwon, O.B.: Modeling and generating context-aware agent-based applications with amended colored Petri nets. Exp. Syst. Appl. 27(4), 609–621 (2004)
18. Moussa, F., Riahi, I., Riahi, M.: A PNML extension for the HCI design. International Journal of Human-Computer Interaction (IJHCI) 5(3) (2011)
19. Reignier, P., Brdiczka, O.: Context-aware environments: from specification to implementation. Exp. Syst. 24(5), 305–320 (2007)
20. Schilit, B., Adams, N., Want, N.L.: Context-aware computing applications. In: IEEE Workshop on Mobile Computing Systems and Applications (1994)
21. Schmidt, A., Laerhoven, K.V.: How to Build Smart Appliances. IEEE Personal Communications (August 2001)
22. Silva, J.L., Campos, J.C., Harrison, M.D.: An infrastructure for experience centered agile prototyping of ambient intelligence. In: EICS 2009: Proceedings of the 1st ACM SIGCHI Symposium on Engineering Interactive Computing Systems, pp. 79–84 (2009)
23. Strang, T., Linnhoffpopien, C.: A context modeling survey. In: Workshop on Advanced Context Modeling, Reasoning and Management, UbiComp 2004 (2004)
24. Sun, J., Zhang, Y., He, K.: A Petri-Net based context representation in smart car environment. In: Bellavista, P., Chang, R.-S., Chao, H.-C., Lin, S.-F., Sloot, P.M.A. (eds.) GPC 2010. LNCS, vol. 6104, pp. 162–173. Springer, Heidelberg (2010)
25. Timmerer, C., Jabornig, J., Hellwagner, H.: Delivery Context Descriptions A Comparison and Mapping Model. In: Proceedings of the 9th Workshop on Multimedia Metadata (WMM 2009) held in Conjunction with the 13th French Multimedia Conference on Compression and Representation of Audiovisual Signals CORESA (2009)
26. Wang, H., Zeng, Q.: Modeling and analysis for workflow constrained by resources and non determined time: an approach based on Petri nets. IEEE Trans. Syst. Man Cybern. A Syst. Hum. 38(4), 802–817 (2008)
27. Ye, J., Coyle, L., Dobson, S., Nixon, P.: Ontology-based models in pervasive computing systems. The Knowledge Engineering Review 22(04), 315–347 (2007)
28. Ye, J., Dobson, S., MacKeeve, S.: Situation identification techniques in pervasive computing: A review. Pervasive and Mobile Computing (8), 36–66 (2011)

Modeling Context Effects in Science Learning: The CLASH Model

Thomas Forissier[1], Jacqueline Bourdeau[2], Yves Mazabraud[1], and Roger Nkambou[3]

[1] Université des Antilles et de la Guyane, Guadeloupe, France
{tforissi,mazab}@iufm.univ-ag.fr
[2] Télé-université du Québec
jacqueline.bourdeau@licef.ca
[3] Université du Québec à Montréal
Nkambou.Roger@uqam.ca

Abstract. In science learning, context is an important dimension of any scientific object or phenomenon, and context-dependent variations prove to be as critical for a deep understanding as are abstract concepts, laws or rules. Our hypothesis is that a context gap can be illuminating to highlight the respective general-particular aspects of an object or phenomenon. Furthermore, provoking a perturbation during the learning process to obtain the emergence of such an event could be a productive tutoring strategy. We introduce the emergence of context effects as a problem space, to be modeled in the system. We propose a model of the contextual dimension, associated with an analytical view of its modeling, based on a metaphor in physics.

Keywords: science education, context effect, model, context, learning scenario.

1 Introduction

A context is defined as a set of objects and events that surround an entity situated in the center and that have structural and functional links with the center. In biology, the context of an animal consists of biotic and abiotic environmental conditions. In science learning, the context of the learner consists of previous knowledge and skills, conceptual models, metacognitive capability, motivation, location and spatial and social environments. A *context effect* is an event that is produced by tension between two contexts. This event is challenging for learners, particularly for their existing mental models. Suddenly, these good old or not so old representations they have no longer account for the new context, and the learners are challenged to proceed to a conceptual change or to accommodate multiple representations. From a scientific viewpoint, each context effect can be isolated to allow for the study, control and manipulation thereof. However, this would mean to study it out of its context, similar to *in vitro* investigations. From a more naturalistic viewpoint, we wish to study the process of the emergence of these events, and consequently the position of an event either on a timeline or in space. We also wish to analyze the correlations among a set of events. Measuring the scientific objects in terms of levels of contextuality might

P. Brézillon, P. Blackburn, and R. Dapoigny (Eds.): CONTEXT 2013, LNAI 8175, pp. 330–335, 2013.

bring valuable information for the understanding and interpretation of the object of study. In this paper, we introduce several issues : the notion of *context effect*, the CLASH Model with the Maz-Calculator, two learning scenarios, and the architecture of a context-aware tutoring system with an authoring service.

2   Context Effects in Science Learning

Science teaching is designed to take into account observations of what is real, as well as experiments. *Authentic* teaching aims to construct students' conceptions on the basis of real situations in both the laboratory [1] and the field for the naturalistic dimensions of the sciences. *Authentic* approaches based on contexts [2] fit into this vein and entail investigations based on the study of environments familiar to the students. The gaps between the contexts of the various actors can lead to misunderstandings, and there are times, in particular when these gaps are significant and when the teaching situation lends itself thereto, that an "event" emerges that renders the gaps explicit. These incidents are called "context effects"[3]. The model we propose here aims to facilitate the identification and description of this phenomenon. Our model possesses a predictive value in that by implementing the parameters of the contexts studied, it indicates the likelihood of the emergence of a context effect.

The objective is to highlight the comparison of learners' conceptions in response to observation results that are different but linked to a single concept,. In biology and geology, the contexts are an integral part of the concepts studied. The concept may be considered as a straight line of which the contexts would be the segments. Situating this context amounts to defining its specificity and representability. The comparison of two unique contexts may be carried out in two ways: 1) through resemblance, which makes it possible in particular to specify the level of generalization of the characters observed to all or a part of the concept; and 2) through dissemblance, which is useful for specifying limitations, singularities and false interpretations.

3   Modeling the Context Effect: The CLASH Model

Context effects are modeled based on a metaphor taken from signal processing (Fig.1). In the case of a multi-frequency signal, which corresponds to a sinusoidal curve with various wavelengths, the law selected by the observer to describe the signal may be different in comparison with his observation thereof. According to the observation scale, he is likely to concentrate his analysis on the wavelength that is the most visible at this scale. Much smaller and much larger variations in wavelength will not be perceived, even though they affect the signal in its entirety. Another parameter, the sample size, influences the effect of the various wavelengths in the general representation. When we attempt to describe the evolution of a measured value by comparing it to a theoretical value, indicators such as the Root Mean Square (RMS) are classically used to quantify the error. It is therefore a question of minimizing the RMS and increasing precision in the course of the process.

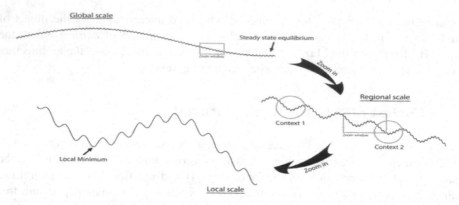

Fig. 1. The Context Effect Model: CLASH

If the observation scale or the sample size is inappropriate, the minimum RMS value might not correspond to the best overall solution. In such a case, the solution is likely to be specific but inexact. This is known as a local minimum. To avoid this possibility, the scales of analysis have to be varied and the sample size increased. Unfortunately, it is not always possible to adjust the scale (technical constraints) or to have a comprehensive view (outcroppings available in geology, for example). In this case, it is best to make observations of the same type but in different contexts through context gap jump-over. By making observations of the same system in different contexts, it is possible to understand how the system evolves (in space, time, society, etc.).

Derived from this model is the *Maz-Calculator*, which indicates the frequency of appearance of context effects based on the gaps of different parameters in two educational contexts. Each context is described in terms of the parameters linked to the teaching objectives, and applying the *Maz-Calculator* to each of these parameters allows it to provide an overall indicator for the contexts selected on the basis of the gaps of each of the parameters.

4   Two Learning Scenarios: *Gounouy* and *Magma*

In order to test our hypothesis on the benefits of context effects, we designed two learning scenarios, one in biology for secondary school learners, the other in geology for university students. Both share the same structure and are based on collaborative learning, direct observation, lab investigation, information exchange, expertise sharing, collaborative reflection and discussions. Both involve two groups of students, one in Guadeloupe, a tropical area, and one in Quebec, Canada. The *Gounouy* scenario leads the students to make fine-grained observations and measurements of the local common frog. The smallest one in the world, the Caribbean frog, is called whistling (*Euleutherodactylus sp.*); in Quebec, the largest one in North America is called bullfrog (*Lithobates catesbeianus*). The scenario is designed in such a way that the learners are stimulated by the contrasting results of their observations and the common ground of the biological concepts. In the *Magma* scenario, the object of study is magmatism; the students are required to compare some of the oldest rocks (Quebec) and the most recent rocks (Caribbean) and to explain the differences based on geophysical concepts. The measurements performed by the learners are quantified to allow for calculation. Each parameter used can be filled either qualitatively or quantitatively [4]. For the *Gounouy* project, the parameters are: frog call, morphologic and taxonomy, the environment, relationship with humans, and developmental nutrition. Parameters used for magma can be classified into different scales: Geochemistry ($\%SiO2$, $\%MgO$ FeO, spectrum REE) Microscopy (presence of minerals, % Quartz, % Plagioclase) snip (texture, mineralogical composition, vacuole, deformation) landscape (hexagonal prismation, relative chronology, particular landscape elements) and regional (cartography, variability, age, seismicity)

For these two scenarios, a simple learning environment is being implemented through a Learning Management System, *Moodle*, to provide access to documents and services (communication, sharing), as well as to capture the data needed to test our hypothesis. In parallel, the modeling of a context-aware tutoring system is underway.

5   The Building Blocks of a System

Several components can provide a structure for the modeling of a context-aware tutoring system: domain, scales, competencies, and context of the animal, the learner and the teacher.

The architecture of a context-aware tutoring system with its' authoring services' is proposed as illustrated in Fig.2. One key issue in developing successful learning environments or tutoring systems is to provide the system with a valid learning scenario. In this authoring system, the Maz-Calculator is a key service, used not only for estimating the context effect frequency but also for highlighting the context parameters that are involved. The author could then use this information to revise the learning scenario. She can be assisted in this adaptation task using CEM tools combined with three scenario management tools (CAS-Edit, CAS-Viz and CAS-Sim) as described in Fig. 2. In this way, it would be possible to iteratively play with the context parameters provided by the Maz-Calculator and adjust the scenario accordingly. The resulting scenario is stored in the CSLS database. As shown in Fig. 2, the Intelligent Tutoring System itself (CAITS) comprises three main components. It is connected to the contexts pool in three ways. The first connection is implemented by the interaction between the Maz-Calculator and the CSDM; this connection makes it possible to provide the ITS with context effects information which will drive the domain model behavior. The second connection is a direct link to the contexts pool which gives access to other contextual parameters to be considered during learners/system interactions; this includes contextual information about the learners' profiles, as well as instructional/learning strategies. The third connection is done through the CSLC database allowing the CAITS to load relevant instructional scenarios that will drive the tutor behavior.

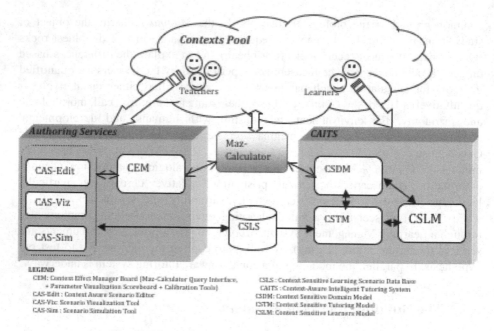

Fig. 2. CAITS Architecture with Its Authoring Services

6   Future Work

Future work consists of: 1) implementing and testing the model; 2) experimenting the scenario *in situ,* in schools and in universities; and 3) designing a context-aware tutoring system with an 'authoring service'. Implementation and testing of the model is under development. The research methodology is Design-Based Research (DBR) [5]. The design of a context-aware tutoring system with an 'authoring service' will be further detailed. Intelligent tutoring systems for science learning have been evolving along the modeling of the student, the domain knowledge and the tutoring knowledge, rarely taking context into account [6]. Context modeling for mobile learning environments focuses mostly on localization and adaptation to rapid changes of user localization. Our work is original and innovative in that it integrates context awareness and provides the author with a scientific foundation for designing an instructional scenario.

7   Conclusion

The CLASH Model makes it possible to validate experimental hypotheses on the emergence of context effects in science teaching both in secondary school and at university. Adapting this model to research on similar teaching at different levels or of different themes appears to be possible and would be particularly useful as an aide to the choice of contexts taken up by the teacher. Measuring the gaps between context effects could also be used in the development of a context-aware digital learning environment.

References

1. Roth, W.M.: Authentic school science: Knowing and learning in open-inquiry science laboratories. Kluwer Academic Publishers (1995)
2. King, D.T., Winner, E., Ginns, I.: Outcomes and implications of one teacher's approach to context-based science in the middle years. Teaching Science 57(2), 26–30 (2011)
3. Leurette, S., Forissier, T.: La contextualisation dans l'enseignement des sciences et techniques en Guadeloupe. InGrand N 83, 19–26 (2009)
4. Galliker, M., Weimer, D.: Context and implicitness: Consequences for qualitative and quantitative context analysis. In: Proceedings of (CONTEXT 1997), Federal University of Rio de Janeiro Ed., pp. 151–163 (1997)
5. Sandoval, W., Bell, P.: Design-Based Research Methods for Studying Learning in Context: Introduction. Educational Psychologist 39(4), 199–201 (2004)
6. Nkambou, R., Bourdeau, J., Mizoguchi, R. (eds.): Advances in Intelligent Tutoring Systems. SCI, vol. 308, 510 p. Springer, Heidelberg (2010)

Context Model for Business Context Sensitive Business Documents

Danijel Novakovic, Christian Huemer, and Christian Pichler

Institute of Software Technology and Interactive Systems
Vienna University of Technology
Favoritenstrasse 9-11/188, A-1040 Vienna, Austria
{novakovic,huemer}@big.tuwien.ac.at, cpichler@ec.tuwien.ac.at
http://www.isis.tuwien.ac.at/

Abstract. One and the same inter-organizational business process - such as e-procurement - may be executed differently in different industries, geopolitical regions, etc. Thus, a standardized reference model for inter-organizational business processes must be customized to the specific business context (industry, region, etc.). In order to share, search, and (partially) re-use context specific adaptations it is essential not only to store the adaptations, but also a business context model where these adaptations are valid. In this paper we describe the Unified Context Model (UCM) introduced by the United Nations Centre for Trade Facilitation and Electronic Business (UN/CEFACT). We explain the shortcomings of the approach and show how these can be undermined by our Enhanced Unified Context Model (E-UCM). The enhanced model serves as a basis for contextualizing business documents which are exchanged between different inter-organizational business processes. Having such an approach at hand, helps prevent negative trends in today's business, such as interoperability issues, inconsistencies and heterogeneous interpretations of the exchanged data contents.

Keywords: business context, business context modeling, annotation method for digital business ecosystems, business context aware e-documents.

1 Introduction

Business processes are essential for fostering collaboration between different partners in inter-organizational business scenarios. In the course of such business processes e-business documents are, amongst other artifacts, exchanged. Thus, defining business processes and their corresponding business documents is a necessary prerequisite for the successful realization of inter-organizational business scenarios. However, this is often a complex, time demanding and expensive task. Therefore, instead of generating new business processes from scratch, it is beneficial to provide concepts and methods for supporting the re-use of the already existing artifacts of the already existing inter-organizational business processes.

One option to support the re-use of existing artifacts of business processes is specifying business context (BC) in which these processes and their encompassed

P. Brézillon, P. Blackburn, and R. Dapoigny (Eds.): CONTEXT 2013, LNAI 8175, pp. 336–342, 2013.

artifacts are or are not valid. However, nowadays, there is not a uniform modeling approach to formally represent BC. Therefore, in this paper we define BC more precisely and present our formal modeling approach to express its structure. The starting foundations of our work originate from the Unified Context Methodology (UCM) [1]. This is the methodology which serves as the theoretical foundation of BC applied under the umbrella of the UN/CEFACT standardization efforts, such as the Core Components based business document standard [2].

However, the UCM business context model has not been applied in real-world scenarios yet. It is, thus, not verified whether the proposed concepts conform to commonly accepted norms, such as interoperability, scalability and re-usability. Furthermore, some of these concepts, such as UCM operands, are incomplete or only partially defined. In this vein, we define extensions of UCM and present our Enhanced Unified Context Model (E-UCM).

The remainder of this paper is structured as follows. Section 2 presents an excerpt of our survey on the definition of BC and introduces the standard UCM methodology. In Section 3 we elaborate on the main shortcomings of UCM. We propose our E-UCM model and highlight the main benefits of its application. Finally, Section 4 concludes the paper and gives an outlook on future work.

2   Related Work

2.1   Business Context

The relevant scientific literature ([3], [4], etc.) describes context as an *enumeration of examples*, such as: location, time, temperature, or in terms of *relevant synonyms*, such as: user's environment, application surroundings, user's situation. Our definition of business context is based on (i) the outcomes of our survey on BC [5] and (ii) by narrowing one of the most applied understandings of context proposed by Dey and Abowd [3] to the domain of business processes. Therefore, we have defined BC in the following way: *BC is any information that can be used to characterize the situation of an entity within a scope where business operates. An entity is a person, place, or object that is considered relevant to the interaction between a business process and a business environment, including the business process and business environments themselves.*

The entities which are introduced by our BC definition can be described by different attributes referred to as primary context categories. Dey and Abowd [3] provide four different context categories, namely location, identity, activity, and time. Considering these four categories, our research [5] shows that only location is applicable in our domain as defined in [3]. We introduced an additional context category named industry as well as redefined activity. For example, Switzerland and the Book industry, Austria and the DVD industry, or France and the Aircraft industry, can be used to locate and describe the situation of the business documents which are involved within a particular user activity, such as invoicing, ordering and confirming goods receipt. Thus, the three primary business context categories that the work presented builds upon are: location, activity, and industry.

2.2   Unified Business Context Model

The Unified Business Context Model (UCM) [1] is the model used to manage representations and applications of BC under the scope of the CCTS business document standard [2]. It is underpinned by two main pillars: (i) the UCM BC Graph (UCM BCG) and (ii) the UCM BC Expression.

The UCM BC Graph (BCG) is defined as a directed acyclic graph (DAG) with organized values to enable normative expressions of multiple BCs. A particular BC Value can be resolved from the BCG by a BC Expression. A BC Value is an atomic piece of information that represents one aspect of the BC (i.e. industry, geopolitical region, or activity). A BC Expression consists of BC Clauses. A Simple BC Clause is a BC Clause used to resolve a set of at least one BC Value from the BCG. Two ordered BC Clauses connected by a UCM operand form a Compound BC Clause. The list of the allowed UCM operands is: Intersection (&&), Union (||), and Exclusion (!!). For instance, the operand && identifies the BC Values from the BCG which are resolved by both related BC Clauses. The other UCM operands can be described analogously.

3   The Enhanced UCM Business Context Model

As part of our research we encountered several shortcomings of the UCM approach which significantly undermined its application. Therefore, in the following we describe these issues more precisely and explain how they can be solved using the Enhanced Unified Context Model (E-UCM). E-UCM is our enhancement of the original UCM approach based on (i) extension of the centralized UCM BCG approach, and on (ii) extension of the set of the UCM operands.

3.1   E-UCM: Business Context Graph

The UCM BCG is the centralized, hierarchical, directed, acyclic graph (DAG) which reflects the BC in which some particular business process is valid. Therefore, it must encompass the complete geopolitical organization, industry classification and all possible user activities. Hence, this graph structure is bewildering complex and usually consists of an overwhelming number of BC Nodes. For example, only the industry classification domain of the UCM BCG, based on the International Standard Industrial Classification (ISIC) [6], covers more than 760 BC Nodes. At the same time, the geopolitical organization of the same graph contains at least as many nodes as the industry classification. Furthermore, the maximal number of potential edges in every DAG depends on its total number of nodes and can be calculated by the following formula: $\max(e) = \frac{1}{2}n(n-1) = f(n^2) \sim O(n^2)$, where n represents a total number of nodes, and e is a total number of edges. Thus, the number of possible edges in the UCM BCG is expressed by millions.

According to graph theory, memory and time complexities of the graph management operations strictly depend on the total number of nodes and edges [7]. Thereby, the representation of BC in the form of the UCM BCG which contains thousands of nodes and millions of possible edges is a significant shortcoming of UCM. This causes the following negative consequences. First, the construction and initialization of a UCM BCG is a laborious and time-consuming task. Second, it is very difficult to efficiently maintain this structure. For example, frequent BC management operations applied on a huge amount of nodes, such as search, remove, or include, are time and memory expensive. Finally, a system based on a centralized UCM BCG shows poor scalability and can be exposed to undesired bottleneck effects.

Conceptual Solution. In contrast to the standard UCM approach, our research shows that it is not necessary to have a complete BC blueprint assembled by thousands of nodes and millions of possible edges. More precisely, the standard UCM BCG covers not only relevant but also a significant amount of superfluous elements which can not be used in the current business scenario. For example, the business document $BDoc_1$, created by an inter-organizational business process p_1, is relevant in the scope of the vehicle production in the European Union. The corresponding BC can be described by only two BC Nodes including one for reflecting the industry, and one for representing the geopolitical region. However, the underlying centralized UCM BCG comprises not only these but thousands of additional BC Nodes as well. For example, the BC Nodes which refer to the Paper Industry of New Zealand represent only a smaller subset of these superfluous elements. Thereby, in practice, it is very probable that these irrelevant pieces of contextual information presented by thousands of BC Nodes will not be considered during any kind of customization of the $BDoc_1$. Therefore, exclusion of the superfluous nodes and edges from the graph will not ruin the relevancy of the graph to the particular business process (p_1 in our example) and will not bring any additional undesired consequences. This is the crux of our E-UCM BCG approach described in the following.

The E-UCM BCG approach represents the transition from the centralized UCM BCG approach to a new, decentralized (distributed) approach. Accordingly, we define a decentralized E-UCM BCG as the subgraph of the centralized UCM BCG. This subgraph comprises only the geopolitical, industry and activity subdomains of BC which are relevant to the scope where a particular inter-organizational business process operates.

Nowadays, business processes are agile, adaptable and prone to changes. Thereby, it is very difficult to know and to detect in advance a complete scope of the relevant BC in which some business process will be valid until its final termination. It is essential that our conceptual solution addresses these issues by establishing the capability to dynamically combine different decentralized BC subgraphs into a unique graph. In other words, it is possible to manipulate with the decentralized BC subgraphs based on the current business needs. For example, a company in the Paper industry located in New Zealand is considered. This company extends its business to the Glass industry in Japan and requires additional e-business documents for new business operations. Consequently, the business environment is changed and these new contextual meanings must be contained by the BCG. Having our decentralized approach at hand, new relevant subgraphs can be

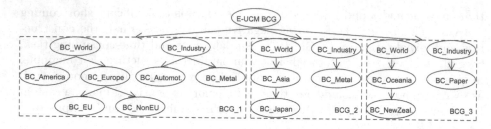

Fig. 1. Decentralized E-UCM BCG

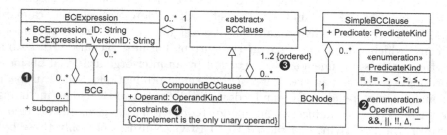

Fig. 2. E-UCM BC Expression Metamodel

dynamically embedded to the existing BCG structure. Furthermore, it is also possible that some BC, which was considered to be relevant for some specific business scenario, can lose its relevancy. In this case, the corresponding subgraphs can be dynamically excluded from the E-UCM BCG.

The example of the E-UCM BCG is presented in Fig. 1. Because of space limitations, the activity primary BC category is excluded from the illustrated graph. For instance, the subgraph BCG_1 shown in Fig. 1 encapsulates the contextual information related to the previously introduced business document $BDoc_1$.

E-UCM Metamodel, Enhancement I. We present our E-UCM metamodel in Fig. 2. It is the extension of the original UCM BC Expression metamodel described in [1]. The proposed E-UCM BCG conceptual solution is implemented by an embedded aggregation which connects BCG entities (Fig. 2, Mark 1). This new relation enables the union of an indefinite number of BC subgraphs into the unique BCG. Thus, the E-UCM BCG is less ramified than the original UCM BCG. Furthermore, we have provided an instrument for its incremental growth and decremental reduction.

Our enhancement of UCM brings the meaningful consequences in the application of this methodology. In a nutshell, a total number of nodes and edges in BCG is significantly reduced. Thereby, decentralized BCG is more memory friendly. Furthermore, this automatically eases graph initialization and decreases complexities of the maintenance operations. Moreover, in order to describe a new target business process, it is now possible to re-use already existing subgraphs and to rebuild them into decentralized BCG structures. Hence, the levels of interoperability, scalability and flexibility are significantly increased. At the same time, the E-UCM BCG approach completely avoids undesired bottleneck effects which are typical in centralized systems.

3.2   E-UCM: Operands

In order to increase the level of BC expressiveness, we formally define two additional UCM operands, namely *Symmetric Exclusion* and *Complement*. Furthermore, negation (complement) belongs to the group of the fundamental operations introduced and widely exploited by computational logic. Therefore, the lack of the Complement operand significantly limits the reasoning capabilities of UCM, which, as shown in [8], can be successfully applied for deriving new knowledge from the already existing contextual knowledge.

Definition 1. *The Symmetric Exclusion of BC Clauses A and B, represented by $A \triangle B$, is the set of all BC Values which are resolved from A or B and are not resolved from both, A and B.*

Definition 2. *The Complement operation of a BC Clause A, represented by $\overline{A}$, is the set of all BC Values which belong to the BCG and are not resolved from A. In contrast to all other UCM operands, complement is a unary operand.*

E-UCM Metamodel, Enhancement II. The unconditional expressiveness of the arbitrary BC and foundations for reasoning are the main prerequisites to model and to exploit BC. We implement these tenets by extending the standard UCM BC Expression metamodel described in [1]. Compared to the original metamodel, the operands Symmetric Exclusion and Complement have been added (Fig. 2, Mark 2) to the list of the allowed operands.

As explained earlier, UCM defines a Compound BC Clause as a BC Clause which consists of two ordered BC Clauses connected by a UCM operand. Therefore, the standard UCM operands are only binary. However, we have enhanced the methodology by the additional unary operand Complement. Thus, a Compound BC Clause can now consist of two ordered BC Clauses connected by the binary operand, or it can consist of only one BC Clause with the assigned Complement operand.

We have implemented the described requirements by changing the multiplicity of 2 to 1..2 of the aggregation which relates Compound BC Clause and BC Clause in the UCM BC Expression metamodel (Fig. 2, Mark 3). Furthermore, as shown in Fig. 2, Mark 4, we have introduced the new constraint that the multiplicity of 1 is only valid for the unary operand. The multiplicity of 2 is valid in case that two ordered BC Clauses are connected by a binary operand. In both situations, a BC Clause can be either a Simple BC Clause or a new, recursive Compound BC Clause. Thus, our enhanced metamodel preserves a mechanism to express BC of an arbitrary complexity.

4   Conclusion and Future Work

In this paper we described our approach to represent and formally define business context. Our research foundations are underpinned by the Unified Context

Methodology. We stipulate that the original UCM approach is not complete and that it is not directly applicable to real-world scenarios. Therefore, we extend this methodology and explain our Enhanced Unified Context Model (E-UCM). The presented work provides two main contributions: the enhancement of the UCM BCG based approach and the extension of the list of the UCM operands. The corresponding enhancements utilize the already known methods which originate from different scientific areas (graph theory, distributed systems, set theory, computational logic, general context understanding, etc.) in the domain of BC.

Our *first contribution* represents a transition from a centralized to a decentralized BCG approach. Consequently, the total number of nodes and edges in the BCG is significantly reduced, which in turn decreases the cost of graph initialization and maintenance operations. Furthermore, this allows re-using existing subgraphs and embedding them into the decentralized BCG. Hence, in contrast to the original approach, the E-UCM addresses the norms, such as interoperability, scalability, consistency and flexibility.

Our *second contribution* provides the formal definition of two new operands (Symmetric Exclusion and Complement). Thus, we enrich the expressiveness of the original UCM and establish the foundations for the BC reasoning.

The described research is financially supported by the Vienna PhD School of Informatics [9].

References

1. UN/CEFACT. Unified Context Methodology technical specification (January 2011), http://www.unece.org/cefact/ (last visit: May 2013)
2. UN/CEFACT. Core Components Technical Specification CCTS, version 3.0 (September 2009), http://www.unece.org/cefact/ (last visit: May 2013)
3. Dey, A.K., Abowd, G.D.: Towards a better understanding of context and context-awareness. In: Workshop on The What, Who, Where, When, and How of Context-Awareness, as part of the 2000 Conference on Human Factors in Computing Systems (CHI 2000) (April 2000)
4. Strang, T., Linnhoff-Popien, C.: A context modeling survey. In: First International Workshop on Advanced Context Modelling, Reasoning and Management, UbiComp, August 18 (2004)
5. Novakovic, D., Huemer, C.: A survey on business context. In: Proceedings of the International Conference on Advanced Computing, Networking, and Informatics (ICACNI), Raipur, Chhattisgarh, India (2013)
6. Department of Economic and Social Affairs Statistics Division. International Standard Industrial Classification of All Economic Activities (ISIC), Revision 4. United Nations Publications (2009)
7. Cormen, T.H., Leiserson, C.E., Rivest, R.L., Stein, C.: Introduction to Algorithms, 3rd edn. MIT Press (2009)
8. Novakovic, D., Huemer, C.: Business context sensitive business documents: Business context aware Core Components modeling using the E-UCM model. In: Proceedings of the 11th IEEE International Conference on Industrial Informatics (INDIN 2013), Bochum, Germany (2013)
9. Vienna PhD School of Informatics, http://www.informatik.tuwien.ac.at/teaching/phdschool

Modelling Behaviour Semantically

David Butt[1], Rebekah Wegener[2], and Jörg Cassens[3]

[1] Department of Linguistics,
Macquarie University NSW 2109,
Sydney, Australia
david.butt@ling.mq.edu.au
[2] First Year Experience Unit,
Macquarie University NSW 2109,
Sydney, Australia
rebekah.wegener@mq.edu.au
[3] Institute for Mathematics and Applied Informatics,
University of Hildesheim,
Hildesheim, Germany
cassens@cs.uni-hildesheim.de

Abstract. Context is only one of several strata of meaning and we can not predict realisation at the lexical or grammatical level from context alone. Yet, there is a tendency to confuse contextual patterning with semantic patterning and allocate patterning to the contextual level that might better be dealt with on other levels. While much work has been done on theorising lexis and grammar and, more recently, on seeing these in context, much remains to be done on theorising semantics as a separate level mediating between context and lexis and grammar. This paper examines the problem of modelling behaviour and the challenge of understanding behaviour in context as well as on a semantic level. By understanding the descriptive responsibilities allocated to each level of language, we are better able to see what remains to be covered by context within a model.

1 Introduction: The Non-isomorphic Nature of Language

A complex phenomenon such as language, or indeed any meaning making system, encompasses different orders of complexity. While some theories of language attempt to deal with this complexity through the notion of components (see summaries in Steinberg and Jakobvits [12]; Lyons [10] and more recently Anderson and Lightfoot [1]), treating language as if it were an engineering problem, others use the notion of stratification or systems of patterning of a particular kind (see for example Lamb [9]).

The Systemic Functional Theory of Language (SFL, [5]) introduces such a stratified model of language. Despite divergence within the SFL community over the details of the argument, SFL generally argues that the meaning making of a group can best be described by the co-interpretation of 4 orders of abstraction (compare e.g. Fig. 1 from Halliday and Matthiessen, [5]): *context* (culture

P. Brézillon, P. Blackburn, and R. Dapoigny (Eds.): CONTEXT 2013, LNAI 8175, pp. 343–349, 2013.

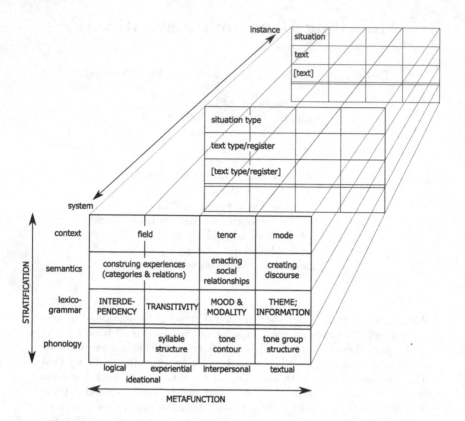

Fig. 1. The dimensions of language - Halliday and Matthiessen (2004)

and situation, or elements of the social structure as they pertain to meaning); *semantics* (systems of meaning); *lexicogrammar* (wordings and structure); and ultimately, of *expression* in various forms e.g. phonology, graphology, gesture, behaviour, art, architecture etc. The meaning bearing level of pragmatics, which can be found in other linguistic theories, belongs to SFL's context strata.

A stratified view of language is not, however, an argument for autonomous strata and, while the relationship between the strata is not isomorphic, certain patternings are descernable. These patterns might best be described as an ensemble effect that can be seen in the way that language functions as a unitary whole. There is perhaps a relative consensus that this ensemble patterning is how the linguistic system operates. It becomes much more problematic when we move beyond the linguistic system to include other meaning making modalities such as behaviour. This is further compounded when we include non-human meaning makers such as animals or smart devices and environments.

While each of the strata is meaning bearing, an account of meaning depends, in particular, on the alignments between the systematic statements of context, semantics and lexicogrammar (or what is known as lexis and syntax in other approaches). The focus in this paper is on the value of a level of semantics, the relationship between semantics and context and the role that this plays in understanding and modelling behaviour. This has consequences for the development of contextualised systems: when we design a system, on which strata do we model different (observable) parameters? For example, if, in an ambient assisted living environment, we model how a person gets up from a chair, is that a parameter of context, or should it be described as a semantic feature?

2   Semantics as a Level of Language

By themselves, statements about context cannot predict realisations in the lexicogrammar for the description of a given situation type. For example, knowing that a text is a "fairy tale" does not, on its own, predict the wording "once upon a time...". What it does predict is the semantics of *temporal distance* and *person particularisation* (see Hasan, [6,7]). Semantic statements such as these, make it possible to establish motivations for the different choices and, thereby, suggest probabilities for each wording.

While all levels of language are meaning bearing and carry meaning in their own right, the semantic stratum acts as a location for statements of what might be called *identifiable meaning*. This repository is important because without a common baseline for meaning, every way of representing an idea becomes unique. Categories such as explanation, question or statement that are typically considered to be at the level of semantics would, if considered as unique, no longer exist, and the commonality on which these terms are based would disappear.

These semantic categories are realised in various ways depending on context. We may, for example, ask a question by declaring or by using final rising intonation for a sentence. Similarly, while the clause "because I say so" may have the lexical and syntactic markers of an explanation (and can serve as one), even a 2 year old child will realise that such a response is not an explanation semantically.

To understand how categories such as questions and explanations work, we need to take a cross stratal slice that shows the ensemble effect that is at work when we make meaning. This is the motivation for setting semantics as a separate stratum between accounts of context and accounts of grammar.

At the semantic stratum, every language user has interpretations of what counts as the relevant units in a way that is less likely as we move into the more technical aspects of, say lexicogrammar. Consequently, there exists a plethora of variously formalised classifications from rhetoric to folklore as to what semantics needs to encompass. Existing proposals are also notable for their diversity of 'scale' from genre to text to semantic feature or atom.

Other proposals for semantics from the theoretical body of SFL include: Rhetorical structure theory (RST, e.g. Halliday and Matthiessen [4]); message semantic networks/cohesive harmony (Hasan, e.g. [7]); Sequence/Figure/Element (Halliday and Matthiessen, e.g. [5]); discourse semantics/Appraisal (Martin); and rhetorical units (Cloran). For non-systemic approaches, we can mention speech act, componentialist, or scripts and plans. These approaches reflect the diversity of interests in meaning and the impact this has on what is considered to be a relevant unit at semantics.

3   What Remains to Be Covered by Semantics?

Semantics needs to make visible the precise contrasts between the discourse under examination and other forms of relevant interaction. Semantics involves comparison, as does linguistics in general. The root of this fundamental aspect of linguistics is the fact that linguistics, as Firth expressed it, is the strange practice of 'turning language back on itself' [3]. This paper proposes that we need to formulate a way of understanding the relationship between different kinds of statements in semantics. Further, it is necessary to form a way of operationalising semantics so that different phenomena of meaning, phenomena at different points along a scale of semantic structures, can be characterised and related to context or text structure (above semantics) and to the most probable systems in the lexicogrammar.

We can identify four problems of semantic description:

1. It must be elaborated to a practical degree of delicacy.
2. It should recognise the usefulness of language turned back on itself in contrast to introducing a metalinguistic description which pretends to exist outside of natural language.
3. It needs to use the full range of terms in the language to provide the basis for characterising Messages/Arguments and Moves.
4. It has to be consistent with Saussure's injunctions against assuming the mental experience of the signs of a language was anything other than the mental experience of the actual signs of a language.

4   Why Semantics Is Important: A Behaviour Example

One of the areas where the need for distinguishing between context and semantics becomes crucial is with the modelling of behaviour. Human behaviour, let alone behaviour of non-human entities, has provided an interesting challenge for many linguists over the centuries. Indeed, while most would concede that behaviour is related and crucial to spoken language, many linguists draw the line at including behaviour within the domain of linguistics. More often behaviour is seen as contextually relevant for spoken language and it is this that causes confusion for the modelling of behaviour.

While behaviour forms the context for spoken language and can be used to explain some of the variation in language, when that behaviour becomes the object of analysis, it is no longer contextual but is in fact textual. Frequently, the challenge of modelling behaviour is treated as a contextual problem when it is a semantic and grammatical problem. To explain this distinction further, we give an example from a smart environments application domain: the example of modelling behaviour for the purpose of building automatic sliding doors.

Kofod-Petersen, Wegener and Cassens [8] put forward the idea that it should be possible to model human behaviour sufficiently clearly to make it possible to distinguish between standing outside a door and talking, walking past a door and going through a door. This, they argue, would be equivalent to modelling intention to go through a door and would allow for the construction of automatic doors that responded to human behaviour rather than to proximity.

The modelling of behaviour for this task took various forms that represent patterning on different strata. Firstly, the components of human behaviour such as visual target, shoulder angle, hip angle, etc were defined. This represents a constituency problem and can be likened to defining the constituency of spoken or written language. Secondly, these elements were combined to form a grammar. This represents a structural problem that might be considered similar to defining a localised grammar for behaviour even if only for a restricted set. This grammar was then addressed to the challenge of defining human intention to walk through a door. This is a semantic problem and looks at how humans display intention behaviourally. Finally, contextual factors impacting on behaviour such as individual and cultural differences in behaviour, placement of doors within the build environment and surrounding features of that environment were also considered with respect to how they would create variation in behaviour.

Of course, research did not necessarily proceed in this linear fashion. As is typically the case with complex meaning systems, it is more usual to range across the strata, so that often we start with a semantic concept such as the display of intention through behaviour and restrict this in some way through context e.g. how is intention to walk through a door displayed in behaviour. This restriction makes establishing the constituency and grammar a much easier task.

In testing the hypothesis outlined in Kofod-Petersen, Wegener and Cassens [8], Solem [11] considered numerous instances of behaviour to establish the accuracy of the key constituents and their most common structural arrangement. In building the doors and moving towards a more commercial application of the idea, Solem [11] restricted the context even further, considering only behaviour relevant to sliding doors located withing a controlled environment such as a corridor. This work produced doors that can respond to human behaviour within the parameters defined for the task. What remains for future work, is to take into account contextual factors and the variation these contextual factors will create to make the doors more robust and generalisable.

Another example where it might prove useful to look at syntax in its own right comes from the area of ambient assisted living. When determining whether an inhabitant is in need of help, it is often necessary to detect falls. But determining whether a person has fallen or is laying on the floor for a different reason is not a context parameter. It is a syntactic parameter in a dialectic relationship with context – e.g., whether the person is doing some yoga exercise both construes the possibility of being on the floor as being on the floor construes the yoga exercise context.

Humans being on the floor, getting up from chairs or moving to go through doors is not context and attempting to solve these modelling problems at the level of context will only result in confusion. Human movement in this case is the text and context is the surrounding or environment that effects that behaviour.

The depth of the chair might shape the movement of getting out of that chair or the area in front of a door influences the angle of the body of a person entering that door. The behaviour itself is a question of semantics.

5   Conclusion and Further Work

This work demonstrates the need to work with a concept of semantics. It is necessary to allocate problems to different strata if we are to properly model in context. It is a definite risk to treat behaviour as a contextual problem, because this belies the fact that context impacts on behaviour.

Behaviour has its own stratal arrangement with constituency, grammar, semantics and context. It remains to be seen how this stratal arrangement is organised and how this relates to spoken and written language.

We have argued for treating the strata of semantics as a separate plane to model, be it when trying to understand the meaning-making system after the fact, or when trying to design contextualised computer systems.

While we have given an example for modelling behaviour on a semantic level, we have not proposed a general model of semantics in this paper. From the theoretical considerations and the lessons learned in practical applications, we find that a model of semantics needs to account for the following aspects:

1. We need to draw on systemic description from context, from semantics, from lexicogrammar, and from the expression plane. This is a stratification of patterns, patterns of different orders of abstraction. Without some systems at all levels, comparisons become 'one off' expositions.
2. We need to group systems according to their dominant semantic contribution, or what is called the metafunction in SFL.
3. We need to enquire as to the role of a rank scale. In lexicogrammar we have morpheme – word – group – clause – (clause complex) in a constituency hierarchy. In phonology we might have phoneme – syllable – foot – tone group. But what about the semantics?
4. We need to think of our work according to 2 different axes of linguistic organisation – as paradigmatic choices (this, and not those options) and as syntagmatic series (given this, what can follow? what predicts the elements which follow?).
5. We need to check our findings against any existing text archives or corpora in order to ground them in natural language.

Further attempts to provide the kinds of statements necessary to carry description between context and lexicogrammar, between lexicogrammar and context have to be made. The non-isomorphic relationship between the levels of language is the basis for separating out the strata or levels of language and provides the main resource for displaying how humans use and develop their meaning potential.

Rhetoric offers us many of the most useful tools for semantic analysis – namely, those that have the greatest consequence for actual analysis. This last claim, however, begs the question of what is consequential, useful, for better or worse in an investigation which depends on a description of meaning. Furthermore, language is a multilayered network of "differences" (inherent comparison). Comparison is, then, at the heart of the concept of sign. Comparisons are also the way to ground semantic projects.

Yet understanding semantics as comparisons both solves problems and raises more questions. If comparison is the key step in the activity of semantics – in the study of meanings for solving problems – then what are the bases of such comparison? Furthermore, how do we go about a linguistic comparison or even a semantic comparison when so many 'relations' may be relevant to the issues under enquiry?

References

1. Anderson, S., Lightfoot, D.: The Language Organ: linguistics as cognitive physiology. Cambridge University Press, Cambridge (2002)
2. Brown, R., Butow, P., Butt, D.G., Moore, A.R., Tattersall, M.H.: Developing ethical strategies to assist oncologists in seeking informed consent to cancer clinical trials. Social Science & Medicine 58, 379–390 (2004)
3. Firth, J.R.: Personality and language in society. Papers in Linguistics 1934-1951, pp. 177–189. Oxford University Press, London (1950, 1957)
4. Halliday, M.A.K., Matthiessen, C.M.I.M.: Construing experience through meaning: a language-based approach to cognition. Cassell, London (1999)
5. Halliday, M.A.K., Matthiessen, C.M.I.M.: An Introduction to Functional Grammar, 3rd edn. Arnold, London (2004)
6. Hasan, R.: Semantic networks: a tool for the analysis of meaning. In: Cloran, C., Butt, D., Williams, G. (eds.) Ways of Saying, Ways of Meaning: Selected Papers of Ruqaiya Hasan. Cassell, London (1996)
7. Hasan, R.: The World in Words: Semiotic Mediation, Tenor, and Ideology. In: Williams, G., Lukin, A. (eds.) The Development of Language: Functional Perspectives on Species and Individuals. Continuum, London (2004)
8. Kofod-Petersen, A., Wegener, R., Cassens, J.: Closed Doors – Modelling Intention in Behavioural Interfaces. In: Proceedings of the Norwegian Artificial Intelligence Society Symposium (NAIS 2009). Tapir Forlag, Trondheim (2009)
9. Lamb, S.: Outline of Stratificational Grammar. Georgetown University Press, Georgetown (1966)
10. Lyons, J.: Introduction to theoretical linguistics. Cambridge University Press, Cambridge (1968)
11. Solem, J.S., Aambø Fosstveit, H., Blake, R., Kofod-Petersen, A.: Intention-based sliding doors. Poster and Demonstration Presented at SCAI 2011. Proceedings SCAI 2011. IOS Press (2011)
12. Steinberg, D., Jakobvits, L.: Semantics: An Interdisciplinary Reader in Philosophy, Linguistics, and Psychology, pp. 18–22. Cambridge University Press, Cambridge (1972, 2004)

Contextual-Ontologies for an AutoE-Learning Process

Nacima Mellal

University Larbi Ben M'hidi, Algeria
Mellal_nassima@yahoo.com

Abstract. According to Brézillon, context is not directly involved in solving a problem, but forced his resolution. In educational community, knowledge is transmitted from tutor to learner(s). However, two main issues are occurred. On one hand, Learner is facing resource bank and s/he has to seek the appropriate information from the relevant resource. To solve this problem, it is required to help learner by providing the context of resources in a pertinent organization. Ontologies represent the essential technology for the organization of eLearning resources. On the other hand, a massive amount of ontologies have spread among eLearning Systems. Our objective is to coordinate these ontologies in order to expand the (re)use, the search, the share of learning resources. For that aim, we propose a method which defines laws to relate automatically relevant parts of different ontologies, based on a mathematical model "Information Flow".

Keywords: E-Learning, Learning Resources, Context-Goal, Contextual Ontologies, Information Flow Model.

1 Introduction

The E-Learning is a new trend towards personalization of learning that is supported by advancements in information technology. It makes access to educational resource very fast, just-in-time and relevance, at any time or place. The main goal of e-learning is to enhance learner autonomy.

According to Jean Houssaye Pedagogical Triangle [1] three essential elements are distinguished in the process of learning: Knowledge, Learner and Tutor. Knowledge represents the learning resources (courses, references, ..). Tutor has the knowledge and transmits it to learner. This last, receives the learning. The e-learning tutor plays a critical role. s/he is the main agent responsible for the delivery of the courses and the support of the learners. Four main tutor roles are distinguished: *Pedagogical roles, Social role, Managerial roles and Technical roles.* For a successful learning, we must follow pedagogical methods. In [3], four pedagogical methods are distinguished: Expositive, Demonstrative, Interrogative and Active. Learner is facing resource bank with unstructured content and s/he has to seek the appropriate information from the relevant resource. This is the active method principle. In our work, we are interesting to the last. However, it is assumed that the tutor is in a difficult position, because s\he does not know the context, learners are different. The tutor should spend much

P. Brézillon, P. Blackburn, and R. Dapoigny (Eds.): CONTEXT 2013, LNAI 8175, pp. 350–356, 2013.

time to create or find new resources to offer online. Thus, it is required on one hand to reduce and/or replace the hard work of tutors by organizing resources in a sound manner to facilitate their access, research by learners.

Recent works propose 'Ontologies' as a great potential in education. They are a mean for description, sharing and reusing information among eLearning systems. They enable confortable research of appropriate resources for learners [3],[4],[5]. However, the proliferation of ontologies causes another issue it becomes necessary to coordinate ontologies in order to perform the interoperability. Thus, there is a need to develop automatic techniques for ontologies connection. The present paper is divided into four sections. In the first one, we define the Contextual-Ontology. In the second section, we present the appropriate part of IF model which serves to automatize the coordination between Ontologies. The third section presents the proposed method. Finally a summary with future research is included in the fourth section.

2   Contextual Ontologies

A considerable amount of the research on knowledge-based systems moves towards ontologies[10],[11],[12],[13]. An Ontology is described in [6], [7] as a formal explicit specification of a shared conceptualization. They find applicability in many domains, in system engineering, knowledge management, eLearning systems. In our approach, and basing on the Pedagogical Triangle principle [1], ontologies are used to serve Learner/Tutor activities. These lasts lead to two types of interactions: Interaction between *Learner* and *Knowledge*: ontologies enable the knowledge acquisition/ retrieval by learner.   Interaction between *Learner* and *Tutor*: to facilitate understanding and interpretation of exchanged resources.

2.1   Context-Goal Notion

The notion of context is important in understanding the world. McCarthy defines context as a generalization of a collection of hypotheses. According to Brézillon, the context is always relative to something: the context of an object, the context of an action, the context of interaction: "what constrains something without intervening in it explicitly." [8]. In our case, we are interested to the context of action. Learner/Tutor activities are represented by actions. Reaching the activity means achieving a goal. Associating an action to a Context represents a Goal.

Different context models are presented in the literature. In [9], a context is expressed by a recording of dependent types which is a sequence of fields in which labels li correspond to certain types Ti. They are modeled by tuples. Inspired by this idea, we formalize contexts distinguishing two categories, Type-Context and Token-Context. *Type-Context*: a type of context C is a set of object types $\{T1, T2, .. Tm\}$ describing entities, properties and/or constraints. We formalize C by the following tuple: $C = [\ l1 : T1\ l2 : T2 ... lm : Tm$ for example, C = [T :Title , A : Author

Token-Context: a token of context is the instantiation of a Type-Context, for example,
   C=[T : Contextual-Ontologies for an Auto-E-Learning Process   A : Mellal Nacima

In our case study, the activities of different actors are expressed by the notion of goal which is defined by the result of an action associated to a particular context, called the context of the action. When the context is a Type-Context, we speak about "type of Goal" and when it is a Token-Context, we speak about Token-Goal. For example,   the tutor adds a title of the learning content, the type of goal is:
          (C1=[T: Title, A: Author, g0], g1 = add(T))

The associated Token-Goal is : (C1=[T : Contextual-Ontologies for an Automatic E-Learning Process, A : Mellal Nacima, g0], g1 = add(Contextual-Ontologies for an Automatic E-Learning Process)). In our work, we aim to success a learning of a course by learner. This course is delivered by tutor. To achieve this goal, we have based on the following course structure The course is divided on 3 elements (subject, course, unit). The unit content is (Goal, Title, lesson). Lesson has a (goal, title, description and references). According to this structure, we propose a set of Context-Goal pairs concerning Learner which aims to search a course and learn it and a set of Context-Goal pairs concerning the Tutor where the purpose is to create and deliver the course.

- Goal pairs concerning the Tutor :

Login (C0, g0),   C0=[T: Tutor, U: Username, P: Password   and g0 = login(T)
Add Title-Lesson(C1, g1),   C1=[T: Title, A: Author, g0 andg1 = addL(T)
Add Reference(C2, g2), C2=[R: Reference, L: Link of reference,g0 and g2 = add(R)
Add Description (C3, g3), C3=[D : Description, K:Key words,g0 and g3 = add(D ,K)
Add Lesson-Goal (C4, g4),C4=[G:Goal, g0 and g4 = add(G)
Add title-Unit(C1, g5)   C1=[T: Title, A: Author, g0 and   g5 = addU(T)
Create lesson(C5,g6),   C5=[L : lesson, g1,g2,g3,g4 and g6 = create(L)
Add Unit-Goal (C4, g7),   C4=[G:Goal, g0 and g7 = add(G)
Create Subject(C6,g8),   C6=[S: Subject, g0 and g8 = create(S)
Create Unit (C7,g9),   C7=[U:Unit, g5,g6,g7 and g9=Create(U)
Create Course (C8,g10), C8=[C:Course,g8,g9 and g10=Create(C)

- Goal pairs concerning the Learner :
login (C0, g0),   C0=[Lr: Learner, U: Username, P: Password and g0 = login(Lr) Search
subject(C1, g1),   C1=[S: Subject, T:Title, A: Author, g0 and g1 = Search(S)
Select lesson(C2,g2),   C2=[L: Lesson, g1 and g2 = Select(L)
DownloadCourse (C3,g3), C3=[C:Course, A: Author,g2 and G3 = download(C)

2.2   Relations between Context Goal Pairs

Causal Dependence. This notion depends on another definition, which is the contextual inclusion.

Definition1. Contextual Inclusion
Let (C, γ) and (C ', γ') two pairs of type contexts and goals (resp. tokens), γ is a type

of goal representing the result of a given action on C. If C ' contains γ, then we say that γ is included in C' and wrote : γ⊆C', For example : g0⊆C1

The validity of the Context-goal pair (C ', γ) depends on the completion of the goal γ. In other words, we say that the pair (C, γ) "causes" the occurrence of (C ', γ). For example, (C0,g0) causes the occurrence of (C1,g1).

Definition2. Causal dependence
A pair Context-Goal (Cl ,γm)i(k) of level i in system k is on causal relationship with the pair (Cl+1, γm+1)i(k) in the same level and same system if γm i(k) ⊆Cl+1 , we note :   (Cl , γm)i(k) ≤ (Cl+1, γm+1)i(k), We give for example: (C0,g0) ≤ (C1,g1)

Subsumption Dependence
Definition3. Subsumption of Context-Goal pairs A pair Context-goal (Cq, γr) i +1 (k) of level i +1 in system k subsumes a plan (Cl, γm) i(k), ..., (Cl+p, γ m+p) i(k) at level i o the same system if the achievement of (γr)i+1(k) depends on the achievement of all the goals of the sequence types (γ m, ..., γ m+p) i (k). We note: (Cl, γ m) i(k). . . (Cl+p, γm+p) i (k) ⟨ (Cq, γr) i +1 (k)

In our example, we have : (C0,g0) , (C1,g1) , ...(C7,g9) ⟨ (C8,g10).

From this, the concepts of the proposed ontology are pairs Context-Goal. Causal and Subsumption dependencies are the relationships between concepts. As a result, the Contextual Ontology is defined by a tuple : O = (CG ,≤,⟨), where CG is a set of Context-Goal pairs. Initially, we propose, two Contextual ontologies: Tutor Ontology (TO), Learner Ontology (LO) (see Fig. 1)

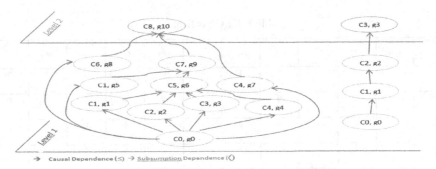

Fig. 1. Tutor and Learner Contextual-Ontologies

3   Information Flow Model

The IF Model describes how information can flow through channels to convey new information under first order logic. Each local component is described by an IF Classification. This last is a very simple mathematical structure. As it is defined in [14], it consists of a set of objects to be classified, called tokens and a set of objects used to classify the tokens. Classifications are linked by applications called Infomorphisms.

Infomorphisms provide a way to move information back and forth between systems. The information flow in a distributed system is expressed in terms of an IF theory of this system, that is a set of laws describing the system. These laws are expressed by a set of types. The theory is specified by a set of sequents, so by a set of types and the relation between them (⊢). The overall "Classification" and "IF theory" constitute what is called a local logic. That is, this system has its own logic expressed by its types. Information Channel is the key for modeling information flow in distributed systems. It is the main step in the process of coordination. The IF theory describes how the different types from different classifications are logically related to each other. For more details, the reader is invited to see the book 'Information Flow: The Logic of Distributed Systems'[14].

4   Process of Ontology Coordination

The process of coordination is summarized into three steps: Identification of possible classifications, Generation of their theories and Construction of the channel.

4.1   Identification of Possible Classifications in System S1 (Tutor), S2 (Learner)

A classification A is a triple $< tok(A), typ(A), \models A>$, which consists of: a set $tok(A)$ of objects to be classified known as the instances of A that carry information, a set $typ(A)$ of objects used to classify the instances, the types of A, a binary relation $\models A$ between $tok(A)$ and $typ(A)$ that tells one which tokens are classified as being of which types.   We have C1 the classification in S1 and C'1 for S2 (see tables 3 and 4)

Table 1. C1 Classification

⊨C1	(C0, G0)	(C1, G1)	(C2, G2)	(C3, G3)	(C4, G4)	(C1, G5)	(C5, G6)	(C4, G7)	(C6, G8)	(C7, G9)	(C8, G10)
G0	1	1	1	1	1	1	0	1	1	0	0
G1	0	1	0	0	0	0	1	0	0	0	0
G2	0	0	1	0	0	0	1	0	0	0	0
G3	0	0	0	1	0	0	1	0	0	0	0
G4	0	0	0	0	1	0	1	0	0	0	0
G5	0	0	0	0	0	1	1	0	0	1	0
G6	0	0	0	0	0	0	1	0	0	1	0
G7	0	0	0	0	0	0	0	1	0	1	0
G8	0	0	0	0	0	0	0	0	1	0	1
G9	0	0	0	0	0	0	0	0	0	1	1
G10	0	0	0	0	0	0	0	0	0	0	1

Table 2. C' Classification

/=C'1	(C0, g0)	(C1, g1)	(C2, g2)	(C3, g3)
g0	1	1	1	1
g1	0	1	1	0
g2	0	0	1	1
g3	0	0	0	1

4.2   Generation of Possible Theories

An IF theory T is a pair $<$ typ(T), $\vdash$-T$>$ where typ(T) is a set of types and $\vdash$-T , a binary relation between subsets of typ(T). For the classification C1 in S1, we have : $\vdash$-C1 (C8,g10); (C0,g0) $\vdash$-C1 (C1,g1), (C2,g2), (C3,g3), (C4,g4), (C1,g5), (C4,g7), (C6,g8); (C1,g1), (C2,g2), (C3,g3), (C4,g4) $\vdash$-C1 (C5,g6);   (C1,g5), (C5,g6) $\vdash$-C1 (C7,g9);

For the classification C'1 in S2, we have: $\vdash$-C'1 (C3,g3); (C0,g0) $\vdash$-C'1 (C1,g1); (C1,g1) $\vdash$-C'1 (C2,g2)

4.3   Construction of the Channel

In our example, the need, to map between ontologies, occurs when the learner searches for a subject in order to download content, we speak about pair (C1, g1) in system S2. To connect this pair with another of the other system we need to define a new classification A which plays the role of a reference in order to compare the types of the distributed classifications (see Table 5).

Table 3. A Classification

/=A	g1
A	0
B	1

We compare the types of C1 with those of C'1, which gives rise to an infomorphism connecting A with C1 and C'1. $I^{(1)} : A \Leftrightarrow C1^{\perp}$ and $I^{(1)} : A \Leftrightarrow C'1^{\perp}$

Applying the property of infomorphism, we have with C1: $I^{(1)\vee}((C0,g0)) = b$; $I^{(1)\vee}((C1,g1)) = a$; $I^{(1)\vee}((C2,g2)) = a$; $I^{(1)\vee}((C3,g3)) = a$; $I^{(1)\vee}((C4,g4)) = a$; $I^{(1)\vee}((C1,g5)) = a$; $I^{(1)\vee}((C5,g6)) = a$; $I^{(1)\vee}((C4,g7)) = a$; $I^{(1)\vee}((C6,g8)) = b$; $I^{(1)\vee}((C7,g9)) = a$; $I^{(1)\vee}((C8,g10)) = a$; We have with C'1: $I^{(1)\wedge}(g1) = g1$

The ontologies coordination allows the generation of the desired channel between C1(S1) and C2(S2). A core classification C is built with a couple of infomorphisms: $I'(1) : C \Leftrightarrow C1$ and $I'(1) : C \Leftrightarrow C'1$. C allows tokens connection of different classifications through the information channel. The theory expresses how the types of C1 are related logically to those of C'. the IF theory relates (C1,g1) with (C0, g0) and (C2,g2) in C1 classification. The constraints in the IF-theory are the following: (C0,g0) $\vdash$- (C1,g1) and (C6,g8) $\vdash$- (C1,g1). The IF logic being defined by a classification and an IF theory gives constraints in terms of sequent, we obtain : $((C0,g0)^{(S1)}, (C1,g1)^{(S2)})$,$((C6,g8)^{(S1)}, (C1,g1)^{(S2)})$ relating Context-Goal pairs of the two systems. According to the initial constraints, the second sequent matches all condition. From this point, the coordination of the two ontologies is based on a mathematic model.

5 Conclusion

In this paper, we have presented a formal method for the coordination of ontologies in an automatic mode, based on the IF model. This facilitates and allows an expanded research and easy manipulation of resources by both Learner and Tutor. Our method contributes to improve the learning process. On one hand, learners learn to be autonomous actors and leaders of their learning. On the other hand, tutor's work is reduced. We aim, in future work, to replace tutors per software agents which behave according to the proposed method. The quest is not to find a miracle solution but improving the quality of learning is our goal.

References

1. Houssaye, J.: Le triangle pédagogique. Peter Lange, Berne (1980)
2. Kalfoglou, Y., Schorlemmer, W.M.: If-map: an ontology mapping method based on information flow theory. In: Spaccapietra, S., March, S., Aberer, K. (eds.) Journal on Data Semantics I. LNCS, vol. 2800, pp. 98–127. Springer, Heidelberg (2003)
3. Snae, C., Brueckner, M.: Ontology-driven e-learning system based on roles and activities for Thai learning environment. Interdisciplinary Journal of Knowledge and Learning Objects 3 (2007)
4. Sridharan, B., Hepu, D., Corbitt, J.: An ontology-driven topic mapping approach to multilevel management of e-learning resources. In: Proc. ECIS 2009 (2009)
5. Gasevic, D., Hatala, M.: Ontology mappings to improve learning resource search. British Journal of Educational Technology 37(3), 375–389
6. Gruber, T.R.: A translation approach to portable ontology specifications. Journal of Knowledge Acquisition, 199–220 (1993)
7. Fikes, R.: Ontologies: What are they, and where's the research? In: Proc. KR 1996, Cambridge, Massachusetts (1996)
8. Brézillon, P., Pomerol, J.-C.: Contextual knowledge sharing and cooperation in intelligent assistant systems. Le Travail Humain 62(3), 223–246 (1999)
9. Dapoigny, R., Barlatier, P.: Deriving behavior from goal structure for the intelligent control of physical systems. In: Informatics in Control, Automation and Robotics (2007)
10. Aroyo, L., Dicheva, D.: Learning and Teaching Support for WWW-based Education. International Journal for Continuing Engineering Education 11(1/2), 152–164 (2001)
11. Aroyo, L., Dicheva, D.: Authoring Support in Concept-based Web Information Systems for Educational Applications. International Journal of Continuous Engineering Education and Life-long Learning 14(3), 297–312 (2004)
12. Devedzic, V.: Next-generation Web-based Education. International Journal for Continuing Engineering Education and Life-long Learning 11(1/2), 232–247 (2003)
13. Dicheva, D., Aroyo, L., Cristea, A.: Cooperative Courseware-Authoring Support. International Journal of Computers and Applications 25(3), 179–187 (2003)
14. Barwise, J.: Information Flow: The Logic of Distributed Systems, vol. (44). Cambridge University Press (1997)

Context Aware Business Documents Modeling

Danijel Novakovic and Christian Huemer

Institute of Software Technology and Interactive Systems
Vienna University of Technology
Favoritenstrasse 9-11/188, A-1040 Vienna, Austria
{novakovic,huemer}@big.tuwien.ac.at
http://www.isis.tuwien.ac.at/

Abstract. The reliable, efficient and seamless exchange of business information is essential for a successful execution of the interwoven business processes. However, development of the contents for electronic data exchange is time consuming and usually can not follow the agile demands of the today's business. If we could contextualize the pieces of the currently valid business information, we could predict its possible context specific variations. Therefore, the business contextual knowledge in which the already existing data contents are valid could be exploited to (semi-) automatically generate new, more homogeneous contents for electronic data interchange.

Keywords: business context, business context model, business context aware documents, (semi-) automatic generation of e-business documents.

1 Introduction

Inter-organizational business processes usually imply a cross-industry collaboration which is established between business enterprises located worldwide. Therefore, the business contextual surrounding, such as the concrete industry branch and geopolitical region, can be used to refine the particular business process and all context dependant scenarios of its possible execution flows.

In the previous phases of our research [1] we have developed the Enhanced Unified Context Model (E-UCM) to formally represent business context (BC). Furthermore, we have established theoretical foundations to exploit the contextual information encompassed by the instances of this model. More precisely, we propose in [2] a theoretical approach to contextualize the already existing implementation guidelines of the business documents which are exchanged between inter-organizational business processes. A business document implementation guideline represents a context specific subset of the underlining document standard which is chosen for the development of the particular business documents. This paper underpins these theoretical concepts and explains how they can be implemented in practice. Thus, the proposed algorithms calculate the content model (subset) of a message implementation guideline which is relevant in a required BC presented by the E-UCM context model.

P. Brézillon, P. Blackburn, and R. Dapoigny (Eds.): CONTEXT 2013, LNAI 8175, pp. 357–363, 2013.
© Springer-Verlag Berlin Heidelberg 2013

The remainder of the paper is structured as follows. First, Section 2 presents our BC definition and gives an overview of the E-UCM BC model. In Section 3 we introduce the UN/CEFACT document standard. Furthermore, we explain our theoretical approach to utilize the contextual information contained by Core Components and to (semi-) automatically generate new implementation guidelines of business documents. In Section 4 we present our implementation of the proposed conceptual solution. We elucidate clearly the key functions of the most important elements of the underlying architecture and show how these elements can be implemented by our described algorithms. Finally, Section 5 concludes the paper and gives an outlook on future research directions.

2   Previous Work

Our research presented in [3] defines business context (BC) as metadata that specify the circumstances in which some particular inter-organizational business process is or is not relevant. Accordingly, business contextual metadata consist of the attributes, where each of these attributes belongs to one of the three primary BC categories, namely location, industry and activity. For instance, the following triple (France, Aircraft industry, Invoice order) defines the BC which geopolitical domain is identified as France, industry domain as the aircraft industry and the activity domain as the invoice ordering.

In the following of this paper we formally represent BC using the Enhanced Unified Context Model (E-UCM) [1]. Accordingly, BC is organized in the form of the E-UCM BC Graph. It is the Directed Acyclic Graph (DAG) with organized values to enable normative expressions of BC. A BC value is an atomic piece of a business contextual knowledge which specifies one aspect of the BC (location, industry or activity). A particular set of BC Values can be resolved from the E-UCM BC Graph using the BC Expression. The corresponding metamodel of the BC Expression is shown and described in [1].

3   BC Aware Core Components Modeling

3.1   Core Components

UN/CEFACT is an intergovernmental Standards Development Organization established by the United Nations. It proposes Core Components Technical Specification (CCTS) [4], the methodology which main aim is the standardization of business documents for electronic interchange.

CCTS defines a Core Component business document modeling approach. Accordingly, every business document consists of business data which are encompassed by semantically interoperable data building blocks. CCTS distinguishes between two primary concepts: Core Components (CCs) and Business Information Entities (BIEs).

CCs represent conceptual data model components for the creation of business documents that are not specific to any particular BC. Thereby, they can be used

in any business scenario. CCs consist of three main entity types: Basic Core
Components (BCCs), Aggregated Core Components (ACCs) and Association
Core Components (ASCCs). A BCC is a piece of information which is located
in a business document. Each ACC represents a collection of BCCs. Relations
between ACCs are established by ASCCs. On the other hand, BIEs are logical
data model components which have assigned BCs. Thereby, they are used in
a context specific business scenario. Each BIE is *derived by restriction* from
a CC. Corresponding to the CC concept, building elements of each BIE are:
Basic Business Information Entities (BBIEs), Aggregated Business Information
Entities (ABIEs) and Association Business Information Entities (ASBIEs).

The runtime BC of a BIE often is not the same as its assigned BC. Thereby, in
the following we refer to runtime BC as overall BC. The overall BC of an ABIE
is dependent and, thus, calculated based on the union of the assigned BCs of the
included BBIEs and on the union of the overall BCs of the included ASBIEs.
This can be expressed by the following Formula:

$$BC\_ABIE_{over} = (||_{i=0}^{k} BC\_BBIE_{assig}) \; || \; (||_{i=0}^{l} BC\_ASBIE_{over}) , \qquad (1)$$

where k and l represent the numbers of the included BBIEs and ASBIEs, respectively. The overall BC of an ASBIE is dependent, and, thus, calculated based on
the intersection of its assigned BC and the overall BC of its associated ABIE.
This can be expressed by the following Formula:

$$BC\_ASBIE_{over} = BC\_ASBIE_{assig} \; \&\& \; BC\_AssociatedABIE_{over} . \qquad (2)$$

3.2 Conceptual Solution

We explain our approach to calculate the content model of a business document
implementation guideline (BDocIG) for a required BC in the following. A BC is
represented by the E-UCM BC model. The corresponding documents conform
to the CCTS business document standard.

In the first step of our approach all already existing business document implementation guidelines (ExistBDocIGs) are selected. Afterwards, all BIEs are
extracted from these guidelines and embedded into a Generic Business Document
Implementation Guideline (GenBDocIG). Therefore, the GenBDocIG comprises
the complete already existing business contextual knowledge. Finally, in respect
to the specific user requirements, only those BIEs which are valid in the required
BC are extracted from the GenBDocIG and embedded into a new Customized
Business Document Implementation Guideline (CustBDocIG). Therefore, the
CustBDocIG is the new BDocIG which is relevant in the BC required by user.

4 Implementation

In this Section we show the implementation of the conceptual solution proposed
in Section 3. First, we describe the XML based representation of contextualized
BDocIGs. Afterwards, we explain the architecture which generates new BDocIGs
valid in the particular BC.

```
<xsd:element name="PostCode" type="bdt:StringType">    <xsd:appInfo>
  <xsd:annotation>                                       <ccts:BC> ❶
    <xsd:documentation>                                    <ccts:IndustryBC>(≤ Aircraft)</ccts:IndustryBC>
      <ccts:AcronymCode>BBIE</ccts:AcronymCode>            <ccts:RegionBC>(~ EU) || (~ CH)</ccts:RegionBC>  ❷
      <ccts:UniqueID>f0e2b9ad-7d05</ccts:UniqueID>         <ccts:ActivityBC>(= Invoice)</ccts:ActivityBC>
      ...                                                <ccts:BC>
    <xsd:documentation>                                  </xsd:appInfo>
                                                       </xsd:annotation>
                                                     </xsd:element>
```

Fig. 1. Example - BDocIG Presented Using the Contextualized NDR Specification

4.1 Representation of BC Aware BDocIGs

The UN/CEFACT XML Naming and Design Rules (NDR) [5] is the specification proposed by UN/CEFACT. It formulates the set of rules necessary to develop XML schemas and XML schema based documents which conform to CCTS.

However, the standard NDR specification can not be directly applied to present contextualized business documents. Therefore, in order to provide an instrument to assign and to process business contextual information, the NDR specification must be enhanced. Our corresponding solution introduces the new XML DOM element which is denoted as: $<ccts:BC>$. It is used to specify the concrete BC in which some specific Core Component presented by the XML NDR schema is valid. The introduced element is integrated in the scope of the application information element ($<xsd:appInfo>$) defined by the standard NDR specification. The relevant example is shown in Fig. 1, Mark 1.

Furthermore, the $<ccts:BC>$ element encompasses the following children elements: $<ccts:IndustryBC>$, $<ccts:RegionBC>$ and $<ccts:ActivityBC>$. These are new XML DOM elements which are correspondent to our primary BC categories industry, geopolitical region and activity, respectively. Thus, the subdomains of the BC in which some specific Core Component is valid can be presented by indicating the relevant E-UCM BC Expression [1] within the corresponding BC category tags. This is shown in the example in Fig. 1, Mark 2.

4.2 Architecture

In the following we describe the simplified architecture which implements our approach to model BDocIGs valid in the required BC. The corresponding blueprint and the explanation of its graphical notation are shown in Fig. 2. All processing units and included libraries are developed using the Java programming language. The BDocIGs (*ExistBDocIGs*, *GenBDocIG* and *CustBDocIG*) conform to the enhanced NDR specification explained in the previous Subsection. Business contextual information is presented using the E-UCM BC model introduced in Section 2.

The core of the architecture is the *Business Context Processing Tool* (Fig. 2, Mark 1). This is the processing unit which initiates, controls and coordinates the execution flows of all other elements in the system.

Input Processing. The following input parameters (Fig. 2, Mark 2) are provided by user: (i) identification of the BC Graph (*E-UCM BC Graph ID*),

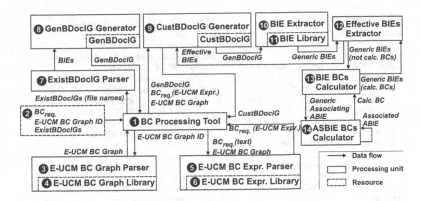

Fig. 2. Architecture

(ii) BC in which the CustBDocIG must be valid (BC_{req}), and (iii) file names of the *ExistBDocIGs*.

The *E-UCM BC Graph ID* is the textual parameter used to unambiguously identify the corresponding E-UCM BC Graph. We present an E-UCM BC Graph as the XML document which underlying schema maps the elements of the E-UCM BC Graph metamodel explained in [1] and [2]. The particular E-UCM BC Graph is resolved by the *E-UCM BC Graph Parser* (Fig. 2, Mark 3). The included *E-UCM BC Graph Library* (Fig. 2, Mark 4) is our Java implementation of the E-UCM BC Graph metamodel.

The BC_{req} is provided as textual data using the BC Expression syntax introduced in Section 2. The *E-UCM BC Expression Parser* (Fig. 2, Mark 5) is the unit which converts this input form of the BC_{req} into the corresponding BC Expression. The resulting form conforms to the BC Expression metamodel [1] which is implemented by the *E-UCM BC Expr. Library* (Fig. 2, Mark 6).

The *ExistBDocIGs* are uniquely identified by their file names provided by user. They are resolved by the *ExistBDocIG Parser*, shown in Fig. 2, Mark 7.

GenBDocIG Generator. The *GenBDocIG Generator* (Fig. 2, Mark 8) is the processing unit used to develop the *GenBDocIG*. It extracts BIEs located in the available *ExistBDocIGs* and embeds them into the generic guideline.

CustBDocIG Generator. The *CustBDocIG Generator* (Fig. 2, Mark 9) is the processing unit used to customize the previously developed *GenBDocIG* and to create the new *CustBDocIG* valid in the BC_{req}. It invokes the *BIE Extractor* (Fig. 2, Mark 10), the processing unit which extracts all BIEs encompassed by the *GenBDocIG*. The included *BIE Library* (Fig. 2, Mark 11) represents our Java implementation of the BIE models defined by CCTS (Section 2).

BIE BCs Calculator. The *BIE BCs Calculator* (Fig. 2, Mark 13) is the processing unit used to calculate the overall BCs in which the generic ABIEs are valid. The corresponding pseudo-code is presented in Alg. 1 and explained in the following.

The ABIEs contained in the list of the generic ABIEs are processed within the loop initiated in Alg. 1, Line 1. According to Formula 1, an ABIE is valid in

Alg. 1. *BIEs BCs Calculator*	Alg. 2. *ASBIE BCs Calculator*

Input: *ABIEList*
  {BIE_overallBCs are not calculated.}
Output: *ABIEList*
  {BIE_overallBCs are calculated.}
 1: **for each** *abie : ABIEList* **do**
 2:    *abie.overallBC = null;*
 3:   **for each** *bbie : abie.BBIEList* **do**
 4:     *abie.overallBC =*
       abie.overallBC || bbie.assignedBC;
 5:   **end for**
 6:   **if** *abie.hasASBIEs* **then**
 7:    **for each** *asbie : abie.ASBIEList* **do**
 8:     *asbie.isOverallBCCalc = false;*
 9:    **end for**
10:    *abie.isOverallBCCalc = false;*
11:   **else**
12:    *abie.isOverallBCCalc = true;*
13:   **end if**
14: **end for**
15: **for each** *abie : ABIEList* **do**
16:   **if** *!abie.isOverallBCCalc* **then**
17:    *abie.overallBC = Alg_2(abie);*
18:    *abie.isOverallBCCalc = true;*
19:   **end if**
20: **end for**
21: **return** *ABIEList;*
	Input: *abie {associating ABIE,*
	  overall BC is not calculated.}
	Output: *abie {associating ABIE,*
	  overall BC is calculated.}
	 1:**if** *!abie.isOverallBCCalc* **then**
	 2: **for each** *asbie : abie.ASBIEList* **do**
	 3: *r = asbie.associatedABIE();*
	 4: **if** *!r.isOverallBCCalc* **then**
	 5: *asbie.overallBC =*
	       asbie.assignedBC && Alg_2(r);
	 6: **else**
	 7: *asbie.overallBC =*
	       asbie.assignedBC && r.overallBC;
	 8: **end if**
	 9: *asbie.isOverallBCCalc = true;*
	10: *abie.overallBC =*
	     abie.overallBC || asbie.overallBC;
	11: **end for**
	12: *abie.isOverallBCCalc = true;*
	13: *ret = abie.overallBC;*
	14:**else**
	15: *ret = abie.overallBC;*
	16:**end if**
	17:**return** *ret;*

the BC which is calculated as the union based on the following two components: (i) the union of the assigned BCs in which its included BBIEs are valid, and (ii) the union of the overall BCs in which its included ASBIEs are valid. The first component of the overall BC of the currently processing ABIE is calculated in Alg. 1, Lines 3-5. If this ABIE does not contain any ASBIE, the second component of its overall BC is null. Thus, its previously calculated component of the BC is equal to its overall BC (Alg. 1, Line 12). However, if the currently processing ABIE contains ASBIEs, the second component of its overall BC is not null, and it is calculated involving the *ASBIE BCs Calculator* (Alg. 1, Line 17).

ASBIE BCs Calculator. The *ASBIE BCs Calculator* (Fig. 2, Mark 14) is the processing unit used to calculate the overall BCs in which the ASBIEs contained by the generic ABIEs are valid. It is implemented by the recursive algorithm which pseudo-code is presented in Alg. 2 and explained in the following.

The ABIE which encompasses the currently processing ASBIEs (associating ABIE) is the input parameter of Alg. 2. The ASBIEs contained by the input ABIE are handled within the loop initiated in Alg. 2, Line 2. According to Formula 2, the overall BC of an ASBIE is dependant and, thus, calculated based on the intersection of its assigned BC and the overall BC of its associated ABIE. Therefore, there are two options (checked in Alg. 2, Line 4) for the following execution steps of Alg. 2 : (i) the overall BC of the associated ABIE is still unknown, and (ii) the overall BC of the associated ABIE has already been calculated.

In this execution phase, the overall BC of the associated ABIE is unknown iff this ABIE contains at least one ASBIE which overall BC has not been processed yet. Therefore, Alg. 2 is recursively called (Alg. 2, Line 5) where the associated ABIE is indicated as the new input parameter. In case that the overall BC of the associated ABIE is already known, the exit condition of the recursion is reached, and the overall BC of the currently processing ASBIE is calculated (Alg. 2, Line 7). Finally, the previously calculated component of the BC in which the associating ABIE is valid is unionised with the overall BC in which the currently processing ASBIE is valid in Alg. 2, Line 10.

Effective BIEs Extractor. The *Effective BIEs Extractor* (Fig. 2, Mark 12) is the processing unit used to extract only those BIEs from the list of the generic BIEs which are valid in BC_{req}. The generic BIEs are relevant in the BCs which are already calculated involving the previously explained *BIE BCs Calculator*.

5   Conclusion and Future Work

In this paper we described the implementation of our approach to calculate the content model of the BC aware BDocIGs. The corresponding e-documents conform to the CCTS standard and they are exchanged between business partners when executing inter-organizational business processes. Our proposed solution uses the contextual knowledge which is represented by our E-UCM model.

We implement our conceptual solution adapting the NDR specification and developing the architecture presented in Fig. 2. The final outcomes of the explained algorithms are new BDocIGs which are valid in the BC required by user. In our current work we evaluate the results achieved by application of the E-UCM model in different real-world business scenarios against the corresponding results achieved in case when our concurrent ontology based BC model [6] is applied. The research described in this paper is financially supported by the Vienna PhD School of Informatics [7].

References

1. Novakovic, D., Huemer, C., Pichler, C.: Context model for business context sensitive business documents. In: Brézillon, P., Blackburn, P., Dapoigny, R. (eds.) CONTEXT 2013. LNCS (LNAI), vol. 8175, pp. 336–342. Springer, Heidelberg (2013)
2. Novakovic, D., Huemer, C.: Business context sensitive business documents: Business context aware Core Components modeling using the E-UCM model. In: Proceedings of the 11th IEEE International Conference on Industrial Informatics (INDIN 2013), Bochum, Germany (2013)
3. Novakovic, D., Huemer, C.: A survey on business context. In: Proceedings of the International Conference on Advanced Computing, Networking, and Informatics (ICACNI), Raipur, Chhattisgarh, India (2013)
4. UN/CEFACT. Core Components Technical Specification CCTS, version 3.0 (September 2009), http://www.unece.org/cefact/ (last visit: May 2013)
5. UN/CEFACT. UN/CEFACT XML Naming and Design Rules technical specification, version 3.0 (2009), http://www.unece.org/cefact/ (last visit: May 2013)
6. Novakovic, D., Huemer, C.: Contextualizing business documents. To Appear in the 10th IEEE Intl. Conf. on e-Business Engineering (ICEBE 2013), United Kingdom (2013)
7. Vienna PhD School of Informatics, http://www.informatik.tuwien.ac.at/teaching/phdschool

Interaction Patterns in a Multi-Agent Organisation to Support Shared Tasks

Moser Silva Fagundes, Felipe Meneguzzi, Renata Vieira, and Rafael H. Bordini

Postgraduate Programme in Computer Science – School of Informatics (FACIN)
Pontifical Catholic University of Rio Grande do Sul (PUCRS) – Porto Alegre – RS, Brazil
{moser.fagundes,felipe.meneguzzi,renata.vieira,
rafael.bordini}@pucrs.br

Abstract. We aim to help the coordination of the activities of groups of users who share certain tasks. In particular, we are working towards automatically predicting the context of each user, in particular which task each user is trying to accomplish. We also intend to predict how probable it is that users will be able to successfully accomplish theirs tasks. In case a failure is likely, we help the users in negotiating task reallocation among group members. This paper presents the interaction patterns we use for information exchange among agents in order to determine the context needed to make those predictions.

1 Introduction

In daily life, groups of people cooperate to successfully complete tasks that are in the interest of their respective members. The members of such groups can be geographically distributed and subject to setbacks which unexpectedly interrupt the progress of their activities. For example, consider a delivery service whose employees pick up and deliver packets in geographically distributed locations. Such activities can be interrupted by traffic jams, cancellations of service orders, mechanical problems in the vehicles, etc. When the activities unfold as planned, coordination requires minimal attention to detail. However, when the plans deviate from the expected courses of action, it is expected that someone estimates how likely it is that the plan will fail. If a plan is expected to fail, then a reallocation of tasks could be made. For example, if an employee gets stuck in a traffic jam and realizes that he will not arrive in time to make a programmed pickup, he can call another employee to perform this task.

In such dynamic and unpredictable environments, the Multi-Agent Systems (MAS) paradigm [3,5,4,6] can be employed to develop complex applications that integrate multiple autonomous entities, both human and computational. Such applications can be designed to facilitate the interaction of users operating several types of devices (e.g., smartphones, tablets, laptops), predicting which tasks each group member is trying to achieve and suggesting possible alternative courses of action that might increase the chances of success in finishing all the group's tasks. However, to make possible the development of predictive multi-agent applications like these, we need to enable autonomous agents to provide and request relevant information to each other so as to reconstruct the *context* of the users.

P. Brézillon, P. Blackburn, and R. Dapoigny (Eds.): CONTEXT 2013, LNAI 8175, pp. 364–370, 2013.
© Springer-Verlag Berlin Heidelberg 2013

In this paper, we put forward a multi-agent organisation to support activities shared among members of a group, focusing on the description of the agent roles and interaction patterns between the roles so as to exchange information in order to gather the context of all the users. We show how these agent interaction patterns can be implemented in the *Jason* agent programming language [1] and we illustrate our approach by means of a scenario related to a delivery service company.

The remainder of this paper is organised as follows. Section 2 describes our proposal for a multi-agent organisation. Section 3 introduces a scenario to illustrate our approach. Finally, Section 4 draws some conclusions and points towards future work directions.

2   A Multi-Agent Organisation to Support Group Activities

A multi-agent organisation consists of a collection of roles and relationships which govern the behaviour of the agents [2]. In such organisations, roles can be employed to determine suitable interaction partners by providing additional information about the individuals. In this section, we employ the notion of organisation to describe a multi-agent system to support the activities of a group of users.

2.1   Roles

There are two roles in our MAS organisation: Interface Agent and Planner Agent. Interface agents operate in devices of the human users (e.g., smartphones, tablets, laptops). These agents encapsulate the methods needed to run properly in particular devices, taking into account their hardware and operating system configurations. An agent playing this role collects information about the human user from different sources (e.g., social networks, calendar, GPS) and provides information to the planner agent (this role is detailed below). An interface agent can deliver information to a planner agent in two ways: (i) *proactively*, when the interface agent believes that the information is relevant to the tasks carried out by the planner agent; and (ii) *reactively*, when the planner agent requests a particular information. Within our organisation, there is one interface agent per device, and this agent interacts with one user and his respective planner agent.

Planner agents operate in "the Cloud" and they interact with interface agents in order to get information about the users. In our multi-agent system, there is one planner agent per user, and this agent can interoperate with the interface agents running on various devices of this user (often a user interacts with several devices such as smartphones, tablets, etc. for the same task, depending on their current context). This way, the planner agents can infer the context of the users on the basis of information from multiple devices. This is fundamental to the type of system that we envision, given that all complex tasks performed by the planner agents (recognition of intentions, negotiation, and task reallocation) are based on the users' context. The agents playing this role are designed to run the reasoning processes that require high computational performance, hence alleviating the burden of the interface agents running on portable devices that have limited computational resources.

In summary, for each user there is one planner agent and a set of interface agents (at least one such agent). Figure 1 illustrates a scenario in which there are three users (userA, userB, and userC) and three planner agents (pa, pb, and pc). The arrows between these agents indicate that they are capable of interacting with each other (in this case, they interact to exchange information about the users). Each planner agent communicates with one or more interface agents of the same user. For instance, pb communicates with three interface agents, namely ib1, ib2, and ib3, running on a laptop, a tablet, and a smartphone, respectively. The arrows between pb and these interface agents indicate that they are capable of interacting. Figure 1 also shows that a single user can have multiple devices (for example, userA has a smartphone and a tablet).

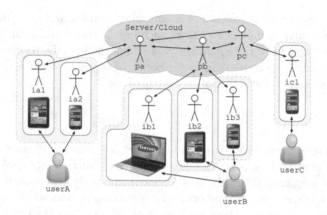

Fig. 1. Scenario with three users, three planner agents, and six interface agents

2.2   Agent Interactions

Within the multi-agent organisation, the following interactions are allowed:

- **Interface Agent– Planner Agent** .

    Interaction #1: An interface agent is capable of proactively sending information to its planner agent. This behaviour is triggered by the arrival of new information that the interface agents believe to be relevant to the construction of the user context. Figure 2(a) shows the protocol for this interaction.

    Interaction #2: A planner agent can tell its respective interface agents about which information it considers to be relevant. Figure 2(b) shows the protocol for this second type of interaction.

    Interaction #3: A planner agent is capable of asking the related interface agents for information in order to construct and update the context of a user. In this interaction, the planner agent asks for specific information, and the interface agent returns such information or tells that it is not available. The protocol for this interaction is specified in Figure 2(c).

- **Planner Agent– Planner Agent** .

  Interaction #4: planner agents are capable of asking other planner agents for information in order to create or update a representation of the users' context. This interaction follows the same protocol as Interaction #3, except that it happens between two planner agents.

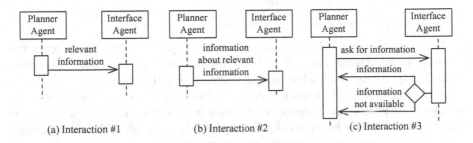

Fig. 2. Interaction protocols

2.3   Jason Implementation

This section shows how to implement in *Jason*[1] the interactions described in the previous subsection. Before describing the implementation of the interactions, we describe the agents' beliefs about the organisation structure. Agents playing the `interface` role know their respective `user` and `planner`. For example, `ia1` in Figure 1 believes that:

```
user(userA).
planner(pa,userA).
```

Agents playing the role `planner` have beliefs about their respective user and interface agents, and about other planners. For example, `pb` in Figure 1 believes that:

```
user(userB).
planner(pa,userA).
planner(pc,userC).
interface([ib1,ib2,ib3]).
```

An interface agent implements **Interaction #1** using the following plan template:

```
@tellXxx[interaction(1)]
+!tellXxx(Y) : user(User) <-
     ?xxx(Y);
     ?planner(Agent,User);
     .send(Agent,tell,xxx(Y)).
```

in which `xxx(Y)` is the belief (information) to be told; the "context part" of the plan instantiates `User`, which is used in the body of the plan to select the name of the planner.

In **Interaction #2**, a planner agent tells its interface agents about which information it considers relevant. We propose an implementation of such interactions using the

---

[1] For the sake of space, this paper assumes that the reader is familiar with the *Jason* programming language. For details about the *Jason* platform, see Bordini et al. [1].

tellHow performative, by means of which the planner informs the interface agents of plans that should be executed when they get to know something that is relevant to the planner. Our implementation uses the following plan template:

```
@tellXxx[interaction(2)]
+!tellXxx : user(User) <-
    ?interface(InterfaceAgents);
    .my_name(Agent);
    .concat("@tellXxx [interaction(2)] ",
            "+xxx(Y) : true <- .send(", Agent, ",tell,xxx(Y)).", Plan);
    .send(InterfaceAgents,tellHow,Plan).
```

in which xxx(Y) is the belief (relevant information) that interface agents are asked to provide to the planner. The plan body consists of retrieving the names of interface agents, and specifying and sending the plan to be executed by them.

Interaction #3 takes place when a planner agents fails to retrieve some information and asks its adjacent interface agents for this information. This third type of interaction is implemented in *Jason* by means of plans triggered by test goals of the planner, which are specified according to the following plan template:

```
@determineXxx[interaction(3)]
+?xxx(Y) : user(User) <-
    ?interface(InterfaceAgents);
    .selectIA(InterfaceAgents,Agent);
    .send(Agent,askOne,xxx(Y),xxx(Y));
    +xxx(Y)[source(Agent)].
```

This plan retrieves the list of interface agents and selects one of them with selectIA. The name of the selected agent is stored in variable Agent. Then, the planner agent sends an askOne message to Agent. If Agent successfully unifies xxx(Y) with its beliefs, then the planner agent adds this predicate to its belief base, which will include an annotation that indicates the source of this information.

Interaction #4 is similar to Interaction #3, except that the planner asks another planner instead of an interface agent. These interactions use the following template:

```
@determineXxx[interaction(4)]
+?xxx(Y) : not user(User) <-
    ?planner(Agent,User);
    .send(Agent,askOne,xxx(Y),xxx(Y));
    +xxx(Y)[source(Agent)].
```

in which xxx(Y) is the belief (information) to be acquired. Note that the context part of this plan is "not user(User)", which indicates that this plan is applicable only when the agent needs to know something about a user that is not its own.

3 Delivery Service Scenario

This section describes a delivery service scenario to illustrate our approach. There are three employees participating in this scenario, and each employee drives a vehicle to make programmed pickups and deliveries. The structure of the organisation is the same used in Figure 1, so we can say that userA corresponds to employeeA, userB corresponds to employeeB, and userC corresponds to employeeC.

Consider a situation in which pa aims to determine the location of employeeA and employeeC. In the code of pa, specified in Listing 1, @someGoal tries to unify

?location(employeeA,LocEA) and fails because it has no beliefs about the location of employeeA. As an attempt to determine this location, agent pa triggers @determineLocation[interaction(3)], which sends an askOne message to one of the other related interface agents [ia1,ia2].

```
────────────────── Listing 1 - pa ──────────────────
user(employeeA).
interface([ia1,ia2]).
planner(pb,employeeB).
planner(pc,employeeC).

@someGoal
+!someGoal : true <-
    ?location(employeeA,LocEA);
    ?location(employeeC,LocEC); ...

@determineLocation[interaction(3)]
+?location(User,Location) : user(User) <-
    ?interface(InterfaceAgents);
    .selectIA(InterfaceAgents,Agent);
    .send(Agent,askOne,location(User,Location),location(User,Location));
    +location(User,Location)[source(Agent)].

@determineLocation[interaction(4)]
+?location(User,Location) : not user(User) <-
    ?planner(Agent,User);
    .send(Agent,askOne,location(User,Location),location(User,Location));
    +location(User,Location)[source(Agent)].
```

Assume that planner agent pa selects the interface agent ia1 (Listing 2) as the receiver of the message. When the agent ia1 receives the message, it attempts to unify location(employeeA,LocEA) and fails to do so. This failure triggers the addition of a test goal, which is handled by plan @determineLocation. This plan reads the current location from the tablet's GPS of employeeA (tablet.getLocation). When location(employeeA,Location) is added to the belief base of ia1, it replies to pa, which resumes the execution of pa's plan.

```
────────────────── Listing 2 - ia1 ──────────────────
user(employeeA).
planner(pa,employeeA).

@determineLocation
+?location(User,Location) : user(User) <-
    tablet.getLocation(Location);
    +location(User,Location).
```

Further, in the body of plan @someGoal, the agent pa tries to unify ?location(employeeC,LocEC) and fails. This failure triggers the plan @determineLocation[interaction(4)], which sends an askOne message to the respective planner agent (in this case, pc), starting an instance of Interaction #4. Sometimes, the planner agents do not have the information requested by other agents. In this case, they have to interact with their interface agent in order to get the requested information. For instance, consider a situation in which pc does not know the location of employeeC. So, when pa asks pc about the location of employeeC, pc asks its interface agents about it (this is Interaction #3 taking place within Interaction #4). This can be seen in Listing 3 and Listing 4, the code for pc and ic1, respectively.

```
─────────────────────────── Listing 3 - pc ───────────────────────────
user(employeeC).
interface([ic1]).
planner(pa,employeeA).
planner(pb,employeeB).

@determineLocation[interaction(3)]
+?location(User,Location) : user(User) <-
    ?interface(InterfaceAgents);
    .selectIA(InterfaceAgents,Agent);
    .send(Agent,askOne,location(User,Location),location(User,Location));
    +location(User,Location).
```

```
─────────────────────────── Listing 4 - ic1 ──────────────────────────
user(employeeC).
planner(pc,employeeC).

@determineLocation
+?location(User,Location) : user(User) <-
    smartphone.getLocation(Location);
    +location(User,Location).
```

4   Conclusion

This paper presented an organisation of agents to support group activities, focusing on the specification and implementation of interaction patterns between the agent roles as an infrastructure to enable the exchange of information about users and their context.

There are three main directions for future work. The investigation and development of plan recognition and negotiation techniques using contextual information for proactive multiuser assistance, as well as the use of ontologies to support the generation of plans for the *Jason* platform using the templates introduced in this paper.

Acknowledgements. Part of the results presented by this paper were obtained through the project named Semantic and Multi-Agent Technologies for Group Interaction, sponsored by Samsung Eletrônica da Amazônia Ltda., under the terms of Brazilian federal law number 8.248/91.

References

1. Bordini, R., Hübner, J.F., Wooldridge, M.: Programming Multi-Agent Systems in AgentSpeak using Jason. Wiley Series in Agent Technology. John Wiley & Sons (2007)
2. Horling, B., Lesser, V.R.: A survey of multi-agent organizational paradigms. Knowledge Eng. Review 19(4), 281–316 (2004)
3. Jennings, N.R.: On agent-based software engineering. Artif. Intell. 117(2), 277–296 (2000)
4. Jennings, N.R.: An agent-based approach for building complex software systems. Commun. ACM 44(4), 35–41 (2001)
5. Jennings, N.R., Sycara, K.P., Wooldridge, M.: A roadmap of agent research and development. Autonomous Agents and Multi-Agent Systems 1(1), 7–38 (1998)
6. Wooldridge, M.: Agent-based software engineering. IEE Proceedings - Software 144(1), 26–37 (1997)

A Trace Analysis Based Approach for Modeling Context Components

Assitan Traoré[1,2], Hélène Tattegrain[1], and Alain Mille[2]

[1] IFSTTAR, LESCOT, 25, avenue François Mitterrand, 69675 Bron cedex France
{assitan.traore,helene.tattegrain}@ifsttar.fr
[2] University of Lyon 1, LIRIS, UMR5205, F-69621, France
{assitan.traore,alain.mille}@univ-lyon1.fr

Abstract. The context is the set circumstances that surround an event or object as reminded by [1]. According to this definition, taking the context into account when analyzing an activity would require having at one's disposal information describing the circumstances that surround each object concerned by this activity. This information is, by definition, difficult to describe precisely at the beginning of the analysis and must be progressively defined during the analysis process. We propose to gradually define the context information surrounding objects concerned by the activity, **based on the interactive learning of activity traces,** revisited by successive interpretations during the analysis. The context model of the components proposed by [1] will be considered as the basis to define the activity components, which are the objects concerned by the activity. The approach by interactive discovery of knowledge from activity traces should allow to discover the values of these components but also new knowledge specific to the observed activity. This approach allows us to **dynamically build the context** useful to the activity analysis. This methodology will be applied in the field of transportation to determine the impact of driving behaviors on fuel consumption.

Keywords: Context, Discovery of knowledge, knowledge representation, Trace-based Analysis, Fuel Consumption.

1 Introduction

Context is a concept used in many fields such as psychology, communication, artificial intelligence, knowledge engineering, design, electronics etc. Every field provides context elements of description. For example, in software engineering, context refers to the interactions between end users and their software environment. In the field of transportation, for the study of the driving activity, context refers to traffic, driving objectives, weather, the road infrastructure etc. Since 1995, several scientific communities have focused on the study of context. In 1999, Patrick Brézillon's synthesis [2] proposed a first view trying to merge several fields using the

P. Brézillon, P. Blackburn, and R. Dapoigny (Eds.): CONTEXT 2013, LNAI 8175, pp. 371–380, 2013.

context. This study led to conclude that there are different context types for knowledge representation, reasoning mechanisms and human-machine interaction. These numerous context definitions have led researchers to seek a general definition of context.

Through these researches some general definitions of context have appeared including that of Anind K. Dey [3], who defines context as "all information that can be used to characterize an entity situation. An entity can be a person, a place or an object that is considered relevant to the interaction between a user and an application, including the user and the applications themselves". This definition can be considered a general definition of context because it allows, whatever the field, to know what relates to context or not. But it does not model the relationships between various context components.

Gaetan Rey and Joëlle Coutaz [7] consider context as a space of infinite and evolving information, which is not frozen and evolves over time. They define context as an infinite space of variables not known in advance by the system. They define the context of interaction as the intersection between the contextual knowledge of the system and the user's context or the idea the user has of his context.

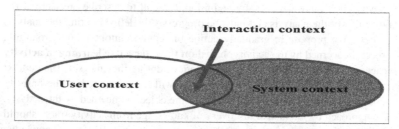

Fig. 1. Definition of interaction context (Source : Gaetan Rey and Joëlle Coutaz [7])

2   Context Model of the Activity Components

The model defined by Bazire and Brézillon [1] intended to represent the components of a situation or an activity that takes into account context and the different relationships between these components. It is based on the assumption that the reason why context definitions diverge depending on the domain, is that they do not have the same center of interest on the components. The components are the entities relating to an activity, which is influenced by the context and each entity has its proper context such as: user's context «Cu», item context «Ci», observer's context «Co» and environmental context «Ce» (see Figure 2 for acronyms). The set of context components of the situation allows defining the context of the situation whatever the domain.

This model helps to identify components and their context; it identifies the activity to be analyzed, defines the relationships that may exist between these components. Relationships are the interactions between the different components necessary for carrying out of the task of the activity. In Figure 2, the context of each component is defined by the relationship r1, r2, r3 and r4. These components interact among themselves through relationships. The components «User» and « Item » interact with each other through relationships r7 and r8. The components «User» and « Item» interacts with the environment represented by the component « Environment » through relationships r5, r6, r9. Component «Observer» interacts with all other components to observe them during the activity. In this study, we will represent these relationships as predicates or properties to be used in logical rules. After defining the components of the activity, the context of the components and their interactions, this model allows to define the context of the activity by taking into account the context of the components and their interactions between the components.

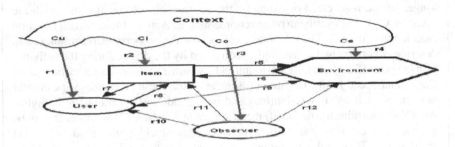

Fig. 2. Model of context (Source : Bazire and Brézillon [1])

Illustration 1: For the driving activity analysis, by using the above context model and the needs of analysis, we can identify the components of the driving activity that will allow us to define the contexts of components and relationships between them. The driving activity is constituted of three context of components and the context of the observer. First is the context of the user (in our case the driver) that corresponds to the component «Cu» of model, and could be defined by the driver's age, gender, attention to driving, driving actions, driving style, driving behavior etc.

The second is the context of the item (in our case the car) that corresponds to the component «Ci», and could be defined by the car conditions, fuel consumption, brand, engine temperature, speed, etc. The third is context «Ce» which corresponds to the context of the environment, and that can be defined by the traffic, the road infrastructure, the density of traffic lights, the weather conditions, etc. The context of the observer «Co» which corresponds to context of analysis could be defined by the objectives of the analysis. Here, the analyst's mission is to observe the components of the driving activity and the relationships that link these components to define the context of the performed driving activity in order to explain the impact of the driving behavior on fuel consumption. The components driver, car and environment interact with each other through relationships. For a person who drives his car on a highway, the relationships r7 and r8 correspond to interactions between the driver and his car, thus to driving actions such as using the brake pedal or acceleration pedal, gear shift, eye glance at the rear-view mirrors etc. Relationships r5 and r6 correspond to interactions between the car and the environment such as the type of road, traffic, other usages of the road etc. For example, the relationship r8 can use the predicate «Action(x, y)» to describe driving actions, such as Action (brake, driver), Action (acceleration, driver). The relationship r4 can use the property «Constraint(x) » to describe environmental constraints encountered by the driver during the activity : Constraint(traffic light), Constraint(bad weather), Constraint(traffic jam), Constraint(speed limit), Constraint(obstacle). With these predicates we can infer new rules such as: if (Action(brake, driver) And(No(Constraint(traffic light)) And(No(Constraint(traffic jam))) then Constraint (obstacle). The obstacle may be a pedestrian crossing the road, a delivery van blocking the road or a road accident etc. These rules represent new knowledge that will allow us to define the context of each component. Among the elements that define the context components of the driving activity, some are easy to fill in such as the speed of the vehicle, its consumption, the driver's age, car brand, engine temperature; but other information, which are unknown, are important to explain the fuel consumption. As the driving behavior of a person in a given driving situation, the situation is defined by the driving objectives, the road infrastructure, traffic, weather etc. This information is unknown in the first instance but can be inferred from the observation of the driving activity and the knowledge of the analyst through a process of transformation of interaction traces *according to a point of view that corresponds to the objective of the analysis*. It should be possible to discover the signature of this person's different driving behaviors in such situations. The study selected to prove this concept aims at determining the impact of driving behavior on fuel consumption. To achieve this goal we will observe the relationship between the components that we have just listed above.

3   The Traces Modeling Approach

This trace based approach was proposed to analyze the activity of an agent (human or artificial) interacting with a complex technical device such as in the driving activity. Said activity is observed to be modeled in the form of modeled traces (M-traces) organized in a transformation graph. The collected trace (primary M-trace) is initially composed of a sequence of event descriptions (Obsels[1]) linked by a sequential relationship. It is then enhanced according to a transformation model in order to build a representation of the activity according to different levels of abstractions associated to different analysis questions. This allows the construction of new knowledge in the form of transformed traces reformulating another observation according to a particular interpretative point of view. The analyst's knowledge allowing the interpretation is encapsulated in the transformation of operations in order to understand and explain a complex situation. In this approach, an M-trace is a succession of observations temporally located, explained by its trace model. All M-trace models comply with a common meta-model. An observed element is any piece of information, labeled and dated, produced by the observation of an activity with the aim to describe it, accompanied by a number of properties that the analyst considers useful for the observation. In order to use this approach during an analysis, two conditions are to be met:

a.   Data about the analyzed activity must be ordered temporally, that is to say that any Obsel[1] has a timestamp.
b.   The produced M-traces are necessarily adapted to the analyst's knowledge, because they can only make sense to him in the context of his prior knowledge. So it is the analyst who guides the M-traces system in transforming collected M-traces into M-traces interesting to him based on such or such interpretation. A platform has been developed for implementing these concepts while, on the one hand, modeling and managing the modeled traces and, on the other hand, specifying and executing transformations. The ABSTRACT platform (Analysis of Behavior and Situation for menTal Representation Assessment and Cognitive actTivity modeling) has an architecture illustrated in the following diagram.

The "collection system" level allows producing a sequence of Obsels[1] from different data sources. In this respect, it regroups various tools for automatic data processing, assistance for manual collection and a merging device. It also includes a visualization tool that allows validating the collected M-trace".

The level of "M-trace based system" constitutes the proper analsysis workshop. It allows manipulating M-traces in the form of RDF graphs [8]. It regroups various functionalities of M-trace transformations: an ontology editor to specify the different M-trace models, a transformation editor to specify the different transformation rules applicable to M-traces, a transformation engine to apply them, a visualization system to visualize the resulting M-traces, a query tool for the search of behavioral patterns signatures occurrences in the traces.

---

[1]   Obsels : Observed Elements.

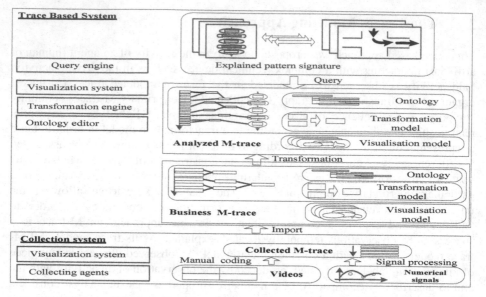

Fig. 3. ABSTRACT Architecture (Source : [4])

Transformation mechanisms consist in introducing new interpretation elements in the observation. The result of a transformation is a transformed M-Trace exhibiting the observed activity in the light of what has already been discovered or what was already known. A discovery process can then be started over until achievement of the analysis objective.

One can, for example, distinguish the levels of transformed M-traces: "Business M-trace" that describes the activity at the operational level (what is available on the interface to make the job), and "analyzed M-trace" that describes the activity in the analyst's language at a certain level of analysis.

4   Methodology for Modeling Context from Traces

The methodology we propose aims to model context according to interactive discovery of knowledge for activity analyze approach. This methodology for modeling context components modeling is constituted of four steps:

1. Definition of Standard Components of Context:

This step allows to define context components and the relationships between them, in relation with the needs and the objectives of the analysis, by using Bazire and Brézillon's [1] proposed model. At this stage of the analysis we identify for each context component the known information defining it, such as driver's age or gender; and those which are not known but could be used to define the context components, for example, a person's driving style, driving actions and behaviors in a given driving situation. This information depends on the situation constraints and the driving situation, therefore on the driving context. At this level of analysis this information is not known but it is very important to help the person reducing his fuel consumption.

A good definition of the activity components and its context will allow for good taking into account of the context and thus ensure quality assistance to a person in achieving the task.

2. Creation of the Ontology and Preparation of the Collected M-Trace:
This step will allow, first, to make a formal description of the context components defined above in an ontology. Each context component will have a class containing the known information defining it and the other unknown information will be discovered thanks to the next step. The activity ontology will be updated progressively along the discovery of knowledge on the context components.

Illustration 2: The collected M-trace contains the raw data from the driving activity collected by means of an instrumented vehicle during driving. This data provides information on the vehicle environment (cameras filming scenes front and rear, speed limits , distance of following vehicle), its dynamics (acceleration, speed records on the CAN bus) its position (GPS antenna, position on the road) and the driver's actions (order status, steering wheel angle, depressing the pedal).

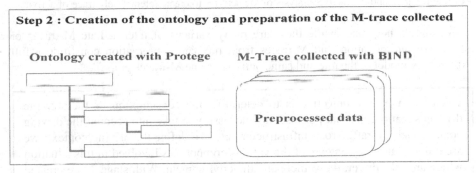

Fig. 4. Ontology and M-trace first collection results

---

3. Observation and Transformations of the Collected Trace:
This objective of this step is to determine the missing information on context components in order to understand or explain an event by defining the circumstances that surrounded it. To define this missing information we reformulate the Obsels[1] sequence from the collected M-trace to construct a transformed M-trace corresponding to this first taking into account of the context recognized at that moment. This transformation is done by inferring new knowledge, observing the event and using the analyst's knowledge to enrich the collected trace from the considered context. In this way, what was the context in step 1 becomes analysis elements in step 2 and the context evolves dynamically in an interactive way. Context models mentioned earlier are then populated specifically to provide elements of capitalization for future analysis and to document the current analysis. In this step the analyst performs in an iterative way several inferences that will transform the trace from the preceding step to generate a new transformed M-trace a the next step of

interpretation. This M-trace is a symbolic and sequential representation of salient facts that are relevant to the analysis objective. Several transformations may be necessary to construct a trace analysis from analysis of traces in order to achieve the analysis objective. Each transformation is a new level of interpretation. The higher the level of interpretation, the more knowledge (including contextual one) is encapsulated in the M-trace model with an explicit, formal and precise interpretation. It is from the most complete trace, in terms of interpretations, that an exploitable model of knowledge for action can be inferred: the analysis objective is then achieved.

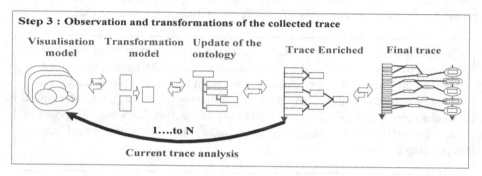

Fig. 5. Iterative and interactive analysis of the activity to create interactively trace of activity

We should note that, while there are many variants of intermediate M-traces or alternative interpretations, all M-traces from the same observation constitute a full explanatory model of the one and same activity (same M-traces graph).

Illustration 3: The objective is to determine the consumption of fuel for the driving situation. For that purpose, it is necessary to take into account the driving context such as traffic, road infrastructure etc. To define the driving context; we are going to use the contexts of the various components involved in this situation which are: the driver, the vehicle and the environment. With stage 2, we created a collected M-trace and an ontology. The collected M-trace represents the known information such as the speed of the vehicle, the GPS position, the driver's actions, etc. The ontology is the formal description of the situation components. The driver component will have a class "Driving actions" with parameters steering angle, pedals positions, etc. The vehicle component will have a class "Vehicle Dynamics" with parameters consumption, acceleration, speed, etc. And the environment component will have a class "Infrastructure" with parameters speed limits, road type, preceding vehicle position, etc.

With the M-trace, and the associated ontology, we proceed to the analysis of the driving situation by observing the video to infer new knowledge. Every inference leads to a new transformation allowing the definition of the situation context. As an example of transformation, the analysis of the position of the preceding vehicle and the road type could allow to deduce the traffic, element of the environment context.

4. Evaluation and Validation of Knowledge from Analysis of M-Traces:

This step allows to evaluate the knowledge discovered progressively and synthesized in the trace which has allowed the achievement of the analysis objective from a collected trace. A comparative approach with sets of analogue traces and different methods will allow to qualify the quality of the discovered patterns (coverage, accuracy in particular). If the error rate exceeds the tolerable threshold with conventional methods, the model will not be validated; otherwise it is subject to the analyst's validation and interpretation.

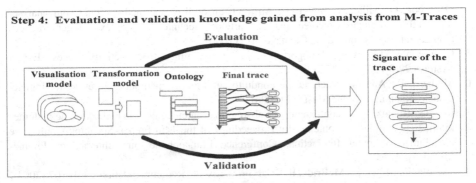

Fig. 6. Evaluation and validation of traces activity

Illustration 4: The trace validation deducing the traffic will be realized by comparing the trace result on data with situation where the traffic was manually coded by an expert (at the moment 70 hours of driving are manually coded).

5 Conclusion and Discussion

The method of analysis from M-traces that we have just presented is based on the method of trace analysis. Interactive knowledge discovery from M-traces is a method of iterative and interactive analysis based on the principle of observation and the usage of the analyst's knowledge for the discovery of new knowledge. We propose to demonstrate that this method can be used to accurately model the missing information for a given object or event, in order to enable its correct representation i.e. its context. This method has been used for example to model two examples of lane change in driving activity [5] by taking into account the progressive context in the process analysis. Now we want to show how generic this approach is. Context is a concept that plays a very important role in many fields; thus our interest in this new way intended to build it dynamically. To test this new way, we will more precisely formalize the method and apply it in the field of transportation, in automobile driving activity in order to assess its relevance and effective usability. In this application, the objective is to model context from the interactive process of knowledge discovery from activity analysis and to apply this approach to the understanding of driving behavior impact on fuel consumption and the prediction that can be made from the observation of behavior.

References

1. Bazire, M., Brézillon, P.: Understanding context before using it. In: Dey, A., Kokinov, B., Leake, D., Turner, R. (eds.) CONTEXT 2005. LNCS (LNAI), vol. 3554, pp. 29–40. Springer, Heidelberg (2005)
2. Brézillon, P.: Context in problem solving: a survey. The Knowledge Engineering Review 14(1), 47–80 (1999)
3. Dey, A.K.: Understanding and using context. Personal and Ubiquitous Computing 5(1), 4–7 (2001)
4. Georgeon, O., Mille, A., Bellet, T.: Abstract: un outil et une méthodologie pour analyser une activité humaine médiée par un artefact technique complexe. Ingéniérie des Connaissances. Semaine de la Connaissance (2006)
5. Georgeon, O.L., et al.: Supporting activity modelling from activity traces. Expert Systems 29(3), 261–275 (2012)
6. Mathern, B.: Analyser l'activité de conduite automobile: méthodologie et atelier logiciel associé. Rapport de Stage Master 2 (2006)
7. Rey, G., Coutaz, J.: Le contexteur: une abstraction logicielle pour la réalisation de systèmes interactifs sensibles au contexte. In: Proceedings of the 14th French-Speaking Conference on Human-Computer Interaction (Conférence Francophone sur l'Interaction Homme-Machine). ACM (2002)
8. Manola, F., Miller, E., McBride, B.: RDF primer. W3C Recommendation 10, 1–107 (2004), http://www.w3.org/TR/rdf-primer/

Author Index